Napoleon Absent, Coalition Ascendant

Napoleon Absent, Coalition Ascendant

The 1799 Campaign in Italy and Switzerland, Volume 1

CARL VON CLAUSEWITZ

Translated and Edited by

NICHOLAS MURRAY
AND
CHRISTOPHER PRINGLE

University Press of Kansas

© 2021 by the University Press of Kansas

All rights reserved

Published by the University Press of Kansas (Lawrence, Kansas 66045), which was organized by the Kansas Board of Regents and is operated and funded by Emporia State University, Fort Hays State University, Kansas State University, Pittsburg State University, the University of Kansas, and Wichita State University

Library of Congress Cataloging-in-Publication Data

Names: Clausewitz, Carl von, 1780–1831. author. | Murray, Nicholas, 1966– editor, translator. | Pringle, Christopher, editor, translator.
Title: The 1799 campaign in Italy and Switzerland / Carl von Clausewitz ; translated and edited by Nicholas Murray and Christopher Pringle.
Other titles: Feldzug von 1799 in Italien und der Schweiz. English | 1799 campaign in Italy and Switzerland
Description: [Lawrence] : [University Press of Kansas], [2020] | Series: The 1799 Campaign in Italy and Switzerland | Translation of: Die Feldzüge von 1799 in Italien und der Schweiz (Berlin: Ferdinand Dümmler, 1833). | Includes bibliographical references and index. | Contents: Vol. 1. Napoleon absent, coalition ascendant — vol. 2 The Coalition Crumbles, Napoleon Returns.
Identifiers: LCCN 2020016440
  ISBN 9780700630240 (vol. 1 ; cloth)
  ISBN 9780700630257 (vol. 1 ; paperback)
  ISBN 9780700630264 (vol. 1 ; epub)
  ISBN 9780700630332 (vol. 2 ; cloth)
  ISBN 9780700630349 (vol. 2 ; paperback)
  ISBN 9780700630356 (vol. 2 ; epub)
Subjects: LCSH: Second Coalition, War of the, 1798–1801—Campaigns—Italy. | Second Coalition, War of the, 1798–1801—Campaigns—Switzerland. | Napoleon I, Emperor of the French, 1769–1821—Military leadership. | France—History—Revolution, 1789–1799.
Classification: LCC DC223.4 .C5613 2020 | DDC 940.2/7420945—dc23
LC record available at https://lccn.loc.gov/2020016440.

British Library Cataloguing-in-Publication Data is available.

Printed in the United States of America

10 9 8 7 6 5 4 3 2 1

The paper used in this publication is recycled and contains 30 percent postconsumer waste. It is acid free and meets the minimum requirements of the American National Standard for Permanence of Paper for Printed Library Materials z39.48–1992.

This series of translations of Clausewitz's work is dedicated to the late Dennis Showalter. Dennis's support and encouragement played an important role in getting this project off the ground, and he will be much missed.

Contents

Translators' Note, ix

Editors' Note, xiii

A Note on Wargaming, xv

Acknowledgments, xvii

Introduction, 1

Original Editor's Note, 5

Clausewitz's Introduction, 7

1. General Situation. Opening of the Campaign in Germany. The French Take Graubündten. Archduke Charles Beats Jourdan at Stockach, 9

2. Opening of the Campaign in Italy. Conquest of Lombardy. The French Are Driven Back to the Apennines, 141

3. Continuation of the Campaign in Switzerland. The Austrians Drive the French out of Graubündten and Cross the Rhine. The Archduke Fights the First Battle of Zurich, 242

4. Continuation of the Campaign in Italy. Suvorov Beats Macdonald on the Trebbia, 318

5. The Allies Take Mantua and Alessandria. Suvorov Defeats Joubert at Novi, 376

Bibliography, 417

Index, 423

A gallery of maps appears after page 227.

Translators' Note

Any translation presents challenges, the most obvious being the tension between adhering to the literal meaning of the author's original words and capturing the spirit of what he is trying to convey. A direct word-for-word translation inevitably sounds cumbersome and clunky, especially if the same sentence structure is retained. Some degree of rephrasing is always necessary, as well as reorganizing sentences and even whole paragraphs to make the work read more fluently. The problem is that the freer the translation, the greater the risk that some important nuance or emphasis may be lost. As we did in Clausewitz's history of the 1796 campaign,[1] we attempted to strike a balance in the translation of the two-volume history of the 1799 campaigns, and we employed a consistent approach and similar style in all three volumes. We hope that in doing so, we have made the entirety of the work more accessible and easier to read while still allowing Clausewitz to make his points as he intended to make them and to speak in his own distinctive voice.

In fact, Clausewitz speaks to us with three different voices. The first is for the bald description of events in chronological order: "A and B did X and Y. C moved to Z. On the nth, W happened." Clausewitz's language here is clear and simple. His sentences are brief. His descriptions are unornamented. That is not to say that this voice is dull. On the contrary, his narration marches briskly and gives us a clear picture of each battle. Furthermore, his selective use of the historic present tense makes certain passages especially vivid. In German as in English, the historic present serves to lend a sense of drama and urgency to descriptions of past events. The effect of this in Clausewitz's history of the 1796 campaign—the battle of Montenotte, when Bonaparte first goes on the offensive—is tremendously powerful. It strikingly conveys the energy and vigor of the youthful Bonaparte bursting onto the scene and emphasizes the contrast between him and his ponderous, elderly Austrian opponent. Napoleon is not present here, but the plodding Austrians are on hand again, and the language helps convey the dynamic differences between the French and the Austrians in particular. Although this change in tense may be disconcerting for the reader,

---

1. See Carl von Clausewitz, *Napoleon's 1796 Italian Campaign*, trans. and ed. Nicholas Murray and Christopher Pringle (Lawrence: University Press of Kansas, 2018).

we have chosen to retain it as far as possible and thus remain consistent across all these three volumes of Clausewitz's campaign histories.

Clausewitz's second voice is for expounding on strategic theory and its implications. Here, his prose is as verbose and florid as his first voice is terse and clipped, as he allows himself lengthy and laborious philosophical discursions. The German language is notorious for its long sentences with multiple nested clauses—the so-called *Bandwurmsatz,* or tapeworm sentence. Clausewitz seems especially fond of the humble tapeworm (though we often felt obliged to cut the creature up). This, together with a penchant for not using a simple word or phrase when a more complicated one will do, results in what our good friend Hartmut "Hardy" Steffin exasperatedly dubbed "Clausewitzification." Clausewitz is not averse to a rather English use of the understated double negative that means "very." If at times the translation seems not inconsiderably long-winded, it is not necessarily our fault nor that of the German language; it is simply Clausewitz in pontificatory mode.

But it is worth putting up with Clausewitz's pontifications for the delight that is his third voice. This is when he wields his quill like a scalpel to dissect the actions of the French, Austrian, and Russian commanders, viewing them through the prism of his strategic analysis and flaying them for their manifold failings. He frequently claims to be baffled by their decisions, and his evaluation is littered with phrases such as "it is incomprehensible," "there seems to be no good reason why," or "it makes no sense." His bafflement often provokes him to lapse from philosophical or scientific language into idiom and vernacular: generals are likened to "feeble-minded beetles," their plans are "egomaniacal," they are "clueless." The remorseless logic he deploys to crush the beetles is a pleasure to read, as he shows step by unarguable step exactly why they were wrong and what they should have done instead.

Identifying geographical locations was not always straightforward. For some, he gives German names that are long obsolete, now that these places are in Italy or Slovenia. That would have been less of a problem if his spellings were not so idiosyncratic, and occasionally a misspelled Italian name directs us to a different part of the country entirely. Near-contemporary maps from the Austrian Second Military Survey of 1806–1869 were helpful and can be found online.[2]

---

2. "Franziszeische Landesaufnahme (1806–1869)," http://mapire.eu/de/map/secondsurvey.

The names of the commanders presented similar challenges. In section 16 of Clausewitz's 1796 history, a chap named "Gugeur" crops up. Later on, we meet a brigadier named "Guyeur." Could these two be one and the same? And if so, could he in turn be related to the French general Jean Joseph Guieu, also known as Guyeux? Then there is the Croat general in Austrian service whom Clausewitz identifies as Wukassowitsch but who, in his native Croatian, would be Vukasovi and appears in other histories variously as Vukasovich, Wukassovich, Vukassevich, or Vukaszovich.

We found similar inconsistencies in this volume and dealt with them in the same way. The convention we used for the names of both places and individuals is as follows: When they first appear, we give Clausewitz's spelling, followed by the modern name in brackets. Thereafter, we use the modern name. For places that have different names in different languages, we give both or all—for example, Botzen [Bozen/Bolzano]—and then use one of those names consistently thereafter.

This translation owes a great deal to the linguistic talents of Hardy Steffin. As a native German speaker with an excellent command of English and an interest in translation and wordplay, Hardy was consulted frequently whenever we encountered an obscure or archaic idiom or a particularly tangled passage of Clausewitzification. His generous help was invaluable in eliminating many misunderstandings and the occasional crass error and in tracking down or teasing out the meanings of phrases we could not find in the dictionary. Still, there were some sentences that even Hardy struggled to make sense of. This is perhaps because Clausewitz's writings are often technical and abrupt, as readers of *On War* can attest, and the original work was published posthumously by Clausewitz's widow, Countess Marie von Clausewitz. Some of the denser Clausewitzifications and ambiguities in his text are probably due to the fact that Clausewitz himself never finished editing his work. A number of obvious mistakes he made (such as referring to the wrong bank of a river) tend to confirm this.

Clausewitz was also fond of emphasizing words or sentences for effect. Where we found instances of this in the original text, we used italic to indicate it. Words or sections emphasized by us, the editors, are identified as such. Foreign words or phrases in Latin or some equivalent are also italicized, following stylistic conventions.

No doubt this work still contains some errors or interpretations that some will find problematic. We request the reader's indulgence, as we were not privy to Clausewitz's thoughts, and the work of translation is as much art as science. If any reader discovers an error, we would welcome being apprised of the correction.

Any such imperfections notwithstanding, we trust that overall we have done Clausewitz justice and prepared a translation that is as faithful and authentic as possible. We hope that you will enjoy reading this work as much as we enjoyed translating it.

Editors' Note

The reader will note that both volumes of the history of the 1799 campaigns contain the same translators' note, note on wargaming, and acknowledgments, which are similar to those in our translation of Clausewitz's history of the 1796 campaign.[1] Not wishing to reinvent the wheel, we also wanted to ensure that readers of either volume had ready access to these thoughts and comments and would not be forced to refer to the other volume. Likewise, each book contains its own index rather than a single index for the two volumes.

The biographic information comes largely from two main sources. For the French, unless otherwise noted, the information comes from Napoléon Bonaparte, *Correspondance Générale*.[2] For the Austrians, unless otherwise noted, the information comes from Dr. Constant von Wurzbach, *Biographisches Lexikon des Kaiserthums Oesterreich*.[3]

Where Clausewitz provides explanatory notes, we include them in the editors' footnotes. For the reader's convenience, we highlighted his name in bold so that his notes stand out.

We hope the reader will find these volumes informative and useful tools for understanding the French Revolutionary Wars and Clausewitz's ideas.

---

1. Carl von Clausewitz, *Napoleon's 1796 Italian Campaign*, trans. and ed. Nicholas Murray and Christopher Pringle (Lawrence: University Press of Kansas, 2018).

2. Napoléon Bonaparte, *Correspondance Générale*, 15 vols. (Paris: Publiée par la Fondation Napoléon, Librairie Arthéme Fayard, 2004–2018).

3. Dr. Constant von Wurzbach, *Biographisches Lexikon des Kaiserthums Oesterreich*, 60 vols. (Vienna: Universitäts Buchruderei von L. E. Zamarski, 1856–1891), http://www.literature.at/collection.alo?from=1&to=50&orderby=author&sortorder=a&objid=11104&page=.

A Note on Wargaming

Clausewitz's theoretical writings are just one symptom of the broader phenomenon of the increasingly systematic approach to war adopted by the Prussian military in the nineteenth century. Another aspect of this was the development of wargaming as a tool for professional military education.[1]

Since then, wargaming has been widely used by militaries around the world. At the time of this writing, there is renewed professional interest in wargaming in the United States in particular,[2] a movement in which the editors are directly involved. Wargaming gives participants the opportunity to practice rapid decision making in conditions of uncertainty, under time pressure, and in a competitive environment, which can offer profound insights and teach enduring lessons. It is "learning by doing," and it can be tremendously powerful. Both of the editors like wargaming because it places students in the role of decision maker and provides opportunities for hands-on problem solving. For example, when "Major Buttercup" is given the role of Suvorov in 1799, students often find that their job is just as frustrating as their historical counterpart's, experiencing their own version of the testy exchanges they have read about. The process of decision making and planning in an uncertain environment is invaluable, and it allows students to see Clausewitz's ideas and concepts in action, so to speak, leading them to exclaim, "That's what a culminating point is!"

As far as the present work is concerned, the editors encourage readers to explore wargaming as a way to gain a deeper appreciation of how and why the campaigns and battles described and analyzed by Clausewitz took the courses they did. To facilitate an understanding of the campaign as a whole, one of us (Nick Murray) has developed a game for his students that is also used by the US Navy, US Army, and US Marine Corps for training and education. A series of games set in 1796–1797 and 1799–1800 allows students to engage with the key problems and war-fighting scenarios of these campaigns, helping them to

---

1. Philipp von Hilgers, *Kriegspiele eine Geschichte der Ausnahmezustände und Unberechenberkeiten* (Munich: Wilhelm Fink Verlag, 2008), 58–71.
2. Deputy Secretary of Defense Robert Work, a memorandum for secretaries of the Military Departments, "Wargaming and Innovation," 9 February 2015.

engage with Clausewitz's key ideas as well.[3] For the grand tactical level, many commercial games are available; we favor *Bloody Big Battles!* (*BBB*), which Nick has also used in class. The scenarios and a set of discussion questions related to the operations are available for free via the discussion group at https://groups.io/g/bloodybigbattles.

3. The wargames have been run largely as elective classes over the last ten years (with thanks to Dr. Tim Schultz and his team in the Electives Department of the US Naval War College). Students take on the role of one of the main theater commanders covered in Clausewitz's history. In that role, they confront many of the problems and choices Clausewitz identifies, making these wargames an excellent tool for understanding his thoughts and for practicing decision making.

Acknowledgments

It is an honor for us to recognize the assistance we received during the completion of this book. In this respect, we would like to thank Dr. Tony Echevarria of the US Army War College for taking the time to discuss Clausewitz's writing. This was a great help in thinking about the meaning of Clausewitz's work. Dr. Chris Bassford of National Defense University and his excellent Clausewitz resource (Clausewitz.com) provided some extremely helpful ideas about the timeline of Clausewitz's writings and what that might mean. Vanya Bellinger, author of the excellent *Marie von Clausewitz: The Woman behind the Making of* On War, was kind enough to provide her guidance and proved to be a great help in identifying nuances in the original writing. Though we were less reliant on his help this time around than for the 1796 volume, Hartmut Steffin again contributed his time and knowledge to assist us with some particularly tricky German idioms. Glenda Pringle provided her valuable expertise in indexing both volumes.

We would like to thank everyone at the University Press of Kansas for their professional assistance in the production of this and our previous work, especially Joyce Harrison for her encouragement and support of the project.

These acknowledgments would not be complete without a word of appreciation for Kara McKamey and Glenda Pringle, whose patience was stretched at times when they were neglected in favor of a long-dead Prussian general. We thank them for indulging us.

In spite of all this help, it is likely that we missed something. Thus, any flaws contained herein are our own.

Napoleon Absent, Coalition Ascendant

Introduction

The writings of Carl von Clausewitz are among the most important works on war ever written. Much of the focus has understandably been on his great theoretical work *On War*, which has been translated and reprinted across the world. That work, however, formed only the first three of the ten volumes of his published writings. This is significant because, despite the importance of *On War*, it can be difficult to understand and decipher. This is where Clausewitz's historical writing and analysis play an exceptionally important role, as he maintained that his foundational writing helped him think through and more clearly form his theoretical understanding of war, and that the process of so doing was difficult.[1] Therefore, our neglect of his historical analysis, when attempting to understand *On War*, impedes our understanding of his main theoretical writing. This is criminally negligent (as Clausewitz might have put it), since he spent a great deal of time analyzing the conflicts he fought in and creating, in the process, the theoretical underpinnings of *On War*. Thus, by reading and analyzing his histories of the series of wars from 1789 to 1815, the reader can hope to understand *On War* more fully.

What Clausewitz tells us about his historical writing is important, and he addresses this in several of his notes. In *To an Unpublished Manuscript on the Theory of War* (according to Howard and Paret, this was written between 1816 and 1818), Clausewitz criticizes past military writers for their lack of effective analysis of the evidence—that is, the history.[2] He goes further in *On the Genesis of His Early Manuscript on the Theory of War*, where he states:

The manner in which Montesquieu dealt with his subject is vaguely in my mind.[3] I thought that such concise, aphoristic chapters, which at the outset

---

1. Jan Willem Honig, "Clausewitz and the Politics of Early Modern Warfare," in *Clausewitz the State and War*, ed. Andreas Herberg-Rothe, Jan Willem Honig, and Daniel Moran (Stuttgart: Franz Steiner Verlag, 2011), 29–48.

2. Carl von Clausewitz, *On War*, ed. and trans. Michael Howard and Peter Paret (Princeton, NJ: Princeton University Press, 1989), 61.

3. If one looks at Montesquieu's *De l'Esprit des Loix*, one can see its resemblance to the structure of *On War*. The work is broken down into multiple smaller books, with each book consisting of multiple smaller chapters, all punctuated with analysis and historical examples.

I simply wanted to call kernels, would attract the intelligent reader by what they suggested as much as by what they expressed; in other words, I had an intelligent reader in mind, who was already familiar with the subject. . . . From the studies I wrote on various topics in order to gain a clear and complete understanding of them, I managed for a time to lift only the most important conclusions and thus concentrate their essence in smaller compass. But eventually my tendency completely ran away with me; I elaborated as much as I could, and of course now had in mind a reader who was not yet acquainted with the subject.[4]

In other words, his histories and other writings were fundamental to the development of his understanding of war, and it seems reasonable to assume that this would also be the case for a reader unfamiliar with the topic. In his *Note of 10 July 1827* and an unfinished note possibly from 1830,[5] Clausewitz again drives home the point about historical study underpinning his work: "If critics would go to the trouble of thinking about the subject for years on end and testing each conclusion against the actual history of war, as I have done, they would undoubtedly be more careful of what they said."[6] With this criticism ringing in our ears, perhaps it is time to introduce Clausewitz's histories to a broader audience so that they too might benefit from his historical analysis and the testing of his theoretical models against the campaigns themselves. Indeed, that is our primary motivation for translating this work.

It is now important to discuss the text we chose to use: the original version published in 1833.[7] We made this choice because it reduced the chance of encountering the changes and errors sometimes found in subsequent publications. It is also the version of the work sanctioned by Clausewitz's widow, Marie von Clausewitz. Although she did not edit the work herself, she did rely on trusted family friend Major Franz August O'Etzel, who was familiar with Clausewitz's writings, to compile them for publication as the fifth and sixth volumes of the planned ten volumes (the first three volumes being *On War* itself).[8] Major O'Etzel stringently denied making edits to the text, so if we take him at his word (and we have no reason not to), the text is largely as

---

4. Clausewitz, *On War*, 63. Howard and Paret date this note between 1816 and 1818.
5. Howard and Paret believe it to be from 1830. See Clausewitz, *On War*, 70.
6. Clausewitz, *On War*, 70.
7. Carl von Clausewitz, *Die Feldzüge von 1799 in Italien und der Schweiz*, 2 vols. (Berlin: Ferdinand Dümmler, 1833).
8. See Marie von Clausewitz's preface in Clausewitz, *On War*, 65–67.

Clausewitz left it.⁹ Thus, it is ideal for our purpose of using it as a tool to better understand *On War*.

For readers interested in digging deeper into Clausewitz's use of history to support his theoretical understanding of war, and perhaps to aid researchers attempting to date the various parts of his work, we would like to suggest some key concepts for cross-referencing: objects and their value, *Anschauung*, culmination, and *Schwerpunkt*. These are key words and ideas in Clausewitz's writing, and they appear here in the context in which he thought about them. As such, their use here is extremely helpful for understanding their actual meaning.

In the translators' note we describe our approach to the translation, and we had much the same ethos when it came to our editors' commentary and analysis. When we use modern terms such as "combat power," the intention is to make the text more accessible rather than to provide an exact replication of Clausewitz's words. We have also cross-referenced the text with *On War* and have attempted to explain what Clausewitz's theoretical ideas mean in relation to the campaign history that is the focus of this work. As such, we hope to make *On War* itself more understandable and usable for students and scholars alike.

For completeness, we have cross-referenced our translation of Clausewitz's campaign history with those of Archduke Charles and Antoine Jomini.[10] These two writers were contemporaries of Clausewitz, and they are considered (both then and now) the other main thinkers about war during the relevant period. Furthermore, Clausewitz used their work to inform his own, and it seemed reasonable to check the veracity of what he claimed they did or said. Thus, comparing their views is illuminating both when they agree and when they do not. We believe that the commentary on and cross-referencing of their work can aid the reader in understanding Clausewitz's history by encouraging critical reflection on Clausewitz's own remarks. In addition, many of the arch-

---

9. Clausewitz, *Die Feldzüge von 1799 in Italien und der Schweiz*, 1:viii. See also Vanya Eftimova Bellinger, *Marie von Clausewitz: The Woman behind the Making of On War* (Oxford: Oxford University Press, 2016), 230; Marie von Clausewitz, "Vorrede zum Dritte Theil," in Carl von Clausewitz, *Vom Kriege*, 3 vols. (Berlin: Ferdinand Dümmler, 1832–1834) 3:v–vi.

10. Karl Erzherzog von Österreich, *Geschichte des Feldzuges von 1799 in Deutschland und in der Schweiz*, 3 vols. (Vienna: Anton Strauss, 1814); Lieutenant-Général [Antoine] Jomini, *Histoire Critique et Militaire des Guerres de la Révolution*, 15 vols. (Paris: Chez Anselin et Pochard, 1819–1824).

duke's and Jomini's notes include valuable historical details that either correct Clausewitz's errors or add information to provide a more complete account.

Editorial commentary is not limited to Clausewitz's theory. We have also tried to make the campaign narrative clearer and, where possible, to fill in gaps in our knowledge of the campaign's history. As part of these efforts, we refer to other published histories to make the narrative more accurate. All of the above was done to help the reader better understand what Clausewitz was really trying to say, both here and in *On War*. Our hope is to encourage discussion of this important historical work and to provide a base so that more people will be able to access Clausewitz's writing and understand his ideas.

Original Editor's Note

The kind mention of my assistance with the publication of this work[1] has occasioned the misapprehension here and there that this constituted a kind of editing. This is by no means the case; the legacy of this immortal gentleman who was held in such high regard, and whose premature demise must fill every Prussian heart with the deepest sorrow, was reproduced *without a single word added or struck out*, and my collaboration consisted entirely in correcting the proofs.

For the printing of the fourth volume (the 1796 campaign)[2] and this present fifth volume, however, I was prevented from doing so by my duties elsewhere, and the business had to be taken care of by a proofreader, who indeed eliminated the actual printing errors with great care, but who, being from another profession, lacked full familiarity with many of the names appearing in these volumes, hence the errors noted here remained.[3]

The publication of the operational maps for these volumes has been delayed by my absence, but they are now close to completion.

O'Etzel[4]

1. See Carl von Clausewitz, *Hinterlassene Werke des Generals Carl von Clausewitz über Krieg und Kriegführung*, 10 vols. (Berlin: Ferdinand Dümmler, 1832), 1:xii.

2. For a recent translation, see Carl von Clausewitz, *Napoleon's 1796 Italian Campaign*, trans. and ed. Nicholas Murray and Christopher Pringle (Lawrence: University Press of Kansas, 2018).

3. The original editor's note included an errata. These errors were mostly typographical and have been corrected in this translation.

4. Major Franz August O'Etzel was a longtime friend of Clausewitz and his wife, Marie, and he assisted her with the publication of her husband's writings after Clausewitz's death in 1831. Major O'Etzel went on to become a key proponent of the use of the telegraph in Prussia and became the first Prussian telegraph director. See Vanya Eftimova Bellinger, *Marie von Clausewitz: The Woman behind the Making of* On War (Oxford: Oxford University Press, 2016), 166.

Clausewitz's Introduction

The two campaigns conducted in Italy and Switzerland in 1799 cannot be separated without depriving them of much of their interest and comprehensibility, because they are so bound together by events and by their effects on each other.[1]

Collectively, they are among the most significant and richest in lessons of any campaigns in the history of warfare. In them, we see four commanders of great repute in action: Suvorov, Archduke Charles, Moreau, and Masséna.[2] Among the generals in the next tier, Lecourbe, Macdonald, Joubert, Soult, Championnet, and Dessoles on the one side and Kray, Melas, Hotze, and Bagration on the other are pretty much the best that both armies had to offer. As for events, we have seven major battles, three opposed river crossings, and a large number of mountain positions in the highest regions of the Alps contested by the most determined attacks and the most steadfast defense. Finally, we have the passage of an army through the St. Gotthard region, held and defended by the enemy, who, after being driven back initially, seals the natural

---

1. It is interesting and enlightening to compare Clausewitz's introduction with Archduke Charles's in his own history of the campaign. The archduke is more concerned with demonstrating that "the laws of a science only become clear and productive when one takes them back to their source—experience, and provides proof of their application in real-life events. Without theory even the most experienced man remains incapable of comprehending the connections between multifarious manifestations from an area of a practical science, to develop its causes and consequences further, to solve apparent contradictions, to identify the leading principle in its entire purity and to honour the deed in line with its true content: but theoretical knowledge alone does not yet teach us to fill in the chasm between knowledge and action." He goes on to state: "Political influences had to be touched on to the extent that they determined the choice and running of the operations but the appraisal of them lies outside this writer's plan. It restricts itself to assessing the war in line with the laws of science involved and the art, and leaves it to the future to one day lift the veil covering the political motivations. Posterity will then decide whether they deserved to take precedence over the military considerations." Karl Erzherzog von Österreich, *Geschichte des Feldzuges von 1799 in Deutschland und in der Schweiz*, 3 vols. (Vienna: Anton Strauss, 1814), 1:iv–vi.

2. Rather than introduce these individuals here, we do so when they first appear in Clausewitz's main text.

exits like a growing avalanche piling up and obliges the army to seek another way out by winding through the steepest of rocky gorges.

These campaigns, born from the fresh force of a new coalition and furious outrage, are notable in that, through the pettifogging political differences that were clearly present, they soon led to tension, then to misfortune, and thereby to the rapid dissolution of the coalition.[3]

---

[3]. We wait until Clausewitz analyzes these campaigns and their political origins in more detail before commenting on his thoughts, except to say that we broadly agree.

1. General Situation
Opening of the Campaign in Germany. The French Take Graubündten. Archduke Charles Beats Jourdan at Stockach.

1 POLITICAL SITUATION AT THE START OF THE CAMPAIGN[1]

In autumn 1797, soon after the peace of Campo Formio,[2] the French had vacated Austrian territory and retreated behind the Rhine in Germany and the Adige in Italy, where it constituted the border between the Austrian states and the Cisalpine Republic.

The Austrians had occupied Venice and its Lombard provinces and deployed their troops in three large bodies. The first was in Italy on the Adige, the second in the Tyrol, and the third, the so-called Reichs-Contingent,[3] between the Isar and the Lech.

This was the situation when negotiations to conclude peace between France and the Holy Roman Empire began at the Second Congress of Rastatt. In a secret article of the Treaty of Campo Formio, the Austrians had agreed

---

1. In a striking contrast with Clausewitz, Archduke Charles wrote roughly 650 words on the political and military strategic situation leading up to war in his history of the campaign. It is largely a narrative description with little in the way of analysis. But he used approximately 7,800 words to describe and analyze the physical terrain and the campaigning options presented by it. In sum, it is very much the product of eighteenth-century military thinking, with lines of operations, secure bases, and a dominant role for fortresses, and with the key to the theater being largely determined by physical geographical considerations. See Karl Erzherzog von Österreich, *Geschichte des Feldzuges von 1799 in Deutschland und in der Schweiz*, 3 vols. (Vienna: Anton Strauss, 1814), 1:1–41, especially 30–33; hereafter cited as Karl.

2. The Treaty of Campo Formio, 27 October 1797, marked a substantial change in the balance of power on Austria's western frontier. For an excellent analysis of Austrian strategy and the role of the frontier and buffer states, see A. Wess Mitchell, *The Grand Strategy of the Habsburg Empire* (Princeton, NJ: Princeton University Press, 2018).

3. This was the name given to the contributory forces of the Holy Roman Empire's states in Germany.

to abandon the left bank of the Rhine and to withhold all their troops, except for the Reichs-Contingent, if the German princes were not willing to consent to the secularization of ecclesiastical territory as substantial compensation for this. The French did not want to hand over the state of Venice to the Austrians until they themselves had occupied Mainz.[4] In December the Austrians relinquished Mainz, and its elector, whose garrison numbered just 3,000 men, found himself obliged to consent to the order to hand it over if he did not want to see his land suffer from enemy action again and find himself driven out of Aschaffenburg. Thus, this German bulwark fell into French hands without a single blow being struck. The surrender of Ehrenbreitstein ensued a few weeks later in similar circumstances.[5]

It is debatable whether Austria just hoped that the peace of Campo Formio would give it time to summon strength for a new war and forge new alliances, bringing such force to bear against France that a positive outcome could be expected, or whether it leaned toward the idea of actually joining with France, of not only making good its losses but even expanding at the expense of lesser princes, or at least putting itself in good shape by forming a temporary alliance with France and developing its power to match that of the French—power that could later be used to either continue alongside them *al pari* [as equals] or take them on again.

---

4. This was a key city and fortress guarding the confluence of the Rhine and Main Rivers, as well as an important bridge across the Rhine.

5. This was an important fortress that guarded the confluence and crossing points of the Moselle and Rhine Rivers, as well as the confluence of the Lahn River and the Rhine. The French siege of this fortress had continued throughout the Congress of Rastatt and culminated in the garrison's surrender at the end of January 1799. This is especially pertinent for a number of reasons. The garrison had resisted almost four years of French attempts to capture the fortress. The position of the fortress gave the French an important crossing point and base of operations on the middle Rhine, which allowed the French to threaten the southern flank of any potential Prussian advance into Holland or to counter any Austrian or Prussian moves into the central or southern German princely states. Baron Franz Maria Thugut, Austria's minister for foreign affairs from 1793 to 1800, considered the fortress extremely important because it formed part of the main defense line against potential French aggression into Germany. Thus its loss was keenly felt. See Karl A. Roider Jr., *Baron Thugut and Austria's Response to the French Revolution* (Princeton, NJ: Princeton University Press, 1987), 128, 193; Piers Macksey, *Statesmen at War: The Strategy of Overthrow 1798–1799* (London: Longman Group, 1974), 64–65, 150–151.

When we consider what kind of men these were, dealing with the emotional impact of a long and unsuccessful war and having failed in their aims by one course and now obliged to pursue a completely opposite one, then it is highly probable that in the Austrian cabinet the former of these two views predominated at first, and the other was preferred later.[6]

6. Here it is worth bringing *On War* into the discussion, as it relates not only to this paragraph but also to those that follow. For consistency, throughout this volume we supply book, chapter, and page references to the most popular translated version—Carl von Clausewitz, *On War*, ed. and trans. Michael Howard and Peter Paret (Princeton, NJ: Princeton University Press, 1989)—so readers can compare other translations or Clausewitz's original version. Clausewitz is referencing the "primordial violence, hatred and enmity, which are to be regarded as a blind natural force" (book 1, chap. 1, p. 89), an element of his wondrous or fickle trinity. This was discussed in Carl von Clausewitz, *Napoleon's 1796 Italian Campaign*, trans. and ed. Nicholas Murray and Christopher Pringle (Lawrence: University Press of Kansas, 2018), 57–58n23. For the reader's convenience, that note is reproduced here: "This section is interesting because it discusses the elements of Clausewitz's 'paradoxical trinity' [see also 44n53]. This is an important discussion, and it is worth quoting Clausewitz at length and from different translators as well as the original German: 'War is more than a true chameleon that slightly adapts characteristics to the given case. As a total phenomenon its dominant tendencies always make war a paradoxical trinity—composed of primordial violence, hatred, and enmity, which are to be regarded as blind natural force; of the play of chance and probability within which the creative spirit is free to roam; and of its element of subordination, as an instrument of policy, which makes it subject to reason alone.' Clausewitz, *On War*, 89. . . . Comparing this with another translation gives the reader a broader understanding of the original language and the variations in translation: 'War is therefore, not only a veritable chameleon, because in each concrete case it changes somewhat its character, but it is also, when regarded as a whole, in relation to the tendencies predominating in it, a strange trinity, composed of the original violence of its essence, the hate and enmity which are to be regarded as a blind, natural impulse, of the play of probabilities and chance, which make it a free activity of the emotions, and of the subordinate character of a political tool, through which it belongs to the province of pure intelligence.' Carl von Clausewitz, *On War*, trans. O. J. Matthijs Jolles (New York: Modern Library, 2000), 282. In the original German, it reads: '*Der Krieg ist also nicht nur ein wahres Chamäleon, weil er in jedem konkreten Falle seine Natur etwas ändert, sondern er ist auch seinen Gesamterscheinungen nach, in Beziehung auf die in ihm herrschenden Tendenzen, eine wunderliche Dreifaltigkeit, zusammengesetzt aus der ursprünglichen Gewaltsamkeit seines Elementes, dem Haß und der Feindschaft, die wie ein blinder Naturtrieb anzusehen sind, aus dem Spiel der Wahrscheinlichkeiten und des Zufalls, die ihn zu einer freien Seelentätigkeit machen, und aus*

The French government, being subject to constant changes in personnel and circumstance, and being prone to passion, could hardly arrive at a consistent view of the political situation and a firm plan. It was always ruled by expediency and the spur of the moment. At the time of the peace of Campo Formio, France showed Prussia the utmost coldness and contemptuous indifference. As for Austria, after its unsuccessful alliance with Prussia, it was only to be expected that its old resentment and envy toward that power would stir anew. Thus, at the start of the Second Congress of Rastatt, it very much appeared as if both belligerents, France and Austria, were occupied with the thought of lording it over Prussia next, and that in this they might find something approaching a common aim. At least, that is the only way one can ex-

---

der untergeordneten Natur eines politischen Werkzeuges, wodurch er dem bloßen Verstande anheimfällt.' Clausewitz, *Vom Kriege*, 1:31. The word *wunderliche* is more closely related to 'wondrous' or 'whimsical' or 'strange' than it is to 'paradoxical.' Although some combination of these terms might provide the best meaning for the purpose of understanding Clausewitz's concept, that would be too clumsy and impractical. Furthermore, the word 'paradox' is often associated with something contradictory or absurd, but we do not think Clausewitz's concept is contradictory. Neither do the words 'strange' and 'wondrous,' in and of themselves, capture the whole meaning in its context. Anders Palmgren recently argued that 'fickle trinity' best conveys Clausewitz's meaning, and his version certainly captures the randomness and arbitrariness of war, albeit without some of the magical connotation of 'wondrous.' In this work, we have chosen to use the phrase 'wondrous or fickle trinity,' as these adjectives together best capture Clausewitz's original meaning, especially if one considers the changeable and unpredictable nature of war itself; when we use the word 'trinity,' we are referring specifically to his wondrous or fickle trinity. Some of Clausewitz's analysis of the political problems in Italy is influenced by his trinity concept. In addition, Clausewitz seems to be poking fun at the Italians for their faith (later to be sadly disappointed) in Napoleon and the promises of the revolution. With these thoughts in mind, it is necessary to provide some degree of clarity: Clausewitz's trinity comprises three parts; these parts are closely related and cannot be separated, hence the trinitarian nature of the concept: that is, they are three in one. For a helpful analysis of Clausewitz's trinity, see Christopher Bassford, 'Tip-Toe through the Trinity: The Strange Persistence of Trinitarian Warfare,' . . . https://www.clausewitz.com/mobile/trinity8.htm. See also Hew Strachan and Andreas Herberg-Rothe, eds., *Clausewitz in the Twenty-First Century* (Oxford: Oxford University Press, 2007); Hew Strachan, *Clausewitz's On War: A Biography* (New York: Atlantic Monthly Press, 2007), 176–190; Anders Palmgren, 'Visions of Strategy: Following Clausewitz's Train of Thought' (doctoral diss., National Defence University, Helsinki, 2014), 352–353."

plain the contempt they both showed for Prussia during the first half of the Rastatt Congress, whereas later they were both soliciting it as an ally.

But as unprincipled and irresponsible as the French government was and had to be, and given the French people's innate arrogance, which was naturally greatly increased by military victories and by their state of elation, there could be no question of the peaceful pursuit of a reasonable aim.[7] Before there could be any thought of a general or continent-wide peace or the definitive establishment of a new political settlement—before the Rastatt Congress had taken even a single significant step—the spirit of the Revolution and the turbulence of the French people led to such steps as in other times any one of them alone would have been sufficient to stir the whole of Europe into action.

As early as January 1798, the French invaded Switzerland to transform that country into a democratic republic, thereby making it a French vassal state and seizing its treasury and arsenals. It is easy to see how this act could have resulted as much from political fanaticism as from a quest for domination. After some battles and bloodshed, the new republic was established (with the exception of Graubündten, which had thrown itself into the arms of Austria), but this generated such a spirit of resistance that the new state could be considered less an ally than a subject, and the slight aid France obtained from the new government was worth less than the hostile tensions that arose everywhere and resulted in bloody unrest in some places.

At the same time, the French general Duphot, from Lucien Bonaparte's delegation in Rome, was murdered during popular unrest, which obliged

---

7. Here the reader can jump straight to book 1, chap. 1, of *On War*, as well as book 1, chap. 2, on "Purpose and Means in War." A reasonable aim implies that at least one side involved in a conflict has an aim that is limited in scope and therefore reasonably achievable in terms of the force required. If the enemy also accepts the reasonable nature of this aim, it is less likely to resist strongly. As such, for a reasonable aim to be truly reasonable, both sides have to agree to its reasonableness. If the understanding of one of the parties differs in any significant way, what seems to be a reasonable aim to one side might require a fight to the death by the other side. For example, the fortress at Ehrenbreitstein was crucial to the defense of the German states and the Hapsburg Empire. As such, even though it was only one fortress among many, its possession had great value, particularly to the Hapsburgs. Thus, it is reasonable to assume that they would be willing to risk and spend more to recapture it than the French would be to keep it. However, as Clausewitz points out, when passion is involved in decision making, reasonable demands and ideas might not be rationally assessed as such. Hence the calculus for war is subject to change, along with the risk for escalation.

Berthier[8] to invade Rome, to let an opposing popular movement proclaim the Roman Republic, and to force the pope himself to retire to Tuscany.

A few months later, in May 1798, Bonaparte set sail with 45,000 men to conquer Egypt. He began this expedition by taking Malta. This did not really affect Austria, and because England was already a hostile power, it did not need to be treated with any particular care. Still, the interests of two hitherto neutral powers—namely, Turkey and Russia—were so damaged by this act that they allied with England in its war against France. Tsar Paul's affection for the Order of Malta, encouraged by his mother Catherine from an early age, led him to declare himself the order's protector. He was so enraged by this conquest of Malta, which breached international law and destroyed the very core of the order's existence, that this sole reason was enough for him to ally against France, and so was perhaps the main foundation of the Second Coalition. It is certainly quite remarkable that this mere accessory to a greater crime—as the seizure of Malta must be seen, in comparison to the conquering of Egypt—gave rise to a much greater series of events than the crime itself.[9] Upon his accession to the throne in 1796, Paul had declined to fulfill the obligation Catherine had incurred to commit 60,000 men to the alliance against France. Thus, when he joined that alliance a year later with 100,000 men, this can only be ascribed to the conquest of Malta, and it is very much an open question whether Austria would have embarked on a new war without Paul's participation.

It is easy to see that these three major acts of arrogance and criminality must have entirely eliminated any chance of peace. Admittedly, the Austrian government tried to reach agreement on the main points of contention in special conferences at Selz in Alsace, initiated by its foreign minister Count

---

8. Léonard Duphot (1763–1797) was killed on 27 December 1797. Alexandre Berthier (1753–1815) went on to become Napoleon's chief of staff. He led the invasion of the Papal States and marched into Rome on 10 February 1798. The biographies of the main French participants are from Napoléon Bonaparte, *Correspondance Générale*, 15 vols. (Paris: Publiée par la Fondation Napoléon, Librairie Arthéme Fayard, 2004–2018). For a brief description of this incident, see Charles J. Esdaile, *The Wars of the French Revolution 1792–1801* (New York: Routledge, 2019), 168–169.

9. This is critical to understanding the meaning of purpose and means in war, as well as the value of the conflict's objectives. Changes in the strategic circumstances that one side might find reasonable can and often do provoke a commensurate response by enemies, real or potential, that are threatened by said change. Any such change requires a reassessment of the object being sought and a recalculation of the value of said object, as well as of the means being used to attain it. *On War*, book 1, chaps. 1 and 2.

Cobenzl[10] with former French director François de Neufchateau in connection with the assault on French emissary General Bernadotte[11] in Vienna in May, but this was unsuccessful. This is not surprising, since the expedition to Egypt did not set off until after the conference had begun, and nothing could have emboldened the Austrians more than this event. On the one hand, the expedition recruited a couple of new enemies for France; on the other, it removed 45,000 of France's best troops, the conquest could be expected to require great effort to secure it, and it took away the commander who was probably perceived as the most direct and effective cause of Austria's total loss of the military balance.[12]

From this time onward, June 1798, one can only regard Austria as being intent on renewing resistance, and the continuation of the Rastatt Congress was a mere charade.

The Austrian government did everything possible to restore its fighting power to a sound footing and concluded a treaty with Russia according to which Suvorov[13] was to join the Austrian army with 50,000 men. The first column of these troops appeared at the Galician frontier in August.

---

10. Clausewitz made an error here, albeit a forgivable one, as Count Cobenzl was foreign minister before and after Baron Thugut, who served from 1793 until 1800. That being said, according to the national biographical dictionary, Cobenzl was directly responsible for negotiations at Campo Formio and Rastatt. When Thugut took over after Cobenzl's short tenure, things were a mess, which makes it even more surprising that Cobenzl apparently had the emperor's ear. This might go some way to explaining the lack of clarity in Austria's thinking about the impending conflict. It also ties in nicely with Clausewitz's thoughts on friction in *On War*, book 1, chap. 7. For all Austrian biographies, see Dr. Constant von Wurzbach, *Biographisches Lexikon des Kaiserthums Oesterreich*, 60 vols. (Vienna: Universitäts Buchruderei von L. E. Zamarski, 1856–1891). See also Roider, *Baron Thugut and Austria's Response*, 97, 126–127.

11. Jean Baptiste Jules Bernadotte (1763–1844) had a distinguished career in the French army before switching his allegiance to Sweden. He was another successful commander who provoked Bonaparte's ire.

12. This ties in nicely with Clausewitz's discussion of the result of war never being final in *On War*, book 1, chap. 1. Austria, threatened by the extension of French power, was looking for an opportunity to right the wrongs against it, and this presented a seemingly perfect opportunity to do so. That the Austrians failed in their endeavors during the War of the Second Coalition, despite apparently ideal conditions for war, should give the reader pause.

13. Alexander Suvorov (1730–1800) is often cited as Russia's greatest military commander. He was an intellectual and dynamic soldier right up to his death in 1800, in

In another treaty concluded with England toward the end of the year, the tsar[14] promised that if Prussia could be persuaded to join the coalition, he would add 45,000 men to its army, but in the event Prussia did not join, the two powers would take other measures to create a diversion. Consequently, they signed a convention in June 1799, under which they would undertake a joint invasion of Holland with 18,000 Russians and 13,000 British troops.

Russia and England now sought to bring about a rapprochement between Austria and Prussia and to persuade the latter power to join a new coalition, but in vain.

Finally, the Russian tsar concluded alliances with the Sublime Porte and the king of Naples, which admittedly had no direct influence on the 1799 campaign. However, after the main French forces quit lower Italy, the fortresses there were retaken from the French, and both of the republics the French had established were overthrown.

Since October 1797, the king of Naples had been at peace with France, but the escalations by that state during the course of 1798, and particularly the establishment of the Roman Republic, naturally must have caused the Neapolitan government very justified concern. It therefore entered into a new alliance with Austria, England, and Russia; decided to take a very active part in the new war; and increased its forces to 60,000 men. Of course, this could not be kept hidden from the French Directory, so the court of Naples feared that it might be attacked at any moment by the French forces in the Roman Republic and on the Po. This seemed even more likely because allowing the victorious Admiral Nelson[15] into Naples harbor on his way back from Aboukir Bay[16] was in breach

---

contrast to many of his contemporaries from Russia and Austria, who seem to have been almost universally slow moving and slow witted. See K. Ospinov, *Alexander Suvorov*, trans. Edith Bone (London: Hutchinson, 1944); Philip Longworth, *The Art of Victory* (New York: Holt, Rinehart & Winston, 1965).

14. This was Paul I of Russia, who reigned from 1796 to 1801, when he was assassinated by former Russian officers. It is quite likely that the assassins were working in conjunction with Paul's son, who became Tsar Alexander I after Paul's murder. It is worth bearing in mind how the conspiratorial nature of Russian court politics affected Russian decision making during the campaigns discussed here.

15. Admiral Horatio Nelson (1758–1805) of Trafalgar fame.

16. This is often referred to as the battle of the Nile, 1–2 August 1798. During this action, Nelson destroyed the French fleet supporting Napoleon's operations in Egypt, thus increasing his already significant influence in Naples. As such, it is no surprise

of one of the terms of the October peace treaty with France. The English, for their part, having thus laid a mine under Naples, considered it to be in their interest to detonate it toward the end of 1798 because they still lacked confidence in the Austrian government and feared that it might reach a new accommodation with France. If, in addition, we consider the forceful personal influence of Nelson, the usual misrepresentation of the great advantages of the offensive, and the prospect—highly attractive to a pious king and a scheming queen, each for reasons of their own—of a glorious restoration of the Papal States, then it is understandable how the king of Naples was persuaded, against the Austrians' advice, to begin the war with an attack on the French troops around Rome at the end of November 1798, even though it could be foreseen that the Austrians would not begin their campaign before April of the following year. We say: seen in this light, this apparently incomprehensible event becomes to some degree explicable, although, of course, far from excusable. Perhaps if the Neapolitan army had been better led and more effective, one might reasonably have expected it to advance victoriously as far as the Po; but there it was bound to encounter an equivalent force, and then, given the superior French morale, which would not be easily lost, and the decisiveness of the French commanders, one could hardly expect the French to settle for equilibrium there. Rather, a powerful reaction could be anticipated, which, given the numerical superiority the French would gradually obtain, must necessarily carry them to Naples and put that state's very existence on the mainland at stake, for which three or four months would be more than long enough.[17]

But as it turned out, the actual events were far worse than the projections above. The 40,000 Neapolitans who went onto the attack under Mack[18] at the end of November were beaten at every point by half their number of French

---

that Nelson was able to persuade the king of Naples to attack the French position in Egypt, given that one of the best French armies, along with its leader, had just been stranded there.

17. The Neapolitan calculation of a relatively easy victory turned into a war for the state's very existence. Hence, Clausewitz's argument for carefully thinking through the objective of the conflict and the likely enemy reaction is critical to achieving success, assuming all things are equal. *On War*, book 1, chaps. 1 and 2.

18. Karl Mack von Leiberich (1752–1828) had seen success prior to 1798 but is most famous for being the officer in charge of Austrian troops at the capitulation of Ulm in 1805, for which he was tried and convicted of cowardice.

under Championnet,[19] without enjoying even the tiniest of victories. After four weeks, the king was obliged to abandon his mainland provinces to the republicanizing French, who established the Parthenopean Republic at the end of January, after a short interlude of *Lazzaroni* rule.[20]

With that, one of the allies and its force of an estimated 40,000 men had already disappeared from the stage. But of course, one might ask whether the French power was not weakened just as much by the extended deployment they were thereby forced to adopt.

In December, while Championnet was putting an end to the kingdom of Naples, the French Directory sent its troops under Joubert to invade Piedmont and effectively forced King Charles Emmanuel[21] to give up his rule over this duchy, transfer his subjects' allegiance to France, and retire with his family to Sardinia. There was no particular political motive for this crime. The French government just felt more comfortable and secure having possession of this natural base for the Italian theater of war, rather than knowing that it was in the hands of a dubious ally.

Since 1795, the grand duchy of Tuscany had not been at war with France and probably would have gladly asserted its neutrality during the impending coalition as well, except that the French did not give it that choice. France declared war on it and Austria at the same time.

Apart from the Grand Duke of Tuscany, the Duke of Parma ruled the only one of the former Italian states that was left. Spain was allied to France, so as a Spanish prince, he likewise counted as one of its allies.

All the rest of the Italian states were fused together as the Cisalpine Republic. This comprised Milan, Mantua, Modena, that part of Venetian territory on the western[22] side of the Adige, the Veltlin, and the three Papal Legations

---

19. Jean-Étienne Vachier Championnet (1762–1800) had a short but distinguished career before dying of disease early in 1800.

20. The *Lazzaroni* were the lowest of the low class and were not particularly supportive of the monarchy in Naples, but they were fiercely anti-French. As such, they ferociously resisted French republican rule, rising up and running bloody riot through Naples for ten days. Esdaile, *Wars of the French Revolution*, 216–217.

21. This is King Charles Emmanuel IV of Sardinia (1751–1819). He had previously surrendered Piedmont to the French in 1796 during Napoleon's campaign in Italy. See Clausewitz, *Napoleon's 1796 Italian Campaign*, 55–59.

22. Clausewitz wrote "the left," but that is clearly wrong: since the Adige flows south, that would be the east side. This was likely a typographical error.

of Bologna, Ferrara, and Ravenna, constituting a state of three or four million people. Of course, its internal organization was still coming into being, and it could do very little as an independent state.

Thus one could regard France as having uncontested possession of the whole of Italy, though of course, not in such a way that it could generate significant combat forces from it.

On the other hand, France had no allies among the European great powers apart from Spain, which had no influence on the 1799 campaign.

Austria, Russia, England, Sicily, and Turkey found themselves in coalition. Of the German [Holy Roman] Empire, all the northern princes had individual peace treaties with France, and since the French army's advance in 1797, so did most of the southern ones as well. The whole extent of the imperial participation comprised a few insignificant Reichs-Contingents, which maintained garrisons in Philippsburg, Mannheim, and Würzburg.[23]

For Russia's part, only 50,000 men belonged to its actual allied contingent. Beyond that, there was what Russia and England would do jointly, but while this brought a similar force into action, it would not have the same weight in the balance, since it was to be used against the extreme flanks (Holland and Naples), where its impact would only take effect later and more uncertainly.

Turkey and Sicily could scarcely be of any account in the 1799 campaign.

Thus, it was only the Austrian forces and the 50,000 Russians that were definitely to be reckoned with.

This was the political situation of the protagonists in the month of February 1799, when both sides had become convinced that war was unavoidable, but Austria still wanted to delay the affair for a while to allow the Russians to arrive.

So, after a two-year cease-fire, the moment for a great European war had arrived once more.

The previous six-year war had cost Austria the loss of Belgium, Holland, the left bank of the Rhine, and the whole of upper Italy. During these six years, there had been no lack of individually successful actions and campaigns, and military honors appeared to be even. The loss of territory could be seen—not without justification—as a consequence of political tensions and differences of interest among the allies.

---

23. Philippsburg and Mannheim formed part of the main defensive line against potential French aggression into Germany. See Roider, *Baron Thugut and Austria's Response*, 128.

The new war seemed to begin in favorable circumstances for Austria and its allies. Austria had raised its effective forces to a level they had never attained in any of the previous campaigns. Two distinguished commanders would lead the armies: Suvorov, famous for his energy, and Archduke Charles, who had elevated himself to the ranks of the most talented commanders by his 1796 campaign. The French, by contrast, had weakened their forces by stretching them hugely in every direction, because the countries they incorporated provided no significant addition to their strength. Their three most distinguished commanders—Pichegru, Moreau, and Bonaparte[24]—were absent, and the Directory was weak and threatened by party strife.

These were certainly very great advantages and sufficient for a successful war, provided there was good housekeeping—that is, if the available means were used with intelligence and energy, and if both time and troops were used economically until the situation changed. But this intensity of operations can be achieved only through two means: either through the energy of one individual who stands at the pinnacle of it all—keeping the aim constantly in sight, he alone supervising and ordering the use of each of the major forces, watching over them all operating simultaneously, and spurring on any that hangs back—or through an enthusiasm for the object of the struggle that sweeps everyone on. Both these means were lacking in the new coalition. The constable's sword was replaced by the quill of the Aulic Council, with "mindless routine" emblazoned on its banner.

---

24. Jean-Charles Pichegru (1761–1804) had distinguished himself in the 1794 campaign in the Netherlands, only to fall from favor later due to his involvement in a royalist plot against the Directory in Paris. He was in exile in French Guyana during the campaigns and eventually died in a French prison (probably murdered). Jean Victor Moreau (1763–1813), a comrade of Pichegru, was also implicated in the plot and had been dismissed from service. He was later reinstated when his talents were required because Napoleon Bonaparte was still absent in Egypt. Moreau was later banished from French service after crossing Bonaparte. Thus, France was missing three good generals when war broke out in earnest.

2 STRENGTHS AND POSITIONS OF THE COMBAT FORCES

The Austrians

[See the accompanying table.][25]

The French

The Army of the Danube under Jourdan's overall command: 38,000 men
The Army of Observation under Bernadotte on the middle Rhine, excluding fortress garrisons: 10,000
   Masséna[26] in Switzerland under Jourdan's overall command: 30,000
   Schérer in upper Italy: 60,000
Total: 138,000 men, of which about 20,000 were cavalry.[27]

This was approximately the situation of those forces that were already in contact and that both sides could bring to bear for a decision. It gives the Austrians a superiority of about 117,000 men overall, but especially in cavalry, of which they had more than twice as many.[28]

---

25. Jomini provides similar numbers to those given by Clausewitz. It is worth pointing out that any discrepancies are relatively minor and might relate to their respective source material, the dates of the army returns themselves, or some combination of the above. Lieutenant-Général [Antoine] Jomini, *Histoire Critique et Militaire des Guerres de la Révolution*, 15 vols. (Paris: Chez Anselin et Pochard, 1819–1824), 11:95–96; hereafter cited as Jomini.

26. André Masséna (1758–1817) was one of Napoleon's best marshals and was a good general in his own right.

27. Here the archduke's numbers differ from Clausewitz's. He credits the French with 174,000 men overall, with 48,000 in fortress garrisons. Karl, 1:52–54.

28. This was potentially very important, given the vital role of cavalry in reconnaissance. However, the extensive use of light infantry by the French probably offset any such Austrian advantage to some extent. In addition, assuming an Austrian advantage in reconnaissance assumes that the Austrians routinely and effectively used their cavalry for this purpose. A more significant difference relates to cavalry's role in the pursuit. This is discussed in depth later, but Clausewitz argues that pursuit is where armies are thoroughly beaten.

The Austrian Army

Sector	Army and Location	Infantry	Cavalry	Total
1	The army of Archduke Charles in winter quarters between the Lech and the Isar	65,000 (61 battalions)	27,000 (158 squadrons)	92,000
2	General Hotze's force in Vorarlberg and Graubündten, under overall command of Archduke Charles	24,600 (23 battalions)	1,400 (8 squadrons)	26,000
3	Under General Bellegarde in the Tyrol	44,400 (50 battalions)	2,600 (14 squadrons)	47,000
4	The army on the Adige in Italy, temporarily under General Kray*	64,000 (82 battalions)	11,000 (76 squadrons)	75,000
	Total	198,000	42,000	240,000
	Plus artillery (approximate)			15,000
	Grand total			255,000**

*General Paul Kray (1735–1804) was in his 60s during the campaigns in Italy and Switzerland. Austrian commander General Johann Conrad Friedrich Ritter von Hotze (1739–1799) was 59 years old when he was killed in action in September 1799. He had a relatively successful career, but it is worth noting that he was one of the younger senior commanders in the Austrian and Russian armies. General Heinrich von Bellegarde (1756–1845) was another fairly young commander who went on to have a relatively successful career through the end of the Napoleonic Wars. Their ages might seem insignificant, but they were, on average, much older than their French counterparts. This might go some way to explaining the lack of dynamism on their part compared with the French. In his thoughts about military genius in *On War*, Clausewitz makes it clear that "war is the realm of physical exertion and suffering" (book 1, chap. 3, 101). He also argues that "four elements make up the climate of war: danger, uncertainty, exertion, and chance" (ibid., 104). Given the Austrian emphasis on bravery as a criterion for promotion and the lack of intellectual curiosity among the Austrian officer corps, it is reasonable to assume that these aspects of military genius were only partially fulfilled by Austrian officers. Younger, more open-minded products of the Enlightenment might have been better equipped to handle uncertainty, chance, and exertion.

**Archduke Charles of Austria gives the numbers for sector 1 as 54,000 infantry and 24,000 cavalry, while the numbers for sectors 2, 3, and 4 are the same as Clausewitz's. He also counts another 73,000 men covering Austrian communications to the rear who were not readily available for campaigning. That being said, the archduke's numbers are broadly in line with Clausewitz's, although it is interesting to note that the archduke states his own forces as totaling nearly 14,000 men fewer than the number given by Clausewitz. Karl, 142–43.

However, if one casts an eye over all the combat forces that could really come into action during the course of this campaign and must therefore be taken into consideration when reflecting on the whole plan of campaign, then on the French side one must also include about 34,000 men in lower Italy; 25,000 in Piedmont, Milan, and Genoa; 20,000 in the Rhine fortresses; and 10,000 in Holland, whereby we reach about 230,000 men. This includes the Swiss, Cisalpine, and Ligurian allied contingents, but they amounted to no more than 10,000. That therefore leaves about 220,000 troops under French colors. This seems very few. But when we consider that 45,000 men had sailed off to Egypt and that, given the state of unrest in France, its very insecure position,[29] and the impending elections, the Directory did not think it feasible to denude the interior of troops—as well as the fact that the coasts had to be guarded to some extent—we no longer have any reason to wonder at the small size of the French army on the frontier. It seems that some 120,000 men remained in the interior for all these various purposes, which together with the troops on the frontier and the army in Egypt, amounts to a total force of about 400,000 men. For France, this is still not a lot, but all the historians agree that the Directory had greatly neglected its armed forces since the peace of Campo Formio.[30] Not until September 1798 did it feel the need for a significant expansion of its combat forces. At the end of that month, it decided to mobilize 200,000 men in accordance with the conscription law that had been introduced in place of the previous impressment law.[31] However, recruiting, clothing, arming, and training these 200,000 men proceeded very slowly, and by February, only about 40,000 of them

---

29. The Directory in Paris had only recently managed to subdue open revolt in the Vendée in 1796, and in 1797 French monarchists were actively agitating for the overthrow of the government in Paris. See William Doyle, *The Oxford History of the French Revolution* (Oxford: Oxford University Press, 2002), 311–340.

30. This was partly due to the severe financial strain wrought by the economic disruption of war and revolution and partly due to the abandonment of conscription. Esdaile, *Wars of the French Revolution,* 127–128, 140, 289.

31. The French had used the *Levée en Masse* from the spring of 1793, but this was extremely unpopular among the French male population. In 1798 a new law with a much less onerous conscription system was enacted. It was named for General Jean Baptiste Jourdan. See Frederick C. Schneid, "The French Army," in *European Armies of the French Revolution: 1789–1802,* ed. Frederick C. Schneid (Norman: University of Oklahoma Press, 2015), 13–33.

were with the armies, so at least 150,000 must be considered a reserve that would join the ranks gradually.

The allied forces that the vassal republics could put in the field were very insignificant. Per its convention with France, Switzerland should have provided 18,000 men but seems never to have mustered more than 3,000–4,000 according to a Swiss author, Haller. Leaving aside the few allied troops that were already with the Army of Italy and are accounted for in the deployments listed above, the only other allied force to add to the total combat forces is the Batavian army, with about 20,000 men.

> Thus we arrive at these totals for the French combat forces.
> On the frontier ready to fight the Austrians: 138,000 men
> Occupying upper Italy: 25,000
> In the Rhine fortresses: 20,000
> In Holland: 10,000
> In lower Italy: 34,000
> Conscript reserves: 150,000
> Batavians: 20,000
> Total: 397,000 men

This total does not include the 120,000[32] men in the interior, of which nevertheless a proportion were able to be used during the course of the campaign.

Thus there were 400,000 men available to use during the campaign.

For the coalition, we must include 50,000 Russians with the Austrian army and another 40,000 allied troops that Russia and England intended to land in Holland, along with 10,000 men that these two powers and Sicily could bring into action in lower Italy during the campaign. If we add perhaps another 30,000 men that the Austrians may have sent to their armies as reinforcements during the campaign, 10,000 Russian reinforcements, and 10,000 men in the Reichs-Contingents, then the total that could be brought to bear for an offensive war was around 390,000 men—that is, just as many as the enemy had available. From this, we can see that, looking at the campaign as a whole, there was no question of any great numerical advantage on the coalition's side. Since the balance of forces given here was not the consequence of later events

---

32. Clausewitz listed this as 150,000, but this appears to be a simple typographical error.

but was already more or less apparent to the governments at the time, we may consider it the foundation for their opposing plans.

We may likewise regard the morale situation as being in equilibrium. Bonaparte and the larger part of his Army of Italy had been taken away to Egypt, Schérer[33] had no great reputation, Jourdan[34] had been roundly beaten by Archduke Charles[35] in 1796, and Moreau was without a command. From Suvorov, at least, something out of the ordinary could always be expected. Thus, the French moral superiority derived from their six mostly successful campaigns had pretty much slipped away, but without being recklessly overconfident, neither could the allies count on any significant advantage of moral force.

As the course of the campaign will show us, though, the value of the troops and their leaders from divisional generals downward was by no means on a par. Rather, the moral constitution of the Austrian infantry in its many new formations, created rapidly one after another, had become very weak. But this could not have been foreseen so clearly, and in such a case, it is natural that a government should somewhat overrate the moral value of its troops.

The French government was poorly constituted and badly insecure, the country wracked by unrest and factional division, and the administration rife with corruption and confusion, its finances in terrible shape. Yet against these disadvantages must be set the by no means extinguished energy of the revolution, the spirit of the nation, the natural and man-made strength of its frontiers, and the unity of its decisions coming from a single source, while the allies' combat forces answered to a will that lived in the three corners of the great triangle of Vienna, St. Petersburg, and London.

---

33. Barthélemy Louis Joseph Schérer (1747–1804), commander of the Army of Italy before Bonaparte and minister of war from 22 July 1797 to 21 February 1799, had a decidedly mixed record, as Clausewitz indicates.

34. Jean Baptiste Jourdan (1762–1833) fared somewhat better than Schérer and was made a marshal of France in 1804.

35. Archduke Charles (1771–1847) was one of Napoleon's great opponents. This is perhaps no accident, given that he was far younger than most of his Austrian contemporaries, many of whom were in their sixties and seventies. He published a couple of histories about his role in the wars of the First and Second Coalitions and wrote widely on military ideas and theory. See Gunther Rothenberg, *Napoleon's Great Adversaries: The Archduke Charles and the Austrian Army, 1792–1814* (Tiptree, UK: Anchor Press, 1982). See also listings in the bibliography of this volume under Karl Erzherzog von Österreich.

It seems to us, therefore, that the general situation offered neither party the basis for any very great success. If one side had had a Bonaparte in charge either overall[36] or of at least two-thirds of its forces, then we think it could reasonably be agreed that had he been leading the French, he would have ended the campaign by threatening Vienna, while if he led the allies, then straightaway he would have advanced triumphantly into the heart of France. Whether that would then have opened up political divisions that made it possible for a march on Paris, bringing about a political revolution that would have both helped and been helped by the military successes, or whether a mighty reaction would have occurred that blunted the allies' victory and forced them to seek shelter behind the Rhine again, that is impossible to calculate now, and it would have been impossible then too. We can only say that, given the nature of people and nations, it would have depended mainly on the scale, the extent, and the brilliance of the victory under the aegis of which the allies entered France. Morale effects have a huge impact here, and as history teaches us, there are some feats of arms that almost nothing can resist.[37]

But neither side had a commander of such greatness, so naturally, neither side could rely on any very great success; nor did either of their plans aim for one.

This is the situation if we are talking about the overall ratios that must come into play during the course of the whole campaign. But it is different if we look at only the ratio of forces involved in the opening phase of the campaign, where, as we have seen, the Austrians had a superiority of about 120,000 men across both theaters of operations, and against their opponents in Germany and Switzerland, they found themselves with a ratio of 180:80.

In the absence of any great disparity between the troops themselves, such numerical superiority should have guaranteed the greatest of victories.[38]

---

36. Here he clearly sets Napoleon above his peers. This ties in with Clausewitz's thoughts on military genius. He writes: "What we must do is survey all those gifts of mind and temperament that in combination bear on military activity. These taken together constitute *the essence of military genius.*" *On War*, book 1, chap. 3, 100. It is worth the reader's time to read this chapter of *On War* in full. In addition, we recommend Clifford J. Rogers, "Clausewitz, Genius, and the Rules," *Journal of Military History* 66 (October 2002): 1167–1176.

37. Thus Clausewitz brings us back to "Purpose and Means in War" (*On War*, book 1, chap. 2).

38. However, as Clausewitz points out in book 3, chaps. 3 and 8 of *On War*, moral

Deployment

We have already indicated the deployments of the main bodies of the combat forces. The boundary between the two sides ran up the Rhine from Mainz to its sources; from there, it was the border of Graubündten (except for the Veltlin, which was held by the French), then the Tyrolese border as far as the Adige, which it followed to the Adriatic Sea.

This position arose simply from political possession, each side thereby demarcating what it had kept or acquired. The one exception was Graubündten. When the French seized Switzerland to forge it into one indivisible republic, it was naturally their intention that this should include Graubündten, apart from the Veltlin, which they had attached to the Cisalpine Republic. At first, even the Graubündtners did not think they could escape this. However, the French had not advanced as far as this remote part of Switzerland, and the political negotiations concerning the new constitution were slow to be concluded. Meanwhile, the French extended their system of pillage and extortion across the country, and the little cantons' resistance led to some very bloody scenes. In August 1798 the Graubündtners therefore plucked up their courage and asked for Austria's aid, basing their request on an old alliance between the League[39] and Austria. This induced the Austrians to send in a corps under General Auffenberg.[40] The Graubündtners now began to arm themselves, and this persuaded the Austrians to incorporate the territory into the Austrian defensive line so as not to leave the Graubündtners in the lurch.

The western border of the Tyrol is practically a straight line from Feldkirch

---

factors and numerical strength are related, and one must consider both to understand the amount of combat power and will a particular force possesses. Hence his point here: if this were simply about numbers, there should have been no contest. But moral will *does* come into play, as do the elements of his wondrous trinity. It is the combination of all these factors that is so hard to calculate, and that is presumably why genius requires a coup d'oeil (book 1, chap. 3) to visualize the course of action despite the lack of clarity or certainty.

39. This was the Grey League region of mostly western Swiss cantons that functioned semi-independently.

40. Franz Xavier Freiherr von Auffenberg (1744–1815) had an undistinguished career and was cashiered for his performance in the 1805 campaign. See http://www.napoleon-series.org/research/biographies/Austria/AustrianGenerals/c_Austrian GeneralsA.html.

to the Adige, except at the town of Nauders; there, where the Engadin enters, it creates an intruding angle. By contrast, the border of Graubündten, which includes the Rhine valleys and the Engadin, constitutes a half-ellipse of which the Ill valley—or, more precisely, the line from Feldkirch via Nauders to the Münster valley—can be considered its base.[41]

Thus, if Graubündten was to be occupied and defended by a dedicated force, this had to be regarded as an advanced corps, and it is easy to appreciate that in this half-elliptical salient projecting into the enemy line, it was necessary to take exceptional care lest this corps be exposed to great danger in the event of a serious enemy attack.

The Austrians did not anticipate the campaign starting soon, and in this respect, the French seem to have positively pulled the wool over their eyes at Rastatt. Consequently, at the end of February their main forces were still in scattered cantonments. The archduke's army was the most concentrated between the Lech and the Isar, but even this was certainly some distance from its actual theater of operations—namely, the region between the Danube and Lake Constance. Bellegarde seems to have been scattered across the whole of the Tyrol, on a front 135 miles across and almost as deep.[42] The army in Italy was spread over 180 miles from the Adige to behind the Murch valley. This was why the Austrian main bodies were slow to come into action.

The precise French positions are not given anywhere, but that is less important for us, since we shall see that, by the beginning of March, they were already concentrated where they wanted to operate on the offensive—namely, on the Rhine and in Switzerland.

---

41. This is difficult to locate on a modern map, but the Ill River that Clausewitz mentions flows through the small town of St. Gallenkirch and northwest through Feldkirch, turning north to empty into Lake Constance. To find its source, go slightly northeast from Piz Buin on a map.

42. The Germans did not standardize distances until 1872, after German unification. Prior to that, each region had its own weights and measures. A league was typically between 2 and 3.5 miles long (in standardized miles), and a Prussian mile was 4.7 standard miles. Given this lack of clarity with regard to distances, we have treated a league as being 3.5 miles and a mile in the original as being 4.5 miles. All distances have been converted to modern miles for the reader's convenience and, to keep things simple, rounded up to the next mile. For more on German historical measures, see "Projekt zur Erschliessung historisch wertvoller Altkartenbestände," http://ikar.sbb.spk-berlin.de/werkzeugkasten/sonderregeln/4_3.htm.

As far as actual fortresses were concerned, apart from Ehrenbreitstein, which was strategically irrelevant,[43] across the whole theater of operations there were only Mainz, Strasbourg, Hüningen, Breisach, and Mantua, all of which were in French hands. They also had the smaller forts of Peschiera, the citadel of Milan, and Pizzighettone. In Germany, the Austrians had only the half-destroyed fortress of Mannheim, the insignificant one at Philippsburg, the citadel of Würzburg, and the hastily fortified cities of Ulm and Ingolstadt. In Italy, Venice was not of much account, for it still lacked a fort on the mainland, and apart from this, they had only the hastily fortified places of Verona and Legnago. In this respect, then, the French had a distinct advantage.

There are no precise details about either side's supply situation, but in fruitful and populous provinces like the ones in this theater of operations, this was not a serious obstacle for either of them. Thus, we will limit ourselves to mentioning that Archduke Charles complained about the delay in organizing the Austrian army and offered this as a reason for its forces being slow to come into action.[44]

3 SWITZERLAND'S INFLUENCE ON THE CAMPAIGN

Before we proceed to further presentation of the campaign and reflections on it, we must spend a moment on the new relationships that Switzerland and lower Italy found themselves in with respect to the war and on the influence that these must have had on the campaign.

In *Histoire Critique et Militaire des Guerres de la Révolution*, Jomini[45] maintains that the French invasion of Switzerland that ended its neutrality was a

---

43. See note 5. This might have been strategically irrelevant to France, but it formed a key part of the Austrian defensive line.

44. In his account of the campaign, the archduke provides more details about these problems—from a lack of concentration of forces prior to the start of the conflict to a dearth of logistical support. His complaints are a regular feature of his campaign history. See Karl, 1:41–61.

45. Lieutenant-General Antoine Henri Jomini (1779–1869) was in many ways the other great military thinker to emerge from the Revolutionary and Napoleonic Wars. He was an intellectual rival of Clausewitz, and the two exhibited a severe enmity for each other's work. Clausewitz was regularly stinging in his rebuke of Jomini's ideas (and those of other theorists such as Maurice de Saxe and Heinrich von Bülow). It is

disadvantage for both the warring parties.[46] We probably do not need to point out that this is a contradiction with itself. If the abolition of Swiss neutrality was a disadvantage for the French, it must thereby be advantageous for the Austrians, since when we are talking about one single dimension of an object, there must always be a polarity of interests. Of course, we can imagine that this ending of neutrality could have disadvantaged the French in one respect and the Austrians in another, but then the disadvantage for one would still have been just as big an advantage for the other, so it comes down to a comparison of the two; if they were the same size, then together they would have no overall effect, making the matter one of indifference to both sides but by no means disadvantageous in the final calculation.

---

worth quoting Clausewitz at length to illustrate this tendency. The following citation comes immediately after an extremely sarcastic detailing of the ideas Clausewitz finds so annoying: "It is only analytically that these attempts at theory can be called advances in the realm of truth; synthetically, in the rules and regulations they offer, they are absolutely useless. They aim at fixed values; but in war everything is uncertain, and calculations have to be made with variable quantities. They direct the inquiry exclusively toward physical quantities, whereas all military action is intertwined with psychological forces and effects. They consider only unilateral action, whereas war consists of a continuous interaction of opposites. THEY EXCLUDE GENIUS FROM THE RULE. Anything that could not be reached by the meager wisdom of such one-sided points of view was held to be beyond scientific control: it lay in the realm of genius, *which rises above all rules*. Pity the soldier who is supposed to crawl among these scraps of rules, not good enough for genius, which genius can ignore, or laugh at. No; what genius does is the best rule, and theory can do no better than show how and why this should be the case." *On War*, book 2, chap. 2, 136. One can see the sarcasm dripping off the page, and it is no wonder that Jomini took such offense. See also Clausewitz, *Napoleon's 1796 Italian Campaign*, 248; Christopher Bassford, "Jomini and Clausewitz: Their Interaction," http://www.clausewitz.com/readings/Bassford/Jomini/JOMINIX.htm.

46. Jomini's argument is indeed an odd one, and it is difficult to support. Apart from claiming, seemingly contradictorily, that there was a potential strategic advantage to moving through Switzerland, the crux of Jomini's argument seems to be that Napoleon did not invade Switzerland in 1805 or 1809, which somehow shows the folly of invading Switzerland in 1799. Apart from the fact that this argument is a fallacy, it does not support the case Jomini made in his history. Furthermore, Jomini is arguing that the invasion of Switzerland was a mistake for the French, and as we shall see later in this section, Clausewitz makes the same argument. Thus, Clausewitz is being extremely picky here and somewhat disingenuous. See this argument in Jomini, 10:276–342.

This mistaken criticism, which arises quite often in such cases, compels us to examine it more closely.

If a third country lies between two belligerents and the question is what consequences its neutrality or its involvement would have, first we must say: neutrality makes the country impassable, and involvement makes it passable, but this passive passability must be distinguished from active involvement in its effects.

Whatever the consequences of such a country's passability might be, they are easily outweighed by its active participation, if that adds any significant weight to the scales. In such a case, there can be no argument about which of the belligerents gains an advantage thereby—it is unarguably the one whose side the third country joins. If the active involvement of Switzerland had only been as significant as its statistical proportions allowed, the ending of its neutrality would have been an undoubted advantage for the French, on whose side it was.

But there are cases where the participation of such countries is utterly insignificant because they are too small or too unwarlike or held back by contrary public opinion, as occurred here with Switzerland. Then the insignificant weight of their active involvement can no longer outweigh the effects of them simply being opened up to military operations. We therefore want to answer the question: what are these effects in general, that is, without regard to particular geographical factors?

We may consider a neutral land between two belligerents as being like a large lake that interrupts the continuity of the terrain and communications. Obviously, two effects arise from this: first, the disadvantage that any interruption in communications brings, and second, the advantage of a shortened frontier.

The disadvantage applies both in offense and defense, since the interruption of parallel lines of communication is equally disadvantageous in both cases, but it applies only to whichever side has this lake behind its line of deployment. If both sides' lines of deployment are such that they run across the middle of the lake, then the disadvantage is equally great for both—that is, it cancels itself out and does not matter.

But the military action of a campaign rarely stays on one line for long, and in most cases, if the neutral country being thought of as a lake is not of very significant extent, the war may soon move from one end of it to the other. Thus, one can say that in the general case, even this disadvantage is the same size for both sides and ultimately is not a disadvantage for either side.

The other effect of the interruption of continuous terrain is the shortening of the frontier. This, however, is obviously an advantage for the defender, as revealed by the simple reflection that a frontier constricted to the width of a single road offers the strongest defense. In most cases, one can avoid the disadvantage of interrupted communications in one way or another; for instance, one can pull either the whole line of deployment or just one end of it further back, thus placing the neutral country partly or entirely in front of the line. So in general, the third country's neutrality is advantageous to the defender.

If we consider Switzerland in terms of these geometrical relationships, we must correct Jomini's assertion, in that Switzerland's neutrality was an advantage for France only so long as it remained on the defensive. Whenever the French went onto the strategic offensive, the opening up of Switzerland must also necessarily be to their advantage, first because it allowed them to have direct communications between their armies in Germany and Italy, and second because it obliged the Austrians to include the stretch of frontier between Basel and the source of the Adige in their defensive system.[47]

One should not imagine that this disadvantage for the Austrians could be nullified by abstaining from local defense. Even the most concentrated defense still has to deal with the size of the area to be defended and, in another way, with the increasing number of possible enemy combinations it has to consider.

If we examine Switzerland's geographical characteristics, we encounter the following two pertinent factors:

First, Switzerland is a mountainous country and as such favors the defense, so that he who holds it has an advantage.

Second, it dominates the whole of the upper Italian plain as far as the foot of the Savoy Alps.

We must consider here what both these factors mean and what their actual effect is.

Elsewhere we have proposed and attempted to prove the principle that a mountainous country favors any relative defense but that it is dangerous and disadvantageous for any absolute defense. We cannot repeat the proof here, but we wish to make our opinion clear.[48]

---

47. This is the region described in section 2 above, running along the Ill valley from the Adige basin to Feldkirch.

48. Clausewitz discusses the idea in more depth elsewhere: "That a mountain region is only advantageous for the defense where a small force needs to put up com-

By "relative resistance" we mean any defense that is meant to last for only a certain time because it does not constitute the decisive battle itself but relates to a decision elsewhere. Any military action takes longer in mountains than on the plain, so even an unsuccessful resistance—that is, one that ends by abandoning the position—always lasts longer than on the plain; thus, if resistance is mainly intended to buy time, as, for example, outposts are meant to, then resistance in the mountains is much more productive for that purpose.

But it is also more effective in that it costs the attackers more in blood. Where a major decision is at stake, the cost in blood does not matter and the price of victory is usually only a secondary consideration. But where it is only a matter of a secondary objective, the price of victory can come very much into play, and because of this, in many cases the attack simply will not happen.

Finally, in the mountains, any small party is infinitely stronger than in the plain because it can never be overrun and because the arm that is most dangerous during the retreat of small parties—the cavalry—loses much of its utility in the mountains.

All these factors mean that weak detachments give very good account of themselves in mountain warfare, since not only can they resist much longer but also they can risk facing a much stronger opponent than in the plain.

But if we are talking about a main army and the major decision it is supposed to deliver, and if the most prolonged resistance is no longer worth anything and no positive result can be expected when it ends in retreat, and if one is no longer fighting for territory but for victory, and if the defender's resistance must therefore be absolute—then a mountainous region is thoroughly disadvantageous for the defender. As we have said, we cannot expound the reasons here in full, but we invoke both the experience and the opinion of the commander with whom we are about to concern ourselves: Archduke Charles. He was the first theorist to express the principle[49] that mountains are

---

paratively long resistance, but in an outright decision between both sides' main bodies it is always unfavorable for the defender, because in the mountains the defender loses the advantage which, in contemporary warfare, he normally derives from being able to respond to the enemy's actions with concealed reserves." Clausewitz, *Napoleon's 1796 Italian Campaign*, 279. Also see *On War*, book 6, chaps. 15–17, book 7, chap. 11.

49. **Clausewitz** notes: "in his work on the campaign of 1796 in Germany." This work is Karl von Österreich Erzherzog, *Grundsätze der Strategie erläutert durch die Darstellung des Feldzugs von 1796 in Deutschland*, 4 vols. (Vienna: Anton Strauss, 1814).

a disadvantage for the defender, to which we, for our part, would however always add: so long as a major battle is sought or feared.

But in examining the case of Switzerland more closely, we must say that its highest parts seem to us less suitable for relative defense than a mountain range of medium height. For if the mountain slopes get so steep and high that one must mount the whole of one's defense in the valley, many of the characteristic advantages offered by mountainous terrain cease, and indeed, disadvantages appear in their place, making it questionable whether such a region is not more favorable to the attack than the defense.

Thus, it is only with this reservation that we attribute to the geographical nature of Switzerland the first of the above effects—namely, great strength in defense.

When we say that a mountain range dominates the plain lying alongside it, this means only that this inaccessible region cannot be controlled by an army advancing into the plain to the same extent it could have been if the region were equally flat and open. In this case, the enemy's flanking forces must fall back to maintain their alignment with their main body, and if they do not, they can easily be forced to do so and punished for it. Thus the mere advance of an army on a plain clears the area to its side to a certain extent without requiring a corps of its own to do so. This is not the case when the area in question is a mountain range.

Simply by virtue of its elevation, any mountainous country cannot be observed from the plain, while those who find themselves in it, that is to say on its outer slopes, have an excellent view over a large part of the plain. But if one is in the interior of a mountainous region, the gorges and forests that pervade it make observation much more difficult than on the plain. Thus, if one is on the plain, with the enemy occupying a mountain ridge alongside it, one is under observation without being able to observe the enemy in return.

An area of vegetated broken ground would achieve a somewhat similar effect but would not offer the same good field of view. Therefore, the element of elevation is not without importance.

Furthermore, any mountainous region is less accessible and, as we have said, very well suited for resistance by subunits and small parties. The combined effect is that the foe can easily keep small forces in such a region and, from there, interrupt our line of communications on the plain if it runs alongside the mountains. We cannot just drive him out of there at any moment as we could in more open country, where an isolated advanced detachment of the enemy can easily be imperiled by sending a superior number of cavalry against it. In the mountains, one can gain control of the area only by a systematic advance—that is, one split into multiple coordinated columns, which always requires a considerably stronger force than that of the enemy. This cannot be done instantly, and once it has been done, it cannot be given up again; one must try to retain possession of the mountain range, so a more or less independent flank corps must advance alongside the main army. Thus we are obliged to take measures we initially sought to avoid. One cannot avoid such measures without seeing one's line of communications threatened in a more or less effective and dangerous way.[50]

In this sense, we must conclude, albeit in a somewhat exaggerated expression: mountains dominate the plains next to them.

If we apply this conclusion to Switzerland, we must say that, by its nature, it is not very well suited to have such an effect on Lombardy. Its southern slopes are too high, steep, and inaccessible, and its communications with Lombardy are restricted to a few difficult passes, making it unsuitable for prolonged and varied action by multiple small forces. Also, the Lombard plain is too wide, and the Po offers too good a means of protection against the mountains. In fact, we shall see that in this very campaign in 1799, the French possession of Switzerland had no perceptible impact on the allies' occupation of upper Italy.

From this double reflection on Switzerland—first, as a mountainous theater of operations in its own right, and second, as a high bulwark flanking the upper Italian plain—it follows that its possession by the French did not actually offer the tactical and strategic advantages the Directory's military advisers might have imagined according to the prevailing views of that time.[51] Indeed, it did the opposite because the French entered Switzerland with one of their three main armies and therefore could suffer decisive blows there. When we also consider that, because of the ratio of forces, the French were reliant on defense and had no justification at all for believing they could go over to the offensive, even though they actually made an attempt to do so initially, then we

---

50. Of course, as Clausewitz is getting at, each of these independent columns is itself vulnerable if the enemy can effect a concentration of force against any one of them.

51. Ross cites this as one of the Directory's reasons for the invasion. See Steven T. Ross, *Quest for Victory: French Military Strategy 1792–1799* (London: Thomas Yoseloff, 1978), 204.

must break ranks with Jomini with respect to this war, in that we consider it a great error by the French Directory to have invaded Switzerland and thereby ended its neutrality.[52]

4 THE INFLUENCE OF LOWER ITALY

We have a further reflection to offer on the influence of the political transformation of lower Italy on the 1799 campaign, which, however, will not divert us so far from the target as did the previous section.[53]

Jomini likewise regards the operation against Naples as a decided disadvantage, in that it disproportionately extended the already insufficient French forces.[54]

The French did not start the war with Naples, and we can blame them for it only insofar as it was definitely their provocations that gave rise to the new coalition, and their contemptuous treatment of the Papal States in particular caused the king of Naples great concern.

The king entered the field with 40,000 men in November 1798; he probably would have fielded an even more considerable force by March 1799, to which another 10,000–15,000 Russian and British troops could subsequently have been added. To be fighting against a force reduced by 60,000 men is clearly not an unimportant advantage, and thus we can probably say that if the king of Naples had not seized the initiative, the French would have made a grave error had they not attacked and crushed him before the other allies entered the field.

The fact that the French left 30,000 men in lower Italy pretty much canceled out this advantage, since one may regard 30,000 Frenchmen as being worth as much as 60,000 Neapolitans. But this measure was required only because of the establishment of the Parthenopean Republic, which was not a

---

52. The problem with Clausewitz's point is that Jomini argued that the Directory made a mistake in invading Switzerland. It is as though Clausewitz missed Jomini's broader point when he focused on the issue of both sides being disadvantaged. See Jomini, 10:276–291.

53. Archduke Charles mentions lower Italy only in terms of military plans, which supports his previous comment about a focus on military affairs. Karl, 1:54.

54. Jomini covers the key points in his history. Jomini, 11:33–86. See also Ross, *Quest for Victory*, 205–208.

necessary consequence of the war with Naples. If the French had simply compelled the king of Naples to reduce his army to a small corps, made him pay a substantial contribution, and obtained a promise of neutrality from him, it would have been unnecessary to leave troops there, and it is highly unlikely that the king would have taken part in the 1799 campaign.

But given the French government's prevailing ambition at that time to republicanize all the second-rank states it could reach, the emergence of this Parthenopean Republic cannot come as any great surprise to us, and the French Directory probably believed that whatever combat forces it had to leave there would be offset to some degree by an allied contingent from the new free state. In any case, France still could have withdrawn its troops four weeks before the likely start of the campaign and added them to the Army of Italy. The fact that it did not do this but was confident that the 80,000 men it had in Italy could occupy the whole peninsula and at the same time withstand an Austrian army on the Adige that was almost as strong must be identified as its major error.[55]

5 RESULTING IMPLICATIONS FOR BOTH SIDES' PLANS OF OPERATIONS

Having studied both sides' situations, we wish to ask ourselves what kinds of plans must arise, given the nature of the matter, and then see how the plans the two sides actually followed acquit themselves when compared with these.

---

55. The Directory's seeming belief that overthrowing monarchies and installing republics would be sufficiently popular to allow this to work was a huge mistake, especially given that, during the fighting in 1796–1797, local populations in some places had taken up arms against their "liberators." This is important because understanding the nature of the war and the means to be employed are crucial parts of Clausewitz's thinking on what is war (*On War*, book 1, chap. 1). Also, all sides in a conflict must accept the result for an effective peace to follow; alternatively, the peace needs to be policed sufficiently to allow stability. Overthrowing the way of life of large numbers of people always creates resistance, even if one accepts the argument regarding the benefits of republicanism. Someone somewhere will lose, and they will likely feel aggrieved. This happened in Milan in 1796, which should have been a clue that there might be a real problem if sufficient force was not available to quell the uprising. As we can see, this occurred in Naples and later, most famously, in Spain from 1808 to 1814. See *On War*, book 1, chap. 1, for the key arguments.

Let us begin with the Austrians.

Basically, the Austrians were the side that wanted the new war,[56] that is, for whom it had a positive purpose.[57] During the peace, the French had engaged in hitherto unprecedented territorial aggrandizement.[58] The Austrians saw the necessity of not just controlling this landgrab but also forcing the French to backtrack on the steps taken toward the subjugation of Europe. As Austria was united with England and Russia on this point, the Second Coalition arose.

This coalition did not command such exceptional resources as to be able to crush France itself, as the alliance of 1813 did. This was not the intention of any of the three main allies, and at the time, perhaps none of them even thought it was really possible, so France's will could not be bent to theirs in that way.[59]

When a state itself cannot be overthrown, he who has a positive purpose has no option but to occupy the objectives he wants or others that may be

---

56. Although Archduke Charles blames the French for the opening of hostilities, his description of events indicates that Austria had the most to gain and implies that France was not looking to renew the war. Thus, although he is not explicit, he seems to be broadly in agreement with Clausewitz. His downplaying of Austrian culpability seems to have more to do with the Austrians' lack of rapid organization and preparation for war than with their intentions and political actions. Karl, 1:36–41. This prompts us to ask whether it was France's fault that Austria proved incompetent in preparing for a war it wanted.

57. Clausewitz argues that "defense has a passive purpose: *preservation*; and attack a positive one: *conquest*." In short, defense is the means to preserve whatever one wants to preserve, and attack is the means to overthrow the status quo. A positive aim might be something as simple as the Austrians capturing the fortress of Ehrenbreitstein from the French. This overturns the current order, albeit in a small way, but achieves a positive aim. The French resisting such an attempt would have the negative aim of keeping the fortress for themselves, thus preserving the status quo. See *On War*, book 6, chap. 1, 357–359. Also see book 8—"War Plans"—more broadly and chaps. 7–9, 611–637, for a closer examination of what this might look like in practice.

58. This brings us back to Clausewitz's idea that the result of a war is never final. He is worth quoting on this: "Lastly, even the ultimate outcome of a war is not always to be regarded as final. The defeated state often considers the outcome merely as a transitory evil, for which a remedy may still be found in political conditions at some later date." *On War*, book 1, chap. 1, pt. 9, 80.

59. Clausewitz is pointing out that this was largely a war of limited aims. It was not about the complete overthrow of the French government, even though the British would have preferred this result. For the British position, see Macksey, *Statesmen at War*, 5.

considered their equivalents and can be traded for them in the peace negotiations.[60]

The territories under the French yoke were in Switzerland and Italy. Austrian operations were therefore initially directed at the conquest of these two countries. The conquest of upper Italy would cause the French creations in lower Italy to collapse of their own accord. At the same time, the Cisalpine Republic could be taken as a bargaining chip to impose a peace on the enemy that much sooner, if one really wanted to use the Treaty of Campo Formio as its basis. But there is little doubt that the three allies intended to obtain a much better peace than that of Campo Formio.[61]

While the allies' activity was accordingly aimed at Italy and Switzerland initially, it does not follow that they would not have taken another French province as their objective if there had been one that was easier to conquer and hold and that could be regarded as effectively equivalent to one of those

---

60. This relates to what Clausewitz discusses in *On War*, book 8, chap. 5, where he talks about *beschränktes Ziel*. Howard and Paret translate this as "limited aims," but that does not match the original. As Christopher Bassford points out, "Such English phrases as 'war of limited aim' and their opposite, 'unlimited war' (which don't appear at all even in the English translations but nonetheless occur frequently in the literature on Clausewitz), are confusing because war is interactive while aims are unilateral, describing only one side's approach." In this case, because it was unlikely that France could be overthrown, the military goals of the various parties were more likely to be achieved by seizing objectives the opponent valued, allowing the parties to negotiate peace from an enhanced position. Had the goal of all the warring parties been to overthrow their opponents, it would be reasonable to argue that they would have deployed far greater efforts to achieve that end, as all the parties would have been fighting for their very existence. See Christopher Bassford, "Clausewitz's Categories of War and the Supersession of 'Absolute War,'" in particular the main text and footnotes on pp. 12–29, http://www.clausewitz.com/mobile/Bassford-Supersession5.pdf#zoom=100. See also "What Is War" and "Purpose and Means in War," *On War*, book 1, chaps. 1 and 2.

61. That is, the allies were looking to overturn the status quo without removing the French government and without causing the French to escalate the violence to an unacceptable level in relation to the allies' objectives. Of course, this assumed the French placed a similar value on the objectives sought by the allies, but it was impossible to accurately predict how the French would react. This idea ties in with the role of chance in Clausewitz's trinity and the likelihood of the level of violence escalating, especially if one side has miscalculated the degree to which the other side will resist. See *On War*, book 1, chap. 1.

two countries. But obviously there were no provinces like that. Previously, the allies had probably thought about carrying the war through Mainz and across the former French frontier to reconquer the left bank of the Rhine, but even if such a conquest had not had the disadvantage of being very difficult to hold, the loss of Mainz made it out of the question.[62]

To take Mainz as the main objective of the attack would have offered a very poor equivalent and would always entail a major difficulty, in that the line of operations from the middle Danube to Mainz is long and oblique and is constantly threatened from the upper Rhine. Any blow the Austrians might strike against France itself would always be more powerful against the upper Rhine, because it is the shortest and most direct route and is completely protected on its left side by the Austrian provinces.

Thus, of all the French-held provinces, Switzerland and upper Italy were the most natural objectives for the Austrian operations. But those objectives consisted of more than simply occupying these provinces; some bounty of victory, some significant destruction of enemy combat forces, was essential.[63] What mattered was victory; conquest was merely its manifestation. Only thus could these conquests be regarded as the means to conquer the enemy's will

---

62. This is key. Had the allies crossed the Rhine, how would this have affected the level of French resistance? If the Directory and those in favor of the republic had thought the French republic's fate was dependent on protecting French soil, they probably would have pursued the conflict with increased vigor, thereby raising the stakes for France and the costs for the allies. As such, the allies would have had to raise their political demands to meet their higher costs, accept the higher costs with no increase in political demands, or renounce their objectives and seek peace because the cost of war now exceeded the value of their objectives, as Clausewitz points out in "Purpose and Means in War," *On War*, book 1, chap. 2. The problem relates to Clausewitz's trinity, where emotion and chance play a role in decision making. Cold rationality does not always win out in decisions; therefore, the consequences of any revision of goals by one party is not easily predictable, especially when emotion and chance are involved. See *On War*, 89.

63. Here again, Clausewitz is discussing his ideas relating to purpose and means in war (*On War*, book 1, chap. 2). Specifically, this relates to his argument that "the fighting forces must be destroyed: that is they must be *put in such a condition that they can no longer carry on the fight*." Furthermore, one must increase the cost of war to the enemy. "The enemy's expenditure of effort consists in the *wastage of his forces*—our *destruction* of them; and in his *loss of territory*—our *conquest*." See in particular *On War*, 90–94.

and bring about an acceptable peace. Now the French army could not possibly be expected to quit these two countries without a single blow being struck or to allow itself to be maneuvered out. Nonetheless, it is important for us to single out this most essential part of the plan from not only a theoretical point of view; rather, it also should have had a significant influence on the development of the plan and on the actions of the commanders in executing it. If occupying territory is regarded as the primary aim, rather than winning a great victory, then bloodless methods will usually be sought, whereby the danger of the whole crisis is not so focused on a single point and does not seem so scary to commander and cabinet; nor does it demand from them both such strength of will, such drive and determination.

As we have seen, the general balance of forces did not give the allies any overall numerical superiority. However, they had a very large superiority at the start of the campaign. This initial superiority alone can therefore be regarded as the means to their end.

If, by means of this numerical superiority, they had inflicted a serious wound on the enemy, defeated and smashed his main army, destroyed confidence in his commanders, damaged the morale of his troops, torn the subjugated countries out of his hands, wrecked his hopes and his plans, aroused a mood of discontent and anxiety in his country, then one might hope that in this campaign at least, he would never recover the parity of forces the general situation had promised him before such a setback. One might hope that by establishing this superiority, either the enemy would be driven to accept suitable peace terms or one's own side would establish the foundation for a second successful campaign.[64]

The situation therefore demanded an early, powerful offensive aimed at striking major blows in Switzerland and Italy.

Let us now turn to France.

Since 1794, France had made steady progress toward the conquest and republicanization of the monarchical rest of Europe. First Belgium; then the left bank of the Rhine, Holland, Lombardy, Switzerland, and the Papal States; and finally both Italian kingdoms fell into its thieving hands. Most of the princes against whom France made war had bowed their heads before its sword, had flown no flag but that of peace, had borne no protective shield other than neutrality. In the end, even Vienna itself had quailed before it.

64. This relates closely to *On War*, book 7, chaps. 1–6, 523–529.

If we consider these successes in combination with the political zeal from which they stemmed, we can easily imagine what a spirit of arrogance, ambition, and contemptuousness they must have induced both in the people and in the government. And this government, which comprised five ephemeral directors who had no inheritance to cherish but had to use their momentary power as much as possible, could only ever be accelerated in its huge momentum by the efforts of these individuals; for they could leave their mark on history only if they gave an extra little push in the direction it was already going, not by pitting their feeble strength against its destructive force.

If the critic casts a cool, calm eye over the mood of such a government, in its cocksure attitude, its proud ambitions, and its excessive expectations, and considers all physical and moral forces as objective quantities, that makes for a very difficult calculation. And so in considering a war plan and a plan of campaign, it is necessary to put oneself exactly in the position of that government, to accept its natural biased tendencies, and to take as the object of criticism only those contradictions of which it is guilty within those limits.[65]

If a man such as Bonaparte had stood at the head of this revolutionary and expansionist power, both in the cabinet and in the field, he would have led it further along this path; on the one hand, he would have prepared the necessary means, and on the other, he would have used them appropriately and successfully. Then, from the domineering position France had adopted, it would not have been difficult to develop grand and successful plans. Subsequent history has shown this to be a fact. But no such man was there. Bonaparte and Carnot[66] were far away, the former because of his expedition to Egypt, and the latter because of the exile imposed on him on 18 *fructidor* 1797.[67] The very poor state of the army in every respect was sufficient evidence that no one in

---

65. Here again, one can relate this to Clausewitz's trinity (*On War*, book 1, chap. 1). Also see book 8, chap. 3B, where Clausewitz points out that this calculation would be "a colossal task.... To master all this complex mass by sheer methodical examination is obviously impossible. Bonaparte was quite right when he said that Newton himself would quail before the algebraic problems it could pose." *On War*, 585–586.

66. Lazare Carnot (1753–1823) was a former member of the Directory. He was nicknamed the Organizer of Victory because of his critical role in raising and reorganizing the French revolutionary army.

67. This refers to the coup of 18 *fructidor* (4 September 1797), when the French Directory seized power and moved France in a more authoritarian direction. Doyle, *Oxford History of the French Revolution*, 330–331.

the government was exercising the necessary forceful judgment. As for the generals put in charge of the four armies, until now, Bernadotte and Masséna had distinguished themselves only as divisional commanders, Schérer still had little basis for his reputation, and Jourdan's had been ruined.[68]

If we consider these factors present at the heart of the French Directory and examine the attitude and position France had taken, in order to offer a plan of campaign for the year 1797 according to our principles, this leads us to the following results.

French domination had been pushed forward broadly as far as the line of the Rhine, the Adige, and the Adriatic. These possessions needed to be held on to against the new coalition.

This was indisputably the political mission at the point in time under consideration. If the French rulers had the idea of extending their system and eventually taking over all of Europe, the moment when a new coalition was forming against what they already had and which they had not yet armed themselves properly to resist was naturally not the time to undertake new projects of this kind, although these could, of course, arise if a very successful war allowed. The political mission was thus a defensive, that is, a negative, one.

At the moment when the initial decisions had to be made, the French forces were obviously by far the weaker; if they had any hope of attaining a degree of parity during the course of the campaign, it would only be by committing their forces from the interior of the country. In this situation, the balance of forces dictated that they remain on the defensive.

Since their conquests had so damaged the political interests of Europe that the Austrians had scarcely paused for breath before deciding on another war, the French could probably expect the allies to aim to strike decisive blows.

---

68. Here, Clausewitz is getting at the idea of genius—that is, someone who has the intuition, temperament, and intellect to deal with such huge problems. Here again, Clausewitz mentions Isaac Newton and Leonard Euler. See *On War*, book 1, chap. 3. Later, Clausewitz discusses the nature of knowledge and points out that "experience, with all its wealth of lessons, will never produce a *Newton* or an *Euler*, but it may well bring forth the higher calculations of a *Condé* or a *Frederick.*" *On War*, book 2, chap. 2, 100–112, 146. He is referring to Louis de Bourbon (1621–1686), who was known the Prince of Condé I, and Frederick the Great, both of whom are often considered military geniuses. As highly as Clausewitz praises them, his choice of words indicates that he does not think of them as military geniuses and that he thinks experience alone is insufficient to produce genius.

They therefore had to organize their defense to oppose these decisive blows by suitable methods. They could not rely on local defense to be effective and useful; they had to keep their forces united in large armies whose victories would defend whatever country they were in.

Everything therefore depended on these victories, and the French could hope that if these repelled the assault, the bonds of the new coalition would soon be loosened, for nothing sows disunion in an alliance so easily as the destruction of its morale.

But could these victories not be won more easily by the offensive?[69]

By the defensive, we mean only strategic defense,[70] which by no means excludes offensive battles. In particular circumstances, these could have been more advantageous, but in general, they were not. We will examine this topic more closely later.

In the above, we believe we have depicted the major outlines within which the two sides had to create their plans.

It is not our intention to expand on these plans more fully, to the point where they could have been approved by the cabinet without unduly constraining the decisions of those on the spot. Even with such broad outlines, such a mass of unknowns comes into the reckoning that our work would be entirely illusory. We just feel that, to avoid misunderstandings of what we have said so far, we need to state more precisely those measures we consider appropriate for both sides and thereby answer some unanswered questions.

If the Austrians intended to conquer Switzerland and upper Italy, they could launch their attack either in both theaters of operations at once or in just one of them initially. The latter would give them the means to arrive at the decisive point with such superiority that success would be quite beyond doubt and would also be much more decisive. If the French were thereby induced to weaken the theater that had not been attacked and to reinforce the threatened one, then the Austrians could go over to the attack in the other one, so as to obtain there the successes that might have been denied them in the first. Given the few and poor communications between Lombardy and Switzerland at that time, mutual support be-

---

69. Ross argues that the French planned for a strategically defensive war with operational offensives to keep the war away from French soil. Ross, *Quest for Victory*, 212–215.

70. Clausewitz points out that the defender should be ready to assume the offensive at any moment in order to "use the advantage to prevent a second onslaught." *On War*, book 6, chap. 5, 370–371.

tween the two French armies was very difficult, and reconnoitering the positions and concentrations of the Austrian forces behind the mountains of the Tyrol and Carniola must have been just as difficult. Because the Austrians could at least be confident of success against the French [if they concentrated their combat power], they should spare no effort to increase the certainty of success and so to mass their offensive forces against one of the two theaters of operations.

As for which of the two provinces should be attacked first, we must say Switzerland, for the following reasons:

Most of the French combat forces were close together in Switzerland and on the upper Rhine; since they could be expected to operate together, bigger victories could be obtained there.

The French army's situation in Switzerland was a very perilous one if a superior enemy wanted to exploit the country's geography to strike decisive blows. If the enemy advanced in greatly superior numbers into its lower region, along the road to Bern, he might be able to get onto the left flank of the French army without much difficulty. The French army would then find itself with its back to the high Alps, in a position hideously perfect for catastrophe. The Austrians would not find such an opportunity to strike such major blows anywhere else.

While the decisive blows were being struck in Switzerland or on the upper Danube, the French in Italy could not undertake any effective operations against the heart of the Austrian monarchy, even if they won a few victories. For an advance like that of March 1797, they would need a Bonaparte, a victorious army, and one with a twofold superiority. All these factors would have been absent. There was significantly more to fear for the heart of the Austrian monarchy, for the effect on its morale, courage, and perseverance, if Austria's main forces operated against Italy and the French generals Jourdan and Masséna succeeded in defeating the forces left in Germany. This rich and open region, the secure French left flank, and the larger French army meant that on this side, the French were much more to be feared.

The bulk of the Austrian army was facing much more toward Switzerland than Italy. The blow could therefore be struck more rapidly, more directly, and more unexpectedly, which must be regarded as major factors for success.

The most natural place to use the Russians when they arrived later would be the theater of operations that temporarily had the fewest troops, and the Italian plains unarguably suited the Russians better than the Swiss mountains.

If we propose Switzerland as the first objective, taking precedence over Italy, it is not because the former country is higher and because occupying it thereby makes conquering the other significantly easier. Although Zurich and Bern do lie 1,000 feet higher than Milan, this is not a lot compared with the 6,000–8,000-foot altitude of the passes between the two provinces, and as the 1799 campaign indeed demonstrates, these passes can be controlled almost as easily from Italy as from Switzerland. To regard the higher altitude of an entire country as a strategically significant factor is a total illusion.[71]

But as far as the dominance (in our sense) of Switzerland over Italy is concerned, we have just shown that its impact is not great.

We have no compunction about our indifference toward geological factors in strategy, as we not only want to use our main force in Switzerland's lower region but actually want to strike our major blows there and thus to some degree work our way up from below. A French main army that is compelled to retreat toward the high Alps is thereby already half destroyed.

According to the views expounded here, without describing these dispositions as standard or as the only possible good ones, we would regard the following as dispositions that could have given rise to a glorious start to the campaign and by which the Austrians could have avoided the disasters that actually befell them:

1. Fifty thousand men form the army in Italy and wait for the arrival of the Russians to open their offensive. They deploy on the Adige, concentrate their forces in masses matching those of the enemy, and accept a major decisive battle only if the circumstances are especially favorable; otherwise, they give way and fall back toward the foot of the Carnolian Alps.
2. One hundred and fifty thousand men form the army in Germany under Archduke Charles. This army concentrates behind Lake Constance and threatens both Graubündten and the Aargau in equal measure.
3. The remaining 26,000 men stay in a chain of observation in the Tyrol, in Graubündten, and on the upper Rhine as far as Strasbourg.
4. The main army is intended to advance across the Rhine into the Aargau with 120,000 men and via Feldkirch against St. Gallen with 30,000 men

---

71. **Clausewitz** notes: "This should not be taken as contradicting what we have said in Section 4 about domination by a mountainous region. The altitude of the country itself has no effect. The two effective factors are the elevation of the first ridges or their slope above the plain, and the inaccessibility of the interior."

and to deliver a decisive battle designed to destroy the main French force in Switzerland.
5. The two bodies separated by Lake Constance unite on its southern shore or at least operate in close cooperation. Their division and their separate advance are intended only:
   a. To facilitate a rapid advance;
   b. To avoid having too large a force in too small a space while crossing the Rhine;
   c. To serve as a demonstration against the right wing of the French army and pin it for a longer time in the higher part of the mountains;
   d. To protect the main army's possible line of retreat toward Bregenz.
6. The western body of the main army advances into the Aargau and seeks to get onto the left flank of the French main army, so that this has its back to the mountains during the battle.
7. If Jourdan's French army on the Danube advances early enough that the Austrian main army can advantageously turn against him first, it leaves 20,000 men behind the Rhine and moves against the Army of the Danube with 100,000 men, with the aim of obtaining a great victory over it, for it does not matter which of the two enemy armies is beaten first.
8. The commander shall endeavor to place himself between the two enemy armies, not so as to deploy in a position between the two but rather to strive to strike the most decisive blows with his momentarily very great superiority and to exploit its results with the utmost energy in Germany, as far as the Rhine, and in Switzerland, as far as the Jura mountains or even beyond them.

Preparations should have been made in such a way that the army was in the initial deployment proposed here by the end of February. Since the French sallied forth at the beginning of March and declared war shortly thereafter, it probably would not have been hard to anticipate this approaching breach of the cease-fire in January; at least by January, the Austrians could no longer have believed there was any chance of peace. Under the prevailing conditions, it surely would not have been a difficult task to organize themselves to preempt the enemy, or at least to be ready to begin their own attack the moment they were threatened by his.

As far as the French are concerned, their system of defense is easily organized according to our principles.

The upper Rhine is much too strong a frontier to be under any threat; the garrisons of Strasbourg, Neu-Breisach, and Hueningen are entirely sufficient for its protection. The 138,000 men available for use in the field could be formed into two armies of 65,000 men each: one behind the Adige and the other behind the Limmat, each so deployed that they could accept battle with their whole force united. The high Alps would then be held by just 8,000 men to allow communications between the two armies.

We split the French forces into two equal parts because it cannot be known which way the Austrian force in the Tyrol will turn, so both theaters of operations appear equally threatened, and also because the transfer of significant numbers of troops from one theater to the other would entail serious difficulties and great loss of time.

Against a deployment of the Austrian forces in the manner we have proposed, the army in Switzerland would have been unable to stand its ground. Then the essential thing would have been for it to escape to Alsace via the Frick valley without being beaten, in which case nothing would have been lost apart from possession of Switzerland. But if the Austrians were too slow in preparing, or if they committed gross errors through unwise division of their forces, this army could seek to exploit those mistakes and achieve a glorious victory over one or other fraction.

In Italy, the opposing forces would have been roughly equal. But as the Russians got closer, or if reverses obliged the French to give up the line of the Adige, it would be high time to withdraw their forces from lower Italy and abandon the new republics to their fate for the time being.

The more negative and unambitious this plan was, the more suitable we think it would have been for minimizing disadvantages against a superior and well-led enemy, while still being ready to take positive and decisive action against a foe who made mistakes and lowered his guard. With this outline, we believe we have merely offered a very simple exposition of the measures to which clear reasoning leads. Our only purpose was to show how we imagined these things being generated. In that we have let this plan emerge from simple logical progression, from a calculation in the broader sense, we submit that it be recognized that in principle it cannot take any other form and that the quest for genius is mostly an unwise one that confuses matters and ruins the whole business. The major outlines of a war or campaign are no place for creative brilliance. The possible configurations for the employment of large masses are few in number and extremely simple; their value is determined mostly through correct principles and a certain astuteness in identifying what matters. Only when either the difficulty of the situation or a commander's own inclination to boldness predominates, allowing subjective judgment to prevail over objective, can this have an influence on the direction and sweep of these outlines; and what the commander accomplishes not just from objective values but by looking into his own heart at the same time, what he grasps and decides as much by instinct as by intellect, that alone—when it does apply—can only be designated with the name of genius, indicating a higher region of intellectual power. No chief of general staff could have expected General Bonaparte to march over the St. Bernard Pass.[72]

6 THE TWO SIDES' ACTUAL PLANS OF CAMPAIGN

The Austrians

As Archduke Charles tells us, when war broke out, the Austrians had not yet settled on any plan of campaign, nor do there seem to have been any contingency plans in case of an unexpected outbreak of war.[73] As a result, the armies did not operate in concert, that is, with a common aim. But such unity is exactly the essential purpose of any plan of campaign.[74] While this need not

---

72. It is worth reminding the reader to compare Clausewitz's ideas here with his thoughts on the attack and the defense in books 6 and 7 of *On War*. The reader is encouraged to use the table of contents (*On War*, viii–x) to identify applicable parts and read small excerpts that relate to Clausewitz's ideas here.

73. Karl, 1:41–42.

74. This already violates Clausewitz's two principles of strategic planning: "Act with the utmost concentration. . . . act with the utmost speed." *On War*, book 8, chap. 4, 617. In that same section, he also argues that the "ultimate substance of enemy strength must be traced back to the fewest possible sources, and ideally to one alone." This idea ties in closely with his concept of *Schwerpunkt*, which is often rendered in English as "center of gravity." See *On War*, 595–596; F. G. Zimmerman, *Military Vocabulary German-English and English German* (London: Hugh Rees, 1915). For a detailed discussion, see Clausewitz, *Napoleon's 1796 Italian Campaign*, 19–22 (the relevant footnote is reproduced later in this volume in chapter 2, note 108). If continued pressure were to be exerted against the enemy's center of gravity in order to achieve success, then it is reasonable to argue that the maximum concentration of effort against this point would ensure the quickest route to victory. This relates to Clausewitz's ideas about

be very specific, and however much it may be felt necessary to leave decisions to the man on the spot, when several armies are involved, this united aim must never be entirely lacking. In this situation, then, the Austrian armies' activity in response to the unexpected opening of hostilities followed no rule other than the general tacit assumption that they should consider themselves assigned to the defense of whichever region they found themselves in. Only Archduke Charles's army seems to have had the provisional instruction to advance into the area between Lake Constance and the Danube, in order, as they put it, to cover the flank of the Army of the Tyrol.

To some extent, one can detect the germ of the intended plan just in how the main bodies were divided up.

Part of the archduke's 92,000-strong army was to observe the French Army of the Rhine, but the main body was to be used against the French Army of the Danube and that part of the French army in Switzerland that was operating west of Lake Constance. Hotze was to hold Vorarlberg and Graubündten, and Bellegarde the Tyrol, as a theater of operations connecting Germany and Italy, and for that purpose, the Austrian cabinet did not think a force of 73,000 men too many. But the actual offensive was to be conducted in Italy after Suvorov's arrival by an army of 100,000–120,000 men (depending on how strong the Russians were). The intention therefore seemed to be a war of active defense in Germany that could possibly also lead to the conquest of Switzerland, a passive defense in Graubündten and the Tyrol, and a true offensive in Italy.[75]

A simple comparison reveals how far this plan deviates from the one we proposed as suitable in the previous section.

---

continuity. See *On War*, 81–83. As such, the Austrians' plan placed their commanders in a difficult position from the start, as they were not concentrated in a way that allowed them to exert their full strength against the French *Schwerpunkt*, whatever that might have been—probably the army, given its close political ties with the Directory.

75. Archduke Charles points out that although the Austrians dedicated 73,000 troops to cover their lines of communication, they never really developed a secure base of operations from which they could operate against the French more effectively. They had no secure base from which to mount attacks and no formidable defensive position against which the French would struggle to act. Thus, those 73,000 troops served no meaningful purpose with regard to executing the campaign. Karl, 1:41–50. For an analysis of the role of a base of operations, see Nicholas Murray, *The Rocky Road to the Great War: The Evolution of Trench Warfare to 1914* (Washington, DC: Potomac Books, 2013), 1–44.

The main idea of making use of the initial great superiority in numbers to strike decisive blows is entirely missing. If the Austrians had had this intention, they would have tried to preempt the enemy by starting the war themselves. We will concede that this could have gone awry, in that, in such cases, it is easy to be a couple of weeks off in one's calculations; we will also acknowledge that the Austrian cabinet might have had some interest in not appearing to be the aggressor. But neither of these factors would have prevented them from having the intention to strike major blows right at the start by means of numerical superiority, since this does not necessarily require that the enemy be strategically surprised. In any case, such an intention would have prevented the Austrians from suffering strategic surprise themselves, as they did in March.[76]

The second piece of evidence that the Austrians had not thought to make decisive use of their initial superiority is the fact that they directed their main offensive against Italy, where they could not exploit their superiority until later, after the arrival of the Russians. This is likewise the second essential point in which the Austrian plan differs from ours.

In all this, though, we must not forget that while the balance of forces now seems clear to our eyes, it can hardly have been known to the Austrian government. Four weeks before the outbreak of war, the French government itself estimated the combat forces of the Armies of Switzerland and the Danube and the Army of Observation at about 140,000 men. After deducting about 20,000 for the Rhine fortresses, the French believed that 120,000 men were available, or 40,000 more than there actually were. If the French government could make this mistake, it is understandable that the Austrians did the same and thought the French army was 40,000–50,000 men stronger than it was. But as always happens, the Austrian government also thought its own army was somewhat stronger than the round numbers we have given for its effective strength, so the imbalance in its favor probably did not seem significantly less. In any case, the error cannot have been so large as to cause any doubt about the very substantial superiority of the Austrian army, and

---

76. Clausewitz seems to be saying that if the Austrians had concentrated their forces as he suggests, they would have been in a position to ward off a direct attack by the French, or they would have been in an advantageous position to take the offensive in the key theater of war, as they defined it. Either way, they would have been better positioned for the conflict.

it was this factor that demanded a decisive offensive right at the start of the campaign.

The third respect in which the Austrian plan differs from ours is the huge force of 73,000 men allocated simply to maintaining communications between the armies in Germany and Italy. We believe that 15,000–20,000 men would have been sufficient for this purpose.[77]

The fact that the Army of the Tyrol would be placed under an independent general meant that the total combat force would be entrusted to three army commanders, while our plan has only two. This apparently simple little fact actually raises a question of very great importance in strategy, because every division of command results in some loss of effectiveness[78] and must therefore be contemplated only as a necessary and nontrivial evil.[79] Here, the situation itself provided so little justification for this division that it must be regarded as having been merely for personal considerations that General Bellegarde was not placed under Archduke Charles's command. Personal considerations are dismissed out of hand by critics far too often and quite unreasonably; all human activity requires them, and in such an activity as war, it is inevitable that

---

77. This matches the archduke's point noted earlier.

78. This is where the Austrians' regulations and prior war experience played a role in their ongoing problems with dividing their force in the face of the enemy and all the command problems this caused (their experience in the 1796–1797 campaigns in Italy is a prime example). The sixth chapter (*Sechstes Kapitel*) of the regulations, explaining how to set out on a march to attack, is particularly enlightening in this regard. It calls for the use of multiple columns setting out independently, as this is more efficient in terms of movement, but it instructs the officers to maintain the strictest secrecy. Should the officer in charge not clearly communicate his intentions, or should circumstances change, it is easy to see how these columns might end up fighting individually and not as part of a greater whole, particularly in difficult terrain. Unlike the later introduction of divisions and corps, Austrian columns were not combined-arms organizations in the same sense, and they varied greatly in size. As such, they would have possessed an inconsistent ability to fight individually. Furthermore, spreading out one's forces leaves them vulnerable to a dynamic and vigorous enemy that could destroy each of these columns in turn. That the Austrians employed this type of deployment seems curious, until one remembers that these rules were written before the immense changes wrought by the French Revolution and the wars studied in this volume. *Generals Reglement* (Vienna: Johann Thoman Edlen von Trattern, 1769), 39–41.

79. Again, Clausewitz is getting at his principle of concentration from *On War*, book 8, chap. 4.

they occasionally become a major factor. Conversely, this justification can also be badly misapplied, and it is often the field on which the most pettifogging opinions run rampant, of which this case in point may serve as an example.

According to these major deviations from our plan, it follows that the archduke's army could not take on any role such as we had envisaged for it. If it were to send a substantial corps against Bernadotte and keep some 70,000 men facing Jourdan and Masséna's left wing, it would still be in a situation not without advantage, but it would not be equipped to strike very major blows.

Since the Austrians could not rely on any morale superiority, and indeed, it was much more to be feared that this lay with the enemy, it was essential for the Austrian plan that, wherever positive results were sought, they should have a healthy numerical superiority—that is, a ratio of between three to two and two to one.

Of course, we cannot say that the seeds of great disasters were already sown in the broad outlines of the Austrian designs, insofar as these were actually indicated; rather, just that they were the reason that a handsome advantage was left unused and a favorable moment passed by without result. The disasters that occurred in March were partly a consequence of strategic surprise, partly the fault of the commanders, and they were actually suffered in the very theater of operations where there was certainly no shortage of combat forces.

The French

As we discover from Jourdan's apologia[80] about his campaign, the French plan of operations referred to an available force of 190,000 men in Germany, Switzerland, and upper Italy, whereas we have taken its true size to be just 138,000. But since the Rhine garrisons must still be deducted from those 190,000 men,

---

80. **Clausewitz** notes: "*Précis des opérations de l'armée du Danube sous les ordres du Général Jourdan. Extrait des mémoires manuscrits de ce général. Paris an VIII.*" Year VIII is the year of the Revolutionary French Republic's calendar, which translates to 1799. Jourdan lists the following numbers for the French: Army of Naples, 60,000; Army of Italy, 80,000; Army of the Tyrol, 40,000; Army of the Danube, 80,000; Army of Observation on the Rhine, 40,000; Army of Observation in Switzerland, 20,000. Général Jourdan, *Précis des opérations de l'armée du Danube sous les ordres du Général Jourdan. Extrait des mémoires manuscrits de ce general* (Paris: Charles, VIII [1799]), 10.

the difference is not so great as to produce any very different conclusions by following the same principles, for it made no difference to the resulting aims or plans whether there were 170,000 men available or only 140,000.

Since the negotiations at Rastatt and the new alliance between Russia and England meant that it could be foreseen that the Austrians would certainly go to war again, the French government decided to seize the initiative and go on the offensive without delay.[81] We find the plan they used as the basis for the start of the campaign word for word in Jourdan's aforementioned self-exculpatory work, in the official form in which it was furnished to General Jourdan, as one of the senior commanders, by the minister of war. We wish to reproduce it here in full:

Orders for the missions and general movements of the field armies upon resumption of hostilities.

In the event of renewed hostilities in Germany and Italy, there shall be five armies, the Army of Mainz, the Army of Helvetia, an Army of Observation on the Rhine, the Army of Italy, and the Army of Rome.

Note: Until further orders, the French army in the Batavian Republic shall be charged with protecting the borders and territory of that republic, but it may be reduced to 15,000–20,000 men, including both field forces and garrisons, and troops of all arms; the remainder of its forces shall be attached to the army of observation.

Dispositions and missions of the field armies.
[Army of Mainz]
[Clausewitz omitted this heading,
which is reinstated here per his source]

As soon as hostilities are renewed, the Army of Mainz, with some 46,000 men of all arms, is tasked with operating in Swabia and Bavaria in particular.

---

81. Ross makes the argument that the French sought an offensive war for four main reasons: (1) They could not strike directly at England or Russia, and they hoped to force the Austrians to the peace table, as they had in 1797. (2) An offensive that removed the approaching Russian forces in western Europe also meant the tsar would be unable to continue the fight effectively against France. (3) The lack of sufficient logistical infrastructure meant the Directory needed to export the war elsewhere in order to pay and feed its own troops. (4) The internal political problems inside France—that is, the counterrevolutionaries—meant that fighting on French soil might result in an uprising. Ross, *Quest for Victory*, 213–215.

This army should immediately be provided with an artillery park, a supply train, transport, equipment, and ambulances in proportion to its size and suitable for its mission, which is to be in constant action in an area that is partly plains, partly hilly, and crossed in places by rivers.

It shall concentrate with the least possible delay between Hüningen and Landau, deployed in such a way as to be able to advance into Swabia via Kehl and Hüningen upon the Directory's order, or upon the first hostile action by Austria.

It shall move rapidly in several columns across the Black Mountains to the sources of the Danube, and from there it shall march between that river and Lake Constance, with its right pushed forward beyond that lake and supporting toward Bregenz.

Assuming that, either because of the enemy forces' strength and positions or by moving more quickly than them, the Army of Mainz is then able to move to the upper Lech, it shall carry out this move, which it shall execute with great speed, so as to prevent the Austrians from crossing this river.

The probability of this expedition's success depends above all on the assumption that it is the French armies that initiate hostilities.

Once the Army of Mainz reaches the Danube, it shall be renamed the Army of the Danube, its right shall be supported by the left of the Army of Helvetia, and in particular it shall aim to facilitate the latter in its march through Graubündten and the Tyrol. The successive moves that it may make to the Lech, the Isar, and the Inn shall depend on the enemy's dispositions, always with the aim of seizing control of the passes between the Tyrol and Bavaria.

Army of Helvetia

The Army of Helvetia, comprising field forces of about 30,000 men of all arms, to which shall be attached those Helvetian demi-brigades fit for service in the field, is to seize Graubündten and the Tyrol.

The left and center of this army shall cross the Rhine between Bregenz and Maienfeld so as to move in part on Chur and in part on Bregenz, and to take these places.

The right of the Army of Helvetia, comprising those demi-brigades which are at Bellinzona and supported by an equal number of troops detached from the Army of Italy in the Veltlin, shall march through the Veltlin upon Glarenz, and from there upon Botzen and Brixen.

The left and center of this army, after taking Bregenz and Chur, shall leave troops to hold these places and then recombine to reach the sources of the Inn, forcing all the crossings as far as Innsbruck and taking that place.

As soon as the army's right reaches Brixen, then according to circumstances, the Army of Italy may withdraw its troops if it is under pressure from a very numerous enemy or if necessary for its own operations.

Once the Army of Helvetia holds Bregenz it shall be renamed the Army of the Tyrol; it is under command of General Masséna, but for major movements and military operations it is subordinated to the commander in chief of the Army of Mainz.

In consequence of this arrangement, the commander in chief may attach a part of the Army of Helvetia to his right and direct its actions, while noting always that it is absolutely vital to the success of the campaign that this army should take the Inn valley and the city of Innsbruck.

Army of Observation

An Army of Observation on the Rhine shall be created and organized as soon as possible.

Its command shall be entrusted to General Bernadotte. This army, comprising 48,000 men of all arms according to the attached table, and including the garrisons in the Rhine fortresses, is to cover all the fortresses and bridges on the Rhine between Hüningen and Düsseldorf, as well as the country on the left bank of that river.

It is charged with continuing the siege of Ehrenbreitstein, undertaking operations against Philippsburg, and at the same time supporting the movements of the Army of Mainz by demonstrating against various points, especially on the Main, the Neckar, and the Enz.

It shall provide garrisons for the Rhine fortresses, adjusting their strengths either for their own defense or else only so much as is necessary to maintain order and protect government offices, according to whether these fortresses are more or less threatened by the relative positions of the French and enemy armies.

It shall leave sufficient troops before Ehrenbreitstein for the siege; the rest of this army, which shall be its field force proper, shall concentrate on the right bank of the Rhine, in front of Mainz between the Lahn and the Main, so as to move through the Landgraviate of Hesse-Darmstadt, before Mannheim and Philippsburg.

This corps shall act according to circumstances on the left and right banks of the Rhine, with the particular aims of supporting the operations of the Army of Mainz, taking Ehrenbreitstein and Philippsburg, and protecting the left bank of the Rhine against invasion.

This army, although commanded by a commander in chief, shall be subordinated to the general commanding the Army of Mainz for major movements and military operations.

Army of Italy

The Army of Italy, comprising some 50,000 men deployed on the Adige and the Po, not counting the Cisalpine, Ligurian, Polish, or Piedmontese troops, shall act to its left against Trient.

The bulk of the army shall cross the Adige toward Verona, which it shall take, and then push the enemy back behind first the Brenta and then the Piave.

The detached corps of this army in the Veltlin shall move on Glarenz, Botzen, and Brixen, in cooperation with that corps of the Army of Helvetia in the canton of Bellinzona.

Once it reaches Brixen, this corps may rejoin the left of the Army of Italy, if the enemy strength makes this essential or if it is necessary for the Army of Italy's further campaign operations.

This army is also to seize Tuscany as soon as it receives the order to do so.

Any French troops that the Army of Italy may have beyond the 50,000 above shall be used to protect Piedmont and the Cisalpine Republic and to feed the field army.

Army of Rome

The Army of Rome shall continue its conquest of the kingdom of Naples; once it takes Naples it shall be renamed the Army of Naples.

It is charged with giving assistance to the islands of Corfu and Malta.

This plan of military operations being entirely decreed and transmitted to the commanders in chief, and indicating to them the course of the operations they should carry out, they are to follow it unless they receive orders to the contrary from the government.

Approved by the Minister of War; signed: Schérer[82]

---

82. In the original French: "*Instruction sur la destination et les mouvemens généraux des armées actives au moment même de la reprise des hostilités.*"

En cas de reprise des hostilités en Allemagne et en Italie, il y aura cinq armées, l'armée de Mayence, l'armée d'Helvétie, une armée d'observation sur le Rhin, l'armée d'Italie at l'armée de Rome.

Nota: L'armée française dans la république batave continuera jusqu'à nouvel ordre à être chargée de couvrir les frontières et le territoire de cette république, mais elle pourra être réduite de quinze à vingt-mille hommes tant en bataillons de campagne que de garnison et en troupes de toutes armes; le surplus de ses forces sera affecté à l'armée d'observation.

Disposition et destination des armées actives.

Armée de Mayence

Au moment de la reprise des hostilités, l'armée de Mayence, composée d'environ 46,000 hommes de toutes armes, est destinée à agir particulièrement en Souabe et en Bavière.

Cette armée devra être immédiatement pourvue d'un parc d'artillerie, et d'un parc de vivres, transports, équipement et ambulances proportionnés à sa force et réglés sur sa destination qui sera d'être constamment agissante dans un pays tantôt de plaines, tantôt de défilés et quelquefois coupé par des rivières.

Elle se rassemblera dans le plus court délai possible entre Huningue et Landau, disposée de maniere à pouvoir déboucher en Souabe par Kehl et Huningue, au premier ordre du directoire, ou au premier acte d'hostilités de l'Autriche.

Elle se portera rapidement par plusieurs colonnes aux sources du Danube en traversant les montagnes noires, marchera de-là entre ce fleuve et le lac de Constance, sa droite poussée en avant de ce lac et venant appuyer vers Bregenz.

Dans la supposition, où par la position et les forces de l'ennemi ou en gagnant de vîtesse sur lui, l'armée de Mayence pourrait se porter de suite sur le Haut-Lech, elle fera ce mouvement, qu'elle exécutera avec une grande rapidité, afin d'empêcher les Autrichiens de passer cette rivière.

La probabilité du succès de cette expédition est surtout applicable à la supposition que les armées françaises commenceraient les hostilités.

L'armée de la Mayence au Danube, prendra le nom de l'armée du Danube, sa droite sera soutenu pa la gauche de l'armée d'Helvétie, elle aura particulièrement en vue de faciliter à cette dernière sa marche dans les Grisons et le Tyrol. Les mouvemens successifs qu'elle pourra faire sur le Lech, l'Isar et l'Inn, se règleront sur les dispositions de l'ennemie, en ayant toujours pour objet de se rendre maitresse des débouchés du Tyrol par la Bavière.

Armée d'Helvétie

L'armée d'Helvétie, composée en troupes de campagne de toutes armes, d'environ 30,000 hommes auxquels se joindront les demi-brigades helvétiques en état d'entrer en campagne, est destinée à s'emparer du pays des Grisons et du Tyrol.

La gauche et le centre de cette armée passeront le Rhin entre Bregenz et Mayenfeld pour se porter partie sur Coire et partie sur Bregenz dont on s'emparera.

La droite est l'armée d'Helvétie, composée des demi-brigades, qui sont à Bellinzona, soutenue par un pareil nombre de troupes, détachées de l'armée d'Italie dans la Walteline, marchera sur Glarenz par la Walteline, et de-là sur Botzen et Brixen.

La gauche et le centre de cette armée, après s'être emparé de Bregenz et de Coire, laisseront des troupes pour garder ces points, se réuniront ensuite pour gagner les sources de l'Inn en forçant tous les passages jusqu'à Inspruck dont elles s'empareront.

Lorsque la droite de l'armée sera arrivée à Brixen, l'armée d'Italie pourra, suivant les circonstances, en retirer ses troupes, si elle était pressée par un ennemi trop nombreux, ou que cela fut nécessaire pour ses opérations.

L'armée d'Helvétie, maitresse de Bregenz, prendra le nom de l'armée du Tyrol; elle est sous le commandement du Général Masséna, mais subordonnée pour les grands mouvemens et opérations de guerre au Général en Chef de l'armée de Mayence.

C'est en conséquence de cette disposition que le Général en Chef de cette dernière armée pourra, suivant les circonstances, attirer à sa droite et faire agir une partie de l'armée d'Helvétie en observant toujours qu'il est absolument nécessaire pour le succès de la campagne, que cette armée s'empare de la vallée de l'Inn et de la ville d'Inspruck.

Armée d'Observation

Il sera formée et organisée le plutôt possible une armée d'Observation sur le Rhin.

Le commendement en est confié au Général Bernadotte. Cette armée, composée d'après le tableau si-joint de 48,000 hommes de troupes de toutes armes y compris les garnisons des places sur le Rhin, est destinée à couvrir toutes les places et les ponts sur le Rhin, depuis Huningue jusqu'à Dusseldorf, ainsi que le pays sur la rive gauche de ce fleuve.

Elle est chargée de la continuation du blocus d'Ehrenbreitstein, des opérations à entreprendre sur Philippsbourg et d'appuyer en même tems les mouvemens de l'armée de Mayence par des démonstrations de troupes sur divers points, particulièrement sur le Main, le Neckar et l'Enz.

Elle fournira les garnisons des places sur le Rhin, en réglant leurs forces, tantôt sur leurs moyens de défense, tantôt sur ce qui est seulement nécessaire pour le maintien de l'ordre et le conservation des établissemens publics, selon que ces places seront plus un moins ménacées par la position respective des armées françaises et ennemies.

Elle détachera devant Ehrenbreitstein les troupes nécessaires au blocus; le surplus de cette armée, qui en sera, à proprement parler, le corps disponible, se formera en grande partie sur la rive droite du Rhin, en avant de Mayence entre la Lahn et le Main, pour se porter par le Landgraviat de Hesse-Darmstadt, en avant de Manheim et de Philippsbourg.

Ce corps agira suivant les circonstances sur la rive droite et la rive gauche du Rhin, ayant particulièrement pour objet d'appuyer les opérations de l'armée de Mayence, s'emparer d'Ehrenbreitstein et de Philippsbourg et de couvrir d'invasion la rive gauche du Rhin.

Cette armée, quoique commandée par un Général en Chef, sera subordonnée au Général commandant l'armée de Mayence pour les grands mouvemens et opérations de guerre.

Armée d'Italie

L'armée d'Italie, composée d'environ cinquante mille hommes de troupes disponibles sur l'Adige et le Po, non compris les troupes cisalpines, liguriennes, polonaises et piémontoises, agira par sa gauche sur Trente.

Le gros de l'armée passera l'Adige vers Vérone, dont il s'emparera et poussera ensuite l'ennemi successivement derrière la Brenta et la Piave.

It is fair to say that what is most striking about this plan of operations is that there is almost no mention of the enemy army, that is, only in passing, and that the stated objective of the three main armies' activity is actually no such thing, because all it consists of throughout is merely aiming for specific geographical locations.[83]

The Army of the Danube is to reach the upper Lech, then the Isar, and then the Inn, and then it is to occupy the exits from the Tyrol; the Army of Helvetia is to take Chur and Bregenz, reach the Inn, and take Innsbruck; the Army of Italy's left wing is to take Trient,[84] and the rest of it is to reach the Brenta and the Piave.

Le corps détaché de cette armée dans la Walteline, se portera sur Glarenz, Botzen et Brixen, de concert avec le corps de l'armée d'Helvétie, dans le canton de Bellinzona.

Arrivé à Brixen, le corps pourra rejoindre la gauche de l'armée d'Italie, si les forces de l'ennemi le rendaient indispensable, ou que cela fut nécessaire pour la suite des opérations de la campagne de l'armée d'Italie.

Cette armée est aussi destinée à s'emparer de la Toscana au premier ordre qu'elle en recevrait.

Le surplus au-delà des 50,000 hommes ci-dessus qui se trouverait à l'armée d'Italie en troupes françaises, servira à couvrir le Piemont et la Cisalpine et à alimenter l'armée active.

Armée de Rome

L'armée de Rome continuera la conquête du royaume de Naples; elle prendra à Naples le nom de l'armée de Naples.

Elle est chargée de donner des secours aux îles de Corfou et de Malte.

Le plan d'opérations de guerre entièrement arrêté et transmis aux généraux en chef, leur indique la suite des opérations à exécuter, ils le suivront, à moins l'ordre contraire du gouvernement.

Approuvé par le Ministre de la guerre; signé: Schérer." Jourdan, *Précis des opérations de l'armée du Danube*, 48–56.

83. If war is in essence a political activity, as Clausewitz argues, then it would be logical to assume that the physical objectives should line up with the political ones and that the utmost concentration of force should be obtained to maximize the chance for success. Here the French plan fails on all counts. It does not provide clear political objectives, nor does it provide military objectives that tie into clear political goals, and the efforts of the armies are not coordinated. This is contrary to Clausewitz's ideas from *On War*, book 1, chap. 1, and book 8, chap. 6. The French offensive plan, however, did fit with Clausewitz's point about increasing the cost to the enemy. By seizing the enemy's territory, one increases his costs and thus forces him to calculate whether the value of the objective being sought is worth the costs imposed. *On War*, 92–94.

84. The original says Trieste, but this must be a typographical error.

This striving for all these points, of course, implies that any opposing enemy should be driven off. If this enemy is only weak, so that driving him off can be regarded as a secondary and inevitable matter, then that is obviously not an objective worthy of the name. But if the enemy might be strong and major battles may ensue, it would be much better to focus on that and to make victory over him the aim of the exercise. Since this was not done, it seems as though the mission can be accomplished just by taking the designated locations, that is, adopting a different position.

The mere attainment of a new position can be the objective of an operation only if this position is much stronger or if the occupied territory gained thereby bestows great advantages. If it is not the former but the latter that is the case, the first question to ask is whether the balance of forces allows us to advance into it.

That is to say, it is a natural and general rule that from the moment one of the two belligerents seeks to change the status quo to his advantage by adopting a new deployment forward of his initial one, he puts pressure on the enemy forces that was not there before, thereby provoking the enemy into action. This therefore changes the situation to his disadvantage and generally reduces his chance of success, even if his power of resistance is no weaker in itself.[85]

The actions of the Austrians against Frederick the Great in Bohemia were very different from those in Silesia.[86]

By the same token, any French deployment in Swabia and the Tyrol would have been much more likely to rouse the superior Austrian forces to action than would one behind the Rhine, and this consideration must be added to the balance.

---

85. Clausewitz is pointing out that by advancing, one is moving further away from one's own base of support and thus becoming weaker, based on his ideas about culmination. However, for the sake of argument, he writes that in this case, the aggressor (the one advancing) is no weaker. Thus, he is saying that this offensive movement increases the likelihood of enhanced enemy resistance. As such, even if the aggressor maintains his strength, the enemy has increased his will to resist, thus changing the balance of power between the two. See *On War*, book 7, chap. 5, 528.

86. Here, Clausewitz is referencing the Silesian wars of the mid-eighteenth century. The campaigns went back and forth across Bohemia and Silesia, but given Silesia's immense wealth, the Austrians made a far greater and more sustained effort to retake it. We cannot know for certain, but we think Clausewitz is making a point about the value of the object to one side. Taking something valuable from an opponent will al-

But even a child can grasp that a French deployment behind the Inn and the Piave is intrinsically much weaker than one behind the Adige and the Rhine.

The first and major mistake in the French plan of campaign is that it makes no mention of where the main bodies of the enemy's combat forces are or can be expected to be or how strong they might be, so as to combine their own forces for large offensive or defensive battles according to these data. Geographical factors could and should come into play in these combinations, but they are just one aspect of the main question, not the main question itself.

We must not make the mistake of thinking that, since we know the execution of this plan gave rise to glorious feats of arms in Graubündten and the Tyrol, the plan relied on these and on strategic surprise. In what follows, it will be very easy for us to show that these military victories were quite independent of the strategic combinations. On the French side, they were founded simply on the merits of the divisional generals and their troops, and nothing about them derived from the effects of strategic surprise.

Also, the plan of operations does not feature strategic surprise as such but is merely intended insofar as they aimed to reach the upper Lech in Swabia before Archduke Charles.

But the French plan of operations cannot even tacitly be said to have as its basis the intention to strike major blows by means of strategic surprise, since only the Austrian troops in Graubündten and Vorarlberg were exposed to such a surprise; those behind the Lech and in the Inn valley were obviously too far away. But these forces comprised only 12,000–15,000 men, a very small fraction of the whole, so the advantages that could be gained over them hardly seemed worth the effort.

Our second remark on the French plan of operations is that, in seeking the new line of deployment, particular importance is attached to the highest places. At the time, a fashionable view had emerged that has still not entirely disappeared: to deduce from the possibility of an individual high point dominating a lower region in a certain sense, a quite generally conceived dominance of higher regions over lower ones.

---

most certainly result in an increased degree of resistance and will potentially raise the political stakes of the conflict, with all the risks inherent in that situation. As such, why do it, unless it is critical to success? Furthermore, the Austrians' effort in those campaigns could reasonably be said to represent the campaigns' relative value to them. See *On War*, book 1, chap. 1. For an account of the Silesian wars, see Dennis E. Showalter, *The Wars of Frederick the Great* (London: Longman, 1996).

We must always limit the reality of this dominance in strategy according to the way in which it actually takes effect, as we explained in our discussion of Switzerland. Any vaguely thought out conclusions from it are entirely illusory.

If the geometrical principle can at least be considered applicable in its strategic outlines if the tactical outcomes are favorable, the operation of that geological principle [the value of using the dominance of higher regions] is completely absent in this case, and everything that was sacrificed for it in terms of military effort was completely wasted.[87]

Thus, in accordance with that illusory notion, the French believed that if they held the sources of the Inn and the Adige, they would undermine the deepest foundations of Austrian resistance in Germany and Italy. It would then be a pure delight to work their way down from top to bottom in a fight they therefore could not lose.

It was simply from this point of view that the occupation of the Tyrol and Graubündten, as the highest terrain, became such an important objective for them.

The operations of the Army of the Danube are entirely subordinated to this conquest, since it is explicitly stated that its primary mission is to facilitate the conquest of the Tyrol.

If we summarize the actions prescribed for Jourdan's and Masséna's armies in a single clear picture, it is this: 12,000 men should wrap around the Tyrol from Italy and 15,000 from Switzerland like left and right arms, while 40,000 men (allowing for the deduction of some detachments) move to the upper Lech as a kind of echelon.

We ask: was that the kind of setup with which to take on the 170,000 Austrians this brought them into contact with?

87. The point Clausewitz is making here relates to his ideas about geometry in war and the role of mountains. He argues that "geometry forms the basis of tactics in the narrower sense—the theory of moving troops. In field fortification and in the theory of entrenched positions and their attack, the lines and angles of geometry rule like judges who will decide the contest." However, he makes it clear that these ideas relate "only faintly in strategy" and have little effect at the strategic level. He is pointing out here that if the rules of geometry do apply, then the rules about the importance of mountains make no sense, as they contradict each other. He is criticizing both the French plan's illogicality and contemporaneous theorists such as Jomini, Saxe, and Bülow. The latter two saw war as being more scientific and mathematical and thus precisely calculable and predictable, particularly Heinrich von Bülow, *Geist des Neuern Kriegssystems* (Hamburg: August Campe, 1835). See *On War*, book 3, chap. 15, 214–215.

This is how the French plan of operations looks if we stop at the document itself. But we can see all too well that this instruction is hardly the result of clear thinking, so we can hardly be surprised that, in the correspondence between the minister of war as an organ of government and one of the senior commanders, General Jourdan, a very different idea emerges as the main aim, which we must consequently also discuss here. This idea is none other than that Jourdan should defeat the archduke in a major battle, and that the aim should be a most decisive strategic offensive. While the troops' numbers might seem insufficient, their spirit and superior morale compared with that of the Austrians should more than compensate.

A letter of 22 *ventôse* (10 February) from the minister of war to Jourdan said:

> To wreak national vengeance on these perfidious governments; the ever-growing national interest which, if we take to the field once more, can only be secured by decisive victories; all these motives will inflame the ardor of the troops and, supported by the skill and wisdom of your military dispositions, must inspire our justified confidence. . . . The Austrians are many, but not to mention our superior boldness and dynamism, it must be noted that they have an immense area to protect and that in advancing against us they are obliged to leave many troops in their rear, whether to occupy Bavaria, or to defend Bohemia, or to guard points in between, and that being so scattered, it seems that the main army which will act against us cannot be very numerically superior to yours.[88]

But in a letter four weeks earlier, after reckoning the Army of Helvetia, the Army of the Danube, and the Army of Observation at 100,000 men, the minister had said, among other things:

> And certainly these forces set in motion by the same mind and following the same plan can well take their chances with 100,000 or 120,000 of the Emperor's troops, especially if these three armies all coordinate their

---

88. In the original French: "*La vengeance nationale à exercer contre les gouvernments perfides; l'intérêt toujours croissant de la paix qui ne pourra plus s'obtenir, si nous rentrons en campagne, que par des triomphes décisifs; tous ces motifs enflammant l'ardeur de nos troupes et secondés par la sagesse et le talent de vos dispositions militaires doivent nous inspirer une sécurité fondée. . . . Les Autrichiens sont nombreux, mais sans parler de la supériorité d'audace et d'activité que nous avons sur eux, il faut observer qu'ils ont un*

respective positions and attacks, which is the most certain method, not to say the most decisive, against the Austrians, who are accustomed to grand maneuvers which in their execution always lack unity, by the very nature of things. *Is it not impossible, anyway, for the enemy to set in motion more than 40,000–50,000 men combined against a single military position?*[89]

From these excerpts, of course, it emerges quite clearly how differently from us the French government saw the situation at that moment. We would have thought the French would have trouble maintaining themselves on the heights of the political position they had taken against the impact of this new coalition, but the Directory has no inkling of that. Rather, it thinks there can be no question of anything other than continuing along its customary path of conquest. There is no trace here of the idea of using the time before the Russians arrived for an early offensive, which Jomini asserts was the basic idea and which he plucks entirely out of thin air; indeed, Jourdan even counts 24,000 Russians among the Austrians' combat forces.[90]

Furthermore, it emerges that the French government estimated the Austrians' combat forces in Germany at only 120,000 men, when in fact they had 170,000. We would, however, certainly be on the wrong track if we thought this error was the reason for their ambitious plans; on the contrary, it is these ambitious plans arising from the spirit of revolution that are the reason they worried so little about the enemy's combat forces. Usually one somewhat overestimates both one's own forces and the enemy's, but to underestimate

---

terrain immense à couvrir qu'en s'avançant vers vous ils sont obligés de laisser beaucoup de troupes derrière eux, soit pour occuper la Bavière, soit pour défendre la Bohême, soit pour garder les points intermédiaires, et qu'étant ainsi disseminée, l'armée principale qui agira contre vous, ne parait pas devoir vous être beaucoup supérieure en force numérique." Jourdan, *Précis des opérations de l'armée du Danube*, 97.

89. In the original French: "*Et certes vos forces mises en mouvement par la même tête et sur le même plan, peuvent bien disputer la fortune à 100,000 or 120,000 des troupes de l'Empereur, sur-tout s ices trois armées se serrent chacune dans leurs positions et dans leurs attaques respectives, ce qui est la méthode la plus sûre, pour ne pas dire decisive, contre les Autrichiens, accoutumés à de grands mouvemens, qui, à l'exécution, manquent toujours dans leur ensemble, par la nature même des choses. N'est il pas impossible, d'ailleurs, que l'ennemi mette en movement, avec ensemble, sur une même position militaire plus de 40 à 50,000 hommes?*" Jourdan, *Précis des opérations de l'armée du Danube*, 66.

90. Clausewitz is harsh but correct. Jomini did point out that the Directory called

them by a whole third can happen only with such a disorganized and fraudulent government as the Directory.[91]

The idea that the archduke would weaken himself significantly by a large number of detachments and thereby offer the opportunity to beat him without being too exposed to his numerical superiority would be tolerable in itself, albeit it did not in fact turn out like that at all, if it were not made completely nonsensical by the dispersal of their own forces, a dispersal that the enemy's could not surpass.

The last sentence we have quoted cannot really be understood unless we remember that the idea of the normal strength of an army[92] was conceived by Montalembert (in his *Correspondance*)[93] and Tempelhof in his *Geschichte des siebenjährigen Krieges in Deutschland, 1783–1801*[94]—a violation of sound common sense, such as war has often had to put up with in his theories.[95]

---

the Russian army's continued advance west a declaration of war. He then stated that the French plan called for a decisive blow before the arrival of the Russian army, which was a logical step if the Directory believed that war had already effectively been declared. Jomini, however, provides no evidence for his claim. See Jomini, 11:33–86. See also Ross, *Quest for Victory*, 28–29, 89–90, 96.

91. This is where Clausewitz's hatred of the French Republic might have influenced his criticism. Although he was technically correct in his criticism of Jomini, he was overly harsh, given that the logical French response was to attack the Austrians before the Russians showed up.

92. This paragraph is virtually identical in tone to its equivalent in *On War*, 196.

93. Marquis de Montalembert, *Correspondance de Monsieur le Marquis de Montalembert, étant employé par le Roi de France à l'Armée Suédoise, avec Mr. le Marquis d'Havrincour . . . pendant les campagnes de 1757, 58, 59, 60 et 61: pour servir à l'histoire de la dernièr guerre*, 3 vols. (London, 1777).

94. Henry Lloyd, *Geschichte des siebenjährigen Krieges in Deutschland zwischen dem Könige von Preussen und der Kaiserin Königin mit ihren Alliirten vom General Lloyd*, trans. Georg Tempelhoff, 6 vols. (Berlin: Gedrukt und verlegt von Johann Friedrich Unger, 1783–1801).

95. See *On War*, book 3, chap. 8, 194–197, particularly the footnote on 196. The idea that there was a maximum usable army size was quite common in the eighteenth century. Given that the mechanism of control of an eighteenth-century army was often limited to a king and one or two trusted subordinates, and given that there were no formal division or corps organizational structures, it is reasonable to believe that an enormous army might be difficult for one person to manage. The reforms in armies' organizational structures that started before the French Revolution would continue during the Revolutionary and Napoleonic Wars. These organizational reforms transformed the utility of large armies and made them much more flexible and control-

Thus the chimera of an irresistible offensive is built on such ignorance and such follies.

But even if we use this chimera as the basis for the instruction quoted above, we must be astonished anew by the latter.

It would be very long and tedious to discuss in full the individual inanities, contradictions, ambiguities, and follies in this instruction, but we must touch on its main traits in passing.

How can one consider such an insignificant river as the upper Lech a good line of defense against a very superior army? What is to prevent this army from crossing the lower Lech? How can the Army of the Danube hold the passes from the Tyrol at the same time it is supposed to be advancing? It would be frittered away.

Masséna was supposed to advance on Chur and Bregenz simultaneously with his center and his left wing, about 16,000–18,000 men, but there is no mention at all of the heavily fortified position at Feldkirch. Then he is supposed to reunite his dispersed center and attain the sources of the Inn, *en forçant tous les passages jusqu'à Inspruck* [forcing all the crossings as far as Innsbruck]. Who could possibly understand that?

The right wing of the Army of Helvetia was supposed to move through the Veltlin on Glarus in the valley of the Adige, then down that valley to Botzen and Brixen, but we cannot tell whether it was supposed to operate against the German border or the Italian one.

The Army of Italy was supposed to act against Trient[96] with its left wing, with its right and center against the Brenta, and to conquer Tuscany in its rear into the bargain, even though the enemy was stronger than it was. It was to cross the Adige near Verona, even though Verona was an enemy fortress and was exactly where the enemy's main army could be expected to be.

If this indescribable nonsense did not lead to great disasters beyond just failing to achieve its aim, this is because, first, it was executed only in very small part, and second, like a man struck by catalepsy who can barely move his

---

lable—that is, as long as the person in charge was willing to delegate control of corps and divisions to subordinates. This was seen in the massive expansion in the size of field armies during the period. Two excellent books on tactical and organizational changes in the French army and in European armies more broadly are Jonathan Abel, *Guibert: Father of Napoleon's Grande Armée* (Norman: University of Oklahoma Press, 2016), and Schneid, *European Armies of the French Revolution*.

96. This was misstated in the original as Trieste.

individual limbs at all, the Austrians dragged themselves forward only gradually and with difficulty and without nerve or muscle power.[97]

7 JOURDAN AND BERNADOTTE BEGIN THE CAMPAIGN

At the opening of the campaign, the Army of the Danube under Jourdan's direct command had the following organization and strength:

Advance guard (Lefebvre): 9,000 men
1st Division (Férino): 8,000
2nd Division (Souham): 7,000
3rd Division (St. Cyr): 6,700
Flanking corps (Vandamme): 3,000
Cavalry reserve (d'Hautpoul): 3,200[98]
Total: 37,000 men[99]

---

97. For similarly harsh and sustained criticism of the Austrians' lack of thought and action, see Clausewitz, *Napoleon's 1796 Italian Campaign*.

98. François-Joseph Lefebvre (1755–1820) went on to become one of the original marshals of France; Pierre Marie Batholomé Férino (1747–1816) had a decent career, but there were suspicions that he remained somewhat of a royalist; Joseph Souham (1760–1837) was another whose career suffered because of suspicions about his royalist leanings; Laurent Gouvion-St. Cyr (1764–1830) probably would have become a marshal of France had he been more openly enthusiastic about the empire; Dominique Joseph René Vandamme (1771–1830) had a good career, but his ill temperament kept him from becoming a marshal of France; Jean Joseph Ange d'Hautpoul (1754–1807) was a good cavalry commander killed at the battle of Eylau. All went on to have successful careers, and it is worth noting the difference in their ages when compared with their Austrian peers.

99. Clausewitz's numbers are virtually identical—albeit rounded up or down—to Jomini's, which indicates that Jomini was his likely source. In contrast, Archduke Charles has Jourdan with 46,000 men. The reason for the archduke's much higher estimate is not clear. Although his tally matches Jourdan's, Jourdan makes it clear that once the campaign starts, he has 38,000 men. As such, it seems disingenuous for the archduke to use the higher figure, and one must be skeptical of his motives for doing so. See Jomini, 11:96–97 (fold-out chart between the pages); Karl, 1:52; Jourdan, *Précis des opérations de l'armée du Danube*, 57, 82.

On 1 March it crossed the Rhine at Kehl and Basel and advanced across the Black Forest in four columns—namely, via the *Waldstädte*,[100] through the Höllen, Kinzig, and Rench valleys, and to the heights of Rothweil and Blomberg—while the advance guard reached Tuttlingen, where it arrived on the 6th and halted to await events in Graubündten.

France had still not formally declared war on Austria. Jourdan, fearing the archduke's superior force, interpreted his order to advance as if he were only supposed to move forward into an advanced position.

However, the orders of 2 *ventôse* (10 February) state: "The commander in chief of the Army of Mayence shall move the army under his command without delay beyond the Black Mountains, and shall occupy the sources of the Neckar and the Danube, and the positions indicated in the above orders."[101] The latter probably means the positions on the Lech, Isar, and Inn, and Jourdan's halt cannot have been what the Directory intended. This is all the more likely because, as we shall see, Jourdan did not wait for the formal declaration of war in his new position.

Jourdan most likely hoped that a large part of the archduke's force would be drawn toward Masséna's invasion of Graubündten and that, at the same time, another part would be drawn to Franconia by Bernadotte's appearance there.[102]

---

100. *Waldstädte*, literally "forest towns," refers to the towns of Rheinfelden, Säckingen (now Bad Säckingen), Laufenburg, and Waldshut (now Waldshut-Tiengen), which lay on the main Austrian route west along the upper Rhine River. Rheinfelden and the part of Laufenburg on the left bank of the Rhine were on the French side of the river following the October 1797 Treaty of Campo Formio, which marked the end of the War of the First Coalition. The strategic location of these towns meant that they were in a much-disputed area between the two main competing states: Austria and France. See Christian Ruch, "Waldstädte," in *Historisches Lexikon Der Schweiz*, http://www.hls-dhs-dss.ch/textes/d/D7350.php.

101. In the original French: "*Le Général en Chef de l'Armée de Mayence portera sans délai l'armée qu'il commande, au delà des montagnes noires[,] et occupera les sources du Necker et du Danube[,] et les positions indiquées par les instructions précédentes.*" Jourdan, *Précis des opérations de l'armée du Danube*, 74.

102. Jourdan was much concerned that the Austrians would flank him to his left and cut his forces off. In a 1 March letter to the Directory, he writes rather dramatically of it being easier to die gloriously than to find laurels in his situation. Jourdan, *Précis des opérations de l'armée du Danube*, 93–94.

Jourdan threw a pontoon bridge across at Breisach and established a bridgehead.

Bernadotte and his so-called Army of Observation—which, however, at the opening of the campaign was still so weak that, after deducting the garrisons of Mainz and Ehrenbreitstein, no more than 8,000 men could have taken the field—likewise crossed the Rhine on 1 March near Mannheim; occupied Mannheim, which the Austrians were unable to provision sufficiently and had therefore evacuated; and laid siege to Philippsburg.

In his headquarters at Friedberg, the archduke learned of the French crossings on 3 March. Since he was fully prepared for this and his army was very concentrated, as early as the 4th, he was able to cross the Lech with his advance guard of no fewer than 9,500 infantry (nine battalions) and 7,800 cavalry (forty-four squadrons) and to have the rest of his troops leave their quarters, so that his 37,800 infantry (thirty-nine battalions) crossed the Lech at Augsburg, Landsberg, and Schongau on the 9th, and his 16,000-strong cavalry (ninety-four squadrons) on the 14th. The cavalry regiments that had been further to the rear only arrived later.

Apart from those troops, another 6,600 men (six battalions) moved to garrison Ulm, 1,500 men (three battalions) came from Bohemia to Ingolstadt, and 9,800 infantry (seven battalions) and 3,500 cavalry (twenty squadrons) under Starray, who had been posted on the left bank of the Danube at Neumarkt, moved toward the Regnitz.

While the advance guard moved in three columns to Biberach, Waldsee, and Ravensburg, the army concentrated behind it in quarters between Memmingen and Leutkirch.

Since there was nothing to be feared from the foe in Franconia, General Starray was moved from the Regnitz to the Danube.

Archduke Charles's intention was to keep to the central axis between the upper Danube and Lake Constance in order to encounter the enemy by the most direct line and fight a major battle against him.

Since this first advance by the French army actually only acted as a demonstration and drew the Austrian main army toward it while Hotze was being attacked in Graubündten and Vorarlberg, and since the decisive events between Jourdan and the archduke only occurred at the same time as the last decisive blows in the Tyrol, by which time those in Graubündten had already happened, let us turn our attention first to Graubündten, from there to the Tyrol, and only then back to the two armies on the Danube.

8 MASSÉNA'S CENTER DESTROYS AUFFENBERG'S CORPS IN THE RHINE VALLEY

As we mentioned earlier, Vorarlberg and Graubündten were occupied by 26,000 men under the command of General Hotze, and Hotze was operating under the overall command of Archduke Charles.

These 26,000 men constituted twenty-three battalions and eight squadrons. The archduke had ordered General Hotze to use his main body to defend the crossing at Bregenz in order to protect the left flank of the archduke's operations between the Danube and Lake Constance. Hence Hotze had occupied Bregenz with thirteen battalions; five battalions were in the Feldkirch position, one battalion was at the Luciensteig, and four battalions and one squadron were under the command of General Auffenberg in Graubündten, specifically, in the Rhine valley. The Engadin was held by a couple of battalions from the Army of the Tyrol.

Before we describe the French attack on General Auffenberg, we must allow ourselves a brief reflection on the nature of the defense among high mountains and give ourselves a clear picture of the shape of the terrain, so as to appreciate General Auffenberg's situation properly.

The defense among high mountains has its own particular difficulties and is obviously less strong than that among medium-sized mountains. It is not easy to maintain actual defensive positions on a high ridge, because even if artillery could be got up there and back down, it cannot be kept there owing to the lack of provisions and the cold in the winter season; besides, the lack of lateral communications makes each position extremely isolated.[103]

103. Clausewitz devotes several sections of *On War* to the issue of defending in mountains (book 6, chaps. 15–17, 417–431). This topic also relates to one of his other important ideas, albeit one that is commonly found in military theory: keeping one's forces concentrated at the decisive point (book 3, chap. 11, 302). Defending in mountains often requires the use of detachments, which may be relatively isolated by the difficult terrain. Each small detachment might be able to defend its position quite effectively, due to the difficulty of an aggressor moving against an individual detachment. This is a great bonus, but said detachment is often at risk of defeat in detail. Thus, as Clausewitz explains, defending a mountain range with several points of access might require a covering force for each access point. The difficulty of moving between these points (typically, mountain valleys) means that these detachments might well be isolated from one another and thus unable to concentrate effectively when the enemy seeks to move a concentrated force through the mountains. Although the use of mountains for a defensive position has many advantages, particularly at the tactical

If what matters is the defense of the valley itself, then there can be even less question of positions on the heights, because its dimensions are usually too large for it to be possible to fire from the top of the ridge down into the valley.

As a consequence, one is obliged either to establish positions in suitable places on the slopes—of which there is not much chance, because these will always be overlooked from another position nearby—or else to put them right down in the valley. If the line of these defensive positions runs parallel to the valley, they are protected by the river and its banks—assuming, of course, that the road running alongside the river happens to be on the defenders' side of it. This obviously does not give the whole line any particular strength, as the rivers and streams are mostly wadable, and their banks are certainly not steep and inaccessible everywhere. But of course, individual places can provide very strong positions, particularly where no progress can be made except along a road that leads over a bridge or a very narrow or steep spot that is suitable for a very strong defense. These individual strongpoints can then become the means for defense of the whole. In particular, even if the enemy marches down into the valley by crossing the high ridge on his side in several columns, he cannot immediately advance any further across the ridge on our side; rather, he must secure the valley and its road above all else. Thus it is not sufficient for him to break through our line; he must gain control of the individual positions. Such a valley defense is therefore like a fortress's covered way, to where the garrison has fallen back behind the traverses and places of arms before the enemy's attack.[104]

Now, if the individual positions are really strong, and if enough support arrives in good time, the enemy who finds himself in a very unfavorable situa-

---

level, there is also the significant danger of being bypassed or outflanked, cut off, and destroyed if the defenders spread their forces too thin or if they are unable to concentrate effectively against an advancing enemy main body.

104. A covered way is a passageway sheltered from enemy fire; typically, this is a walkway dug behind a parapet of a fortress or a temporary field position. See Murray, *The Rocky Road to the Great War*, 245. This serves the purpose of providing the defense with cover, so that fewer soldiers can be used to man a particular section of line, thus freeing up men for use elsewhere. In addition, soldiers can use the parapet as cover to retreat to another defensive position or to shield concentrated defensive forces seeking to counterattack. Again, this works only if there is a concentrated force to fall back on or if the defense can buy sufficient time for such a force to be concentrated in front of the enemy. Otherwise, all this does is provide a tactically difficult problem for the attacker who can throw his whole force against an isolated enemy.

tion can easily be driven back again, which will happen with not insignificant loss. But these positions are usually not as strong as people think; they rest on steep mountain slopes that can be scaled by detours at the cost of some time and effort. These positions can be seriously overlooked, fired on from the rear, and so forth, which usually results in their loss. But the major flaw in such a defensive line is that if it becomes necessary to retreat, the line of retreat is already lost for a portion of these positions. The retreat is usually along transverse valleys, so the key positions are usually sought at the mouths of these valleys; but because these do not always coincide, and because entrances into the valleys are few and other footpaths over the ridges are just as rare, so it can easily happen that part of the force is captured by the enemy. This is the situation when the line of defense runs along the length of the valley.

If the line of deployment runs perpendicular to the direction of the main valleys and ridges, the defense will obviously be stronger, for the enemy is now restricted to far fewer points of attack and, for most of the positions, the line of retreat is not threatened. But in this case, either the positions are very isolated because communications have to run across the ridges, or else if they run through transverse valleys, the previous case applies once again.

The result of these considerations is that the defense among very high mountains achieves less than that among those of more moderate height. In particular, instead of the great advantage of prolonged resistance in which one contests every inch of the ground, and instead of the advantage of relatively light losses when disengaging, which makes mountain defense so very valuable for small bodies of troops, here we find exactly the opposite.

Graubündten consists of two long valleys—the Anterior Rhine and the Inn—and several transverse ones. The left slope of the Rhine valley and the right slope of the Inn create its northwestern and southeastern borders, while the southwestern border is formed by the high ridge of the Alps that divides the Italian rivers, the Ticino and the Maira, from the German Rhine and Inn.

Crossing all these mountain ranges are just a few small mountain paths passable only on foot. Their highest points, the so-called passes, are given individual names. They can be crossed by infantry only slowly and with difficulty and by light artillery, at best, if specially equipped. That northern edge of the Rhine valley has only a few more passable roads from Maienfeld down toward the Walensee and in Appenzell Canton, because there the massif is cloven by wide valleys.

The troops based in the Rhine valley had no perpendicular line of retreat other than the Inn valley, since the valleys on the Italian slopes were in French hands. But from the Rhine to the Inn valley, paths lead through the following transverse valleys:

1. From Reichenau through the Posterior Rhine and Albula valley across the Julierberg and the Albula River.
2. From Chur [Coire] through the Schanfigg[105] valley over the Strelenberg to Davos and then across the Scaletta and the Flülen.
3. From Maienfeld through the Prettigau and likewise across the Flülen.
4. From Feldkirch through the Montafu to Martinsbrück.

But in fact, the main line of retreat for these troops was to Feldkirch, which was an extension of their front.

General Auffenberg established his main position at Chur, occupied Reichenau and Maienfeld from there, and used a battalion together with the armed peasants to occupy all the passes across the northwestern edge of the Rhine valley and those over the main alpine ridge as far as the Splügen. These positions were probably mainly held only by the locals. The St. Gotthard Pass lies outside Graubündten's borders and was held by the French, so the Austrian position on this side of it was at Disentis.[106]

The St. Luciensteig is an old Graubündten fort comprising a hornwork[107] and two flanking redoubts facing the Vorarlberg, that is, toward Austria. It blocks the main road from Feldkirch between Balzers and Maienfeld where it crosses the foot of the mountain through a gorge formed by the steep rocky massif of the Falkenisberg on one side and the Fläschnerberg on the other. The redoubts rested against these mountains. This work was held by one battalion with five guns. Thus it secured the right flank of General Auffenberg's deploy-

---

105. The original had Schalsick (presumably Schälsick), which means the "wrong" side of the valley. The Schanfigg valley is the one that matches the physical geographical location.

106. If one looks at a map of the region, it is clear why Clausewitz makes the point about a mountain defense and concentration. To cover each pass with a force strong enough to delay an advancing enemy would probably mean that other routes of advance were left undermanned or that small parts of the army could be isolated and defeated in detail.

107. This was a pair of demi-bastions or a pair of connected redans. Its profile resembled the horns and head of an animal. See Murray, *The Rocky Road to the Great War*, 246.

ment and protected him against any force that might advance across the Rhine below the Luciensteig. The outpost at Reichenau was at the twin bridges over the Rhine there. At Chur there were advantageous heights for a central position. The stretch of the Rhine from Reichenau to the Luciensteig was crossed by the two bridges at Reichenau and by the so-called lower toll bridge at the confluence of the Lanquart; there were also a few fords, but because of the high water level at this time, these were not very usable.

It can be seen at a glance that this situation did not allow a strong defense and that some losses were to be feared, even though things turned out quite differently from the way one might have expected. Since the French deployment meant that they largely enveloped General Auffenberg's left flank as far as the Splügen, it was especially to be feared that first the position at Reichenau and then also that at Chur would be taken in rear, cut off from the Engadin, and therefore driven back on the Luciensteig and Feldkirch; then it all depended on whether the two positions at Feldkirch and the Luciensteig could hold out long enough for Hotze to arrive in sufficient force to drive off the French from whatever places they might have occupied between the two. If the Luciensteig fell before then, Auffenberg's corps would be lost. We shall see that things turned out somewhat differently, but no less unfortunately.[108]

Masséna's army was organized as follows:

Division Xaintrailles (left wing): Brigades Ruby, Oudinot
Division Ménard (center): Brigades Lorge, Chabran
Division Lecourbe (right wing): Brigades Loison, Ainoni[109]

The first two divisions stood on Lake Zurich and Lake Walen, while the third was on the Italian side of the Alps near Bellinzona, with outposts in the alpine passes.

---

108. This is the key to Clausewitz's idea. The forces spread out across the mountains are effective only if they are able to hold up the French advance long enough to allow the Austrians to concentrate. If this fails to happen, the individual forces are, in essence, wasted.

109. Charles Xaintrailles (1769–1833), Nicolas Charles Oudinot (1767–1847), Jean François Xavier Ménard (1756–1831), Jean Thomas Guillaume Lorge (1767–1826), Joseph Chabran (1763–1843), Claude Jacques Lecourbe (1758–1815), and Louis Henri Loison (1771–1866) all went on to hold division command or higher in the French army, with Chabran being described as a brilliant division commander. Again, it is worth noting their respective ages at the time of the campaign.

If we take the confused French plan of operations as we have just described it[110] and interpret it in the simplest way, Masséna was supposed to advance with two divisions across the Rhine above Lake Constance into Swabia between the Lech and Lake Constance, while one division moved through the Inn valley. With this division, he was to seize the entrances to the Adige valley, which would threaten the right flank of the Austrian army in Italy. Masséna's first task was therefore to drive General Auffenberg out of his positions in the Rhine valley, then to take the Feldkirch position, and finally to drive the Austrians out of the upper and lower Engadin beyond the Adige valley entrance. This would bring Masséna into a kind of alignment with Jourdan's army, and for the time being, the general plan of operations intended no more than that. Along the way to this aim, the scattered Austrian deployment and the still unready state of part of the Austrian army offered the opportunity to collect some trophies, and the French generals did not miss this chance to reap a rich harvest and thus compensate for the defects in the government's plan.[111]

The Action at the St. Luciensteig on 6 March

On 5 March Masséna concentrated his troops with his center in the Rhine valley between Ragaz [Bad Ragaz] and Werdenberg. On the 6th, from his headquarters at Azmos [Azmoos], he informed General Auffenberg that the truce was ended and demanded that he vacate Graubündten; he then immediately proceeded to attack.

Ruby's brigade of Xaintrailles's division stayed at Schafhausen to maintain communications with the Army of the Danube. The other brigade under Oudinot joined the center.

As for the division on the right wing, General Loison led one brigade from Urseren over the Crispalt [the westernmost range of the Glarus Alps] down to Disentis and attacked the position there, which was held by a few thousand peasants and perhaps a company of infantry, but he could not overcome them.[112]

---

110. **Clausewitz** notes: "According to Jomini." This is Jomini, 11:87–144.
111. It should be noted that this was true despite the lack of a French concentration of force and clear objectives, as already discussed.
112. This highlights the tactically useful strength of defensive positions in the

Masséna himself was in the center, which comprised three brigades. General Demont was sent through the small lateral valley from Ragaz and Vettis [Vättis] to march through the Kunkel Pass opposite Reichenau and attack there.

General Oudinot was to cross the Rhine with one brigade at a ford near Bendern, below Werdenberg, to observe Feldkirch with part of his force and move to the right with the rest of it to support Masséna. Masséna himself, with Lorge's and Chabran's brigades from Ménard's division, was to attempt to wade across the Rhine above the Luciensteig at Fläsch and Maienfeld, while a detached battalion was to cross below the Luciensteig at Azmoos by means of a trestle bridge. This battalion was to threaten the fort frontally, while Masséna, after driving off the troops opposing him in the field, was then to attack it from the rear.

General Demont overwhelmed the Austrian outpost in the Kunkel Pass. He had a company with two guns above Tamin seize Reichenau and its two bridges over the Rhine, and he then sent a detachment against the rear of the outpost at Disentis, which was therefore caught between two fires and captured. He himself [Demont] turned toward Ems [Domat/Ems] at 7:00 a.m. Here the Austrians received reinforcements from Chur and threw Loison back to Reichenau, but they were unable to regain possession of that place.

General Oudinot encountered many difficulties during his crossing and could do no more than occupy the Schellenberg facing Feldkirch, without joining in the action fought by the French center.

General Auffenberg had taken General Hotze's nearest battalion under his own command, and as we have seen, he had detached some troops toward Ems and Reichenau. With the remaining two battalions and half a squadron he took position along the Rhine from the lower toll bridge at the confluence of the Lanquart as far as Fläsch, a frontage of more than 5 miles. Nonetheless, because the Rhine's waters were high, he was able to render futile all French efforts to cross it by the fords at Fläsch and Maienfeld.

On the other hand, the bridge at Azmoos had been completed, and Masséna now decided to march off to the left with Lorge's brigade and cross at this bridge to attack the Luciensteig frontally, while Ménard with Chabran's brigade kept General Auffenberg occupied and pinned him. Crossing this

---

mountains, but it is worth noting that this position was apparently defended mainly by locals rather than large numbers of Austrian army units.

weak trestle bridge took some time, and it was not until three in the afternoon that Masséna appeared in front of the Luciensteig. He decided to take this position whatever the cost because, unless he held it, he could not remain in the narrow Rhine valley with such a woeful bridge behind him and his forces divided.[113]

Masséna had a column of grenadiers scale the Falkenisberg, on which the right-hand flanking redoubt rested. Another column scaled the unoccupied Fläschnerberg to the left of the work, and a third assaulted its front. After four hours of fighting, the position was taken. That is to say, the column that had climbed the Falkenisberg was able to fire down into the right-flank redoubt with great effect, a frontal assault charged home, and as night fell, the redoubt was lost. Now the French got around behind the hornwork, killed or captured its garrison, and opened its gates to the column advancing against its front. One may assume that few of the garrison escaped.

The Action at Chur on 7 March

After this day's dire outcome, General Auffenberg decided to withdraw behind the Lanquart and posted himself with two battalions and half a squadron at the upper toll bridge across the Lanquart, while one battalion and half a squadron remained at Ems.

On the 7th Masséna advanced against him again, while bringing up Chabran's brigade across the lower toll bridge.

When Masséna attacked, the upper toll bridge was soon lost, and a second position at Zizers and then a third close to Chur at Masans were likewise quickly overwhelmed, which one can easily imagine when one remembers that there were 7,000–8,000 men pressing forward against 2,000.[114] General Auffenberg seems to have been in a bad situation at this point. When he arrived at Chur and formed up once again on the heights there, probably just so that he could bring in the battalion from Ems, his right flank was bypassed

---

113. This seems reasonable in the circumstances. He had no realistic route of retreat should he be hard-pressed and possessed no reasonable position to secure his defense.

114. Again, this comes back to Clausewitz's arguments about concentration and defense in mountains. When the defender seeks to cover multiple passes, at least one is likely to be vulnerable to an enemy concentration of force.

by troops that Masséna had sent left into the mountains, his last line of retreat through the Albula valley was cut off, and his front was broken through. As a result, he fell into the hands of the French with all his troops and the battalion at Ems. A few weak remnants of this 6,000-strong corps escaped over footpaths into the upper Engadin.

When the Luciensteig was attacked, Hotze's troops were still in cantonments, and Oudinot was already scaling the Schellenberg, which is only separated from the Feldkirch position by a single meadow valley that opens out into the Ill. Hotze hastily gathered the closest battalions, 2,000–3,000 men, and led them against Oudinot on the Schellenberg on the 7th, intending to gain time to muster the rest of his troops.

Oudinot had been further reinforced by part of Lorge's brigade, so it was easy for him to repulse the advancing Austrians, who lost their artillery and half their men, and himself to capture the outer works of the Feldkirch entrenchments. It was only with the greatest difficulty that Hotze was able to wrest these back from the French at nightfall and thus keep possession of the entire Feldkirch position.

This concluded the first part of Masséna's attack. The result was that he had gained possession of the Rhine valley, annihilated an Austrian corps of some 6,000 men, taken 5,000 prisoners and fourteen guns, and put the Graubündten militia out of action.

It is clear that this glorious outcome was due not to the plan of attack but to the energy with which it was conducted. The strongest point of the whole position, the Luciensteig, was the very place where Auffenberg suffered disaster, whereas one might much sooner have expected that to occur on the left [other] flank.

The Luciensteig is evidence again of how dangerous it is when fortifications in such narrow defiles seek to support themselves on mountainsides.

The fact that General Auffenberg lost his line of retreat in this way was certainly not due to the characteristics of the position. If he had abandoned his artillery, then, as the course of the battle turned out, the route through the Albula valley could not have been denied him had it not been for his own negligence.

Masséna now masses his center in front of the Feldkirch position and stays quietly in the Rhine valley for a few weeks, without anything significant occurring, while he waits for the results of the actions of his right wing and of the Army of the Danube.

9 LECOURBE CONQUERS THE ENGADIN

The Engadin is a valley in Graubündten, so the two Austrian battalions that pushed forward into it were part of the Graubündten garrison. But these troops came from the Army of the Tyrol, whereas Auffenberg belonged to Hotze and the archduke. In any case, the Engadin can be regarded as one of the main entrances to the Tyrol. Therefore, before we can describe Lecourbe's attack clearly, we must review the situation of the Tyrol and its army.

Once Auffenberg was wiped out and the Rhine valley in Graubündten was lost, there could no longer be any thought of a proper defense of the Engadin. We may therefore consider the army in the Tyrol, which was 47,000 strong, as being independent and confined to the Tyrol.

Bellegarde apparently did not anticipate the impending outbreak of war as well as Archduke Charles did. The latter was closer to the seat of negotiations and better informed. The archduke states several times that the Tyrol was completely unprepared, and indeed, it seems that ten or twelve days passed before the troops carried out any sort of strategic approach march.[115]

One does not obtain a clear overview of the deployment of the Austrian combat forces in the Tyrol from the archduke's work. Although he gives many figures and names many places that seem to lead toward it, there is always something missing: either the time is not given exactly, or the forces are not listed exhaustively, or the purpose of the individual forces is not clear, or else there are even contradictions.[116] What we can glean from it about the situation at the start of the campaign is the following:

On the Tyrol's northern border, in the lower-altitude regions: 29 battalions, 5 squadrons

In the southern Tyrol, no doubt in the Adige and Puster valleys: 10 battalions, 2 squadrons

---

115. Karl, 1:41–56.

116. This is a reasonable criticism. Although the archduke provides a number of figures, it is not always clear where all the forces are or what they are doing. He allocates specific numbers of troops to specific commanders (Karl, 1:43, 44) but does not consistently explain who is doing what or where. For example, on page 44 he mentions 75,000 men moving into the "plains of Italy" (Po valley), but the reader is left to guess who this might be. Almost certainly it was Kray's force gathered in the Adige valley. Karl, 1:41–43.

These were the two major forces. Pushed forward into the approaches were:

In the Sulz valley facing the Tonnal: 3 battalions, ½ squadron
In the Vintschgau (upper Adige valley): 3 battalions, ½ squadron
In the Engadin: 2 battalions, 1 squadron
Innsbruck garrison: 1 battalion
Landeck garrison: 1 battalion
Total: 49 battalions, 9 squadrons

Thus, only one battalion and five squadrons are omitted.[117]

When the war broke out in Graubündten, which Bellegarde probably would not have learned about until the 8th, he set his troops in motion. Again, we do not learn exactly according to what plan, nor in what manner. But after twelve days, that is, around 18 March, the archduke gives the following deployment for the Tyrol army:

In the Sulz valley: 4 battalions, ½ squadron
In the Münster valley at Taufers: 8 battalions, 1½ squadrons
In the Inn valley at Martinsbrück: 4 battalions, ½ squadron
In Montafu [Montafon valley] and the Kloster valley: 6 battalions
Reserve in the Adige valley at Laatsch: 9½ battalions, 2½ squadrons
Reserve in the Inn valley at Landeck: 10,000 men
Total: 10,000 men, 31½ battalions, 5 squadrons

If we take the 10,000 men to be ten battalions and nine squadrons and add the two battalions that, by this time, had already been lost in the Engadin, we have evidence for forty-three and a half battalions and fourteen squadrons. Thus, there are still six and a half battalions missing, some of which may have been used as garrisons and others omitted.[118]

From this, it seems that of the twenty-nine battalions in the northern Tyrol, five had marched to the Münster valley to establish the outpost at Taufers, together with the three battalions from the Vintschgau; six to Montafon and

---

117. The archduke lists fifty battalions and fourteen squadrons under Bellegarde in the Inn valley and southern Tyrol. Karl, 1:43.

118. These numbers are contained largely in chapters 3 and 4 of the archduke's history of the campaigns. Karl 1:41–93.

the Kloster valley; and four to Martinsbrück. About ten were posted in reserve at Landeck, but the reserve now posted in the Vintschgau at Laatsch was made up of the ten battalions that had been in the southern Tyrol.

Therefore, while the first actions were being fought between Laudon and Lecourbe, we must assume that the Tyrol army was in transition from the first of these states to the second.

Bellegarde was under orders to defend the Tyrol, and the same attitude prevailed there as in Graubündten: that the defense should be organized as locally as possible so that the Tyrolese would be protected everywhere and would support the mobilization. Thus Bellegarde saw his mission as purely to defend this province, and according to a comment from the archduke, he seems to have been all the happier to limit himself to this idea, as he knew very well how much value was attached to the defense of this province in Vienna.[119]

What folly it was to commit 50,000 men specifically to defend this province and thereby cut them off in isolation from the overall coordinated action, and to do so because the province is very inaccessible and has a warlike armed population, reasons that actually should have led to leaving them to rely on their own forces to some degree. That cannot be disregarded, however fleetingly one touches on this point.[120]

If we consider the Tyrol as a country that has to be defended against the west, it has four main approaches, that is, where the mule trails over the passes have already joined up into passable roads: (1) from Feldkirch through the

---

119. This is not strictly true, and Clausewitz would have known this. The archduke comments on this in two main places: "Food supplies and all requirements could not be lacking thereby as one obtained free communication with Swabia rich in sources of assistance and for the Tyrol it would have been a blessing to be relieved of troops, who lacked everything, who were too many for a meaningful defense and yet too weak when one distributed them. The mismatch of a defensive stance with lavish means was too striking not to be recognized soon and Bellegarde received the order from Vienna to re-conquer Graubündten." And later: "Bellegarde, who had been entrusted with the defense of the Tyrol and who knew the value being placed in Vienna on holding onto this province, believed he had to secure himself against liability by setting off directly from the threatened border and in the direction in which it was threatened. Hotze was supposed to cover the rear and the flank of the army in Germany. He [Bellegarde] feared therefore that he would lay it bare through a march up the Rhine and was worried for his withdrawal." Karl 1:114–115.

120. Following the criticism of Clausewitz earlier, it is reasonable to point out that he is correct here.

Montafon, (2) the Engadin, (3) the Münster valley (the southern source of the Adige), and (4) the Sulz valley. More or less arduous passes led to each of these valleys over the high ridges across which one descends into them. Defending these passes was not feasible for the reasons laid out earlier, so it came down to a defense of the valleys. Thus, the line of defense began at the Feldkirch position, which, as we know, was still in Austrian hands; ran up through the Montafon valley along its length; but cut straight across the Inn, Münster, and Sulz valleys. At Lake Garda it rested on the Austrian army in Italy, whose first outposts were at the lake's northern tip.

This depiction of the approaches indeed renders the second deployment given above entirely understandable, even if one does not otherwise agree with it. The nine battalions at Laatsch may be regarded as the reserve for the Sulz and Münster valleys, as well as for the outpost at Martinsbrück in the Inn valley, if need be, because from the Vintschgau, one can easily come through the valley of the northern source of the Adige to Nauders. The 10,000 men at Landeck are the designated reserve for the Inn and Ill valleys.

The strength of the mobilized militia is not given anywhere. In one place in the history of the 1796 campaign,[121] it is given as 7,000, but in 1799 we must assume it was twice as many. Not only do we find that the advanced outposts are often reinforced by several thousand militia, but also, on one occasion, Laudon uses 6,000–7,000 of them in a single place.

Having thus given a clear picture of the situation of the Tyrol and its combat forces, so far as we are able, and having shown its relation to the Engadin, which depended on it, we now know the shape of the object against which Lecourbe and Dessalus [Dessolles][122] direct their attack. We hope our description of that attack will therefore be somewhat more comprehensible and satisfactory.

---

121. Presumably, Clausewitz is referring to the Archduke Charles's four-volume 1796 campaign history: *Grundsätze der Strategie erläutert durch die Darstellung des Feldzugs von 1796 in Deutschland.*

122. We could find no verifiable biographical information for Dessalus. He is not mentioned in Napoleon's *Correspondance Générale*; nor is he found in Georges Six, *Dictionnaire Biographique des Généraux & Amiraux de la Révolution et de L'Empire (1792–1814)*, 2 vols. (Paris: Libraire Historique et Nobiliaire, 1934). Presumably, this is Jean-Joseph Marquis de Dessolles (1767–1828), who is referred to in Jomini's account. Jomini, 11:104. Dessolles had a distinguished career as an officer and administrator. Note that Napoleon's *Correspondance Générale* spells this Dessolle, but Dessolles seems to be ubiquitous in English, so we retained that spelling.

According to the French plan of operations as we have presented it, the attack by these two detachments on the Italian side of the Alps formed part of the general attack that Masséna was supposed to launch against the Austrian combat forces in Graubündten. But it was natural that the boundary of this operation should not be drawn to follow the Graubündten border. Instead, Lecourbe and Dessolles were to advance into the Tyrol and seize the entrances to the Adige valley (Vintschgau). This was seen as a kind of strategic alignment, a way of thinking that was very much in vogue among the French at that time. That is, if Masséna advanced to the Rhine above Lake Constance, the French line of deployment would run either through the Montafon (if they happened to take Feldkirch) or through the Prettigau to the lower Engadin at Nauders and from there into the Adige valley and Vintschgau. The French believed they could either hold this position or consider it a step along the way to further advances. By pushing the right wing of the Army of Helvetia forward in this way, they intended to threaten the right flank of the Austrian army in Italy via the Adige valley and interrupt its direct line of communications with the army in Germany—that is, through the Vintschgau—restricting it to the line over the Brenner Pass. But if they succeeded in advancing as far as Botzen, the Austrians would lose their communications over the Brenner Pass as well. For the French strategists of that time, the prospect of gaining possession of the highest points and working their way steadily downward from top to bottom from the Umbrail Pass was a pleasant one. We will present our reflections on this offensive aim later and content ourselves here with merely making it clear.

We cannot discover why Lecourbe did not set off from Bellinzona until the 7th and Dessolles did not arrive in Worms until the 17th. If we assume that these columns were intended to act simultaneously with those on the Rhine, then, given their respective positions, it is obvious that Lecourbe arrived two to three days too late and Dessolles eight to ten days late. Mishaps and misunderstandings were probably to blame.[123]

---

123. This fits in with Clausewitz's ideas about the role of chance in war and his concept of the trinity, discussed earlier. This also connects with his concept of friction, referenced earlier but not discussed. It is worth quoting him to illustrate his meaning: "Everything in war is very simple, but the simplest thing is difficult. The difficulties accumulate and end by producing a kind of friction that is inconceivable unless one has experienced war. Imagine a traveler who late in the day decides to cover two more stages before nightfall. Only four or five hours more, on a paved highway with relays

On 7 March Lecourbe began his march from Bellinzona with ten battalions and some cavalry, crossed the snow-covered Bernhardin ridge, and went down the Posterior Rhine to Tufis. From there, he turned through the Albula valley and moved in two columns—one under his personal command across the Albula to Pant, and the other under General Ainoni over the Julierberg to Silva Plana in the Inn valley. On the 10th both columns encountered Austrian outposts on the heights and drove them off.

The route given here is 45 miles long across the highest alpine ridges. To cover this in four days scarcely seems possible, but we are not entitled to change this figure provided by the historians.[124] Not one author says a word about why General Lecourbe took this detour through the Posterior Rhine valley to get to the Engadin. If the purpose was to arrive in the rear of the two advanced battalions in the Engadin and cut them off, these battalions had to be holding a strong and important position at the entrance to the Engadin; any other mere deployment of these troops could not have been a reason for anyone in Zurich or Bellinzona to prescribe such a maneuver, as it was highly uncertain whether these battalions would still be there by the time it was executed. But there is no question of it being a strong position; on the contrary, Archduke Charles says these two battalions were spread out in far-flung quar-

---

of horses: it should be an easy trip. But at the next station he finds no fresh horses, or only poor ones; the country grows hilly, the road bad, night falls, and finally after many difficulties he is only too glad to reach a resting place with any kind of primitive accommodation. It is much the same in war." *On War*, book 1, chap. 7, 119. This is an important point, as even the best plans can overlook some minor detail, or something completely unanticipated can cause a major hiccup. In more recent times, the battle of Mogadishu on 3–4 October 1993 witnessed such a chain of events, and a brief description is worthwhile to aid in understanding Clausewitz's point. One of the helicopters carrying soldiers for the raid landed in the wrong place, delaying the mission. This problem was compounded when a soldier fell while trying to fast-rope to the ground. The subsequent delays allowed the locals to concentrate men in the area. As a result, what was intended to be a quick raid to arrest people wanted by UN forces in Somalia turned into a major incident with several hundred casualties and long-standing political consequences. For details, see Mark Bowden, *Black Hawk Down: A Story of Modern War* (Berkeley, CA: Atlantic Monthly Press, 1999).

124. Both Jomini and Archduke Charles have Lecourbe leaving on 7 March. That being said, it is worth pondering whether the sources Clausewitz refers to are merely citing the archduke—all using the same date without knowing whether that date was correct to begin with. Jomini, 11:103; Karl, 1:80.

ters, part of them as far as the Puschiaver valley. However, one can hardly resist the idea that Lecourbe was tasked with first taking Auffenberg's position in the Rhine valley in rear and then later turning toward the Engadin, and that he would not have learned of the success in the Anterior Rhine valley on the 7th until the 8th, when he had already descended to the Posterior Rhine. But of course, it would be astonishing if such an essential provision of the plan had eluded the major historians.[125]

The battalions pushed forward in the upper Engadin were cut off and the majority of them taken prisoner.

Upon the first report of the outbreak of hostilities, several battalions in the Inn valley on the border of the Engadin were collected under General Laudon, together with the battalions in the Vintschgau, so that on the 10th he had three battalions and one squadron at Nauders and five battalions and a squadron in the Münster valley between Taufers and St. Maria. With these and another four battalions—which it seems were not among the first eight—he set off to meet the foe. During the night of the 10th and 11th he arrived with these at Zernetz.

According to the archduke's account, the remnants that had retreated from the Rhine valley were covering the passes of the Scaletta and the Flülenberg, which are on the left slope of the Engadin; one battalion advanced from St. Maria in the Münster valley to Bormio, and one occupied the Tschirfser Joch [Ofen Pass], which the path from Zernetz to Bormio crosses. This last battalion was probably one of the four that Laudon had brought with him to Zernetz. It was probably with the remaining three battalions that Laudon advanced against

---

125. Again, Clausewitz is being unreasonably snide. He is sarcastically referring to Archduke Charles's and Jomini's failure to address the reasons for Lecourbe's actions. But Clausewitz does not provide the reason either. Instead, he analyzes what he *thinks* Lecourbe was doing. In fact, the archduke does comment on this: "Le Courbe gave in completely to his bold impetuous coarse character: he gave preference to the speed of the operation over its security and did not pay heed to loss of life if he hoped to purchase an advantage thereby. He only trusted the superiority of the offensive as well as taking the initiative in movement which is not as predominant in any terrain as it is in the high mountains. Due to the difficulty in communications and obtaining consent, the combining and determining of a counter-manoeuvre incurs losing so much time that usually before the plan can be executed, the entire situation, upon which the plan was drawn up, changes. This means that the attacker achieves a whole series of advantages, one after the other, which he exploits inexorably and which cannot be so easily wrested back from him." Karl, 1:84–85. See also Jomini, 11:103–107.

Pont on the 12th, drove the French out of there, and seized part of the Albula valley. But Lecourbe held on to the high ground with part of his force, while the rest marched off to the left through the Davos valley, which runs parallel to the Inn valley in this area; took the outposts at the Scaletta and the Flülenberg in rear; drove them off; and came down into the Engadin from there. As soon as Laudon realized this, all he could do was beat a hasty retreat, and it was already too late for him to do this without a large number of his men being cut off.[126] Laudon abandoned Zernetz during the night and continued his retreat to Martinsbrück on the 13th. On the 14th the French followed as far as Remüs.

Lecourbe now obviously found himself isolated in the Engadin. There was no word of General Dessolles, and on his left, there was no significant body of French troops for a very long way. The Austrians held the upper Adige valleys right on his right flank with 5,000–6,000 regular soldiers and probably a similar number of militia; there was a similar-sized force in the Montafon on his left. Lecourbe recognized the danger of his situation but, driven on by the courage and one might say the fanatical determination that inspired the French generals of the time,[127] could not resist making an attempt against the Martinsbrück position. To protect himself to some degree against the threat to his rear, he left detachments from his division in Zernetz and Schuols [Scuol].

The Action at Martinsbrück on 14 March

The Martinsbrück position is a narrow passage formed by the cliffs and the river. It was easy to defend with the three battalions and three guns the Austrians had posted there, but at the cost of a little time, it could be outflanked on its left by a footpath that ran along the high ridge. The impetuous Lecourbe did not allow himself the time to do so but tried to storm the position on the 14th by frontal assault. He was repulsed and took position at Remüs again. When he was about to renew his attack on the 15th, he heard fire from his rear at Zernetz and Scuol.

---

126. **Clausewitz** notes: "Erzherzog, volume 1 page 81." Karl, 1:81.

127. The archduke writes: "Le Courbe gave in completely to his bold impetuous coarse character." Karl, 1:84.

The Actions at Zernetz, Scuol, and Remüs on 15 March

General Laudon decided to beat Lecourbe by attacking these points; we put it that way because there seems to have been no expectation of completely destroying him. Laudon, for his part, had retired through the Münster valley and gathered 7,000 militia on the 15th. Reinforced by three companies of regular infantry, these militia marched over the Tschirfser Joch [Ofen Pass] against Zernetz, while General Laudon himself advanced from Santa Maria over the Schärljoch [Scharl Pass] against Scuol. The Martinsbrück outpost was ordered to attack General Lecourbe frontally at Remüs at the same time.

The outcome of this attack was as follows: The first column crossed the mountain but was attacked by the French battalion in Zernetz and driven back over the mountain again. The second column penetrated into Scuol and so surprised the force there that General Ainoni himself was taken prisoner. But this column too was attacked by Lecourbe's main body returning from Remüs and was likewise obliged to retreat over the mountains. Thus, three companies of the first column were cut off. The attack made by the two battalions from Martinsbrück against Remüs could not break through, even against the weak detachment Lecourbe had left there.[128]

This is how Archduke Charles describes this action. Unless some error occurred in the editing, it is indeed striking that General Laudon was not with the major column of 7,000–8,000 men but instead was with the one of just three companies, and that this large column could be repelled by one French battalion. If it really did happen that way, then of course it is no wonder that, when Lecourbe returned from Remüs with perhaps three or four battalions, he was able to drive off General Laudon and his three companies. It is equally unsurprising that the two battalions advancing from Martinsbrück against the position at Remüs did not break through; since the latter probably had similarly advantageous terrain to that at Martinsbrück, and since Scuol is only about 5 miles from it, they probably feared that Lecourbe might return from there at any moment.[129]

---

128. Karl, 1:86–89.
129. Clausewitz lists the distance as being half a mile (about 2.25 miles). This is wrong, as the distance from Martinsbrück to Remüs is just about 6 miles, and the distance from Remüs to Scuol is another 5 miles.

Be that as it may, it is certain that, given the Austrians' superior numbers and the situation they found themselves in, something better might have been expected. Lecourbe probably had no more than 6,000 men, some thousands of whom would have been posted at Remüs and elsewhere, so he would have been just 3,000–4,000 strong in the valley when he faced 7,000–8,000 Austrians and Tyrolese coming down from the mountains on the 7th; if the latter could not break through in such circumstances, it was probably simply because of leadership.

Archduke Charles criticizes General Laudon[130] for using only six regular companies for this operation. From a general point of view, this criticism is entirely justified, for if one wants to go on the counterattack in mountain warfare, this can happen only if one temporarily abandons the defense of all nonvital places to obtain forces for the attack. But at that time, the Austrians absolutely did not hold this view; it was always their first principle that not one single point of the whole defensive system should ever be exposed for even a moment. Given this point of view, it is at least understandable why Laudon might have had reservations about weakening the Münster valley position by more than six companies, for as the archduke recognizes, he probably could not have known for certain that he was not threatened there, since two days later, Dessolles actually did cross the Wormser Joch.

The Action at Martinsbrück on 17 March

After his victory of the 15th, Lecourbe felt he could renew his attack on Martinsbrück; he let his troops rest for a day and then attacked the position frontally on 17 March, while at the same time using the track leading over the left edge of the valley to outflank it. But the frontal attack was beaten off, and the Austrians, who had meanwhile been reinforced, had posted a reserve at Finstermünz, where the path known as the Novellasteg descends to join the road, so the outflanking French battalion was captured.

This loss, on top of the attrition Lecourbe had suffered in the other ten days his attack had now lasted, finally convinced him that it would be wise to wait for General Dessolles to arrive in the Münster valley.

---

130. Karl, 1:87–93.

10 DESSOLLES DESTROYS LAUDON'S CORPS AT TAUFERS AND LECOURBE DEFEATS ANOTHER AT NAUDERS

General Dessolles and his brigade of 5,000 or so men arrived at Worms on the 17th and captured the Austrian outpost there.

That such a thing could still happen now, when the war was already eleven days old, can only be explained by gross negligence or incompetence on the part of the Austrians. The Austrian army probably lacked that stern discipline and that internal organization that compensate for the weaknesses and follies of human nature and that prevent the thousands and thousands of errors and omissions to which an army's operations are always vulnerable, being like a machine composed of so many individual parts. The moral discipline of the French was much worse, and their own internal regulation was hardly well organized, but at least on their side the positive efforts of their leaders[131] and of the soldiery made up for their deficiencies; and the body can go rot, so long as the spirit lives on.[132]

---

131. Perhaps Archduke Charles's criticism of Lecourbe cited in the previous section is an indication of what was fundamentally wrong with the Austrians. That is, they were fundamentally lacking dynamism. "Le Courbe gave in completely to his bold impetuous coarse character: he gave preference to the speed of the operation over its security and did not pay heed to loss of life if he hoped to purchase an advantage thereby." Karl, 1:84.

132. This criticism is interesting, as it appears to undermine Clausewitz's own ideas about critical analysis, as well as his comments in his history of the 1796 campaign in Italy. In that work Clausewitz noted: "After all, one can say in general that whenever unfortunate military operations result from a succession of mistakes, in their internal interactions these are never constituted in quite the way the public thinks. The men responsible, even if they were among the worst of field commanders, were not without sound common sense and would never perpetrate such outright absurdities as the public and critical historians impute to them. Most of these latter would be astonished if they only knew the specific reasons for these actions, and most probably would be just as easily misguided by these as was the commander who until then looked like a half-wit to them. Of course there will always be mistakes, but these usually only lie deeper, in errors of judgement or weakness of character, which do not appear as such at first glance, but which one only discovers and recognizes clearly if one compares the outcome with all the reasons which influenced the actions of the defeated party. Such historical hindsight is permissible in criticism and should not be accused of being mockery, as this is its essential concern, though of course it is far easier than doing the right thing at the time the action was taken. In fact it is therefore folly, when we see

On the 17th, upon Dessolles's advance, General Laudon withdrew from St. Maria into the entrenchments of the prepared position at Taufers.

On the 18th Dessolles advanced to St. Maria.

Both the French generals, Dessolles and Lecourbe, now stay put for eight days, the former at St. Maria facing the Taufers position, and the latter at Remüs before the Martinsbrück position, without the historians telling us any reason for this pause.[133] If we were to hazard a guess, we might say that Lecourbe was waiting for reinforcements and that they wanted to both attack on the same day. In the subsequent actions of 25 March, we do find Generals Loison and Demont in Lecourbe's division. It is therefore probable that, during these eight days, he called the former up to him from the Rhine valley and that he was reinforced with the latter by Masséna.

As we have already said, General Masséna himself had suspended the attack by his center since 7 March. Around the time we are looking at now, he was prompted to renewed action by Jourdan, who was beginning to be worried about his own situation. So he decided to make new attempts against the Feldkirch position and at the same time ordered Lecourbe and Dessolles to attack.

Thus this new attack by the French right wing coincides with the center's renewed activity, and in that sense, we can consider this as part of a second attack by the French Army of Helvetia. But this concurrence is actually not the essential point of the matter, since this right wing's original mission was to gain possession of the line of communications between the Inn valley and the Adige valley at Nauders, and this objective of their offensive had not yet been achieved.

Lecourbe and Dessolles therefore decided to attack on 25 March.

---

almost every army abiding by the principle of revealing as little as possible about their military disasters; such affairs always look better if they are understood in detail than in superficial overview." Clausewitz, *Napoleon's 1796 Italian Campaign*, 43–44n51. The topic of critical analysis is explored in *On War*, book 2, chaps. 5 and 6.

133. Clausewitz is wrong. Although the archduke does not explicitly explain the delay, he does indicate that Masséna's position was somewhat exposed, with his units being isolated from one another, and that the supply situation in the mountains was tenuous. Later, he points out that Lecourbe and Dessolles had been prevented from continuing their operations due to a lack of food and their troops' exhaustion. Karl, 1:94–95, 127–128.

The Action at Taufers on 25 March

After the loss of Graubündten, the Austrians had conceived the notion of advancing aggressively out of the Tyrol and reconquering Graubündten, because as the archduke says, "the incongruity of a defensive posture with such fulsome resources was too obvious."[134] General Bellegarde, who received the order from Vienna,[135] took the view that this advance on his part could be carried out only if it kept all the approaches to the Tyrol covered, and he felt that it needed the cooperation of Hotze's corps and of the army in Italy. All this required extensive discussions and extensive supply arrangements, so its execution was postponed until 2 April. Thus, we must imagine the Austrians in the Tyrol as preparing for this offensive and the troop dispositions of 18 March given in the previous section as a consequence of this. On the 25th we find no change in this situation, other than that four battalions have been posted at Nauders to support the Martinsbrück position. These seem to have been taken from the reserve at Landeck, which was still nine battalions strong. The reserve in the Vintschgau, which comprised ten and a half battalions on the 18th by the archduke's account, must surely have been very scattered by the 25th, for it tried to rush only two battalions to the aid of the Taufers position. Bellegarde had his headquarters in Botzen, so it is probable that he too had troops in this part of the Adige valley that could only have come from this reserve.

Thus, on 25 March we find General Laudon in position at Taufers with eight battalions comprising 6,200 men and sixteen guns. There is a reserve in the Vintschgau, but it is too far away to support him effectively during the battle.[136]

The position at Taufers was not chosen in the narrowest part of the valley at all—that would have been 2.5 miles further back than it actually was—but rather in a place where the valley broadens out. This is where the Vallavola stream running down from the Schärljoch (i.e., from the area of Scuol) flows into the Rambach, which is the southern source of the Adige, the watercourse in the Münster valley. This broadening out of the valley on the left bank of the Rambach is a few thousand paces across. However, it is not a flat meadow but undulating ground. The Vallavolabach, flowing between steep, high banks like

---

134. Although not cited by Clausewitz, this is Karl, 1:113.
135. Although not cited by Clausewitz, this is Karl, 1:115.
136. It was located almost 6 miles away, too far to provide an effective tactical reserve because the distance precluded timely assistance.

a deep gutter, was considered a frontal obstacle. The right wing rested on the cliffs on the left edge of the valley, and the left wing on the Rambach, which likewise flowed between deep, steep banks. Both streams were so dried up that one could walk along the streambeds. The village of Taufers, which extends along the length of the valley, was in the rear of the position; Münster was a few thousand paces in front of it at a fairly narrow point in the valley.

Archduke Charles thinks this position was chosen mainly in connection with the intended offensive,[137] because of the fear that if they deployed in the narrowest part, they would not be able to get out. However, the real reason seems to have been that the village of Taufers provided shelter for the troops, whereas further to the rear, there was none until the Adige valley. Perhaps those who decided on the location of the position also saw it as a tactical advantage, in that it permitted a considerable development of frontage, while the enemy had to come through a narrow gap at Münster 2,000 paces away. If this defile had been 500 paces in front of the position, we might have accepted this reasoning, but for such a small corps at 2,000 paces, this advantageous relationship entirely ceases.

The position at Taufers was fortified. Three open redoubts[138] connected by two long lines occupied a stretch of 1,000 paces right behind the Vallavolabach, resting their left on the Rambach, but they could not look down into the bottom of either stream.

En échelon 500 paces behind the right of this line of entrenchments lay a second line about 500 paces long, likewise behind a small steep-sided stream, and comprising two enclosed redoubts connected by a long line.

Although these entrenchments certainly had some defects in their situation—partly in that they did not command the gullies of the Vallavola and Rambach, and partly in the open redoubts and the useless long lines connecting them—still, if attacked from the front and properly defended, they probably would have withstood an enemy who had almost no artillery. That left only the option of outflanking over the mountains, but these were occupied by light troops and militia; any outflanking move would therefore be discovered and impeded, which would gain time to bring reserves against it.

Dessolles had spent eight days in front of the Austrian entrenchments, and there were bound to have been places on the high ridges between which they lay

137. Karl, 1:138.
138. The archduke cites two redoubts. Karl, 1:129.

from where he could see them perfectly and discover their weaknesses. On the night of 24–25 March he moved through Münster with 4,500 men and two guns. At daybreak he drove back the enemy outposts and immediately threw himself at the entrenchments, having three battalions advance along the bed of the Rambach, protected from any enemy fire, and attacking frontally with the rest. The Austrians appear to have been totally surprised, since the three battalions that advanced along the Rambach, marching more than 1,000 paces in it, met no opposition. They got into the entrenchments from behind, and into the village of Taufers, while at the same time sending a detachment down the Rambach to block the valley lower down. For lack of order and composure, there seems to have been almost no resistance; confusion reigned,[139] as we can well believe from the fact that out of the whole corps, only 300–400 men escaped with General Laudon and sought refuge in the mountains on the left side of the valley—although we cannot understand how three battalions were able to bar the way against eight in a valley that was not narrow enough at that point to explain it.

Thus, here 4,500 men with two cannon had captured 5,000–6,000 men and sixteen guns. General Laudon and his handful of men crossed the massif separating the two sources of the Adige to escape through Nauders; but when not far from Reschen, he learned that Nauders was already in Lecourbe's hands, so he threw himself into the mountains that follow the right bank of the Inn and escaped with unspeakable dangers and difficulties over the Gebatschferner to Landeck.

On the 26th Dessolles moved to Glurns, where he took position facing the reserve in the Vintschgau. Its two battalions and three squadrons sent to support the Taufers position ran into the French vanguard at Schlanders.

The Action at Nauders on 25 March

On that same day, 25 March, Lecourbe attacked his opponent as well. Who this was—that is, who was in command at Martinsbrück and Nauders—we do not know. But we have already said that the first of these two positions was held by two battalions and the other by four that acted as a reserve. There were probably also some troops at Finstermünz.

This time, Lecourbe sent a sizable part of his division under General Loison over the mountain ridge on the right bank of the Inn. Part of this force

---

139. This provides a classic example of friction. See *On War*, book 1, chap. 7.

was able to get onto the road leading to the Adige and thus onto the left flank of the reserves at Nauders, while another part of Loison's force came down the mountain further to the left and attacked them frontally. Thus these four battalions, which were probably stronger than General Loison's force, were beaten and hurled in precipitate retreat toward Finstermünz, whereby the two battalions that still held Martinsbrück lost their own line of retreat and were captured along with nine guns.

Now the Austrians also abandoned Finstermünz and withdrew to Landeck, where they joined up with their reserve.

Lecourbe stayed at Nauders. Because of the reverse Jourdan had suffered at Osterach on the 18th, both the French generals had been ordered by Masséna not to advance any further.

Thus, this French attack on the Inn and Münster valleys had succeeded far better than they had hoped or expected. Instead of pointlessly occupying a tangle of roads and mountains that they would necessarily have had to leave again because of the general situation, they had once again totally wiped out one Austrian corps of similar strength to that in the Rhine valley and defeated another. With perhaps 15,000 men, they had taken twenty-five guns and between 10,000 and 12,000 prisoners in just a few days.

It is strikingly obvious that this glorious result owed even less than the one in the Rhine valley to strategic combinations. Once again, it was the energy of the French commanders and the courage and indefatigability of their soldiers, against the perversity of the Austrian generals and the poor morale of the Austrian troops, that had brought them victory. In fact, however hard we try to explain this repeated cutting off and capturing of whole battalions and this annihilation of entire corps, which is essential if we are to salvage the honor of the Austrian colors at these points, it is impossible to do so without assuming that the Austrians were guilty of extraordinary slackness and blunders.

11 MASSÉNA ATTACKS THE FELDKIRCH POSITION IN VAIN

The strategic significance of the position at Feldkirch that this war made so well known rests on three different elements. It lies where the Ill valley opens out into the Rhine valley, and although it is 3.5 miles away from the Rhine, it is on the road that comes out of Swabia from Bregenz and goes through the

Rhine valley over the Splügen toward Italy. It thereby controls the Rhine valley, and naturally likewise the Ill valley in which it lies and through which the last convenient line of communications between the Rhine and the Inn runs through Bludenz to Landeck, in that the more southern ones mostly go over very difficult passes that are unsuitable for wagons. Furthermore, Feldkirch is only about 20 miles from Lake Constance, and since the ground in between is fairly flat and open, especially on the right bank of the Rhine, it is not hard for the position to have an influence on this area too.

The Feldkirch position, whose tactical configuration we will describe in more detail below, is capable of being defended by a force of from 8,000–10,000 up to 20,000 men, depending on the force attacking them, in such a way that there is little fear of it being overcome. In these circumstances, the three elements that constitute the strategic significance of the position are the following:

It defends the exit from Graubündten into Swabia and repels any enemy advancing up the Inn valley, on the road through the Tyrol.
It blocks the line of communications between the Rhine and the Inn through the Montafon and the Kloster valley.
It can serve as a flank position against an enemy advancing between it and Lake Constance, since its defenders' line of retreat through the Montafon cannot easily be cut.

Because of these three factors, the Austrians always kept a corps of 8,000–10,000 men there, but at the point in time that concerns us here, the effect of the third factor did not seem strong enough to them. They therefore specifically occupied Bregenz as well, and in fact, with more troops than at Feldkirch itself, and there certainly were important reasons for that. If 18,000 men (for that is how strong Hotze was) posted at Feldkirch could not have defended the area as far as Lake Constance against a similar force—that is, prevented the enemy from penetrating a significant distance into this area—then in the whole of strategic theory, there cannot be any way to defend an area indirectly; that is surely beyond doubt.[140] But first and foremost, if the Feldkirch position was vulnerable to being isolated from Swabia, arrangements should have been made for it to be supplied with provisions via the Inn valley and through Bludenz, which had perhaps not been done; second, if instead of hav-

---

140. We cannot help but think that Clausewitz is being sarcastic here.

ing all 18,000 men at Feldkirch there were just 6,000 there and 12,000 at Bregenz, there was the possibility of using the latter in Swabia. This route could have been taken all the more readily because the Austrians had the Tyrol and Vorarlberg militias available, which could always send several thousand men to the aid of the Feldkirch position, and because General Masséna had barely 10,000–12,000 men left with which to attack Feldkirch or Bregenz after his right wing had moved into the Engadin and since his left could not abandon Schafhausen. Against such a force, Feldkirch could still be held with 6,000 men, and in any case, from Bregenz there was still the line of retreat to Swabia.

As far as the tactical nature of this position is concerned, it is one of those lower foothills that are often found at the narrow end of high mountain ridges, which arise where the steep slope of the great ridge suddenly levels off and then becomes undulating and much less steep for some distance so that it creates a kind of plateau, which, however, usually ends in steep slopes again down to the plain. These slopes then present a difficult approach to the plateau and provide the position's frontal obstacle, behind which one can maneuver easily with the rear protected by the high mountain. Where it rises up particularly steeply, it may be considered impassable. This, of course, is never entirely true, but it is usually effectively so for artillery and for large bodies of troops. If it is wooded, an abatis[141] may be used to make it even more inaccessible. If, despite this, a few enemy light troops are able to work their way through there, these may be opposed by a similar force and thereby neutralized. In this situation, the fact that the high ridge dominates the position is of no great importance.

The Feldkirch position is just such an end of the high ridge that runs between the Samina valley and the Rhine and slopes steeply down toward the Ill. It is in the form of a plateau, which derives even greater strength from the fact that, at its foot, it is partly surrounded by a marshy area known as the Great Marsh, which empties into the Rhine at Bendern. On the far side of this meadow valley is another very significant ridge, the Schellenberg, which separates it from the Rhine and is significantly higher than the Feldkirch position, but since its dominating peaks are 1,800–2,000 paces away, this does not create any real disadvantage for the position. That part of the

---

141. A line of felled trees with the branches pointing in the direction of an enemy. This would be used to delay or stop the movement of enemy troops and animals. For a glossary of technical fortification terms, see Murray, *The Rocky Road to the Great War*, 245.

lower foothill that serves as the actual position is at the angle of the ridge facing toward the Rhine, and as well as the foot of the ridge it comprises a fairly long mountain running parallel to it called the Blassenberg, which is roughly the same height as the foot of the great ridge and is connected to its center. The actual front of the position faces toward Graubündten, with its left resting against the high ridge, and is about 2,000 paces long; the right flank runs along the Blassenberg to the Ill in a straight line comprised in part of impassable cliffs and is 2,500 paces long. At the Ill, the position is mostly enclosed by a steep wall of unscalable cliffs. On the right bank of the Ill, the main ridge that follows the river rises extremely steeply, as does another ridge separated from it by a valley 600–800 paces wide in which the town of Feldkirch lies. This is the Arzenberg, which may be regarded as a continuation of the Blassenberg, since the Ill lies in a narrow gorge between these two mountains. The road from the Rhine along the left bank of the Ill runs through this gorge into the position. But the main road from Bregenz runs through the valley that separates the Arzenberg from the great ridge and, consequently, through the town of Feldkirch. In order to block the roads coming from the Rhine and from Bregenz, one does not need the heights on the right bank at all, since from the Ill side, the position may be regarded as very strong. But if one does not want to be denied the road to Bregenz oneself, the ridge on the right side of the Ill must be secured as far as Altstätten.

The road from Chur comes through Nendeln and is squeezed into a defile between the high ridge and the mire of the Great Marsh as far as the Nendeln Mill, 1,000 paces in front of the position, where the terrain opens out somewhat. This factor provides the main strength of the actual front of the position, because it prevents the enemy from deploying many guns against it.

The Austrians had used only that part of the position on the left bank of the Ill and surrounded it with a mostly continuous line of entrenchments, with some of the individual works echeloned next to or behind each other, according to the terrain.[142]

142. **Clausewitz** notes: "The Archduke says in his account that they included redoubts, but none are given in his plan apart from a couple of individual flèches or crescent works." The plan to which Clausewitz refers shows five lines of fortifications along with six to seven flèches. In total, the works are approximately 1.6 miles long, without including the individual works. Karl, 3:plan II. Technically, the fortifications described and drawn are not redoubts, as they are not closed works. That being said,

Six to eight thousand men in this position could hardly be overcome by 10,000–12,000; if it were defended by 20,000 with numerous artillery, perhaps even 50,000 could not take it.

Let us turn now to Masséna's attack on it.

The Attack on Feldkirch on 23 May

After Oudinot first threatened the position by his attack of 7 March, it seems that General Hotze occupied it with a considerable part of his force—eight or ten battalions. But ten or twelve days later, when Jourdan's new advance into Swabia brought Férino's division into the region of Markdorf on the north side of Lake Constance, Hotze began to worry about his strategic right flank. On the 19th he therefore moved part of his force out of the Feldkirch position, leaving General Jellachich[143] in it with five battalions and two squadrons, another five battalions and four and a half squadrons in Bregenz, and one battalion and a squadron in Dornbirn, and took position behind the Senblach [Clausewitz presumably means the Leiblach], east of Lindau, with eight battalions and six squadrons.

Spurred into action again by Jourdan, Masséna tried to take advantage of Hotze's absence by attacking Feldkirch.

On 22 March he concentrated Ménard's division and Oudinot's brigade, about 12,000–15,000 men.

On the 23rd he advanced to the attack in four columns.

Three small columns, each of a couple of battalions, approached from the Schellenberg. The leftmost was supposed to cross the Ill at Noffels, 1.5 miles below Feldkirch at the foot of the Schellenberg, but was unable to do so because there was no bridge and an Austrian outpost was entrenched there. The second column advanced along the Ill road to the gorge separating the Blas-

---

Clausewitz's criticism is unreasonable, as he is arguing over a relatively minor technicality to undermine the archduke. One can only assume that Clausewitz's enmity for the archduke got in the way of his own critical analysis. Perhaps it would behoove the reader to remember Clausewitz's trinity and call for rational analysis rather than emotion.

143. Franz Jellachich (1746–1810) had a long if undistinguished career in the Austrian army and was the victor at Feldkirch in 1799.

senberg and the Arzenberg, where it suffered so much from Austrian fire and from hurled rocks that it abandoned its attack. The third column, crossing the Great Marsh at the other end of the Blassenberg, achieved equally little. Masséna himself led the main attack by Ménard's division and the grenadiers along the main road from the Nendeln Mill against the front.

He attacked the line of entrenchments frontally, but at the same time, he sent several battalions off to the right, which were to work their way forward through the abatis on the slopes of the high ridge and thereby outflank the position on its left.

Jellachich had only five battalions and two squadrons, so probably no more than 4,500 regular troops. But he also had several thousand militia available, so his force could be assumed to number as many as 6,000–7,000 men.

Although the frontal attacks were carried out with great determination, and an audacious cavalry detachment even burst into the middle of the entrenchments along the main road, they achieved nothing. However, the French troops in the woods made good progress at first, until at 4:00 p.m. Jellachich sent four companies of his reserve against them and ordered the militia to come down from the peak of the main ridge, known as the Rojaberg, and move against the flank of the advancing French. This was a complete success; the advanced detachments had to fall back. While Masséna got ever more involved and engrossed in this action on his right wing, his frontal attack slackened off, and now Jellachich mustered all the troops he had nearby and counterattacked the French front, which decided the French commander to retreat.

Masséna lost 3,000 men, perhaps a quarter of those in action. He withdrew to Chur, where he took position and held the Luciensteig, while Oudinot had to post himself at Rheineck.

12 ARCHDUKE CHARLES DEFEATS JOURDAN IN THE ENCOUNTER AT OSTERACH

We left Archduke Charles and the French Army of the Danube under Jourdan facing each other. On 7 March Jourdan and his army had halted on the heights of Rothweil, Tuttlingen, and Blomberg. Archduke Charles used this halt to concentrate his own army, for as we have said, his infantry only crossed the Lech on the 9th and the cavalry on the 14th; the archduke's advance guard had moved to Biberach, Waldsee, and Ravensburg, and the army mustered behind this position. Thus, when Jourdan began to move again on 14 March, the two armies' main bodies were still four or five days' march apart, and the Austrian army had not had any real rest.

Masséna had been successful in Graubündten, and he now urged Jourdan to advance in turn. The Directory also seemed to find its commander in chief too tentative, and it had the minister of war prompt him to advance. The minister sent him a letter on 10 February from which we have already shared some excerpts, discussing the plan of operations.[144] But these urgings contained no single clear and definite idea, and until now, there had been no suggestion of a battle against the archduke. To some extent, it seems as though they did not have the heart to explicitly demand such a thing of General Jourdan. This was the sorry half-measure, confusion, and sloppiness with which the strategic leadership of the campaign was conducted.

The prior nebulous idea of primarily seeking to establish the Army of the Danube in position on the upper Lech and considering it as merely cooperating with the conquest of the Tyrol soon evaporated when the archduke turned up.

Even though he always underestimates the Austrians' total forces and seems to have had only too small and confused an assessment of Bellegarde's 50,000-strong army and the 25,000 men under Hotze, nevertheless, from extensive reports, Jourdan clearly knows that he is facing the archduke and 80,000 men and that some 20,000 more have been sent to Franconia. He thus sees that he is going to have to contend with these 80,000 and that, most likely, none of them will be sent to Vorarlberg against Masséna.

In this situation, General Jourdan was not happy. He could not and would not leave Masséna in the lurch by complete inactivity, yet any further advance risked a blow from a force of more than twice his strength.

Jourdan learned of Masséna's victories on 11 March; he began to move on the 12th but decided to advance only until he was level with the Army of Helvetia, as he put it, by which he apparently meant in the vicinity of Osterach, and he asked the Directory urgently "to let me know its latest intention."[145] In the meantime, he conducted his march slowly, halting on alternate days.

---

144. See the text at note 88 of this chapter.

145. Clausewitz transcribed this as *"de lui faire connaître ses dernières intentions."* In Jourdan's original, it is *"de me faire connaître ses dernières intentions."* See Jourdan, *Précis des opérations de l'armée du Danube*, 103. This might be attributable to the German convention of converting first person to third person in reported speech.

Jourdan's advance proceeded so that his left wing was on the Danube, his right on Lake Constance, and his center on the road that leads through Stockach and Pfullendorf to Munich. Vandamme was to follow along the left flank of the Danube with a flanking detachment.

On the 17th Jourdan arrived at Pfullendorf with his center. He had his advance guard at Osterach, his left wing under St. Cyr at Mengen, and the right under Férino at Überlingen. Vandamme was facing Sigmaringen.

Jourdan remained in this position on the 18th and 19th. He did not dare advance any further because, in his view, he could not give up the support of Lake Constance and the Danube, and because with every forward step he took, these got further apart from each other, which would have put him in a very extended position.

On the 19th Jourdan received the news of the French government's declaration of war against Austria, though we can see that this made no difference to his movements or decisions.

During the course of his continued advance, Jourdan had transferred his main line of communications from Kehl to Neu-Breisach and Basel. This measure had the peculiar result that, like a picture reflected in multiple mirrors, it turned into a nightmare vision for him. As is so common in such cases, the inhabitants of the Black Forest had concluded that the line of communications he had given up must be threatened by the Austrians, and general alarm spread all through the Rhine towns. The governor of Strasbourg, General Châteauneuf-Randon, reported this to Jourdan, who in turn was induced to send General Vandamme and his detachment back to the Neckar.[146]

The Action at Osterach[147] on 21 March

On 17 March the archduke concentrated his army in a compact cantonment between Ochsenhausen and Wurzach, and on the 18th he moved into a camp at Biberach. The archduke recalled four of the six battalions he had

---

146. This is an excellent example of friction in war. Jourdan was forced to change his plan due to a circumstance completely out of his control.

147. This is written as Osterach in both Clausewitz's and the archduke's writings on the campaign. On modern maps, Ostrach is the name of the town, and Osterach is the name of the small river flowing through the valley.

sent to Ulm, so his army in Swabia (i.e., excluding Starray's corps) had 52 battalions and 138 squadrons. It is uncertain whether this includes the three cavalry regiments that had been further to the rear. In this case, by his own account, the archduke's army would have had 76,000 men, 24,000 of which were cavalry. This was twice the number his opponent fielded, and threefold in cavalry.

Jourdan was very aware of his dangerous situation and knew it would be prudent to retreat from the archduke, but he feared being held responsible if he did not support Masséna. On the 18th he therefore wrote to the Directory from Pfullendorf, saying that he would stay there until 30 March (the day Bernadotte should be in a position to act with significant force) and operate offensively then, but that if the archduke should advance on him before then, he would attack regardless of the enemy's superior numbers.

The fatuous Directory was entirely in favor of a decisive offensive, since on 19 March the minister of war wrote to Jourdan: "Citizen General, the Executive Directory, while leaving to your total discretion the manner in which your forces and those of the Army of Helvetia should execute this, charges me to advise you that it believes it to be of the utmost importance that you should thwart the enemy's plans by attacking them as soon as possible, and before they shall have united all their forces."[148] And on the 23rd, in reply to Jourdan's letter of the 18th, he wrote:

> Citizen General, the Executive Directory has read your letter of 28 *ventôse* [18 March] carefully. It charges me to observe to you that, regarding the Army of Helvetia as an integral part of that which you command and which you may use in the most convenient and useful manner, it is important that you should not lose a moment in attacking the enemy, who can only accrue greater resources every day while yours constantly remain the same.
>
> With your army organized thus being strong, veteran and electrified by the success of the Army of Helvetia, and the enemy's troops necessarily

---

148. In the original French: "*Le directoire exécutif, en vous laissant, citoyen général, toute la latitude sur les moyens d'exécution, que vous offrent vos forces et celles de l'armée d'Helvétie, me charge de vous mander qu'il croit de la plus haute importance que vous préveniez les ennemis dans leurs projets, en les attaquant au plutôt, et avant qu'ils n'aient réunis tous leurs moyens.*" Jourdan, *Précis des opérations de l'armée du Danube*, 114.

being discouraged, the Directory thinks that you must have nothing to fear for your left, and should attack immediately.[149]

We cannot help but be amazed anew each time by the stupidity with which such affairs are conducted. When the Directory had this letter sent, Masséna's right wing was on the sources of the Adige, 110 miles from Pfullendorf, and his center and half of the left wing were in front of Feldkirch, 55 miles from Pfullendorf; only Ruby's brigade was nearby. The right wing had to deal with an army of 50,000 in the Tyrol and the center with 20,000 men, but the archduke and his 76,000 men were one day's march away from Jourdan! This is what happens when one does not consider the enemy's combat forces to be the major factor and does not keep an eye firmly on each of his major formations right from the start.[150]

This letter probably vindicates General Jourdan sufficiently against the criticism that has been leveled against him since: that he attacked without orders. But another serious criticism of this general strikes home: that on 20 March he thought the archduke was still behind the Mindel[151] and that he had only one

---

149. In the original French: "*Le directoire exécutif, citoyen Général, a lu avec attention votre lettre du 28 ventôse. Il me charge de vous observer que devant regarder l'armée d'Helvétie comme partie intégrante de celle que vous commandez, et pouvant en disposer de la manière la plus convenable et la plus utile, il importe que vous ne perdiez pas un instant pour attaquer les ennemis, qui ne peuvent chaque jour qu'accroître leur moyens, lorsque les vôtres restent constamment les mêmes. Votre armée, ainsi composée, étant forte, aguerrie, électrisée par les succès de l'armée d'Helvétie, le découragement devant être dans les troupes enemies: le directoire pense que vous ne devez rien craindre pour votre gauche, et attaquer sur-le-champ.*" Jourdan, *Précis des opérations de l'armée du Danube*, 115–116. It is worth pointing out that Clausewitz lists the date of this letter as 23 March. It should be 22 March, as Jourdan dates it 2 *Germinal* in the French revolutionary calendar. The reader should be aware that not all dates will match up exactly, as there were three different calendars in use in Europe at the time: the French revolutionary calendar, the Gregorian, and the Julian.

150. This illustrates Clausewitz's emphasis on tying purpose to means in war. A discussion of this topic would take far too much space, so the reader is encouraged to read the sections of *On War* dealing with purpose and means (book 1, chap. 2) and war plans (book 8). Clausewitz spells out what he sees as the mechanism for achieving the political purpose of the war. In a campaign theater, destruction of the enemy's forces is often highlighted.

151. **Clausewitz** notes: "Jourdan, 127."

vanguard corps in front of him, whereas the Austrian commander had already advanced to the Schussen on the 19th and set up two camps at Rheinhardsweiler and Alschhausen on the 20th, concealed behind the forests there.

The archduke definitely intended a battle.[152] Therefore, on the 20th he had the French outposts driven in to about 5 miles from the Osterach, so as to attack the foe the next day in his position behind the Osterach before Jourdan should have had time to establish himself there.[153]

On the 21st the archduke advanced to the attack in three columns.[154]

The first column on the right wing, comprising eleven battalions and twenty squadrons (15,000–16,000 men) under the command of General Fürstenberg, was to drive the French out of Friedberg, then advance on Mengen and from there in the direction of Pfullendorf.

The second, comprising twenty-two battalions and fifty squadrons (32,000–33,000 men) accompanied by the archduke, moved through Saulgau on Osterach.

The third, of fifteen battalions and twenty-two squadrons (20,000–21,000 men) under General Wallis, likewise moved on Osterach through Hoskirch.

Both the second and third columns were to cross the stream there and mount the attack on the enemy center.[155] Six to eight thousand of the archduke's men are unaccounted for and were probably sent to the Danube and Lake Constance.

Thus, there were 53,000–54,000 men combined against the village of Ostrach.

---

152. Although the archduke mentions this, the language is somewhat vague: "The mismatch of a defensive stance with lavish means was too striking not to be recognized soon and Bellegarde received the order from Vienna to re-conquer Graubünden. The plan for a general assault was worked out but done in such a comprehensive manner and with so many kinds of preparations with regard to supplies as well as the disposition and combining of the movements that one had to postpone the period for conducting the operation from 19th March to the 2nd April." Thus, the Austrians planned to attack, but almost by default. The archduke himself gives the impression that he was more focused: "The archduke's plan was appropriate to his circumstances. He wanted to move against the enemy with his entire strength and open the campaign with a decisive victory." Karl, 1:154.

153. See Karl, 1:162.

154. For a full description of Archduke Charles's plans, see Karl, 1:151–183. It is worth pointing out that the restricted nature of the terrain meant that the archduke had the cavalry follow the tail end of the advancing columns.

155. These two columns were forced to use some of the same approach roads. Karl, 1:163.

Jourdan's position on the 21st was essentially unchanged.

His left wing under St. Cyr was at Mengen. Because Vandamme had not yet returned from the Neckar, he had two squadrons on the far side of the Danube, one battalion in Sigmaringen and Scheer at the Danube bridges there, and one battalion and three squadrons on the road to Ulm.

The advance guard under Lefebvre had its main body behind Osterach and deployed to defend the stream.

The actual center under Souham and the cavalry reserve under d'Hautpoul were at Pfullendorf, which is about 7 miles from Osterach.

Férino was pushed forward toward the Ach, much too far away to take part in any decisive action in the area of Osterach.

Thus Jourdan had spread his army out across 30 to 35 miles, while his opponent, who was twice as strong, struck his center on a front of not much more than 5 miles.

Admittedly, the position behind the Osterach offers a steep-sided valley, advantageous heights, and marshy meadows along the stream as obstacles to a frontal approach, while its left rests on the Danube and its right on the great marsh that separates the sources of the Ach from those of the Osterach. But these buttressing locations did not offer great protection[156] because they still had to be specially guarded, and also the distance of 9 miles from the marsh to the Danube was far too great an extent for the few troops Jourdan had here to oppose the archduke.

When the French commander received Lefebvre's warning of the Austrians' approach on the morning of the 21st, he sent Decaen's brigade from Souham's division to defend the ways across the marsh between the sources of the Ach and Osterach, because he thought it likely that he would be outflanked there. He sent a demi-brigade with a horse artillery battery from the same division to reinforce Lefebvre.

Souham stayed at Pfullendorf with the weak force he had left and d'Hautpoul's cavalry reserve.

Thus Jourdan had perhaps 15,000 men extended along the Osterach on a 9-mile front, while some 70,000 advanced against them.

But these 15,000 men were by no means simply deployed behind the Osterach. Rather, Lefebvre still had a considerable portion of his troops on the

---

156. Archduke Charles certainly thought this. See Karl, 1:160–161.

right bank,[157] so that during the Austrian advance, Adjutant-Commandant Fontaine with two battalions and six squadrons was cut off from Osterach and was obliged to retreat to join General Decaen at Riedhausen, thereby depriving Lefebvre of this part of his division.

Still less did St. Cyr stand behind the Osterach. On the contrary, he had only one brigade at Mengen, while he himself was with the rest of his troops in the area of Hohentengen, with the idea of acting offensively against the Austrians' right flank.

So General Lefebvre was left with about 7,000–8,000 men to defend 7 miles of the Osterach from the marsh to Einhart.[158]

The Austrian columns began their march at 3:00 a.m., concealed initially by thick fog. The first column divided its advance guard into two detachments, one of which moved on Hohentengen, and the other on Friedberg and Rappertsweiler against Einhart. The forward units of St. Cyr's division were driven back everywhere. As we have said, this general did not want to await the attack behind the Osterach; instead, he gathered his available troops and counterattacked Hohentengen. He drove off the Austrian vanguard and now advanced against the right flank of the first column itself, which was heading not for Hohentengen but for Einhart and had just arrived on the heights there. General Fürstenberg sent five battalions and twelve squadrons against General St. Cyr, who soon gave way, and then pursued him to Hohentengen. Possession of that place was contested for a long time until the French finally withdrew behind the Osterach.

The right-wing column itself met little resistance at Einhart, so it crossed the Osterach there, advanced to Habsthal, and then turned toward Magen-

---

157. Clausewitz identifies this as the left bank, but the river flows north to the Danube, so Lefebvre's troops would have been across the river on the east (right) bank and behind the river on the west (left) bank.

158. It is worthwhile to read what Clausewitz has to say about the defense of river lines and mountains. See *On War*, book 6, chaps. 15–20. If defending forces are concentrated too close to a river, it can be difficult to prevent an enemy from crossing at another location; if they are deployed too far away, the enemy cannot be prevented from crossing at all. Combine this with the problems of moving in mountains, and the large-scale defense of a river line is even more difficult. Pushing sufficient troops forward to defend a specific locale risks their defeat in detail by a concentrated enemy, and deploying too far back makes the defensive line easy to breach, as defending forces struggle to concentrate at the enemy's crossing point.

buch against the center. Meanwhile, the archduke had arrived here with the second column and General Wallis with the third, after driving the French advanced posts back across the Osterach. This was accomplished not without stubborn resistance, in the course of which, as already mentioned, one and a half battalions and six squadrons were driven away from Osterach along the marsh through Riedhausen and were obliged to join General Decaen.

Jourdan himself had hurried to Lefebvre's division, and the two battalions, eight guns, and six squadrons he had ordered up from Pfullendorf as reinforcements likewise moved up. But what could such feeble support achieve? In such a situation, 7,000–8,000 men could not withstand a force of 50,000 for long. The Austrians forced crossings everywhere and scaled the heights on the far side. Lefebvre himself was wounded and lost a couple of thousand men, as well as three guns, whereupon Jourdan realized he had to retreat. Lefebvre's division retreated to Pfullendorf, while St. Cyr's division went to Möskirch.

The archduke followed only as far as Pfullendorf, without making any attempt to cross the Andelbach.

We can probably say that, on the part of the archduke, this was a mountain that gave birth to a mouse. It is pointless to list the ways in which the archduke could have achieved greater results: it is enough to say that he was twice as strong as his opponent, had three times as many cavalry, and found the enemy spread across 36 miles. These are conditions that enable glorious successes and virtually guarantee them, provided operations do not lack energy. The simplest blow against the enemy center would have provided success, perhaps even without any planning or forethought.

But the archduke acted not just cautiously but timidly.[159]

---

159. We find it difficult to disagree with Clausewitz. The archduke could have been more aggressive and sought a more decisive blow, given the relative strengths of the two armies and the favorable deployments. In the archduke's defense, Clausewitz's criticism is harsh: the terrain meant that the archduke could not easily get his cavalry forward, and the early-morning fog hindered the Austrian advance as much as the French defense. This slowed down the Austrians, prolonging the fight and making it more difficult than expected. But as the archduke noted above, terrain can just as easily favor the attacker, and he certainly had a large numerical advantage. The archduke also notes numerous errors by Jourdan in terms of the latter's deployment. Curiously, the archduke does not explain why he did not capitalize on these errors more effectively, and the chapter on the battle at Osterach hints at his own caution. See Karl, 1:151–183. Thus, it is easy to agree with Clausewitz's rather acerbic take. In contrast, Jo-

On the night of the 21st and 22nd Jourdan continues his retreat to Stockach and is joined there by Férino. General St. Cyr moves to Tuttlingen. Vandamme has returned from his march to the Neckar and moves to Friedingen.

On the 22nd the archduke moves across the Andelbach into the camp abandoned by the French and has his advance guard pursue in several columns.

The archduke designates the 23rd yet another rest day.[160]

On this day, Jourdan continued the retreat of his center and right wing for several miles. He had the latter move to Singen, posting himself with the center at Engen, while his left stayed in its position at Tuttlingen and Friedingen. He remained here on the 24th.

13 THE BATTLE OF STOCKACH ON 25 MARCH

On the 24th the archduke moved into a camp at Stockach and had his advance guard push ahead a few leagues in three columns. The first column, consisting of three battalions and six squadrons under General Meerfeld, advanced on the Tuttlingen road; the second, of six battalions and sixteen squadrons under General Nauendorf, on the Engen road; and the third, of two battalions and twelve squadrons under General Schwarzenberg, on the road to Singen, thus directly conforming with the positions of the French main bodies.

The first column encountered the enemy in Liptingen and in Neuhausen ob Eck, driving them out. The column pursued as far as Liptingen, where Meerfeld formed up and was reinforced with another five battalions from the archduke. In the afternoon St. Cyr advanced against this part of the Austrian advance guard with reinforcements of his own, initially driving Meerfeld's forward troops back on Liptingen, but when the five battalions sent by the archduke

---

mini broadly overlooks errors by Archduke Charles and points out that the archduke gained a good result only a few days later at Stockach. That argument ignores the fact that a more aggressive attack at Osterach might well have removed the need for the later battle. See Jomini, 11:119–144.

160. In the archduke's defense, his troops had marched quite rapidly to Osterach and had fought an action there, and they surely needed the rest. Then again, his great surplus of troops in comparison to Jourdan meant that he had men who were fresher than their opponents, and they could have been used to press the French and prevent them from re-forming.

arrived, St. Cyr was thrown back in turn through Emmingen ob dem Eck and into the Danube valley. In this place the Austrians captured three cannon.[161]

The second column of the Austrian advance guard reached Eigeltingen and pushed its forward elements toward Aach.

On the left wing, Prince Schwarzenberg had driven Férino's outposts back through Steusslingen and Friedingen (not to be confused with the one on the Danube) toward Singen. But Férino reinforced them, and Schwarzenberg had to fall back behind Steusslingen. Here he received four battalions of reinforcements and was then able to reoccupy the forest in front of Singen.

Apart from these three advance guards, the archduke also had a detachment of one and a half battalions and eight squadrons advance toward Constance through Radolfzell between Lake Constance's two bosoms, the Überlingensee and the Untersee, as they are known.

The archduke chose the main army's camp so that the left wing with thirteen battalions and twenty-four squadrons was on the tongue of land created by the sharp northward bend of the Stockach stream between Stockach and Lake Constance and rested on the marsh of Lake Constance. The center and right wing, with twenty-four battalions and thirty-six squadrons, were posted in front of Stockach with the stream to their rear. This position was very poor in many respects and was chosen by the archduke simply to put the Stockach defile behind him, so that it would not delay his further advance.

Thus, at least as far as the infantry is concerned, we find the archduke's army fairly concentrated here.

That is to say, there are forty-eight battalions in this position, and one and a half sent toward Constance; of the cavalry, ninety-four squadrons are immediately at hand, and eight sent toward Constance. This still leaves twenty-six squadrons unaccounted for, with no word of their whereabouts. Perhaps the three cavalry regiments that started further back had not yet arrived. We must assume there were at least 70,000 men present.

As the archduke himself says, he was not satisfied with the success obtained at Osterach; indeed, there is no conceivable way that he could have been content with it. Therefore, as he puts it, he wanted to bring about a decisive battle.[162] This expression allows us a glimpse into the somewhat irresolute soul of

---

161. Broadly speaking, this narrative lines up well with that of the archduke. See Karl, 1:183–193.

162. Karl, 1:191–192.

the archduke. When one is twice as strong as one's opponent, one does not need to instigate the battle with any great caution and complexity; the main thing is simply to go for it. If the archduke thought Jourdan might fall back again, his slow and tentative pursuit was the least suitable way of achieving the aim, whereas a decisive thrust into Jourdan's line of deployment could at least have made him retreat immediately, thus causing all kinds of other complications for Jourdan that would have been just as bad for him as losing a battle.[163]

But although the archduke's deployment of the 24th at Stockach was in front of a defile, it was much more like a defensive deployment than one from which he was determined to march forth to battle the next day. The archduke does not actually do this on the 25th either—instead, he decides upon a general reconnaissance. This is an age-old favorite practice of the Austrians whenever they lack the spirit of enterprise and begin to feel embarrassed about it. Daun was constantly ordering general reconnaissances,[164] and later we see

---

163. This ties in with two of Clausewitz's ideas. The first is the role of numerical superiority: "But superiority varies in degree. It can be two to one, or three or four to one, and so on; it can obviously reach the point where it is overwhelming. . . . When we observe that the skill of the greatest commanders may be counterbalanced by a two-to-one ratio in the fighting forces, we cannot doubt that in ordinary cases, whether the engagement be great or small, a significant superiority in numbers (it does not have to be more than double) will suffice to assure victory, however adverse the other circumstances. . . . We believe then that in our circumstances and all similar ones, a main factor is the possession of strength at the really vital point. Usually it is actually the most important factor. To achieve strength at the decisive point depends on the strength of the army and on the skill with which this strength is employed. The first rule, therefore, should be: put the largest possible army into the field. This may sound a platitude, but in reality it is not." *On War*, book 3, chap. 8, 194–195. The second is Clausewitz's thought on military genius and the need for both physical and moral courage (*On War*, book 1, chap. 3, 100–101). One can see why his criticism of the archduke is so scathing. The archduke possessed roughly double the numbers of his opponent, he had just beaten the enemy at Osterach, and he claimed to be seeking a decisive blow. Yet he chose to conduct a reconnaissance, and he had previously failed to pursue Jourdan vigorously. Despite the archduke's success at Stockach, his irresolute decision making surely cost him a more complete victory.

164. Count Leopold Joseph von Daun had a long career in the Austrian army and was best known for his service during the Seven Years' War of 1756–1763. Daun's record was mixed but included some prominent successes, such as at the battle of Hochkirch in 1758. Clausewitz is most likely referring to the battle of Liegnitz (1760), where Daun arrived late and did not press into action despite his great numerical superiority

Schwarzenberg carry this bashful gesture to the point of ridiculousness.[165] As to the reason for this diversion, the archduke cites his uncertainty about where he would encounter the enemy army and the danger of being attacked in the flank by it if he headed in the wrong direction.

Of course, attackers often find themselves in such situations, especially at the start of a campaign, when they do not yet have the enemy in sight and cannot follow his every move. But even then, this problem is usually solved not by reconnaissance but by a decisive advance on that line where the enemy has to be unless he has made a mistake. Even if he does not meet the defender there, at least the attacker is in the right place himself and can be sure that his opponent will have to come and find him.

But the present case really cannot be considered such an instance. We maintain that we find the archduke's reason for reconnoitering and for postponing his attack to be only half sincere; it was the rationale he tried to reassure himself with, but in short, it was an act of indecision. Ever since the 21st, the Austrian commander could not have lost sight of his opponent, since he was generally quite close to the enemy's center and never more than 10 miles from it. The allocation of his own advance guard to the three axes of Tuttlingen, Engen, and Singen is sufficient evidence that he knew very well the position of the French army on the 23rd and 24th and that if he wanted to encounter its main body, he just needed to head boldly for Engen. But to the archduke—who, like the strategists of his time, attached infinitely more value to the geometric form of a deployment than to the ratio of forces—the idea of piling in against 20,000 men with 70,000, when 10,000 on his right and 10,000 on his left might move against his flanks, was a moral impossibility.

---

over the Prussians. Clausewitz criticized Karl Philipp, Prince of Schwarzenberg, for his lack of vigor during the 1812 campaign. Schwarzenberg had a mixed record as a senior commander, despite his success as a more junior officer. Carl von Clausewitz, *The Campaign of 1812 in Russia*, trans. Francis Egerton (London: John Murray, 1843), https://www.clausewitz.com/readings/1812/Clausewitz-CampaignOf1812inRussia-Ellesmere Translation.pdf.

165. This favorite Austrian practice persisted for at least another fifty years. During the Hungarian War of Independence in 1848–1849, Austrian Feldmarschall Fürst Windisch-Grätz was a prime exponent of the reconnaissance in force as a substitute for decisive action. See Johann Nobili, *Hungary 1848: The Winter Campaign*, trans. and ed. Christopher Pringle (Solihull, UK: Helion, 2021).

The archduke therefore decided, as we have said, to undertake a general reconnaissance on the 25th, which was organized as follows.[166]

The advance guard led by General Meerfeld was reinforced by two battalions so that it now had ten battalions and six squadrons (11,000–12,000 men). It was tasked with attacking the enemy at Emmendingen ob dem Eck.

The advance guard under Nauendorf at Eigeltingen was reinforced by three battalions and twelve squadrons, bringing it to nine battalions and twenty-eight squadrons, 14,000–15,000 strong. The archduke posted himself at the head of this corps, which was to advance on the road toward Engen.

The advance guard on the left wing under Schwarzenberg was unchanged and could not really have been asked to advance any further, as it was fairly close to Férino's division.

While the archduke was busy with these half-measures, the French commander had decided to attack his opponent again. Jourdan had called Ruby's brigade over to him from Masséna's army and attached it to Férino; if he fell back any further, he would have to send it to Schafhausen again and would then lose communications with the army in Switzerland. Besides, he had instructed Masséna to attack Feldkirch, and Masséna had replied the same day that he would attack that position on the 24th. In these circumstances, it seemed morally impossible to continue his retreat and appear to desert General Masséna. Finally, the French commander still did not think victory was impossible, and on the other hand, he thought that given the proximity of the

---

166. This caution can also be explained, but not justified, by the possibility that the archduke was considering a march into Switzerland rather than to the source of the Danube. Jomini notes the archduke's uncertainty in this regard. Jomini, 11:126–127. If Jomini is correct, Clausewitz's argument is shaky, but the archduke still deserves criticism for not being clear about what he was trying to achieve and how. Surely, having clear intentions is the minimum expected of a commander. If Jomini is wrong, however, then Clausewitz is right. Archduke Charles notes in his memoirs of the campaign that he was taken ill after the battle and that the Viennese court had pressured him to stop the advance, which it thought had already advanced "far too far." Karl, 1:231–232. That being said, this does not excuse the archduke's lack of dynamism at Osterach or the faffing around prior to Stockach. He could have delivered a much greater blow to Jourdan before ceasing his advance west, thus removing much of the French threat from the Danube valley and satisfying his own political masters.

Rhine, the Black Forest, and the Danube and in such broken ground, losing a battle might not incur any great disadvantage.[167]

These are the reasons that determined him to seek out and attack the enemy decisively on the 25th.

Since the French government had put General Jourdan and his army in a position where it was impossible to succeed, these appear to be pretty good reasons. But it is still no more than an appearance and not the truly intrinsic content of the reasoning that makes them valid.

Jourdan always had the vague idea that he would gain an advantage by attacking, first, just by the principle of the offensive in general, and second, because he would strike just a portion of the enemy force. The first of these notions rests on a quite common misconception for which we do not wish to make any special criticism of him, but the other was quite without foundation. He must have known that the archduke had not detached any significant part of his force, and as we shall see, the dispositions he made for the attack of the 25th entailed his columns converging on the enemy position at Stockach. He therefore had no reason to expect to defeat the Austrian commander in detail, and even less so since Jourdan advanced very divided and on an extended front, so he lacked the means to be a serious threat to an isolated corps of Austrians, even if he did actually find one somewhere. If we look at it in the cold light of day, Jourdan had no prospect at all of victory, so he went to incur a defeat simply to avoid appearing inactive. This is a practice that criticism can never tolerate.[168]

---

167. The broken ground would preclude an easy pursuit, and it would facilitate a rearguard defense.

168. This ties in with Clausewitz's trinity, in that hate (passion), reason, and chance are all at play in war, and no one element (the people, the government, or the military) can be clearly ascribed to any one part of the whole. This is where the corruption of his trinity as simply people, government, and military is so misleading. This corruption implies that one can divorce these elements from the raw emotions and blind luck that often constitute a major part of any instance of violence, let alone war itself. Clausewitz is pointing out that, in essence, the three parts of his trinity make one whole, and war is the binding force. One cannot assume that rationality is a given, even for otherwise rational people. As such, Jourdan's decision to attack is one of those inexplicable events in war that illustrates Clausewitz's broader point. It also ties into his idea of genius, whereby such a person needs both physical and moral courage as well as the ability to see through uncertainty yet still make clear decisions. See *On War*, book 1, chaps. 1 and 3. For a more detailed explanation, see Hew Strachan, "A Clausewitz for

We could accept the reasoning that a lost battle could bring no great disadvantage under the prevailing circumstances if it were based on the character of the archduke, which could have been known to General Jourdan as one from which there was not much to fear. But given the enemy's great superiority in numbers, the road to the Rhine was not short enough to prevent heavy losses. It is seven days' march from Stockach to Kehl, and when the victor has great superiority, his beaten opponent can lose more on this road than on one three times as long with a less unequal balance of forces.

If General Jourdan had stayed constantly in sight of the archduke but remained on the defensive—that is, if he had contested every inch of ground, as the saying goes—the danger of an actual crisis, such as is found in every battle, would have been entirely avoided. The archduke would have been kept just as busy, and it is quite possible that Jourdan would have held on somewhere around the entrances to the Black Forest on that side of the Rhine. Indeed, that is probably what would have happened, considering the Austrian government had already rebuked the archduke for advancing as far as Donaueschingen. So it is likely that the effect of the defensive would have been successfully demonstrated here in the same way it is nine times out of ten—that is, the opponent decides not to attack.[169]

This must be our objective verdict. But of course, in the French commander's defense, we can say that fear of blame drove him to act. However much wiser and more useful a protracted fighting withdrawal might have been, among the windbag members of the Directory, it would have been construed as the product of cowardice and incompetence, and it was quite possible that they would look more favorably on an outright defeat.

Jourdan's dispositions for the attack of the 25th were as follows:

Every Season," *American Interest* 2, 6 (1 July 2007), https://www.the-american-interest.com/2007/07/01/a-clausewitz-for-every-season/.

169. Clausewitz argues in *On War*, book 6, chap. 1, that the object of defense is preservation—whether of time, space, or combat power. As such, Jourdan, knowing the archduke's cautious nature, might have been better off conducting a fighting withdrawal. That being said, he was under immense pressure from the Directory in Paris to achieve success, so whatever he did, Jourdan could not win. He did not have the manpower to win decisively, and a strictly defensive campaign might have got him sacked and possibly executed by the Directory. Thus, it is hard to criticize him too harshly.

Férino and Ruby's brigade, about 12,000 men, were to advance on Stockach via Steusslingen and Örsingen.

Souham was also to head there with 6,000 men via Eigeltingen, so the two were to combine in front of Stockach.

Lefebvre's division (led by Soult,[170] as Lefebvre was wounded) and the cavalry reserve, perhaps 10,000 men altogether, were to move through Emmingen ob dem Eck against Liptingen, which lay 5 miles from the archduke's position, virtually as an extension of his right wing.

St. Cyr and Vandamme with another 10,000 men were likewise to advance against Liptingen.

Thus the two armies were on the move against each other: the French with their full force of about 38,000 strong, and the Austrians with less than half of theirs, so in absolute terms, not much weaker than their opponent at about 30,000 men.

At daybreak the archduke's central reconnaissance column found itself on the march from Eigeltingen toward Aach. Its vanguard had already taken that place from the French when Souham arrived with his division and threw the head of the column back across the Aach again, taking a whole battalion prisoner. At that moment, the archduke received word that several columns were advancing against Liptingen and that a major attack seemed to be directed there. The archduke handed over command of the central advance guard corps to General Nauendorf, directing him to withdraw slowly through Eigeltingen on the Stockach position, so that the left wing's advance guard under General Schwarzenberg should have enough time to complete its retreat through Örsingen. Then the archduke himself hastened back to the position, to betake himself from there to Liptingen.

General Nauendorf carried out his instructions appropriately. He did not leave Eigeltingen until midday, by which time Schwarzenberg had moved through Örsingen while under attack by Férino. He then took up an intermediate position halfway back and did not arrive in front of the position of the center and right wing until 3:00 in the afternoon, without being pressed hard by the enemy.

---

170. Jean-de-Dieu Soult (1769–1851) had a distinguished career as a French soldier and politician. He became a marshal of France and had an excellent record of command throughout much of the period.

As for the French, only Férino and his division had pursued as far as the Stockach at Nennzingen, in front of the Austrian left wing. Souham had contented himself with sending Decaen's brigade after General Nauendorf, while he himself remained at Eigeltingen. Férino's division on its own was much too weak to mount a serious attack on the Austrian left wing in its very strong position, so nothing else significant happened there.

Thus, here the Austrian left wing and Schwarzenberg's advance guard, fifteen battalions and thirty-six squadrons altogether, or about 20,000 men, are pinned by Férino's division, which is perhaps 12,000 strong. Likewise, Nauendorf's corps of 15,000 men is pinned by the perhaps 3,000–4,000 men of Decaen's brigade.

General Meerfeld had collected nine battalions and fourteen squadrons of the right wing's advance guard, about 12,000 men, between Liptingen and Nennhausen ob dem Eck, and two more battalions were on their way from the main body of the army. He wanted to advance with these troops against Emmingen ob dem Eck, and his lead elements had already driven the French out of that place at 5:00 a.m. when he saw their main body approaching in several columns. Meerfeld abandoned his attack and intended to withdraw to Liptingen and take up position there. But through heaven knows what mistakes in his orders, he failed to get there. Soult's division pressed in on his columns from several directions, the French cavalry repulsed the Austrian cavalry, and his force fell into great disorder. Since St. Cyr's columns appeared from Tuttlingen at the same time, there could be no thought of trying to make a stand at Liptingen. Not until he was a mile behind Liptingen, in the Grauenwald,[171] was Meerfeld able to rally the two battalions and three squadrons he still had. But, under attack by a couple of French cavalry and infantry regiments, these did not stand for long here either and retreated in disorder toward the right wing of the position. Meerfeld had sent part of his cavalry toward Schwandorf and Möskirch to cover this area through which the army's line of retreat ran.

Thus, here we see General Meerfeld, who has 12,000 men (according to the archduke's account), driven back by Soult and d'Hautpoul, who are probably no stronger, for 7 miles, until his force lost any semblance of order and could

---

171. This is a large, sprawling area of forest on the main road between Stockach and Liptingen. Although only one part of the forest is identified as Grauenwald on contemporary maps, the term seems to be applicable to the large forest in its entirety.

no longer fight. St. Cyr's division took part merely by making an appearance, for it was still not in cannon range. It is remarkable that Meerfeld only lost two howitzers during all this, from which it virtually follows that it was more rout than disorder, and that in any case, the main blame for this shameful episode rests with General Meerfeld himself.

To General Jourdan, this looked like a decisive success by his center against the enemy's right wing. Presumably, he took General Meerfeld to be not the advance guard but the wing itself, since, by his own testimony, he thought Meerfeld had 25,000 men. As soon as he saw this, he decided to have Generals St. Cyr and Vandamme move on Möskirch to cut off the Austrian army's retreat. In doing so, he partly intended to make the battle, which he thought had been won, that much more decisive; he also wanted to threaten the cautious archduke's line of retreat to persuade him to abandon any further resistance, because Jourdan himself did not think his victory was that emphatic. This is how General Jourdan himself explains it.[172] Other writers have always presented St. Cyr's maneuver as though it were only a tactical outflanking for the action between Liptingen and Stockach. But this view is obviously wrong, for how could Jourdan have directed General St. Cyr to Möskirch, 10 miles from the battlefield, for such a purpose! Thus, St. Cyr and Vandamme headed off to the left, away from the battlefield, and only Soult and d'Hautpoul pursued the defeated Meerfeld toward the right wing of the Austrian position.

It is not easy to get a clear picture of the organization and positions of the Austrian combat forces at this decisive moment, since, like most people who describe battles, the archduke attaches little value to this information and so does not structure his account accordingly; yet we consider this to be most essential in a battle whose geometric form is so convoluted. We will try to compile what we can about this but will confine ourselves mainly to the infantry because the position and use of the cavalry are known with even less certainty.

The three advance guards had taken twenty-six battalions and fifty-two squadrons with them, so twenty-two battalions and fifty-four squadrons would have been left in the position. The archduke says that when Meerfeld was thrown back on the right wing of the army, there were eight intact battalions there and six grenadier battalions on or rather behind the Nellenberg in the center. This then leaves eight battalions for the left wing on the far side of the Stockach. Thus, from its thirteen battalions, this left wing had prob-

---

172. **Clausewitz** notes: "Jourdan, 162."

ably provided the reinforcements Prince Schwarzenberg received on the 24th. When the archduke criticizes himself for not having used the thirteen battalions and twenty-four squadrons on the left wing properly, he is reckoning it at its original strength, which it must indeed have returned to when Schwarzenberg retreated upon it.

In any case, we see that with the fourteen battalions (14,000–15,000 men) the archduke had on the right bank of the Stockach, he would have had no trouble renewing the fight against Soult, and even if St. Cyr and Vandamme had turned up, their success at this point could not be considered guaranteed and probably would have been doubtful.

We must assume that at this time Generals Nauendorf and Schwarzenberg were still at Eigeltingen and Örsingen.

The eight battalions of the right wing at Mahlspüren were under the command of General Wallis; when the defeated Meerfeld approached them, they executed a quarter turn to the right and deployed between Rierhalden and Raithaslach, from where they advanced to the attack. This attack too was going awry, especially on the road to Liptingen, where the French were strongest and the Austrian troops were beginning to waver when the archduke arrived in person. By his personal influence, he was able to rally the troops forward again and continue the action there. This now lasted for several hours of bloody exertion by both sides, without further result. The archduke had sent an order to the six grenadier battalions from the Nellenberg with twelve squadrons of cuirassiers to hurry to the aid of the right wing, but since these had to march almost 5 miles, it must have taken them a couple of hours to get there. When these 9,000 fresh troops arrived, it was impossible for the French to resist them, even though they fought for every inch of ground, so they withdrew to Liptingen. As the battle turned here, Jourdan recognized his error in having sent St. Cyr and Vandamme so far away, and he dispatched an order for them to speed up and send a demi-brigade to their right to support Soult's division directly. But although the archduke was informed, just as his grenadiers arrived, that St. Cyr and Vandamme were heading toward his rear, he paid little heed to this measure that had become a mere demonstration and instead resolutely piled into his opponent. The demi-brigade that St. Cyr sent against the Austrian right flank as direct support to Soult came too late and was largely captured by the Austrian cavalry. Soult was therefore thrown back upon Liptingen, and the action at this point was decided beyond doubt. Férino on the right wing was facing an enemy position against which he could achieve nothing; the center had not dared to move beyond Eigeltingen with its main body. Jourdan felt that, given doubtful success in two places and defeat in the third, and with his army spread out again over 13 to 18 miles and facing a numerically superior enemy, there could be no further thought of victory. He therefore decided to retreat.

The archduke saw matters the same way, and the belief that he had achieved this result was enough for him. For the archduke, it was always about the idea of victory, not the extent of it. Thus, instead of striking at Soult and d'Hautpoul with the full force of his victory and his superior numbers and pursuing them to twist the knife in their ribs for as long as daylight allowed, the archduke let them remain in possession of Liptingen. "Evening was approaching," he says, "satisfied with having won a victory, [I] did not risk sallying forth onto the plain." And what is the use of an army having 27,000 cavalry if they are not in a position to annihilate a defeated division after twelve hours of fighting and to drive an enemy cavalry reserve of 3,000 horse from the field? Of the fifty-four squadrons that ought still to have been in the archduke's position, twenty-four were on the far side of the Stockach with the left wing, six had been sent toward Möskirch, and twelve had been left behind Stockach through an excess of caution, so the archduke had only twelve to move up to the decisive point.[173]

So the battle was won, but without any trophies, without the destruction of enemy combat forces, and with almost no morale effect. The Austrians took one single gun, against which they lost two; the two sides' losses in dead, wounded, and prisoners would have been fairly equal at about 4,000–5,000 men each.

The French right wing stayed where it was from the night of the 25th until midday on the 26th, and the center remained until the evening, without the archduke having the courage to attempt any kind of operation against them. Early on the 26th St. Cyr and Vandamme even undertook some demonstration attacks against the Austrian cavalry in the area of Wahlwies, to make their

---

173. It is worth reminding the reader of the archduke's intention to secure a decisive battle and his subsequent failure to do so. It is also worth quoting him on the art of generalship: "The battle of Stockach was, like most great battles, won by a reserve. Using such a reserve at the right time to deliver the decisive blow with it is the art of the general. When the *corps de bataille* is no longer able to overcome the press of the enemy or his maneuvers or his resistance at the crucial moment of the battle then the reserve must take part in the battle. Its mission is actually only to replace the depletion in the forces which are necessary to win an objective, as the troops which first come into the melee are mostly dispersed or scattered or weakened, and victory goes to the remaining strength at the last." Karl, 1:225–226.

extraction through there easier. One might say that it was an abstract victory without corporeal form.[174]

The French commander even claimed the honor of victory for himself, and it is true that there are cases of commanders before and after him who have claimed victory with far less justification. However, all claims of this kind are designed not to gain the moral weight of victory for themselves but to reduce it.

The question of whether the strategic purpose of a battle was achieved or had to be abandoned decides otherwise doubtful cases in an incontrovertible way.

The French army withdrew across the Rhine, and even if, as it happened, this cannot be considered a direct and entirely necessary consequence of the battle of Stockach, that was indeed its underlying cause. It happened because of concern about what else might befall, and it was the battle of Stockach that laid the foundation for that concern.

Let us postpone what we have to say about the character of this battle as a whole until the reflections we offer at the end of this section about its larger context.

14 JOURDAN AND BERNADOTTE RETREAT ACROSS THE RHINE

Jourdan therefore left the area of the Stockach battlefield on 26 March and began his retreat toward the Black Forest. If the situation obliged him to cross it, he wanted to do so in three columns through the Höllen, Kinzig, and Rench valleys. Even if he had preferred to retreat to the Rhine between Basel and Lake Constance, this was no longer possible because of St. Cyr's division, which would thereby have been in danger of being lost completely.

Generals St. Cyr and Vandamme felt they could no longer return safely from their position between Möskirch and Stockach to the points on the Danube from which they had come, namely, Tuttlingen, Mühlheim, and Friedingen. They therefore decided to march on Sigmaringen, seize the bridges there that were only weakly held by the Austrians, and cross the Danube there. They had to cover about 15 miles to get there and carried out this march on the 26th without hindrance.

Soult and d'Hautpoul stayed at Liptingen and Emmingen on the 26th.

---

174. It does not seem to be a "great battle" either. See note 173 above.

Souham fell back to Aach; Férino fell back to Singen, and from there he sent Ruby's brigade back to Schafhausen and Stein again.

On the 27th St. Cyr was on the march to Rothweil.

D'Hautpoul crossed the Danube at Tuttlingen.

Soult and Souham moved to Geisingen on the Danube, and Férino moved to Blomberg.

On the 28th Jourdan moved into another position in front of the Black Forest with his right wing at Löffingen on the road to Neustadt and his left at Rothweil on the road to Freudenstadt, thus on a front of 25 miles. He remained in this position for three days, that is, until 31 March.

The Austrian advance guard did not follow the French toward Singen, Engen, and Tuttlingen until the 27th.

The archduke stood fast with his main army because he intended to turn against Switzerland, but when he learned that the French had not continued their march through the Black Forest but had halted in the positions described above, he decided to march toward the Danube first in order to push Jourdan completely back over the Rhine. He therefore concentrated his army at Liptingen and Emmingen on the 29th, after sending five and a half battalions and eighteen squadrons toward the Rhine and reinforcing his advance guard again. But still the archduke did not set his army itself in motion. He waited for General Starray, whom he had summoned to him and who did not get beyond Ulm until the 27th. It is not until 3 April that we see the archduke arrive at Donaueschingen.[175]

When the Austrian lead elements approached the French position, Jourdan feared they might seize one or other of the passes behind him. He therefore retreated into the Black Forest on the 31st so that Férino held the entrances to the Höllen valley, his center held the Kinzig, and his left wing the Rench.

He stayed in this position for four days, until the leading Austrian troops began to penetrate his line in one or two places. Jourdan himself had fallen ill and left the army, so General Ernouf, who was temporarily in command, decided to retreat across the Rhine. Férino's division did so at Alt-Breisach on 5 April, and the rest crossed at Kehl on the 6th.

On 3 April the archduke halted in Donaueschingen. When he learned that the French army was crossing the Rhine, he left General Starray behind to

---

175. It is worth reminding the reader that the Viennese court had pressured the archduke to stop his advance. See note 166 in this chapter.

observe the Rhine with eighteen battalions and sixty-four squadrons, or about 30,000 men, while he turned toward Switzerland with the main army.

It is remarkable that General Starray was not supposed to go into the Rhine valley with these troops. Instead, he was ordered to hold the exits from the Black Forest with eight battalions and thirty-six squadrons and to keep a reserve of ten battalions and twenty-eight squadrons around Villingen. The former, together with the armed inhabitants of the Black Forest, conducted a constant guerrilla war against the frequent French parties infiltrating into the Black Forest from the right bank of the Rhine.

Thus, in the last scene of this act, the archduke seems to repudiate his own claim to victory. While he justifiably saw no important purpose in a strict defense of the Rhine, the freedom of action he left to his opponent would merit approval only if he had marched away with his whole army and left just a corps of observation of a couple of thousand men facing the Black Forest. To leave 30,000 men there and still allow the French the freedom for their parties to operate on this side of the Rhine was inexcusable, an offense of the highest order against the honor of arms and a strategic error to boot.

As a result of the Army of the Danube's retreat across the Rhine, General Bernadotte also abandoned the siege of Philippsburg and fell back behind the Rhine, so the French had only two garrisons remaining on the right bank, namely, those in Mannheim and Heidelberg.

15 REFLECTIONS

If we ask ourselves what the result of this first section was, it is the following:

The French gained possession of Graubündten, took 12,000–13,000 prisoners and forty guns, and thereby struck such a blow against the moral strength of Austrian arms, particularly the army in the Tyrol, that its effects would be difficult to recover from.

Conversely, their Army of the Danube was repulsed across the Rhine and thereby lost some of its own moral strength. The impact of this setback counted somewhat more than just the tally of lost trophies because it involved their main army and their commander in chief. Also, in terms of public opinion, from the theater of operations all the way to Paris and Vienna, the glorious French feats of arms in Graubündten were more than outweighed by this hollow victory. Lecourbe had annihilated one Austrian corps and Dessolles another, but Archduke Charles had beaten Jourdan, and that rang louder and more resonantly, even though it could not be compared with those victories.[176]

And the French had attained these fine victories while the 73,000 men of their combat forces (Jourdan's army of 38,000, Masséna's 30,000, and Dessolles's brigade of 5,000 men) were engaged against 148,000 Austrians (the archduke's army of 76,000, Hotze's corps of 24,000, and Bellegarde's army of 50,000).[177] They attained these victories under the influence of an absolutely preposterous plan on the part of their own government,[178] whereas the Austrian government at least did not obstruct its forces by actively interfering in their commonsense operation.[179] The solution to this contradiction lies in the course of events, which we must therefore accompany with our reflections.

In terms of the opposite directions they took, the events of this first section on the two wings of the theater of war may be considered like weights in a scale, striving to balance each other. We will look first at the weights, then at the balance arm and its pivot point.

Let us first consider the events in Graubündten.

The fact that the Austrians occupied this territory in 1798 when asked to do so by its inhabitants, who were under threat, will probably not be condemned by anyone who regards the honor of a government as anything more than a matter of complete indifference. If they occupied it, then they would also have to defend it, in the event that the political fact of its occupation should not suffice to deter the French from invading it. But the necessity of defending it followed only insofar as it was a question of a partial attack by the French on this little country, that is, with a proportionate fraction of their force. The

---

176. The archduke's success at Stockach threatened Masséna's offensive in Switzerland. Masséna's forces captured the important town of Martinsbrück on 26 March, but he was forced to pull back to avoid the risk of encirclement as the archduke's forces moved west. See Ross, *Quest for Victory*, 232.

177. These numbers add up to 150,000; the discrepancy is probably a typographical error.

178. Clausewitz is referring to the French decision to attack on all fronts. See Ross, *Quest for Victory*, 225–230. Also see Georges Lefebvre, *The French Revolution from 1793 to 1799*, trans. John Hall Stewart and James Friguglietti (New York: Columbia University Press, 1964), 2:236–238; A. B. Rodger, *The War of the Second Coalition 1798–1801* (Oxford: Clarendon Press, 1964), 158.

179. This is not strictly true, as the archduke claims he was pressured not to advance too far. See note 166 in this chapter.

Austrians had 6,000–8,000 men there. Assuming that, before the outbreak of general war, the French had threatened to move 20,000 men into this territory if the Austrians did not withdraw their 6,000–8,000, the Austrian government would have had no choice but to move in 20,000 men to support these 8,000, for no one can think that, in response to such a threat, the Austrian government should have withdrawn its 8,000 men and vacated the country. Also, it is hard to see what disadvantages the Austrians would have accrued if they had sent as many combat forces to Graubündten as the French did. But all this is true only if we are talking about a local dispute and struggle over Graubündten, without a general outbreak of war. This local struggle did not happen; nor was it to be expected. We would not even remark on such a notion were it not that the Austrians' refusal to abandon the Graubündtners obviously arose from this point of view. Thus, for purely political considerations that apparently emerged from a sense of fairness and honor, they were forced to defend this territory, all of which projected beyond their line of deployment.[180]

We say: any obligation as a matter of honor could apply only while the powers of France and Austria were at peace, for only in that case does honor dictate that one power cannot tolerate the other's advance. In war, one asks not whether opposing an advance is a matter of honor but whether it is useful; thus, a commitment to defending Graubündten in case of war would have been extremely foolish. The Austrians should have told the Graubündtners: So long as there is peace, we will protect you against any French violation, but if war breaks out, it is up to you whether you want to be our allies or not. In any case, we cannot undertake any special obligation to defend your country, but we must leave that to the general course of events in the war. So long as we have not achieved a victory in Germany or Switzerland and shifted our line of deployment to the Limmat, we cannot commit to any sustained defense of

---

180. This is an interesting argument that relates to a number of ideas in *On War*, book 1, chap. 1, particularly sections 6–10. In book 1, chap. 2, Clausewitz examines purpose and means in war and discusses the need to identify the object of the conflict, its value, and the level of effort required to attain it. In turn, the enemy makes a similar calculation, setting up an interaction between the two. The fact that war is not an isolated act (book 1, chap. 1, section 7) means that Austria had to consider what protecting this part of Europe meant for its power and influence elsewhere. If the Austrians ceded control of a region they had agreed to protect to France, they risked having other states question their honor and integrity. They also risked having other states look elsewhere for assistance, thereby weakening their influence and power.

Graubündten.[181] If, after this explanation, the Graubündtners had thought it too risky to organize a popular mobilization, that had to be left up to them; it would have been no great loss.

Actually, throughout the whole war, the Austrian government held this fundamentally mistaken view concerning the Tyrol as well: that any province that armed itself for its own defense also had to be so strongly occupied and protected by the regular army that there was no fear of the enemy conquering it. If a popular mobilization produces this result, governments would do better to expressly prohibit them, since there are few cases in which a war under such obligations would not lead to unhappy outcomes.

But this implication is by no means tied to popular mobilization in and of itself; rather, it arises from the ambiguity of the concept. If a country wants to arm itself, two essentially different measures can follow: a true nation in arms, or the establishment of corps of volunteers. In the first case, all brave inhabitants who are fit to fight arm themselves as best they can to resist the invading enemy in detachments large or small, wherever he does not appear in force. Where the enemy is too powerful, all resistance is suspended, and those who have armed themselves either fall back to other areas or conceal their weapons and return peacefully to their homes for the time being.[182] It is of course unquestionably the case that, as we have seen in Spain,[183] such popular resistance is always associated with all manner of risks and sacrifices for the people resisting, and a people that commits itself to this path must be ready to make these sacrifices. The second measure, the creation of organized corps of volunteers, has the aim of reinforcing the fighting strength of the regular army either overall, without any local considerations, or for the defense of only the province that creates them. In the first case, these corps attach themselves to the army and follow it forward or back, wherever it may go. However, in the

---

181. This also relates to the sections mentioned above. Clausewitz's position is based on reason and seems perfectly sensible. The problem is that, as Clausewitz knows, war is subject not to reason alone but also to chance and passion.

182. This relates to another idea from *On War*: "Lastly, even the ultimate outcome of a war is not always to be regarded as final. The defeated state often considers the outcome merely as a transitory evil, for which a remedy may still be found in political conditions at some later date." *On War*, book 1, chap. 1, 80.

183. Clausewitz is referring to the frequently brutal and sustained fighting in Spain from 1808 to 1814. Jourdan, interestingly, was one of the more important French commanders during that conflict.

second case, if the army advances, the corps may remain in their own province, and so long as the province is part of the general line of deployment and line of defense, they belong to that place itself in particular; but if the general situation requires a retrograde movement, they must join this movement to avoid being at odds with their very purpose, for if they remain in the province, the enemy would disarm them or take them prisoner. Whether it is feasible for the corps of volunteers to remain in the province along with a detachment of the army to defend the province like a strategic castle (the idea that frequently comes up concerning the Tyrol) must only be judged according to the other strategic conditions; by no means should it be seen as a necessary consequence of the popular mobilization and implemented when it is contrary to the nature of the situation, thus at the expense of wider success.[184]

This digression, like many others, is part of our plan for this work. Throughout it we want to clarify the vague notions that occur in the higher conduct of war. Thus we must not shy away from frequently straying from our topic, even at the risk that some readers may think we ourselves are too vague to see the wood for the trees.

Returning to Graubündten, it is our view that, in the event of a new outbreak of war, the popular mobilization there did not in any way oblige the Austrians to commit to a dogged defense of the province that did not otherwise suit their situation.

Since the French did not threaten Graubündten any further from the moment the Austrians moved into it, the latter would have had no obligation to deploy stronger forces nearby for its support. In these circumstances, naturally General Auffenberg should have been ordered to withdraw in the face of any superior force, since he had five battalions, or about 5,000 men, and if we gauge the whole front on which an enemy might move against him—from the St. Luciensteig via Disentis, the St. Bernard Pass, and the Splügen to the Septimer—it is at least 110 miles. Given this huge extent of his outpost line and the dangerous position of his main body in the Rhine valley itself, naturally, General Auffenberg could not have been expected to offer serious resistance in all circumstances, but only if he did not see himself threatened by too large a force.

---

184. This section clearly shows how Clausewitz used his historical writing as a direct aid to understanding his theory of war. As such, it is surprising that so little of this work was translated into English until relatively recently.

Since his outpost at Disentis had held, there was no reason for him not to defend himself against Masséna initially. Even when the outpost at Reichenau fell, resistance could still have continued at Maienfeld. However, General Auffenberg had to abandon the idea of retreating via Chur because he could not know whether the single battalion posted at Ems between Chur and Reichenau would hold; moreover, Chur could easily be reached from Reichenau by another path across the Heid, and the route via Chur runs through the Schalsick valley over two high ridges and leads to the upper Engadin, so at any point, he could have run into a French column advancing from Italy. General Auffenberg and his main body therefore had to direct their retreat through the Prettigau and send only the battalion at Ems along the road via Chur and Davos.

After the strongest post in the entire Rhine valley, the St. Luciensteig, was lost on the evening of the 6th and Masséna's force was now united, any further resistance must have seemed extremely unwise. General Auffenberg should have begun his retreat through the Prettigau that night, after putting up a fight all day. Then he would have got away with just the loss of those troops taken prisoner at Disentis and the Luciensteig, perhaps 1,000 in number. He chose to retreat on Chur, so it is no surprise that, after being vigorously pursued for 10 miles by a force four times as strong, he arrived in the most dire condition, and that any attempt to deploy there was punished by the loss of his line of retreat; for what could be easier, when one is four times as strong, than to deny a line of retreat that relies on one single road, and furthermore one that runs at a ninety-degree angle from its previous direction?

Thus, when we see an entire corps of 6,000 men totally wiped out here, it is not because it got into a tricky situation and lost its line of retreat through the enemy's strategic combinations. Rather, it resisted a vastly superior enemy for too long and then chose the wrong line of retreat.

What is most striking about the events in the Engadin, and what we see repeating itself soon after, is that the Austrian generals did not use all the troops they had available for the defense. On 10 March General Laudon goes to Zernetz with four battalions, when there were at least eight battalions, if not twelve, at Nauders and Taufers.[185] On the 15th he falls on the flank and rear of

---

185. **Clausewitz** notes: "The relevant part of the Archduke's history is ambiguous." Clausewitz is correct. It is not entirely clear whether there were eight or twelve battalions; nor is it clear exactly what the plan of defense was. See Karl, 1:80–81.

General Lecourbe with 7,000–8,000 militia but only six companies of his own corps. Even the archduke remarks on the fact that he did not use more here.[186] It would be easier to understand this false economy of force if the rest of the troops had been split up in defensive positions off to the side, but this was not at all the case; rather, they were held in reserve in the valleys to be used defensively or offensively according to eventualities. But if one wants to conduct the resistance mainly through offensive action against the enemy, as General Laudon intended on 10 and 15 March, one must be decisive enough to denude the other unthreatened places temporarily and hope that a decisive blow at the place in the most immediate danger will compensate for whatever might be lost elsewhere. If, on the 15th, instead of six companies General Laudon had marched with six battalions[187] and the militia to the support of the general commanding at Martinsbrück, he would have had a fine chance of destroying General Lecourbe or at least forcing him to retreat. Instead, because the battalions posted forward at the sources of the Inn were recalled too late, and because of the half measures undertaken on 10 and 15 March, several thousand prisoners were donated to the French as trophies. Besides, it is hard to understand how these two battalions came to be cut off, since General Lecourbe advanced against the Inn valley only after the alarm had been raised everywhere and everyone was stood to; what was the use of all these militia if they could not even warn of this general's approach?

The action at Taufers, or rather the glorious victory there, offers nothing strategically noteworthy in itself. For 6,000–7,000 men to be attacked frontally by 4,000–5,000 is a quite common occurrence, but the fact that they were captured without any other assistance can only be attributed to tactical errors; strategy did not play the slightest part in it. But this incident does have one important strategic aspect, insofar as we must ask what detained General Bellegarde for the whole of these eight days from 17 to 25 March, preventing him from supporting the most definitely threatened position at Martinsbrück with the designated reserves from Finstermünz and Nauders on the one side and Taufers on the other. These reserves were so close that they could have arrived within a couple of hours, the usual duration of such an action. Behind the former there were nine battalions in reserve at Landeck, 18 miles from

---

186. Karl, 1:81–89.

187. These were certainly available if he had been willing to concentrate and assume more risk. See Karl, 1:81–89.

Martinsbrück and Nauders. Since the Feldkirch position had not yet fallen and there were six battalions in the Montafon, the Landeck position was of no importance, so these nine battalions could have been at Finstermünz and then been used against Lecourbe on the 25th without any disadvantage to be expected from it. As for the troops in the Adige valley, no other place was threatened apart from Taufers, and not a single Frenchman had shown himself at any other point, which was probably reason enough to give particular consideration to keeping a reserve at the Taufers position. Thus we find Bellegarde repeating Laudon's error on a larger scale and arranging things in such a way that three weeks after the opening of hostilities, no more than 6,000–7,000 of his 47,000 men fight at each of the two places under attack; all the rest are occupying or being held in reserve for positions that are not threatened at all. Incidentally, this strategic error by Bellegarde did not bring about Dessolles's and Lecourbe's glorious victories, since they had no strategic foundation; it just allowed them to go unpunished.[188]

If the glorious French victories can be attributed in part to the shameful conduct of the Austrians, they must also be ascribed, in equal part, to the energy of the French generals and the courage of their troops. Only when a force is driven forward by such thirst for victory and such determination is the moral weakness of an opponent brought fully to light,[189] and it is only through such blazing execution that such victories are made possible as one could otherwise expect only from great numerical superiority and enveloping attacks.

Thus, the development of French ascendancy on the southern flank is to be sought only in the course of the events themselves—that is, in the execution, not in the conception. Let us now turn to the northern flank.

Here we see an army of fewer than 40,000 men move against one of 92,000 in three columns several miles apart. The commander of the latter sends 16,000 men against an enemy who has not yet even appeared on the battlefield, but he moves against his scattered opponent with his remaining 76,000 men

---

188. Clausewitz's criticism is reasonable, as the Austrians failed to deploy a thin screen of troops with forces behind and ready to move and concentrate where needed—in other words, a classic defensive line in the mountains. In *On War*, book 6, chap. 6, "Scope of the Means of Defense," Clausewitz discusses the role of militia and of a people in arms. If one then reads chaps. 15–17 regarding the defense in mountain warfare, one can see why Clausewitz is so critical of the Austrian commanders.

189. This ties in, again, with his thoughts on military genius and with the problems identified earlier caused by senior Austrian commanders' age and lack of dynamism.

so concentrated that his whole force can take part in one and the same battle, and his intention is to deliver this battle. Such a situation seems to offer the foundation for the most magnificently decisive results; nevertheless, its effect is only enough to repel the strategic offensive, without any positive impact.

There is not much for us to explain here. It was in the archduke's power to smash his opponent at any moment, but he did not do so. The reason for that is to be found in him alone, in two respects.

First, he was lacking in spirit of endeavor and thirst for victory.

Second, as we have already said, in a telling verdict elsewhere, he exhibits a fundamentally wrong view of strategy: he mistakes the means for the end and the end for the means. The destruction of enemy combat forces—which every action in war should be geared toward—does not exist as an objective in its own right in his sequence of ideas; for him, it exists only as a means to drive the enemy from this or that place. On the contrary, he sees all success solely and only in terms of gaining particular lines and areas, even though these can never be anything more than a means for victory—that is, for the destruction of the enemy's physical and moral force.[190]

How far the archduke goes in that wrong direction can be seen by his failure to inflict any notable losses in prisoners and captured guns on his enemy in a single one of his victorious battles at Amberg, Würzburg, Stockach, and Caldiero: they are almost devoid of trophies. But we see it even more in his account of them, in that the archduke does not once mention the losses suffered by the enemy in any of them.

The consequence of this erroneous direction is that the archduke not only neglects the actual fighting; he is also so constantly preoccupied with combinations of time and space and with the directions of roads, rivers, and moun-

---

190. The archduke's own words capture this best: "The advantage won at Osterach did not satisfy the archduke: he wanted to bring about a decisive battle but also not to venture anything unless there were justifiable grounds for doing so based on the probability of victory. Faithful to the principle of not dividing his forces, and never to set off on two routes at the same time before a battle fought for and won, at Stockach he found himself at the crossroads of either heading towards Switzerland or turning towards the sources of the Danube. He viewed heading towards Switzerland as the decisive direction to take for both parties but, without knowledge of the enemy position, it was impossible to make purposeful arrangements and he would run the danger of marching somewhere and the enemy not being there thus exposing his flank." Karl, 1:191–192.

tain ranges that he attributes a value to these things in their tiniest forms that they would warrant, at the very most, only in their largest. He forgets that small obstacles of this kind are easily overcome and small disadvantages easily evened out. To give an example of this, we should like to point out that, as he himself admits, at Stockach he obviously made his left wing too strong. We now present in his own words the criticism he directs at himself:

> The probability based on an appropriate calculation that Jourdan would direct his retreat towards Switzerland, and the decision to follow him in this direction and not to wait in a defensive position against any attack (that is to say in case Jourdan did not retreat but instead attacked), misled the archduke to neglect his right and to disproportionately reinforce his left wing, from which the onward advance was to be developed. Thus he committed a certain error in order to facilitate the execution of an uncertain project, one that depended not just on his own will but on his opponent's decision; and this facilitation for his troops in saving them a march of at most a couple of hours, if they had to return from the right wing to the left again as anticipated, was quite insignificant.[191]

Is it possible to accord any more excessive influence to the principle of direction and of the route one generally has in mind? Because the thrust was to be directed generally to the left—and for that reason alone, without any necessity imposed by the terrain—making his left wing disproportionately strong in a prepared position is roughly the same as stepping out of the house with one's left foot first to go around a left-hand corner, even though doing so runs the risk of falling off the step.

By this example, we wanted to show how far such guiding ideas, we might even say bad mental habits, penetrate into how one operates and can gradually bar the way to sound common sense, even in making major moves.

This insight into the Austrian commander thus provides sufficient explanation of what transpired between the two armies.

Jourdan's advance on a front several days' march across was based on the

---

191. **Clausewitz** notes: "Archduke, 1:222." It is worth reading the part immediately preceding this quotation too, as the archduke notes that he had thirteen battalions defending a position that could have been held by four to six—a criticism that is entirely accurate. See Karl, 1:220–222.

then-fashionable view that any attack must be carried out in the form of an envelopment. What the archduke says, however, is entirely true, except that, when he allows that it was possible for General Jourdan to resist the archduke successfully with his force concentrated by a good choice of line of operations and of positions, we simply see again how little value the archduke attaches to the actual fighting. If a commander with more than twice the strength seeks a decisive battle, there are very few cases in which the choice of lines of operations and positions could carry so much weight as to prevent that decision, and it could hardly have enough influence to compensate for great numerical superiority if the decisive battle were delivered. Anyway, in the end, what the archduke means here by the correctly chosen line of operations is, as usual, nothing more than the straightest and therefore shortest path to the enemy, whereby the line of retreat is best protected.[192]

Jourdan's weakness was mitigated to some extent by his twin bases. Since he could equally well retreat to Alsace at Strasbourg or to Switzerland at Stein or even Constance, he did not need to worry very much about being outflanked on one side. This put him in a position to advance in the center on the Stockach road with his force concentrated and to just have small observation detachments on the Danube and Lake Constance. If his opponent came up with the idea of outflanking him on both sides, he would have been superior to each of these outflanking columns and could consequently have thrown himself on one of them. But the French commander was nowhere close to having this idea. On the contrary, the weaker he was, the more compelled he felt to secure his flanks even more. He would have been justified in doing so if he wanted to avoid any decisive battle, since, on a strategic front that is too narrow, a very numerically superior opponent can force us into a decisive battle because of the situation. But because General Jourdan was seeking a decisive battle in spite of his weakness, there was no option but to stay concentrated, give up one of the two lines of retreat completely, and smash through on the other side by a determined attack if necessary. The advantage of being able to stay concentrated and thereby attain the possibility of victory must naturally be paid for in some way, since nothing comes for free.

---

192. What Clausewitz is getting at here is that the archduke seems more interested in a cautious approach, despite possessing a significant numerical advantage, especially when one considers that the archduke has also concentrated much of his force, which prevents him from inflicting the decisive blow he claims to desire.

The great concentration of forces with which the archduke advances is highly commendable and quite clearly derives from the lessons he drew from the 1796 campaign,[193] about which he is his own sternest critic for his dissipation of forces. He allows himself only one detachment, sending General Starray to observe Bernadotte, and even this he frowns on, and justifiably so; on the Danube, this general would have been perfectly able to cover the right flank of the theater of operations against any possible advance by Bernadotte and at the same time assist with the decision against Jourdan.

Contemplating the opposing dispositions at the battle of Stockach grants us little satisfaction. It has the idiosyncrasy that the far weaker commander, who could have achieved success only by the maximum concentration of his forces, strikes in the form of an envelopment by widely separated columns, while the commander with greatly superior numbers, who could have destroyed his opponent by means of an envelopment, advances on three eccentrically divergent radii, a form that does not allow any major success. The result should have been a battle in which victory for the latter was scarcely in doubt, but the margin of success was actually very narrow. This outcome therefore really must be reflected upon. If it really did appear to be in doubt for a moment, and if one might even believe that Jourdan could have been the victor had St. Cyr not been detached, we must ascribe this to the rout in column, as one might call Meerfeld's retreat. But it is a rout across 7 miles by 12,000 men fleeing from 12,000 men, finishing with their complete disintegration—just as exceptional a case among European troops as the capture of a corps of 7,000 men by one of 6,000 (at Taufers)—and we must certainly leave such outliers out of consideration if we want to discover something about the value of particular forms.

We say then: if even an event like this could not deprive the archduke of victory, that victory must have been as certain as it could possibly be.

The fact that the archduke entered the fight in this form is certainly an accident, as we know, because he chose it for his reconnaissance, not for battle. We do not wish to rack our brains over how it would have turned out if the archduke had found himself sitting quietly in his position at Stockach, though we suppose it would not have been very different. Anyone who accepts battle

---

193. See Karl von Österreich Erzherzog, *Der Strategie Erläuert durch die Darstellung des Feldzugs von 1796 in Deutschland und in der Schweiz*, 4 vols. (Vienna: Anton Strauss, 1814).

in a prepared position with great superiority can achieve great results proportionate to his superiority only through large reserves echeloned to his rear, with which he moves against the enemy's flank and rear at the crisis of the battle. But the archduke had made no such arrangements.[194]

Nevertheless, it is beyond doubt that the archduke could have made more of the victory at Stockach than he did. Even without a favorable form, superiority in numbers remains a means that can enable the taking of significant trophies, especially when that superiority consists in exactly the arm needed for pursuit.

We cannot refrain from saying a word here about the Austrians' numerous cavalry.

Cavalry is a very expensive arm. Allowing for both equipment and maintenance, one cavalryman costs as much as four infantry. One should therefore consider carefully how many of that arm one needs and not keep any more than that. Without getting involved in theoretical analyses here, there is really no doubt that, after an army's basic requirements for cavalry are met, 40,000 infantry will achieve more in the conduct of a war than 10,000 cavalry. The need for cavalry is different in different situations; it is worth more to someone who is certain of his victories and has a lot of pursuing to do than it is to a Fabius,[195] who is inclined to caution and trundles from one position to the next. Cavalry is also worth more in a flat, open area than in mountains and broken ground.

If we now think about the role the Austrians had to play in this war and the regions in which their theater of operations lay, we cannot grasp how they came to have a mass of cavalry far in excess of any normal proportions. The most probable reason may have been that the moral constitution of this arm

---

194. To be fair, the archduke had a reserve, but it is not clear he intended to use it as a flanking or enveloping force. Rather, he states that it was to be used "only to replace the depletion in the forces" engaged in battle. Karl, 1:225–226.

195. Here Clausewitz is referring to Quintus Fabius Maximus Verrucosus, who fought against Hannibal during the Second Punic War, 218–201 BCE. His strategy is famous because he avoided direct confrontation with his opponent, as he rightly feared the Carthaginians' superiority in cavalry and tried to outlast them. The failure to confront Hannibal directly led to Fabius's sacking, after which Hannibal crushed Fabius's replacement at Cannae. The parallels can be seen here, except that the Austrians were superior in both overall numbers and cavalry. Hence the sarcastic tone of Clausewitz's comments.

in the Austrian army is so much better than that of their foot troops, but that does not at all make up for the disparity.[196]

Be that as it may, since the archduke had so horrendously many cavalry that he himself did not know what to do with them, he should have used them at any cost, despite the forested terrain. Instead of immediately sending off a couple of thousand horse whenever he found any half-decent reason to observe an area, he should have constantly outflanked the French columns on left and right with a few cavalry regiments; even if these regiments took some losses here and there, that certainly would have been richly rewarded by the fear they spread. In this way, even a strong force of cavalry could still be usefully employed in a not altogether impenetrable region, but of course, not so usefully as the fourfold infantry he could have had instead.

Now we must give special consideration to the outflanking that Jourdan ordered during the course of the battle, sending St. Cyr and Vandamme toward Möskirch, because this is more a strategic measure than a tactical one and could therefore have various motivations. General Jourdan describes his reasons in the following way:

> Assuming that the archduke would decide to retire reeling from this rout [i.e., that of Meerfeld] and under pressure from the 1st and 2nd divisions [Férino and Souham], which I assumed must have arrived near Stockach, I ordered General Soult to push his division into the Stockach woods and to vigorously pursue the enemy who was in total rout. I left the cavalry reserve on the plains by Liptingen, and I ordered General St. Cyr to move on Moeskirch, with a view to turning the enemy army in such a way as to fall upon it when it fell back to Pfullendorf. This maneuver may appear bold, perhaps even reckless to some military men, but I invite them to reflect on the situation I found myself in. The enemy army was twice as large as mine; the success that I had just won was far from being of a kind that could restore the balance between the two armies, and assuming that the enemy effected his retreat, he could calmly fall back on Pfullendorf and

---

196. This can be partly explained by the Austrians' experience fighting the Ottomans, where they were regularly outnumbered by the latter's numerous cavalry. In addition, the Austrian cavalry was fully maintained during peacetime, which meant that large numbers of cavalrymen were available most of the time. Lee Eysturlid, "The Austrian Army," in Schneid, *European Armies of the French Revolution*, 64–85.

even behind the Osterach where I would certainly not have been in any state to attack him. Instead I favored this maneuver on Moeskirch, which should have contributed powerfully to forcing him to withdraw; I had the hope that General St. Cyr would fall on his baggage train and on the flank of his army, whose rear I would have pressed vigorously with the main body of the army. Thus I hoped to complete the rout of the enemy and to capture a large part of his army, which would have ensured my success for the whole campaign.[197]

The detachment of General St. Cyr to Möskirch may be considered from two quite different points of view. It could be intended either to convince the archduke to finally retreat, at the moment when one of his corps had suffered a severe blow, or to inflict very heavy losses on the already beaten archduke, to escalate it from a lost battle to an utter defeat.

But the two points of view cannot be combined, since they rest on quite different premises.

In the first case, the archduke is not considered beaten but only somewhat shaken,[198] and the French army is assumed to be too weak to turn this into a

---

197. **Clausewitz** notes: "Jourdan, 161" (it should read "Jourdan, 161–162"). In the original French: "*Présumant que l'Archiduc, frappé de cette déroute et pressé par la première et deuxième division [Férino and Souham], que je supposais devoir être arrives près de Stockach, se déciderait à faire sa retraite, j'ordonnai au Général Soult de pénétrer dans les bois de Stockach avec sa division, et de suivre avec vigueur l'ennemi qui était en pleine déroute. Je laissai la reserve de cavalerie dans les plaines de Liptingen, et j'ordonnai au Général St. Cyr de se porter sur Moeskirch, dans la vue de tourner l'armée ennemie de manière à tomber sur elle au moment où elle se retirerait sur Pfullendorf. Ce mouvement paraîtra audacieux, peut-être même téméraire à quelques militaires, mais je les invite à réfléchir sur la situation dans laquelle je me trouvais. L'armée ennemie était la double plus nombreuse que la mienne; le succès que je venais de remporter n'était pas à beaucoup près de nature à retablir la balance entre les deux armées, et en supposant que l'ennemi effectuât sa retraite, il pouvait se retirer tranquillement sur Pfullendorf et même derrière l'Osterach où je n'aurais certainement pas été en état de l'attaquer; au lieu qu'à la faveur de ce mouvement sur Moeskirch, qui devait fortement contribuer à le forcer à se retirer; j'avais l'espérance que le Général St. Cyr tomberait sur les équipages et sur le flanc de son armée, que j'aurais vigoureusement poussée en queue, avec le corps d'armée. Je pouvais donc espérer de completer la déroute de son armée, ce qui aurait assure mes succès pour toute la campagne.*" Jourdan, *Précis des opérations de l'armée du Danube*, 161–162.

198. As mentioned previously, he had lost only a relatively small portion of his army.

decisive victory. In this case, St. Cyr's march should be considered a true maneuver whose operative principle is seated in the archduke's shaken morale. It is a threat to the enemy's line of retreat in a situation in which it is believed he cannot restore it. In this case, the whole episode becomes not a true battle but a maneuver, and the notion of vanquishing the opponent must be abandoned.

In the circumstances at the time, such a maneuver was certainly not reprehensible; it was a test of the enemy's *courage d'esprit* [mental fortitude]. This sort of thing often succeeds, and indeed, the battle of Dresden in 1813 was something of that kind. There, by threatening the line of retreat from both flanks, Napoleon brought about the retreat of 180,000 men between the Weisseritz and the Elbe, in the face of 60,000.[199]

If that had been all General Jourdan intended from St. Cyr's maneuver, the criticism leveled against him many times would be very unreasonable; but then he should not have had Soult's division press on but instead satisfied himself with the successes at Emmingen and Liptingen and let his outflanking move do the rest.

But at the same time, General Jourdan mainly held the second point of view: he thought the archduke was beaten, and he wanted to increase the scale of the victory by means of the outflanking maneuver. Seen in that way, his action was a huge mistake.

For a start, it is a very major error that he took Meerfeld's 12,000 men to be twice as many and therefore thought he had actually beaten a column of the main army.

But even if he really had defeated 25,000 men, he still would have had to fear that the other 50,000 could cause him a lot of trouble, especially since any prisoner could have told him that the archduke himself was not with that detachment. It was therefore extremely rash to regard the affair as having been decided at Liptingen, to already be thinking about enhancing his victory and thereby to deprive himself of all the means to continue the battle at the decisive point.

But the fact that General Jourdan held both points of view at the same time generates the stark contradiction that, on the one hand, he does not think he is strong enough to truly defeat the archduke, while on the other, he is thinking

---

199. The 1813 battle of Dresden was one of Napoleon's last great victories. Interestingly, it came against Prince Schwarzenberg, mentioned earlier.

about wiping out half his forces. That is how we must describe the intention "to complete the rout of the enemy and to capture a large part of his army."

If, having considered the outcome on the northern flank, we now turn our gaze upon the balance of our strategic scales and the relationship of events in the north and south of the theater of operations, both to each other and to the whole, the situation presents itself as follows.

After the actions at Taufers and Nauders, the encounter at Feldkirch, and the battle of Stockach have made their impacts, the opposing lines of deployment are shaped so that they follow the Rhine as far as the Feldkirch position, extend up the Ill as far as the sources of the Adige, and then run across the high ridges to Lake Garda. On this curved line of deployment, Jourdan's army finds itself behind the Rhine between Strasbourg and Hüningen without a commander, awaiting new organization and instructions from Paris and consequently unfit for full and decisive action of any kind for some weeks. Masséna's army was spread out from Schafhausen to Finstermünz, across more than 100 miles of the most mountainous country in Europe.

On the Austrian side, Hotze's 18,000-strong corps pins the center, Masséna's main body, between Bregenz and Feldkirch; Bellegarde's 40,000 men threaten the 12,000-strong right wing at the sources of the Adige, standing significantly on its right flank thanks to the Sulz valley and also on its left by virtue of the Montafon. The archduke and his 90,000 men must be regarded as being fully available as soon as he has driven Jourdan back across the Rhine, which must easily have been done five or six days after the battle of Stockach, so by the end of March.

What results could have been expected, we ask ourselves, if immediately after Jourdan's retreat across the Rhine, the archduke had flank-marched his whole force to the left, crossed the Rhine between Basel and Schafhausen and then the Aar, left a corps of observation on the latter, and gone for Masséna with his army moving through Zurich, while Bellegarde simultaneously hurled himself on Lecourbe and Dessolles?[200]

We do not wish to lose ourselves in guesses and speculation about the situations in which the opposing sides would have met and fought. We can

---

200. It is curious that the archduke considered this line of operations to be the decisive one, yet he failed to vigorously pursue this plan of action. For a thorough explanation of the archduke's options, see Karl, 1:210–256.

maintain that this quite simple, direct blow by these superior forces would have compelled the French either into an immediate evacuation of the Tyrol, Graubündten, and Switzerland or else into a very perilous situation, and in any case, would have caused them heavy losses. It seems to us that this is self-evident.

Thus, despite the incredible wealth of victories the French had obtained in the south, and despite the incredibly empty Austrian victory at Stockach, at the end of March, matters were in such a state that if the Austrian forces just carried on normal activity and continued to act through the sheer weight of their numbers, within a few weeks, the French would have lost all of Switzerland and seen their army defending it destroyed.

If we do not see these results occur in the second period, that is the fault of the Austrians. To what extent it was the fault of their commanders, or of their subordinates, or of their troops, or of their government will only gradually be revealed to our eyes; but of course, in the absence of any positive explicit plan, we cannot help but remember the influence the government's intentions must have had on the commanders' actions. It would be a great illusion to believe that commanders who have not been expressly prescribed any plan are free to act according to their own judgment and their view of things. Only very rarely will a single individual at the head of an army be in this situation. We must therefore imagine that Archduke Charles and Bellegarde aimed more or less for what Vienna wanted. For the critic of modern history, it is naturally very difficult to reflect on the will of government when that is not known from any document. However, if we consider just two details in the archduke's history of the campaign—namely, that according to the government's wishes, Bellegarde was not to leave the Tyrol, and that disapproval of the archduke had been expressed because he had advanced too far and thereby exposed the Tyrol—it seems that where at first glance we just think we find an absence of a plan, a carte blanche, in fact a wide range of idiocies is revealed that lets us suspect all the difficulties under which the commanders must have labored.

2. Opening of the Campaign in Italy
Conquest of Lombardy. The French Are Driven Back to the Apennines.

16 STRENGTHS AND DISPOSITIONS OF THE TWO ARMIES

According to its detailed returns, the Austrian army in Italy comprised eighty-seven battalions and sixty squadrons with a total strength of 69,000 infantry and 12,000 cavalry. To these, 3,000[1] artillerymen must be added, making 84,000 men altogether. Thus they may be reckoned at about 800 men per infantry battalion and 200 per squadron. The total number of guns was 350.

In February their organization and dispositions were:

1. Kaim's[2] division on the upper Adige.
2. Hohenzollern's[3] division (actually under Kray) between Verona and the Piave.
3. Mercantin's division on the lower Adige.
4. Montfrault's division in Venice and along the coast.
5. Fröhlich's division between the Piave and the Tagliamento.
6. Ott's[4] division in Carniola, Carinthia, Croatia, and Dalmatia.
7. Zoph's division ditto.

---

1. **Clausewitz** notes: "The small number of artillery crews is due to the fact that half of the cannon were battalion guns." The crews of battalion guns were normally part of the infantry. For more detail on the Austrian army, see Eysturlid, "The Austrian Army," in Schneid, *European Armies of the French Revolution*, 64–85.

2. Konrad Valentin Ritter von Kaim (1737–1801) was fairly typical in terms of age and lack of distinction. He held brigade and division commands during the French Revolutionary Wars. He was wounded and later died during the fighting in Italy after the Austrian defeat at Marengo.

3. In contrast to Kaim, Friedrich Prince of Hohenzollern-Hechingen (1757–1844) was one of the few younger Austrian commanders. He went on to have a good career, becoming a corps commander and eventually president of the Aulic War Council.

4. The military career of Peter Karl von Ott (1738–1809) began during the Seven Years' War. He served with distinction, demonstrating his bravery on a number of

The first five divisions constituted the army proper in Italy, while the last two, with 25,000 men altogether, were regarded as a reserve, but one that should join the army in Italy.

When news of the opening of hostilities reached the headquarters in Padua on 7 March, General Kray, who was in temporary command, moved Hohenzollern's division closer to Verona, Fröhlich's up to the Brenta, Zoph's to between the Piave and the Tagliamento, and Ott's between the latter and the Isonzo.

Montfrault's division seems to have stayed in Venice and on the coast.

The Austrians remained in these positions until 21 March, that is, for fourteen days and until shortly before the outbreak of hostilities, which were initiated by the French on the 24th.

In the way of fortresses, the Austrians held Verona and Legnago.

The front of their line of deployment was defined by the Adige, only crossing that river at Polo so as to close up to Lake Garda at Lacise.

The first column of the Russian auxiliary army, 24,000 strong, was expected at the beginning of April, but its arrival was delayed until mid-April by the swollen rivers. When it did arrive, it numbered no more than 17,000 men.

Overall command was entrusted to the famed Suvorov, whom England and Austria had proposed for the role. He was therefore summoned back from semiexile by Tsar Paul and appointed an Austrian field marshal by Emperor Franz. Beneath him, General Melas[5] was to command the Austrians. Because of his age and illness, Melas was traveling in short marches to join the army.[6]

General Kray, the eldest of the generals posted to the army in Italy, had taken over command in the interim, and since Melas and Suvorov did not arrive until later, Kray was in charge at the opening of the campaign and in the first decisive days.

---

occasions. He was in charge of the Austrian left wing during the defeat at Marengo in 1800 and retired in 1805.

5. Michael Friedrich Benedikt Freiherr von Melas (1729–1806) had served in the Austrian army since he was a teenager. He did well until his defeat by Napoleon at Marengo on 14 June 1800.

6. **Clausewitz** notes: "It is characteristic of the conduct of the business of war by the Austrian Aulic Council that when Melas wanted to decline the command because of his infirmity, it was explained to him that he could travel to the army in a sufficiently leisurely and unhurried way, which he duly did."

He was a spry, brave, and decisive man, in whom the troops had great confidence.

General Chasteler was designated chief of the general staff.

Including allied contingents, the strength of the French army in Italy came to 116,000 men. Of these, 34,000 were in lower Italy, and 24,000 were employed occupying Lombardy, the state of Genoa, and Piedmont. This left about 58,000 for the Army of Italy proper, of which about 7,000 were cavalry. Their organization was:

1. Division Montrichard: 9,500
2. Division Victor:[7] 8,200
3. Division Grenier:[8] 7,400
4. Division Sérurier:[9] 7,300
6. Division Delmas (advance guard): 7,700
7. Division Hatry (reserve): 6,300
   Subtotal: 46,400 men
8. Division Gauthier: 6,400
9. Brigade Dessolles: 5,000
   Total: 57,800 men

However, by order of the Directory, immediately upon the outbreak of war, these troops were to disarm and occupy the grand duchy of Tuscany. Little resistance was expected, but General Schérer still thought he would need all of Gauthier's division for it, so it was foreseeable that this division would be unavailable during the first few weeks for events on the Mincio or the Adige.

Furthermore, as we know, Dessolles's brigade was also absent, as it had set off for the upper Adige valley, so the force with which the French had to oppose 84,000 Austrians came to just 46,400 men.

This does not include the garrisons of Mantua and Peschiera. But since these were very weak—the one in Mantua, for example, being just 2,400

---

[7]. Claude Victor (1764–1841) excelled as a commander and went on to become a marshal of France.

[8]. Paul Grenier (1768–1827) proved an excellent division commander and served Napoleon until 1815.

[9]. Jean-Mathieu-Philibert Sérurier (1742–1819) also excelled and became a marshal of France.

men—it can easily be considered that if this fortress should have been in the least threatened, at least another 5,000–6,000 men would have been needed to reinforce its garrison.

The French had two fortresses that came into the reckoning for the moment, Mantua and Peschiera. They also occupied five or six citadels in Lombardy and the Piedmontese fortresses at the alpine passes into Piedmont.

The Mincio may be regarded as their front line.

General Joubert[10] had previously been nominated to command of the Army of Italy, but he fell out with the Directory and demanded to be recalled; the Directory asked him to designate his successor. He named Moreau, who was with the Army of Italy as its inspector of infantry and had made a name for himself during the 1796 campaign, especially by his victorious battle against Starray at Biberach during the retreat. However, opinion about the value of this reputation was divided. Jourdan and his party in particular believed that Moreau had not supported the Army of the Sambre and Meuse adequately, while the Directory considered Moreau suspect because of his political views. It therefore did not act on this recommendation but named Schérer, the former minister of war, who had commanded in the Apennines in 1795 with some success.[11] This nomination could not fail to displease the army, first because a war minister rarely has many friends, and second because Joubert's and Moreau's reputations dated from 1796 and were therefore fresher and were acquired at a time when Schérer was already associated with a corrupt government and an administration that was held in contempt. Apart from that, Schérer was brave and skillful, but without any great qualities or strength of character. For such a man in such a situation, it was not possible to raise himself above the common herd in terms of the influence that the merit of a commander has on the operations of war, and thereby to make up for the combat forces he lacked. On the contrary, the lack of confidence in or respect for Schérer naturally weakened such powers as he did have. His weakness of character led him to choose the wrong path. He wanted to win everyone's affection by considerate handling of his subordinates and especially by show-

---

10. Barthélemy Joubert (1769–1799) had excelled under Napoleon in 1796–1797. He was killed at the Battle of Novi on 15 August 1799.

11. This highlights the problems mentioned previously with regard to the political stability of the Directory. Because of extensive unrest, it is reasonable to think that loyalty was required as much as competence in command.

ing confidence in Moreau. What could have been accepted in a man of great renown as evidence of self-confidence seemed like weakness in Schérer and only made things worse.

17 SCHÉRER ATTACKS KRAY: THE ACTIONS AT PASTRENGO, VERONA, LEGNAGO, AND PARONA

Schérer arrived in Milan on 11 March. On the 21st he transferred his headquarters to Mantua, and on the 22nd he received the order to commence hostilities with the plan of operations we discussed above.

No explanation is given anywhere for why the campaign in Italy began three weeks later than that in Germany and Switzerland.[12]

Since Jourdan got the order to cross the Rhine on 1 March, and Masséna received his order on the 6th to drive the Austrians out of Graubündten, it almost seems as though the Directory had in mind a kind of alignment of the three armies and therefore considered the movements of the two other armies a preparatory operation. In fact, around 22 March, the three armies found themselves roughly in line with the direction of the Mincio.

General Schérer hereupon concentrated his army on the Mincio between Mantua and Lake Garda. Since it was already prescribed that he should cross at Verona and that his left wing should operate toward Brixen, he was not given the option of advancing from Ferrara and Bologna, which would have been particularly difficult anyway because of the flooding of the Po.

---

12. The archduke does not mention a reason for the delay. It was well known, however, that Schérer was unpopular with his subordinates, and he had been described as indecisive and weak. This might be enough to explain the delay. Of course, such conjecture does not provide sufficient evidence to make a solid claim. That being said, Jomini notes that political problems in the Italian states were exacerbated by French actions. This is something Clausewitz should have been aware of, having read Jomini. Thus, Clausewitz's comments are somewhat disingenuous. More recently, Ross writes that Schérer was afraid of a popular uprising against French governance and notes that parts of the Italian nobility, peasantry, middle classes, and priests were alienated from French rule. As such, it is hard to believe that Clausewitz was completely unaware of these factors when making his statement. Yet it is also reasonable to suppose that Schérer was simply waiting for formal orders from Vienna. See Jomini, 11:150–160; Ross, *Quest for Victory*, 237–238.

Before anything else, he sent General Gauthier with his 6,000-strong division to conquer Tuscany. To this end, Gauthier marched in two columns on Florence and Livorno, disarmed and took prisoner the grand duchy's couple of thousand troops without any resistance, occupied Florence on 26 March, and governed the country in the name of the French Republic for the time being.[13]

On the 24th Schérer had the main body of the army cross the Mincio and take up position on its left bank between Peschiera and Sanguinetto.

On 21 March General Chasteler[14] had joined General Kray and given him the plan of operations for the Austrian army in Italy, which read:

> It should drive on the Adda with its entire force via Brescia and Bergamo, and should take in rear the valleys leading toward the Tyrol, Graubündten and the Veltlin; the first step should be the crossing of the Tartaro and the Tione; Peschiera should be invested as part of this operation. The bridges at Goito and Valeggio are to be seized and the army is to cross the Mincio; a considerable force should remain at Goito to observe Mantua and maintain communications up the Mincio; Peschiera is then to be besieged, the army should occupy Lonato and march to the Chiese, while General St. Julien shall attack the enemy in the valley of the Chiese. The operation should continue as far as Brescia and Crema. From Brescia one corps shall be detached via Palazzolo along the Oglio toward Edolo and Monte Tonale, a second corps via Bergamo, Lecco, along Lake Como, and the Adda into the Veltlin and toward Chiavenna. Wherever the enemy may be found concentrated, a major battle is to be delivered. By this plan, the Tyrol may be freed without a mountain war.[15]

---

13. This paragraph almost certainly confirms that Clausewitz had read the relevant section of Jomini with regard to the point in the preceding note, as this description is very close to Jomini's. Furthermore, it describes exactly the type of French behavior that was so odious to many Italians. See Jomini, 11:155.

14. Johann Gabriel Marquis de Chasteler-Courcelles (1763–1825) proved to be a good commander and an excellent liaison officer with the Russian army in Italy.

15. This quote is virtually identical to one found in Jomini (given the vagaries of language). Clausewitz does not cite the source, but Jomini cites Chasteler-Courcelles's memoirs: "*L'armée impériale se portera en forces sur l'Adda, par Brescia et Bergame, afin de prendre à revers les vallées qui versent dans le Tyrol, les Grisons et la Valteline. Le premier pas à faire est le passage du Tartaro et du Thione, combiné avec l'investissement*

We will present our actual reflections on this plan later, but we cannot avoid remarking on the awful way in which these things were wont to be prescribed! What a mass of pointless, tiny, detailed instructions overwhelms the main idea, making a mockery of any clear unifying mission, as if it came from someone who had taken a bang on the head. Why did it not quite simply say: the Austrian army shall attack the French main body in a decisive battle; if victorious, it shall advance on the road through Peschiera to the Adda, besiege the fortresses listed above, and send detachments into the valleys of the Oglio and the Adda toward Monte Tonale and into the Veltlin to threaten the rear of the French in the Tyrol and to establish communications with Bellegarde. Everything else is either implicit or must remain a matter of execution.[16]

Anyway, this plan of operations was not accompanied by any order to concentrate the army, and it did not even say when it should be carried out; on the contrary, it expressly forbade initiating hostilities. Most likely it was thought that Melas, Suvorov, and the Russian troops must necessarily be present before the curtain was raised.[17]

Around this time, General Kray received news of the French army's first moves, so he thought it was high time he mustered his own. He therefore had Fröhlich's division move from the Brenta to the Adige, transferred his headquarters to Bevilacqua, and ordered Zoph and Ott to get there as soon

---

de Peschiera. On emportera donc de vive force les ponts de Goito et de Valeggio; après quoi l'armée passera le Mincio, en laissant un corps de troupes à Goito pour observer Mantoue. On commencera ensuite le siége de Peschiera. Aussitôt après l'occupation de Lonato, l'armée marchera sur la Chiese, d'où le génaéral St.-Julien chassera de son côté les Français, en descendant la vallée, tandis que le gros de l'armée s'avancera jusqu'à Brescia h et Crema. De Brescia, un corps sera détaché par Palazzuolo, le long de l'Oglio, vers Edolo et le Tonal; un autre par Bergame sur Lecco, le long du lac de Como, pour pénétrer dans la Valteline jusqu'à Chiavenna. On livrera bataille aux Français partout où on les trouvera réunis; de cette manière le Tyrol sera délivré par le moyen le plus prompt, et sans engager une guerre de montagne." Jomini, 11:156–157.

16. Clausewitz's emphasis on simplicity is important because war has so many variables and so much friction. The more complicated something is, the more likely it is that something will go wrong. Thus, keeping things simple increases the chance of success purely by reducing the number of things that can go wrong. See Sir Michael Howard's essay on the influence of Clausewitz in *On War*, 34. See, for example, *On War*, book 1, chap. 7, on friction; book 3, chap. 1; book 4, chap. 3.

17. Ross makes the same argument. Ross, *Quest for Victory*, 238.

as possible. But, in accordance with the instructions contained in the plan of operations, he ordered Fröhlich to detach General St. Julien with six battalions and some cavalry through the Brenta valley to the Val Sobia (Chiuse valley) to maintain communications between the army in Italy and the one in the Tyrol, whose left wing was in the Sulz valley.

General Kray thought that an entrenched camp between the Adige and Lake Garda in the vicinity of Pastrengo would do him excellent service, both deterring the French from crossing the Adige and making it easier for him to do the same. Pastrengo is on the southern slopes of Monte Baldo, where the Adige is at its closest to Lake Garda, 5 miles from it. Such a position would also cover the approach to the Adige valley and the Tyrol road as far as the northern tip of Lake Garda, where St. Julien's brigade was headed, and it would give the position behind the Adige proper support on Lake Garda.

General Kray had therefore sent General Gottesheim from Kaim's division there with 7,800 men, who constructed fourteen redoubts and four flèches there, and two pontoon bridges over the Adige at Pol di Piovezzano and Pol di Pastrengo.[18]

At this time, the Austrian army seems to have altered its organization somewhat, so it was now as follows:

Division Kaim: 15,800 men
Division Hohenzollern: 12,000
Division Fröhlich: 14,000
Division Mercantin: 15,000
Division Zoph: 10,200
Division Ott (cavalry reserve): 4,500
Garrisons in rear areas: 12,500
Total: 84,000 men

Whether the 12,500 men left in garrisons to the rear of the theater of operations were indispensable there must remain open to question, but in any

---

18. Clausewitz had these labeled incorrectly as Pol di Sopra and Sotto Percantin. Jomini has this as Pastrengo, which he too notes is entrenched. Jomini, 11:155–156. Pol di Piovezzano and Pol di Pastrengo are east of Piovezzano and Pastrengo, respectively, and on the Adige River. The archduke notes that the entrenched position is at Pastrengo. Karl, 1:244.

case, they were not with the active army, which can therefore be assumed to number only 72,000 men. The 5,000 men under General St. Julien who had been sent away from the theater of operations on the Adige to the Val Sabia must also be deducted for the time being, leaving 67,000.

Accordingly, the Austrian army had the following positions on 25 March:

Gottesheim at Pastrengo: 7,800 men[19]
Kaim's and Hohenzollern's divisions at Verona: 20,000[20]
Fröhlich's and Mercantin's divisions at Bevilacqua: 20,000
General Klenau (from Mercantin's division) at Acqua in the vicinity of Rovigo: 4,500
Total: 52,300 men
Ott's and Zoph's divisions on the march: 14,500
General St. Julien: 5,000

From this, it emerges that the troops ready to resist in the first instance no longer had any significant numerical superiority over the French army advancing to the attack. The ratio was 52 to 46, a difference that can easily be lost, given the uncertain estimates on both sides.

General Kray had only decided to concentrate on the 21st, and until then, Fröhlich's division on the Brenta was three days' march from the Adige, Zoph was five days away behind the Piave, and Ott was seven days' march away behind the Tagliamento. However, the French could burst forth from one day to the next, so it is clear that at the start of the campaign, at most Kray could rely on the effective cooperation of [Fröhlich]. Thus, the Austrian army had been deployed unnecessarily in such depth that, in the event of a French advance, it had to either withdraw behind the Adige or fight the initial battles with just four-fifths of its strength.

The first option did not remotely occur to the courageous Kray; rather, indignant at the French advances in Graubündten and the Tyrol, he was eager to make up on his side for the losses there. The desire to use his short time in command to make a name for himself probably played a part in motivating

19. Jomini says 8,000. Jomini, 11:156.
20. The original hard copy says 29,000, but 20,000 more closely matches the total strength, as well as Jomini's claim, so we presume this was a typographical error. See Jomini, 11:146 (plan).

him as well. He therefore decided to attack the French immediately, and on the 25th he wrote to the Aulic Council:

> It seems irresponsible to me to stay inactive in Italy so long as to allow the enemy time to execute his aims in other directions. Austrian advances in Italy would thwart the enemy's main plan and oblige him to withdraw from the Tyrol and Graubündten. I am planning to attack the enemy on the day after tomorrow, the 27th, which promises me the advantage of striking the enemy on this side of the Mincio.[21]

The intention to attack seems to have been based on the French being on the left bank of the Mincio. If the French were headed for Verona, as General Kray thought probable, he intended to advance offensively against the French flank with the two divisions from Legnago, while General Kaim made a stand with the other two divisions in a position right in front of Verona. Although this was a lopsided plan that, in many cases, would not have been suitable, we find no mention of any other. This was probably because the French did not leave Kray much time to think about it, since they attacked the next day.

General Schérer had definite orders to attack, and as the situation had developed—namely, given the Austrian army's delay in concentrating—an attack was indeed entirely appropriate. Schérer knew that the Austrians were not all together and that the Russians had not yet arrived, and he could calculate that, in the circumstances, he would not have to deal with any significantly superior numbers, and he would probably not be presented with a better balance of forces in the whole campaign.[22] Furthermore, the designated commanders, Melas and Suvorov, had not yet arrived, a factor that was certainly not insignificant; as a result, the Austrian army would likely be subject to various uncertainties that would hinder its properly coordinated action. General Schérer therefore had some prospect of victory, even though this could not lead very far because, in advancing, he would bump into the arriving reinforcements and find himself facing a force twice his size. Still, the positive results of a victory and the weakening of the enemy's combat forces both physically and

---

21. Clausewitz does not cite the source, and we are uncertain where this quotation came from, as neither Jomini nor the archduke cites it.
22. In fact, with the arrival of Russian forces, Schérer would likely be heavily outnumbered, so an attack made sense.

morally were by no means inconsequential, and indeed, this would stand him in good stead for a later defense of the Adige or the Mincio.

Once the decision to attack was made, there was not a moment to lose. With every day, the momentary advantages of the balance of forces could diminish significantly. The French commander therefore decided to attack the next day, the 26th.

The Action at Pastrengo on 26 March

General Schérer had received false reports about the camp at Pastrengo. For a start, he thought it was occupied by a more substantial force than it actually was. In addition, he thought that only the advance guard was at Pastrengo and that the main body was at Rivoli. He believed he had to take this position [the camp at Pastrengo] first, hoping he would then be able to cross the Adige above Verona without difficulty. His plan of attack was therefore as follows:

He himself would attack the entrenched camp at Pastrengo with Sérurier's, Delmas's, and Grenier's divisions, 22,000 strong. After taking it, he would cross the Adige and advance on its left bank across the Verona plain. Moreau was to attack the Austrian position in front of Verona with the 15,000 men of Victor's and Hatry's divisions, pin the Austrians there, and, if the situation allowed, try to penetrate into the fortress. Meanwhile, Montrichard's division, 9,000 strong, was to advance against Legnago, observe that place and the Adige below it for the time being, and build a bridge across the Adige when ordered to do so.

The precise dispositions of the three divisions on the left wing were predicated entirely on an enemy position being at Rivoli. Accordingly, Sérurier was to advance along Lake Garda via Lacise to Bardolino and from there upon Incaffi, where Schérer thought the right wing of the enemy position was probably located because of the terrain. Delmas was to move against its center via Campara and Camporengo, while Grenier moved via Bussolengo to combine with Delmas for the attack.[23]

---

23. There were three problematic place names in this section of text. Clausewitz named Illasi, Caprino, and Campo Reggio, but we chose to use the places that make sense based on the map: Incaffi, Campara, and Camporengo, respectively. Incaffi is transcribed as Incassi in Jomini, 11:161, and it could certainly be easily confused when

Just before the start of hostilities, General Kaim had sent three battalions to support the Austrian camp at Pastrengo (where General Elsnitz had taken over command), but when they arrived, the fighting was already at its fiercest.

General Sérurier found only outposts in his way, which he drove back without any trouble and then continued on his course for Rivoli. On Lake Garda itself, the Austrian flotilla was driven northward by the stronger French one.

Delmas's division, with Schérer himself, seized the half-finished works at Pastrengo itself without major effort but encountered strong resistance at Piovezzano,[24] somewhat to the north. It was about to be defeated when Grenier hurried to its aid. He had driven back the Austrian outpost at Bussolengo, sent one brigade to the Adige, and turned toward Delmas with the other. Now the Austrians at Piovezzano[25] were all the more overwhelmed, as Sérurier's advance must have caused them to worry about their retreat. Judging by their heavy losses, this was carried out not in the best of order toward the bridges at Polo. They demolished one bridge immediately but left the other standing to be used by their rear guard.[26] When the rear guard crossed, the French imme-

---

looking at older maps. Jomini also has Campara as Compara, but the small hamlet of Campara better matches the location, which would have been on the flank of the Austrian positions in Piovezzano. If the reader looks just north of Piovezzano, there is a small farm of this name that lines up almost identically with near-contemporary maps. Camporengo also has a small farm that lines up with said maps, and the area just to the north is now named Zona Industriale Camporeggio. As such, in all three cases, it seemed reasonable to make the change. See also note 32 in this chapter.

24. Here, Clausewitz calls the town Palazzolo, which does not make sense, given where the French were moving and where the Austrians were deployed. There is a hamlet named Palazzina in approximately the right area, but it is so small as to be inconsequential. Thus, Piovezzano seems to be the most likely location, given its proximity to everything else that was going on.

25. The sheer scale of the battle area and the difficulties with place names make it all the more difficult to clarify what was really happening during this part of the action—if that is ever truly possible with any battle. There was fighting all the way from just south of Rivoli to the outskirts of Verona at the villages of St. Lucia and St. Massimo, and the main writers are not in agreement as to where the fighting took place. Jomini notes fighting at Palazzuolo (Palazzo), and the archduke has fighting taking place at "St. Lucia and San Massimo." See, respectively, Jomini, 11:164; Karl, 1:244.

26. It is not certain which bridges these are, but their most likely location is near Pol di Piovezzano and Pol di Pastrengo, which are east of Piovezzano and Pastrengo, respectively. See note 18 of this chapter.

diately poured such intense fire on the bridge that it could not be demolished. General Elsnitz withdrew behind the Barona [Parona] valley, halfway to Verona. The whole action was over by 8:00 in the morning.

The Austrians give their losses as 2,000 dead and wounded and 1,500 prisoners, to which twelve guns must be added, a fact they withhold. This is more than a third of the corps that was in action here.

According to the Austrian account, this feeble resistance and these heavy losses were due to two main factors: first, that the entrenchments had not been completed; and second and much more important, however, that the Austrians had still kept their strong chain of outposts along the border defined by the peace of Campo Formio, which had been considered necessary until now during the state between peace and war. The corps' forces were scattered along this strong outpost chain, so there were not enough left to occupy the works. Because the French commenced hostilities without any notification, the Austrians were supposedly surprised in this not fully battle-ready state, which explains the weak resistance in the works and the large number of prisoners.[27]

We did not want to incorporate this story into our account because too much of it is implausible. The chain of outposts may well have been too strong, but probably not because of the earlier truce arrangements; more likely it was because of mistaken opinions and misguided measures. Kray was marching his divisions up pell-mell, and Kaim had already found it necessary to send three battalions of reinforcements the day before. How could these outposts be unprepared to resist?

It therefore seems likely that this action was one of those utter failures caused by such egregious mistakes that people prefer not to talk about them.

Schérer did not pursue across the Adige. Instead, he just guarded the bridge with a couple of battalions on the left bank and stayed at Rivoli with Sérurier's division, while Delmas was at the bridge at Polo and Grenier at Pastrengo.

27. In addition to Clausewitz's points, it is worth pointing out that the Austrians had time to construct these works and failed to do so, if they are to be believed. In and of itself, that is a failing, given that they expected to fight the French sooner rather than later. Furthermore, that the Austrians were collaborating with the Russians should give us pause when considering whether this excuse is believable. Given that fact, Clausewitz's point about their incompetence seems perfectly reasonable. If they were not ready for a fight, that demonstrates incompetence because they were preparing for one. And if they were ready for a fight, why were their troops spread out over such a large area? Either way, the Austrians demonstrated little competence.

The Action at Verona on 26 March

We do not know exactly what the Austrian plans and arrangements at Verona were. It seems that they entrenched themselves there as well, but there is only incidental mention of this. What we can say with more certainty is that General Liptay commanded the outposts and occupied them with three battalions and one and a half squadrons in a semicircle 2 miles from Verona, running from Tomba via Tombetta, St. Lucia, San Massimo, and Croce-Bianca to Chieva [Chievo]. Two battalions and two squadrons stood on the glacis ready to support them, and another six battalions and eleven squadrons at the city gates.

General Kaim's available strength after detaching General Elsnitz can be assumed to be about 16,000 men. He thought the best way for him to resist—or, to put it better, to take part in the battle—was to move against the enemy and counterattack as soon as General Liptay was attacked. He made his arrangements accordingly.

At daybreak Moreau launched his attack with Victor's division against St. Lucia and Hatry's against San Massimo. Victor came into action first and drove General Liptay back upon the glacis outside Verona. But when Prince Hohenzollern moved to support him, the battle moved back to St. Lucia again; this outpost was fought over inconclusively for the whole day but remained in French hands. Hatry's division had advanced as far as San Massimo when Kaim himself moved against it; now at this point, the fighting was just as heavy as at St. Lucia, but here it was the Austrians who ended up in possession.

Night put an end to the fighting. Its intensity can be judged from the fact that three of the Austrian generals were wounded: first Liptay at St. Lucia, then Minkwitz, and finally Kray himself at San Massimo.

The Austrians give their losses as 1,500 dead and wounded and 1,000 missing. Against those they took 300 prisoners. The French losses would not have been much lower.

It is hard to find another action in such equilibrium in terms of its situation, its course of events, and its outcome.

Both sides were divided into two divisions, under the orders of a general who was not the commander in chief; both were equally strong; both advanced to the attack; neither could drive the other off the position. We can say that here one force completely neutralized the other, while neither of them contributed to general success. The result was virtually zero.

The Action at Legnago on 26 March

We turn now to the third battle of the day, which was delivered on the French right flank. Here General Montrichard and the advance guard had advanced to in front of Legnago and skirmished with its garrison. But Vigne's brigade moved to Anghiari on the Adige 3 miles above Legnago and was wastefully deployed observing the river as far as Albaredo. General Montrichard kept Gardanne's brigade in reserve at San Pietro on the road to Mantua, 2 miles from Legnago.

In the camp at Bevilacqua, General Kray had Mercantin's and Fröhlich's divisions. The latter had only just arrived, so he let them both rest for a bit and cook a meal. Then he began his march on Legnago at midday and debouched from there with Fröhlich's division at 4:00 p.m., leaving Mercantin behind Legnago. He advanced in three columns: the first and strongest on the main road against San Pietro, the second on Gallo, the third on Anghiari. The first two overcame the advance guard and Gardanne's brigade in a series of tough fights and drove them back through San Pietro with the loss of nine guns. The troops with which General Vigne opposed the third column led by Colonel Sommariva were thrown back across the Menago; their losses were all the heavier and their disorder all the greater because General Vigne had been mortally wounded almost immediately.

Defeated and having lost fourteen guns and 500 prisoners, Montrichard therefore continued his retreat to Torre, 13 miles from Legnago on the road from Mantua, and spent the night there.

The total losses on this day as admitted by the two sides were:

For the Austrians: 4,300 dead and wounded, 2,600 prisoners, and 12 guns.
For the French: 3,000 dead and wounded, 1,000 prisoners, and 15 guns.

Thus the Austrians had lost some 3,000 more men than the French, which stems from their disarray in the action at Pastrengo.

Despite this modest advantage, the French could not regard the day's overall result as a victory; at most, it was preparation for a victory. The tension between the two sides—that is, the state of crisis—was not yet past; it seemed that events of the following day would determine the victor in this still unresolved battle.[28]

28. The actions described are found in Jomini, 11:158–163; Karl, 1:242–252.

But on this following day, 27 March, the tension still did not resolve. Instead, to our astonishment, we see that both commanders had second thoughts about their plans in the middle of executing them, tried to change the direction of their main thrusts, and thus abandoned their original plans—not because unexpected events forced them to do so but because they realized the impracticality of those plans while carrying them out.

Although the first blow General Schérer struck with his main body had been completely successful, and although he had already seized a crossing over the Adige before noon and had nothing in front of him except General Elsnitz's half-destroyed force at Parona, Schérer lacked the courage to cross the Adige and advance against Verona. It had suddenly become clear to him that he would then have to attack Verona itself, since there was no road across the spurs of Monte Molare,[29] and the general staff therefore regarded it as quite unfeasible to cross them and advance onto the Verona plain in sight of a significant enemy force.

This extremely important geographical datum, which had constituted the pivot around which Bonaparte's famous campaign of 1796 largely turned, had been so ignored that it was not properly considered until a council of war on the 29th.

This factor could not have been unknown, since a whole crowd of officers on the general staff of the Army of Italy had served in the 1796 campaign, including General Chasseloup, who was the chief engineer at the time. It is indeed highly unlikely that this had never been discussed at all, but in the vague strategic terminology that was fashionable then, everyone meant something different by the expression *tourner la position des ennemis*. Those who knew that one could not reach the plain without going through Verona either imagined an attack on Verona itself (which both sides must have regarded as possible, since it is not a proper fortress) or thought this maneuver would produce an Austrian position in front of Verona facing the Tyrol [northward], which could then be taken in its right flank by individual detachments sent through the mountains. Others, though, certainly including Schérer himself, must really have believed that the army could descend to the plain across Monte Molare. If the main body's mission had been indicated in simple terms right from the start, this misunderstanding would have come to light sooner, and a major factor affecting the

---

29. They had done this in 1796. See Clausewitz, *Napoleon's 1796 Italian Campaign*, 112–113, 149, 201.

whole operation would not have waited until the fourth day (the 29th) to be properly considered, to the great shame of the high command.

If we consider the state in which General Elsnitz would have reached Verona if Schérer had pursued him without pause and that, at that time, both of Kaim's divisions were engaged in heavy fighting with Moreau, then it is very possible or even probable that the French would have taken Verona. They could have done so by pressing right behind Elsnitz and risking an assault, or even if Kaim had refused battle against Moreau in such circumstances and evacuated Verona. This was not actually necessary, for if Kaim had withdrawn on both banks of the Adige in the face of the French forces and concentrated entirely in Verona, he would have had some 20,000 men for the defense of the fortress and probably could not have been overwhelmed there. But then he would have been totally cut off from Kray, and this is a situation he might have been unwilling to expose himself to.

Furthermore, the notion that it would have been impossible to advance across the spurs of Monte Molare onto the Italian plain seems exaggerated to us. If the French army had arrived victoriously in front of Verona, it would have found the means to advance further across the mountains. We therefore see Schérer's failure to achieve his aim as the consequence of a mere lack of determination.[30]

Having thus considered the aim that Schérer set himself initially and that then eluded him, let us recount what he did next.

As we have seen already, he did not pursue on the 26th, even though the action at Pastrengo was already over by 8:00 in the morning, but instead literally called a halt. On the 27th Moreau proposes crossing the Adige immediately at Polo; then, without waiting for an answer, he sets off with Hatry's and Victor's divisions to march to Bussolengo and sends an order to Montrichard to leave one brigade in Isola della Scala and move the other one up in front of Verona.

But Schérer cannot bring himself to commit to a crossing, seemingly for fear of what the army in the Tyrol might undertake against his rear.[31] He spends the 27th and 28th dithering in his headquarters in Villafranca, and then on the 29th he calls a council of war to put an end to this state of affairs. Here

---

30. Here it is worth reminding the reader of Clausewitz's take on military genius and the role of determination. See *On War*, book 1, chap. 3, particularly 102–103.

31. As he moved east, he might have been vulnerable to a counterthrust down the Adige valley from the Tyrol.

his generals express great indignation at the lost opportunity of the 26th and are unanimous in their opinion that they should cross the Adige immediately. Since the general staff hereupon explicitly declared that it was impossible to attain the Verona plain without going through the city itself, it is decided to march to the right and cross the Adige below Verona at Ronco or Albaredo. Before we describe this march and the circumstances associated with it, we must take a look at the Austrian commander.

As we have said, Kray had intended to fall on the right flank of the French with half his army from Legnago while they were advancing on Verona. That evening, after beating General Montrichard at every point, he found himself with Fröhlich's division at Cerea and Anghiari and Mercantin's behind it in reserve. He could now have carried out his plan on the 27th and marched on Verona, where either he would have met a substantial body of the enemy that he could have attacked, as the plan implied, or, if the enemy had marched away to the Polo bridge, he could have united with Kaim. Then his combined force would have stood astride all the French lines of communication, and in that situation, they would hardly choose to march on Verona via Polo.[32] Even if Kray had learned on the evening of the 26th about the outcome of the action at Pastrengo and the loss of the bridge, this still should not have caused him to change his mind, for this turn of events was actually more positive than negative for his plan. But it was not even that news that made him decide to change his plan. Rather, it seems that while carrying it out, it struck him just how risky and unsafe it was.[33] The area between Legnago and Verona is crisscrossed by

---

32. This description matches the location of Piovezzano in note 23 of this chapter.

33. Clausewitz uses the German word *Anschauung*, which we have translated as "struck him" because this fits the context in which the word is used here. However, *Anschauung* is often translated as "intuition." This is an important word for scholars of the philosopher Immanuel Kant, particularly his *Critique of Pure Reason*, trans. and ed. Paul Guyer and Allen W. Wood (Cambridge: Cambridge University Press, 2000), 757. In simple terms (and any budding philosophy majors will need to cover their ears), Kant is using *Anschauung* to mean a combination of intuition and inference. Clausewitz uses the word a number of times in *On War* too; see *On War*, 106, 115, 140, 192, 274, 352, 365, 396. For those checking the original German, see book 1, chaps. 3 and 5; book 2, chap. 2; book 3, chap. 6; book 4, chap. 14; book 5, chap. 18; and book 6, chaps. 3 and 10. See also his use of the concept of *coup d'oeil* and military genius, particular in book 1, chap. 3. Essentially, a great commander can visualize (intuit) what is unseen, despite the fog and friction of war. See also volume 2, chapter 7.

a mass of small marshy rivers and ditches, so even if the enemy opposed him with just a weak corps, he could advance only very slowly; in addition, Montrichard's division remained on the Mantua road on his left flank, and he had to leave a significant force to face it because it threatened his line of retreat. Verona was in great danger, and everything depended on supporting General Kaim quickly; if he did this directly—that is, not via a detour but by marching up the right bank—he could accomplish it during the night and be there at daybreak.

Could anyone fail to heed so many reasons for common sense? Kray was probably all the less able to ignore these reasons because the chief of the general staff, General Chasteler, had been opposed to the original plan's division of forces from the start. Thus, as a result of this wiser decision, General Kray marched to Verona during the night with Mercantin's division, which had not been in action. Zoph's division headed for Verona as well, and Fröhlich followed on the 27th. Only three squadrons and the five battalions of the garrison remained in Legnago, so apart from these, the whole Austrian force was united at Verona.

Matters remained that way on the 28th and 29th. On this day, Zoph's division arrived in the camp at Verona.

Kray had also sent an order to General St. Julien not to go around Lake Garda to the Chiese valley but to march down the Adige valley to maintain communications between the armies in Italy and the Tyrol. As we shall see, this measure to achieve the greater unification of his forces had the beneficial result of enabling St. Julien to take part in the decisive battle.

The Action at Parona on 30 March

Kray had reinforced General Elsnitz at Parona with three battalions and four squadrons, and on the 29th he charged Elsnitz with driving off the two French battalions guarding the bridge on the left bank. Misunderstandings prevented the execution of this order.

This was the situation when Schérer began his march to the right. On 30 March, Sérurier's division was to mount a diversion against Verona on the left bank of the Adige to cover the march; Delmas's division was to be relieved by a detachment from Victor's division and march with Grenier's division to Porcarizza [Isola Rizza] and Sanguinetto; the other divisions were to follow between the Tartaro and the Menago, and a bridging train was to be sent from Peschiera down the Mincio and the Molinella to Castellaro [Castel d'Ario].

Sérurier's planned diversion gave rise to a significant action at Parona on the 30th, so let us examine that first.

Sérurier had been ordered not to get involved in any serious fighting. Despite this, he did not content himself with driving back General Elsnitz's advance guard but attacked Elsnitz's main body and even made moves to outflank him. When General Kray received the first reports of the French advance in the Adige valley, he had immediately set off with seven battalions and four squadrons to reinforce General Elsnitz and now moved out of Elsnitz's position to the attack with fourteen battalions and four squadrons in three columns. Sérurier, who had some 6,000 men and was about half as strong, could not resist for long and began to retreat, reaching the bridge by the skin of his teeth. The bridge had to be demolished before the last 1,100 men could get across it, so they fell into the hands of the Austrians. Altogether this day cost Sérurier 1,500 men.

Already threatened on his right flank by a detachment from Hohenzollern's division at Bussolengo, Sérurier retreated toward Peschiera. He received an order from Schérer to follow the army and take up position behind Delmas's and Grenier's divisions at Bovolone.

While Kray was busy with this, the French army carried out its flank march a few miles from Verona. But even without that distraction, it seems unlikely that it would have occurred to the Austrian commander to attack the enemy army while it was on the march with his whole force—partly because he probably did not know about this march, and partly because, given that his subsequent advance did not happen until three days later, we can conclude that he was not ready for such a quick decision anyway. However, the French army could not rely on that, so the diversion on the left bank cannot be criticized at all, and indeed, the losses it incurred were perhaps not too high a price. Some 30,000 men in five separate divisions on a flank march with neither plan nor intention to engage in battle, who suddenly find themselves attacked by 45,000, are certainly caught in a bad position, and throughout history, such operations have been regarded as among the most difficult in the conduct of war. Whatever special arrangements Schérer made for security on the march are not given in Jomini's account, which in this section is very poor. That author is too eagerly engaged in criticizing Schérer's countermarch that had Delmas's and Grenier's divisions marching off first from his left wing toward

Legnago, which meant they had the furthest to march—that is, they ended up on his right wing.[34] But this measure is actually utterly natural, because meanwhile, Moreau could maintain his front against Verona with both his divisions, and this measure is the only indication of any attempt to protect the march against Kray.

Without having any clear and precise knowledge of the French army's movements, on 2 April we find it in the following positions:

Right wing:
    Division Grenier: Porcarizza [Isola Rizza]
    Division Delmas: Sanguinetto
    Division Sérurier: Bovolone
Left wing:
    Division Hatry: Azzano [Castel d'Azzano]
    Division Montrichard: Magnano [by Marchesino]
    Division Victor: Mazzagato[35]

Schérer's headquarters was at Isola della Scala; Moreau's was at Settimo, behind Magnano and Azzano.

The French must have taken 30 and 31 March to reach these places, and perhaps 1 April as well, as the roads were very bad. Now they seem to have been waiting for the bridging train.

18 KRAY GOES OVER TO THE ATTACK: THE BATTLE OF MAGNANO ON 5 APRIL

When General Kray learned that the French were marching off to their right, he contented himself with sending three battalions to Albaredo to guard the Adige in that area, so he would know for sure when the enemy was engaged in crossing there. But he decided not to oppose the crossing directly with his main army; instead, he planned to cross to the right bank and attack the French army before it had finished crossing. He ordered General St. Julien to move to Castelnuovo and thereby invest Peschiera from the east; he sent

---

34. See Jomini, 11:169–182.
35. We are unable to identify this location.

Hohenzollern's division to Sonna on the road from Peschiera. On 2 April he established a camp in front of Verona with Kaim's, Mercantin's, and Zoph's divisions, with his left flank on the Adige at Tomba and his right at St. Lucia. Fröhlich's division seems to have been posted in Verona and toward Polo.

During this advance, Major Fulda with three squadrons of hussars surprised a French detachment in Villafranca and took 500 prisoners, captured two guns, and seized the order to the commandant of Peschiera to send the bridging train. This incident therefore probably happened on 1 April.

Since the French had completely deserted the area between Peschiera and Verona, Kray had Hohenzollern move closer to the army and take position on the road from Verona to Villafranca at Dossobono.

These moves by Kray disturbed Moreau; the army was spread out across 13 miles, and Moreau urged Schérer to close up on its left wing in order to face front toward Kray. Schérer therefore abandoned the idea of crossing the Adige and decided to attack Kray instead. General Victor was to position himself on the right flank of Hatry's and Montrichard's divisions, Sérurier was to move to Vigasio to form the left flank again, and Delmas and Grenier were to move to Buttapredo [Buttapietra] behind the divisions in the center. These moves were to be carried out on 3 and 4 April.

On 3 April the Austrian commander had several general staff officers reconnoiter the enemy position. They drove back the enemy outposts and discovered large enemy camps at Magnano, Buttapietra, and Raldon. However, on the road from Villafranca toward Mantua and Goito, enemy cavalry were not encountered until Mezzecane [Mozzecane], 5 miles from Villafranca.

From this, General Kray conceived the idea that, in the event of a battle, the aim should be to drive the French away from the Mincio and even from the road to Mantua. His plan of attack was therefore to advance in breadth, matching the French front, with his focus on obtaining a position for his army between the Tartaro and the Tione at Isola della Scala if successful.

With this in mind, he made the following arrangements:

First column (Division Mercantin), 6 battalions, 10 squadrons: Move against Pozzo and attack the French right wing

Second column (Division Kaim), 8 battalions, 2 squadrons: Move against Magnano and attack the enemy center

Third column (Division Zoph), 8 battalions, 2 squadrons: Move against Azzano to attack the left wing

Fourth column (Division Fröhlich), 13 battalions, 6 squadrons: Follow the second column in reserve

Fifth column (Division Hohenzollern), 12 battalions, 12 squadrons: Advance through Villafranca against Isola Alta [Isolalta]

Total: 47 battalions, 32 squadrons

The second column was to initiate the attack and provide direction for the first and third to conform to. In case of a reverse, the camp at Verona was designated the rallying point; but if the enemy should be defeated, the army was to shift to the right and rest its right wing on Isola della Scala. Mercantin's division was to advance to Isola della Scala that same evening, Kaim's division was to follow it there through Buttapietra and deploy between Isola della Scala and Trevenzole [Trevenzuolo], Zoph's division was to link up with Kaim's and extend to Bagnolo, and Fröhlich was to camp in the second line at Isola della Scala. General Hohenzollern was to probe forward through Villafranca to Isolalta, observing the Mantua road at the same time.

Colonel Szenasy was ordered to move with four battalions from the Verona garrison along the Adige to San Giovanni, which is roughly as far down as Magnano. Colonel Schusteck was to cross the river with two battalions and two squadrons from the troops that had been sent to Albaredo to defend the Adige, so as to harass the enemy's right flank.

According to these dispositions, it seems that Hohenzollern's division was held back to some extent and deployed in echelon to the right, which we can only ascribe to a concern that enemy detachments might approach from Roverbella or Valeggio and threaten the line of retreat to Verona. This was now extremely unlikely, and such regard to that remote possibility was not particularly consistent with the plan to drive the enemy away from the Mincio. Overall, the dispositions have a very cautious character, which indeed we cannot criticize, as the Austrians were not especially superior to their opponent, but of course, this did not allow any expectation of large-scale results.[36] We will see that this caution also reveals itself in the conduct of the battle.

Kray's initial intention was for this plan to be carried out on 4 April, but on the 3rd there was already concern that the column commanders would not

---

36. Therein lies the nub, for if one concentrates for a decisive blow, one assumes more risk elsewhere. See Clausewitz's thoughts on boldness in *On War*, book 3, chap. 6, 190–193.

have enough time to make their preparations, so the attack was postponed until the 5th.

Since all five divisions were next to one another in front of Verona, it is hard to see why this postponement was necessary. But because of it, the French gained precious time, for on the 4th, their right wing was still on its approach march. Of course, Kray could not have known this, but in war, it is certainly a very good rule that anything that needs to be done should not be postponed unless there are very important reasons to do so.

It is always especially important to identify the combat forces available at the start of a battle. In this instance, it is all the more necessary for us to look around for the Austrians, since of the eighty-seven battalions and sixty squadrons they had in Italy, forty battalions and twenty-eight squadrons were absent from the decisive battle.

Of the infantry, thirteen battalions were in garrisons in the rear areas, four were with General Klenau, and three were at Albaredo, for twenty in total.

Thus, there are still twenty battalions missing. General St. Julien, who had been detached in the Adige valley with six battalions, had rejoined the army and was with Hohenzollern's division, as we shall see from the course of the battle. But these two generals had probably left some of their troops outside Peschiera. If we reckon those at six battalions and estimate that another two might have been lost in the action at Pastrengo, that still leaves twelve battalions for the garrisons of Verona and Legnago, which is probably too many and leads us to suspect that there must have been another detachment as well.

The missing cavalry does not surprise us, since Ott's division had not yet arrived. But this is, of course, difficult to understand, since Zoph's division had already been with the army for five days, and Ott had only been a couple of days' march further away.

In any case, the Austrian commander's economy of force does not have much to commend it. If we include the detachments under Colonels Szenasy and Schusteck, Kray fights his battle with just 46,000 men, even though, after allowing for losses incurred, there were 77,000 in Italy. With strict economy of force, by which it would have been appropriate to bring in von Klenau's detachment in particular, at least 60,000 would have been available for the battle.

The French commander chose the same day, 5 April, for his attack on the Austrian army.

According to his dispositions, Moreau was supposed to move with Montrichard's and Hatry's divisions to Sommacampagna, where he thought a substantial part of the Austrian force would be. Sérurier's division was to move to Villafranca, where 7,000–8,000 Austrians were supposed to be, while Victor's and Grenier's divisions (with no common commander) were to march via Pozzo on Verona and attack the Austrians there. Delmas was to move on Dossobono [Dossobuono] as a kind of reserve between Moreau and the right wing.

The whole French force came to some 41,000 men.

Without dwelling too long on the essential idea behind these dispositions, which were more suitable for a mere advance than an actual attack, let us remark that the columns have divergent directions and finish up spread out across 9 miles, while in the Austrian dispositions, at least the columns' directions converge. Since the two sides bumped into each other halfway, as we shall see, it follows that they met on roughly the same frontage.

The French set off early on the 5th, the Austrian columns only began their march at around 10:00 a.m., and they ran into each other at about 11:00 a.m.

The outcome at the various points was as follows.

On the road from Verona and Porcarizza, between San Giovanni and Raldon, 7 miles from Verona, Mercantin's 7,000-strong Austrian division ran into Victor's and Grenier's French divisions, which were over 14,000 strong. Very heavy fighting quickly developed, the natural consequence being that the Austrian division was driven back with heavy losses as far as the area of Tomba on the way to Verona. General Mercantin himself was mortally wounded.

Kaim's Austrian division, 4,500 strong, did not find any enemy at Magnano because Montrichard's division had already marched off in its designated direction toward Sommacampagna and Delmas's division had not yet arrived. It was only 1.5 miles further south, at Buttapietra, that Kaim met this 6,500-strong division.

Fröhlich's division was following in reserve in the same column as Kaim's, but the defeat of the left wing had persuaded General Kray to head there with the majority of the reserve, so Kaim was supported by only a small part of it. In this situation, he was unable to achieve anything decisive against Delmas, as the latter was supported by a brigade from Montrichard's division, which Moreau sent against the Austrians' right flank.

Near Castel d'Azzano, the 6,500 men of Zoph's Austrian division met Hatry's and Montrichard's divisions, which, after deducting the brigade detached against Kaim, would have been about 10,000 strong. In these circumstances the Austrian division had to fall back as far as Scudo Orlando [Scuderlando, on the road north out of Castel d'Azzano], 5 miles from Verona. The action then continued here because, on one side, General Hohenzollern had sent some battalions under General St. Julien to help, and on the other, Kray arrived with a few battalions and some cavalry from the reserve.

Hohenzollern's Austrian division, 12,000 strong, had to deal with Sérurier's French division, which was only 6,500 strong. In this situation, General Hohenzollern surely would have prevailed had he not been assigned the role more of a reserve covering the right flank. This had led him to send General Gottesheim with a detachment to Villafranca and to push another detachment under General Döller forward to Povegliano, while St. Julien was sent off with a third to Alpo to support Zoph's hard-pressed division at Scuderlando. In these circumstances, General Hohenzollern probably cannot have had much left. Where he was with the rest of his troops we are not told, but most probably between Villafranca and Dossobuono.

General Döller advanced to Isolalta, where he met Sérurier's division and immediately detached a battalion to Vigasio against its left [right] flank.[37] He soon got involved in heavy fighting and achieved some initial success, but it ended with him suffering heavy losses, including the capture of most of the detached battalion. General Hohenzollern's forces were thus scattered over many miles, and in spite of their numerical superiority over Sérurier, they could not make any impact. On the contrary, given the state of Zoph's division's action, by 5:00 in the evening, General Hohenzollern felt he had to withdraw to Dossobuono. Sérurier advanced to Villafranca and the area around it.

While the two columns of the French left wing had undoubtedly made progress (albeit without any glorious results), Delmas had reached complete stalemate, and on the French right wing, their victory had been transformed into defeat.

For when Mercantin's division continued its retreat verging on rout to Tomba, thus as far as the camp at Verona, it met the four battalions of the garrison under Colonel Szenasy that were supposed to advance along the Adige together with eight squadrons of hussars. This considerable reinforcement rallied the routers again.

The Austrian commander was with Fröhlich's division. When he perceived

---

37. We think this should state right flank, as this would be the right of Sérurier's force, which made up the left flank of the French force more broadly.

his left wing's defeat and saw the fighting approach ever nearer to Verona, he took nine of Fröhlich's battalions and six squadrons that were at Citta di David and fell on Victor's and Grenier's left flank. We cannot describe in any more detail how the course of the battle then unfolded, because both sides' accounts are too vague and incomplete.[38] It seems that Victor's division was in the lead and attacking toward Tomba with Grenier behind him, and that Kray attacked Grenier in the area of San Giovanni. According to the Austrian account, Grenier was quickly beaten, and only the village of San Giovanni held out for a while. If so, it is hard to understand how Victor was still able to get through, since San Giovanni is more than 4 miles from Tomba, and indeed, it is difficult to see how Grenier was not driven into the Adige. In any case, the success against these two divisions was a very decided and therefore very decisive one. While Kray moved against their left flank with 8,000–9,000 men, General Chasteler advanced from Tomba with perhaps as many men again from the remnants of Mercantin's division and Colonel Szenasy's detachment. The French had to beat a hasty retreat, losing 3,000 prisoners and eight guns, and were driven through Raldon, Valese, and Mazzagette as far as Villa Fontana on the Menago by the pursuing Austrian columns, which were joined by Colonel Schusteck's detachment arriving from Albaredo. The Austrians halted for the night at the Menago, while the French divisions continued their retreat to Isola della Scala, where they spent the night in a state of complete disorder.

General Kray had left the pursuit to his subordinates and returned to the center (probably with part of the reserve), as we have already described, in order to come to the aid of Zoph's division at Scuderlando with a few battalions.

When disaster struck the French right wing, Victor asked for support from Schérer, who was with Delmas's division, which had originally been his reserve. But Delmas was already fully occupied with Kaim.[39] Schérer therefore sent an order to Moreau to go to the aid of the right wing by a flank march to the right. In a battle, help can be given only by reserves; General Moreau was already tangled up in serious fighting, so it was not up to him whether he wanted to move to the right. Even if he had kept enough reserves out of the

---

38. Jomini covers the battle, but not in great detail, and the archduke hardly mentions it. See Jomini, 11:180–202; Karl, 1:247.

39. This indicates that the division was not being used as a reserve, given that it was already in action or had already been committed.

firing line to be able to send any substantial support, this would have arrived much too late, since he was more than 4 miles away from Victor's battlefield. When Schérer realized that the cannon fire was moving more and more into his rear and that his right wing had been totally defeated, he ordered General Moreau and the four divisions of the left wing to retreat toward Vigasio behind the Tartaro, even though Moreau would have preferred to remain on the battlefield and avoid a night march.

Schérer himself led the rearguard action by Delmas's division and moved to Isola della Scala.

The result of the battle was that the Austrians lost 3,800 dead and wounded, 1,900 prisoners, and some guns. The French lost about the same number of dead and wounded, 4,500 prisoners, and twenty-three guns.

19 THE FRENCH RETREAT ACROSS THE ADDA

The French army's losses, its damaged morale, and its total loss of confidence in its commanders meant there could be no question of it remaining on that side of the Mincio. The French army withdrew behind the Molinella on the 6th and then crossed the Mincio at Goito and Pozzolo on the 7th.

Kray did not pursue; on 6 March [sic][40] his lead elements occupied Isola della Scala, Isolalta, Villafranca, and Valeggio, while the army went into camp behind Villafranca.

The proximity of the Mincio and the arrival of General Melas were probably the reasons for the Austrian commander's sudden immobility. Melas arrived on the 9th, and it was understandable that Kray did not want to gamble his newly won fame on a crossing of the Mincio, even though the bridge at Valeggio lay open to him. If he had known the poor state of the French army, and especially its high command, he probably would not have hesitated to drive the French back beyond the Oglio or the Adda. He surely was not deterred by a lack of authority. A few days before the battle, he had received the explicit order to attack, and an advance to the Adda would have been entirely in line with the advance intended in the Tyrol.

But after four days, the French commander also abandoned his position behind the Mincio in order to withdraw behind the Adda. Several factors

40. This should read April.

motivated him to do this. While the events on the Adige were taking place, General Klenau had crossed that river and marched up the Po as far as Governolo. From here he raided up both sides of the Po with great success, not only destroying the French flotilla on the Po that had been constructed with operations against Venice in mind but also capturing masses of artillery, ammunition, and grain, some on boats and some in various other places.

On the other side [of the theater of operations], General Wukassowitsch had advanced from the Tyrol into the Chiese valley as far as Idro, and Colonel Strauch had moved through the Tonnal into Val Camonica (the upper Oglio valley) to threaten Brescia, the French strategic left flank, and even Milan.

Finally, because of the inverted strategic front of the two armies at the time of the battle of Magnano, the Austrians were able to seize Valeggio, where they apparently found the bridge intact. Thus, they were already in possession of a crossing point.

It seemed to General Schérer that all these factors made an effective defense of the Mincio impossible. Rather than stopping at a half measure, he decided to continue his retreat to the Adda right away.

On 12 April, after reinforcing the garrisons of Peschiera and Mantua with 8,000 men and asking General Macdonald[41] to prepare to withdraw from lower Italy, Schérer began his retreat in two columns. Moreau was to move with the left wing via Brescia to Cassano, while Schérer went with the right wing via Marcaria to Cremona. However, after receiving worrisome reports about the Austrians advancing from the Tyrol, he ordered Moreau not to retreat on the Brescia highway but instead to march via Asola (on the Chiese) to Pontevico (on the Oglio). Since there was no highway there and the roads were in a very poor state because of the rainy season, Moreau's units became seriously disarrayed during this march. This resulted in heavy losses of all kinds and turned the army against Schérer even more.[42]

---

41. Jacques Macdonald (1765–1840) was from an émigré family from Scotland and eventually rose to the rank of marshal of France.

42. See *On War*, book 1, chaps. 5 and 7, on physical effort and friction in war, respectively. This is a classic example of how chance, friction, and the need for physical effort can interact in negative and unforeseen ways. The sheer physical effort required for underfed and exhausted soldiers to march on bad roads in poor weather should not be underestimated. It is not surprising that Clausewitz notes the losses. In such circumstances, hundreds if not thousands of soldiers might die of exhaustion, and those who could not keep up might desert, fall prey to locals out for vengeance, or be

20 REFLECTIONS

The Austrians held the fortresses of Verona and Legnago, which made their position behind the Adige very strong. For the French to cross below Legnago was scarcely feasible, at least under the prevailing conditions in 1799. There were marshes all along the right bank of the Adige, making it impassable as far as the confluence of the Tantaro [this is the confluence at Castagnaro, where the Tartaro–Canalbianco–Po di Levante joins the Adige], while below this point they no longer had just one watercourse to cross but four or five, giving the Austrians plenty of time to oppose them at one of these crossings with their whole force. Besides, they would have had their back to the Apennines and would have completely exposed Lombardy, Milan, and their line of communications. There could therefore be no question of doing this.

Crossing above Verona was even more dangerous as far as the line of communications was concerned, because how easily the Austrians could have cut off any retreat just by moving from Verona toward Peschiera![43] Such a crossing was therefore possible only by dividing the force, so that half the army stayed in front of Verona to defend against any debouchment by the Austrians. Now, even if the other half of the French army really did manage to cross somewhere and appeared on the left bank before Verona, and even if it really did also manage to bring down its pontoon bridge to quite close above the city, still it is quite clear that in these circumstances the Austrians would retain the most decisive advantage: undivided, with a secure base in Verona, in the middle of the divided French army. This was not a strategic result one could reasonably strive for.

But besides, the view of the French general staff was that it was impossible to reach the plain on the left bank of the Adige without passing through Verona. We maintain that this seems to be a strategic exaggeration. In strategy, because there are so few certain datum points, one tends to turn difficulties into absolute impossibilities, so that anything that serves as a guide for a while eventually becomes a firm axiom for reasoning. It may be difficult to get from

---

taken prisoner by the enemy. Of course, such losses would include horses, equipment, and supplies as well.

43. In addition, the mountains to the north meant there would be little space to maneuver for such an attempt. However, as Clausewitz points out, there were viable options for such an approach.

the Roveredo [Rovereto] road to the Verona plain without going through the city itself, but it is naturally not impossible, which had already been proved in 1796 when the French crossed Monte Molare off-road several times in divisional strength.[44] Even though this was not in exactly the same direction, it does allow the conclusion that the nature of the terrain does not make maneuvers with all arms impossible. But even if we see it this way, we must still accept that this difficulty is such that it must make the idea of a crossing above Verona even more remote.

There is just one case in which one might expect such a crossing to have a better result: namely, if the enemy's main body is not at Verona but at Legnago. One then has the prospect of some kind of operation against Verona itself, or at least the possibility of advancing onto the plain before the enemy army arrives.

It follows, then, that the only place left to cross is the 30-mile stretch between Verona and Legnago. But since part of this stretch is covered by marshes, as at Arcole, and since throwing a bridge across close to Verona or Legnago itself is not possible either, the available crossings are virtually limited to two individual places: around Zevio and Albaredo. For an army to force a crossing in such a situation against a superior enemy is against all strategic probability and would be tactically possible only with very great moral superiority.

We say this just to give more precise justification for our judgment that the French army in Italy should have adopted a defensive posture, all the more so because its position behind the Mincio was also very strong and could have compensated for the imbalance of forces.

But some people find it quite impossible[45] to distinguish the advantages

---

44. See Clausewitz, *Napoleon's 1796 Italian Campaign*, 112–113, 149, 201.

45. Clausewitz is calling out Jomini, although he is somewhat misrepresenting Jomini's argument. Jomini did not call for only offensives; he argued that the offense was more advantageous because it allowed an aggressor to use the initiative to strike at the decisive point at the moment of its choosing. His description of the defense implies that it is relatively passive by comparison. Later, Jomini revised his ideas, and they became far more nuanced. It is worth quoting Jomini on this: "*Les opérations de la guerre ont un but ou un objet, soit offensif, soit défensif. L'offensive est, en général, la plus avantageuse, surtout en stratégie. En effet, si l'art de la guerre consiste à porter ses forces au point décisif, on comprend que le premier moyen d'appliquer ce principe sera de prendre l'initiative des mouvemens, c'est-à-dire l'offensive. Celui qui a pris cette initiative, sait d'avance ce qu'il fait et ce qu'il veut; il arrive avec ses masses au point où il lui*

that lie with the offensive by virtue of its positive purpose from the effectiveness of its form and to recognize that the advantages of the latter are weaker. Not that they really deny the matter, since after lost battles, when they find themselves in a powerless position, they often remain on the defensive of their

---

convient de frapper. Celui qui attend est prévenu partout; l'ennemi tombe sur des fractions de son armée; il ne sait ni où son adversaire veut porter ses efforts, ni les moyens qu'il doit lui opposer. En tactique, l'offensive a aussi des avantages; mais ils sont moins positifs, parce que les opérations n'étant pas sur un rayon aussi vaste, celui qui a l'initiative ne peut pas les cacher à l'ennemi, qui, le découvrant à l'instant, peut, à l'aide de bonnes réserves, y remédier sur-le-champ. Outre cela, celui qui marche à l'ennemi a contre lui tous les désavantages résultant des obstacles du terrain à franchir pour aborder la ligne de son adversaire: quelque plate que soit une contrée, il y a toujours des inégalités dans le terrain, de petits ravins, des buissons, des haies, des métairies, des villages à emporter ou à dépasser: qu'on ajoute, à ces obstacles naturels, les batteries ennemies à enlever, et le désordre qui s'introduit toujours plus ou moins dans une troupe exposée long-temps au feu d'artillerie ou de mousqueterie, et l'on conviendra qu'en tactique du moins l'avantage de l'initiative est balancé." [Military operations always have some aim or objective, either offensive or defensive. The offensive is generally the most advantageous, especially at the strategic level. In fact, if the art of war consists in bringing one's forces to bear on the decisive point, we understand that the first means of applying this principle is to seize the initiative by maneuver—that is, by the offensive. Whoever thus seizes the initiative knows in advance what he is doing and what he wants to achieve; he arrives with his forces massed at the point where it suits him to strike. He who waits is on the defensive everywhere; his army is attacked in detail; he does not know where his adversary intends to make his main effort, nor what measures he needs to take to oppose it. The offensive also has advantages at the tactical level, but they are less positive. Since tactical operations are not carried out over such a large area as strategic ones, he who has the initiative cannot conceal them from the enemy who, discovering them right away, can respond right away if he has sufficient reserves to use. Besides, the attacker faces all the disadvantages of having to cross terrain obstacles to reach the enemy's line: whatever the country, there are always undulations in the ground, small ravines, copses, hedges, farms, villages to be taken or bypassed; add to these natural obstacles the enemy batteries to be carried, and the disorder which is always caused to some degree in units exposed to artillery fire or musketry for a long time, and it will be agreed that at the tactical level at least, this compensates for the advantage of the initiative.] Antoine Baron de Jomini, *Tableau Analytique des Principales Combinaisons de la Guerre, et de leurs apports avec la politique des états pour servir d'introduction au Traité des grandes opérations militaires*, 3rd ed. (Paris: Chez Anselin, 1830), 71–72. For a broader discussion of Jomini, see the excellent essay by John Shy, "Jomini," in *Makers of Modern Strategy: From Machiavelli to the Nuclear Age*, ed. Peter Paret, 143–185 (Princeton, NJ: Princeton University Press, 1986), 143–185.

own accord because of rational instinct. But because they hate clear concepts, it always seems to them as though the result of a victory has to be weighed in the scales along with its probability. To stay voluntarily on the defensive anywhere seems absurd to these people, even though there is no greater absurdity than to want to attack in every situation.

Here there were two reasons that are sufficient to excuse General Schérer's decision to attack.

The first is that the government expressly ordered him to do so, and the second is that he thought, not without justification, that he would catch the Austrians before they concentrated and thus, in the first moment, he might have superiority over their forward bodies of troops and thereby have the probability of victory. A victory is *toujours bon à quelque chose* [always good for something], as the French say; if there is the prospect of effecting one, there are very few cases where one should not try to do so, even if one does not really know what to do with it. We must therefore picture General Schérer as determined to cross the Adige and hoping to find an enemy force on this river that was at least not significantly superior to his.[46]

If we now ask ourselves what to advise a French general to do in such a situation, it would be to attempt a rapid maneuver to attain a crossing between Legnago and Albaredo, to leave a few troops to encircle Legnago, and, with an otherwise united force, to seek battle with the enemy's main body. If the latter gives way so that the French commander cannot engage it in battle within a short day's march, he should stop and concern himself first with taking Legnago; as he does not have great numerical superiority, nobody could think it feasible for him to go far beyond the Adige without holding one of the two fortresses on it.

But if the Austrian main army was encamped in the vicinity of Legnago, a crossing could not be forced there but could only be attempted above Verona.

This is also the case even if only a significant fraction of the Austrian army was close to Legnago. The stretch from Legnago to Albaredo is just 10 miles, and an assault crossing here can probably be defended against by 20,000 men, even if the means for crossing are readily available.

When he had to make his decision about where to cross, Schérer found the Austrian commander with his headquarters and one division already at Bevi-

---

46. It is also worth reminding the reader of the problems in France and of the need for victories to provide legitimacy and kudos to the Directory.

lacqua, close by Legnago, and this alone must have been sufficient to make him abandon any idea of crossing there.

Besides, the Directory had expressly charged him with operating up the Adige with his left wing to link up with Lecourbe, which was another reason to seek to cross higher up.[47]

Finally, above Verona the Austrians had a corps on the right bank of the Adige, which could therefore be beaten without getting involved in the difficulties of a river crossing. It could be imagined that it would then be easier to cross in the wake of this initial success. Admittedly, this corps was in an entrenched camp, but the Austrians had only decided quite late to construct it, so one could expect that it would not be impregnable if it were attacked by very superior numbers.

In this way, Schérer's attack of the 26th seems to us fully justified, and the losses the Austrians suffered at Pastrengo were in the nature of the business and by no means a trivial result.

The fact that Schérer did not pursue the beaten Elsnitz to Verona on the 26th was attributable to a lack of judgment and decisiveness. He had thought the Austrians' main camp was at Rivoli, so his blow was actually aimed in that direction. When he beat the corps at Pastrengo and it retreated toward the two bridges at Polo rather than Rivoli, he easily could have gambled that there was no significant Austrian force at Rivoli; otherwise, Elsnitz would have retreated toward there from Pastrengo.[48] He should therefore have checked his blow against Rivoli and sent just a reconnaissance in that direction; then, after finding nothing there, he should have recalled Sérurier's division and advanced against Verona that same day. Since the action at Pastrengo was already over

---

47. This point also illustrates that although each campaign theater was ostensibly a single theater of operations, the campaigns in Switzerland and Germany could have a direct bearing on circumstances in Italy. This is where Napoleon's genius in 1796–1797 came to the fore. He had been able to make his subsidiary theater the decisive one largely through his own force of character, dynamic leadership, and skillful campaigning. For a full analysis of this campaign, see Clausewitz, *Napoleon's 1796 Italian Campaign*.

48. This would have matched Clausewitz's argument for a commander to possess a coup d'oeil to see through the fog and friction of war, as well as his arguments about weighing chance and probability as part of his trinity. See *On War*, book 1, chap. 3, and book 1, chap. 1, pts. 18–21 and 28, respectively. See also book 2, chap. 5, for his take on the role of chance, and book 4, chap. 9, for its role in battle.

by 8:00 a.m., there was still enough time to do all that, and he probably could have made an attempt against Verona on the evening of the 26th. But if he did not attempt anything until early on the 27th, either moving against Verona or advancing onto the plain, by then, he could have been all the more certain of not having to deal with the Austrian force that had been at Bevilacqua, as he must have heard the gunfire and been informed that it was still fighting Montrichard near Legnago late on the evening of the 26th. In fact, as we now know, for the whole of the 26th and probably until midday on the 27th, he would have had only General Elsnitz to deal with, since Mercantin's division did not set off until dusk and had 30 miles to cover, which it probably could not have done in less than fifteen to eighteen hours.

Schérer's idea of a flank march to the right to find a crossing near Legnago (because crossing above Verona seemed too problematic) can be excused on the following grounds:

1. The Austrians had completely deserted the Legnago area and therefore probably did not expect a crossing there.
2. The unfortunate action at Pastrengo would still have affected them and made them cautious.
3. He still had to try something to satisfy the Directory.[49]

But if there was to be any hope of success from this decision, the flank march should have happened immediately on the 28th (i.e., after Schérer fully understood his situation on the 27th) and the crossing on the 29th. The longer Schérer waited, the more time the wound of Pastrengo had to heal and the more Austrian forces arrived from the rear. His flank march on the 30th could no longer achieve its intended aim.[50]

---

49. As noted earlier, although a particular act might not clearly match up with the logic of *On War*, book 1, chap. 1, it might well be politically necessary; thus, it is encompassed within Clausewitz's idea that war is merely an extension of politics. As such, an act might meet a political objective even if it does not conform directly with a military one.

50. See Clausewitz's ideas on the strategic means of exploiting victory in *On War*, book 4, chap. 12. Here, he drives home the point about the role of pursuit and its use to prevent the enemy from reorganizing and re-forming after a battle. Continuous pressure can have the same effect, and if Schérer wanted to avoid an organized Austrian attack, it might have behooved him to maintain pressure on the Austrian army.

176 Napoleon Absent, Coalition Ascendant

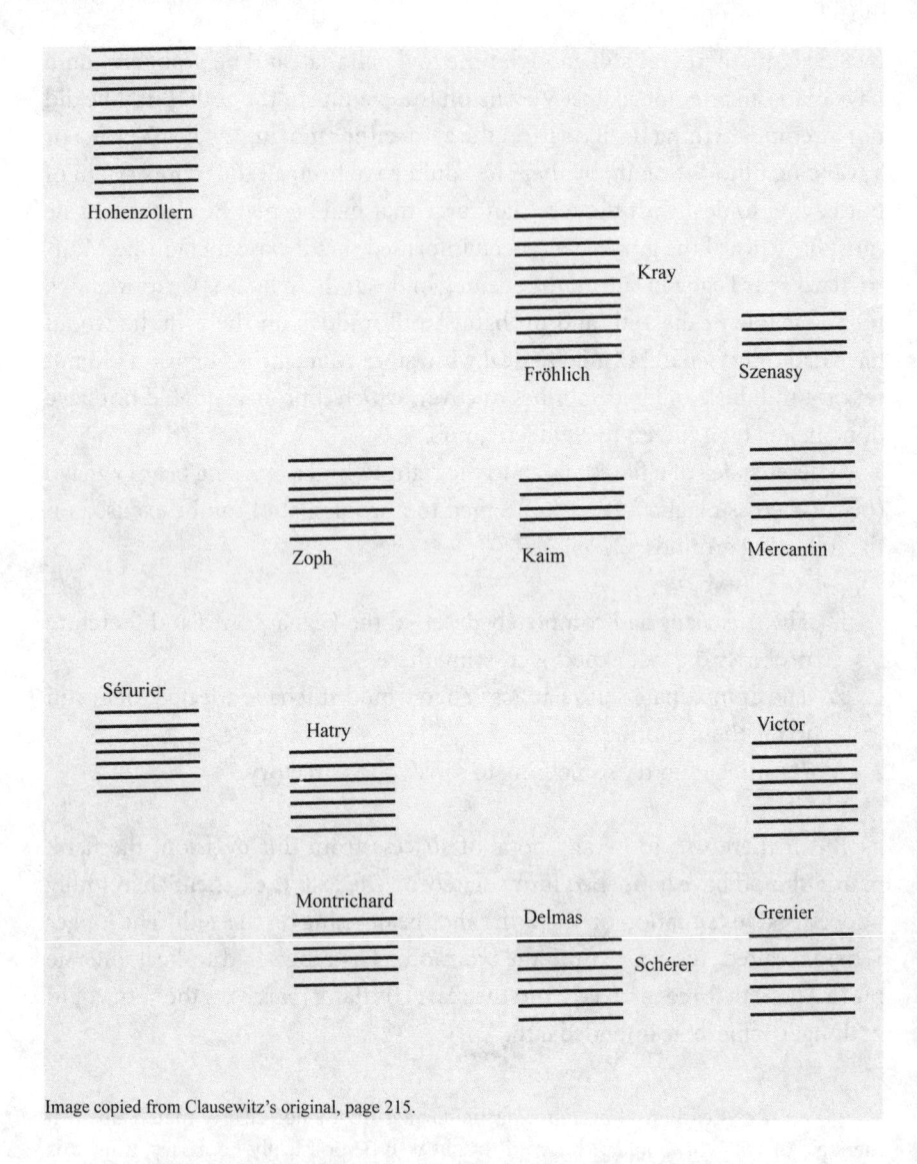

[Diagram showing troop formations with labels: Hohenzollern, Kray, Fröhlich, Szenasy, Zoph, Kaim, Mercantin, Sérurier, Hatry, Victor, Montrichard, Delmas, Grenier, Schérer]

Image copied from Clausewitz's original, page 215.

We therefore believe that, after the French commander had let the favorable moment for an advance disappear, the best he could do was to take position at Villafranca merely to keep his opponent guessing and exploit any careless enemy advance, but otherwise avoid any decisive action by withdrawing behind the Mincio.

There is very little to say about the Austrians' conduct. The most natural thing would have been to advance through Verona on the 26th to attack the

French with all available forces. Kray would have run into Moreau's two divisions and met them with the whole of his superior force.

The battle of Magnano is indisputably a quite remarkable episode in tactical terms.

Both armies again found themselves in very similar situations. The two were of roughly equal strength, both were advancing to the attack, and both were deployed in four columns whose strengths varied between one and two divisions. Both had turned their fronts so sharply that their last lines of retreat—Verona for the one and Mantua for the other—lay obliquely behind their left wings.

But one essential difference in favor of the Austrians lay in the fact that they were closer than the French to a secure base—namely, Verona.

The main proportions of the forces in the battle can be seen from the accompanying figure, in which each line signifies 1,000 men, so that the strength ratios are visible.

If we contemplate the main causes of the French losing the battle, we must cite the proximity of Verona and the differences between the two sides' dispositions.

Considering them individually, these causes were the following.

1. The units the Austrians brought into action against Victor and Grenier totaled 18,000 men. But these two French divisions were only about 15,000 strong. This superiority of 3,000 men has to be taken into consideration, but it certainly would not have been sufficient to obtain such a decisive victory over these two divisions if it had not been combined with the following factors.
2. The 8,000 men of Fröhlich's division that Kray led against Grenier and Victor, and the 3,000 men under Colonel Szenasy who joined Mercantin near Tomba, appeared here as fresh reserves directed later on against an enemy who was already in that weakened state that is always caused by having been in action. Delayed commitment of reserves—or outflanking through time, to put it another way—is always a very effective principle in modern warfare.[51]

---

51. Here, Clausewitz is discussing the concentration of forces in space (*On War*, book 3, chap. 11) and, more particularly, the unification of forces in time (book 3, chap. 12). He argues that using reserves is extremely effective if one feeds them into the fight

3. Furthermore, the proximity of Verona must have adversely affected both French divisions. If the fortress had not been there, it is very possible that Mercantin's division would not have rallied behind Colonel Szenasy at Tomba, and instead, this weak reserve would have been overrun with the rest before Kray could bring Fröhlich's troops into action.
4. Likewise, the proximity of the Adige had a disadvantageous effect, for when Grenier and Victor needed to present a common front to fight Kray, they could not extend their resistance to the utmost because of the danger of being driven into the Adige.

Thus, while the right wing of the French army was defeated because of a combination of all these factors, the left wing could not compensate for this, even though it was advancing, for the following reasons:

1. Sérurier's division was headed for Villafranca, while Moreau and the two other divisions moved on Scuderlando against Zoph's division; these directions are noticeably divergent.
2. Conversely, Hohenzollern's Austrian division came closer to Zoph by moving on Dossobuono and had also detached General St. Julien against the French left flank. Finally, Kray himself arrived with a couple of battalions from Fröhlich's division. Thus, General Moreau became disadvantaged in both numbers and situation and could not expect to obtain similar advantages to those Kray had already obtained.

All these causes have their origin in the two sides' dispositions.

As we have already said, Schérer's dispositions were more suitable for a preliminary advance than for a battle. In dispositions for battle, one would do the following:

---

and does not hold them back. They provide fresh impetus to the fight and will not be disordered or tired, as they would be if they had been in the fight from the start. He also points out that having a fresh reserve enables the pursuit, which is where armies are destroyed. He sees outflanking as "taking the initiative" (*On War*, book 7, chap. 7, 530). With this in mind, if one uses a reserve in battle, one is, over time, seizing the initiative. As the battle goes on, the commander who uses his reserve will have more fresh troops, causing his enemy to wear out more quickly (assuming the latter is not using his reserves) and thus increasing the chance of decisive success.

1. Not direct the main blow against a point where one could not fully apply all one's force. But here, Victor's and Grenier's attack constituted this main blow, whether intentionally or not, in that it was the most successful, and we have listed above the disadvantageous factors that weakened it.
2. Not put the reserve in a position to find itself in the first line right from the start. But Schérer's reserve was Delmas's division, and he had let it follow on between the two wings so that it could support either one. This would not have been unsuitable for a mere advance, but it was highly unsuitable for an actual battle, since a body of troops cannot simultaneously act as a reserve and maintain communications between two quite separate columns. Yet Delmas would still have had the latter role even if the Austrians had not advanced.

As we have said, the Austrian dispositions were characterized by great caution, and this served them well when they encountered quite unexpected circumstances. This caution manifested itself mainly in Hohenzollern's division being held back; this thereby became a reserve that only came into action later, bringing General Moreau to a halt after he had already dispersed his forces in their divergent directions and his beaten right wing was causing him concern. If Zoph and Hohenzollern combined had run into Moreau's three divisions earlier, perhaps he would have achieved a decisive victory over both of them that would have either prevented or compensated for the defeat of the right wing.

When we consider that Hohenzollern and Fröhlich had 12,000 men each, it follows that Kray had the majority of his force in his second line in reserve. As it happened, Szenasy also acted as a reserve, so that out of 46,000 men, 27,000 were reserves.

The caution on General Kray's part in his conduct of the battle lay in the fact that, after beating Victor and Grenier, he did not then turn against Delmas's division that was fighting at Buttapietra. He undoubtedly would have beaten that division as well, and then his success would have been incomparably greater. Instead of thus indirectly resisting the French left wing's success, he turned back toward the center to operate directly against the French left wing. That was unarguably more cautious.

Although both sides intended to attack, if we examine the major outlines of the battle, we cannot ignore the fact that the Austrians became the defenders and that elements of the defense, combined with how they operated, led to their victory. For instance:

1. The French right wing was beaten as a result of its own advance, not the Austrians'. Kray's attack on this wing with part of his reserve is totally in character with attacks arising during the defense. It was actually made more effective by the French advance.
2. The influence of the proximity of Verona is a purely defensive element.
3. The whole Austrian right wing put up its effective resistance against Moreau while on the defensive. The time gained by Zoph giving way and by Hohenzollern's rearward deployment was a characteristic element of the defense, and this proved to be the main and very effective contribution to the Austrians' overall success.

21 SUVOROV ATTACKS THE FRENCH BEHIND THE ADDA. THE BATTLE OF CASSANO

We have already said that Melas reached the Austrian army on 9 April; Ott's division arrived on the 11th. But the army stayed in its position at Villafranca until the 14th. On that day it crossed at Valeggio and took position 5 miles beyond at Castellaro.

The army had been reorganized. Mercantin's division was dissolved and divided up among the others. The main army now comprised the advance guard under General Ott and three divisions under Zoph, Kaim, and Fröhlich.

Hohenzollern's division crossed the Mincio at Goito and was to act as an independent corps. Eleven thousand men under General Elsnitz were left outside Mantua, and a corps of 6,000 was situated before Peschiera.

The total effective strength of the Austrian army now, having received some reinforcements from the rear, is given as 50,600 men, including Wukassowitsch's 4,000-strong corps.[52] But we will soon see that this is contradicted by a later account, according to which it must have been close to 60,000 strong.

The Austrian army was waiting for the first column of the Russian allied

---

52. Joseph Philipp von Wukassowitsch (Vukassovich) had fought in the 1796–1797 campaigns and was one of the younger Austrian commanders, being in his 40s. See Clausewitz, *Napoleon's 1796 Italian Campaign*, 28.

army. This had paraded for Emperor Franz at Olmütz in December, 22,600 strong. On 14 April it arrived in Verona under the command of General Rosenberg, but its effective strength was now only 17,000 men. It rested in Verona for a few days.

On the 15th General Ott and the Austrian advance guard advanced to the Chiese and established communications with Wukassowitsch, while Hohenzollern moved to Marcaria on the Oglio.

On this day Suvorov arrived at the headquarters in Valeggio. We will not indulge ourselves by depicting the character of this famous man, since the general features of his appearance are sufficiently well known, and we do not feel equipped to provide a detailed description and discussion of his remarkable individuality. We must just touch on what is unanimously agreed: that he was a person of burning will, great strength of character, and much natural good sense who had learned his trade in a hard school in the wars against the Turks.[53] While this school could not entirely provide him with what was needed to fight a war against French armies, and his crude eccentricity must often have caused problems for the simple sensible conduct of such a complex activity as a war between civilized nations, everyone knows that this eccentricity was mostly an affectation that his penetrating intellect allowed to influence only superficial matters and not major decisions. If we also assume that the Austrian general staff, headed by a very educated and distinguished man (General Chasteler), would have contributed something in respect of the more complex factors and forms of war between civilized nations, that is not to take anything away from Suvorov's individual merit. The most accomplished general staff with the most correct of views and principles is not enough to guarantee the excellent leadership of an army if the soul of a great commander is lacking; but the innate vision and will of a great commander's nature are also excellent correctives against a scholarly general staff engrossed in its own plans, even if he cannot do without them as an instrument. While the Austrians under Kray won a victory at Magnano that brought honor to their arms, without Suvorov, they would not have won the battles from Cassano to the Trebbia and at Novi. In these, the particular character of his energy and his clarity of vision must not be underestimated.

---

53. Suvorov had served as a general in the Russo-Turkish Wars of 1768–1774 and 1787–1792.

Another four days passed before Suvorov set his army in motion. He used this time to have Russian officers teach the Austrian infantry how to assault with the bayonet. We may well imagine that this went down badly with the Austrians. Some saw it as an insult, others as stupidity. It was certainly a rebuke. Bonaparte expressed this in a different way in his 1796 campaign when he marched his headquarters under the guns of the English fleet. There might have been a more effective way of expressing his exhortation to be courageous, but it was surely justified. Great commanders often attach exaggerated worth to details and mention odd things in their orders for great battles that really belong in a drill book. Thus, these assault exercises squeezed in between two great battles cannot be entirely credited to eccentricity.

While Suvorov conducted these exercises, Hohenzollern advanced to Pontevico on the Oglio. Like Klenau before him, Hohenzollern took rich booty in vessels laden with supplies of all kinds, including an especially valuable prize in the form of the forty-five-wagon pontoon train retreating from Mantua.

General Ott crossed the Chiese on the 17th, and Suvorov himself set off on the 19th.

By the Austrian account, the numbers of allied troops when they set off were as follows:

Austrians: 35,600 men
Russians: 17,000
Total: 52,600 men, of which 6,000–7,000 were cavalry

Hohenzollern's division is not included in this figure. Its strength is unknown.

The Austrian force was organized roughly as follows:

With the allied army: 36,000 men
General Elsnitz before Mantua: 11,000[54]
General St. Julien before Peschiera: 6,000
General Klenau on the lower Po: 4,000
Total: 57,000 men
If we estimate Hohenzollern's division at: 6,000

---

54. **Clausewitz** notes: "This is as stated by the Austrians; but since eleven battalions and eight squadrons could not have amounted to this many, some troops from the Legnago garrison may have been attached as well."

And the losses in the battles on the Adige at: 13,000
Total force: 84,000 men

The Austrian force had been 84,000 strong, and another 4,000 had arrived under Wukassowitsch, so we estimate that this left about 12,000 men sick and in garrisons in the rear.

Although Schérer had decided to retreat behind the Adda, for the time being, the French had retreated only behind the Oglio. In fact, when Moreau and the left wing reached this river at Pontevico and saw that the Austrians were not pursuing, he not only felt it would be highly detrimental to the honor and spirit of the army to retreat any further but also summoned the hope that it could halt on the Oglio. He therefore moved his divisions up the river to Calcio and Palazzolo. But since, meanwhile, Schérer and his column had already left the Oglio behind and Hohenzollern had secured the crossing at Marcaria, the French right wing could only post itself at Pieve San Giacomo, halfway between Cremona and the Oglio.

The French army in this position was still 28,000 strong. Since it had been 40,000 strong in the battle of Magnano and had lost 8,000 there and sent 8,000 to reinforce Peschiera and Mantua, it must have drawn 4,000 men in reinforcements from units in its rear.

It was divided into three divisions under Sérurier, Grenier, and Victor, each consisting of ten battalions and ten squadrons. It had left an advance guard of five battalions and seven squadrons on the left bank of the Oglio and a detachment of several thousand men under General Montrichard on the right bank of the Po to keep in check the insurrectionist movements aroused by the appearance of Klenau's troops in that region.

Suvorov set off on 19 April. When General Chasteler proposed that he should first carry out a reconnaissance, Suvorov replied: "Reconnaissance! I have no need of it; it is of use only to timid men, and to warn the enemy of one's arrival; you can always find the enemy if you really want to. Columns, the bayonet, the sword, to attack, to get stuck in—these are my reconnaissances!"[55]

---

55. In the original French: "*Des reconnaissances! Je n'en veux pas; elles ne servent qu'aux gens timides et pour avertir l'ennemi qu'on arrive, on trouve toujours l'ennemi quand on veut. Des colonnes, la baïonette, l'arme blanche, attaquer, enferrer, voilà mes reconnaissances!*" This exact quote is also contained in Jomini, 11:261–262.

We offer Suvorov's own words here partly because they are very characteristic of him[56]—even though any commander with a desire for decisive action would have thought essentially the same—and partly because, as we have said elsewhere, we regard these endless reconnaissances as a peculiar malady of the Austrian army.

On the 19th the advance guard moved to Castenedolo. The army followed in three columns to Lonato, Calcinato, and Montechiaro on the Chiese. Hohenzollern moved out through Bozzolo.

On the 20th the allied army halted.

During the night of the 21st it set off again. The advance guard under Ott, supported by Zoph's division and Wukassowitsch's brigade, was to approach Brescia from several directions and attack if the French tried to hold it. General Kray was in overall command of these formations.

The army itself was to direct its march on Chiari, which Suvorov expected to reach on the 21st.

Since the direct route from Montechiaro to Chiari is at least 30 miles, this means he intended a very rapid maneuver against the Oglio.

When Kray appeared before Brescia, he summoned General Bouzet and his garrison of 1,100 men to surrender. When Bouzet did not respond, Kray bombarded Brescia for an hour and a half, whereupon General Bouzet withdrew into the citadel. Kray was under orders to storm it and massacre the garrison: "This must be done," said Suvorov, "for if the enemy is allowed honorable surrender, he will defend every blockhouse, and this will cost us time and men." This clearly smacks somewhat of the Russo-Turkish theater of war, especially as the citadel was a regular work of permanent fortification.[57]

However, this fortification was not in a particularly good state; on this occasion, the serious preparations for an assault on the one hand and the threat of massacre on the other proved effective; the French general surrendered at 4:00 in the afternoon. Ott's division then continued its march to Ospedaletto [Ospitaletto].

Because of the very bad muddy roads and some navigational errors by his marching columns, Melas got only as far as the Mella, half the distance he should have gone, before halting for the night. Presumably the Austrians com-

---

56. For an accessible biography of Suvorov, see Longworth, *Art of Victory*.
57. As noted earlier, Suvorov had regularly fought the Turks.

plained a lot about their men having to march in the wet.[58] Suvorov was so incensed that he wrote the following letter to General Melas:

> I hear there are complaints that the infantry have got wet feet. Well, that is just how the weather happened to be on the day. Dry days are for women, dandies and layabouts. The march was undertaken in the service of the supreme Emperor. Any selfish loudmouth who objects to that noble service shall be dismissed immediately. Operations must be carried out quickly, without the slightest loss of time, so that the enemy is never allowed to recover. Anyone who is in poor health can stay behind.[59] Italy must be freed from the yoke of the godless French. Any honorable officer should be willing to sacrifice himself for that. Quibblers cannot be tolerated in any army. A good eye (namely *coup d'oeil*),[60] speed, and vigor! That is all that is needed here.[61]

There is nothing to criticize in this letter except its coarseness, and even that can be faulted only insofar as there are other ways to express the power of the commander in chief. But of course, those would not have suited such a man as Suvorov.

---

58. According to Duffy, Melas had written on 21 April complaining about his men's suffering in the bad weather. Christopher Duffy, *Eagles over the Alps: Suvorov in Italy and Switzerland, 1799* (Chicago: Emperor's Press, 1999), 23.

59. **Clausewitz** notes that Melas had been ill while on his way to join the army.

60. This is one of Clausewitz's key ideas in relation to military genius. Given that war is a mix of passion, reason, and chance and that fog and friction can obscure events, Clausewitz notes: "If the mind is to emerge unscathed from this relentless struggle with the unforeseen, two qualities are indispensable: *first, an intellect that, even in the darkest hour, retains some glimmerings of the inner light which leads to truth; and second, the courage to follow this faint light wherever it may lead.* The first of these qualities is described by the French term, *coup d'oeil;* the second is *determination.*" On *War*, 102 (emphasis in original). For use of the term *coup d'oeil,* see *On War*, book 1, chap. 3, and book 8, chap. 1.

61. For the letter, see D. A. Milyutin, *Geschichte des Krieges Russlands mit Frankreich unter der Regierung Kaiser Pauls I. im Jahre 1799*, 5 vols. (Munich: Commission der Jos. Lindauer'schen Buchhandlung, 1856–1858), 1:229–230. It is also cited in Ospinov, *Alexander Suvorov*, 140. Duffy writes that "Chasteler (Suvorov's Austrian chief of staff) had to summon up all of his powers of persuasion to convince Suvorov that he could not possibly send such a message." Duffy, *Eagles over the Alps*, 23.

On the day the allies reached the Mella and took Brescia, the French army began its retreat behind the Adda because, in the opinion of the French commander, Colonel Strauch's descent down the Val Camonica made any defense of the Oglio impossible. Sérurier's division moved to Lecco on Lake Como, Grenier to Cassano, and Victor and the advance guard to Lodi. Victor had to abandon thirty guns at Crema because of the boggy roads and inadequate limber teams.[62]

The French had all kinds of stores at Cremona and should have evacuated it right away, but the necessary measures were taken too late. On the 21st Hohenzollern arrived there and seized the place, along with eleven vessels laden with supplies, and captured the 200 men of the garrison.

The allied army continued its march to the Oglio in the vicinity of Chiari. Wukassowitsch moved to Lovere at the northern tip of Lake Iseo.

An action was fought with the enemy rear guard at Palazzolo.

From this position, Suvorov sent General Kray back to take over command of the units outside Mantua and Peschiera from General Klenau.

The Battle at Cassano on 27 April

The allied army could not resume its march until the evening of the 23rd, after the bridges had been repaired. The crossing of the Serio caused another halt, and again, some of the march columns went astray. As a result, on 24 April the army still had not covered the roughly 18 miles between the Oglio and the Adda, and the corps only arrived at the following locations on the 25th:

> The Russians at Lecco on Lake Como. Thus, they had been pushed across from the extreme left wing, where they had started, to the extreme right.
> Wukassowitsch opposite Brivio on the Adda. He therefore must have been called back from his very divergent path to Lovere.
> Ott facing Trezzo.
> Zoph facing Vaprio.
> Melas with Kaim's and Fröhlich's divisions at Treviglio on the road to Cassano.
> A detachment under General Seckendorff was sent to Lodi via Crema.

---

62. This is a classic case of friction and luck. Had it not rained so much or rained just a couple of days later, these guns might well have been available to the French.

Thus the allied army threatened a 45-mile stretch of the Adda from Lodi to Lecco. But its main strength of perhaps 20,000 men was concentrated in an area 7 miles across between Treviglio and Trezzo.

There is no suitable explanation in any of the accounts as to why Suvorov sent the whole Russian corps, more than a third of his entire army, to force a crossing at Lecco, precisely where it was hardest to do so because of the lakes.

The French had chosen their position behind the Adda to gain time. By defending this river, they hoped to allow reinforcements expected from France and lower Italy to reach them.

At that time,[63] the Adda could be crossed only by bridges. Its course from Lake Lecco to the Po is 75 miles long. The main bridges are at Lecco, Cassano, Lodi, and Pizzighettone. Of course, apart from these, there are others that are not on the main highways. In addition, throwing a pontoon bridge across a river of such modest width does not entail any great loss of time.[64] What increases the difficulty of crossing it to some degree is the fact that as far as Cassano, the Adda's banks are quite high, with the right bank dominating the left; below Cassano, there are several branches of the river, canals, or ditches everywhere, presenting many watercourses to cross. However, it is clear that these difficulties do not make the Adda a river obstacle suitable for defending; at most, it is a break in the terrain that would enable good combinations in a battle against an enemy who was not superior.[65] If the French commander had deployed his army in the area around Cassano (on the road that leads most directly to Milan), destroyed every one of the bridges, and had at most a brigade at Lodi and Trezzo to make it appear that these places were defended, then, against a cautious opponent, he might have gained time. In the event of a careless advance, he might have had the opportunity to fight at an advantage, either at the river itself or somewhat further back from it. In any case, if the situation got too disadvantageous, he would have been in a position to begin

---

63. This could mean the time of year, as spring is generally a season of heavy rains. Alternatively, it could just refer to the recent heavy rains the Austrians had been complaining about, which swelled the rivers and made them unfordable.

64. This would have been a much more difficult proposition if heavy rains had swollen the river. For an examination of the topic, see Major-General Sir Howard Douglas, *An Essay on the Principles and Construction of Military Bridges, and the Passage of Rivers in Military Operations* (London: T. Egerton, 1816), https://books.google.com.

65. See *On War*, book 6, chaps. 18 and 19, on the defense of rivers and streams.

his retreat to Milan without loss. Such a stand on the Adda was therefore not just feasible but indeed advisable, since in war, one must always expect the opponent to be cautious at significant rivers, and one must therefore not lightly omit at least making a show of intending to defend them.

But what did General Schérer do? He spread his force out along the whole 70-mile stretch from Pizzighettone to Lecco. He sent his advance guard under Laboissière to the Pizzighettone area, from where it extended even as far as Piacenza; he deployed Victor around Lodi and Grenier around Cassano; and he had Sérurier hold the crossing at Lecco and keep the river under observation as far as Trezzo. We have already said that there was a detachment under Montrichard on the right bank of the Po, but another detachment of four battalions was also posted in the Veltlin, where the Oglio and Adda valleys are connected by the Apriga Pass, another 45 miles from the extreme left wing of the line of deployment given above.[66]

The French had fortified bridgeheads at Cassano, Lecco, and Lodi, a measure that is suitable when intending to attack but, in the present case, just made the job more difficult because now it obliged local defense of these places.[67]

Such a division of forces really guaranteed the allies' progress, and whether the French could get away without serious losses would be down to luck and chance.

It was in this position that Schérer provisionally handed over command of the army to General Moreau the day before the allied attack; but Moreau's definitive nomination to the command arrived on the very day of the battle.

Suvorov used 25 and 26 April to obtain reports on the French army's positions, as well as on the river and its crossing places.

The Russians had already tried to drive the French back across the bridge at Lecco on the 25th, but in vain.

On the 26th Suvorov issued his orders for the crossing, according to which:

1. Wukassowitsch was to try to cross at Brivio using local boats.
2. Ott's and Zoph's divisions were to cross at Trezzo using pontoons.
3. Melas was to try to force the crossing at Cassano with Kaim's and Fröhlich's divisions by attacking the bridgehead and pushing across the bridge.

---

66. Combined with the poor weather and bad roads, this would have made a concentration to repel an enemy crossing virtually impossible.
67. This is where fixing a defense can aid an attacker, as per Jomini's ideas outlined

4. Rosenberg was to force the crossing at Lecco, send a detachment to Como and march down the Adda with his main body as far as Vaprio, and then head for Milan.

Since Lecco is 20 miles from Vaprio, it is self-evident that unless General Rosenberg took Lecco at least a day earlier, he could have no effect on the other divisions' crossings; nor could he join them to deliver a decisive battle straight after crossing. But attacking Lecco a day earlier had the disadvantage that then nothing would keep the enemy forces spread out, so forcing a crossing would become harder. Even so, the plan must be praised for instructing General Rosenberg to take the shortest path to the rest of the army straight after crossing, rather than heading directly to cut the enemy off, for example, toward Milan. Having 17,000 men so far away from the rest of the army was undesirable and had to be rectified as soon as possible.[68]

Suvorov's orders were carried out successfully at all points.

By the afternoon of the 26th, General Wukassowitsch succeeded in getting his troops across the Adda at Brivio by means of a quickly constructed flying bridge.[69] He then deployed them so advantageously that he was able to repel two attacks by the local commander, Adjutant-General Guillet, and pursue him up the Adda to Olginate.

---

earlier. If the attacker concentrates on one of these points, it will be able to overwhelm the defender and safely ignore the other crossing points. Once the attacker has achieved the aim of gaining a river crossing, it can cross the barrier in concentrated force should it wish to do so.

68. Although the broad outline agrees, if the reader is interested in the action from a Russian perspective, see Duffy, *Eagles over the Alps*, 58–69.

69. "A FLYING BRIDGE is formed by suspending a floating body in a river, so as to receive the action of the stream obliquely; from which a force is derived to move the vessel across the river. . . . These are particularly useful in all enterprizes of a bold, desultory character; and are essential in attempting to pass a river in [the] face of an enemy, either by stratagem, or by a combination of force with it." This type of bridge is a little unusual, but it is extremely useful when there is no bridge and the crossing might be opposed. An anchor is placed in the river, and a narrow barge is tied to it. The flow of the water provides the energy to move the barge across the river in a manner similar to a pendulum. See Douglas, *Essay on the Principles and Construction of Military Bridges*, 94–102.

According to General Jomini's account, at this time, General Sérurier was on the march to Vaprio, where the road from Bergamo crosses the Adda. General Jomini does not tell us what this maneuver by Sérurier with 4,000 men (half his division) signified; it was probably induced by earlier concerns about the Cassano area. At 6:00 p.m. on the 26th, when Moreau learned of General Wukassowitsch's crossing, he sent an order to Sérurier to turn back to Brivio and leave just one battalion at Trezzo. At the same time, Moreau decided to concentrate the army more toward that area, so he ordered General Grenier to march to Vaprio, Victor to Cassano, and Laboissière to Lodi.[70]

Thus we must picture the French divisions engaged in these maneuvers with their main forces, while detachments held the bridgeheads at Lodi, Cassano, and Lecco.

General Chasteler had Zoph's and Ott's divisions start building a pontoon bridge at Trezzo during the night. Although it needed only seven pontoons, because of the riverbank's steep cliff, its construction took until 6:00 a.m.; but since the French had no pickets on the riverbank itself, they did not notice this construction until daybreak. The Austrians crossed over and drove the battalion of Sérurier's division posted there back to Pozzo on the road to Milan. Here, the battalion met Grenier's division moving up, which soon prevented any further advance by the Austrian advance guard. Ott's division was still filing through and was brought up as quickly as possible, one battalion at a time, to join the serious fighting that had developed with Sérurier's division between Pozzo and Vaprio. It seemed that victory had already been decided in favor of the French. The Austrians had lost the entire Hentsch grenadier battalion to the enemy cavalry when General Chasteler arrived with the first brigade of Zoph's division and renewed the fight.

When Moreau learned of the Austrian crossing at Trezzo, he soon recognized that this was the main attack and that the attack at Brivio was just a secondary one. He repented of having sent General Sérurier in the wrong direction and ordered him to halt at Verderio (halfway between Brivio and Trezzo). He ordered Victor's division to quicken its march and betook himself with all haste to join Grenier. Here, he found the battle still hanging in the balance, and although successive increases in the Austrian forces had given them a numerical superiority that made a French retreat advisable, Moreau's newly announced promotion to commander in chief had generated a kind of giddy

---

70. Jomini, 11:264–277.

enthusiasm that led to new efforts. Moreau himself may well have been carried away by this for a moment,[71] but then he realized that Victor would arrive too late and that no further orders could reach Sérurier. He decided on a retreat just as the last brigade of Zoph's division arrived, and the Austrians struck a new blow that threw some of the French into disorder and forced them to retreat to Inzago and Gropello, near Cassano, with the loss of thirteen guns and 2,800 prisoners.[72]

Meanwhile, Melas had also attacked at Cassano.

The French had a demi-brigade behind the Ritorto Canal, in front of the actual bridgehead. This unit withstood the Austrians for a long time and was only finally forced to withdraw into the bridgehead itself by the fire of thirty cannon. Here, it had already withstood one attack when Argod's brigade of Victor's division arrived and moved into the bridgehead at 4:00 p.m. But the Austrians were not deterred by this; they crossed the Ritorto Canal with their full force and successfully stormed the bridgehead, which was bitterly contested, General Argod himself being killed there.

It is not known whether Suvorov was at this place, but it is very likely, and that would explain the unusual vigor of this attack.[73]

When the French retreated, they did not have time to set fire to the incendiary material they had piled on the bridges.

After this double defeat of a force that had originally been perhaps 10,000 strong, Moreau really could do nothing but retreat toward Milan. This was no longer possible on the highway from Bergamo, so he had to retreat through Melzo.

As probably could have been foreseen, Victor was relieved at Lodi by a

---

71. Again, we see the elements of Clausewitz's trinity (*On War*, book 1, chap. 1) at play: a commander pushed to do something because of emotion rather than strict logic.

72. **Clausewitz** notes: "General Jomini reports just 1,000 prisoners and no guns lost; but in such cases he is often afraid to tell the truth; and since he does not explicitly object to the Austrian account, we are probably justified in regarding that as essentially accurate, even if, as quite often happens, it has led the wounded to be counted in among the prisoners." Jomini, 11:275. Duffy cites "Moreau's figure of 2,452," which probably excludes the captured French, and he has some estimates as high as 6,900 for the few days of fighting counted together. Duffy, *Eagles over the Alps*, 68. Duffy also cites Suvorov's 1 May correspondence with Tsar Paul regarding this matter; see Milyutin, *Geschichte des Krieges Russlands*, 1:581.

73. According to Duffy, Suvorov was present and was urging the men to advance. Duffy, *Eagles over the Alps*, 66.

brigade of the advance guard, but it was so late that he could no longer march to the battlefield with his second brigade. He had to start his retreat to Milan via Melegnano on the Lambro.

It went still worse for the French on their left wing.

We have seen that Sérurier and his 4,000 men were supposed to halt at Verderio, while we find the rest of his division holding the outposts at Lecco, Brivio, and Trezzo. We can assume that, in the circumstances, the one at Lecco would have comprised at most one demi-brigade. Brigadier Soyez, who was in command there, knew that the Austrians had crossed at Brivio and driven Adjutant-General Guillet back to Olginate and that, for fear of finding that the outpost at Lecco was no longer in French hands, Guillet had begun to retreat to Como. In this situation, Soyez believed that if his own bridgehead fell, he himself would no longer be able to get to Como. Since General Rosenberg was now making serious preparations for an assault and since, ultimately, no bridgehead can withstand six- to eightfold odds, he thought it wisest not to sacrifice his entire detachment in futile resistance. He therefore sent his artillery under escort back to Como, while he and his infantry sailed across Lake Lecco. Since Como was actually abandoned before he got there, he landed at Menaggio; from there, he traveled by land via Polezza and Lugano to Luvino on Lake Maggiore, embarked there again, and joined the French army via Arona.

Thus, over the course of the 27th, the Russians gained possession of the bridge at Lecco.

The Action at Verderio: Sérurier Lays Down His Arms on 28 April

Sérurier and his 4,000 men stayed quietly at Verderio all day, 7 miles from Brivio on the road to Milan between the Adda and the Molgora. Here, he had found a very strong position at the confluence of two streams, where he planned to await the enemy arriving from Brivio. He probably thought that in this way he could cover Moreau's left flank while the latter drove back the Austrians crossing at Trezzo. This is the only way to explain him loitering here so imperturbably while the battle was being waged in front of and behind him all day.[74] He probably believed that the rest of the army was in a suitable state to resist successfully and that he was the only one separated and surrounded

---

74. It is possible that the exhausted troops simply needed rest.

by enemy columns; and it therefore seemed to him that what mattered most was to organize himself to be strong on all sides and to resist the storm breaking over him like a rock in the sea. This convinced him to hold firm in position, to strengthen his position by constructing earthworks, and to make it quite unapproachable on three sides by opening a mill sluice.

But the Austrians who had crossed at Trezzo turned down the Adda toward Cassano, and it seems that Wukassowitsch headed upriver toward Olginate. So it turned out that for the whole of the 27th, Sérurier remained not just unengaged but undiscovered.

On 28 April Suvorov directed all his columns to head for Milan. When Wukassowitsch tried to march in that direction via Verderio that morning, he was the first to discover Sérurier's position.

Wukassowitsch could conclude from the success of the action on the 27th that Sérurier had generally lost his line of retreat and that the nature of Sérurier's position made it easy to deny him any escape. Despite his own modest strength of just 3,500 men, Wukassowitsch decided to encircle Sérurier entirely, using his infantry and some artillery to surround Sérurier's flank and rear while the cavalry and most of the artillery remained facing the impassable front. In this situation, the two sides bombarded each other all day, Sérurier waiting to be relieved, and Wukassowitsch recognizing that this loss of time meant his opponent's downfall. Once Sérurier had had time to appreciate both the general situation and his own, he asked to surrender that evening. So it happened that the loss of around 3,500 Austrians in the action at Taufers was avenged here, as two generals, 250 officers, and around 4,000 men with fifteen cannon laid down their arms. For the Austrians, the total losses in the battle of Cassano that ended here were 3,700 dead and wounded and 1,200 prisoners; on the French side, probably the same number of dead and wounded, around 7,000 prisoners, and some thirty guns.

The allies' main army had taken position at Gorgonzola on the 28th and entered Milan on the 30th. General Rosenberg arrived there via Monza, and General Wukassowitsch via Vimercate.

22 REFLECTIONS

We have only a little to say about the actions of the two sides since the Russians' arrival.

We have already said that the French could not hold out for a serious defense of the Adda, but the first principle of a feigned defense[75] or a simple forward position behind a river is that it should not be widely extended, to avoid becoming completely separated or losing individual corps and so that advantageous circumstances can be exploited.

If instead of one division at Cassano the French had had two, perhaps they would have been able to drive back the column that crossed at Trezzo and hold the bridgehead at Cassano; this possibility would have arisen from their opponent's unsuitable plan for the crossing. We cannot criticize Moreau for trying to drive back the Austrians with Grenier's division alone, as he could not see the full picture initially, but it does seem that he prolonged his resistance a little too far. An action that is of very uncertain character as an operation, one that is very speculative by nature, must be conducted with great caution and broken off in good time. Thus, it is absolutely not just a matter of fighting on so long as there is still a possibility of success. It was extremely unlikely that Victor would meet the enemy in time, since he had to wait for General Laboissière; it was also very unlikely that one demi-brigade left behind the Ritorto and in the bridgehead could withstand a force of 10,000–12,000 men for long. But these were the factors that would dictate whether anything could be expected from the attack against the Austrians who had crossed at Trezzo. Thus Moreau should have considered his action against this force as merely a probe, and when he saw new forces constantly arriving, he should have withdrawn before he was properly beaten.[76] Strategy does not cease and leave the job to tactics as soon as the fighting begins; on the contrary, there are battles during which some degree of strategic maneuvering is constantly required, and a commander should be expected to understand this.

---

75. This form of defense is discussed in some detail by Clausewitz in *On War*, book 6, chap. 18, 443–444: "A feigned defense requires that the main force should deploy along the river in approximately the same way as it would in the case of a real defense. However, the intention of a mere feint proves that circumstances are not favorable enough for a real defense. It follows that the positions you take up—which are inevitably more or less extended and scattered—may well give rise to serious losses if the units really get involved in resistance, on however limited a scale. That would actually be a half measure." Thus, the main defensive force would be concentrated much further back, with the intention of resisting along the river only long enough to allow a disengagement.

76. Here it is clear that Clausewitz's use of historical analysis is closely related to his theoretical ideas.

Despite all the reasons for it that we have tried to put forward, General Sérurier's conduct is inexcusable. To adopt a strong position to the rear when it is a matter of defending a river line is always a strange measure; if the attack ever has any value, it is in a case such as this. Even if Sérurier had thought himself chained to Verderio for a while by Moreau's order, still, after several hours during which no enemy had approached him and he heard cannon fire on all sides, his whole position must have appeared highly dubious and inappropriate. But in such cases—that is, when the original mission becomes wasteful—one must hasten to the nearest battlefield to operate on a less well-chosen spot rather than not at all. This principle would have led General Sérurier to Vaprio, where he would have been much too late to give a favorable turn to the action there, but not too late to protect his honor and reputation.

Although the allied army lost a few days after the Russians' arrival and did not begin to move until 19 April, we should not judge that too severely. A foreign commander such as Suvorov would certainly have needed a couple of days to meet people and orient himself somewhat.

In the nine days from the 19th to the 27th (the day of the battle of Cassano), the allies covered 70 miles, crossed five rivers—the Chiese, the Mella, the Oglio, the Serio, and the Adda—and fought a battle. So we really cannot complain about them being slow.[77]

It is very commendable that a corps under Hohenzollern was detached in the direction of Cremona, for the battle had already been fought and no resistance was expected nearby. What mattered now was to reap the benefits of the victory that had been won. A quite essential part of this was to rapidly seize those places where one could expect the enemy to have masses of supplies of all kinds. Besides, this corps could reasonably expect to be used to outflank any river defenses the enemy might intend.

The rest of the combat forces constituting the main allied army were kept very close together, except for the Russians sent to Lecco.

This detachment was entailed by the deployment for the river crossing, and it certainly does not seem to be exempt from criticism. If Suvorov felt sure of forcing a crossing at Lecco through superior numbers, this should have

---

77. It is worth pointing out that they were led by Suvorov and that the Austrians complained about the exhaustion of their troops. Even if the Austrians were right to do so, it indicates what can be accomplished by dynamism, even at the expense of the loss of troops.

happened by the 26th at the latest, so that this column could already have approached the Trezzo area on the 27th.[78]

If there was any way that the French could have resisted successfully, it probably lay in the fact that, with this march on Lecco, the allies put 17,000 men completely out of action on the 27th and, at the same time, moved with 12,000 men against a bridgehead they certainly could not have taken if it had been held by Victor's division. The Russians reasonably could have crossed at Trezzo as well, and the storming of the bridgehead at Cassano itself can be excused only because they knew it was held so weakly.

But another and more important question is whether the allies would not have done better to move on Cremona and the lower Adda with their main body and cross the Po as soon as possible. In this situation, the French army would have been unable to mount any resistance on the Adda, and instead, the war would have been carried into the area of Alessandria by a single day's march. The French would thereby have been cut off from lower Italy and even from Genoa and separated from all the combat forces they had in those areas. Lombardy and a large part of Piedmont would then have fallen of their own accord, and a corps like Hohenzollern's would have sufficed to complete the conquest of these provinces. The major battle could then have been delivered in the vicinity of Alessandria in the first days of May.[79] In this battle, the allies would have had about 40,000 men and the French certainly no more than 20,000 because, far from drawing in all their troops from Lombardy—for which they would not have had time—they most likely would have reinforced the garrisons of the individual citadels, probably leaving Sérurier's division behind to do this. This weight of numbers alone would have decided victory. One might perhaps think that, between the Po and the Tanaro at Alessandria or wherever else it might have tried to confront the allies, the French army would have found itself in a very strong and concentrated position and therefore less easy to defeat than it was behind the Adda. But in the first place, this

---

78. Clausewitz contradicts his own argument from section 21 above.

79. In wargames examining the 1799–1800 campaigns in Italy, Germany, and Switzerland (run by Dr. Murray, Commander Krivacs, and Lieutenant Colonel O'Gorman at the US Naval War College in 2018–2019), players often sought to use the Po River in this fashion for many of the reasons Clausewitz outlines. Clearly, this is not scientific, but Dr. Murray has run dozens of games set in the Po valley during the wars of the French Revolution and has found that players try this strategy, but often not at the first opportunity.

battle of Cassano, with all its successes, was a real stroke of luck for Suvorov, not something on which he could rely with any certainty, because a serious stand on the Adda was so unlikely; and then if the French had tried to fight on the Bormida or the Tanaro, they would have had plenty of reasons to dissipate their forces. In any position they might take facing east, their line of retreat to the passes in the county of Nice lay behind their right flank and would have to be protected, meaning that they would certainly be obliged to occupy the spurs of the Apennines as far as the crest. It was extremely likely that by mid-May, the French army in upper Italy would have been beaten and would have arrived in the county of Nice with 10,000–15,000 men left. As for what would then have happened to Macdonald, who was near Rome at that time, let us not distract ourselves in speculation about that.

Of course, Suvorov could not know all that we know now; he could not know for sure whether the French had been reinforced by 8,000–10,000 men in the course of their retreat, whether the troops in Tuscany might have been recalled in time, or even whether those stationed in lower Italy might have begun moving earlier. But this last was very unlikely, and the first would not essentially change the situation, and in war, one must sometimes trust a little in luck. The allies were the stronger, and they had already won a battle; the provinces in the French rear were in such a state that they could not be held without the French army covering them; and finally, the French army's main line of communications with France—that is, the one with the county of Nice—ran not directly behind it but obliquely behind its right flank. All these reasons warranted the allied commander to perform a major strategic outflanking of his opponent in order to separate him completely from lower Italy and drive him away from his natural line of communications, or else force him to retreat so far before giving battle (which he was still in a state to be able to do) that, in the event of victory, he would be driven entirely out of Italy.

23 SUVOROV MARCHES TO THE PO

After the battle of Cassano, the French army withdrew across the Ticino: Grenier to Buffalora, after putting 2,400 men into the citadel of Milan, and Victor and Laboissière to Pavia. Moreau thought that, once he was behind the Ticino, he could be rejoined by Sérurier's division, having still had no news of its fate.

With this retreat behind the Ticino, the Cisalpine Republic could be regarded as dissolved.[80] Whatever supplies could be salvaged were hastily removed, and the officials the French had installed, along with their most fervent supporters, fled with their families and belongings. All the highways and roads were filled with long wagon trains, and all the bridges were jammed with them. The whole ephemeral state seemed to wash away in little pieces like a mass of ice breaking up in springtime. This sight, and the appearance of a beaten army hastening to the Ticino and the Po in the most parlous state, quickly fanned the flames of hatred and partisan rage already stirring in the people. Thus, inevitably, the popular insurrection that had broken out in the Ferrara region after the first French reverses now spread across the whole theater of operations in upper Italy all at once. Wherever weak French forces presented the opportunity, insurrectionist corps sprang up and fought them vigorously. If the French invading Lombardy in 1796 and Genoa and Piedmont in 1798 had flattered themselves that they were breaking the chains of an oppressed people, now it appeared a thousand times more as though the change in the fortunes of war had broken the shackles keeping the people's hopes and feelings forcibly restrained. This necessarily had a most decisive influence on the French commander's whole situation.[81]

This situation was a very difficult one anyway, because of the following particular factors:

1. The French were occupying a country by holding citadels inside a large number of populous cities, which themselves also offered a kind of fortification but were in a very neglected and unarmed state and could

---

80. The Cisalpine Republic had been formed by the French after their success in the war of the First Coalition in 1797. This lines up nicely with Clausewitz's point about the result of a war never being final. See *On War*, book 1, chap. 1, sec. 9.

81. This illustrates the value of the object being sought (see *On War*, book 1, chap. 2). In this case, the allies have demonstrated their willingness to overturn a republic founded by the French. As such, the French have little choice but to seek the reestablishment of the republic, as failure of the revolution would be a catastrophe for its supporters. Thus, if the revolution itself is threatened by the allies, the French have little option but to resist to the maximum degree to which they are able, thereby increasing the degree of effort required by the allies to subdue them. Unless the allies are willing to raise their efforts to the same level, it is unlikely that they will be able to beat France and maintain a lasting peace. Of course, French rule was not necessarily popular, as can be seen in this section, and the same logic can be applied to the subject Italian population to gauge their reaction.

not be held owing to a lack of sufficient garrisons. In many of these places, there were substantial supplies of rations, weapons, ammunition, bridging equipment, and the like. Among these were Peschiera, Ferrara, Pizzighettone, Milan, Orci, Pavia, Tortona, Alessandria, Turin, Valenza, Ceva, Cuneo, and a host of other places. Mantua was the only proper fortress they occupied. By their sheer number, these citadels swallowed up a large combat force in garrisons, yet it could be foreseen that as soon as the people rose up against the French everywhere, these garrisons would not be able to hold out for very long.

2. The French army's main line of communications ran through the county of Nice, leaving Turin and Piedmont off to one side, and then wended its way in a crooked line through the narrow valleys of the Apennines to the sea. In this part of the Apennines, a kind of guerrilla war had never completely ended, and it was to be expected that it would now flare up with renewed force. In the narrow mountain valleys on the main line of communications, it would be easy for such a guerrilla war to have a major effect.[82]

3. Macdonald was expected to arrive with the army from lower Italy. Of course, when Moreau arrived behind the Ticino, Macdonald had not yet set off, but Moreau could not know that for sure. And even if he did, he had to try to keep a line of retreat open for Macdonald along the Riviera, to maintain possession of the eastern Apennines for as long as possible. Here again, the popular uprisings necessarily had a major influence, for it is in a war of small parties spread across a large area that they are truly effective.

If we take these factors into account, there can be no question of General Moreau making a stand behind the Ticino. But it is hard to say where he could have taken a position at all that would still allow the possibility of joining up with Macdonald without getting into a dangerous situation.

In this situation, and after learning of the loss of Sérurier's division, Moreau made the decision that seems the simplest and most natural. He wanted to withdraw to Turin and Alessandria, halt his main body between these two places, and try to hold the eastern Apennines with Montrichard's and Gauthier's troops. In this way, he hoped to prevent Turin from breaking

---

82. See *On War*, book 6, chap. 26, "The People in Arms."

away entirely, and he even deluded himself that by mobilizing the national guard there, he could keep the people chained to the French banner and all the better secure for himself this place, which was very important because of the many kinds of supplies it provided.

After having the remnants of Sérurier's division return from the lakes and join him at Novara, Moreau set off for Turin with Grenier's division and had the divisions of his right wing retreat across the Po at Valenza. On 7 May the French divisions arrived behind the Po.

In Turin, which Moreau could not garrison sufficiently due to a lack of troops, he moved the majority of the means of defense into the citadel and prepared it suitably for defense. He left 3,400 men there under General Fiorella to serve as a garrison for the citadel in case of attack and now took position with the main army between Alessandria and Valenza.

General Pérignon, who had recently arrived in Genoa, was put in command of the troops stationed in the Ligurian Republic and was supposed to link up with Montrichard and Gauthier right away.

At this time, the French main army was 20,000 strong. Since the battle of Cassano, when it numbered 28,000 men, it had been weakened by the loss of 12,000 in that battle and another 5,000 after detaching Montrichard and garrisoning Milan, so 17,000 overall. It had probably lost more men during its retreat as well; on the other hand, it had incorporated some 8,000 men from the troops stationed in the province of Milan and had received perhaps a few thousand men from the interior.

Apart from the main army, the French combat forces included:

In the Piedmontese fortresses: 9,000 men
In the province of Genoa: 5,000
Montrichard in the eastern Apennines: 2,600
Gauthier in the eastern Apennines: 6,400
Total: 23,000 men

Together with the main army, this constituted a force of 43,000 men. Adding Macdonald's army of some 20,000 would have brought the total to about 65,000 men.

While Moreau was reorganizing in this way, not so much to renew resistance as to await further events, Suvorov squandered precious time, for time is always precious immediately after winning a battle. Cassano is only 18 miles from Milan, so he could have appeared outside that city on the 28th but did not arrive there with the army until the 29th. He did not set off again with the main body until 1 May.[83]

Since uniting the two French armies from upper and lower Italy had to be a major objective of the French operations, Suvorov decided to carry the war across to the south bank of the Po with his main force immediately. He considered Piacenza the most suitable crossing point because, given his lack of appropriate bridging equipment, that was the first place where a bridge could be constructed from local boats, and there was no fear of the enemy making a stand there. Therefore, on the 30th he just sent Ott's division forward toward the Ticino on the Buffalora road and had Zoph's and Kaim's divisions march half a day along the Lodi road. Fröhlich and the Russians remained in Milan.[84]

Colonel Prince Rohan[85] was sent to Lecco with four battalions and one squadron because, since the Russians' departure, no allied forces were left in that area. He was supposed to link up with Colonel Strauch of the Tyrol army coming through the Oglio valley. The latter was instructed to march on Monbegno in the Adda valley, and the two of them were to clear the enemy out of Chiavenna and Bellinzona and try to seize the St. Gotthard Pass and thus take the French position in Graubündten in rear.

On this day the 500-strong garrison of the small fortress of Orci surrendered.

On 1 May, after leaving General Lattermann behind with 4,500 men to besiege the citadel of Milan, Suvorov set off in two columns. The first, com-

---

83. Suvorov's arrival on this date is confirmed in Milyutin, *Geschichte des Krieges Russlands*, 1:248–250. Also see Duffy, *Eagles over the Alps*, 69–70.

84. Melas noted the ruthless pillaging by the Russian Cossacks. See Duffy, *Eagles over the Alps*, 69. This behavior did not encourage civilians to welcome the army with open arms as liberators. Nor did Suvorov's comments: "I have been sent to restore the Pope's ancient throne, and to return the people to obedience to their monarch. Help me to finish this sacred work." [*Ich bin gesendet, um den alten Thron des Papstes wieder aufzurichten, und das Volk zum Gehorsame gegen seinen Monarchen zurückzuführen. Helfet mir, dieß heilige Werk zu vollbringen.*] Milyutin, *Geschichte des Krieges Russlands*, 1:249; cited in English in Duffy, *Eagles over the Alps*, 70.

85. Prince Ludwig Victor of Rohan (1766–1846) was a French nobleman who had fled the revolution and was now fighting against it. He had a distinguished career in the Austrian army before retiring after being severely wounded at the battle of Wagram in 1809.

prising the three Austrian divisions, moved to Lodi; the second, formed by the Russians, headed to San Angelo.

Wukassowitsch, with a division of 8,000 men, was to replace General Ott on the Buffalora road, while General Ott and his 4,500-strong division moved into Pavia, where he found substantial supplies of all kinds. General Hohenzollern was busy besieging the fortresses of Orci and Pizzighettone.

Suvorov's army had thus spread out across Milan along the radii of a circle. About 3,000 men moved toward the Swiss Alps, 8,000 along the road to Turin, 4,600 to Pavia, 17,000 headed for the Po between Pavia and Piacenza, and 14,500 were moving toward Piacenza.

This crippling dispersion of forces was compounded by wasting both time and effort on pointless maneuvers. The whole army moved forward from Cassano to Milan and then back to Piacenza. Ott was first pushed forward along the road to Buffalora (Pavia province) and then had to turn toward Pavia after that, at a time when it still seemed so important to reach Pavia as soon as possible.[86] Directing the Russian column via San Angelo implied that it would also have to make a detour to move to either Pavia or Piacenza.

This pointless waste of time and effort is impossible to condone, for even if weak reasons for each of these maneuvers could have been found, they all would have been outweighed by a simple forceful pursuit of the aim. That could have entailed sending 10,000 men to Pavia as soon as possible and setting off for Piacenza with the main army.

The bridge at Piacenza was not ready until 6 May. In 1796 Bonaparte had needed about forty-eight hours to complete his bridge, so it can reasonably be asserted that if the allies had busied themselves with preparing this crossing right after the battle of Cassano, the bridge would have been finished by 2 or 3 May.

But as if he had not squandered enough time already, while the bridge at Piacenza was being built, Suvorov swapped the missions of his divisions again. He had set off for Pavia with the Russians and had sent General Ott to Piacenza, where he was tasked with advancing against Parma. This division had thus been gradually shunted from the right wing to the left and had described an arc of more than 100 degrees around the headquarters.[87]

---

86. Jomini comments that Ott was heading to Pavia, where he "found a considerable train of abandoned French artillery along with stores and supplies." It is not clear whether he knew of its existence before marching there. Jomini, 11:284–285.

87. This is curious, as Suvorov had declared the objective to be Piedmont. His words

Kaim's Austrian division was to advance to Pizzighettone, which the French were trying to defend with inadequate means. He was to besiege the place together with Hohenzollern's division.

On 6 May the Austrians crossed the Po. Zoph's and Fröhlich's divisions were on the road to Tortona; Ott's division was headed toward Parma to operate against General Montrichard and to link up with General Klenau, who was partly besieging Ferrara and partly covering the siege of Mantua. Ott and Klenau were to move to Modena and Bologna together to observe the exits from the Apennines for Macdonald's approach.

While Zoph and Fröhlich advanced on Tortona, Suvorov had the Russians move to Lomello on the Cogna. Wukassowitsch had pushed forward to Vercelli on 8 May, after thirty guns the French had left parked in Novara fell into his hands.

On 7 May Peschiera had capitulated on condition of safe conduct for its garrison, and on the 10th, the 600-strong garrison of Pizzighettone surrendered. In the latter place, a very considerable magazine was captured.

After taking Pizzighettone, General Hohenzollern marched off to Milan with three battalions to take over command outside the citadel. General Kaim and the rest of their troops followed Zoph and Fröhlich.

These two divisions had arrived outside Tortona on 9 May, taking possession of the city that same day with the support of the inhabitants, and had

---

are interesting too, as they do not fully match his actions: "We cross the Po. Our objective is Piedmont. We *must* [emphasis added] have artillery—as has often been said—for the conquest of its fortresses, as much as possible from captured pieces, since our own is being used at Mantua and Peschiera. Only after that [the sieges of Mantua and Peschiera] can our artillery be brought forward to reinforce us for important sieges. Other conquests toward Parma, etc., do not help us with the main object. They are pointless; we cannot hold them until a later more opportune time without weakening ourselves. As for food! We will find that as we advance—like Bonaparte, who got none from France." [*Wir gehen über den Po. Unser Ziel ist gegen Piemont. Zur Eroberung der Festungen muß, wie schon oftmals beredet worden, Artillerie geschafft werden,—so viel wie möglich von den eroberten Stücken, in so weit die eigene Artillerie wegen Mantua und Peschiera gebraucht sein wird,—welche erst nachher uns verstärken kann zu wichtigen Belagerungen—die übrigen Eroberungen gegen Parma u. s. w. können in der großen Sache (Hauptsache) uns nichts helfen, sie sind umsonst; wir können sie nicht behalten, bis auf künftige gelegenere Zeit ohne uns zu schwächen,—Lebensmittel! Werden wir im Vorrücken antreffen,—wie Bonaparte, der keine derselben aus Frankreich bekommen hat.*] Milyutin, *Geschichte des Krieges Russlands*, 2:369. Duffy includes only the first part of the quote from Milyutin and cites it as being from volume 1. See Duffy, *Eagles over the Alps*, 72.

obliged the French to withdraw into the citadel. Suvorov himself established his headquarters in the city, even though most of its streets were commanded by fire from the citadel. The Austrian divisions crossed the Scrivia and took position at Garoffoldo.

The advance guard under Generals Karaczay and Bagration was deployed at San Giuliano. It patrolled along the Bormida and the Tanaro from Acqui to their confluence with the Po.

Suvorov himself did not leave Tortona until the 12th.

During this time, the second Russian column of 6,000 men under General Förster joined the army, increasing Suvorov's force in the vicinity of Alessandria (i.e., not including Wukassowitsch) to some 30,000 men.

Meanwhile, Wukassowitsch had advanced from Buffalora [probably Boffalora Sopra Ticino] to the Po; occupied the crossings at Casale, Ponte Stura, and Trino; and was patrolling into the Doro valley as far as Ivrea to support the insurrection that had broken out in that area.

The Po, the Tanaro, and the Bormida were lightly held by French troops, but the main body of Grenier's division was between Valenza and Pezzetti, and the main body of Victor's was at Alessandria.

On 11 May Suvorov ordered General Rosenberg, who was at Lomello, to cross the Po near Valenza with part of his corps and seize the city of Valenza.

The Action at Bassignana on 12 May

This mission was certainly not a demonstration to facilitate the main army's crossing of the Tanaro; conversely, neither was it supported by any demonstration by the main army. Rather, it constituted a sheer part-operation that, carried out so close to the French main army, could not possibly succeed; at best, it could only result in digging in behind entrenchments on the right bank of the Po. It is therefore impossible to know what this operation was supposed to achieve, and we can only suggest that it smacks very strongly of the Turkish theater of war, where battles usually had no purpose beyond mutual slaughter.[88]

88. Duffy indicates that one of the subordinate commanders, General Andrei Rosenberg (1739–1813), had "almost certainly" been influenced to attack by the presence or prodding of Russian Grand Prince Constantine (who was accompanying the army). Duffy, *Eagles over the Alps*, 76.

Rosenberg found himself opposite the area of Borgo Franco between Valenza and the Tanaro. He marched there with about 10,000 men, and during the night of the 11th and 12th he had 4,000 men under General Tschuberof ferried across to an island at Mugarone.[89]

Since the arm of the river separating the island from the right bank was wadable and the troops appeared very eager to attack, Tschuberof crossed all the way over, attacked the French pickets, and drove them back through Pezzetti. He was soon attacked in the right flank by 4,000 men from Grenier's division, led there from Valenza by General Colli.[90] Tschuberof was thrown back to his island in great haste and disorder and found himself in a dire situation. The island was packed tight with men and wagons, and the distance between the island and the right bank was so narrow that even muskets could fire across it with great effect. The flying bridge, which was his one connection with the left bank, had been interrupted when the rope snapped.

The French, naturally worried that this might be a mere demonstration, wanted to keep their forces concentrated to oppose the main crossing they expected over the Tanaro. Therefore, they did not take any further advantage of the Russians' dire situation. The flying bridge was repaired, and during the night [of 12–13 May] Tschuberof's brigade, whose commander had fallen, retreated to the left bank. Rosenberg thereupon marched across the Cogna to San Nazaro, crossed the Po on the road from Pavia to Casteggio on the 13th, and then moved through Voghera to Sale. Tschuberof's brigade had lost 2,500 men dead and wounded and all its artillery.

When Suvorov learned of the danger Rosenberg's troops found themselves in, he marched toward Sale with Fröhlich's and Förster's divisions but returned to his position on the 13th.[91]

---

89. General Rosenberg had orders from Suvorov to "march quickly across the Po and join him at Tortona." See letter from Suvorov to Rosenberg, 11 May 1799, in Milyutin, *Geschichte des Krieges Russlands*, 2:41.

90. **Clausewitz** notes: "This general, who commanded the Sardinian allied forces in Beaulieu's army in 1796 and left Sardinian service after the armistice to enter Austrian service, must also have left the Austrian army again since; for when Moreau arrived in Turin, he found himself there and offered Moreau his services, which the latter naturally happily made use of, because he thought this would tie a new bond with the Piedmontese."

91. Duffy's account of the battle fills in some of the gaps here. Duffy, *Eagles over the Alps*, 73–79.

On 14 May Kaim's division joined the main army from Pizzighettone, increasing it to 35,000 men (excluding Wukassowitsch).

24 MOREAU RETREATS INTO THE APENNINES. THE ENCOUNTER AT MARENGO ON 16 MAY

The French commander did not think he could hang on very long in his position. His opponent was constantly being reinforced, and General Rosenberg's attempt to cross the Po seemed to be just the precursor of a serious attack. The popular insurrection in his rear was spreading further every day across all the entrances to the Apennines. General Pérignon, whose troops were mostly Ligurian, could easily be overwhelmed, and then Moreau would lose his lines of communications not only with France but also with the corps stationed in the Apennines and with Macdonald.

Moreau therefore decided to reinforce General Pérignon with some of his combat forces and to flank-march to the left with the rest and set himself astride the road from Turin toward Nice through the Col de Tende. He intended to cover this road and Cuneo and to prepare his retreat into the Apennines, so as to be able to march off unhindered at the right time to join Macdonald, who by this time had reached the border of Tuscany.

Meanwhile, Wukassowitsch had started to bombard Casale. This and Rosenberg's attempted crossing led Moreau to believe that Suvorov and the Russians might have moved up the Po and that there might be nothing but an Austrian corps left at Tortona. If so, it could not be very strong, especially if Kaim's division coming from Pizzighettone had not yet arrived. Moreau therefore decided that before marching away he would attempt a crossing of the Bormida and an attack on the enemy corps between the Bormida and the Scrivia. If his guess was proved right, he might be able to defeat this corps, relieve Tortona, and then await Macdonald's approach on the road leading to the Bocchetta, in order to unite with him north of the Apennines.

General Jomini calls Moreau's attack a reconnaissance;[92] Archduke Charles says he wanted to gain the road to the Bocchetta.[93] If we take each of these reasons by itself, the first is somewhat incomplete, and the second is somewhat

---

92. Jomini, 11:295.
93. Karl, 2:43.

incomprehensible, since to gain the Bocchetta road he only needed to march to Novi. However, both these reasons occur together in the view that we have offered of Moreau's motivation for his maneuver, and that has led us to present this view as a likely one.

To carry out his plan, Moreau concentrated both his divisions at Alessandria, threw a bridge across the Bormida at Marengo during the night of the 15th–16th, and crossed it with Victor's 5,000-strong division and 2,000 cavalry, while leaving Grenier at the river. He drove back the Austrian outposts and advanced against San Giuliano. But here he encountered Fröhlich's division, which had been rushed up under General Lusignan's[94] command, and General Bagration's Russian brigade of the advance guard, which had already been ordered to march off to Sale but did not fail to support the Austrians in this situation. These two formations had eleven battalions and nine squadrons altogether, with which they made a successful stand. Since Moreau now saw more enemy troops hurrying up from Garoffoldo (the camp in the area of Tortona), he felt he had to give up on his plan. He therefore began to retreat and reached the left bank of the Bormida again after losing 500 men.

Moreau had probably left Grenier's division behind because of a report that there was an enemy corps at Sale.

As far as the Austrians are concerned, it is striking that neither Suvorov nor Melas was present at this action, even though the former's headquarters was a few leagues away in Castelnuovo and Melas's was certainly no further. Also, by the Austrian account, Zoph's division took no part in it; rather, the troops that hurried up from the camp at Garoffoldo were from Kaim's division, which had just arrived. Zoph's division was probably being used outside Tortona and to furnish detachments toward the Apennines.

After this abortive attempt, on the night of the 16th–17th,[95] Moreau sent Victor's division of ten battalions and four squadrons, minus its artillery, through Acqui and Cairo into the Apennines to reinforce General Pérignon at the Bocchetta. He also formed a couple of mobile columns to send ahead into the western part of the Apennines and disperse the rebellious locals. He left General Gardanne in Alessandria with 3,000 men, while, with Grenier's divi-

---

94. Franz Joseph Marquis de Lusignan (1753–1832) was a Spaniard in Austrian service. He was a skilled and brave commander and was captured or wounded more than once in action against the French.

95. The archduke confirms the French retreat safely across the Bormida. Karl, 2:45.

sion, the cavalry, and the artillery—some 8,000 strong—he began his march via Asti to the area of Villanova and Moncaglieri.[96]

Suvorov, for his part, thought he could not achieve anything against Moreau on the Bormida and the Tanaro, so he decided to head toward Turin along the left bank of the Po, which offered fewer advantageous positions for the enemy. Besides, it would be hard for the French to defend this sprawling city if they did not want to be completely besieged in Turin. But if the allies could gain possession of it, the benefits associated with that would not be insignificant. Furthermore, it is extremely likely that the Austrian government attached great value to it.[97] Since the Austrians had just repelled one attack by Moreau, it did not seem likely that he would disturb the siege of the citadel of Tortona with a second. Anyway, Suvorov probably thought that his opponent would have to follow him to the Turin area, and the idea that Moreau might exploit his absence to unite with Macdonald on the northern foothills of the Apennines was apparently far from his thoughts, just as it was from those of the French commander himself.

Suvorov therefore set off at about the same time as Moreau on the 17th, moving through Casteggio on the Pavia road with his main body. He had a corps cross the Po at Cambio by means of a bridge of boats; he left General Alcaini outside the Tortona citadel; after discovering Moreau's departure, he sent General Schweikowsky to Alessandria; and he himself moved with the main army along the left bank to Turin in a maneuver that was somewhat delayed by the swollen rivers, arriving in the area on the 26th. Thus, in ten days he had covered some 90 miles. General Wukassowitsch moved along the right bank in order to invest the city on that side.

These maneuvers by the two armies obviously had no reciprocal connection with each other, as we can see from their simultaneity.[98] We may regard

---

96. Duffy has Moreau effectively choosing to cede the region. Duffy, *Eagles over the Alps*, 80.

97. Given that the results of war are never final (*On War*, book 1, chap. 1), and considering the value of the object (book 1, chap. 2), it seems reasonable to assume that Piedmont, much like the recently created Cisalpine Republic, might want to throw off the recently imposed French yoke and that the Austrians might want to liberate a former ally.

98. The reciprocal connection relates to an important concept in *On War* (see book 1, chap. 1, secs. 3–8; book 2, chap. 2; book 6, chap. 30, particularly p. 511; and book 8, chaps. 3–4). This is far too complex to discuss in full here, but in essence, the idea is

what had taken place in the previous three weeks, up until the appearance of the two sides' approaching armies, in the same way. Thus, a precise synchronistic treatment of the two sides' actions would make an overview of them unnecessarily difficult.

In fact, in connection with Macdonald's approach, Suvorov had proposed reinforcing the allied army in Italy with part of the army in the Tyrol. As we shall relate in the next section, in the second half of May, the Austrian government ordered Bellegarde to set off for Piedmont, where he was consequently expected to arrive in early June.

Until this new configuration of the balance of forces, all the allies' efforts are devoted to conquering the upper Italian fortresses. After the fall of Pizzighettone on 11 May, they are still busy investing and besieging the fortress of Mantua and the citadels of Tortona, Milan, Alessandria, Turin, Ferrara, and Ravenna, as well as taking the more important walled cities in Piedmont.

The French spend this time carrying out their retreat to the Riviera.

We therefore have to place these isolated events alongside one another only in terms of their historical sequence. Let us first relate what went on with the allied army and then follow the French commander's move to the Riviera.

We have already said that the allied army advanced to Turin on the 27th, after Wukassowitsch appeared outside the city on the right bank of the Po the day before. He quickly reached an agreement with the inhabitants, and on 27 May, after the Austrian howitzers had set a few houses on fire, the people of Turin overpowered the French guards on the Po gate, opening the city to the Austrians and obliging General Fiorelli to withdraw into the citadel.

The allied army thereby came into possession of a large amount of war materiel, including 261 cannon, 80 mortars, 60,000 firearms of various types, and 300 tons of gunpowder.

While the allied army now stayed around Turin, waiting for Bellegarde and intending to make itself master of the Piedmontese fortresses, Kaim's division was tasked with besieging the Turin citadel; General Fröhlich, with part of his

---

that each action in war provokes a reciprocal action from an opponent. That response, in turn, provokes another from the original party, and so on and so forth. Unless one side overthrows the other sufficiently to attain its goals, this interaction continues, with neither side fully in control. Hence the tendency for escalation, as the amount of effort increases to attain one's end, leading to a corresponding increase in the opponent's effort to gain its goal in the face of escalating force from the other side.

division, was posted at Savigliano and Fossano facing Cuneo; Wukassowitsch was sent via Cherasco to the area of Ceva and Mondovi; and, from the units left outside Tortona, General Seckendorff was pushed forward with a weak brigade between the Erro and the Scrivia toward the Apennines to cover the siege of Alessandria from that side.

The inhabitants of the exits on the Italian side of the Alps from Mont Blanc to the Po valley had attached themselves to the French cause with the same zeal as those in the Apennines had embraced the Austrian cause, and they had formed considerable armed bands. General Lusignan was therefore detached to Fenestrella with part of Fröhlich's division, a Russian detachment under Colonel Zuccato was sent to Pignerol, and Prince Bagration went to Susa. Of these places that bar the roads from Grenelle over Mont Cenis and from Briançon over Mont Genèvre, only Fenestrella stood firm and still held out, while the others fell into the Russians' hands.

In the rear of the allied army, the following events occurred around this time.

As a result of the offensive undertaken by the Austrians in Graubündten, which we will describe in the next section, Loison's[99] brigade (formerly Dessolles's) and Lecourbe's division were chased out of the Veltlin and pushed back to the Italian slope of the Alps. In this situation, they hurled themselves with greatly superior numbers on Prince Rohan, who had advanced with his detachment from Lecco, where we last left him, to the Bellinzona area and was therefore threatening their rear. On 13 May they threw him back with significant loss behind the Tresa, which connects Lake Maggiore to Lake Lugano. Since the news of this development arrived right when the Russians suffered a blow at Bassignana, the impact of this intrinsically insignificant event seems thereby to have been increased above its true weight and to have generated a kind of concern for flank and rear. Suvorov ordered General Hohenzollern, who was besieging the citadel of Milan, to set off immediately with half his troops to support Prince Rohan. General Hohenzollern headed there with five battalions and one squadron and joined up with Prince Rohan on the 17th, but now he had only one brigade under General Loison to deal with, since Lecourbe had turned toward the St. Gotthard Pass. He easily drove Loison

99. Here, Clausewitz has Souson in charge of the brigade, although he switches to Loison partway through the paragraph. Archduke Charles and Jomini both have it as Loison. See Karl, 1:277; Jomini, 11:217. As such, we thought it best to change this.

back to Bellinzona with the loss of 500–600 men, after which he returned to Milan.

Although these events took place in the Italian theater, that is, on the southern slopes of the Alps, and the allied troops involved were predominantly from the allied army in Italy, the events themselves undoubtedly belong to the Swiss theater of operations, so we must defer a detailed presentation of them until later.

On 21 May, as soon as he returned to face the Milan citadel, General Hohenzollern had the approach saps begun.[100] The fortress surrendered soon after, on the 23rd, on condition of free passage for its 2,200-strong garrison. General Hohenzollern then marched off to reinforce Kray outside Mantua.

The siege of Mantua had not yet properly begun owing to a lack of means. General Kray now had the place surrounded, and he tried to extend along the right bank of the Po and establish himself there with part of his force. General Klenau and a few battalions advanced to Ferrara, which the insurgents had already been investing for a while. He soon seized the city, and after he had bombarded the citadel for a couple of days, the 1,500-man garrison surrendered it on 24 May on condition of free passage. The citadel of Ravenna was taken at the same time and in the same way by a detachment sent by sea from Venice, in cooperation with the insurgents.

The uprising in central Italy spread ever further. In mid-May General Lahoz, an Italian who had joined the ranks of the French in 1796 and was commanding at Pesaro under Montrichard, went over to the insurgents and provided a core for the popular uprising on the eastern slopes of the Roman Apennines. Its stronghold was Fermo; on one side it kept the French garrison at Ancona in check, and on the other it established communications with the insurgents in the Abruzzo, as well as with the Russian and Turkish warships off the coast. This took place on the eastern slopes of the Apennines at the time when Macdonald was west of Rome, moving toward Florence with some 20,000 men.

Thus, through force of arms and the insurrection, the allies became masters of more and more of upper and central Italy, while on both sides new forces were arriving at roughly the same time and in roughly the same strength

---

100. Approach saps are entrenchments dug to approach a fortress. Typically, they zigzag to prevent enfilading fire, and they allow a besieger to move closer to an enemy fortress in relative safety.

to make each army fit for new battles. At the same time as Bellegarde was embarking on to Lake Como with about 15,000 men to join up with Suvorov, Macdonald had reached Florence on his way to unite with Moreau.

Let us turn now to Moreau.

As we said, immediately after his abortive action at Marengo, on 17 May Moreau had begun his march to Turin via Asti with 8,000 men, including Grenier's division, the majority of the cavalry, the artillery, and the baggage train. Victor, with six battalions and four squadrons, had marched via Aqui, Spigno, and Dego to the Genoese Apennines, where he linked up with General Pérignon on the 19th. When Moreau arrived in Asti on the 18th, he learned that the garrison of Ceva, a few hundred men strong, had surrendered to the insurgents. He therefore ordered Adjutant-General Garreau to march swiftly to Ceva with four battalions and recapture it with the support of a detachment from the Cuneo garrison. Moreau marched with his corps to Villanova on the road to Turin, without approaching the latter place too closely. From here, taking advantage of the allies' absence, he sent the baggage train as well as the heavy artillery with an escort commanded by General Drouot along the road through Fenestrella and over Mont Genèvre to Briançon. He thereby freed his corps of a major encumbrance and made it capable of moving through the smaller Apennine passes to the Riviera, where he apparently felt it would be most feasible to unite with Macdonald, who by now had arrived in Tuscany. Upon the Russians' approach, Moreau retreated from Villanova through Carmagnola to Savigliano. Garreau's operation against Ceva was unsuccessful; the high water of the Tanaro had obliged him to march up the left bank of the river,[101] which gave an Austrian detachment, probably from General Seckendorff's command, time to occupy the place. Moreau now sent Grouchy, his chief of general staff, to take over command of Garreau's detachment; Grouchy gathered several other detachments that had been dispatched to drive off the local insurgents, but even he only managed to seize Mondovi, which had likewise been occupied by the insurgents. Since he did not want to commit himself to a bloody assault, he had to withdraw from Ceva.

As far as his continued retreat is concerned, the French commander's situation at this point has been described as extremely dangerous—indeed, desperate—although it is the writers who are to blame for that. Even if General Moreau did not care to march through the Col di Tenda because he was wor-

---

101. This episode is recounted in Jomini, 11:302–308.

ried about taking a detour that put him 70 to 80 miles away from the corps posted in the Genoese Apennines, there was still nothing intrinsically desperate about this predicament. The Austrian account maintains that just then the road through the Col di Tenda was completely blocked by a rockfall, but as General Jomini testifies, the French operations journal makes no mention of this. We must therefore assume that it was a false or exaggerated rumor that had spread among the Austrians. Be that as it may, General Moreau decided not to use the road through Cuneo but tried to march down via Ceva, which he still hoped to retake, through the Col San Bernardo to Loano on the Riviera. He therefore marched via Mondovi on the road to Ceva as far as Lesegno, where the Cursaglia flows into the Tanaro below Ceva. Since mere threats and bombardment had not sufficed to recapture the latter place, and since Moreau's force was so weak that he was unwilling to stake the number of men an assault could cost him, he arrived at the idea of having laborers build a road for his field artillery from the valley of the Cursaglia across the mountains into the Tanaro valley at Garessio. Several thousand laborers managed to do this without any particular difficulty, so Moreau and his corps moved via Garessio, leaving a detachment facing Ceva, and descended through the Col San Bernardo to the Riviera at Loano on 6 June.

From this, we can see that there is no question of his retreat being a desperate situation, because in that case, he would not have cared about the couple of hundred men the storming of Ceva would have cost him. Besides, the French and Austrians had traversed this part of the Apennines in all directions in 1796, so the obstacles to maneuvering with field artillery cannot have been that insuperable.

It is not until the end of this march, when Moreau descends to the Riviera on 6 June, that we discover when it was carried out, because otherwise, Jomini's very fleeting and superficial account does not give one single date for the period of almost three weeks from 18 May to 6 June. The road that Moreau covered during these eighteen days from Asti via Villanova, Savigliano, Mondovi, and Garessio to Loano is about 90 miles long; assuming that a few days were lost around Lesegno while the new road was being constructed, we can suppose that he stayed close to the Po for seven or eight days, roughly until the time the allied army approached Turin and news could have been received of Macdonald's arrival in Florence on 25 May. Thus, we can conclude that these two events caused Moreau's retreat.

25 REFLECTIONS

The French

The French commander was too weak to let it come to a new decisive battle before Macdonald had arrived or until he had received significant reinforcements. Macdonald could not be expected to arrive before the end of May, since his recall was prompted by the battle of Magnano (5 April). The road from Napolitania to the Po valley is 320 miles long, which would have taken him about four weeks to traverse; another three weeks had to be allowed for communications, discussions, and all kinds of delay.

Moreau reached the Po at the beginning of May, so he still had four weeks to wait for Macdonald to arrive. He could not expect substantial reinforcements from the interior before then, as experience shows, since they did not arrive in significant numbers until July. The French commander's immediate aim had to be to put off any decisive battle for these four weeks. But the success of such an endeavor depended primarily on the allied commander not going about his business with any great energy, and Moreau therefore had to constantly ask himself what he should do if the opposite case arose. However many citadels Suvorov found to storm along his way, his remaining force would still be larger than Moreau's main army, so there was nothing to prevent him from continuing his strike against Moreau, so long as the latter did not escape him completely. Where could Moreau fall back to then? What could he do in the worst case?

First option: Reinforce the Genoese troops somewhat; leave garrisons in the citadels of Turin, Tortona, and Alessandria; and fall back behind the Var with the army itself, which by then still would have been perhaps 12,000 strong. Naturally, Suvorov would not have followed across this river.

Second option: Head the army not toward Nice and the Var but toward Genoa, with the intention of barricading himself inside Genoa if he should be defeated in the Apennines.

Third option: Withdraw with the army itself to Turin, hold out as long as possible outside the walls of the city, and finally barricade himself inside it.

Fourth option: Put only about 10,000 men in Turin and, if need be, retreat across the Var with the cavalry and a couple of thousand infantry to form the core of a new army.

Whichever of these four courses Moreau might choose in extremis, the temporary position between Valenza and Alessandria was still a suitable measure to await what came next, because from there, he could take any of the four options described above. We must therefore declare ourselves absolutely in complete agreement with this first position of Moreau's. Suvorov did not continue his attack against Moreau's army itself to the maximum, but he obliged Moreau to abandon the Alessandria area and withdraw into the Apennines. This proves that Moreau did not want to take the third or fourth of the options we presented; however, it remains uncertain whether, in the event of a continued attack, he would have retreated into Genoa with his main body or withdrawn to the Var, since from his position behind the Apennines, he could still do either. In any case, it is necessary for our critical consideration to establish the value of each of the above four possible courses of action.[102]

The first and second options had the advantage that General Moreau could still take a position in the Apennines that the foe might treat with respect, as indeed he did. As long as Moreau occupied this position, directly joining up with Macdonald remained feasible. This advantage probably inclined the French commander in that direction. If Suvorov had attacked him in the Apennines, the choice between the first and second options would have come into play.

Since Genoa would have been adequately garrisoned by the troops under Generals Pérignon and Victor, there was no reason for General Moreau to put himself in there as well, unless his ultimate intention was that, by doing so, he would have been in a position to hold on longer in the Apennines. That is, it is clear that if he wanted to retreat to Nice and the Var, he would have to keep one eye constantly on the road in that direction and adopt a much more extended position than if he allowed himself to be pushed back into Genoa. If he let himself and his whole corps be driven into Genoa, there was no danger of

---

102. Again, it is worth reminding the reader of Clausewitz's concept of critical analysis. He argues that "three different intellectual activities may be contained in the critical approach. First, the discovery and interpretation of equivocal facts. This is historical research proper, and has nothing in common with theory. Second, the tracing of effects back to their causes. This is *critical analysis proper*. It is essential for theory; for whatever in theory is to be defined, supported, or simply described by reference to experience can only be dealt with in this manner. Third, the investigation and evaluation of means employed. This last is criticism proper, involving praise and censure. Here theory serves history, or rather the lessons to be drawn from history." *On War*, book 1, chap. 5, 156 (emphasis in original).

being besieged and finally captured there; Macdonald's approach soon would have broken his shackles, since Suvorov was not strong enough—nor could he become so—to keep 20,000 men blockaded in Genoa and fight 30,000 men under Macdonald (which is how strong he certainly would have been after joining up with Montrichard and Gauthier). However, if Moreau let himself be locked up in Genoa, he would no longer be able to unite directly with Macdonald, and each of them would have to operate independently, in which case it was actually a disadvantage that they were much closer to each other than if Moreau had fallen back to the Var with the core of his army. When the enemy stands between separated forces and there is no chance of uniting, the closer the separate forces are to each other, the greater the disadvantage of separation, until the point where the distance between them is so small that it can serve as a single battlefield, because in this case, combined operation becomes possible. The reason for this relationship is that the smaller the distance between separated forces at the moment of decision, the easier it becomes for the enemy between them to use the majority of his force against one of them first and then turn against the other.[103]

For these reasons, General Moreau must have regarded it as disadvantageous to be obliged to shut himself up in Genoa;[104] naturally, it was in this respect but also in another, in that he would not be able to incorporate any reinforcements arriving from the interior and bring them into action quickly, and finally because once an army is enclosed in a fortress, operations always become much more restricted.

In this situation, General Moreau must have regarded retreat behind the Var as the most natural course of action. Being driven into Genoa was a necessary evil he would expose himself to only in exchange for the probability that it would not go that far. Rather, he hoped that this greater concentration of his forces would prevent General Suvorov from driving him to that extremity. In other words, the choice between the two measures depended on the energy he

---

103. See Napoleon's initial attacks described in Clausewitz, *Napoleon's 1796 Italian Campaign*, 17–59.

104. Being confined in a fort often means that the army is stuck there. As such, staying outside Genoa or Turin offered the French the ability to maneuver and not get pinned down in one place. Note the problems the Austrians had in Mantua in 1796–1797, where they had an army largely stuck in the fortress, and where they felt forced to make several major attempts to relieve the fortress, all of which failed. See Clausewitz, *Napoleon's 1796 Italian Campaign*.

could expect from his opponent, and this expectation in turn had to be based on the measures the opponent had taken so far.

The third and fourth options give up sooner on the possibility of directly linking up with Macdonald, but they also neutralize the enemy's main body sooner, before it can conquer the Apennines. If we imagine Turin being held by 12,000–15,000 French and 10,000 Piedmontese, nearly the whole allied army, around 50,000 strong after General Förster's arrival, would have been required to invest the fortress, since the two rivers divide the area into three separate sectors, making the investment more difficult. Thus, it is clear that after the investment of Turin and the most minimal observation of the Alessandria and Tortona citadels, Suvorov would scarcely have had enough troops left to even observe the Apennines, let alone threaten them. Admittedly, General Bellegarde and his 15,000-man army arrived about four weeks later, but Macdonald arrived at exactly the same time, so this was not the time to be thinking about conquering the Apennines. We believe that if Moreau had decided to put the majority of his combat forces into Turin, that would have granted the French the advantages of:

1. Being in no danger of losing the Apennines and the Riviera, and
2. Remaining in possession of a fairly large area and a very important territory.

Now of course, Moreau could not have united with Macdonald, but the latter's approach would put Suvorov in a very awkward situation. If he wanted to continue the investment of the three fortresses, most likely he could not march away with a large enough force to face Macdonald, but if he raised the siege, he would have 20,000 men in his rear and right away would have to think about establishing a new line of retreat across the Po.

When someone stands with his force united between two separate enemy forces, the natural advantage this gives him is reduced if one of these enemy forces is in a fortress from which it is not too difficult to sally forth. This takes away half his effectiveness, as he cannot use his superior numbers against that force.

We therefore believe that such a decision by Moreau would have created better strategic conditions than the retreat into the Apennines could have afforded, if Suvorov had not paused his attack. Besides, if we assess the importance of Turin in particular in terms of its political and moral consequence, we again find ourselves required most emphatically to prefer this course of action over the others. We maintain that even by comparison with the factors that arose after Suvorov did not continue his attack, those conditions just touched on still retain the advantage. We will return to this again in our reflections on the next section.

As far as the choice between the third and fourth options is concerned, the third would certainly merit preference if the means were available to fodder the cavalry's 2,000–3,000 horses in Turin for six weeks. This would keep together the combat force with which to carry out the counterblow in Suvorov's rear; it would not lack the necessary cavalry, and that would make everything easier.

In the event the fourth course had to be taken, we imagine that General Moreau would have found himself with the small corps that fell back toward the Var, for in this case, the force collected in Turin would not be suited to active operations. Moreau's talent could then be displayed to full effect with the corps that remained in the field, which, with some reinforcements from the interior and by combining with the troops left in Genoa, could have grown to 12,000–15,000 men again.

But this idea that the main body of Moreau's army should seek refuge in Turin, that it should seriously defend the place and make it a base for strategically turning the campaign around, is of course subject to the condition that it could have survived for six weeks in Turin. Whether there were sufficient provisions for that, and whether there were enough other essential supplies such as ammunition, we cannot establish, but we believe that if Moreau had made this decision in time and prepared actively, these difficulties would not have been insuperable.[105]

These four different courses of action the French commander ultimately could have followed have been discussed here in such detail partly because they must have affected his earlier actions and partly because the distinctive factors related to this question are too important not to deserve a meticulous examination in the interest of theory. Suvorov did not continue his offensive, so the critic must now assess the French commander's conduct from a quite different standpoint again. There are three voluntary actions of his for us to

---

105. As noted earlier, he would have rendered himself effectively immobile, and he would have been reliant on a French army coming to his rescue, which was not certain.

examine: his withdrawal to the Turin area, the combat at Marengo, and his retreat over the Apennines.

Whether Moreau's withdrawal to the Cuneo road was entirely necessary, we cannot judge; at least the reasons given for it in the history are not entirely unsatisfactory. But in any case, this withdrawal was a disaster for the French. If Moreau had known that Suvorov would set off for Turin that same day, thus voluntarily giving up his position between Moreau and Macdonald, then nothing in the world should have taken Moreau away from Alessandria. Since he did not intend to retreat into Turin, there was no need to follow his opponent there, and now at Tortona, he had the perfect opportunity to land a lucky blow because the corps that Suvorov left in that area was not strong enough to resist him. If he had waited a few days to attack that corps, this success would have coincided with Macdonald's arrival in Florence, and then everything would have taken a very desirable turn.

However, while we do not venture to disapprove of the French commander's withdrawal, and we find the attempt against the Austrians at Marengo sufficiently motivated in the way, of course, only speculatively presented in our account; yet we can only regard the actual retreat to the Riviera as having arisen from one-eyed timidity.

Jomini says that it had been Moreau's intention to move into the mountains as soon as the main body of the Russians appeared at Turin.[106] This reason is really just something Jomini has made up to fill the gap, for Suvorov at Turin was hardly the head of the Medusa. If fear of being attacked is what caused Moreau to retreat, he could have at least waited until the attack was being prepared.

We therefore believe that the French commander was preoccupied solely with the idea of opening his line of retreat to the Riviera and engrossed in the difficulties that lay in his path. He had sent part of his remaining force as a patrol corps into the mountains against the insurgency, and another part to Fenestrella as escort for his heavy artillery and baggage train. Thus, he was no longer thinking about the possibility of joining up with Macdonald north of the Apennines, even though, at the time Moreau began his retreat, Macdonald had already arrived in Florence and could have been in Parma in eight days, while there was actually nothing to prevent General Moreau from marching back to the Alessandria area and calling Victor back to him there.

---

106. Jomini, 11:303.

Thus, we can perhaps say that Moreau did not consider this possibility sufficiently and that he committed an error in not staying at Savigliano so long as Suvorov tolerated him there. Then he might have gained time to bring in all his detachments and to have the necessary discussions with Macdonald. In our account, we have given Macdonald's arrival in Florence as the reason for Moreau marching away so that Macdonald would not have to wait unnecessarily, but this reasoning rests precisely on Moreau no longer having his eye on the alternative of joining up on the plain.

We therefore believe that a more truly judicious commander and one more adept at strategic calculation, such as Turenne, with whom people are so keen to compare Moreau,[107] would either have returned to Tortona immediately to punish his opponent for quitting the area with his main army, making do with Genoa as a base for the time being, or else at least have hung on in the Savigliano area for as long as possible.

The Allies

In section 21 we opined that Suvorov should not have attacked the French at the Adda but instead crossed the Po immediately at Cremona to throw himself on their strategic right flank. But after he had sought them out them behind the Adda and advanced to Milan with his army, the route via Piacenza was a significant detour, and it would have been fundamentally more natural to carry on to Pavia with his main body. Still, we do not wish to criticize him for heading for Piacenza, for the advantage of crossing the Po there undisturbed was worth a lot. Pushing General Ott and his 5,000–6,000 men forward into the Apennines right after crossing was unavoidably necessary, since the French had Gauthier's and Montrichard's corps there, and the left flank of the main army had to be protected against them, as did the bridge. Thus Suvorov arrived on the line of the Tanaro and the Po some 30,000 strong. For a truly

---

107. Although it is not entirely clear to whom Clausewitz is referring, the comparison was made by contemporary writers, and Jomini regularly praised Moreau. See, for example, Jomini, 13:370. See also Officer of the Staff, *The Life and Campaigns of Victor Moreau: Comprehending His Trial, Justification and Other Events, till the Period of His Embarkation for the United States*, trans. John Davis (New York: I. Riley, 1806), vii–viii, 22, 249–250, https://books.google.com.

decisive commander who aimed his operations right at the *Schwerpunkt*[108] of the enemy's resistance, this force easily would have been sufficient to attack General Moreau again on the spot and drive him across the Apennines into the county of Nice. Even if our estimate of the allied army is too high and Suvorov was really only about 25,000 strong, he still would have had numerical superiority, as well as being armed with the force of earlier victories. A decisive army commander would have needed no more than this.

But we still do not wish to disapprove of Suvorov advancing only to the Tortona area for the time being, with the intention of holding himself ready to keep the two French armies separated while waiting for his imminent reinforcement by Förster's column and by the corps surrounding the weaker fortresses before continuing his offensive. But after he was joined by General

---

108. This is discussed at length in Clausewitz, *Napoleon's 1796 Campaign in Italy*, 19n5. That note is reproduced here in its entirety for the reader's convenience: "Clausewitz's term *Schwerpunkt* is often rendered as 'center of gravity.' See Clausewitz, *On War*, 595–596; F. G. Zimmerman, *Military Vocabulary German-English and English German* (London: Hugh Rees, 1915). Some dispute this, arguing that it really means 'weight (or focus) of effort.' See Milan Vego, 'Clausewitz's Schwerpunkt: Mistranslated from German, Misunderstood in English,' *Military Review* 87, 1 (January–February 2007): 101–109. In the context of this work, center of gravity is the better definition. *Schwerpunkt* is a German word used in early-nineteenth-century physics to describe a center of gravity, and Clausewitz often used scientific analogies in *On War* to illustrate his thinking. For example, see book 1, chap. 1, pt. 28, for his analogy of the use of magnets and his 'paradoxical [wondrous, fickle, whimsical, or strange] trinity' (89), and book 4, chap. 11, for comments on the effects of concentrated sun rays (258). In the original German (book 1, chap. 1, sec. 8), this is '*Die Aufgabe ist also, daß sich die Theorie zwischen diesen drei Tendenzen, wie zwischen drei Anziehungspunkten Schwebend erhalte.*' Carl von Clausewitz, *Vom Kriege*, 3 vols. (Berlin: Ferdinand Dümmler, 1832–1834) 1:31–32. Although it is possible to translate *zwischen drei Anziehungspunkten schwebend erhalte* as 'suspended between three points of attraction,' the magnet analogy also makes sense. This view is reinforced by Clausewitz's own experience observing the classes of German physicist Paul Erman and his interaction with Erman's son, Adolph, who was studying magnetism. See Paret, *Clausewitz and the State*, 310–311, 310n. Therefore, it seems reasonable that Clausewitz is using the word *Schwerpunkt* as it might be understood by scientists. But in *On War* he also uses it differently, depending on which level of war he is discussing. See Christopher Bassford, 'Clausewitz and His Works,' accessed 23 February 2017, http://www.clausewitz.com/readings/Bassford/Cworks/Works.htm. For purpose of this translation, we have chosen the word or phrase that makes most sense in the context."

Förster and Kaim's division, he was some 40,000 strong. Also, he must have learned enough about Macdonald's movements to know that, at that time, he must still be on the other side of Rome. If Suvorov now shifted his line of communications to the left bank of the Po through Pavia, he could even call General Ott back to him and thus have an army of 45,000–50,000 men at his disposal facing Moreau. With that, he should have gone for General Moreau in the second half of May, attacked him wherever he made a stand, breached any possible defense of the Apennines Moreau might intend, and driven him into Genoa or back across the Var.

This is how we believe a more decisive general, hungrier for success and with more clarity of vision, would have acted. Suvorov did not act this way, and while we are far from regarding him as a man of the utmost decisiveness, still we are really very surprised by this and at a loss to explain it. For all his talents as a commander, Suvorov was not capable of conducting the campaign in Italy with full clarity of understanding merely from his own insight, in the way Bonaparte, Frederick the Great, or Turenne could have in his situation. Leading an army when three-quarters of its combat forces belong to a foreign monarch is a task of a quite different kind from leading an army either as its sovereign or at least with the authority earned gradually by commanding it for a while. Who does not feel a quite different master in someone else's house rather than in one's own, whatever powers may have been bestowed![109]

Furthermore, we should not overlook what has already been pointed out: that the conduct of a campaign between large armies of civilized nations in a very cultivated country and under the various influences of political and personal connections demands more substantial knowledge of men and matters than we may expect from such a man as Suvorov. If we leave aside his affected eccentricity, Suvorov can quite reasonably be compared with Blücher. In both of them, their subjective side as a commander was quite outstanding, but both lacked clear understanding of the objective world, so both needed

---

109. Both Duffy and Jomini have the Austrian government putting pressure on Suvorov regarding the course of action for the liberation of Piedmont. It is reasonable to suppose that this played a role in his action, although it is by no means certain. See Duffy, *Eagles over the Alps*, 80–81; Jomini, 11:309–310. Suvorov, it must be remembered, was in command of an allied army and had to temper his instincts and plans to the allies' stated goals as well as Russia's. Thus, when thinking about means and ends in war, one has to take into account all the players involved, and this might call for a different objective or a different level of effort than one ally is able or willing to make.

advice and guidance. In the circumstances, however highly one ranks Suvorov, it was quite inevitable that the Austrian general staff—and not only the so-called headquarters general staff [quartermaster-general's staff] but also all the generals and other individuals who had a say in such matters—assumed a much more important position in the leadership of the army than is the case under great commanders. It is easy to understand how Suvorov's decisiveness and spirit of enterprise were largely lost in this machinery.

Finally, from among these aggravating circumstances, we must single out the effect of the political element, which had its origin in the difference of views and intentions between the Austrian cabinet and Suvorov. Within a short time, these differences laid the foundations of the discord in this campaign that put an end to the coalition. We do not know very much about exactly what each party did or did not want, but the disunity that arose at this time is a certain fact, and it is understandable that this prevented the war from taking a swift and decisive course.

If we bear all this in mind—after the half-prepared Austrians successfully withstood the first French blow on the Adige and even won a battle against them at Magnano, won a decisive victory on the Adda, and then, as a result of this threefold success, marched triumphantly through all of upper Italy to the foot of the Apennines and the Alps—we cannot possibly be very surprised that the allies thought they had fought and won enough for the time being and wanted to concentrate on harvesting the fruits of their victories by seizing all the citadels and walled cities so they could regard themselves as the masters of all Italy. Although we think it would have been very feasible to expel General Moreau from Italy completely and conquer Genoa, this was still no easy matter; nor have we presented it as such. It would have required great economy of force, something that not everyone is good at, because there are always many concerns standing in its way that can be overcome only by uncommon decisiveness. It is therefore quite understandable that such an operation might seem far too extensive and uncertain to the commander of the allied army (we are deliberately not just talking about General Suvorov here), who might be worried about failing to conquer the country before Macdonald arrived and involved his combat forces in another major battle.

In this mind-set inspired mainly by the Austrian government, it came to pass that the allies' combat forces spread radially outward from Milan to every corner of Lombardy to besiege every citadel, occupy the major cities, threaten the forts on the French border and summon them to surrender, and encourage insurrection across the whole country by their approach. This was supposed to bring about the rapid and complete occupation of the country, which we can therefore regard as the overall objective of their operations after the battle of Cassano.

If, however, the allies had wanted to continue their offensive against Moreau's army itself as far as the Var, they would have had to keep their forces more concentrated, leaving only weak forces observing the citadels and not worrying about popular uprisings; everything in their flanks and rear would have been left alone for the time being.

We regard this alternative of continuing the offensive immediately as the more energetic and more effective measure. But if this is to be anything more than the usual empty rhetoric, it is incumbent on us to present the essential advantage of this course of action.

"Throwing General Moreau out of Italy" is empty rhetoric as soon as it is assumed to mean anything more than the operation itself, for one cannot throw an enemy out of a country as one would throw him out of a house, locking the door behind him. As far as the decisive battle that had to be fought against Macdonald is concerned, General Moreau with 12,000 men behind the Var is of no less value than General Moreau with 12,000 men behind the Bormida. According to our principles, the fact that the Var is some 90 miles further away than Alessandria from the point where the Austrians will have to fight Macdonald is an advantage for Moreau, because then he may be all the more certain that he will not be held up by a small number of troops. Also, when it comes down to it, the Var and the Apennines are certainly not the kind of obstacles that would do much to impede the return of Moreau's army and whose possession could provide any major advantage.

The advantage of continuing the offensive, the real point of chasing Moreau out, must be found in the impact of obtaining yet another victory while doing so.[110] The enemy combat forces that would be destroyed in such a victory, the new shock to the enemy's spirits, the shattering of his confidence, the moral impression made on Macdonald and his army and on the French government and people, the apprehension it would awaken about the next point to be threatened, the worries that would quickly mount everywhere else—these are the reasons that would have crippled the cooperation between

---

110. This brings us back to Clausewitz's point about continuous pressure. See *On War*, book 1, chap. 1, secs. 12–14, and book 1, chap. 2.

Macdonald and Moreau and paved the way to new victories for the allies. Now the French commander could have largely avoided these disadvantages if he had known how to skillfully evade any decisive battle, if he had retreated just as far as Suvorov advanced against him and brought his little army back across the Var intact. Certainly, if he had done this, Suvorov would not have entirely achieved his aim. But such evasion is pretty difficult without having it degenerate into a rout, and in this case, the allied commander still had the option of striking his blow with such weight and energy as to give his opponent's retreat the virtual character of a rout, thus not missing out completely on success in terms of its material and morale effects.

We imagine that this unspectacular result of continuing the offensive may leave many of our readers surprised, frustrated, and annoyed because they have been spoiled by the conventional kind of reasoning and can only be satisfied by the most glaring contrast between the advantages of one course of action and the disadvantages of another. But such critical braggadocio works only by making assertions that are like acts of terrorism, in that they are quite untrue and totally unrealistic but shock the mind like a thunderbolt. We do not present results so that they look good; we present them as they are. Therefore, we have not said that Suvorov should have annihilated his opponent, hurled him into the sea, laid France open, threatened its heartland, and so forth, because that would have been quite unrealistic.

Until now, we have been considering the alternatives as a choice between either subjugating Italy or driving Moreau out of the country. But even if we find it understandable that Suvorov preferred the first of these two objectives, we cannot condone the individual measures he took against Moreau; indeed, we can scarcely understand them. These include Rosenberg's attempted crossing of the Po and the main army's march away to Turin before Moreau had begun his retreat. Even if Suvorov did not want to pursue Moreau all the way to the Var, what could have been more natural than to drive him from the plain by attacking him with concentrated force and thus make besieging the citadels easier! It cannot possibly have been believed that the French army would have been strong enough to defend the full extent of the Bormida and the Po and to make a well-prepared and organized crossing impossible or even at all dangerous.

Some reports say that it was mainly the Austrian government, disinclined to take any further decisive action, that pressured Suvorov into turning toward Turin and making himself master of that fortress.

If we take another overview of the allied allocation of forces in the Italian campaign so far, it reveals:

1. Of the 84,000 men the allies had in Italy, Carinthia, and Carniola originally, 48,000 fought the first battle on the Adige, 12,000 stayed in Venice as a garrison, 15,000 were still on the march, 5,000 were maintaining communications with the Tyrol, and 4,000 were detached to observe the lower Adige.
2. Of the 77,000 men left after the battles on the Adige, 46,000 fought the second battle at Magnano, 4,000 were still on the march, and 27,000 were detached, even though there was not a single fortification to besiege apart from Peschiera, which was invested by a few thousand men. In addition to the 12,000 men they had in Venice and the 4,000 under Klenau, they left another 11,000 on the Adige and outside Peschiera.
3. Of the 92,000 men the allies had after the battle of Magnano and the arrival of the Russians and General Wukassowitsch, 52,000 men advanced for the battle on the Adda, but only 35,000 fought it, since 17,000 Russians were sent to Lecco. The other 40,000 men were divided roughly as follows: 20,000 remained on the Mincio and the Po, 6,000 under Hohenzollern headed for the lower Adda, and 14,000 made up the garrisons in the rear and the sick list, since 52,000 men is the stated strength of those that moved out.
4. Of the 47,000 men remaining to the main army after the battle of Cassano, 32,000 moved to the Po to fight another battle there if necessary, 3,000 were sent toward the Alps and 6,000 toward the Apennines, and 6,000 were left with Hohenzollern outside Milan and Pizzighettone.

Of course, we can find no obvious waste of forces in these figures, especially since we do not know the exact numbers or the precise reasons for some of these detachments, other than that the French garrisons that found themselves behind the allied army after its crossing of the Po and had to be invested amounted to some 20,000 men. But neither can we find in these numbers any great economy of force of the kind we so admire in Bonaparte. He probably could have made do with half as many detachments and struck with three-quarters of his entire force, as he constantly did in 1796, even though simply investing Mantua seemed to require his whole army.

We can see that how much room for maneuver the commander has left here depends on whether he is content to follow the usual rules and leave forces everywhere, as these rules require, or whether he feels the need to fight major battles and consequently keeps his main army constantly concentrated and strong, in which case, by his energy and industry, he will then always find the means to reduce the need for detachments markedly.

In the six weeks from the end of March to mid-May, the allied army's losses in dead, wounded, and sick seem to have come to scarcely 20,000, or a fifth of its original 105,000 men—a modest figure, given that there were three major battles in this period.

Worms
Saarlouis
Mannheim
Neckar river
Heidelberg
Metz
Landau
Philippsburg
Anspach
Heilbronn
Hall
Karlsruhe
Rhine river
Durlach
Nancy
Stuttgart
Donauw
Strasbourg
Kehl
Danube river
Offenburg
Tübingen
Ulm
Augsb
Colmar
Freiburg
Rottweil
Biberach
Iller river
Rhine river
Osterach
Black Forest region
Stockach
Menninge
Schaffhausen
Lake Constance
Kempfe
Lauffenburg
Basel
Constance
Lindau
Bregenz
Brugg
Winterthur
Aare river
Aarau
Zurich
St. Gallen
Rhine river
Besançon
Aarburg
Lake Bieler
Lake Zurich
Feldkirch
Wallenstadt
Lucerne
Lake Lucerne
Glarus
Sargans
Maienfeld
Berne
Lake Neuenburger
Altdorf
Nauders
Thun
Chur
Brienz
Lausanne
Splugen
Glurns
Lake Geneva
St. Gotthard Pass
Maloja Pass
San Bernardino Pass
Rhone river
Nufenen Pass
Geneva
Bellinzona
Chiavenna
Simplon Pass
Lake Maggiore
Lake Como
Great St. Bernard Pass
Lake Garda
Dora river
Sesia river
Como
Bard
Brescia
Little St. Bernard Pass
Ticino river
Milan
Novara
Peschiera
Mont Cenis Pass
Adda river
Oglio river
Mincio river
Chivasso
Turin
Po river
Piacenza
Montgenèvre Pass
Tanaro river
Alessandria
Gap
Col Angel
Parma
Maddalena Pass
Cuneo
Genoa
© Nicholas Murray
Mediterranean Sea

Main Geographical Features

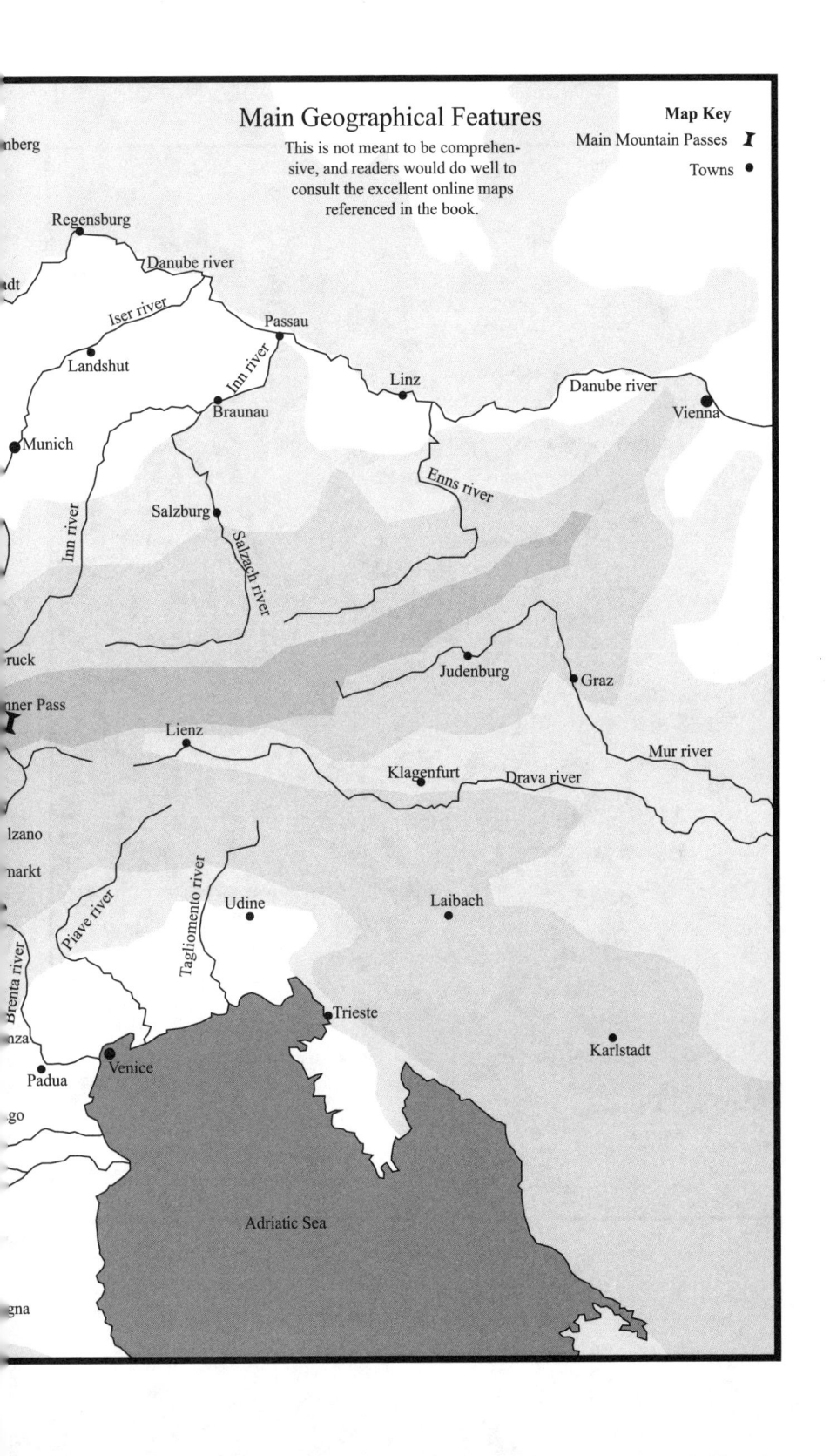

This is not meant to be comprehensive, and readers would do well to consult the excellent online maps referenced in the book.

Map Key
Main Mountain Passes ⛰
Towns ●

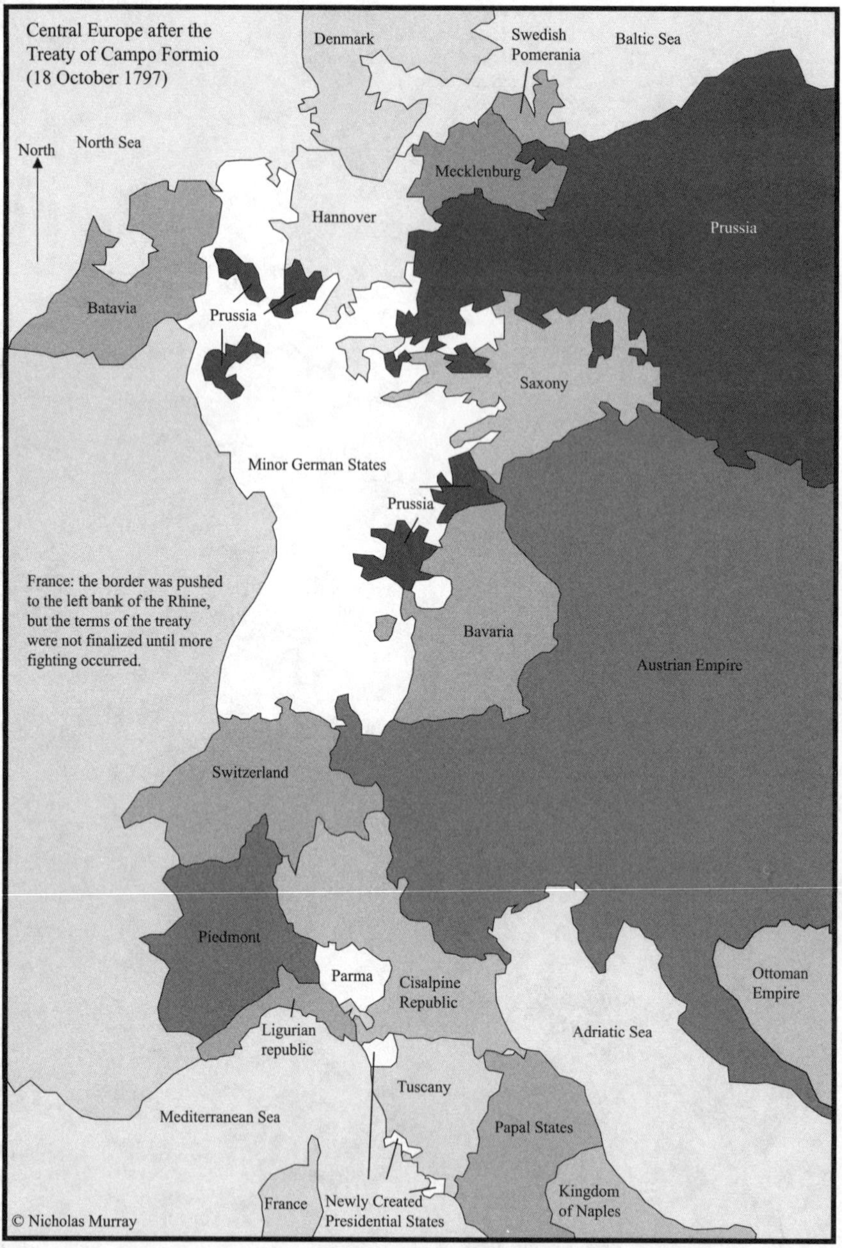
Central Europe after the
Treaty of Campo Formio
(18 October 1797)
North
North Sea
Denmark
Swedish
Pomerania
Baltic Sea
Mecklenburg
Hannover
Prussia
Batavia
Prussia
Saxony
Minor German States
Prussia
France: the border was pushed
to the left bank of the Rhine,
but the terms of the treaty
were not finalized until more
fighting occurred.
Bavaria
Austrian Empire
Switzerland
Piedmont
Parma
Cisalpine
Republic
Ottoman
Empire
Ligurian
republic
Adriatic Sea
Tuscany
Mediterranean Sea
Papal States
Kingdom
of Naples
France
Newly Created
Presidential States
© Nicholas Murray

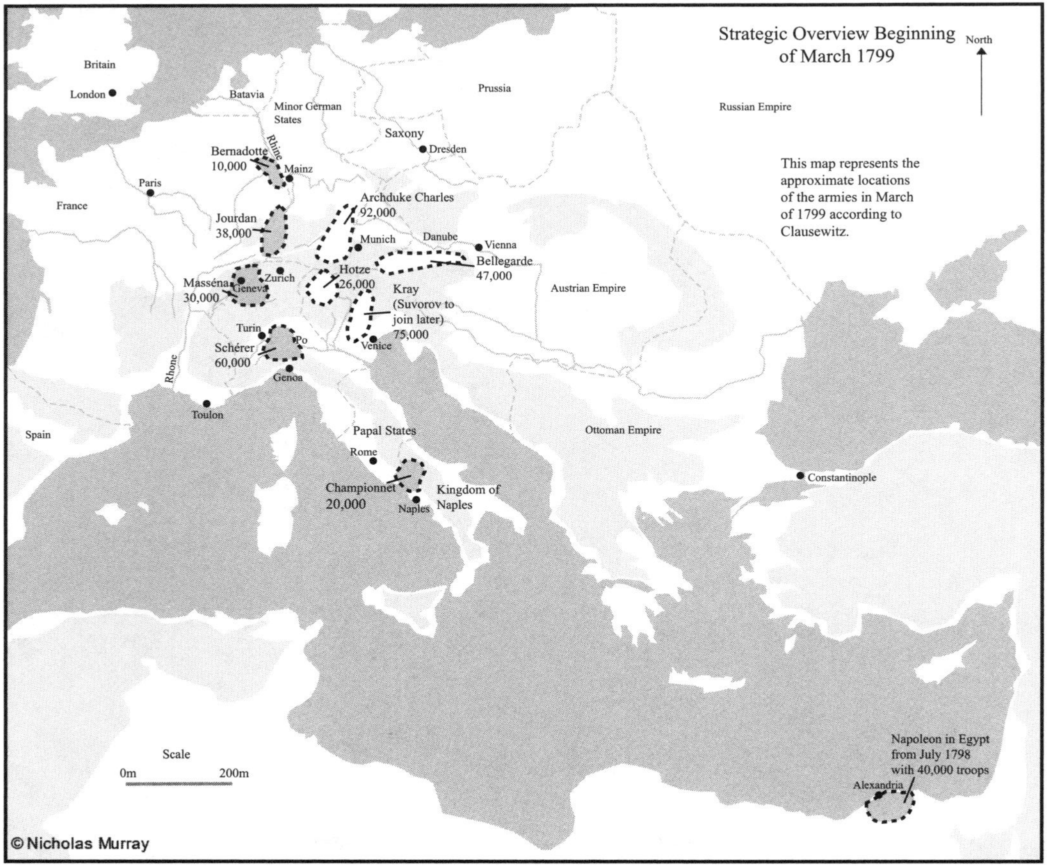
Strategic Overview Beginning of March 1799
North
Russian Empire
This map represents the approximate locations of the armies in March of 1799 according to Clausewitz.
Britain
London
Batavia
Minor German States
Prussia
Saxony
Dresden
Rhine
Bernadotte 10,000
Mainz
Paris
France
Jourdan 38,000
Archduke Charles 92,000
Munich
Danube
Vienna
Bellegarde 47,000
Hotze 26,000
Zurich
Masséna 30,000
Geneva
Kray (Suvorov to join later) 75,000
Austrian Empire
Turin
Po
Schérer 60,000
Venice
Genoa
Rhone
Toulon
Spain
Papal States
Ottoman Empire
Rome
Championnet 20,000
Naples
Kingdom of Naples
Constantinople
Napoleon in Egypt from July 1798 with 40,000 troops
Alexandria
Scale
0m
200m
© Nicholas Murray

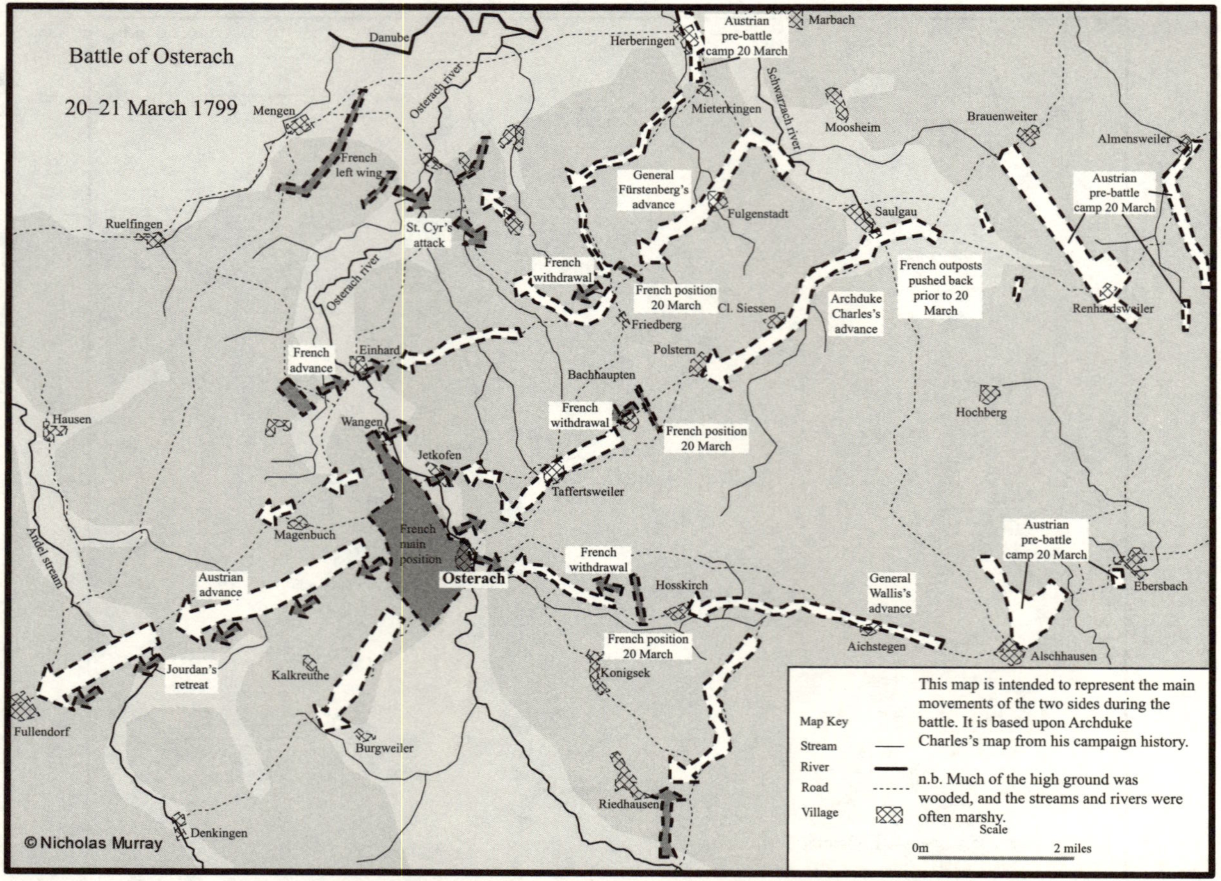
Battle of Osterach
20–21 March 1799
Danube
Mengen
Osterach river
French left wing
Ruelfingen
St. Cyr's attack
Osterach river
French advance
Einhard
Hausen
Wangen
Jetkofen
Magenbuch
French main position
Osterach
Andel stream
Austrian advance
Jourdan's retreat
Kalkreuthe
Fullendorf
Burgweiler
Denkingen
© Nicholas Murray
Herberingen
Austrian pre-battle camp 20 March
Marbach
Schwarzach river
Mieterkingen
Moosheim
General Fürstenberg's advance
Fulgenstadt
French withdrawal
French position 20 March
Friedberg
Cl. Siessen
Bachhaupten
Polstern
French withdrawal
French position 20 March
Taffertsweiler
French withdrawal
Hosskirch
French position 20 March
Konigsek
Riedhausen
Saulgau
French outposts pushed back prior to 20 March
Archduke Charles's advance
Hochberg
Brauenweiter
Almensweiler
Austrian pre-battle camp 20 March
Renhardsweiler
Austrian pre-battle camp 20 March
Ebersbach
General Wallis's advance
Aichstegen
Alschhausen
Map Key
Stream
River
Road
Village
This map is intended to represent the main movements of the two sides during the battle. It is based upon Archduke Charles's map from his campaign history.
n.b. Much of the high ground was wooded, and the streams and rivers were often marshy.
Scale
0m
2 miles

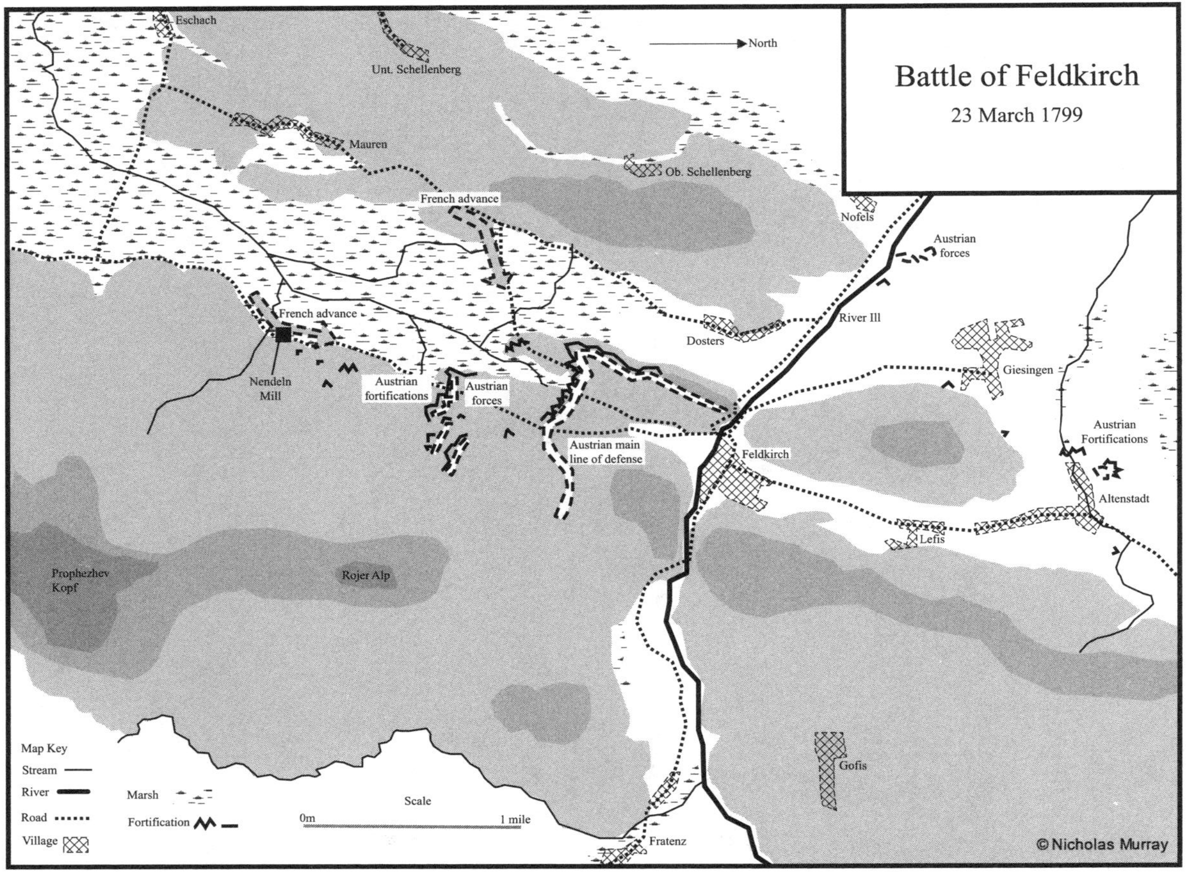
Battle of Feldkirch
23 March 1799
North
Eschach
Unt. Schellenberg
Mauren
Ob. Schellenberg
Nofels
French advance
Austrian forces
River Ill
Dosters
French advance
Giesingen
Nendeln Mill
Austrian fortifications
Austrian forces
Austrian main line of defense
Austrian Fortifications
Feldkirch
Altenstadt
Lefis
Prophezhev Kopf
Rojer Alp
Gofis
Map Key
Stream
River
Road
Village
Marsh
Fortification
Scale
0m
1 mile
Fratenz
© Nicholas Murray

Battle of Taufers
25 March 1799

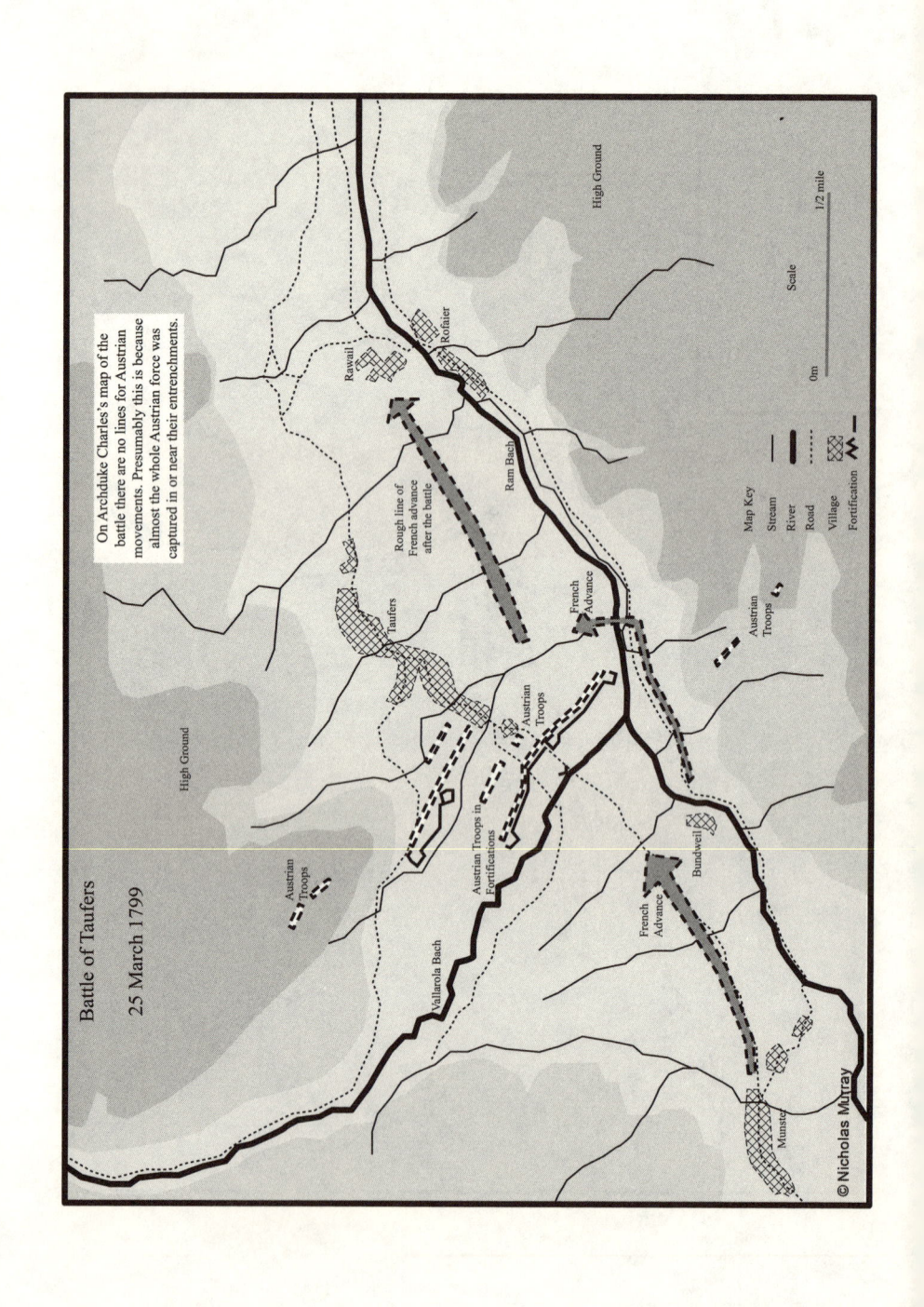

On Archduke Charles's map of the battle there are no lines for Austrian movements. Presumably this is because almost the whole Austrian force was captured in or near their entrenchments.

Map Key
- Stream
- River
- Road
- Village
- Fortification

Scale: 0m — 1/2 mile

Locations: Rawill, Rofaier, Ram Bach, Taufers, Vallarola Bach, Austrian Troops, Austrian Troops in Fortifications, French Advance, Bundweil, Munster, High Ground

© Nicholas Murray

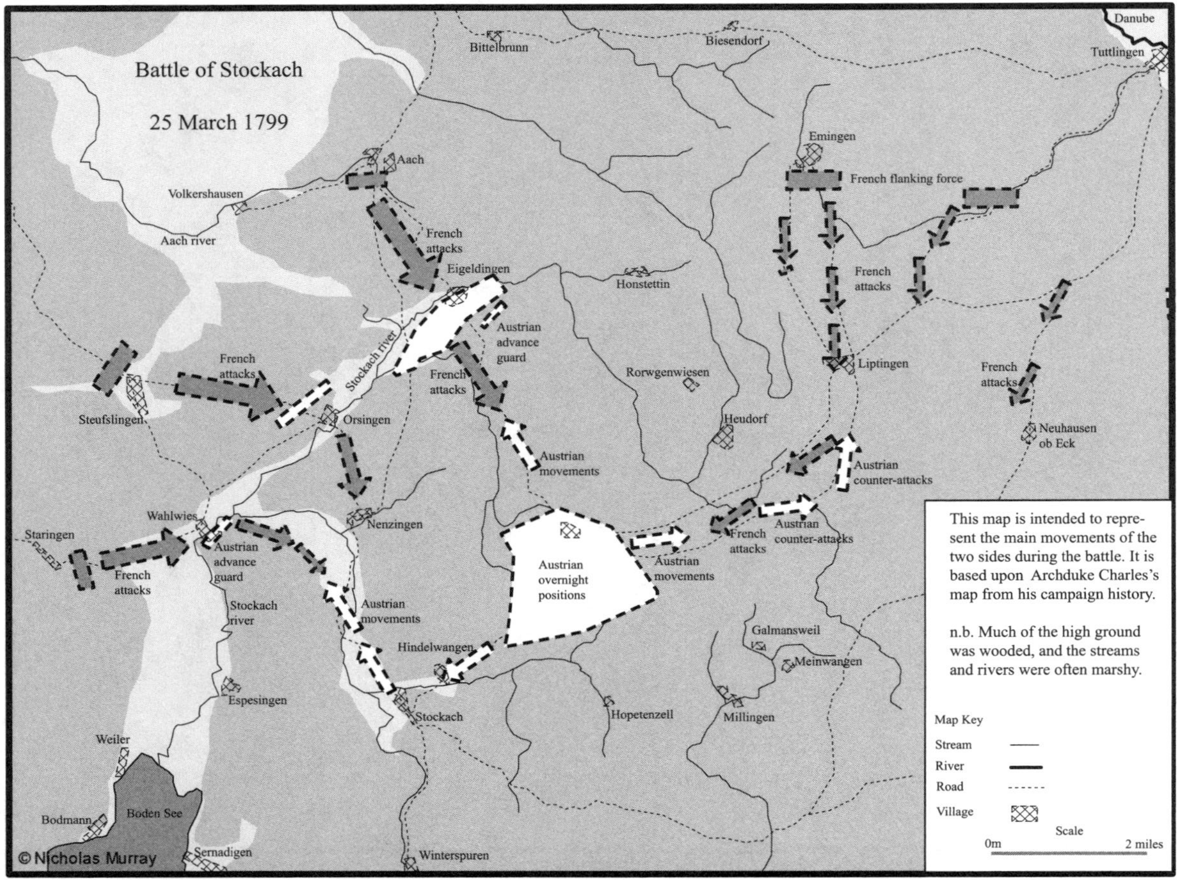

Battle of Stockach
25 March 1799
Danube
Tuttlingen
Bittelbrunn
Biesendorf
Emingen
French flanking force
Aach
Volkershausen
Aach river
French attacks
Eigeldingen
Honstettin
French attacks
Liptingen
French attacks
Neuhausen ob Eck
Austrian advance guard
Stockach river
French attacks
French attacks
Steufslingen
Orsingen
Rorwgenwiesen
Heudorf
Austrian movements
Austrian counter-attacks
Wahlwies
Staringen
Nenzingen
Austrian advance guard
French attacks
Stockach river
Austrian movements
Austrian overnight positions
Austrian movements
French attacks
Austrian counter-attacks
Galmansweil
Meinwangen
Hindelwangen
Espesingen
Stockach
Hopetenzell
Millingen
Weiler
Boden See
Bodmann
Sernadigen
Winterspuren
© Nicholas Murray
This map is intended to represent the main movements of the two sides during the battle. It is based upon Archduke Charles's map from his campaign history.
n.b. Much of the high ground was wooded, and the streams and rivers were often marshy.
Map Key
Stream
River
Road
Village
Scale
0m
2 miles

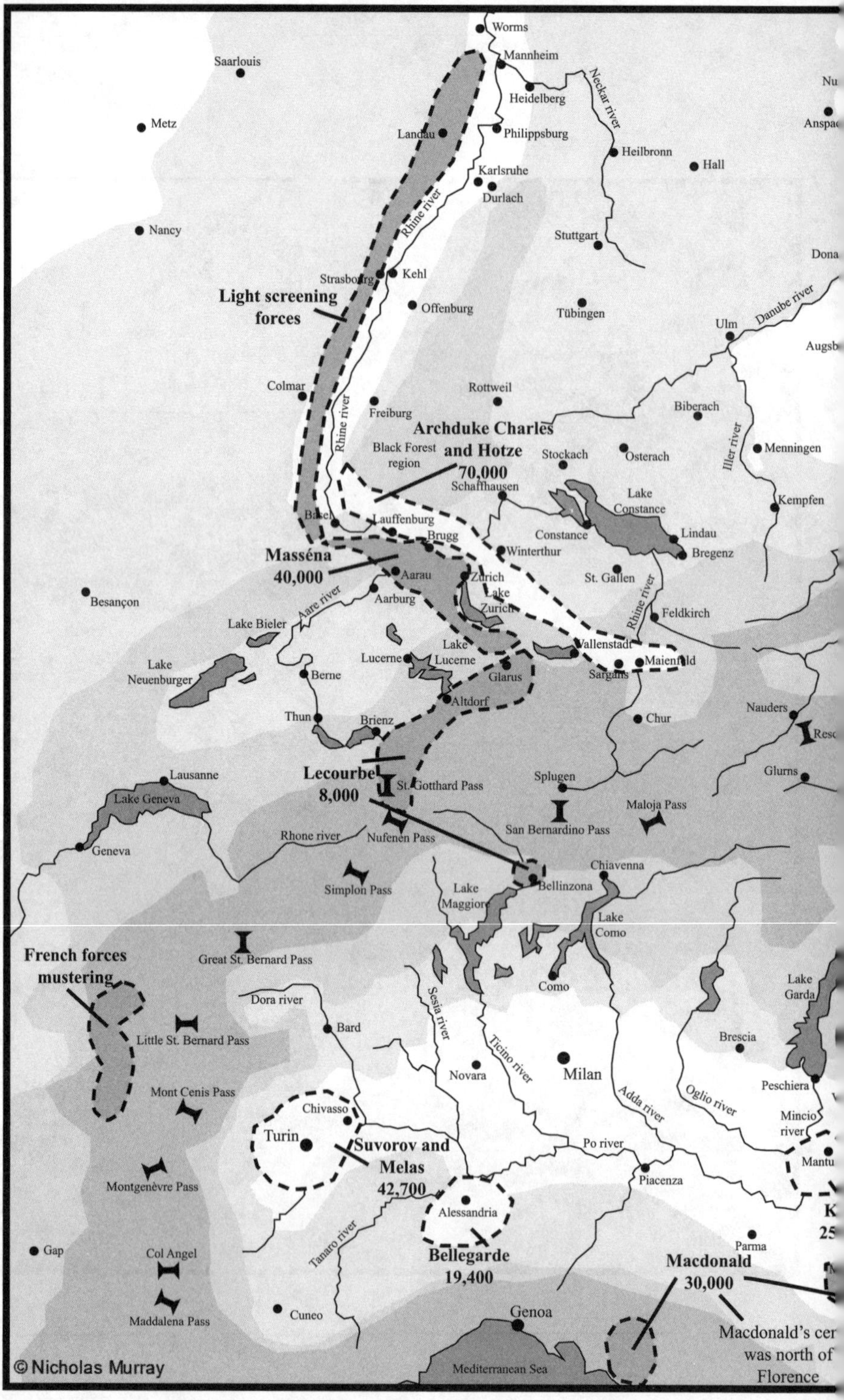

Worms
Mannheim
Saarlouis
Heidelberg
Neckar river
Metz
Landau
Philippsburg
Heilbronn
Hall
Karlsruhe
Durlach
Rhine river
Nancy
Stuttgart
Strasbourg
Kehl
Light screening forces
Offenburg
Tübingen
Ulm
Danube river
Colmar
Rottweil
Biberach
Freiburg
Rhine river
Archduke Charles and Hotze 70,000
Black Forest region
Stockach
Osterach
Iller river
Menningen
Schaffhausen
Lake Constance
Kempfen
Basel
Lauffenburg
Constance
Lindau
Brugg
Bregenz
Masséna 40,000
Winterthur
Aarau
Zurich
St. Gallen
Besançon
Aare river
Aarburg
Lake Zurich
Rhine river
Feldkirch
Lake Bieler
Lake Lucerne
Vallenstadt
Lucerne
Maienfeld
Lake Neuenburger
Berne
Glarus
Sargans
Altdorf
Nauders
Thun
Brienz
Chur
Lecourbe 8,000
Lausanne
St. Gotthard Pass
Splugen
Glurns
Lake Geneva
Maloja Pass
San Bernardino Pass
Rhone river
Nufenen Pass
Geneva
Chiavenna
Simplon Pass
Lake Maggiore
Bellinzona
Lake Como
French forces mustering
Great St. Bernard Pass
Como
Lake Garda
Dora river
Sesia river
Bard
Little St. Bernard Pass
Brescia
Ticino river
Novara
Milan
Mont Cenis Pass
Adda river
Oglio river
Peschiera
Chivasso
Mincio river
Turin
Suvorov and Melas 42,700
Po river
Montgenèvre Pass
Piacenza
Alessandria
Tanaro river
Gap
Col Angel
Bellegarde 19,400
Parma
Macdonald 30,000
Maddalena Pass
Cuneo
Genoa
Mediterranean Sea
© Nicholas Murray

Strategic Situation First Week of June 1799

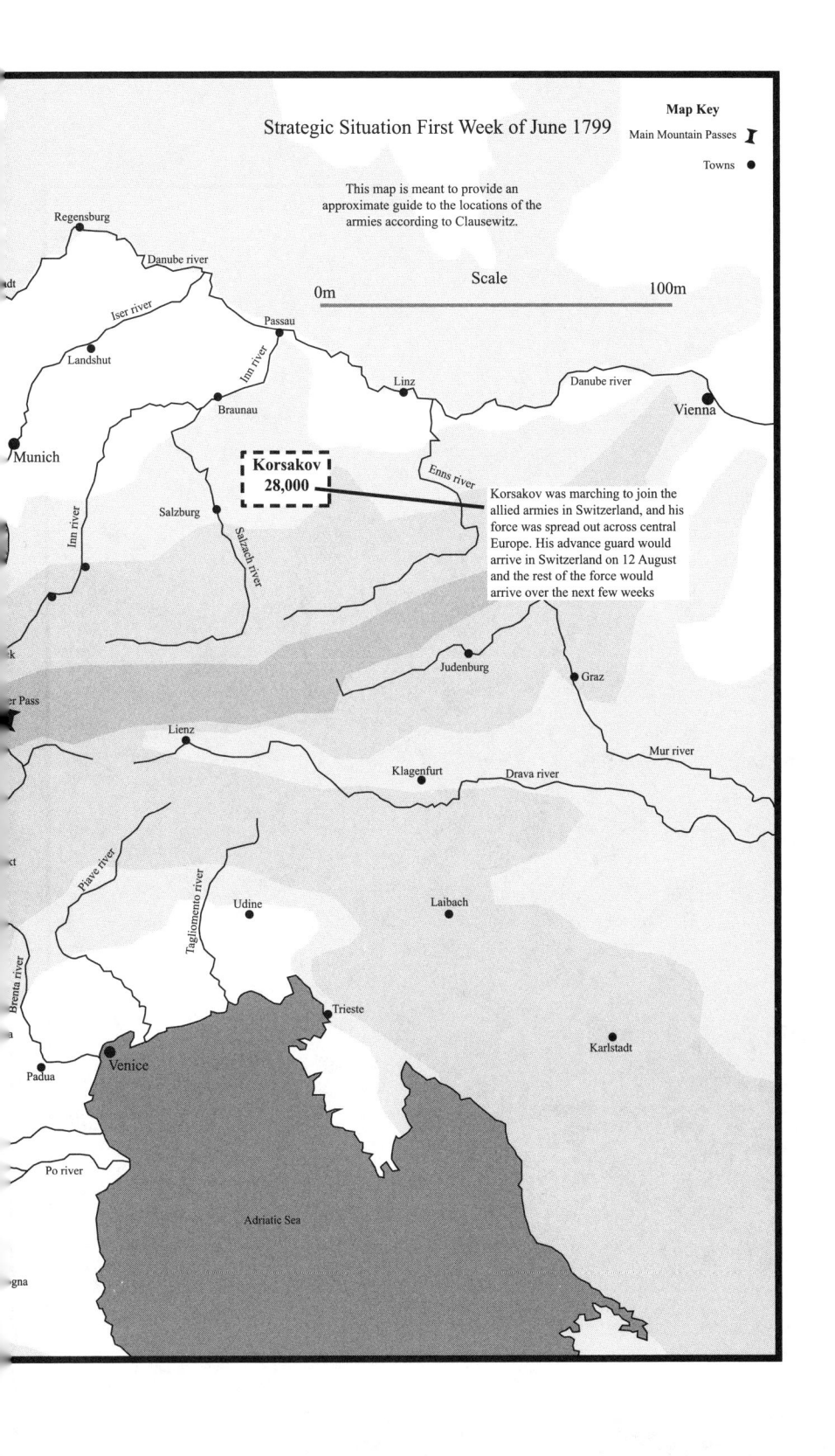

Map Key
Main Mountain Passes ✕
Towns ●

This map is meant to provide an approximate guide to the locations of the armies according to Clausewitz.

Scale
0m — 100m

Towns and features labeled: Regensburg, Danube river, Iser river, Landshut, Passau, Inn river, Braunau, Linz, Danube river, Vienna, Munich, Salzburg, Salzach river, Enns river, Inn river, Pass, Lienz, Judenburg, Graz, Klagenfurt, Drava river, Mur river, Piave river, Tagliomento river, Udine, Laibach, Brenta river, Trieste, Karlstadt, Padua, Venice, Po river, Adriatic Sea

Korsakov 28,000

Korsakov was marching to join the allied armies in Switzerland, and his force was spread out across central Europe. His advance guard would arrive in Switzerland on 12 August and the rest of the force would arrive over the next few weeks

Battle of First Zürich

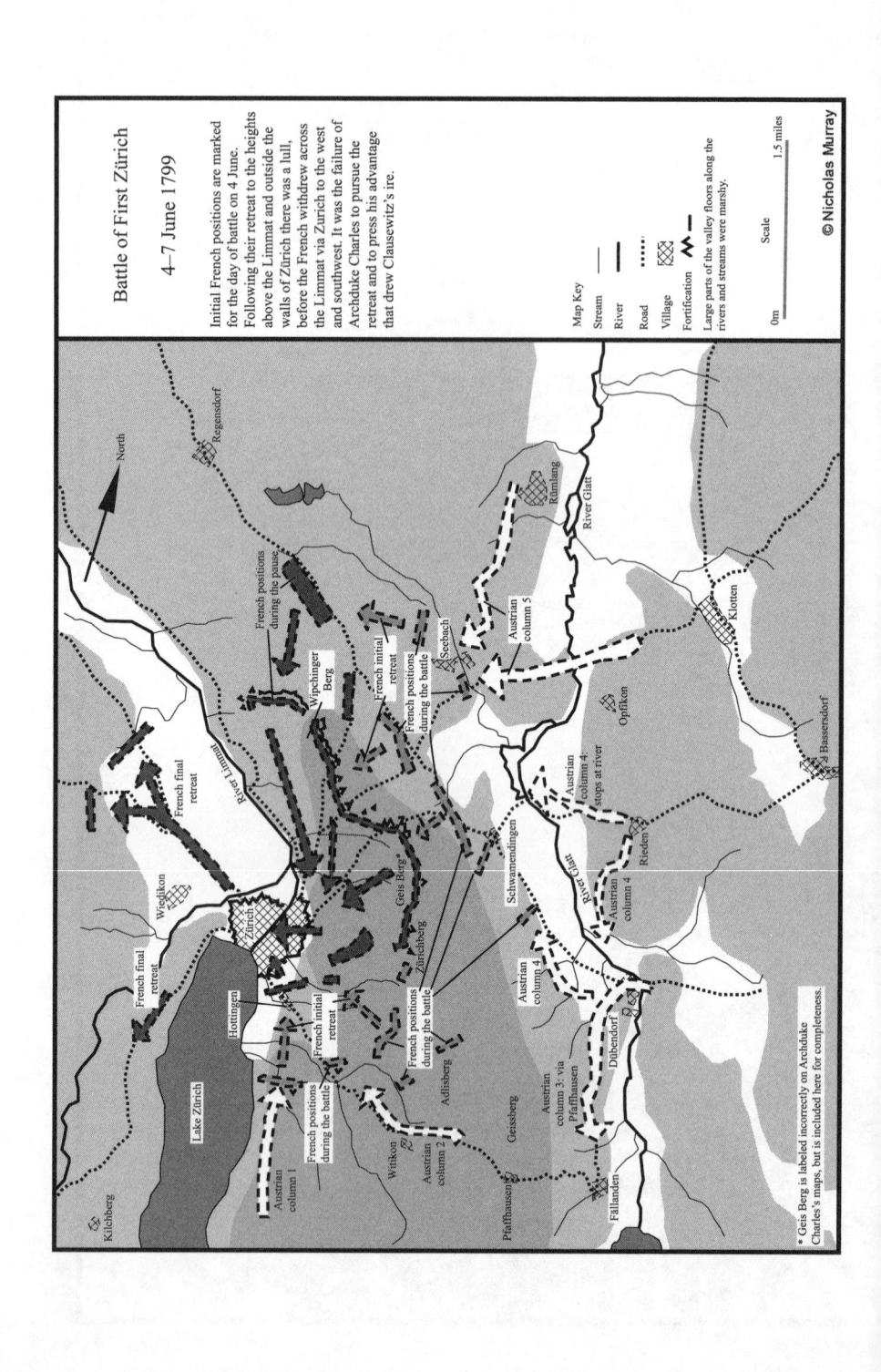

4–7 June 1799

Initial French positions are marked for the day of battle on 4 June. Following their retreat to the heights above the Limmat and outside the walls of Zürich there was a lull, before the French withdrew across the Limmat via Zurich to the west and southwest. It was the failure of Archduke Charles to pursue the retreat and to press his advantage that drew Clausewitz's ire.

Map Key
Stream
River
Road
Village
Fortification

Scale
0m   1.5 miles

© Nicholas Murray

* Geis Berg is labeled incorrectly on Archduke Charles's maps, but is included here for completeness.

Battle of Novi
15 August 1799

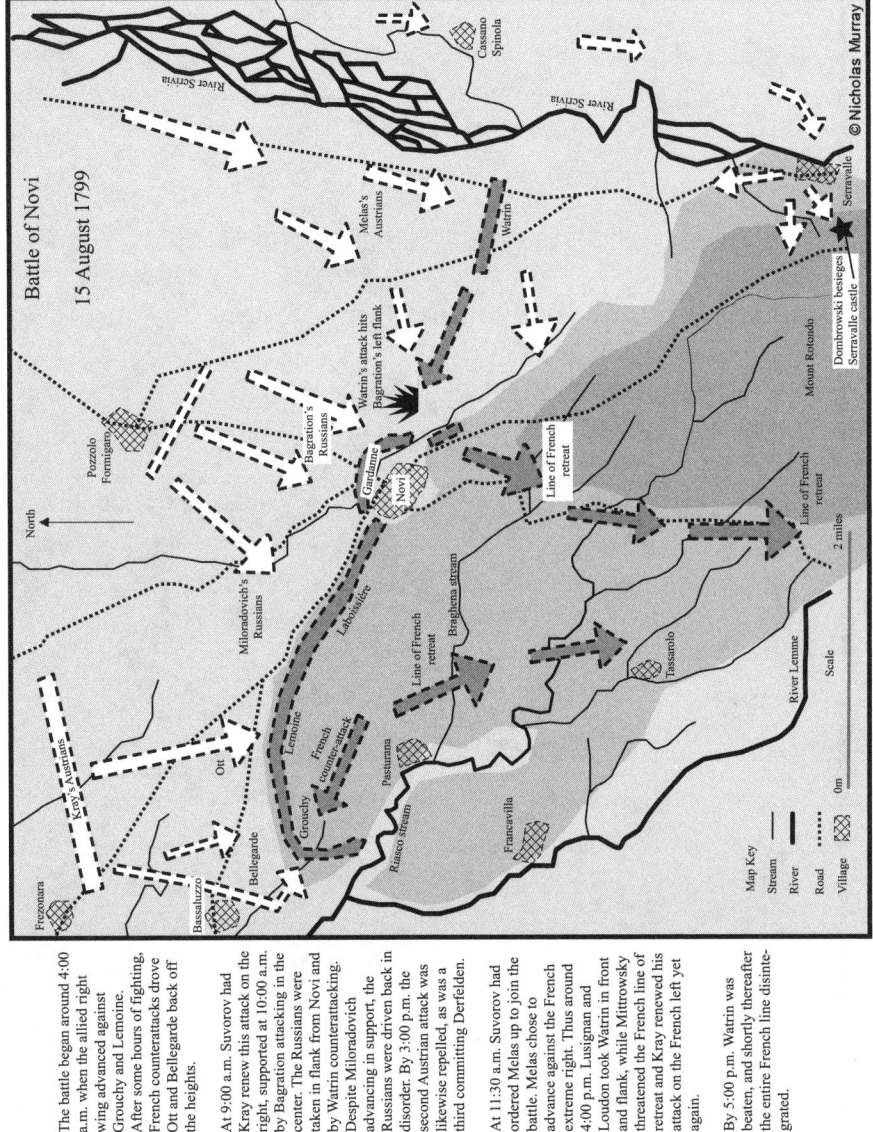

The battle began around 4:00 a.m. when the allied right wing advanced against Grouchy and Lemoine. After some hours of fighting, French counterattacks drove Ott and Bellegarde back off the heights.

At 9:00 a.m. Suvorov had Kray renew this attack on the right, supported at 10:00 a.m. by Bagration attacking in the center. The Russians were taken in flank from Novi and by Watrin counterattacking. Despite Miloradovich advancing in support, the Russians were driven back in disorder. By 3:00 p.m. the second Austrian attack was likewise repelled, as was a third committing Derfelden.

At 11:30 a.m. Suvorov had ordered Melas up to join the battle. Melas chose to advance against the French extreme right. Thus around 4:00 p.m. Lusignan and Loudon took Watrin in front and flank, while Mittrowsky threatened the French line of retreat and Kray renewed his attack on the French left yet again.

By 5:00 p.m. Watrin was beaten, and shortly thereafter the entire French line disintegrated.

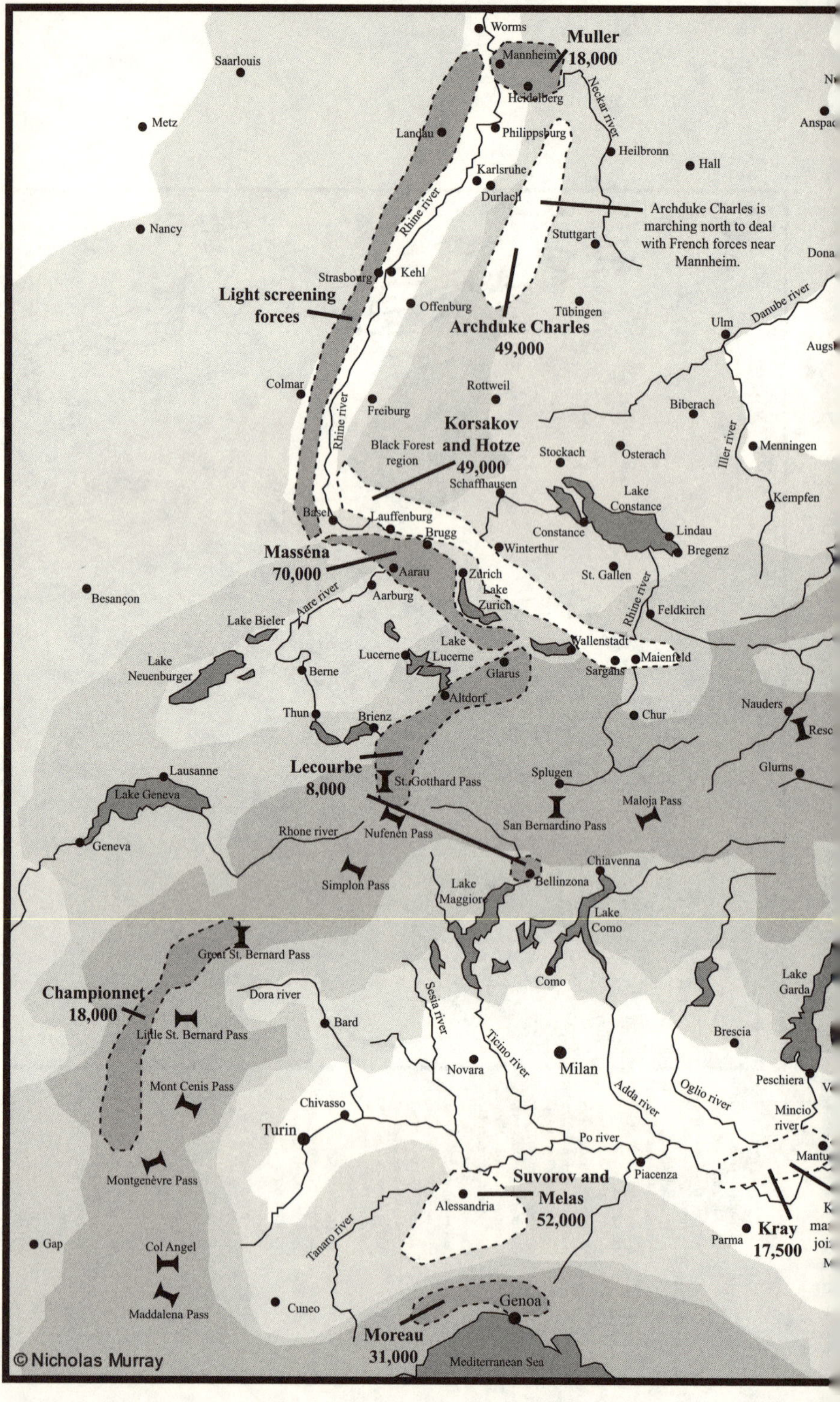
Worms
Muller
18,000
Mannheim
Heidelberg
Neckar river
Saarlouis
Metz
Landau
Philippsburg
Heilbronn
Hall
Karlsruhe
Durlach
Rhine river
Archduke Charles is marching north to deal with French forces near Mannheim.
Nancy
Stuttgart
Strasbourg
Kehl
Light screening forces
Offenburg
Tübingen
Archduke Charles
49,000
Ulm
Danube river
Colmar
Rottweil
Freiburg
Biberach
Iller river
Korsakov and Hotze
49,000
Black Forest region
Stockach
Osterach
Menningen
Schaffhausen
Lake Constance
Kempfen
Basel
Lauffenburg
Brugg
Constance
Lindau
Bregenz
Masséna
70,000
Winterthur
Aarau
Zurich
Lake Zurich
St. Gallen
Besançon
Aare river
Aarburg
Feldkirch
Lake Bieler
Lake Lucerne
Wallenstadt
Lake Neuenburger
Lucerne
Maienfeld
Berne
Glarus
Sargans
Altdorf
Thun
Brienz
Chur
Nauders
Lecourbe
8,000
Lausanne
St. Gotthard Pass
Splugen
Glurns
Lake Geneva
Maloja Pass
San Bernardino Pass
Geneva
Rhone river
Nufenen Pass
Chiavenna
Simplon Pass
Lake Maggiore
Bellinzona
Lake Como
Great St. Bernard Pass
Lake Garda
Championnet
18,000
Dora river
Como
Bard
Little St. Bernard Pass
Sesia river
Ticino river
Brescia
Milan
Novara
Mont Cenis Pass
Adda river
Oglio river
Peschiera
Chivasso
Mincio river
Turin
Po river
Montgenèvre Pass
Piacenza
Suvorov and Melas
52,000
Alessandria
Kray
17,500
Parma
Gap
Col Angel
Tanaro river
Cuneo
Maddalena Pass
Genoa
Moreau
31,000
Mediterranean Sea
© Nicholas Murray

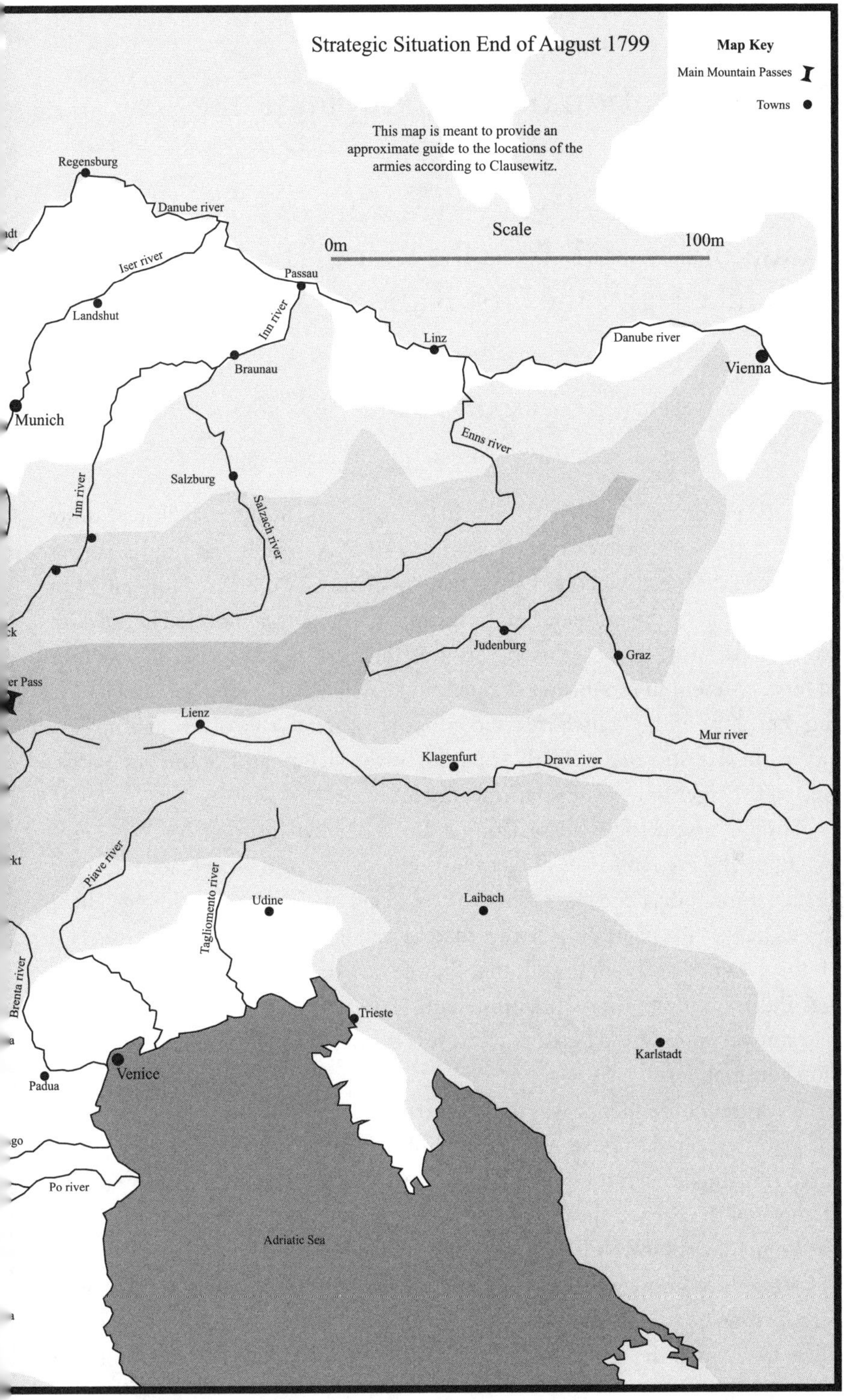
Strategic Situation End of August 1799
Map Key
Main Mountain Passes
Towns
This map is meant to provide an approximate guide to the locations of the armies according to Clausewitz.
Scale
0m
100m
Regensburg
Danube river
Iser river
Passau
Landshut
Inn river
Linz
Danube river
Vienna
Braunau
Munich
Enns river
Salzburg
Inn river
Salzach river
Judenburg
Graz
Lienz
Mur river
Klagenfurt
Drava river
Piave river
Tagliomento river
Udine
Laibach
Brenta river
Trieste
Karlstadt
Venice
Padua
Po river
Adriatic Sea

3. Continuation of the Campaign in Switzerland
The Austrians Drive the French out of Graubündten and Cross the Rhine. The Archduke Fights the First Battle of Zurich.

26 NEW SITUATION IN GERMANY AND SWITZERLAND

After the victory at Stockach, the war in Germany and Switzerland took a quite different turn. This victory was the cause, but of course, it was not like other decisive battles that, whether by the hand of chance or the prevailing talent of a commander or the influence of the moment, untangle a knot tied in the dark womb of destiny. Rather, this victory was the pure expression of the balance of forces present in the theater of operations, which had been obscured by the foggy notions of the French rulers, confused by their vortex of conflicting passions, but was now made clearly apparent by the victory and, at the same time, earned the right to assert its natural consequences.

Three consequences arose from it immediately: Jourdan lost his command, all the French forces in Germany and Switzerland were placed under a single commander, and the offensive was called off for the time being. These three changes may certainly be regarded as major steps to improve results. Of all the generals of the first rank that France had to offer at the time, Jourdan was indisputably the most incompetent. He was replaced by Masséna, who had not yet commanded an army but was probably the foremost of the division commanders.

A further consequence was that the Army of Observation and the Army of the Danube ceased to exist. Along the whole of the Rhine, only an insignificant force remained; everything else was sent to Switzerland, so that the natural strength of the French theater of operations on the Rhine came into play, and the French forces were much more concentrated in Switzerland.

We do not know whether this fundamental change in the distribution of forces emanated from the government or from General Masséna. It is more likely that it was the latter, for in his position, it was natural above all else to ensure successful resistance in Switzerland, for whose defense he had been made responsible.

These changes in the distribution of the French forces, as well as moving up significant reinforcements to the Army of Helvetia, took two to three weeks. Thus, if the archduke had exploited his victory at Stockach with suitable hunger for success, first to quickly chase Jourdan across the Rhine and then to turn against Switzerland without a pause, these changes on his opponent's part could not have taken effect before the new decisive battles the archduke could have forced on him in the first half of April. But we have already seen that, after the battle of Stockach, the archduke let his army remain in the area and rest for a couple of days because he wanted to head for Switzerland. He then concentrated on the 29th to go after Jourdan once more, because Jourdan had halted on the near side of the Black Forest, but he then found it necessary to wait for the arrival of General Starray from Franconia, who by the 27th had only reached Ulm. So the archduke did not get to Donaueschingen until 3 April, a full eight days after the battle, even though this place is not more than one hard day's march away from the battlefield. From Donaueschingen to Schafhausen is just one hard march more. Thus the archduke still could have crossed the Rhine in the first eight days of April and would then have found Masséna still in his previous situation, without having received any reinforcements. But as we shall see, the archduke let the whole of April pass by, so the French commander had plenty of time to reorganize.

27 BELLEGARDE DRIVES DESSOLLES OUT OF THE MÜNSTER VALLEY. THE ACTION AT TAUFERS AND MÜNSTER ON 4 APRIL

Before we present Masséna's and the archduke's actions in more detail, we must describe Bellegarde's attack on General Dessolles.

As we related in the first section, as a result of their successful actions at Nauders and Taufers, Lecourbe had advanced to Nauders and Dessolles to Mals in the Adige valley. Following the encounter at Osterach, Masséna ordered them not to advance any further, so Lecourbe remained at Nauders, while Dessolles withdrew to Taufers and began to entrench himself there.

After the Austrian defeats in those two actions, General Bellegarde had concentrated his army to the extent that he felt his situation allowed in two places: 10,000 men at Latsch, 13,000 at Landeck. This was roughly half his original strength. He had sent 4,000 men under General Wukassowitsch to join the army in Italy. If we assume that he had already lost 10,000 men in battle, that a number of battalions were probably posted in the Montafon valley, that he had not entirely vacated the Sulz valley, and that a few individual battalions were scattered in the passes, we can understand to some degree how it came to be that the main body of the Army of the Tyrol was no larger than this, especially when we consider that sickness and desertion could easily have reduced its effective strength by a couple of thousand men below the original 47,000 reckoned by its strength returns.

In any case, with those 23,000 men, General Bellegarde would have been strong enough to drive the two French generals, who certainly could not have been more than half as strong, out of the Münster valley and the Engadin and thereby, to some extent, restore parity of military success on that side. Alternatively, one could say that, since the two French generals had moved a little way backward and revealed that they were going to pause their offensive for the moment, it might have been in General Bellegarde's interest to delay his own offensive until he could be joined in Switzerland by the archduke, who had meanwhile beaten Jourdan and seemed to be in the process of driving him across the Rhine. But General Bellegarde did neither of these things: he did not wait for the archduke, nor did he seek to obtain a decisive advantage over the French right wing. He did only as much as he felt obliged to do as the defender of the Tyrol and attacked Dessolles at Taufers. According to the Austrian account, this was because Dessolles was entrenching himself there, but obviously it was because Taufers was on Tyrolean soil, whereas Remüs, where Lecourbe was also entrenching, was merely on allied territory.[1]

On 4 April Bellegarde attacked General Dessolles with the 10,000 men he had mustered at Latsch. How strong Dessolles was, or how his forces were deployed, does not emerge clearly from the accounts. He seems to have been reinforced by a detachment of Cisalpine troops since the action at Taufers. In

---

1. Archduke Charles does not mention this. He notes that orders were issued (he does not state when) by the Viennese court and that Suvorov "was keen for the enemy to be driven out of the bordering parts of Switzerland with his advance in the plains of Italy, [and] Bellegarde decided on 22nd April to penetrate into the Engadin." Karl, 1:270–271. As such, it is not clear whether this relates to the attack at Taufers, but it does show that the Austrians were keen on the broader idea of pushing the French back.

anticipation of the need to retreat, his deployment seems to have been organized more to protect that than to put up strong resistance, as he apparently had troops in Münster and in St. Maria.

Bellegarde's main column of eight battalions and three squadrons attacked straight up the road, while small columns of a couple of battalions each advanced along the slopes of the mountain range on each side. A detachment of 300–400 men had been sent the day before through the Drofuger valley via Stilfs against the Wormser Joch to deny General Dessolles a line of retreat there. Dessolles resisted only to the extent necessary to secure his retreat. Since the Austrian detachment sent to the Wormser Joch made the route through that long, narrow defile even more dangerous for him, he decided to turn off at St. Maria through the Tschirfser Joch into the Inn valley and then to descend through the Puschiaver valley into the Veltlin again. This retreat cost him 300 men taken prisoner and apparently the whole of his artillery, since the Austrians captured three guns, fourteen ammunition wagons, and eleven gun carriages whose gun barrels had been either buried or dragged away on sleds.

Bellegarde contented himself with this success, and in this area, both sides now stayed quiet for the time being.

28 THE NEW BALANCE OF FORCES AND POSITIONS OF THE TWO SIDES

During this general lull, Masséna concentrated his forces in Switzerland. On 11 April Vandamme crossed the Aare with a division from the Rhine army, followed by Férino and Soult. We are not in a position to present in detail the individual changes that took place in the French army's strength, organization, and deployment. However, we believe it would not be far from the truth to say that at this time Masséna's former army had some 20,000 men, that roughly 15,000 men had been moved to Switzerland from the former Army of the Danube, and that the reinforcements drawn from the interior by the end of April, supposedly comprising sixteen infantry regiments and thirteen cavalry regiments, totaled some 30,000 men. Masséna's force in Switzerland would thereby have been increased to about 70,000 men, to which Dessolles's brigade with its 4,000–5,000 men may be added. This also tallies with Jomini's order of battle, according to which Masséna had 72,000 men three months later, provided one assumes that Masséna received as many reinforcements during June as he had lost in those three months.[2]

This force was deployed as follows:

Right wing:
    Dessolles's division in the Veltlin
    Lecourbe in the Engadin
    Ménard in the Rhine valley above Feldkirch
    Lorge on the Rhine below Feldkirch as far as Lake Constance

Center:
    Oudinot, Vandamme, and Tharreau on the Rhine between Lake Constance and the Aar
    Soult in reserve
    Klein with the cavalry reserve behind the center

Left wing:
    Souham in Basel
    Legrand in Breisach and Kehl
    Galland in Mannheim

As well as these, a division under General Nouvion was in the Swiss interior to intimidate the locals; another under Xaintrailles had been sent to Wallis to disperse the insurrection there.

In addition, Jomini tells us that General Baraguey-d'Hilliers was in command in Mainz and General Dufour in the newly gained provinces on the left bank of the Rhine.[3] That as good as tells us that there was another small corps in these areas besides the Mainz garrison. Jomini gives the total as around 100,000 men, excluding Dessolles, which likewise tallies with our account above, since we must naturally count Souham in with the troops in Switzerland, and Legrand, Galland, Baraguey-d'Hilliers, and Dufour certainly had no more than 30,000 men.

Throughout this calculation we have omitted the allied Swiss troops, partly because there were only 12,000 of them, most of whom were cursed with such poor morale that little assistance could be expected from them, and partly because the Austrians also had some Swiss formations in their army whose

2. See the chart in Jomini, 12:60–61.
3. Jomini, 11:211–214.

strengths we cannot estimate precisely and which, being well motivated, would have pretty much balanced out their counterparts.

If we group the 70,000 men of the French army in Switzerland according to their main missions, about 12,000 men under Dessolles and Lecourbe may be regarded as detached against Bellegarde, 12,000 were in a cordon deployment 45 miles long from Chur to Lake Constance to defend the Rhine against Hotze's corps and some of Bellegarde's troops, 28,000 were concentrated between Lake Constance and the Aar to oppose the Austrian main army if it crossed the Rhine, about 12,000 were on the far side of the Aar to observe the Rhine there, and 10,000 were in the canton of Wallis and the rest of Switzerland, neutralized by the inhabitants.

From this it emerges that, even if General Masséna could add some of his other troops to his center through maneuvers leading up to a battle, still, hardly more than 35,000–36,000 men could come into action for a major blow against the archduke.

The full extent of the line from the Adda valley to Basel was some 180 miles long.

Let us turn now to the Austrians. Here we find ourselves in the kind of awkward situation that often arises in military histories written from a strategic point of view when we pay more attention to strength returns: namely, that a significant portion of the combat forces suddenly disappears from the account, and we are unable to see where it went. This is something quite normal for the Austrians and especially for their commander-author the archduke.

Those same three armies that the archduke lists most precisely as having 92,000, 26,000, and 47,000 men at the start of the campaign are supposedly only 118,000 strong by the end of March, according to his passing remark.[4] If we estimate the losses in the Tyrol, Graubündten, and the encounters at Osterach and Stockach at roughly 25,000 men dead, wounded, and prisoners, as revealed by the individual accounts, and if we deduct the 5,000 men of Wukassowitsch's corps, there are no fewer than 17,000 men missing. To assume these all went absent through sickness and desertion in the space of five weeks would be very unusual, to say the least. We know of no other way to explain this contradiction than to assume that the archduke did not include individual detachments like Strauch's brigade on the extreme left flank and perhaps a detachment left in the Mannheim area, as well as individual garrisons in the

---

4. **Clausewitz** notes: "Vol. 1, pp 253 and 256." This is Karl, 1:253–256.

army's rear. We are all the more compelled to think this because he reckons the corps of eighteen battalions and sixty-four squadrons left behind the Black Forest under Starray at only 20,000 men, whereas, according to the strengths the archduke himself assumed at the start of the campaign, it must have had at least 30,000, and it is quite impossible that it could have lost a full third in action and to sickness. It also emerges in some accounts that the Austrians patrolled as far as Frankfurt, which naturally could not have happened unless Starray dedicated a corps of several thousand men to do so.[5]

Furthermore, we find that the first two armies, which the archduke seems to take to be just 68,000 combined, still had some 70,000 men six weeks later after losing several thousand in action, without any mention of them receiving reinforcements.[6]

Even if this situation compels us to assume the Austrian army's total strength at 10,000 more, many of the wounded would have returned to the ranks, so this is still a loss of 10,000 sick and deserters.[7]

We regard this army's rapid melting away from 165,000 men to 128,000 within five weeks as a consequence of its own characteristics. Its hastily created formations with few officers and even fewer good ones, the disproportionately large battalions and cavalry regiments that are, in a way, intrinsically wasteful of men, and the Cossack-style character of its Slavonian units are all reasons why the Austrian army of this period must be considered a much less cohesive and stable mass than the French army.

If we go by the archduke's account, the 118,000 Austrians facing the 100,000 French were divided roughly so that 30,000 were in the Tyrol, 28,000 in Vorarlberg, 40,000 under the archduke between Lake Constance and the Rhine, and 20,000 under Starray toward the Black Forest and Alsace.

From this, it seems to follow that if the archduke had turned toward Switzerland, he could not have done so with any marked superiority, and he would

---

5. For a list of the archduke's forces, see the chart in Jomini, 12:60–61.

6. To further confuse matters, a letter (156) from Count Tolstoy to General Suvorov on 6 May (it is not clear whether this is the Julian or Gregorian calendar, but the chronological sequence of the letters indicates that it is probably Gregorian) claims that the strength of the archduke's army, including Bellegarde's forces, is 90,000 men. See Milyutin, *Geschichte des Krieges Russlands*, 1:604.

7. For an in-depth look at the issue of desertion in old-regime armies, see Ilya Berkovich, *Motivation in War: The Experience of Common Soldiers in Old-Regime Europe* (Cambridge: Cambridge University Press, 2017), 55–94.

have needed very complex combinations merely to unite south of Lake Constance with 10,000–12,000 of Hotze's 28,000 men. The archduke indisputably saw the matter this way too, and all the disapproval he voices of the Austrians, the Aulic Council, Bellegarde, and himself is perhaps only half serious, since it is blurred by such general expressions of criticism intermingled with excuses that we must thoroughly doubt how strongly he held this view.[8]

We estimated Masséna's army at about 105,000 men, including Dessolles. But this does not mean the Austrians outnumber the French by only 13,000; rather, if we deduct from the latter the 30,000 men on the lower Rhine and the 5,000 in the Swiss interior, as we naturally must do, the Austrians outnumber them by 48,000—in other words, they are almost twice as strong. The French would reach this strength only gradually, as the divisions from the Rhine and the reinforcements from the interior arrived. But of course, this Austrian superiority cannot be brought into play while 20,000 men are left standing in and behind the Black Forest with nothing to do, when a body of 2,000 horse would have been entirely sufficient for the time being, and while that superiority is almost threefold on secondary fronts like the Tyrol and Vorarlberg, as a result of which it is almost absent on the main front. In this situation, the Austrian army appears to us like a weary giant who stretches out his great hulking limbs far from his body but lacks the resolve to move even one of them powerfully, let alone all at the same time.

How much of the blame for this lethargy and clumsiness attaches to the archduke and how much to the Aulic Council we do not care to judge. But if we ignore the force in the Tyrol, the archduke must still remain answerable to criticism for the division of the rest of the combat forces, unless the Aulic Council's original orders prove that he was instructed to leave 28,000 men in Vorarlberg and 20,000 behind the Black Forest.[9]

We are dwelling for a moment on this division of the Austrian forces because it is obviously the main reason why the archduke does not immediately renew his offensive with new heart and urgent desire. After the battle of Stockach, instead of having himself a ball—concentrating his forces and using his great numerical superiority to crush and smash General Masséna, as any general who loved major battles would have done—all the archduke sees in the offensive against Masséna is another miserable task of doubtful outcome

8. Karl, 1:265–267.
9. Karl, 1:265–267.

in which the fresh laurels of Stockach could easily wither and die. We are by no means sure that, besides the archduke's erroneous view, the cause of this division of forces was not a deliberate attempt to weaken his main body and thus limit the scale of the task he could accomplish.

The reasons the archduke offers for his six weeks of continued inaction are incomplete supply arrangements; his own illness, which obliged him to hand over command to Wallis for a while (he does not say how long); the long uncertainty about whether the French Army of the Danube might go on the offensive again, given the reinforcements joining it on the Rhine from the Low Countries; the Vienna court's concern that an operation against Switzerland below Lake Constance would expose the Tyrol and Vorarlberg, making it preferable to operate from there against Graubündten; later on, the intention to wait for the 40,000 Russians under Korsakov who were on the march and destined for Swabia but could not arrive before July; Bellegarde's difficulty surviving with a substantial body of troops in the high mountains of Graubündten; the prevalent lack of indispensable necessities in the army in the Tyrol, because it had been considerably expanded right before the war, and which still prevented it acting with the whole of its force; lack of unity of command (insofar as the commander of the army in the Tyrol was completely independent, and even Hotze seems to have been not so much under the archduke's orders as under his general guidance); and failure to reach quick agreement among the commanders.[10] While the archduke is listing these excuses

---

10. To understand Clausewitz's criticism, it is worth quoting the archduke at length: "The Austrians did not exploit the overwhelming advantage of their situation and spent the entire month of April in inaction. . . . After Jourdan's retreat was complete, the Austrian army had turned towards the Swiss border. The archduke decided on the 10th April for the start of an operation in the direction of Zurich. . . . Meanwhile, the victualling commissioner declared that it was impossible to get in place the necessary stores of food at the moment of the imminent move. The mentality then ruling this important branch of military administration did not fit in with that of the new system of warfare. . . . [H]owever other causes hindered the course of the victorious Austrian arms. The archduke fell ill and transferred the command to general of artillery Wallis. . . . [T]he Viennese court found an operation into Switzerland below Lake Constance as too bold, repeatedly recommending that the Tyrol and the Vorarlberg were not to be exposed and expressly stated that the main operation had to be directed from there to Graubünden. Later on the arrival of 40,000 Russians who, however, were only able to reach the Rhine in July, was to be awaited in order to break out of Swabia into Switzerland with more security for Germany. In this manner several obstacles gradually

Continuation of the Campaign in Switzerland 251

for indecision, he does not refrain from refuting them himself and then says in conclusion:

> The commanders in Swabia and the Tyrol, with their very superior forces, were both impotent. In both of them their conviction of the need to act and of the possibility of doing so struggled with the obstacles surrounding them. Appalled at their own involuntary inaction, they themselves *sought to magnify these problems as a means of avoiding admitting that they had stayed immobile when they should and could have acted.* Neither wanted to start an offensive operation without being sure of the other's active cooperation; and yet each was strong enough to have operated independently. If only one of them had dipped his toe in the water,[11] the other would not have stayed behind. But there arose between them an extensive correspondence—queries, exchange of proposed plans, brief negotiations—of the kind that has never produced a definite result for as long as war has been waged, and had not the slightest chance of doing so here, given the great distance between their headquarters.[12]

While this confession does not justify the Austrians' inactivity, it does at least explain it. Indeed, it explains their entire conduct of the rest of the campaign, not so much through the objective causes it lists as through the insight the author allows us into the commander. It seems that, in addition to the erroneous views that crippled the momentum of the archduke's own operations, at that time a kind of malady of indecision and ill feeling had weakened his resolve.

This is why the time up to the middle of April passes by completely unexploited when the Austrians were so very superior not only in numbers but also in the situation, allowing the French to be reinforced daily up until May. Thus, it is no wonder that when the operation finally did start under self-inflicted

---

occurred, draining the archduke's energy." Karl, 1:265–267. Thus, there were multiple excuses, and Clausewitz is not being unduly harsh here.

11. In the original, this is: "*Hatte nur einer das Eis gebrochen*" [if only one of them had broken the ice]. However, we believe that our interpretation better fits the contextual intent.

12. Karl, 1:269.

handicaps, it progressed laboriously and with difficulty to dubious and meager results.[13]

On 5 and 6 April the archduke returned from Donaueschingen to quarters between Engen and Stockach, with his advance guard at Singen. He wanted to begin his operation against Masséna on the 10th, but his commissariat advised against it.[14] He therefore contented himself with driving away the French outposts from the left bank of the Rhine at the bridges at Schafhausen, Petershausen (Constance), and Eglisau on the 13th, 14th, and 17th. During this action, the beautiful bridge at Schafhausen was burned down by the French.

Prompted by Suvorov's march to the Oglio, General Bellegarde also tried to start tentative[15] operations against the French right wing on 22 April, but a fresh snowfall on the 21st obliged him to countermand the orders he had already issued. Because of this, most of a detachment of one regular battalion and six companies of Tyrolean militia riflemen [*Landesschützen*] was lost, as they had already begun their march and did not receive the counterorder. They had set off from Yssel in the Paznauner valley (a western tributary valley of the Inn), climbed over the Fimpenberg down into the Engadin, and fallen unexpectedly upon the French cantonments at Remüs. Twice they took this place, and twice they were driven out again. Naturally, this episode ended with French troops rushing up from all directions, overwhelming the two battalions, and taking most of them prisoner. Bellegarde's operations were now suspended for another eight days.

13. This brings us back to Clausewitz's point about the application of continuous pressure. See *On War*, book 1, chap. 1, secs. 12–14, and book 1, chap. 2.

14. The Austrian general staff was originally the quartermaster general's staff, and it seems that logistical considerations dominated Austrian thinking. Part of the problem was that local requisitions could cause rising prices, which meant that obtaining local goods could be expensive and unpredictable. For example, the prices of corn, rye, barley, butter, and lard all increased, sometimes by as much as 40 to 50 percent, over the first year of war in Bregenz (near Lake Constance). E. J. Zwirner, *Die Kriegerischen Ereignisse in Vorarlberg zu Beginn des Zweiten Koalitionskriegs 1799* (Feldkirch: Druck von L. Sausgruber, 1912), 103.

15. **Clausewitz** notes: "Politisch-militärische Geschichte des merkwürdigen Feldzugs von 1799, vom Freiherrn Seida von Landensberg, p136." This is Franz Eugen Joseph Anton von Seida und Landensberg, *Politisch-militärische Geschichte des merkwürdigen Feldzugs von 1799* (Stettin, 1801), 136, https://books.google.com.

29 BELLEGARDE DRIVES LECOURBE OUT OF THE ENGADIN

Now we arrive at the actual period of the Austrian operation. But unlike what we are accustomed to from Bonaparte when he is intent on a decisive battle, this operation is not a simultaneous effort by all forces toward a common aim but individual operations against individual places, and even then, with only a portion of the forces available. It is as though the Austrians were generally content with their situation and it was merely a matter of maneuvering to become somewhat better organized or to tidy things up here or there—in short, the kind of operation undertaken when there is no prospect of a decisive battle. But did the Austrians really care to seek such a battle? We dare not say so for sure, but we may well maintain that it was a major strategic sin if they did not. The numerical superiority they still had in Switzerland, the progress of the allied army in Italy to the foot of the Cottian Alps, the scattered deployment of the French combat forces in Switzerland, and the hostile anti-French attitude of its inhabitants, who had taken up arms against them in many places, were such strong reasons for a decisive attack or, rather, were such favorable opportunities to let the very reason for the war itself take effect [i.e., the temporary superiority of forces the coalition could muster], that we can regard this omission as the most important reason why this Second Coalition also had a poor outcome.[16]

Thus, it was not the archduke and Bellegarde who seized their swords with both hands to attack their opponent; for the time being, it was just Bellegarde and Hotze. Nor did the entire forces of both these generals participate, but again, only part of them. It is their operations we deal with first.

On 30 April Bellegarde finally marched out to drive General Lecourbe from the Engadin.

---

16. Both Clausewitz and Jomini argue that a concentration of force is necessary to achieve decisive results, a concept that is so well known as to be almost a cliché. The subject repeatedly shows up in their works, far too frequently to cite. A simple Internet search demonstrates the point.

The Action at Remüs on 30 April

Lecourbe had entrenched himself behind Remüs on one of the lower foothills that join the great mountain ridge (the Fimpenberg) to the left bank of the Inn. The Varana stream (Ramoschbach) and the villages of Manos and Remüs were to his front. Thus, the right of the position rested on the Inn, whose left bank strongly dominated its right at this point; the left of the position rested on the high ridge. To counter the inevitable outflanking maneuvers, the adjacent passes on both sides of the Inn valley were blocked with abatis or otherwise rendered impassable and occupied by a few infantry. In addition, some reserves were stationed in the rear in the Inn valley itself; that is, Lecourbe was echeloned, as the French call it.

This seems to have been the fairly typical deployment adopted by the French in such cases, and in fact, we cannot suggest a better one. In this way, the very short front of the position could be made quite strong, any outflanking through the passes would be discovered soon enough and held up long enough to respond suitably in the valley, and the reserves posted in the rear (the echelons) provided the best means of opposing the outflanking enemy early on or even taking him between two fires.

Bellegarde arranged his attack in eight columns, strictly speaking.[17] He advanced with nine battalions in the valley itself; six of them went directly up the road, and two small columns advanced on its right and left—one on the mountain slope, and the other on the right bank of the Inn. These two flank columns were intended to directly outflank the obstacles found in front.

General Haddick[18] advanced from the Münster valley with seven battalions likewise in three columns over the high ridge into the Inn valley. He crossed the Schärljoch with four and a half battalions against Tarap and Schuls, one battalion to his right moved over the Rosenkopf to the bridge at Blattamoda, and one and a half battalions on the left moved over the Tschirfser Joch against Zernetz.

---

17. After the earlier talk about the need for concentration, we again find the Austrians marching in multiple columns, per Austrian army regulations. See chapter 1, note 78, of this volume.

18. Karl Jospeh Haddick (1756–1800) had a distinguished record as a regimental commander in the Austrian army. He was mortally wounded at the battle of Margeno in 1800.

Besides these six columns, three battalions remained at St. Maria observing the Wormser Joch; they were supposed to follow the column through the Tschirfser Joch later. Finally, on the extreme right flank, one battalion moved from Yschyl in the Paznaun valley back over the Fimpenberg, to turn the position's left flank.

The outcome of these dispositions was:

1. Bellegarde himself gradually took the forward ravines held by the French outposts, not without some effort, and drove the French out of Remüs and from the left bank of the Varana, but his assaults against their main position were in vain. The battalion arriving over the Fimpenberg did appear on the enemy's left flank but was too weak to break through. Thus the day passed and nightfall brought the action here to a close.

2. General Haddick had great difficulty on the snow- and ice-covered paths. The French had not limited themselves to establishing just one outpost in the strongest part of the passes but had set up a whole series of them, one behind the other. Since the nature of the terrain made each of these outposts very strong, the Austrians could take them only by outflanking maneuvers, each of which cost them much time and effort. For some of these outflanking maneuvers, the Austrians used crampons to move across the glaciers, and the columns were provided with mountain guns. The French also had a few guns in their high defensive positions. In this way, the French outposts' resistance in their successive positions lasted so long that although General Haddick had marched through the night and attacked the first French outpost at 4:00 a.m., he was unable to participate in the attack on Remüs on the 30th. Apparently, he only arrived at Schuls on the Inn at nightfall, where the French then destroyed the bridge. So, for the time being, their main body's retreat from Remüs was indeed threatened but not cut off.

3. General Haddick's left column, which was moving through the Tschirfser Joch against Zernetz, was attacked and defeated by the French outpost there, with the loss of 500 prisoners. It is unknown whether this involved just the one and a half battalions that took this route first or whether the three from St. Maria fought as well. We must assume they did, since in his report, Masséna says this column was five battalions

strong; the number of prisoners, which included Lieutenant Colonel Prince von Ligne, also makes it likely. On the other hand, it is 25 miles from St. Maria to Zernetz, so it is inconceivable that the three battalions posted there to observe the Wormser Joch could have advanced as far as Zernetz. It therefore seems as though this last attack was more of a demonstration and that Colonel Weissenwolf, who was in command, brought only his advance guard into contact with the enemy and left it rather too exposed in doing so.

Despite the day's defensive action turning out so well for the French, General Lecourbe must have thought it unfeasible to remain in his position, either on general grounds or because of some particular local disadvantages we do not know about. He began his retreat at midnight and continued as far as Süss in the vicinity of Zernetz. General Haddick's appearance at Schuls cannot be regarded as sufficient reason for Lecourbe's retreat; we know this from the example Lecourbe gave in March, when he drove Laudon back into the mountains at Schuls with some of his troops while he held out at Martinsbrück with the rest.

Lecourbe's retreat was undisturbed by the Austrians, and on 1 May Bellegarde followed only as far as Fettau, 7 miles from Remüs, probably because of his troops' fatigue and the delays imposed by destroyed bridges, as well as the resistance of the French rear guard.

On 2 May Bellegarde advanced to the attack again and drove back the French rear guard, always with difficulty and usually only by outflanking the positions it took on ravines. On this occasion, Brigadier Demont was taken prisoner. Lecourbe made a stand again at Süss but had to withdraw to Zernetz, during which he himself was slightly wounded. Lecourbe left a rear guard at Zernetz and continued his retreat to Pont on the 2nd. He stayed there on the 3rd to prepare his retreat across the Albula into the valley of the Posterior Rhine, while his rear guard retreated to Pont after demolishing the bridge at Zernetz. Lecourbe chose to retreat into the Albula valley to get closer to the army again, whereas continuing his retreat straight across the Maloja into the Maira valley to Chiavenna would have taken him still further away from it. Since the artillery could not cross the Albula, the gun barrels had to be removed from their carriages and transported on sleds, and the gun carriages were burned. Lecourbe crossed the Albula during the night of 3–4 May and arrived at Lenz on the 4th, where the road forks toward Chur and Reichenau. While Lecourbe stayed there for a few days, his rear guard followed and occupied the passes over the mountain ridge. Bellegarde stayed at Süss on the 3rd, sent his advance guard along the roads across the Albula and the Maloja, and took position at Zernetz on the 6th.

30 DESSOLLES ABANDONS THE VELTLIN

Meanwhile, what had transpired with Dessolles's brigade, so far as it can be pieced together from the extremely incomplete accounts, is as follows. As we have described according to Jomini, after the action at Taufers on the 4th it had moved through the Tschirfser Joch and Puschiaver valley, with a detour into the Adda valley, to Tirano, where Dessolles himself left to join the Army of Italy and Loison took over command.[19] It seems the division now remained in the upper Veltlin for the entire month of April and, because the Austrians did not pursue over the Wormser Joch at all, deployed more toward the units of the Tyrol army that were in the Sulz valley beyond the Tonnal. Among those units was Colonel Strauch's brigade, which we have already mentioned in connection with the Italian theater of operations.

These units comprised nine battalions and one and a half squadrons. When Suvorov joined the allied army in Italy and wanted to advance into Lombardy, he required Bellegarde to establish communications with the army in Italy by means of a detachment in the Val Camonica. Bellegarde entrusted Colonel Strauch with five battalions and a half-squadron for that purpose, while four battalions and one squadron were left on the Tonnal as support (as it was put).

Consequently, Strauch had arrived at Ponte di Legno at the source of the Oglio on 28 April. Before the destiny of upper Italy was decided by the battle of Cassano, Suvorov had wanted to draw Colonel Strauch to his right flank, so on 1 May, Strauch came to Severa at the northern end of Lake Iseo. After his victorious battle, Suvorov changed Colonel Strauch's mission and ordered him to move via Ponte di Nossa through the Brembo valley and the Brembo Pass to Morbegno in the Veltlin and join up with Prince Rohan to drive the French out of there. We must therefore imagine that at the end of April and the beginning of May, Loison's brigade was in position on the Adda between Tirano and Morbegno.

19. Jomini does not note Loison's position until he reappears at Monte Ceneri in mid to late May. Jomini, 11:298.

After the action at Süss, Bellegarde's advance guard moved through the Puschiaver valley against the Veltlin from one direction while, at the same time, that is, on 5 May, Bellegarde ordered the four battalions and one squadron left on the Tonnal to advance from the other direction. Loison then hastily began his retreat via Morbegno to Chiavenna. Strauch and Prince Rohan's advance guard pursued him through Fort Fuentes to Chiavenna, arriving there on the 8th, whereupon Loison withdrew into the Misoccer [Moesa] valley to San Giacomo [Pian San Giacomo] and apparently sent a few battalions to occupy the Splügen Pass and secure his communications with Lecourbe. According to some accounts, Loison himself crossed the Splügen, but other reports that are much more plausible say that he stayed on the Italian slopes and Lecourbe joined him there.

In Chiavenna the Austrians found twenty-six bronze cannon and ten iron ones that Loison had not had time to remove.

Before we follow Lecourbe's and Loison's movements any further, we must relate what Hotze had been doing in the Rhine valley meanwhile.

31 HOTZE ATTACKS THE ST. LUCIENSTEIG IN VAIN.
THE ACTION AT ST. LUCIENSTEIG ON 1 MAY

If Bellegarde advanced into the Inn valley, he would have to be concerned about his right flank, which could be outflanked by Ménard's troops from the Prettigau. He had therefore agreed with General Hotze that on 1 May, one day after the attack on Lecourbe, Hotze should take the St. Luciensteig. For that purpose, he transferred five battalions to Hotze that were in the Montafon and Paznaun under the command of Colonel St. Julien.[20] These troops would then seize control of the Prettigau and establish communications with Bellegarde via Davos.

For this operation, Hotze set ten and a half battalions and two squadrons in motion, including five and a half battalions and two squadrons of his own troops. He divided this force into five columns.[21]

The first column, consisting of one and a half battalions, set off for the Gamperthon valley on 29 April and was supposed to take the St. Luciensteig fortifications in rear from the Maienfeld Alps.

20. **Clausewitz** notes: "It seems that this officer who led a brigade of the army in Italy at the battle of Magnano had been transferred to the army in the Tyrol."
21. Again, we see an Austrian commander divide his force into multiple columns.

The second, consisting of one battalion, was to scale the Falknissberg during the night of 1 May, take the small village of Guschen at dawn, and descend on the right flank of the fortifications.

The third, consisting of one battalion and one squadron, was to demonstrate against the front of the fortifications on the road from Balzers.

The fourth, consisting of three and a half battalions under Colonel St. Julien, was to set off from the village of Mels and take the Fläschnerberg. Separated from the high mountains by the deep saddle in which the fort lay, and provided with its own entrenchments, this height constituted the position's support on the Rhine. This column was then to unite with the first column in the rear of the St. Luciensteig.

Two battalions and one squadron stayed in reserve at Balzers.

Finally, the fifth column, consisting of one and a half battalions, was sent from the Montafon on the Gargellasteig over the Schlapiner Joch into the Prettigau. Whether this was intended to merely create a diversion and draw French forces away from the point of attack or indeed to attack them in the rear during the Austrian advance into the Prettigau does not emerge clearly from the accounts.

The result of this operation was that it failed completely.[22]

The first column did not arrive at all; the second achieved nothing; the third [actually, the fourth] took the Fläschnerberg and the village of Fläsch with great effort, but as it had left some troops behind to protect its line of retreat and set others to pursue the French withdrawing to Maienfeld, it was too weak to attempt an assault on the rear of the works. While it was rallying its troops and waiting in vain until midday for the first column, General Ménard had time to bring up his own troops from Chur. Now St. Julien was attacked in his turn and escaped only with difficulty across the Fläschnerberg after one and a half battalions had laid down their arms, according to the archduke. Another author (Seyda von Landensberg) says his whole detachment was lost and only he and a few routers got away.[23]

On 2 May St. Julien moved to Bludenz. Bellegarde called him in from there, along with what was left of his troops.

The fifth column had actually taken the French outpost at Klosters and remained in possession of it throughout 2 May, but naturally, after hearing

---

22. See Jomini, 11:217–219.
23. The archduke recounts the episode in Karl, 1:282–286.

that the attack had failed, during the night of 2–3 May it went back the way it had come.

We see here that, as the archduke says, fewer than 8,000 of the 28,000 Austrians facing the French between Paznaun and Bregenz were employed to try to take the St. Luciensteig. The reason is that Hotze and Bellegarde felt that they could not at any point completely denude the 70-mile cordon they had strung from Bregenz via Feldkirch through the Montafon and Paznaun to the Inn. But the fact that even these 8,000 men were in no position to take the St. Luciensteig, and that Ménard, with perhaps half as many troops, captured whole battalions of them, is, of course, just as bad as previous events in the Rhine valley.[24]

32 THE INSURRECTIONS

The Swiss in the cantons of Schwyz and Uri, the Bündnerland [Graubündten], and Wallis, who had long been ready to rebel, were actually prompted to take up arms by the Austrians' plan for an attack on the French position in Graubündten at the end of April. What part the Austrian government played

---

24. The archduke makes an interesting comment on the character of the two armies that is worth quoting: "The selection of the officers, to whom the command of individual units is entrusted is never more important than in mountain warfare because the success of great undertakings is often dependent on them and because the nature of the terrain often deprives the general of a rapid overview of errors committed and the means to rectify them on the spot. It is worth noting that in the recent wars incompetent leadership generated quite opposite effects among the Germans and the French; in the former it produced vacillation, in the latter, rashness. The French, inclined by the spirit of the Revolution to breach all boundaries and expecting every gamble to produce results, followed this impulse whenever they saw no other way out. The Germans, trained to subordinate their will, accustomed to rules and bound by responsibility, were paralyzed by indecision. Hence the French superiority whenever it concerned the simultaneous action of several men left to their own devices, while their adversaries obtained advantages when they were under the direct leadership of their commanders. Hence the agility of the French in mountain warfare and the dependability of the Germans in the open field." Karl, 1:286–287. Given the fragmented nature of mountain battlefields, this seems reasonable, as the quality of French commanders had improved immensely during the Revolution, when merit played a far greater role in their selection.

in this is unknown.[25] The [Swiss] émigrés who had formed three Swiss battalions of the Austrian army naturally played a major role because of their many strong connections and agitation. Also, it cannot have been entirely irrelevant that General Hotze was a Swiss by birth and a man of ardent spirit, of whom it is certainly known that he strongly exhorted his compatriots to a general insurrection; it was that very general who found himself facing the French here.

On the day the Austrians attacked the St. Luciensteig, 10,000 men from the Oberbund[26] attacked the French outposts at Disentis, Ilanz, and Reichenau and drove them off. Thus, if General Hotze's attack had succeeded, General Ménard might have been forced to lay down his arms, for 6,000 armed peasants were massed at the bridge at Reichenau.

The insurrection broke out in the smaller cantons on 28 April, whereupon 3,000 armed men gathered in Schwyz.

In Wallis, the number of insurgents was twice that. It was now high time to act against this insurrection.

After defeating St. Julien, on 3 May Ménard turned against the insurgents in the Rhine valley. He gradually drove them out of Reichenau through Ilanz to Disentis. Here they tried to make a stand; he attacked them on 5 May and scattered them after not insignificant resistance.

At the same time, Soult was sent against the small cantons with part of the

25. The archduke implies that the inhabitants knew: "The accident on the pass [the action at St. Luciensteig detailed above] brought disaster on a number of inhabitants of Switzerland. Many of their most respected men had joined the Austrians and set up 3 battalions of auxiliary troops. Having left the bosom of their family they had continuously entertained secret understandings with the malcontents, particularly in Graubünden and in the small cantons and processed them with that fervor and confidence, which are shared with the dispossessed of all nations because they have nothing to lose and everything to gain. This is why when the news spread that the Austrians' operations would commence on the 1st of May and, optimistically confident of their favorable success, the 10,000 inhabitants of the upper and grey federation and then the cantons of Glarus and Schwyz picked up their arms." Karl, 1:287.

26. The Oberbund (Grey League) was an alliance of local groups that had existed since the sixteenth century. It had effectively controlled the region until the French incorporated the region into the Helvetian Republic in April 1799. Given the groups' long history of independence or semi-independence, it is not surprising they chose to revolt. This brings us back to the point that the result of conflict is never final; see *On War*, book 1, chap. 1. Clearly, many locals were not happy with the previous result and sought to change it.

reserve division. First he encountered an armed party at Rothenturm in the canton of Schwyz on 8 May, but these voluntarily laid down their arms when summoned to do so. Soult then sailed across the Vierwaldstättersee [Lake Lucerne] on the 9th to Altorff in the canton of Uri. Here he found 3,000 men with four guns who tried in vain to stop him from landing. They were defeated, lost their artillery, and had to retreat up the Reuss valley, where they were completely dispersed after running into a detachment sent there by Lecourbe.

Only in Wallis were the French unable to bring the insurgents under control right away; these formed a corps of 6,000 men with seven guns and took position at Leuk, blocking the valley of the Rhone. General Xaintrailles, who was supposed to suppress them, was assembling his division at the exit from the Rhone valley, partly from troops arriving from the interior, and did not commence operations until several weeks later.[27]

By defeating the main insurgent groups, Switzerland was pacified, and the discontent was transformed into fear.

This outcome of their insurrection demonstrated that the Swiss were no longer capable of such a serious and persistent popular uprising in the enemy army's rear that, overcome more by the circumstances than by its opponent, it would decide to leave the country. Nonetheless, if this eruption by the Swiss had coincided with an emphatic Austrian attack, it could have resulted in the conquest of the whole of Switzerland. Given the difficult position Masséna was in, without any need for complex combinations by the Austrians but just through the sheer energetic pressure of superior numbers, Dessolles's, Lecourbe's, and Ménard's divisions inevitably would have found themselves in very bad situations; and because the whole of the Lombard side of the Alps was already in the hands of the allies, they would have been partly captured and partly driven into Wallis, where they first would have had to cut a way through with sword in hand.[28] With such success, the uprising in Masséna's rear would have spread quickly, and he might not have had the confidence to make a stand against the archduke's main body.

---

27. See *On War*, book 6, chap. 26, "The People in Arms," for a more detailed description of the unique problems faced in this type of fight.

28. It is worth pointing out that in Spain during the Peninsular War of 1808–1814—that is, after the 1799 campaign but before the time Clausewitz was writing—where the British, Portuguese, and Spanish armies fought in parallel with guerrillas, this approach paid off enormously against the French invaders.

Instead, the only result was bloody reaction by the French, giving the Swiss a terrifying example to remember in future, and inevitably, the victims blamed the Austrians for their misfortune.

33 LECOURBE AND LOISON DRIVE PRINCE ROHAN BACK TO THE TRESA BRIDGE

After Lecourbe had been driven out of the Engadin and the operation against the St. Luciensteig had failed, there ensued another fourteen-day lull while the Austrian prepared for new operations. Before we present these new operations, we must describe the intermezzo that Lecourbe and Loison performed on the southern slopes of the Alps toward mid-May, which we have already noted in passing in connection with the Italian theater of operations.

As we said, Lecourbe arrived in Lenz on 4 May, and Loison in the Moesa valley four days later. The former's opponent, Bellegarde, halted at Zernetz; the latter's, Strauch, in Chiavenna and before the Splügen Pass, where there were a couple of battalions from Lecourbe's division.

Lecourbe had withdrawn into the Rhine valley to close up toward the center of Masséna's army, but Masséna did not want to shorten his line by that much. He felt he could not abandon the St. Gotthard Pass because, first, according to the conventional view, it served as the last point of support for his right wing once the entire Inn valley and the Splügen were lost, and second, as soon as the insurgents had been cleared out of the Wallis valley, it was the means of maintaining communications with the Army of Italy by a shorter route than if communications had to run behind Lake Geneva through Savoy. Since Lecourbe's retreat from the Engadin into the Rhine valley happened just as news arrived of the allied army's entry into Milan on 30 April, Prince Rohan's march to Lake Como, and Colonel Strauch's push into the Val Camonica, Masséna was justifiably worried about the St. Gotthard. He therefore ordered General Lecourbe to leave one demi-brigade behind in the Rhine valley and descend with the rest of his division to the Italian slopes of the Alps again to cover the approaches to the St. Gotthard.

After spending a few days at Lenz, Lecourbe marched from there across the St. Bernard Pass and back into the Moesa valley. He joined Loison at San Giacomo on the 10th and then marched to Bellinzona with 8,000 men, arriving there on the 11th.

Prince von Rohan had initially headed for Chiavenna; when the French vacated the Veltlin, he turned toward Porlezzo at the northern tip of Lake Lugano, sailed across the lake, landed at Lugano, and advanced to Bironico on the 12th, while his advance guard drove the French off Monte Cenere [Ceneri], taking 300 prisoners.

The Action on Monte Ceneri on 13 May

When Prince von Rohan took position on Monte Ceneri himself on the 13th, he was attacked by Lecourbe. Since the latter was roughly twice as strong, the prince was hurled violently back, with heavy losses, to behind the Tresa, which links Lake Maggiore to Lake Lugano. He would not have been able to stop even there if a detachment of Colonel Strauch's force had not advanced into the Moesa valley, causing General Lecourbe to worry about his rear.

Strauch himself had taken position at Chiavenna, where he was observing the Splügen and the Moesa valley and presumably did not think he could move far enough from Bellegarde to come to Prince Rohan's aid. Also, because of his frequent changes of route, the last of his troops arrived in Chiavenna only on 12 May.

Presumably after learning of the new Austrian attack in Graubündten, Lecourbe left General Loison facing Prince Rohan and headed for the St. Gotthard with the larger part of his division. As we have seen, this overwhelming attack on Prince Rohan spread a kind of strategic terror in Suvorov's army, and General Hohenzollern, outside the citadel of Milan, was ordered to hurry to Prince Rohan's aid.

The Action at Taverno on 18 May

General Hohenzollern arrived at the Tresa bridge with five battalions on the 17th; on the 18th, as we have already said, he attacked Loison at Taverno in the Val d'Agno and drove him out of there and back through Bellinzona, with the loss of 460 prisoners. Hohenzollern then reinforced Prince Rohan with one battalion and returned to Milan. In Bellinzona, the Austrians found ten guns left behind by the French.

Around this time, Colonel Strauch joined Prince Rohan. The two of them now stayed in Bellinzona for about eight days, that is, until Haddick arrived on 26 May. Loison stayed at Biasca, where the Breno joins the Ticino.

This is where Haddick's operations against the St. Gotthard begin, as we shall describe in due course.

34 BELLEGARDE AND HOTZE DRIVE THE FRENCH OUT OF GRAUBÜNDTEN

After Lecourbe's departure, the French forces from Feldkirch upward and in Graubündten consisted of Ménard's division plus one demi-brigade of Lecourbe's, or perhaps 8,000 men. Their main forces were in the Rhine valley, but their forward line of defense established in the passes ran along the right slope of the Lanquart valley to its source and, from there, along the left slope of the Inn valley via the Flülen [Flüela], Albula, Septimer, Splügen, and St. Bernhard Passes, constituting a line about 70 miles long. The 30 miles from the St. Luciensteig down to Lake Constance were held by Lorge's division.

We are tired of pointing out what forces were still available of the original 73,000 Austrians in the Tyrol and Vorarlberg that the 18,000 French had to face. But we must note that the archduke, Bellegarde, and Hotze did not think them sufficient to destroy the flimsy cobweb of the French right wing; instead, the archduke sent off yet another reinforcement to Hotze. He does not say how strong this was, but it was probably was not more than 4,000–5,000 men.[29] Hotze undoubtedly felt embarrassed about his unsuccessful attack on the St. Luciensteig on 1 May; Bellegarde, for his part, felt that he had not yet done enough and was not in a very good position because his line of retreat in the Inn valley was an extension of his right flank, and the French still held the Prettigau. Of course, as we know the balance of forces, we find it difficult to refrain from a degree of displeasure when we see the constant recurrence of such apprehensive geostrategic considerations. But because the Austrian generals most likely overestimated the enemy forces, we can at least understand the source of their concerns. Hotze and Bellegarde, for their part, now decided on a renewed combined offensive that was supposed to drive the French out of

---

29. The archduke states that he "reinforced Hotze to 34 battalions and 26 squadrons." Karl, 1:291. Jomini mentions the reinforcement but does not give specifics. Jomini, 11:223.

the Rhine valley, but the discussions between the two Austrian commanders took so long that it was not executed until 14 May.[30]

The archduke, getting ever further away from the idea of one great decisive battle for the reconquest of Switzerland, sees this operation by his left wing as his most advantageous form of action: first, because it is the only way Bellegarde can be moved to cooperate; second, because Masséna's right wing is clearly his weakest spot; third, because the Austrian government is constantly worried that Graubündten and the Tyrol might be too exposed; and finally, we might add, because he himself has no desire to do anything decisive. He fears the four divisions Masséna has concentrated behind the Rhine below Lake Constance, and he hopes that an offensive by his left wing will be the means of advancing that carries the least risk overall. He is therefore very willing to send reinforcements to strengthen this new operation even further.

The Actions in Graubündten on 14 May

After this reinforcement had arrived, then, a plan of attack for 14 May was devised according to which Hotze, with nineteen battalions and eight and a half squadrons, was to seize the St. Luciensteig, take the Lanquart valley, and advance up the Rhine to drive the French out of the Rhine valley, while Bellegarde, with twenty and a half battalions, was to advance on the Rhine over the mountains that separate it from the Inn.

We only deduce this plan for the whole operation from the specific dispositions and from what transpired, since the plan itself is not provided anywhere. If we therefore do not attribute to General Bellegarde the very natural intention to advance into the Anterior Rhine valley to cut off the French from their line of retreat and to unite with Hotze, this is because we see him halt in the parallel valleys of the Posterior Rhine and the Landwasser. However, we cannot say that this might not have been his original intention, since just as he was executing it, he received the order to march away to Italy.

Thus we see two large bodies, each of 17,000–18,000 men, set in motion

---

30. The archduke notes: "As usually happens when two free wills are to join together, the undertaking was delayed and the joint operation against Graubündten was not set to start until the 14th of May." Karl, 1:291.

from two sides against Ménard's division of about 8,000 men. We are therefore entitled to expect great results.

Hotze divided his force into four columns.

The first, of six battalions, eight squadrons, and twenty-one guns led by him in person, formed up at Balzers on 14 May and advanced against the front of the St. Luciensteig. It was mainly intended to combat any French forces that might hurry up the Rhine on the road from Werdenberg to Ragaz, which it could do thanks to its numerous artillery that commanded the far bank of the Rhine. But it was also provided with scaling ladders to assault the fortifications directly, if necessary.

The second column of three battalions under General Jellachich had already moved off into the Gamperthon valley on the 12th, scaled the Maienfeld Alps on the 13th, and was supposed to seize the villages of Maienfeld, Jenins, and Malans on the 14th. One battalion of this column was tasked with attacking the St. Luciensteig from the rear.

The third column of five battalions under General Hiller was likewise supposed to advance through the Gamperthon valley but descend from the high ground not to the Rhine but to the Lanquart, take the French outposts there, and march down the valley, rolling up the French.

The fourth column, four and a half battalions and a half-squadron under Colonel Plunket, was to advance over the Gargellasteig and seize the upper part of the Lanquart valley.

This attack succeeded at all points, and its results were satisfactory if not particularly glorious.

We know nothing about the French positions other than that two battalions occupied the St. Luciensteig.[31] It seems that one brigade (Chabran) may have been in the Lanquart valley and in the Rhine valley at the confluence of the Lanquart, and the other under Suchet[32] further up the Rhine valley, probably at Chur, since we find Chabran concentrated at Ragaz and Suchet at Reichenau.

Of Hotze's four columns, the second had the most effect. It took the vil-

---

31. Both the archduke and Jomini are short on specifics in this regard. Karl, 1:289–300; Jomini, 11:221–226.

32. Louis Suchet (1770–1826) was another excellent French commander who rose to the rank of marhsal. Again, it is worth noting his young age in comparison to his opponents.

lages of Maienfeld, Jenins, and Malans with two battalions, while the third battalion took the St. Luciensteig itself with an attack up the gorge. The French apparently put up little resistance, as the Austrians' losses were quite negligible. After the St. Luciensteig had been opened by this battalion from the second column, Hotze advanced through it with the first column as the third column arrived from the Lanquart valley. Some of the victorious Austrians pursued the French up the Rhine, while the rest stayed at the St. Luciensteig and at Maienfeld, facing the French concentrating at Ragaz.

The fourth column advanced into the Lanquart valley without difficulty and likewise marched down it to the Rhine valley, so that Hotze's whole force was now united there.

The trophies of this day were fifteen guns, twenty-two ammunition wagons, and 3,000 prisoners.[33] About 1,000 prisoners were taken in the St. Luciensteig, 1,100 from the outposts cut off in the Prettigau, and the rest during the pursuit.

To explain why the French resistance was so much weaker than usual, we need to know something about the measures they took. We can, of course, guess that their forces were much more scattered than on 1 May, since at that time, because of Lecourbe's position in the Inn valley, they had nothing to fear for the upper region of the Rhine valley. But still, we must imagine that the majority of their force was at the St. Luciensteig and in Maienfeld, and even if these forces were overwhelmed by the Austrians' superior numbers, the small numbers of dead and wounded on the Austrian side prove that the resistance was not very determined. Furthermore, General Ménard disappears from the ranks of the division commanders for a while, which suggests there was some unhappiness with the measures he had taken.

The second part of the operation, Bellegarde's attack, naturally could not be so rich in trophies, since he had nothing but a weak chain of outposts to break through.

He too divided his force into four columns.

The first column, of one and a half battalions, set off on the 13th from Galthür in the Paznaun valley for Gargella to establish communications with General Hotze; it met Hotze's fourth column there. While the latter moved down the Lanquart, the former headed up it to the outpost at Kloster, which the French abandoned without a fight. This column then moved to Davos in the Landwasser valley and joined up with the second column.

---

33. These numbers are identical to the archduke's. Karl, 1:297.

This second column, consisting of seven battalions, set off from Süss in the Engadin [Sils im Engadin] on 13 May, drove out the French outpost in the Flüela Pass, and moved to the nearby village of Tschuggen. On the 14th it attacked Davos and drove the French from behind their barricades without much difficulty. On the 15th it sent two battalions to Langenwies [Langwies] toward the Plesser, and the rest took the Lenz road as far as Alveneu, where they stayed on the 16th.

The third column, of eight battalions led by Bellegarde himself, already held the Albula. It did not move out from there until the 15th, when it went to Bergün; then on the 16th it moved to the Landwasser River at Fillisur. A couple of French battalions hastily retreated into the Rhine valley.

The fourth column moved in two contingents—one over the Julierberg, and the other over the Maloja and Septimerberg. It reunited on the 14th at Mühlen in the Oberhalbsteiner valley and moved to Tiefenkasten on the 15th, facing Lenz; from there it sent detachments into the Rhine valley.

The French detachments in all these areas retreated hastily without a fight, mostly through the Posterior Rhine valley across the Splügen Pass to join Lecourbe and Loison at Bellinzona.

The trophies consisted of two guns that the enemy could not get away and a few prisoners.[34]

Thus Bellegarde and his twenty battalions spent the 14th and 15th advancing about 13 miles from the Inn valley over the mountains through the weak line of enemy outposts to Lenz. He had now united all his columns around that place.

On the same day, that is, 15 May, Hotze had advanced to Chur and reconnoitered Reichenau, where Suchet was collecting 4,000 men. Hotze allowed him the necessary time and opportunity to do so, as well as to withdraw further to Disentis and from there into the Reuss valley, in that he pursued Suchet weakly and only as far as Ilanz because he wanted to turn his corps around and prepare to join up with the archduke.

Since Suchet could not take his artillery with him along this route, he threw the gun barrels into the Rhine and destroyed their carriages; he reached Urseren on the 19th.

---

34. Clausewitz mentions light Austrian casualties for the two days' fighting. The archduke notes, "The days of the 14th and 15th May only cost all four columns of Hotze's corps no more than 4 officers and 67 men in dead and wounded." Karl, 1:301.

Ménard's left wing had concentrated at Ragaz and was driven out of there on the 15th through Pfaeffers, up the Tamina valley, with the loss of two guns.

Another small French corps, probably the right wing of Lorge's division, had concentrated at Sargans. On the 16th its infantry retreated from there to Wallenstadt, and its cavalry to Werdenberg.

At this point this joint operation ends. Hotze turns right, and Bellegarde, having received the order to march away with 25,000 men to join Suvorov in Italy, stays put to prepare for his departure.[35]

At first glance, we may be amazed to see the Army of the Tyrol stated as 25,000 strong, when the archduke reported that it had 47,000 men, in his estimate, for the campaign. But we need to deduct five battalions that stayed in the Rhine valley under St. Julien, two as garrisons in Innsbruck and Kufstein, and five under Wukassowitsch that joined Suvorov at the beginning of April. These twelve battalions would have had about 9,000 men. That leaves 13,000 men as casualties, but we can scarcely assume there were any fewer than that when we compile the list of Bellegarde's sins. If we enumerate the individual battalions that, according to the archduke's account, were cut off or otherwise captured, they are:

1. In the upper Engadin at the start of the campaign: 2 battalions
2. When Laudon moved against Lecourbe with four battalions, he lost the majority of his men during his retreat, so let us say: 2 battalions
3. When he attacks Lecourbe's rear at Scuol, he again loses: about 1 battalion

35. The archduke describes the order and situation: "The undertaking on Graubündten was the last one in which Bellegarde took part in Switzerland. Souwarow [Suvorov] demanded that he join up with him in Italy where the French army weakened, disorganized, supported by poorly equipped and even more poorly defended fortresses, subject to attacks by the enraged local population, was no longer in the position of being able to put up a proportionate defense. The fortunate general found himself in the position of only being able to base his operations on the superior numbers and on physical strength of his troops and was able to flatter himself that he would achieve possession of the whole of Italy within a short space of time for which the most renowned army commanders had often fought through several bloody campaigns. Germany and Switzerland were only important to Austria from a defensive consideration, namely due to the security of its own states and due to the close and protected link with the army operating in Italy. A further operation leading to lasting results was not feasible from that region at that time." Karl, 1:305.

4. At Taufers: 8 battalions
5. On the same day, cut off at Martinsbrück after the action at Nauders: 2 battalions
6. In Bellegarde's abandoned attack on the Engadin on 22 April: 1 battalion
7. In St. Julien's unsuccessful attack on the St. Luciensteig: 1½ battalions
8. Total: 17½ battalions

If we add to these a number of other prisoners, dead, and wounded who did not return to the ranks, it is easy to see that, because an Austrian battalion was originally 800 to 1,000 strong, a good number of men from these seventeen and a half battalions must still have escaped along byways if the total losses in the three months of March, April, and May came to only 13,000 men.

The figure of 25,000 men also tallies with the fact that, as we shall see later, Bellegarde sent 10,000 men under Haddick against the St. Gotthard and joined Suvorov with 15,000.

35 BELLEGARDE MARCHES TO ITALY

This departure [of Bellegarde] took place amidst such particular strategic complications that we must consider it not merely a route march, or a girder underpinning the wider implementation of a strategic principle, but as an actual strategic action in its own right.[36]

It seems that Bellegarde received the order to depart when he arrived in Lenz on 15 May. We can probably suppose that this new mission for his army did not just appear all of a sudden but that Bellegarde could have anticipated it; however, we cannot assume it, since none of the authors says so.[37] This makes a crucial difference: if Bellegarde had anticipated this impending march, it would have been all the more important for him to advance into the Anterior Rhine valley and make himself master of the St. Gotthard Pass, but if the order arrived completely unexpectedly, it is understandable that he would be obliged to halt momentarily. We must put ourselves exactly in his place.

36. Although Count Tolstoy (Suvorov's liaison to the archduke) was with the Austrians, it is not clear that the two parties had agreed to a specific course of action in advance; indeed, his letter (157) of 13 May (Gregorian) indicates that Tolstoy was ignorant of the Austrian objectives. See Milyutin, *Geschichte des Krieges Russlands*, 1:604–605.

37. See note 35 in this chapter.

On 13 May Lecourbe had driven Prince Rohan back to the Tresa bridge; the news of this probably reached Bellegarde on the 15th. This had a very strong impact on Bellegarde's departure. If he saw General Lecourbe as just having a weak, isolated division wandering across the southern slopes of the Alps with no communications with the Army of Italy and connected with the army in Switzerland only through the St. Gotthard, a continued march into the Anterior Rhine valley as far as the St. Gotthard would have cut off this division and, since the whole of Wallis was in insurrection, inflicted disaster on it. But if Bellegarde thought the French were in strength on the Ticino, in strength at the St. Gotthard, and in strength in the Anterior Rhine valley, and if he thought that continuing his march to the St. Gotthard would get him involved in a dubious operation, it would be natural for him to halt in the Posterior Rhine valley, make his preparations, and march away via Chiavenna. The order to march from one theater of operations to another is not an order for an attack, and it is not in the spirit of such an order to march over the body of one's opponent. An enterprising general who is eager for success and who sees things as easier than they are rather than more difficult would have been drawn to the St. Gotthard without any great misgivings by the glorious success that could be gained in a real sense *chemin faisant* [along the way]. The weak defense of the St. Luciensteig alone showed that the French in the Rhine valley were not in great shape. But Bellegarde had always been known as an extremely cautious man,[38] and it is not surprising that he chose the more cautious path if we bear in mind all the genuine concerns that actually arose from the other route.

First, Suchet was in the Anterior Rhine valley with half of Ménard's division, while Hotze was in the process of turning away from him toward the archduke. Thus, it would still take one more fight to reach the St. Gotthard.

Second, it was probably scarcely feasible for Bellegarde to go for him with his whole force, as he may have lacked the provisions to do so. If Suchet and Lecourbe combined, they would have matched him to some degree; of course, that would then have forced them away from Masséna, but not without a line of retreat, for while the insurrection in the Rhone valley would probably make this more difficult, it was not enough to make it impossible.

Third, if General Bellegarde had got involved in such an operation, he would

---

38. More broadly, the Austrians had been cautious and slow for much of the campaign, and in Count Tolstoy's letter referenced earlier, he commented on their "army's complete inactivity." See Milyutin, *Geschichte des Krieges Russlands*, 1:604–605.

have been unable to concentrate his army beforehand to begin its designated march to Piedmont united; instead, he would have had to let his other columns make their way there, while he himself attacked and pursued the enemy with his right wing. It is easy to imagine what incidents, uncertainty, and loss of time could have arisen during that action; thus, if he did follow this course of action instead of joining Suvorov quickly and punctually with his force united, Bellegarde ran the risk of voluntarily embroiling himself in a situation with no clear result. The time he might thereby save through shortening his route and avoiding the need to sail across Lake Como would not count for much.

It is very easy to see that if Bellegarde had considered not only taking the St. Gotthard and beating Lecourbe but also driving him back to Wallis, as General Jomini advocates, these concerns and difficulties would have become even greater, and such a notion may certainly be regarded as completely impractical.[39]

Lecourbe's victory over Prince Rohan and the news that Suchet, driven back by Hotze, had concentrated a French force that was, of course, only 4,000 strong but could easily be taken for 6,000–8,000 apparently impressed General Bellegarde, and thus he abandoned any idea of continuing his operations.

After these reflections, we can accept the archduke's criticism of Bellegarde on this occasion as a judgment based on better-informed hindsight. But to evaluate Bellegarde's decision fairly, we must note that he was a cautious general rather than an enterprising one, that his decision was by no means unreasonable, and that in this situation, most generals—probably including the archduke—would not have acted any differently.[40]

General Bellegarde began his march as early as the 18th, which certainly indicates his desire to avoid getting involved in any further action in the Swiss theater of operations. The French outposts that were still in the Splügen and St. Bernard Passes were abandoned around this time, and Bellegarde went through the former to Chiavenna, where he arrived on 21 May.

To hold the approaches from Italy to Graubündten and thus secure communications between the army in Italy and the archduke, at Hotze's request, Bellegarde had left Colonel St. Julien's brigade in the Posterior Rhine valley and had also tasked Colonel Strauch to stay with Prince Rohan facing the St. Gotthard together.

---

39. Clausewitz is disagreeing with Jomini, but Jomini too is critical of Bellegarde's inactivity and his failure to take the St. Gotthard. See Jomini, 11:228–230.

40. For the archduke's take, see Karl, 1:307–315.

With the rest of his troops, perhaps 20,000 men, he embarked at Riva,[41] for which purpose 200 boats had been held in readiness. Since these could not hold the whole force, a large portion of the infantry was transported to Gera to march by land to Como. The ferrying could not be completed until the 27th, but on the 28th the whole corps was concentrated at Como. Only the heavy artillery and the baggage train had taken the road through the Adige valley, with probably a few thousand men as escort.[42]

Bellegarde had been ordered to transfer command of the troops left facing the St. Gotthard to General Haddick, and in Como he received a new order to bring Haddick's corps up to 10,000 men so that it could take the St. Gotthard and relieve the insurgents in Wallis. He therefore sent Debrie's and Lamarcelle's brigades from Como to Bellinzona to join Rohan and Strauch and form the corps intended to operate against Lecourbe. Nobili's brigade stayed behind at Varese between Lake Maggiore and Lake Como in support, or rather to maintain communications. Bellegarde marched through Milan to Pavia with the rest of his corps and reached Suvorov about 15,000 strong.

36 THE ARCHDUKE CROSSES THE RHINE

The archduke had finally decided to meddle in military matters himself again. He saw the operations by Generals Hotze and Bellegarde as preparation for this, and after the Rhine valley in Graubündten had been taken, he wanted to

---

41. There was a small village, Riva di Chiavenna, in the present-day commune of Samolaco on the northern shore of the Pozzo di Riva. This small lake was a large bay on Lake Como in 1799. The troops could have sailed from here directly to Como itself. The rest of the troops marched to modern-day Gera Lario.

42. The heavy artillery might have been too big for the available boats, but that does not explain the baggage train. It is not entirely clear why they traveled this far east, unless Clausewitz is referring to a separate force: the mention of heavy artillery might indicate that this was intended as a siege train for the Italian campaign. This view is supported by the archduke's comments: "The Russian general had encircled so many objects [in Italy] at the same time that he was only able to control and implement the system he had adopted through numerous reinforcements. The Viennese court's concerns for the Tyrol had evaporated: in contrast, its entire attention had turned to Italy, where it wished to hold on to the conquests made and increase them with new ones." Karl, 2:49–51. Given that many of the objects were fortified Italian cities, the dispatch of siege artillery makes sense.

cross the Rhine himself, position General Hotze and most of his troops between Lake Zurich and Lake Constance, and operate united with him against Masséna's main body. Whether this would lead to a battle—and if so, how it would be decided—was impossible for a man like the archduke to predict, especially as it seemed that he would not have a decisive superiority of forces.[43] The archduke apparently had no specific objective for his operation, at least he makes no mention of one in his history; rather, he describes his crossing of the Rhine as being like the natural progress of a clock mechanism whose pendulum has been set in motion again.[44]

The archduke's and Hotze's maneuvers to join up, and Masséna's attempt to prevent them, take up the last quarter of the month of May and are the prelude to the first battle of Zurich.

The loss of the St. Luciensteig and the associated losses of combat forces left Masséna in no position to hold the Rhine valley for long. This led him to concentrate his forces and await further developments in a position between the Rhine and the Limmat. Meanwhile, he constructed an entrenched camp in the rear of his position, in front of Zurich and between the Limmat and the Glatt, into which he could withdraw if his opponent advanced decisively; it also seemed well suited to secure the rest of Switzerland against a not too decisive opponent. Since the archduke was separated from Hotze by Lake Con-

---

43. The archduke seems more interested in the position of Zurich as "the strategically decisive point" than in seeking a decisive battle. Karl, 1:346–347. Indeed, his thoughts on planning, as he looked back at the first battle of Zurich on 4–7 June 1799, are worth reading: "No operation is drawn up thoroughly and executable with caution if, in addition to the inviolability of its base, it does not also guarantee the safety of the communications with the same. This security consists in the impossibility of the enemy aiming early on at the lines of communication of the army operating in front or to the side when this can be prevented. One can reach it either through protective positions close to one's own communications or through such that threaten those of the opponent or through incapacitating the enemy operations through prior use of arms." Karl, 2:1. From this, which is his opening paragraph of the second volume on the war, it is clear that securing his lines of communication and his base was at the forefront of his thinking. That sums up his cautious approach better than anything else.

44. This entire section (13) of the archduke's history is riddled with comments about lines: lines of operation, lines of retreat, lines of communication. It struck us as being extremely geometric and an exact description of the ideas Clausewitz so detested. Karl, 1:315–350. See *On War*, book 3, chap. 2, "Elements of Strategy," and book 3, chap. 15, "The Geometrical Factor."

stance, it seemed that they might have some trouble linking up in Masséna's vicinity, which might offer Masséna the opportunity to make an advantageous combination for battle.

The left wing of Ménard's division had already abandoned the Sargans area on 16 May and withdrawn to Wallenstadt. However, the right of Lorge's division remained in its position at Azmoos until Hotze came to drive it out.

Hotze had reconnoitered Ménard's right wing under Suchet at Reichenau on the 15th and decided to leave just a few troops to pursue him. Hotze turned back to Maienfeld with his main body.

The 16th, 17th, and 18th then elapsed.

On the 19th Hotze sent a detachment under Colonel Gavasini through the Siez valley toward Wallenstadt and another toward Werdenberg. The latter drove the French out of Azmoos and Werdenberg, taking five guns. Part of the right wing of Lorge's division moved to Lichtensteg, and the other part went down the Rhine.

Gavasini pressed on to Flums and Berschis and was attacked there by Ménard at midday on the 19th. The support of armed locals and of a battalion sent by Hotze enabled him to hurl the enemy back to Murg on the southern shore of Lake Wallenstadt.

On 20 May the French abandoned all their outposts on the Rhine above and below Lake Constance as far as the confluence of the Thur and withdrew behind that river. Lorge's division took position at St. Gallen, Lichtensteg, and Uznach.

On the 21st they abandoned the Thur as well and moved behind the Töss. On this day their positions were:

Thurreau's division as advance guard at Winterthur.
Oudinot's, Vandamme's, and Soult's divisions and the cavalry reserve at Klotten and Bassersdorf.
Lorge remained in his position.
Ménard, reunited with Suchet, at Bilten between Lake Wallenstadt and Lake Zurich on the southern bank of the Linth.

During this time, the entrenchments of the Zurich position were worked on industriously.

On the 20th the Austrians were busy building bridges for Hotze at Balzers and Meinungen and for the archduke at Stein.

On the 21st General Nauendorf crossed at Stein with the archduke's advance guard of twenty-one battalions and thirty squadrons, while a small detachment crossed at Constanz.

Hotze did not finish his bridge building until the 21st. On the 22nd he crossed at Balzers and Meinungen with eighteen battalions and thirteen squadrons, followed later by another four battalions from Vorarlberg, while five battalions remained in the Anterior Rhine valley to maintain communications with Haddick.

Of the archduke's army, Nauendorf advanced against the Thur on this day and took position around Örlingen on the road from Zurich to Schafhausen. The archduke had the pontoon bridge from Stein brought to Kloster Paradies near Schafhausen so as to cross there.

Nauendorf was under orders to push his detachments forward toward the Töss, not to get involved in any serious fighting but to make it easier for him to file across the Thur. Nauendorf therefore posted an outpost line of 500–600 men beyond the Thur.

The French advance guard was at Winterthur and had an outpost line just 2 miles in front of it. The Austrians pushed their outposts right up to the French, even taking the village of Hettlingen from them. Thus, the Austrian outpost line was pushed a full 5 miles out beyond the Thur and extended in a convex arc many miles across from the confluence of the Thur and the Rhine up to Frauenfeld, while on the 18-mile stretch of the Thur from Pfyn to its mouth, there were only two bridges at Adelfingen and Pfyn on the roads from Schafhausen and Frauenfeld, and apart from these, the Thur could be crossed only at two fords. While Nauendorf sought to use a weak chain of outposts in this way to gain room for the archduke to link up with Hotze, on the 22nd the Austrians posted some detachments across the Rhine at Eglisau to threaten the French left flank and draw their attention and their forces in that direction. On the 23rd more and stronger detachments followed through Kaiserstuhl, Zirzach, and Koblenz. The result of these demonstrations was that on the 22nd Masséna sent a few thousand men against Eglisau, who were repelled by the Austrians, and on the 23rd he transferred General Thurreau to Baden with part of his division to observe that stretch of the Rhine between the Töss and the Aar and to serve as an echelon for the army's left flank. General Ney[45] took over from General Thurreau in command of the advance guard at Winterthur.

45. Michel Ney (1769–1815) was probably the most famous of Napoleon's com-

On the 23rd Archduke Charles and his army crossed the Rhine at Kloster Paradies, apparently leaving a corps of 6,000–8,000 men on the right bank to observe the Rhine between Schafhausen and Basel. On this day he took position at Kloster Paradies.[46]

General Hotze marched to St. Gallen on the 23rd and sent his advance guard along the road to Bischofszell and Frauenfeld.

On the same day, Colonel Gavasini moved to Mollis at the exit from the Klöntal into the Linth valley.

On the 24th the Austrian main army had a quiet day, as neither its outposts nor the main body changed position. The archduke was awaiting Hotze's approach, but this general was likewise standing still on the 24th at St. Gallen, against the archduke's wishes and fearing for his left flank, or so the archduke says. Hotze contented himself with sending General Petrasch to Frauenfeld with six battalions and six squadrons.

It seems that both Austrian commanders shied away from moving sideways to link up, for fear of having Lake Constance behind them at the moment of a decisive battle.[47] Hotze presumably thought the archduke could at least come as far toward him as the road to Constanz, but the archduke did not want to leave the Schafhausen road. This was still the main road, and if the French did risk an offensive, they could be expected to launch it along this road.

Thus the French commander was granted the three days between 21 and 25 May to make his dispositions for attacking one of his opponents with his force united. If he beat him, the other would inevitably give up his attack and retreat across the Rhine.

Masséna did actually make moves on the 24th for an attack to be carried out on the 25th, but of course, most of the French commander's forces were

---

manders, largely for his incredible bravery. He was an able commander and was made a marshal in 1804. He was executed in the counterrevolution following the fall of Napoleon in 1815.

46. Karl, 1:322–323.

47. The archduke addresses this point: "Appropriately, this general [the archduke] selected the road via Andelfingen to Zürich as his line of operation. If he went further to the right then he would move further away from Hotze, and would delay joining up with him. If he kept closer to Lake Constance, then he could run the risk of being pressed back against it and losing the line of retreat to his main position of Stockach." Karl, 1:323.

still so scattered that he lacked the means to carry this plan through to a decisive result.[48] The remnants of Ménard's division were south of the Linth; Chabran, who was now in command of Lorge's division, had concentrated toward Uznach and had apparently left only observation posts facing St. Gallen; Masséna felt he could not take General Souham away from Basel to observe the Rhine and Frick valleys; and, as we have seen, Thurreau had been sent to Baden with 3,000–4,000 men to cover the rear. Thus, all he had left behind the Töss was Vandamme's, Soult's, and Oudinot's divisions, part of Thurreau's division, and the cavalry reserve, which constituted a force of perhaps 25,000 men combined. The Swiss contingent should also be added to these; its total strength was probably close to 10,000 men, of whom, however, the majority were used as labor and direct protection for the entrenched camp.

The French commander could probably tell himself that Hotze would not take any more southerly route than the one to Frauenfeld, which was closest to the archduke; he must also have been aware that Hotze and his corps could have reached Frauenfeld on the 25th, and there was nothing to prevent the archduke from arriving at Andelfingen on the same day. These two places are less than 10 miles apart, so Masséna could not move against one of the two enemy generals without sending a significant force against the other at the same time; otherwise, he ran the risk of being attacked in flank and rear by one while he was fighting the other, thus getting entangled in a fight of a very unfavorable kind and at the same time seeing his retreat to Zurich threatened. The French commander would have estimated General Hotze at about 20,000 strong and the archduke at 40,000, so there was no prospect of him meeting one of them with superior numbers.

In any case, Hotze was the weaker of the two; his position at Frauenfeld was strategically weaker than the archduke's at Andelfingen, if he wanted to retreat the same way he had come; and Frauenfeld is not much further from Winterthur than Andelfingen is. Thus, it is quite natural that Mas-

---

48. Again, the archduke's thoughts are enlightening: "It [an attack] must, just like every offensive move without exception, be based on the security of the retreat and conducted in the only favorable moment so that one does not arrive too late to thwart the opponent's combinations and not get too far from one's own pivot so as to be able to suddenly switch from one line of march to the other." Karl, 1:324–325. Here again is an example of caution and of the eighteenth-century military thinking that Clausewitz was rebelling against.

séna turned against Hotze with his main body and only sent as much force against Andelfingen as was necessary to protect himself against a crossing there for a while.

If Masséna had known that Hotze had stood still in St. Gallen on the 24th, the combination would have been a different one. If need be, he could then have considered marching against the archduke with his whole force of 25,000 men, and even if the archduke was not yet to be found at Andelfingen, Masséna could have sought him out at Kloster Paradies and made him fight a decisive battle. Of course, the archduke probably still would have had superior numbers, even if he had not yet concentrated all his forces in the same spot; still, there were such possibilities of good results here that the French commander would have had to prefer this course of action over any other. Both the archduke[49] and General Jomini[50] have therefore criticized him for this; they have not made allowance for the fact that on the evening of the 24th, when Masséna was in Winterthur making his plans for the next day, he had even less reason to think that Hotze was sitting in St. Gallen, as Petrasch was already on the march from there to Frauenfeld [sent as an advance detachment by Hotze].

But while we thus exempt the French commander from a criticism that, in our opinion, is itself based on a defective view, we certainly cannot find that the dispositions he made on the 25th could have produced any result that was worth the trouble.

General Thurreau remained in his position at Baden. One brigade under General Paillard was to drive back the Austrian right wing's outposts and move to Andelfingen. General Ney, with a second column whose strength is not stated anywhere, was to head for Altikon close to the Thur, halfway between Frauenfeld and Andelfingen; Oudinot and his division were to head for Frauenfeld; and Soult with the reserve was to support the various columns. Here, for the first time, we note the absence of General Vandamme from among the leadership. As we see from the correspondence in *le Moniteur*,[51] at

---

49. Karl, 1:340.
50. Jomini, 11:232–236.
51. Napoleon made *Le Moniteur Universel,* an important French newspaper, an official one in December 1799. The relevant year of this newspaper is available online through the French National Library: https://gallica.bnf.fr/ark:/12148/bpt6k49333r.image.

the time of the first battle of Zurich, he was being tried for extortion.[52] So it is likely that there had been a reorganization.

This whole disposition for battle does not even remotely resemble a decisive blow, and if we go by the meager report that General Masséna sent to the Directory,[53] he had no aim beyond driving the Austrians back behind the Thur again. But this serves no sensible purpose and seems almost like a way to merely pass the time. The tactical dispositions are entirely in accordance with this view, since the center column had no specific objective and, incredibly, the reserve was tasked with supporting all three columns, so that absolutely nothing decisive could happen at any one point. If Hotze had turned up at Frauenfeld or the archduke at Andelfingen, Masséna would have got himself into roughly the same situation as Jourdan at Stockach; that is, he would have lost a battle despite all the archduke's caution.

At daybreak on the 25th, General Paillard crossed the Töss at Rorbas and outflanked the right wing of the Austrian outpost line while pinning it frontally. From the other side, Ney breached the center of this line, and detachments from his column advanced on Andelfingen. This double outflanking put the Austrian right wing in a critical position, and it had to fight its way out through the streets of Andelfingen while its cavalry swam the Thur, during which it necessarily incurred significant losses. But the support that Nauendorf rushed up from Örlingen, and the burning of the bridge, easily put a stop to any further French advance.

At Frauenfeld, Oudinot ran into Petrasch, who was just arriving there and who found a strong position behind the town that enabled him to hold out stubbornly until 7:00 in the evening. However, reinforcements brought up by Soult then obliged the exhausted Austrians to withdraw to Mazingen.

Ney advanced with the main body of his column to Pfyn, so they say, and

---

52. "Vandamme was accused of imposing contributions from the citizens of Wurttemberg for his own personal profit and tolerating the misappropriations of others under his command." Six, *Dictionnaire Biographique*, 2:528. He was brought back to Paris for trial, which never happened. Vandamme's correspondence lists some of the appropriations levied and many of the supporting letters and documents. See A. du Casse, *Le Général Vandamme: et sa correspondence*, 2 vols. (Paris: Librairie et Cte, 1870), 1:452–518.

53. **Clausewitz** notes: "See the *Moniteur*." See https://gallica.bnf.fr/ark:/12148/bpt 6k49333r.image.

seized the crossing there without difficulty. But after darkness had already fallen, a brigade sent by Nauendorf arrived, crossed at a ford, and drove off the French.

At daybreak another nine battalions and six squadrons sent by the archduke arrived.

Besides the many dead and wounded they suffered on this day, the Austrians lost two guns and 2,000 prisoners.

While this fighting was going on, Hotze marched to Schwarzenbach, halfway from St. Gallen to Frauenfeld.

Masséna felt that he could not exploit his advantage in either direction, so on the 26th he withdrew into his previous position behind the Töss.

The Austrians used the 26th to prepare for the advance set for the 27th. The bridges over the Thur were mended, and the archduke joined Nauendorf with six battalions and sent some more cavalry to Hotze, who deployed in two camps at Frauenfeld and Duttwyl on the road from St. Gallen to Winterthur.

On the 27th the Austrians advanced: Hotze in the direction of Winterthur, and the archduke on Nestenbach close to the Töss on the direct road to Zurich. Hotze arrived first, drove the French advance guard out of Winterthur with the loss of four guns, and seized the crossing over the Töss at the village of that name. The archduke arrived later, delayed by the bridge construction at Andelfingen, and likewise drove the enemy outposts back across the Töss and established himself in occupation of the village of Pfungen on the left bank.

Early on the 28th Masséna abandoned his strong position at Breiten and withdrew to the area of Klotten. Here, Masséna again presented a front with his main body while Soult and the reserve were already retreating across the Glatt, but Thurreau turned around, collected all his troops spread along the Rhine, and advanced to Bülach. From there he threatened the right flank of the Austrians as they followed, driving their light troops back across the Töss and occupying Rorbas. We do not know how far Hotze and the archduke advanced on this day, but in any case, the archduke was so close to this isolated attack of Thurreau's that it could have no further effect. It is hard to say what the point was supposed to be: all of Masséna's actions look as if he wanted to gain one day of time, but again, we cannot see the importance of this.

On the 29th Masséna retreated entirely behind the Glatt, apart from a few small outposts; on the 30th these outposts followed as well.

On the 29th Hotze took position at Bassersdorf with his advance guard at Klotten, and the archduke was at Pfungen with his advance guard at Embrach.

On the 30th the Austrians stood still; on the 31st the archduke moved to Embrach.

During this slow advance, the archduke yet again tested the effect of demonstrating against both his opponent's flanks, perhaps to maneuver him backward strategically and avoid having to fight the decisive battle that was approaching.

On the right flank, he used the troops left behind on the right bank of the Rhine, having three battalions and one squadron renew the demonstration against the Rhine between Eglisau and Waldshut. We do not know if any actual crossing was attempted.

Masséna had four battalions move from Basel to Kaiserstuhl to reinforce his army from the detachments hitherto left to observe the Rhine.

The archduke thought to achieve his aim on his left flank by reinforcing Colonel Gavasini.[54] To that end, he had sent General Jellachich to Uznach with six battalions and four squadrons to combine with Gavasini and clear the enemy from both sides of the Linth and the upper end of Lake Zurich and advance along the road to Zurich; a few squadrons of the cavalry left in Graubündten were also brought up for this purpose. The archduke describes this measure as simple prudence, but even he cannot hold back from criticizing his own exaggerated caution.

Gavasini and his five battalions and one squadron had stayed at Glarus and Näfels until the 25th, Chabran was at Uznach, and Ménard was on the left bank of the Linth between Lake Zurich and Lake Wallenstadt. On this day, Gavasini carried out a reconnaissance toward Reichenburg, but this was repelled by Ménard with the loss of two guns.

The Action in the Muotta Valley on 28 May

Now on the 28th Gavasini tried to outflank Ménard by means of a detachment sent through the Klön and Muotta valleys via Einsiedeln. By ill luck, part of Lecourbe's division, which Masséna had brought to Altorf from the St. Gotthard, landed at Brunnen at the same time. Gavasini's detachment was thrown back to Glarus again and lost another two guns. After this, he stayed quietly at Mollis.

On the 28th Chabran's division moved from Uznach to Rapperschwyl.

54. For his take on the battle as a whole, see Karl, 1:350–387.

Then on the 29th one part of it went to Zurich, and the other took the Rapperschwyl track to the left bank. On the 31st Jellachich went to Rapperschwyl, and on 1 and 2 June he moved in three columns between Lake Zurich and Lake Greiffen and to the east of the latter. When he reached the area of Wytikon, Fällanden, and Schwerzenbach, Masséna attacked him with part of Soult's division and repulsed him as far as Zollikon.

On this day the archduke moved to Klotten with the main army.

We find ourselves at the threshold of the first battle of Zurich. Before we describe this, we must learn of the events that had taken place at the St. Gotthard between Generals Haddick and Lecourbe.

37 GENERAL HADDICK DRIVES LECOURBE OUT OF THE ST. GOTTHARD PASS

When we last left the corps fighting each other on the southern slopes of the Alps between the Swiss and Italian theaters of operations, Lecourbe was at the St. Gotthard, General Loison at Biasco where the Bregno joins the Ticino, and the Austrian colonels Strauch and Rohan at Bellinzona.

On 26 May General Haddick joined these latter. Following Bellegarde's departure, Haddick was tasked with forming a corps to maintain communications between Suvorov and the archduke and with taking the St. Gotthard to shorten the line of communications. Initially, only Rohan's, Strauch's, and St. Julien's three brigades seem to have been designated for this task, with the latter remaining in the Anterior Rhine valley, as we know. But at Como on 28 May, Bellegarde received the order to leave 10,000 men facing the St. Gotthard.[55] Hence, on that very day he had Debrie's and Lamarcelle's brigades march there, while ordering Nobili's brigade to deploy as a communications outpost at Varese between Lake Maggiore and Lake Como.

Around 27 May, when the maneuvers and combat in this sector of the theater of operations began after eight days' rest, the composition and distribution of the combat forces were as follows.

---

55. **Clausewitz** notes: "*Neue militärische Zeitschrift*; 1812. 5th volume, p58." A number of the early editions of this journal are digitized and available via the Bavarian state library: https://www.bsb-muenchen.de/. Unfortunately, at the time of writing, the volume to which Clausewitz refers is not one of them.

On the 26th, Loison withdraws from Biasco to Dazio in the Ticino valley with one brigade. Lecourbe has an outpost in the St. Gotthard Pass but is with the main body of his division at Urseren, facing Graubündten. Suchet, who initially retreated out of the Rhine valley toward him, has marched straight off again and joined Ménard by Lake Wallenstadt.

On the Austrian side, Haddick's corps was supposed to comprise six brigades, or about 15,000 strong: St. Julien, Rohan, Strauch, Nobili, Debrie, and Lamarcelle. But of these, the first was in the Anterior Rhine valley, and the last three were still with Bellegarde and had not yet arrived at Como.

Thus, Haddick had only Rohan's and Strauch's brigades at hand. On the 26th they pursued General Loison to Giornico. On the 27th Haddick attacked and fought him all day but could not take Airolo.

On this day Lecourbe received the order from Masséna to draw closer to him; he therefore marched to Altorf but sent five battalions through the St. Gotthard to reinforce Loison.

Haddick, for his part, sent an order to General St. Julien to advance over the Crispalt into the Reuss valley and attack the St. Gotthard from that side. Haddick himself attacked Loison again on the evening of the 28th, and this time, Loison had to give way. Perhaps this retreat was actually voluntary and the action just a fighting withdrawal, for the main purpose of Loison's stubborn resistance had been to protect General Lecourbe's departure to Altorf.

The Action at the Devil's Bridge on 29 May

Loison had moved through the St. Gotthard on the 28th, and on the 29th he continued his retreat across the Devil's Bridge. Right at the moment he reached it, St. Julien arrived at Urseren. The French main body still escaped across the bridge, only 600 men being cut off and forced to lay down their arms.

The archduke remarks that General St. Julien was tardy, but it was probably well-judged caution that prevented him from appearing until after he had heard that Lecourbe had left for Altorf.[56]

While Loison was thus barely eluding the Austrian columns, Lecourbe

---

56. Karl, 1:312.

and part of his division, as we have said, had sailed across the Vierwaldstättersee [Lake Lucerne] and beaten Colonel Gavasini in the Muota valley on the 28th.

General Haddick had not bothered to climb over and beyond the St. Gotthard, which would have been so important, as we shall see shortly. Rather, on the 29th he had remained at Airolo with Strauch's brigade, while, per Suvorov's order, he sent Prince Rohan to Domo d'Ossola, presumably to watch the Simplon Pass and maintain communications with Nobili's brigade at Varese.

Thus, the breach of the French right wing effected by Hotze on 14 May, whereby Suchet, Lecourbe, and Loison were apparently completely cut off from Masséna, caused none of these corps any trouble. Instead, Suchet unhurriedly rejoined Masséna, Lecourbe found his way to Lake Lucerne, and even Loison escaped without significant loss, albeit not without difficulty. Indeed, the result could not really have been otherwise, so long as only General St. Julien's five battalions from the Rhine valley were tasked with separating this force of close to 15,000 men from the rest of the army. It was natural that General St. Julien should be wary of getting too close to General Lecourbe, hence he did not enter the Reuss valley until he knew Lecourbe had left; thus it is not surprising that he arrived too late to cut off Loison as he followed after.

After this conquest of the St. Gotthard, we find General Haddick's force with:

Nobili's brigade at Varese
Rohan's brigade at Domo d'Ossola
Strauch's brigade at Airolo
St. Julien's brigade on the march toward Altorf following Loison
Lamarcelle's and Debrie's brigades on the march to Airolo

Thus the whole force was spread across some 90 miles.

The Actions at Am-Steg on 31 May and the Devil's Bridge on 1 June

Such a deployment to maintain communications not only dissipated forces to such an extent that it neutralized 15,000 men; it also resulted in an outright loss. General St. Julien had advanced to Am-Steg in the Reuss valley because he probably did not count on a quick about-face by Lecourbe. However, when the latter learned of the Austrian general's approach, he turned around to reinforce Loison with some of his troops and attacked St. Julien at Am-Steg on 31 May. Lecourbe beat St. Julien on two days in succession after stubborn resistance and drove him back up the Reuss valley and across the Devil's Bridge so violently that, in prisoners alone, St. Julien lost three entire battalions that had to lay down their arms. He was able to salvage the wreckage of his corps only by demolishing one of the arches leading to the Devil's Bridge. The support of one battalion sent to his aid from the St. Gotthard by Haddick was of no great help.

While the Austrians were thus alternately victors and vanquished, they made themselves masters of the St. Gotthard. Meanwhile, the French bent their efforts toward regaining control of the Wallis valley in which, as we have said, the insurrection had formed a substantial corps of 6,000 men with five guns. General Xaintrailles had been ordered to form a division of fourteen battalions and three cavalry regiments out of the troops arriving from France, with which he was first to disperse the insurrection in Wallis and then march away to reinforce the Army of Italy. He and his troops had entered the Rhone valley via Martigny and driven the insurgents back to Leuk, where they took position while he remained at Siders and awaited the last of his troops. Xaintrailles moved into Wallis, but how long he held his position facing the insurgents and what transpired there remain untold by the French history of the war. Another couple of thousand men joined his corps from the *pays de Vaud*, which we must assume brought him up to 10,000 men.

On 27 May the insurgents made an attempt against the camp at Siders, which was repelled. On the 28th Xaintrailles attacked the insurgents himself, beat them, took all their artillery, and drove them up the Rhone, some toward the Simplon Pass and some toward the Furka. Thus, these poor people were left to the mercy of a superior enemy while the Austrians sat quietly at Airolo and Domo d'Ossola. In particular, it seems that Prince Rohan did not support their attack of the 27th, or certainly not in any significant way; General Haddick cared even less about their situation, as he remained halted at Airolo on the 28th and 29th.

These twin French successes against St. Julien and in Wallis caused Haddick to send Colonel Strauch to Oberwald at the entrance to that valley, while he himself remained at Airolo with Debrie's and Lamarcelle's brigades, which had arrived in the meantime. Before we spin the yarn any further of the secondary and basically very insignificant events between the intermediary corps, we must turn to the main armies in Switzerland, on whose subsequent deployments that which follows depends.

38 THE FIRST BATTLE OF ZURICH ON 4 JUNE.[57]
MASSÉNA MOVES BACK ACROSS THE LIMMAT

We left the two main armies at the point where Masséna had occupied his entrenched position between the Limmat and the Glatt and the archduke was approaching.

Masséna's plan was to deploy his army at Zurich and accept a decisive battle there. Zurich itself was certainly strategically significant.[58] Specifically, Zurich lies at a crossroads from which major highways radiate out toward Bern, Basel, Schafhausen, Constance, Bregenz, Feldkirch, and the minor cantons. With the 30-mile-long Lake Zurich on one side and the Glatt, Limmat, Reuss, Aare, and Rhine clustered together on the other, detouring around this place would be a difficult and complex operation for the enemy. Finally, Zurich is a city of 11,000 inhabitants and thus one of the largest in Switzerland, and it is a fortress (albeit a weak one) that was distinguished, at the time, by a richly endowed arsenal.[59] Retaining total control of this place was therefore a not unimportant aim for the French commander.

Masséna decided to take position *in front* of Zurich rather than *behind* it, for the following not unimportant reasons:

1. Because the area there offered a very advantageous position.
2. Because this was even stronger toward the Limmat, and if it fell into the Austrians' hands, it would blockade the town of Zurich.
3. Because the weakness of the fortifications was a reason to deploy in front of them; although they were protected against escalade, they were seriously overlooked and could be defended against numerous enemy artillery only at a great cost in men.
4. Given the still very unfavorable mood of the Swiss, it was not unim-

---

57. The archduke's account is detailed and worth the reader's time. Karl, 1:350–387. Also see Jomini, 11:246–253.
58. The archduke saw it as the decisive strategic point. See note 43 of this chapter.
59. The archduke claims that 149 cannon of various calibers were there. Karl, 1:380.

portant to protect Zurich from bombardment. The outcome proves this, since after Masséna's retreat across the Limmat, ten battalions of the Swiss contingent dispersed.

All these reasons had obliged General Masséna to establish an entrenched camp next to Zurich in which to deploy his main body. It would thus become unassailable, would be a constant offensive threat to the enemy, and could therefore constantly keep him in check, because there was no way the enemy would be strong enough to surround the camp completely and cut off all its lines of communication.

Unlike the other authors,[60] we do not say that Masséna was doing this to try to wait for the considerable reinforcements that were supposed to be coming from the interior. The Austrians found themselves in the same situation, as General Korsakov was on his way to them.

However, the French commander felt he could not unite his force in this position to such a degree that he could leave the area below it as far as the Rhine merely under observation, and still less so that area on the west side of Lake Zurich. Instead, as is usually the case in a war of mutual observation between evenly matched forces, he kept suitable forces ready to resist everywhere.

Thus he kept one strong division covering the area below the position—not behind the Limmat, as one might expect at first glance, but between the Glatt and the Limmat in the direction of Kaiserstuhl. He obviously chose this position for his left wing because it was shorter than the one behind the Limmat and the Aare as far as Koblenz.

On the other side, General Ménard was on the western shore of Lake Zurich and had drawn General Suchet back to him, as we said.

We do not know exactly what had become of Lorge's division under Chabran's command. It seems that the right wing of the French combat forces was reorganized, and from now on, it comprised just two divisions. Lecourbe's division had probably been reinforced somewhat, and perhaps some of Lorge's troops had been moved to the center. At the time of the first battle of Zurich, we find General Ménard in command on the western side of Lake Zurich, but Chabran is in his place after that.

---

60. See Karl, 1:377–379; Jomini, 11:253–254.

Only Oudinot's and Soult's divisions are mentioned as being in the entrenched camp, along with a reserve of grenadiers.

Here again, we must therefore make do with guesswork, according to which it may be broadly assumed that Tharreau was below the position, between it and the Rhine, with 8,000–10,000 men; Ménard was by Lake Zurich with 5,000–6,000 men; and there were 20,000–25,000 men in the position itself. This makes 40,000 men altogether for the six original divisions (Tharreau, Lorge, Ménard, Vandamme, Soult, and Oudinot), not counting the 6,000–8,000 Swiss troops.

The position Masséna had chosen was on the crest of the high ridge that runs between the Limmat and the Glatt toward the Rhine.[61] In the vicinity of Zurich, the base of this ridge is 3,000–4,000 paces wide, but its crest is mostly only a few hundred paces across, while its height varies from 500 to 600 feet. It draws close to Zurich, with its western slope encamped hard by the Limmat, whereby it forms the strong position facing Zurich to which we have alluded; its eastern slope faces the Glatt, but in some places it leaves a plain 1,500 paces wide between its foot and the river, and in others, such as below Schwamendingen where the Glatt turns east, it is undulating open country.

The eastern slope of the ridge that provides the front of the position is fairly steep, and in many places it is completely impassable. It is cut up by a host of small, sharply indented, partly forested valleys, and the crest itself is also partly forested and impassable. Such a slope naturally provided a very strong obstacle to approaching the position, though of course, this could not be covered adequately by fire everywhere. A major strength of this front was that the enemy's approach to his chosen crossing points over the Glatt could be observed very easily, while it was necessarily very difficult for an attacker to assess the position and its troop dispositions to any degree.

The entrenched position on this ridge was such that it lay in the form of an elliptical arc about 2,000 paces from Zurich. The right flank reached Lake Zurich 1,000 paces from the city walls, the left rested on the Limmat at the village of Höngg a mile below the city, and the front was about 4 miles in extent.

The front proper of the entrenched camp may be divided into three sectors. The Züricherberg, on the line from Schwamendingen to Zurich, formed

---

61. It is worth looking at the archduke's maps in Karl, vol. 3, particularly map VI. These maps (along with the entire history) are available online at https://www.e-rara.ch/zut/content/pageview/10433846.

the right wing; the Wipkingerberg, on the line from the Katzensee to Zurich, the left. Both are forested hilltops a few thousand paces long. Between these two and a bit further back lies a somewhat lower ridge, a few thousand paces longer and more open and accessible, so that the first two hills seem like bastions, with the third as their curtain wall. The part of the line that curved back toward the lake from the Züricherberg naturally lay on the western slope of the ridge and was dominated in some places by the terrain in front of it; by contrast, the Wipkingerberg reached to within 1,000 paces of the Limmat and completely dominated its own foothills as far as the river.

So far as we can tell from Archduke Charles's map,[62] which is hardly totally reliable in this respect, the entrenchments were composed partly of individual redoubts and flèche-type works a few hundred paces apart, partly of continuous lines up to 1,000 paces long, and extensive abatis wherever there were woods. The 4,000 paces of the line from the Züricherberg to the lake had far fewer works, for in this whole stretch there were only three or four flèches. But an actual position as such was not really necessary there anyway, since unstormable Zurich was behind it. It should therefore be considered just a reinforced outpost line.

The entrenchments were still not quite complete, even though they had been under construction for six weeks. This must have been a major reason why Masséna abandoned the position after the battle.

A major defect of the position, which Masséna may have realized too late—that is, not until the critical moment of the battle on the 4th—was its lack of alternative crossings over the Limmat other than through Zurich, which naturally meant that the line of retreat of the center and left flank could come under significant threat. Besides, even in Zurich itself there were only three bridges across the Limmat, only one of which could be used by wheeled transport.

Masséna had deployed twenty-eight guns from the Zurich arsenal in the position, but according to the archduke,[63] he had already moved part of his own artillery across the Limmat to safety, as well as the baggage train. If this is true, then the latter measure—which Jomini also mentions,[64] though with deliberate ambiguity—combined with the ensuing voluntary evacuation of the

62. See Karl, vol. 3, map VI.
63. Karl, 1:357.
64. Jomini, 11:252–253.

position on the 6th, leads us to suppose that ultimately Masséna was not really serious about defending it.

Such was the French commander's situation when the archduke pushed forward as far as the Glatt on 3 June with the intention of fighting a decisive battle.

According to the archduke, the force that he and Hotze had under command on the spot consisted of 53 battalions and 67 squadrons. The combat forces of these two commanders had originally comprised 87 battalions and 176 squadrons. Eighteen battalions and 64 squadrons were under Starray in the Black Forest, and 5 battalions and 6 squadrons were in Graubündten. That still leaves 59 battalions and somewhat more than 100 squadrons; if Auffenberg's misadventures had not reduced the number of battalions, there would have been another 6 battalions and 40 squadrons on the right bank of the Rhine.[65] It is fairly certain that matters stood this way as far as the infantry are concerned, but as for the 40 squadrons, there had presumably been other detachments sent off that the archduke has forgotten to mention; in particular, it seems that Bellegarde arrived in Italy with rather more cavalry than he started with.

We may assume these fifty-three battalions and sixty-seven squadrons came to around 60,000 men, which General Masséna could oppose only with his main body and Tharreau's and Ménard's divisions, or 45,000 men all told, and it is likely that even some of these could not be brought up in time. Thus the archduke would have had at least a third more men.

While its considerable extent for the number of troops he had means that Masséna's position cannot be considered impregnable, it still looked very strong. Attacking it therefore seemed to be a course of action that promised little success and one that could be chosen only if there were no other way. Thus it seemed natural that the archduke should attack General Tharreau first, drive him across the Limmat, and then await the consequences; if his opponent did not abandon his position, perhaps a crossing of the Limmat could be attempted, which, if successful, would oblige Masséna to either abandon the position or at least fight the archduke outside it.

---

65. Clausewitz's arithmetic seems faulty here. If the forces in the Black Forest and Graubündten totaled 23 battalions and 70 squadrons, deducting these from the original 87 and 176 leaves 64 and 106. Subtracting the archduke's and Hotze's 53 and 67 leaves 11 battalions and 39 squadrons unaccounted for, not the 6 and 40 that Clausewitz states.

It seems that the archduke did not give proper consideration to this natural direction for his operation. He assumed that a strategic outflanking of the position on its left side required a much greater superiority than he possessed. What he says about the danger to his line of retreat while outflanking the left wing really relates to a tactical outflanking, undertaken with the aim of attacking the camp on its left wing and left flank. He imagined that, in such an attack, he would have his rear toward Kaiserstuhl, where he would have no bridge over the Rhine and only difficult roads; from this, he concluded that prudence left him no option other than a frontal attack.

We wish to defer our examination of this reasoning to the end of this section, having raised it here only because it belongs to the course of events.

Thus the archduke decided not only to attack Masséna's position but also to attack with his main body directly against its front. His dispositions were the following.

The attack was to be carried out in five columns:

1. Jellachich with five battalions and three squadrons along the lake road against the right wing of the enemy's right flank line.
2. General Bey with four battalions and three squadrons from Wytikon toward Hirslanden against the center of the right flank line.
3. Prince von Lothringen with four battalions and four squadrons from Dubendorf.
4. General Hotze with seven battalions and twelve squadrons from Schwamendingen; thus eleven battalions and sixteen squadrons combined were to attack the Züricherberg, which was the right wing of the front and its key point.
5. Prince Reuss with ten battalions and twenty squadrons was to advance via Seebach and Orlikon against the center of the enemy position.

Eight battalions and sixteen squadrons were placed in reserve at Optikon on the Glatt.

Nauendorf remained on the lower Glatt with fifteen battalions and nine squadrons to observe General Tharreau.

According to these dispositions, nine battalions and six squadrons were to engage the enemy's right flank. We may view this as merely a diversion, since even if these troops did break through, they would hit the fortifications of Zurich, which they could not simply take *chemin faisant* [along the way].

But the attack on the enemy right wing and center was carried out by twenty-one battalions and thirty-six squadrons. This is not an insignificant mass, but because they were directed against an area of the enemy position 4,000 paces across, they may again be regarded as being very split up and extended.

The reserve at Optikon, 2 miles from the enemy position, may be considered more a strategic reserve than a tactical one. To that extent, it was not part of the attacking force, whose thirty battalions and forty-two squadrons we may estimate at 33,000 men, though of course, it should be remarked that the 6,000–7,000 cavalry could be of little use in an attack on such a position.

It is really self-evident that such an attack could not break through anywhere,[66] and it is likewise no surprise that it never reached the position proper, being repulsed at the foot of the mountain ridge. It was a futile blow, half strength and halfhearted.

The outcome conformed entirely with how it had been set up.

Jellachich drove the French from their position on the right flank to beneath the walls of Zurich, was repulsed from there, advanced again, and finished up taking position at Riedsbach, 1,500 paces from the fortifications.

General Bey advanced through Hirslanden against Holtingen but had to fall back some way again and took position level with Jellachich.

Prince von Lothringen, who was actually supposed to advance via Stettbach directly against the entrenchments on the Züricherberg, felt that he could make no progress through the difficult, broken terrain of its slopes and took a huge detour through Fällanden behind the second column, then turned right from Praffenhausen. He reached the Attisberg and Topelhof, 1,500 paces from the Züricherberg entrenchments, but then foundered on the abatis in front of these redoubts, and at 2:00 p.m. he withdrew out of range of the enemy's fire.

General Hotze could not force a crossing at Schwamendingen. He therefore moved through Dübendorf but had great difficulty taking the villages of Stettbach and Schwamendingen, which lay 2,000–3,000 paces in front of the position proper. He himself was wounded during this attempt and had to give up his corps; Petrasch, who took over command, got no further than the foot of the heights.

66. There was insufficient strength at any one point to achieve a breakthrough of the French lines.

Prince Reuss moved his left wing to Orlikon, thus, like Hotze, reaching the foot of the main ridge. However, as the archduke says, with the rest of his force he adopted a position in the shape of an arc with his right wing at Rümlang, but that village is on the Glatt, 3 miles from Orlikon. This therefore obviously had an entirely defensive character, as though he feared an attack by the enemy's left wing; yet that was threatened by a greatly superior corps and, in any case, could have been repulsed by the strategic reserve waiting at Optikon.

At 1:00 p.m., by which time the Austrian attack had roughly taken shape, the archduke still thought he could break through with a reinforcement of five battalions under General Wallis, which he brought up from the reserve. He had Wallis advance between Hotze and Lothringen via Schwamendingen and the brickworks against the Züricherberg, and he ordered Prince von Lothringen to renew his attack on the mountain. Wallis left one battalion at the Schwamendingen bridge and advanced with the other four against the French position. He actually got closer than any of the other columns; he took an abatis and even one of the enemy batteries but was met there with such superior force and devastating fire that he had to retreat with heavy losses. Generals Wallis and Hiller were wounded there. This column's deeper penetration is easily explained, since it arrived so much later than the others and the enemy could not remain equally strong everywhere along his extended battle line, so this point was probably only weakly held. But when the column penetrated into the position, it was the reserve of grenadiers under Masséna's personal command that hurled it back.

Prince von Lothringen's renewed attack was no more successful than his first one, and at the end of the day, he and his main body retreated to the Wytikon heights.

We know nothing of the French dispositions. The course of events tells us that Soult commanded on the right wing, Oudinot on the left, and Masséna himself was on the Züricherberg. On this day, the French were mostly fighting not in their entrenchments on the high ridge but in the abatis at its foot, where individual units frequently went over to the offensive.

The day's result was therefore that, including General Wallis's force, 35,000 men fought against 25,000, and that the latter, favored by very strong terrain and supported by the redoubts behind them, repulsed the attack everywhere, and the Austrians lost 3,000–4,000 men. The ferocity of the fighting at certain points is proved by the large number of wounded generals: Oudinot and Humbert on the French side, and Hotze, Wallis, and Hiller for the Austrians.

Masséna could count himself the victor, yet the archduke still did not want to abandon the attack. The archduke himself says, "he occupied himself by using the vantage points that had been gained to reconnoiter a position that could neither be seen into nor gauged from a distance, and decided to base a new plan of attack on what he thus discovered."[67]

We confess that we do not understand this first sentence, which has perhaps turned out to be so obscure by accident: "Cost what it may, the enemy had to be driven out of his occupation of Zurich, without which there was nowhere the Austrians could deploy to cover the area of Stockach, the Vorarlberg and their line of communications with Italy all at the same time."[68]

The archduke's next attempt was a surprise attack on the night of 5–6 June.[69] He mustered two columns of eight battalions each, probably of picked troops, one at Schwamendingen and the other between Orlikon and Seebach; the first was to advance against the Geisberg, the second against the center. At the same time, the archduke moved his right wing from the lower Glatt toward the center and replaced it with four battalions he brought up from the troops that were still on the right bank of the Rhine. These troops set off at 2:00 a.m. The archduke forbade them to load their muskets. He therefore envisaged actually overrunning the enemy and was very much counting on all the advantages of surprise that this unusual and thus certainly unexpected measure could provide. Especially, he reckoned that the garrison of this strongest point of the position might have been weakened the most, which was justified by the character of the fighting on the 4th.[70]

But while the Austrian commander was moving to execute this new plan, on that very night of 5–6 June, the French commander had already vacated his position, abandoned the twenty-eight guns from the Zurich arsenal, and retreated behind the Limmat with his army. The city of Zurich was vacated at midday on the 6th by agreement, and its 150 guns were left for the Austrians.

There is naturally something very surprising about Masséna's retreat. He had been working on this position's entrenchments for several months, constructing thirty or forty redoubts, felling abatis 1,000–1,500 paces across, and emplacing twenty-eight guns from Zurich there. He had accepted a battle

67. Karl, 1:374.
68. Karl, 1:374.
69. Karl, 1:374.
70. Karl, 1:375–376.

there, and the enemy had not reached the main position at all, except for one single point where he was repulsed with heavy losses. Despite this, and without any external reason, the French commander retreats, abandoning his position, his redoubts, his artillery, his victory, and the city of Zurich. This striking inconsistency has naturally drawn the critic's gaze. General Jomini[71] believes there were three reasons motivating the retreat—namely, the incomplete state of the entrenchments; the danger to the line of retreat if one individual point was lost, since everything had to go through Zurich; and finally, the fact that the Zurich position was of only secondary importance, merely a bridgehead.[72]

We must respond to these three reasons by asking, if this position had so little strategic importance, why did General Masséna establish it, and if it was so untenable, why did he accept battle there? We make this remark simply to show that the retreat cannot be motivated by these reasons in any natural way, and in fact, military history still lacks a cause for this extremely unexpected step, of which no report is to be found in the *Moniteur*. Since there is not the remotest suggestion of any external reason, obviously, we can seek this cause only in the course of the battle. This was thoroughly favorable for the French, and their success on the 4th was so total that their situation was never in doubt, so far as we can judge from the outside. Yet on 4 June Masséna must have felt that he was too weak for the extent of his position. He must have known that on the 4th the archduke had not attacked with his full strength; so when the archduke remained in position on the 5th, with one foot raised for the next step, as it were, Masséna probably feared that he was concentrating his army and planned to attack him with full force, and perhaps he thought he could not withstand such a concentrated attack. It therefore seems that precisely because the archduke *held on in his attack position* on the 5th, Masséna was prompted to retreat.

Now, whatever circumstances may have appeared worrying to the French commander in the course of a battle that, it seems to us, turned out so entirely favorably, nonetheless it remains an unresolved inconsistency to have abandoned a position that was still completely intact and whose key features had not even come into action yet. We are compelled to say that either the position

---

71. **Clausewitz** notes: "Jomini, 11:253." Jomini writes: "Some writers have reproached Massena for prematurely abandoning his camp at Zurich." Jomini, 11:252–254.

72. Jomini, 11:253–254.

was no good from the start, or else it must have been good enough for 6 June as well.

As far as Switzerland was concerned, Masséna's action had immediate consequences: the seat of government moved from Lucerne to Zurich, and almost the whole Swiss contingent with Masséna's army dispersed.

Masséna now deployed his army on that section of the Albis that runs behind the Limmat and is known as the Ütli.

The archduke had his army move onto the heights between the Limmat and the Glatt, pushed a small advance guard across the Sihl from Zurich, occupied Zurich with five battalions, and established his headquarters in Klotten.

Masséna's headquarters was in Bremgarten on the Reuss. General Tharreau withdrew behind the Aare.

39 HADDICK IS RECALLED TO ITALY FROM HIS OFFENSIVE AGAINST XAINTRAILLES

At the St. Gotthard Pass, we left General Xaintrailles advancing toward the source of the Rhone, General Lecourbe pursuing St. Julien, and Haddick in the Reuss valley. The two French generals seem to have been endeavoring to link up at the St. Gotthard, but it appears that the demolition of part of the Devil's Bridge in front of Lecourbe and the deployment of Strauch's brigade facing Xaintrailles at Oberwald had the effect of bringing them both to a halt. The fact that Haddick was between the sources of the Reuss, the Rhone, and the Ticino with 10,000–12,000 men probably helps explain it as well. However, they might not have been deterred for long from conducting a joint attack on the St. Gotthard had the archduke's advance on Zurich not obliged General Masséna to withdraw his right wing to Altorf and Lake Lucerne again.

There is no record of when General Lecourbe marched off with the troops he had used against St. Julien, nor of where he and his entire division were for the first eight days of June.[73] It is clear that his move to Lake Lucerne was a half-measure, since he could not take part in the battle at Zurich, and while Lecourbe was apparently away from the action, Haddick could have attacked

---

73. The archduke mentions him marching toward Brig on 4 June. Karl, 1:383–384.

General Xaintrailles in greatly superior force and seized control of the whole of Wallis.

Yet this did not happen, and through order and counterorder, a most reprehensible neutralization of forces arose on the Austrian side. First, General Haddick seemingly sat idle at Airolo until 9 June. On that day he crossed the St. Gotthard to Oberwald with Debrie's and Lamarcelle's brigades, nine battalions strong, while at the same time ordering Rohan's and Nobili's brigades to advance on the Simplon Pass. This made Xaintrailles withdraw to Brig and Naters. By 13 June, both the latter brigades had reached the Simplon, and Haddick had advanced to Münster. It seemed the moment had arrived when Xaintrailles would be forced to quit Wallis completely. But to give Suvorov's conquests in Italy a truly decisive character through great numerical superiority, the court of Vienna had now decided that General Haddick should join him as well. Thus, on the 13th Haddick received the order from Suvorov that, as decreed by the emperor in person, he should instigate the relief of his troops by General Hotze and then send them in detachments by forced marches to Alessandria. This order of Suvorov's arose from Macdonald's approach and Suvorov's concern that he would not be strong enough to withstand the combined operations of both French commanders. Now Haddick could and should have continued his offensive against Xaintrailles,[74] for that would soon have given him control of the route through the Simplon Pass, and a successful outcome would have made him all the more ready to march away and put him in a position to take the shorter route. This case obviously has much in common with General Bellegarde's departure from Graubündten, except that here, continuing the attack would have made everything much easier and less uncertain, while on the other hand, waiting for his troops to be relieved before leaving made Haddick's departure dependent on others. Thus, while many reasons of normal prudence may be offered for General Bellegarde's decision, there is no such excuse for General Haddick calling off his offensive. But this general acted like all those who act as ordered for fear of responsibility rather than following their own desires at such moments: he used the order he had received as a pretext for abandoning his plan of attack. A detachment under General Bey, sent by General Jellachich to support General St. Julien, had arrived at the St. Gotthard, and Haddick handed over the position at the Devil's

---

74. This reminds us of Clausewitz's point about continuity in *On War*, book 1, chap. 1. See also book 3, chap. 16, on the suspension of action in war.

Bridge to Bey. Haddick had Strauch's troops advance a little further against Xaintrailles as a demonstration to cover his departure, and he began concentrating the rest of his troops at Airolo in preparation to leave. Before he set off, a letter from the archduke arrived, insisting that there could be no question of Hotze's troops relieving him and that his departure from Wallis would have the most adverse consequences. Both statements by the archduke betray his great anxiety and the exaggerated value he attached to the occupation of high regions, his later assertions notwithstanding. Just after Haddick received this letter, a repeated and indeed duplicated order arrived from Suvorov and Melas, instructing Haddick to expedite his march. He began it immediately (presumably on 15 June), leaving Colonel Strauch in the Wallis valley, and had reached Bellinzona on the 17th when he received a counterorder to continue his operations in Wallis.

One might have expected General Haddick to return to the Rhone valley without delay, but he apparently did not find Suvorov's later order sufficient to cancel Melas's earlier one. He therefore consulted his former commander, General Bellegarde, whom he was supposed to join, and stayed at Bellinzona meanwhile. Here, on the 23rd, he received a demand from the chief of staff of the army in Italy, General Chasteler, that he should betake himself on a forced march to Alessandria, again contradicting the previous order. This order had obviously been prepared for dispatch after the battle of the Trebbia, demonstrating yet again how worried the army in Italy was about the supposed French superiority. Even after the most glorious victory over one of the two French commanders, the Austrians still did not believe they could match the French strength.

On the 24th Haddick began his march via Milan, where he got the order to hasten his troops' march but to return in person to Wallis. But even this order was amended again. The archduke had refused outright[75] to extend himself far enough to the south to take over the positions held by Haddick, and General Bey would not extend any further than the Devil's Bridge. Suvorov therefore assigned Haddick's corps to observe General Xaintrailles. Strauch remained in the Rhone valley, Prince Rohan occupied the Simplon Pass, and Haddick posted himself at Aosta to observe the two St. Bernard Passes.

Thus, three weeks of June passed by, during which Haddick's 12,000 men

---

75. Karl, 2:10.

facing an enemy force of about 8,000 were kept inactive by indecision and contradictory orders, at a time when they were thought to be urgently needed in Italy.

Meanwhile, as we have said, Masséna deemed it sensible to draw his right wing still closer in, to abandon the St. Gotthard completely for the time being, and to content himself with a position between the lakes.

On 8 June Lecourbe vacated Altorf and Schwyz; his main body went by water from Altorf to Lucerne, while the detachment from Schwyz moved to Arth on Lake Zug.

Since the archduke anticipated that the positions adopted by the opposing armies on 6 June would last for a while and would lead to a war of observation, it seemed to him that his left wing, which was supposed to maintain communications with Haddick 80 miles away, was not strong enough. This left wing had consisted of five battalions and one squadron under Gavasini and five battalions and six squadrons in the Rhine valley. These last units had partly reinforced Gavasini and partly St. Julien, but as we have described, Gavasini had suffered significant losses against Lecourbe. This therefore left only about 5,000–6,000 men, of which probably several battalions were still in the upper part of the Anterior Rhine valley. On 6 June, two days after the battle, the archduke therefore sent General Jellachich with nine battalions and several squadrons to Uznach to unite with Gavasini, which brought Jellachich's corps up to 12,000 men. He linked this reinforcement of his left flank with the idea of using it in combination with Haddick's corps to drive the French right wing further back. This last aim was thwarted by Haddick's departure.

General Jellachich sent General Bey with four and a half battalions and one squadron from Uznach into the Anterior Rhine valley to advance into the Reuss valley and come to the aid of St. Julien, whom he believed to be hard pressed by Lecourbe. But we have seen that it was too late for that, and this detachment served to relieve General Haddick's outpost at the Devil's Bridge. Jellachich himself advanced with six battalions and five squadrons down the right side of Lake Zurich to Rapperswil, and had three battalions move through the Klön and Muotta valleys to Schwyz to establish an outpost there; communications posts were established at Schindelegi and Einsiedeln.[76]

---

76. The archduke's dispositions are detailed in Karl, 2:11–12.

The French under Lecourbe were on both sides of Lake Lucerne from Lake Sarnen to Lake Zug.[77] Lecourbe's headquarters was in Lucerne.

At this time, the other division, hitherto commanded by Ménard, was under Chabran's orders, but we do not know what had happened to Ménard. On 12 June it was deployed with its right wing at Sattel; from there, its line ran via Rothenturm, over the Höhrohnen (a mountain ridge on the river Sihl), to Richterswil on Lake Zurich.

Thus we leave the 40,000-strong French army in a cordon deployment 70 miles long from Lake Sarnen to the Rhine.

The Austrians, about 55,000 strong, are similarly spread out facing them.

40 REFLECTIONS ON THIS CHAPTER

The Austrians

We have already woven many of our reflections into our account, partly because they were needed to explain individual operations, and partly because we were able to introduce them very naturally that way. We still have three things on our mind that we want to talk through: the need to make the conquest of Switzerland the object of the campaign, the attack on Graubündten by Generals Hotze and Bellegarde, and the archduke's attack on Masséna at Zurich.

It is not our intention merely to reiterate our complaints about the Austrians' timidity and lack of enterprise; rather, we wish to draw the reader's gaze back to the position that the conquest of Switzerland actually had in the strategic situation. In section 5 [chapter 1] we demonstrated that upper Italy and Switzerland were the two natural objectives of the offensive and that if one was to be attacked before the other, it had to be Switzerland—not because occupying it would be more important than occupying Lombardy, of course, but simply because *this form of offensive promised greater success overall.* Just because the available forces must have been considered sufficient to conquer both countries, was there no reason to ask which of the two conquests was more valuable? Because of the lack of nerve or strength of will with which the

---

77. Clausewitz states Lake Thun, which makes no sense and is almost certainly an error of transcription. The archduke has it as Lake Zug. See Karl, 2:17–18.

Austrians conducted the war in the German theater of operations, it turned out that they conquered Italy but not Switzerland. The Austrian government seems to have been reconciled to that, as it gave decided preference to upper Italy and had a quarter of the combat forces from the German theater of operations go there under Bellegarde.

This preference for upper Italy was indisputably thoroughly justified; Switzerland was basically not an objective of the war as an asset in its own right. The Austrians could never have any thought of making it an Austrian province, and even the French only wanted to rule it indirectly. By contrast, Lombardy was a former Austrian province, and the French had made it a vassal state that, for the time being, they could regard as their own territory. This was actually just some real estate for political compensation. But a country that one can use directly in a political dispute therefore also has a higher value strategically.[78] Furthermore, the fate of lower Italy depended on the conquest of upper Italy, and finally, because of its size and population, the upper Italian plain alone was more important than Switzerland. Therefore, if one of these two countries had to remain in French hands, it was correct for the Austrian government to prefer that this be Switzerland's lot.

But having acknowledged this, we must still say that the Austrian government unduly overlooked Switzerland's importance to Italy.

The subjugation of Switzerland was not only the first but also the most arrogant of the French actions leading to this armed conflict. France had already been more or less in a state of war with the Italian states, but Switzerland had constantly observed the most meticulous neutrality; the Italian states had been embroiled in every previous war, while Switzerland had stayed aloof from Europe's affairs for centuries. It therefore certainly took much greater arrogance, and more resolute contempt for all old relationships, to decide on this intrusion into Switzerland than it did to overwhelm the Italian states; hence, in this sense, Switzerland was a real point of political honor for Austria and the European powers, which was emphasized yet more by the Swiss people's resistance to the French constitutional reforms.

---

78. This ties in directly with the value of the object of the conflict (*On War*, book 1, chaps. 1 and 2). If the value of the object is high, greater efforts must be expected, especially if the object is of high value to both sides. Here again, it is clear that Clausewitz is using his analysis of history to better understand and explain his theoretical ideas.

For these reasons, without the conquest of Switzerland, the object of the war could never be regarded as having been achieved.[79]

But even the outcome of the campaign seems only half satisfactory without the conquest of Switzerland. The cooperation of a power like Russia in a war against France for many years could not be relied on. The great distance between the theater of war and Russia's borders, the huge costs this entailed, Russia's indirect involvement in the whole business, and the eccentricity of its ruler caused the Austrian government to worry that the alliance would not last long; it therefore felt the need to reach a stage in the first campaign that promised to lead to peace, either directly or at least as a result of success in the second campaign.[80] The mere conquest of Italy was not such a stage. A French force on the Rhine was a greater threat to Austria than an Austrian one at the foot of the Cottian Alps was to France; however excellent Italy may have been as a pledge or a bargaining chip for peace, it was of little consequence when it came to intimidating the French government. With Switzerland, it was quite the reverse; it was of very little value as a pledge but far more valuable as a base for attack, because its occupation threatened the heart of France with invasion without having to leave two-thirds of one's army before the Rhine fortresses.[81] Thus if, during the course of the campaign, the allies showed that they were in fact incapable of conquering Switzerland, then indeed one could see no reason for the French government to be especially worried about the year 1800.

These considerations should not have left the Austrian government and its commanders so indifferent toward Switzerland.

But now yet another point arises that relates not directly to Switzerland but to the need for sufficient action. When a power wages war on its own, it can use time and forces as it pleases, or at least no secondary disadvantage

---

79. This is because the two sides would have been at war without achieving the initial aim: sorting out the control or neutrality of Switzerland.

80. For Russia, the war was not an immediate and direct threat, so the Russians were less likely to increase their effort than the Austrians, for whom the war was far more important.

81. **Clausewitz** notes: "This certainly does not mean that we think it would have been sensible for the great allied army of 1814 to take a route through Switzerland. At that time it was not a question just of invasion but of the conquest of France, and their armies were not at the Swiss border but at Mainz; but their opponent had fled to France with his sword shattered, and it was only a matter of striking the shard from his hand before he could sharpen its point again."

arises from doing so. But in an alliance, it is invariably the case that conspicuous inactivity by one ally either obliges the other to follow suit or causes such irritation that it leads to an early collapse of the alliance.[82] The latter was the case here. The Austrians themselves cannot deny it, and the archduke frankly admits that they sat on their hands when they could and should have been acting. The Austrian government probably could have told itself that the Russians would not forgive them for this. Thus, if the Austrian councils and commanders had kept this in mind, they would have been stricken with strategic remorse and avoided strolling vacantly around the Rhine and Lake Constance with their superior combat forces as if they could not decide how to kill the time.

We will wait until the end of the campaign, when all the individual episodes of attack and defense of mountain regions have been revealed, to put forward the conclusions that can be drawn from these events, as much to highlight the characteristic behaviors of the two armies as to obtain a general result for theory.[83]

What we have to say now about the attack by Generals Bellegarde and Hotze against Graubündten at the end of April and mid-May concerns only its overall strategic value.

The idea of attacking the Inn and Rhine valleys simultaneously is certainly a very natural one, since they lie parallel to each other and are connected via the Prettigau in the area where the main positions were—namely, the St. Luciensteig and the position at Remüs. But it cannot be asserted that it was therefore completely unfeasible to attack just one of these two valleys. After all, in such high mountains, there is no pressing need for the strategic front to follow a straight line because flanking operations cannot take effect so quickly and unexpectedly that an attack on one's rear could not be countered, as the French repeatedly demonstrated. The outcome of the attacks undertaken at

---

82. It is likely that each member of an alliance has its own objectives, and even if the objectives are the same, the value placed on them differs. Logically, this means that each ally weighs its own effort against what it wants from the conflict. Thus, the degree of effort is rarely the same for each alliance member unless they are all threatened existentially, in which case their options are (one would hope) obvious: fight or die.

83. If the value of Switzerland and Italy was high for the Austrians, they should have put more effort into their conquest. That they seemingly made only a halfhearted effort indicates that they placed a low value on these countries or that they misunderstood what was at stake in the conflict.

the end of April also sufficiently proves what has been said here, since the attack in the Rhine valley failed utterly without preventing Bellegarde from driving Lecourbe out of the Inn valley.

Thus, when we see these two generals discuss the attack for four weeks initially and then for another fourteen days, resulting in a long postponement, we can only ascribe this to a mistaken view and a lack of decisiveness. This criticism applies mainly to General Bellegarde, who was almost twice as strong as Hotze and, unlike him, did not have to hold a long line that was threatened by the enemy's main body. This case, like a thousand others, shows that the good intentions, ambition, and spirit of enterprise of subordinate commanders can powerfully support action in war and that one should not think everything must come from above. This is even more true in the mountains than on the plain, because their situation is necessarily more independent there. The fact that the Austrian commanders, especially General Bellegarde, were as lacking in these qualities as the French division commanders Lecourbe and Dessolles were distinguished by them may be regarded as one of the main reasons why the Austrians' campaign in Germany did not turn out well, despite their great superiority.[84]

When these two generals finally set their attack in motion with 35,000–36,000 men on 14 May, with the goal of driving some 10,000 men out of the Rhine valleys, their plan did not even dare to consider destroying this weak corps. Instead of advancing into the Posterior Rhine valley first with Bellegarde's corps and then into the Anterior Rhine valley, while Hotze advanced into the Prettigau and against the St. Luciensteig to overwhelm the Kunkel Pass with a detachment and then advanced down the Rhine and the Tamina against Maienfeld, whereby the whole French right wing and everything the French had in the Prettigau would have been cut off from retreat, on the contrary, Bellegarde only crossed the Albula on the 15th, a day later, and did not risk advancing any further than the Posterior Rhine. At the time and on the spot, there were no doubt a thousand minor reasons for this, but even without knowing any of them, we may venture to direct the harshest criticism against this timorous half measure, since there was no danger of any kind to justify it.

Finally, as far as the archduke's attack on Masséna's main body is con-

---

84. This lack of dynamism is not attributable to just their respective ages. For example, Suvorov was old but still pretty dynamic and bold, in comparison to the Austrians.

cerned, we must pick out two topics: the archduke's advance, and the assault on the entrenched position.

The archduke's and Hotze's combined forces totaled some 70,000 men. What Masséna actually had against them was some 40,000 French troops; he could have brought up most of the troops at Basel, which would have brought his force up to 50,000 men, or 60,000 if we include the Swiss. Also, one could not know how close General Lecourbe was, as he had returned to the St. Gotthard from the Tresa when the archduke crossed the Rhine. If we add another 8,000 men for Lecourbe, Masséna would also have been close to 70,000 strong. It is natural that when the archduke crossed the Rhine, he would have been looking at this total number of troops, and he must have thought to himself that however they might be deployed, they were still around, and he could not be sure that some of them would be completely neutralized. Thus, while the Austrians as the attackers could hope to be stronger at the decisive point, they could not rely on their superiority to achieve such a decisive success there that they could ignore all the other points entirely. But when one is no longer certain of success, concentration of one's entire force becomes dangerous, and such a cautious commander as the archduke was not the man to expose himself to that danger. As a consequence, on one side a corps of 6,000–8,000 men was left behind to cover Feldkirch and the St. Luciensteig and to observe the French right wing; on the other side, a force of similar size was left to observe the French at Basel and between Basel and Schafhausen to protect the rear and the bridges. This meant the attack could no longer be undertaken with 70,000 men but with only about 56,000, without knowing for sure whether they would have to deal with a force of similar size or even greater.

In such circumstances, and with a cautious commander, there could be no thought of the Austrians making the only suitable use of their enveloping deployment—namely, bringing the whole force to bear with a thoroughly determined advance by the separate columns, gaining in one place whatever might be lost in the other. The separate columns were the archduke's and Hotze's: the former was about 38,000 strong, the latter 18,000; the former was based on Schafhausen and Stein, the latter on the area between Rheineck and Feldkirch. If they had been able to follow their natural directions, Hotze would have moved via Lichtenstein, and the archduke via Andelfingen to Zurich. But then Hotze would have been in danger of being attacked and beaten by superior numbers, and the archduke would have been unsure whether he himself could remain unharmed. For example, he might have run into 20,000 men in the entrenched position, which he could not have overcome before Masséna returned.[85]

In order to deny his opponent this advantageous game of interior lines as soon as possible, he needed to link up with Hotze at the first opportunity, thus somewhere near the Thur.

This linking up in the face of the enemy and with lines of retreat very constricted by Lake Constance was certainly not without difficulty. It constitutes one of those problems that often arise in military history and that earlier strategic theory dealt with so well, although the whole business was usually begun with a pointless separation, like a quadrille.[86] This was certainly not the case here, since a junction between the archduke and Hotze north of Lake Constance would have cost a lot of time, and if it had been accomplished, Graubündten would have been very exposed meanwhile.

The two Austrian generals may have decided on a feint crossing on the 21st, since on that day, Nauendorf crossed with the archduke's advance guard, the larger part of his corps crossing at Stein and a detachment crossing at Constance. Meanwhile, it is said that Hotze's bridge had not yet been completed. The French did not abandon the Rhine until the 20th, so the arrangement made with Hotze cannot have been for a mere march to link up; it must have been geared toward forcing a crossing against the enemy cordon. Thus, it was to be expected that all the subsequent maneuvers would involve more or less significant fighting, hence allowing only short marches. The French had retreated behind the Thur; the Austrians controlled only the area as far as the Thur, and beyond that river, they might run into the enemy's main body, that is to say, some 40,000 men. But the Thur is only about 5 miles from Stein, whereas Meiningen is 50 miles from there. It was all the more difficult to join up in this small oblong because the main army could not meet General Hotze halfway, since its own crossing point would then be much too exposed, and it would have been too dangerous to base itself on the crossing point at Constance. If the French commander had done everything possible to take the 32,000 men

---

85. The archduke's own words in note 43 of this chapter reinforce Clausewitz's points. He was as interested in his own lines of operation and the physical strategic location of Zurich as he was in defeating the enemy forces. See also notes 44, 47, and 48 of this chapter.

86. Again, it is worth reminding the reader of the Austrian regulations of 1769 and their guidance regarding the use of multiple columns.

between Lake Constance and the Aare and concentrate them behind the Thur, which reasonably could have been done on the 22nd, and if he had left just a light chain of troops facing Hotze and drawn the main body of Lorge's division to him, then, including the Swiss, he could have moved against the archduke with some 40,000 men on the 23rd. On that day, it was highly likely that Hotze would have advanced only as far as the area of Bischofszell, where he still would have been more than a day's march away from the archduke. This calculation shows that if the archduke had crossed on the 21st and advanced to the Thur, he risked having to fight without Hotze for three whole days, that is, the 22nd, 23rd, and 24th. On the other hand, he could not do it much later, since he had to cross to pin the enemy's main body and prevent it from falling on Hotze. This caused the archduke to cross with his strong advance guard on the 21st and move to the Thur on the 22nd, pushing a strong outpost line across it, but not to cross with the rest of his troops until the 23rd.

Hotze easily could have been in Bischofszell by the 23rd, but he stayed in St. Gallen for the whole of the 24th, which delayed the linkup by another couple of days. This was indisputably not the fault of the archduke, so we cannot criticize him for not crossing the Thur until the 25th. But of course, it is hard to see why he failed to move the rest of his troops up to the Thur and why, instead of pushing out the extended chain of outposts that resulted in the losses of the 25th, he did not prefer to occupy Andelfingen and Frauenfeld in force and hasten General Hotze's march by the most urgent orders. He should have regarded the village of Frauenfeld as his left hand, which he was holding out to join up with General Hotze. Since Frauenfeld is only 9 miles away from Andelfingen, both their forces could have been used in the same decisive battle.

Thus, in general, we must say that the two Austrian commanders did not solve the problem particularly well of meeting up under the eyes of their opponent, and although the enemy did not obtain a decisive success over them before they met up, that is no credit to them.[87]

Between 26 May, when the French retreat to Winterthur, and 4 June, the day of the battle of Zurich, there are nine days when nothing much happens,

---

87. Again, the archduke seems to regard Zurich as the decisive strategic location, as though simply moving there would somehow be sufficient. If he were correct in his thinking, a cautious march to Zurich made sense. That he arrived there and captured the city without beating the French, or without them giving up, greatly undermines his logic and choice of action.

other than the archduke pushing the French back across the Glatt into the entrenched position at Zurich, which reasonably could have been done in just two days. Thus, the archduke allowed his opponent a whole week to reinforce himself from both wings and to perfect his entrenched position. If it was the archduke's intention to attack this, then every day lost must be regarded as highly detrimental. We do not actually know whether General Masséna really was reinforced during this time, but from his point of view, the archduke must necessarily have assumed so.

We do not regard the archduke's decision to attack the entrenched position as justified in any way by the reasons he gives in his account.

General Masséna takes a position between the Limmat and the Glatt about 13 miles long from Zurich to the Rhine. The right wing of this position has two-thirds of his force in a very strong entrenched position 3 miles long; the other part is a line of outposts 10 miles long with very few bridges over the Limmat and the Aare behind it or down toward the Rhine. Was it easier to attack the entrenched position or these outposts? Certainly, if the archduke had tried to turn against General Tharreau with the majority of his force, he would have put his line of retreat in an awkward situation so long as there was no bridge at Eglisau; but for a start, restoring the bridge at Eglisau would not have been a major problem, and there was no question of the archduke needing to use the majority of his force against Tharreau. He had 56,000 men massed on the 27th. If, instead of pointlessly sending Jellachich off to Pfaffikon, he had remained at Klotten with 30,000 men to cover his main line of communications with Andelfingen and had sent 26,000 men to drive General Tharreau back over the Limmat, that corps would not have needed to move more than 10 miles away from him. Thus, there was really no fear that, while that corps was driving off General Tharreau, the archduke would be forced to retreat by Masséna in such a way as to leave it in the lurch. If General Tharreau's retreat behind the Limmat and the Aare still did not prompt General Masséna to vacate the position in front of Zurich, then driving Tharreau back would be the best preparation for an attack on the position itself, if that was what the archduke wanted. But even then, we would not regard attacking this position as necessary; rather, in the archduke's position, we would have preferred to build some bridges between Eglisau and Kaiserstuhl and proceed to maneuver our opponent out of his entrenched position by putting pressure on the Limmat with our right wing. If this did not succeed and gradually led to a dangerous situation, then of course we would have to think about an attack on the position itself. But Masséna's retreat on the 6th indeed demonstrates that he attached no special value to holding this position and that attacking it would therefore not have been necessary.

It would have been quite a different matter if the archduke had decided to attack the position because he knew it was basically weak and incomplete or that the number of troops defending it was much too small and he did not want to give his opponent any time to get better organized, and because he wanted a great and glorious victory of the kind that can be obtained only against the enemy's main body. But if these reasons had really been in effect, the archduke would have cited them, and besides, he would not have wasted eight days. Instead of that, he presents this attack as though it were a necessary evil.

If we see the archduke's decision crowned with success, insofar as General Masséna feels obliged by the course of the fighting on the 4th to abandon the position on the 6th, we can only regard this as the result of two contradictions colliding.

41 REFLECTIONS ON THIS CHAPTER: THE FRENCH

We have seen that the operational plan prescribed a forward movement north of Switzerland for Masséna's army. The battle of Stockach brought this maneuver to a sudden halt, and we must consider the course of events and the connections between them from then on.

This maneuver had taken Dessolles into the Münster valley, Lecourbe into the Engadin, and Ménard into the Anterior Rhine valley and the Prettigau. The whole French deployment now looked like one continuous line from Rheineck along the Rhine to Maienfeld, then along the Lanquart into the Inn valley and through the Münster valley to the Adige, so that the right wing covered the entrance into the Adda valley through the Wurmser Joch and established communications of a kind with the Army of Italy via the Veltlin. The positions at Taufers, Remüs, and the St. Luciensteig may be regarded as the key points in this line, and it is quite understandable that after Masséna took over this extended line resulting from previous arrangements, he too regarded them this way and failed to do what the archduke thinks he should have[88] and give up the positions at Taufers and Remüs and, with them, half of Graubündten

---

88. See Karl, 1:127–150.

in order to post his right wing between Maienfeld, Chur, and Lenz. By this, we do not mean to say that Dessolles's and Lecourbe's position was not very risky, because Bellegarde with three times their strength surely could have enveloped them both; rather, we mean that it was no more dangerous to remain in this position than to advance, and if the French thought they could do the latter against the Austrians, they would have had no great concerns about doing the former. The idea of retaining some kind of direct communications with the Army of Italy in this way was too much in keeping with the conventional views of the time to surprise us.[89]

Bellegarde's first operation was to drive General Dessolles out of the Münster valley at the start of April; this shortened Masséna's line because it now reached only as far as Remüs, but it did not strengthen the line because Dessolles did not stay with Lecourbe but moved into the Veltlin to provide a kind of corps of communication with the Army of Italy. The right flank was therefore bent back, making Lecourbe's position so dangerous that he surely would have been destroyed if Bellegarde had not acted so timidly.

The French remained in this position for four weeks, that is, until the start of May. Meanwhile, the French Army of Italy had already lost its battles on the Adige and the Adda and had vacated Lombardy as far as the Ticino; as a result, the rationale for this position, based on maintaining communications with that army, had entirely disappeared, and the shortest line of communications now ran through the St. Gotthard Pass. The French left Dessolles in the Veltlin and Lecourbe in the Engadin merely with the aim of not giving up any more territory than could be taken from them by force of arms. They also banked on the Austrians' inactivity and perhaps thought to obtain an advantage if Suvorov thought his right flank might be threatened by this position and felt obliged to make significant detachments. This last idea basically failed, since he might just as well have had Rohan's weak brigade face the St. Gotthard, and Prince Hohenzollern's rapid return meant that detaching him had no tangible impact on operations in Italy.

89. This is something students have found when participating in wargames involving the campaign. The link between the armies in Germany and Italy via Switzerland is exceedingly important, as this region effectively protects the flanks of the French forces operating to the north and south. Furthermore, it is an excellent route into France, as there is a geographical gap running west from Lake Constance via Basel and into France. See Main Geographical Features Map located on pages 228–229 of this volume.

After the Austrians had spent four weeks sitting back and watching, they finally drove Lecourbe out of the Engadin. This general did not draw closer to Masséna's right wing nor into the upper Rhine valley to occupy the St. Gotthard Pass; instead, he went straight over the St. Bernard Pass to the Italian side of the Alps to join up with General Loison, who was now commanding Dessolles's brigade, and to retake the area of Bellinzona by attacking Prince Rohan.

While Lecourbe was involved in this attacking display, Bellegarde and Hotze attacked Masséna's right wing, and General Ménard would have had to duly pay the price if Bellegarde had not halted in the Posterior Rhine valley, to some degree because of the specter of Lecourbe. This Austrian attack captured the third of General Masséna's key positions—namely, the St. Luciensteig—and this resulted in two major changes: first, he had to abandon the line of the Rhine above Lake Constance, which in turn dictated abandoning the Rhine below the lake; and second, he had to let his line to the St. Gotthard Pass run through the Reuss valley past Lake Lucerne and Lake Zug. Thus, in six weeks the French were driven out of their long and dangerous deployment by three very timidly conducted Austrian offensives, without suffering any particular harm.

General Lecourbe was unable to pursue his offensive any further toward the Italian lakes. Instead, upon hearing the news of the loss of Graubündten, he hurried back to the St. Gotthard Pass, where he arrived at the same time as Hotze and Bellegarde were seizing the Rhine valleys. He could not stay there either, since an intermediate position was needed to cover the long line between the St. Gotthard and Lake Zurich, so he left some of his troops at the St. Gotthard and moved to Altorf. But Loison also had to give way before Haddick and quit the St. Gotthard. Now Lecourbe turned about to strike at General St. Julien, half wiping him out, and was in the process of retaking the St. Gotthard when the battle of Zurich on 4 June—even though the French could not in any way be said to have lost it—persuaded Masséna to draw Lecourbe closer to him again, that is, between Lake Lucerne and Lake Zug.

Thus, in the four weeks of May, we see General Lecourbe perform a five-legged maneuver, from Pont via Lenz, the St. Bernard Pass, Bellinzona, and the St. Gotthard Pass to Altorf, without achieving any real strategic objective, since the small victory over Prince Rohan was too insignificant and indecisive to count. No sooner had he met up with Loison than he had to leave for the St. Gotthard; no sooner had he arrived there than Masséna ordered him to Altorf.

Of course, we have offered one reason for Lecourbe's move to Bellinzona: to cover the approaches to the St. Gotthard. Here we are questioning not Masséna's motives but rather what use this maneuver really turned out to be, for this is the only way we can judge whether his reasons were justified. Lecourbe's maneuver demonstrates that Masséna could not hold the St. Gotthard, much less the Bellinzona area. Yet Bellegarde had departed and left just 15,000 or so men from his army facing the French army in Switzerland, so Masséna's aim was even less justifiable, since he knew nothing of Bellegarde's departure!

Even though General Lecourbe won three small but quite distinct victories during these four weeks—against Rohan at Monte Ceneri south of Bellinzona on 13 May, against Gavasini in the Muotta valley by Lake Lucerne on the 28th, and against St. Julien in the Reuss valley on the 31st—again, these are attributable only to that general's inimitable energy and great determination. Between 4 and 31 May he covered some 180 miles, crossing the chain of the high Alps three times and sailing across the southern part of Lake Lucerne twice. The French colors must certainly be indebted to General Masséna for giving General Lecourbe the opportunity for this most brilliant and admirable episode of the campaign.[90]

A question is in order here: what value did possession of the St. Gotthard Pass have for either side? We make so bold as to assert that, as shocking as it may seem to general staffs in every army, it was *quite insignificant.*

We absolutely deny that it can derive any value from its geological significance as the highest point in Switzerland and as the dividing point of the great European watershed. We do so without seeking to justify ourselves, since we are of the opinion that it is those who have attributed this illusory and *largely figurative* significance to the notion of dominant terrain who are under an obligation to prove its reality, which they have yet to do.

That is to say, this whole concept has hitherto only ever been expressed as phraseology. There is no evidence that it would be unfeasible or even markedly more difficult to hold an outpost at Disentis or Am-Steg than in the St. Gotthard merely because the latter lies 3,000–4,000 feet higher; on the contrary, this is disproved by the very examples given in this history of the war. But of course, the St. Gotthard is also a dividing point for the roads, since it

---

90. Lecourbe's dynamism provides a telling contrast to the lack of energy displayed by most of the allied commanders.

is usable by horses and pack animals. Roads run from it to Chur and Altorf on the one side and to Brieg in Wallis, Domodossola, and Bellinzona on the other. A road nexus can certainly be very significant strategically, but only if the roads themselves are significant, such as when they lead to an objective that has a strong connection with the military operations and an army there uses them in some situation or another.[91] The roads to Domodossola and Bellinzona no longer had any value to the French for communications between their two armies, since the Army of Italy had retreated behind the Apennines; thus their only value would be if the French were thinking of using them to threaten the rear of the allied army in Italy, but that could not reasonably have been their aim at that moment when Masséna's army in Switzerland was itself under such direct threat. The route through the Wallis valley was in the hands of the insurgents, and even if it had been open, there were still other ways than the St. Gotthard to reach the Great St. Bernard Pass, which was the one line of communications of any value at the time. The road over the Crispalt to Chur led to the Austrians in the Rhine valley, while the Altorf road led to Masséna's army. Although possession of the St. Gotthard made possession of the Crispalt easier, it did not in any way guarantee it. In addition, it is just as much of an exaggeration to say that the Crispalt exercised dominance over the Rhine valley; we must insist on returning to the fact that, regardless of the local terrain, one could hold an outpost at Disentis or elsewhere just as well as at the St. Gotthard, and the French could cover the route to Masséna against the Austrians just as easily without being at the St. Gotthard. Accordingly, we believe that after Moreau lost Lombardy, the St. Gotthard no longer had any value as a point for communications between the two armies; to anyone who claims that it would have had some indirect value by making communications between the two Austrian armies more difficult, we reply that there were enough routes leading to Italy via the Julierberg, the Splügen, and the St. Ber-

---

91. Again, this is where wargames have proved helpful in understanding what Clausewitz is getting at. In games covering this campaign and that of 1796–1797 (wargames run as electives at the Naval War College and at Fort Leavenworth, Kansas, from 2011 to 2019), the players have found the St. Gotthard Pass to be no more or less important than the other valleys through the Alps. One valley becomes truly significant only when the others are unavailable or blocked. Thus, Clausewitz's point is well taken. Obviously, wargames are only as good as their design, but when using the original maps as a base, the players wrestle with many of the same problems as the original protagonists.

nard Passes, entailing only a small detour, for a whole army like Bellegarde's to get there without hindrance.

Thus, we believe that the way things stood in May and June, possession of the St. Gotthard was of no particular significance, and even if holding these mountains did provide some advantages, these were not worth extending oneself any further than was advisable. In fact, at the end of the section in which we find ourselves, we even see Masséna abandoning the St. Gotthard, together with the high mountains, and General Lecourbe posting his main body north of Lake Lucerne without making his situation any worse.

We turn now to Masséna's attack of 25 May on the advancing Austrians. Although the moment was suitable for offensive action, and although such action was demanded here according to the system of interior lines[92] and must be considered the most essential principle of the defense, it is hard to see Masséna's attack from this point of view. We cannot be under any illusions; he envisaged nothing more than driving back the Austrian troops by a roughly parallel attack, and we do not know what he actually hoped to achieve with respect to the overall situation. His report to the Directory says: "The enemy's most recent movements, and the definite information I had about him concentrating on the left bank of the Thur, revealed that he was planning to attack. *To disrupt his preparations,* I felt I must preempt him and order a general attack on this line to tumble him back beyond the river."[93]

In this rationale for the attack we can find hardly any intention of a battle or an action that could be considered the equivalent of one. What General Masséna did seems to us such a half measure, without character and without any clear purpose, that we are at a loss to explain what coherent idea it could be part of.

Furthermore, when we see from General Masséna's reports that he thought the archduke's demonstration across the Rhine with a few isolated detach-

---

92. **Clausewitz** notes: "We choose this expression, not for its role in Jominian theory, but because it is a very well known way of operating that has naturally been around for a very long time."

93. **Clausewitz** notes: "*Moniteur* of 13 *prairial,* year VII [1 June 1799]." ["*Les derniers mouvemens de l'ennemi, et les avis certains que j'avais des ressemblemens qu'il faisait sur la rive gauche de la Thur, annonçaient de sa part le projet de nous attaquer. Pour romper ses mesures, j'ai cru devoir le devancer et ordonner une attaque générale sur cette ligne pour la culbuter au-delà de la rivière.*"]

ments on the 23rd and 24th was a serious attack, and when we see him still accept battle on the far side of the Glatt on the 27th even though his intention was to withdraw into the entrenched camp at Zurich, and finally, when General Tharreau undertakes a quite meaningless attack against the archduke's right flank on the 28th that bears no relation to any larger operation, we are certainly very strongly confirmed in our suspicion that General Masséna was more accustomed to operate according to the momentary impressions and inspirations on which a division commander bases his decisions than according to a plan directed at a distant goal.

This lack of a plan results in the complete contradiction we observed in the French commander's latest act—namely, in the battle of Zurich. We have already said that Masséna's reasons for his retreat on 6 June must have been based on the battle of the 4th; yet we assume this only because it lacks a motive, and we cannot acknowledge these unknown reasons as valid. More than one stark inconsistency emerges here. To work on an entrenched position for several months, only to fight in front of it rather than within it, indicates that the works were not completed or had turned out so badly that it was better not to rely on them. But if the position was so poor, why did Masséna not retreat over the Limmat straight away? And how weak his reasons for accepting battle on the right bank of the Limmat must have been if circumstances that entirely elude the searching eye of history convinced the French commander to retreat.

4. Continuation of the Campaign in Italy
Suvorov Beats Macdonald on the Trebbia

42 MACDONALD ADVANCES FROM LOWER ITALY TOWARD THE APENNINES

As we described in the first section, in January the French had moved into Naples and had begun to turn the country into a republic like their own. It was inevitable that besides those inhabitants who were averse to the reforms and the republican system anyway, a discontented crowd soon arose even among their fairly numerous former supporters in the middle class who were unhappy with the nature and manner of the reforms and with the war-related charges imposed on the country.[1] Neither the French Directory nor its representative in Naples, Commissar Faypoult, felt they owed the slightest consideration to local attitudes or interests, and thus as far as confiscations, extortion, and the new institutions were concerned, they came to operate in a way that turned public opinion against the French and was bound to lead to open resistance.[2]

Championnet, who was in command of the French army, felt he had to put a check to these measures by the government commissar, but within the Directory he lost his battle against Faypoult[3] and was recalled, hauled in front

---

1. After the French conquest, Naples was declared a republic in January 1799: the Parthenopean Republic. Despite good intentions and attempts to bring the bulk of the locals on board, "the Parthenopean Republic was a disaster" from the start. The French-imposed "indemnity of 17,500,000 ducats" was enough to kill all hope of success. Furthermore, regular bad behavior by French troops and additional attempts to extract cash thwarted the formation of a republic. See Esdaile, *Wars of the French Revolution*, 170–171. See also Lefebvre, *French Revolution from 1793 to 1799*, 233.

2. This again returns to the idea of the result of war not being final (*On War*, book 1, chap. 1). This is especially so when severe penalties are imposed on the defeated and the victors are not strong enough to enforce the peace. In such circumstances, the defeated have little choice but to throw off the rule of the victors and seek a new result.

3. Guillaume Faypoult was the French Directory's representative in the republic and was bitterly opposed to Championnet's governance. When Championnet went too far and had Faypoult arrested, the Directory intervened and sacked Championnet. Esdaile, *Wars of the French Revolution*, 171.

of a commission of inquiry, and replaced by Macdonald. The latter naturally had no option but to let this business carry on.

Twenty-five men were appointed to draft the new constitution, and until this was finished, the government was administered provisionally. All the executive means it possessed in terms of its own troops and gendarmerie were dissolved as instruments of the previous regime because, given the poor popular mood, none of these corps could be relied on. This mistrust also hampered and delayed the new formations and the establishment of the national guard; as a result, while the new government, for its part, was not equipped with a force of any kind, a mass of hungry, unemployed men was only too keen to be taken into service by those contemplating reaction. No country is so suited for reaction as Naples, so long as one is not also master of Sicily. Calabria, a wild country with wild inhabitants who cannot be ruled by the power of [ideological] concepts and slogans, naturally offered a very suitable theater for nearby Sicily to sow the first seeds of resistance around which the popular uprising could quickly crystallize; the long extent of the country and its inaccessibility afforded it time to gain inner strength and solidity.

In Cardinal Ruffo,[4] who had transferred from the service of Rome to that of the court of Sicily, the court found an enterprising spirit, more warlike than ecclesiastical and well suited to serve as the instigator and head of the bands that mustered around him partly from the elements of the dissolved units and partly from stirred-up fanatical peasants. He had landed at the start of February and, without any authorization from the Sicilian government, by his own hand in a way, had soon put together a force of 10,000–15,000 men with which he seized the city of Monteleone. Soon thereafter the king officially named him governor and supported him with small detachments of troops. An uprising also broke out in Apulia at the same time, and its consuming flames approached ever closer to the vicinity of the capital, where Macdonald had concentrated his army. Thus, in February Macdonald was obliged to combat the insurrection. Columns were sent to Apulia and Calabria, with Duherau's French division forming the first column and new Neapolitan formations the second. The war with these factions lasted through March and April. The

---

4. Cardinal Fabrizio Ruffo led the revolt against French rule. Esdaile, *Wars of the French Revolution*, 219–221. Ruffo's behavior was strikingly similar to that of many clergy in the later war in Spain, where there was a strong connection between many rural clergy and the local population.

French were successful in Apulia, but in Calabria it was the other way around, to the disadvantage of the republicans. Thus Ruffo's faction, among whose commanders Fra Diavolo distinguished himself, grew stronger day by day, and he was ready to march on Apulia. At this moment, that is, at the end of April, Macdonald received the order to set off with his army for upper Italy after leaving garrisons in the Neapolitan and Papal fortresses. This task was not an easy one. Macdonald used every means to conceal this intention until the moment of its execution, while expediting to the utmost the arming of the new regime, particularly the formation of the national guard. But neither of these endeavors had sufficient effect. Duherau had great difficulty cutting his way through back to Capua, and the new formations could not be brought up to the appropriate level. The British landed 600 men in the Gulf of Salerno, a detachment of Russian troops landed in Apulia, and Ruffo was advancing with an army of 25,000 men.

In this way, even before Macdonald actually left, everything was made ready to administer the coup de grâce within a few weeks to this ephemeral state created by the French upheaval[5] and to establish a new theater of operations for the allied Sicilians, Russians, and British.

At the start of May, Macdonald had concentrated his 24,000-strong army around Naples, detached 5,000 men from it to serve as garrisons for Capua and Gaeta, and on 7 and 8 May set off for Rome with the other 19,000. Since the uprising had already spread to the Papal States, and General Garnier, who was stationed there, was having trouble concentrating his division, Macdonald had a mobile column of 4,000 men under General Dombrowsky[6] clear the way. The main army followed in four columns, two each with a day's interval between them on two roads, namely, via the Pontine Marshes and via San

---

5. There was much turmoil here in southern Italy and elsewhere too. Where old orders had been removed from power, new orders sought to emerge. Once the French left, there were reckonings all over Italy. This pattern followed the revolution through its course and sparked a great deal of the resistance to it. The old order knew that opposing the revolution was likely a matter of life and death, hence its willingness to increase the level of resistance, which brought a corresponding increase in violence by the other side. Thus, in theory, they were both likely to continue escalating to the maximum amount of force at their disposal. See *On War*, book 1, chap. 1, and book 6, chap. 26, "The People in Arms."

6. General Jean Henri Dombrowsky (1755–1818) was a Polish general in French service. He left Poland after the Third Partition and served with the Cisalpine Republic.

Germano, arriving in Rome on 16 and 17 May. Here Macdonald reinforced himself with a few thousand men, leaving the rest of Garnier's division behind as garrisons for San Angelo, Civitavecchia, and Ancona. He continued his march on the Perugia and Siena highways to Florence and arrived on the 25th, having covered some 250 miles in eighteen days. There he joined up with Gauthier's and Montrichard's divisions, which had been fighting a war against the partisans, the former on the border with Bologna and the latter on the border with Modena. Only a few battalions of these divisions remained behind in Tuscany under Generals Gauthier and Miollis, partly to control the popular insurrection that was spreading all around them and partly to defend Livorno against the British. The rest formed an army of 27,000 foot and 3,000 horse and were organized as follows:

Division Salm (advance guard): 3,000 men
Division Olivier: 6,000 men
Division Montrichard: 6,000 men
Division Rusca: 5,400 men
Division Watrin: 6,000 men
Division Dombrowsky: 3,600 men
Total: 30,000 men

On 29 May Macdonald transferred his headquarters to Lucca and deployed his army so that Dombrowsky's division on the left wing was in the valley of the Magra at Sarzana and Aulla, Rusca's and Montrichard's divisions formed the right wing and held the Apennine passes from the Modena highway to the Bologna one, and the center stood behind the two wings between Florence and Pistoia.

In this position, Macdonald established secure communications for the first time with Moreau, who at this time was beginning his retreat into the Apennines, whereas hitherto most of the couriers they had sent to each other had been captured by the enemy or the insurgents. This tardy communication with Moreau was probably the reason why Macdonald did not advance without delay as far as the plain of the Po, nor continue on his path along the coast, but instead let a period of ten days elapse during which he remained in his position on the southern slope of the Apennines. Before we examine the start of his operation, we must cast an eye over how the allied forces in Italy were distributed.

43 THE ALLIES' POSITION

After the battle of Magnano, the allies were 92,000 strong (section 25); since then, they had been reinforced by some 5,000 Russians under General Förster and were expecting General Bellegarde with 15,000 men in early June, making 112,000 in total. According to the overview given in the Austrian account, at the start of June they were 98,000 strong including Haddick's corps or 88,000 without it. Thus, 24,000 of the 112,000 are unaccounted for; their losses in the battle of Cassano and other actions may have run to 10,000 men, so that would leave 14,000 for the garrisons of the fortified places, which is not an unlikely figure.

On 7 June, shortly before Macdonald began his operations, these 88,000 men were deployed and engaged as follows:

1. The main army under Melas and Rosenberg—42,700 men—was besieging the Turin citadel and had detachments facing the Piedmontese Alps. Its advance guard under Wukassowitsch was at Montcaglieri, with outposts from Pinerolo to Asti.
2. Bellegarde's corps—11,400 men—was blockading the Tortona and Alessandria citadels and observing the Apennines toward Genoa. Ott's division[7]—8,000 men—was attached to Bellegarde and was in Modenese territory facing the Apennines.
3. General Kray's corps—19,800 men—was besieging Mantua. Klenau's division—6,100 men—was attached to Kray and was in Bolognese territory observing the Apennines and covering the siege of Mantua.

The fortified places occupied by the allies west of the Mincio were Peschiera, Orcinovi, Pizzighettone, Forea, and Ceva, as well as the citadels of Milan, Piacenza, Ferrara, and Valenza and the Bordo and Arona castles.

The allies had made Valenza their main depot and prepared it for defense; they had bridges over the Po there and at Bassignano and were busy entrenching and arming the Bassignano bridgehead. A third bridge was at Piacenza,

---

7. **Clausewitz** notes: "The Austrian military journal gives Bellegarde and Ott 19,400 men, and later says of General Ott that he was 8,000 strong. Thus General Bellegarde must have left some of his 15,000 men with the main army. *Jahrgang 1812*, Vol. 6, p74." The *Jahrgang* is the *Österreichische Militärische Zeitschrift*.

and this place, whose citadel had been prepared for defense, could be regarded as its bridgehead.

During the crossing of the Po, when General Ott was sent off against Montrichard, he was tasked with driving him from the plain and securing the highway via Pontremoli and Sarzana, which is the only major highway cutting through the mountains except for the roads from Modena and Bologna to Florence. In addition, he was to maintain communications with Klenau, who was advancing toward Bologna and Fort Urban.

The Austrian account[8] says General Ott's general mission was to prevent Moreau and Macdonald from joining up, and it quotes an order handwritten by Suvorov himself that says: "I hear that Moreau and Macdonald want to join up on the Riviera. You, sir general, shall do your best to get stuck into them and hurl them both into the sea."[9]

Given his strength and his position, General Ott could have no other mission than to observe the Apennines, and if need be and a favorable enough situation arose, to place himself on the road that General Macdonald wanted to march along and halt his progress so that the main army could rush up in good time. Thus he could be most effective in obstructing a junction of the two French armies north of the Apennines. As for a junction south of the Apennines on the Riviera, from his position General Ott could, of course, obstruct it on his own, but when it is a question of two masses of 20,000 and 30,000 men trying to link up, no one could imagine that 8,000 men could prevent this. We must therefore very much doubt that the allies' commander really gave General Ott such a mission, and in Suvorov's letter quoted above, all the more so since it is in his own hand, we can see nothing but a jocular exhortation to action emerging from the actual mission. General Ott probably would have read nothing more from this than that Suvorov regarded him as a capable fellow who would go for his opponent if the situation allowed.

General Ott was occupying that part of the mountains that lay closest to the line of communications between the two French armies and through whose passes they could best advance united onto the plain of the Po, that is, through the valleys of the Taro, the Nura, and the Trebbia on the northern slope and the Magra on the southern one. He had detachments posted at Bobbio in the

---

8. **Clausewitz** notes: "Östreich. Militär. Zeitschrift. 1812. Vol. 6, p76."

9. For a deeper look at Suvorov's plan, see Milyutin, *Geschichte des Krieges Russlands*, 2:1–2.

Trebbia valley, at Bardi in the Zeno valley, at Campiano in the Taro valley, at Pontremoli on the Magra, and at Fivizano on a tributary of the Magra, with orders to patrol as far as the coast. He had had to capture some of these places from the French first. He posted himself with his reserve at Reggio and sent a few hundred men toward the Panaro, partly to maintain communications with Klenau and partly to observe Fort Urbino from the west, while Klenau invested it from the east and stood outside Bologna with the rest of his corps.

From this deployment by Generals Ott and Klenau, we see that the French held the Bologna and Modena roads across the Apennines and that the Austrians held the mountains further west, but only with patrol detachments that were sufficient to interrupt communications between the two enemy armies so long as they had not approached close together, but too weak to offer any kind of resistance. The detachments that had been pushed south of the Apennines to Pontremoli and Fivizzano were themselves in a dangerous position.

From the main army, General Lusignan and Prince Bagration[10] had a few thousand men in the Pinerolo and Susa valleys to observe the roads from Grenoble and Briançon. Lusignan was blockading Fenestrella; Bagration was occupying the pass from Sesane to Mount Geneva, Fort Brunette at Susa, and the so-called Camp de l'Assiette, an old entrenched position that lies on the ridge separating the Susa and Pinerolo valleys.

There seems to have been no significant force facing the passes leading over the Cottian Alps between Pinerolo and Cuneo. In any case, these are mostly only mule tracks.

Fröhlich's division, about 4,000 strong, was at Fossano facing Cuneo.

Next was Wukassowitsch, 5,000–6,000 strong, who was occupying Mondovi, Ceva, and Salicetto.

Linking with Wukassowitsch were Seckendorff's outposts. Seckendorff had taken position forward of Acqui with a few thousand men.

Thus we can regard Generals Bagration, Lusignan, Fröhlich, Wukassowitsch, and Seckendorff as Suvorov's and Bellegarde's advance guards, extended in a long chain of outposts.

This still left Kaim's and Zoph's divisions alongside the Russians at Turin,

---

10. Prince Peter Bagration (1765–1812) was a skillful and successful Russian commander of the French Revolutionary and Napoleonic Wars. He is perhaps most famous for his defense of the Russian left flank at the battle of Borodino in 1812, where he was mortally wounded.

about 30,000 strong altogether, and Bellegarde's corps of about 8,000 men at Tortona and Alessandria.

Thus, while the allies were besieging six fortifications in a line from Fenestrella to Mantua—namely, Fenestrella, Turin, the citadels of Alessandria and Tortona, Bologna, and Mantua—their main body was extended over more than 180 miles, and they had dispersed 25,000 men in weak detachments in the mountains. Although the original objective of their operations since reaching this area had been to prevent the two French armies from uniting, they themselves were now much more divided than the French.

44 REFLECTIONS ON THE FRENCH PLAN OF ATTACK

The allies have missed their chance of driving Moreau's army so far away before Macdonald arrives that it would become very difficult for the former to operate in coordination with the latter. Macdonald has arrived, and after Moreau has received a few thousand reinforcements from the interior, the French force comes to some 50,000 men who are ready for a decisive battle: that is to say, 30,000 under Macdonald in Tuscany and 20,000 under Moreau in Genoese territory, after deducting the necessary garrisons for Genoa and Cuneo.

Even if the allies abandon one or other of their many sieges, it is unlikely that they can put an equivalent force on the battlefield. The French are thus in a position to seek a major decision and are obliged to do so because the allied offensive is progressing intensively by means of their sieges, and their situation becomes more advantageous every day. Meanwhile, the French army's situation, with so little territory to its rear, is such that it cannot tarry there long, even if it really wants to defer any positive reaction for the time being. Thus we find ourselves at the threshold of a major decisive battle.

The operation that is supposed to lead to this battle arises from very unusual circumstances, so theory must regard it as an interesting problem, and in solving it, no relevant notion should be overlooked. We must therefore allow ourselves an exhaustive exploration of the questions to be found here.

So long as Macdonald was in Naples and Moreau in Genoa or Piedmont, we think of the two as strategically separated or, more accurately, divorced; that is, separated not only by distance but also by a region they do not control. But this was basically only an expectation, in that one thinks of the allies intending to take a position between the two, and one imagines that the French could do nothing to stop this; but so long as this did not happen, no real division between them existed. Suvorov certainly could have achieved this if he had gained control of Tuscany in good time, and nothing prevented him from doing so save the action elsewhere that he found and preferred on the Piedmontese plain. But since Suvorov did not do this, and since, as we have seen, the Apennines constituted all but a minor part of the dividing line between the two sides, in short, given the two sides' positions at the end of May, the idea that the two French armies were divorced—that is, so separated that they could not unite without first fighting a decisive battle—is completely false; there was no enemy between them other than the couple of groups that Ott had at Pontremoli and Fivizzano, and as we shall see shortly, these were soon driven off. Thus the two French armies had communications, and the only thing that must be conceded is that this was through difficult terrain.

If Macdonald simply wanted to join his army with Moreau's, he could do so by the coast road. This road was fit for wheeled traffic only as far as Levici, but in these campaigns we frequently see sizable French corps march along roads that are not considered fit for traffic,[11] and later we even see Macdonald take this same road after the battle of the Trebbia, so we cannot regard this coast road as entirely unusable. Light field artillery and ammunition could be carried on pack animals, and for the siege train and heavy baggage, there was still the option of travel by sea, for right at this time, Admiral Bruix's squadron arrived in Vado harbor, so there was nothing to fear from the English [Royal Navy].[12] Whether such a junction with Moreau was the best thing he could do is a different question; all we want to do here is establish that it was not impossible and that one therefore cannot use this impossibility as the foundation for the whole rationale.

While it was within the power of the French commanders to meet up along the coast without engaging in a decisive action first, which would be merely a route march and not an operation as such, even the various routes that did require an operation were not intrinsically difficult. For the purpose of simply joining up, far from being separated by the main enemy army, the two com-

---

11. It is worth contrasting this with the Austrian complaints to Suvorov noted in section 21 of chapter 2 in this volume.

12. Just because Admiral Bruix's squadron had arrived did not mean there was nothing to fear from the Royal Navy, as he had to slip through the Royal Navy's blockade to get there in the first place. For an overview of the war in the Mediterranean and Bruix's cruise, see Rodger, *War of the Second Coalition*, 81–122.

manders only had to overcome such weak corps that there could be no doubt of the outcome.

Thus, from the moment Macdonald entered Florence, the two French armies may be regarded as already united, and this union could no longer be considered as an objective for a dedicated operation unless one wanted deliberately to confuse matters.

But the junction of the two armies meant nothing in itself. As we have already said, they could not remain in their position, nor was it in their interest to keep quiet. They had to seek a decisive battle, but the question therefore arose, how could they best go about it?

The minimum goal the French commanders could set for themselves was to throw the allies back across the Po and thus relieve the besieged citadels. For such a success to be achieved, either a victory had to be obtained over Suvorov himself or a serious defeat had to be inflicted on one of his corps.

If we now look more closely at the two armies' situations in relation to such a goal, there are two points of view available, depending on whether we take matters as they could have been at the end of May or as they actually were because of Moreau's mistakes.

That is, it is quite obvious that simply by reason of the distribution of forces, such a union of the two French armies reasonably could have taken place in the northern foothills of the Apennines, which at the same time would have been very advantageous preparation for a decisive battle.

Macdonald entered Florence on 25 May. At that time, Bellegarde had not yet embarked to cross Lake Como, and Hohenzollern had just set off from Milan; thus the allied forces ready for action were 20,000 men weaker than they were fourteen days later, when the blow was actually struck. At the same time, Suvorov was still on the march to Turin, which had not yet fallen, and Moreau was still on the plain of the Po close to that city. Macdonald was facing only Ott and Klenau, whose 12,000–13,000 men were dispersed in small detachments; within a few days, he could have concentrated up to 25,000 men and had just 65 miles to cover to reach the highway from Piacenza to Bologna, by which point, at the latest, he would surely have encountered Ott's and Klenau's main forces. Thus, at least the way we see matters now, there was not the slightest doubt that within eight days, by 1 June,[13] Macdonald could

---

13. The original said July, but we think this is a typographical error, as 1 June makes more sense in context.

have hurled this corps back across the Po and been on the march to Piacenza. Just then Moreau was busy with preparations for his retreat into the Apennines, that is to say, with the vain attempts to recapture Ceva, suppressing the insurgent peasantry, and opening a new route to the Riviera. It seems there was nothing to prevent him from returning to the vicinity of Alessandria and calling Victor back to him. It is hard to see what obstacles could have been put in the way of such a union of the two armies, whereby they would have had Genoa in their rear. Tortona and Alessandria would then have been relieved, and if they established a bridge at Valenza, it is very much in question whether Suvorov would have risked giving them battle on the right bank of the Po.

But this solution to the problem was lacking the necessary preparation. When Macdonald entered Florence, Moreau was so fixed on the idea of reestablishing his lost line of communications with the Riviera and retreating there that he entirely lost sight of the possibility of a junction north of the Apennines. If Macdonald crossed the mountain range on his own initiative, he ran the risk that General Moreau would be descending its southern slopes at the very moment he himself arrived near Tortona at its northern foot. There was no time for discussion if the allies were to be denied the opportunity to take countermeasures. Moreau's mistakes that prevented this solution to the problem lay in the preceding section of the campaign; when Macdonald arrived, there was no longer time to correct them, and the critic must therefore refrain from using this viewpoint, which would otherwise be the most natural one. But we cannot ignore it, first, because it deserves consideration in itself and needs to be eliminated, and second, because it shows Moreau's mistakes in their proper light.

The other viewpoint, then, is that we consider General Moreau as having arrived in the Riviera and think about the operations of the two armies arising from this situation.

The essential difference between this situation and the one above is not that Moreau was now also obliged to descend to the plain again first, like Macdonald, but that the whole operation happens ten to twelve days later. Since at the start of June, Moreau was still stuck in the Tanaro valleys, totally obsessed with regaining control of Ceva and winning through on the road to Loano on the Riviera, and this crisis was not over until 6 June, so we can very well understand how Macdonald was checked in the execution of his own operation, which, as we shall see, he only begins on the 9th. But during this interlude, Bellegarde and Hohenzollern arrived, and Suvorov had already begun to concentrate his force and prepare for his departure to Alessandria. This changed everything: what in the first case could have been carried out with spontaneous ease, because Suvorov himself lent a helping hand by leaving the Alessandria region, now had to be sought through a combination of maneuvers that the enemy could adequately oppose, meaning that all the difficulties of the French commanders' own situation now came into play.

The unusual situations of the two armies, of which we have already spoken, consisted of the following:

1. In their strategic deployment, both of them had their fronts rotated by 90 degrees, so their true lines of retreat and communications lay behind their left flanks. This already very significant factor became all the more so because of the next point.
2. The allies' line of deployment stretched from Fenestrella to Genoa and covered some 180 miles, while the French line was close to 180 miles long from Cuneo to Lucca. Naturally, the anomaly of their situation was greatly exacerbated by the length of the line of deployment. It is very unusual to see such long and such sharply rotated lines of deployment.
3. The sea was immediately in the rear of the French line of deployment, because they could not treat lower Italy as a base. The allies at least had the whole of Lombardy behind them.[14]
4. The two French armies had the Apennines in front of and between them, but in these mountains, only the two highways from Florence to Modena and Bologna provide good passes. To the east, in the direction of their linking up, only the poor roads along the coast to Genoa and through Pontremoli to Parma and Piacenza were available.

The French were therefore subjected to many disadvantageous circumstances that were only compensated to some degree by the fact that the allies' numerous sieges had extended them along a very long line and occupied a large portion of their forces.

We turn now to the question: what could the French have done in this situation?

14. Despite Clausewitz's earlier comment about the Royal Navy, there was no guarantee that the French would have unfettered access to the advantages of waterborne transportation.

Of the various allied force groupings, Kray and his siege corps could not be reached because he was covered by the Po.

Confronting their main army itself at Turin was advisable only with the French forces united. Macdonald therefore would have had to traverse the entire length of the strategic front, which could be done only behind the Apennines, thus along the coast roads. Although this was certainly not impossible, it was the form of strategic offensive that required the most time to prepare and was thus the least able to achieve surprise; in addition, because it would strike the enemy's main body frontally and at the extreme end of the strategic front, it would have the least decisive effect. These disadvantages could not be compensated for by the fact that the line of retreat would be best protected by this form of attack.

Nor could an attack with a united force be effected in any advantageous way against either Bellegarde's corps on one side or Ott and Klenau on the other. Combining against the former would have required ten to twelve days, since the distance from Lucca to Alessandria is nearly 140 miles through mountains all the way. But this time would have been more than sufficient for Suvorov to concentrate his whole force at Alessandria. Combining against Ott and Klenau was simply not possible, for if Moreau had marched off to his right for that purpose, he would have had to abandon his line of communications with Nice, and that with Genoa would have been very much at risk; the French army would have been hanging in the air, as they say. The question therefore arises: what could be achieved against these two corps without uniting, that is, along twin lines of operations?

We must first note that when the two French commanders had to make their plan, at the beginning of June, Bellegarde had not yet arrived. At that time, there could only have been about one weak division at Alessandria and Tortona, but it can well be imagined that Moreau knew of Bellegarde's approach, since the orders for it had been given three or four weeks earlier. In that case, he would have had to be prepared to meet this corps at Alessandria, that is, to encounter a force of perhaps 20,000 men there, or roughly the same number he could bring into action even with the strictest economy of force. This possibility could not entirely deter him from considering an attack on the allies at Alessandria, since at the moment of its execution, he would necessarily be better informed and thus could still abandon the attack if circumstances were too unfavorable; however, this reasoning shows that Moreau's army could not rely with any certainty on achieving a decisive result against Alessandria and Tortona. Even assuming that Moreau found a weaker force there than he could bring against it, and assuming he could be sure of raising both sieges and driving the allies back across the Tanaro, he still had to be prepared for Suvorov appearing with his main army a couple of days later, that is, much sooner than Macdonald could come to his aid if the latter had begun to move at roughly the same time he did. But if Macdonald's operations had had a head start of eight or ten days, then Suvorov too would have started moving earlier, and then Moreau probably would have encountered him between Tortona and Alessandria. It follows from this that a blow by Moreau in the Alessandria area, that is, against Bellegarde, would not lead to a favorable situation for the ensuing decisive battle.[15]

By contrast, there were no such reservations about a rapid attack on Macdonald's part against Ott's and Klenau's corps. Macdonald greatly outnumbered them, even if they received reinforcements during the course of his attack, as could probably be expected; at least eight days were bound to elapse before the main army could arrive to support them. But of course, this blow by Macdonald against Ott and Klenau could not be expected to produce a significant result. Both of them could fall back across the Po or toward the main army. Therefore, after the French had made whatever they could out of this first blow, they had to be prepared to survive a fight with Suvorov himself; in other words, immediately after Macdonald struck Ott and Klenau, the two French commanders had to unite the main mass of their combat forces, preferably in such a way that some of the Austrian forces were pushed away from Suvorov. In this way, it could be hoped that beyond their successes against individual corps, by breaking through the center of the enemy line of deployment, the French commanders would also obtain an advantage that would set up the main decisive battle well. Then Suvorov, separated from part of his force and at the same time obliged to leave corps outside Turin, Alessandria, and Tortona, would most likely appear on the battlefield with a weaker force than the French could oppose him with. He could thereby easily be taken in his right flank so that, in the event of a retreat, he would have to head straight for Pavia and thus for the time being allow himself to be cut off from his right wing.

---

15. Given that each side would have had only a portion of its strength present, it is unlikely any such battle would have been truly decisive.

It would have been in accordance with this general aim for Macdonald to advance through the Pontremoli Pass either against Parma or even directly on Piacenza. He could be sure of finding General Ott between Parma and Piacenza. If Moreau advanced at the same time from Gavi to Bobbio on the Trebbia, he would be in a position to keep an eye on any possible operations by Suvorov against the Bocchetta Pass and Genoa, thereby protecting the point of retreat of both French armies. If Suvorov crossed the Scrivia, Moreau would be ready to join up with Macdonald to throw themselves upon him.

It would have been impossible to determine in advance the next steps the two armies should take, the point where they should meet up, and whether they should attack Suvorov or await him in position. These decisions would have had to be made according to the enemy's movements.

It seems that all our reflections on the plans of the two French commanders lead to one very simple result. But we are not embarrassed about this. It is the ruin of so many critical reflections and designs that they strive for brilliant results where the situation does not provide them.[16] It is never difficult to design a one-sided, apparently brilliant combination with great words and phrases at the expense of all logic and probability, but it is also never instructive. If we compare our plan with the one the French commanders actually decided on and carried out, this demonstrates their mistaken views and misguided efforts and how the outcome inevitably suffered because of them; this is exactly what we have served up here. The French commanders' plan was for Macdonald to advance on Modena and from there up the Po via Parma and Piacenza to Tortona, with his right wing resting on the river and his left on the Apennines, and for Moreau to break through via Gavi and Serravalle. Since Macdonald had the tougher task, Victor was to advance through the Taro valley toward Parma with 6,000–7,000 men and be placed under his command, while an intermediate corps under Lapoype was to move to Bobbio on the Trebbia to maintain communications and cover Macdonald's left wing.

So says Jomini.[17] If we again find this plan totally lacking in clarity or

---

16. Again, using the anecdotal evidence of classroom wargames, the students have found that there is often a succession of bad choices, and the solution is often the least bad option.

17. Jomini, 11:341–346.

proper precision, this should come as no great surprise, since we find its like recurring all too often in the history of warfare. Also, in the end, what the commanders really thought and decided may well have been rather different from how General Jomini represents it; but of course, it does not show that author's theory in a very good light when his account contains so little critical analysis and at important points leaves him incapable of tearing himself away from the usual vague phraseology.

A mere route march, which is how he [Jomini] presents Macdonald's operation, is not an effective action in itself and so cannot be given as the objective of his operation. Using the Apennines for support on one side and the Po on the other is an imprecise idea that does not work in practice; furthermore, it would have had no value for Macdonald's situation and aim, since he did not intend to conduct positional warfare on the plain of the Po but was seeking a decisive battle, for which he would have to remain concentrated and could not seek support from points that were 30 miles apart. Associating these advantages with Macdonald's advance is supposed to make the whole thing look a bit better. The purpose of Moreau's advance against Tortona is not stated. We do not know whether the French commanders were thinking that they would deliver a major decisive battle at Tortona together, which they had no right to expect; whether Moreau was just supposed to advance in order to pin part of the allied force there, so that not too much could move against Macdonald; or whether Moreau was supposed to fight his own decisive battle at Tortona in the event the main body moved against Macdonald. Any of these could have been the aim, but it is not made explicit. It seems to us that in this unclear plan, two erroneous ideas are causing trouble:

1. That separate action by the two commanders was necessary and indeed preferable.
2. That the so-called debouchment onto the plain should be regarded as a major action by which much was already to be gained.

If the French commanders were convinced of the difficulty of carrying out their attack with their forces united, that was completely justified by the circumstances we have described, but it does not follow that it was necessary to operate entirely separately. They could and should have joined up during the course of the operation.

One might say that General Victor had been ordered to join Macdonald with 6,000–7,000 men,[18] and if Moreau himself had done so, perhaps he would have brought only 10,000–12,000 more, so it might not have made much difference. However, for a start, in a battle delivered by 40,000 men, another 4,000–5,000 is not an insignificant number, and second, the whole battle would have taken on a different character if Moreau were there. He was the commander in chief to whom Macdonald's army was entrusted; he could regard himself as the most experienced and talented commander. Above all, it is essential to our idea of uniting forces during the operation that this should *be sought from the outset* and that securing it *should be made a major objective*, which thus excluded any divergent blow by Macdonald against Modena and Bologna. We shall see from its execution that the French commanders' plan did not lead in that direction.

But the French commanders most likely thought of this separate action not as just a necessary evil but actually as an advantageous form of attack, a force multiplier. The principle of attacking an enemy from several points and on several sides at the same time wherever possible has been dragged across from tactics into strategy, even though it is actually the opposite that applies here. At that time, this principle was very much in fashion,[19] and it therefore seems very likely that the French regarded Macdonald's march as a strategic attack against the allied flank and as something advantageous precisely because of that.

We infer this idea from an excerpt of Jomini's concerning the question of a junction on the southern slopes of the Apennines, which states:[20] "after uniting at Genoa he would have had to debouch a second time through the Ligurian Alps." Since debouching into the duchy of Modena seemed much easier, that was a reason for General Macdonald to advance onto the plain; the idea was that this would break the ice, and one would then be able to see what to do next.

But this so-called debouchment onto the plain, *thought of as a kind of cri-*

---

18. Jomini, 11:342.

19. See the discussion of Austrian regulations in chapter 1, note 78, which called for the use of multiple columns to enable movement and facilitate the attack. Of course, all the columns need to arrive nearly simultaneously to have the desired effect. A lack of effective communications makes this extremely difficult to accomplish in practice.

20. **Clausewitz** notes: "Vol. XI, p341" [*"après la reunion à Gènes il eut fallu déboucher une seconde fois par les Monts Liguriens"*]. This is Jomini, 11:341.

sis, is empty terminology in most cases, since there are very few situations in which the enemy can make this into a crisis.

We therefore believe that how the French could most easily descend to the plain did not matter at all; instead, what mattered was how to create the best conditions for the decisive battles. A united breakout from the Genoa region had to be avoided only because it could not be expected to produce these conditions, not because the effects of geography and topography made a breakout from that region with the whole force too difficult. We need only recall 1796, when Bonaparte had so little difficulty breaking out from a place from which there was not a single highway.[21]

The importance attached to the breakout made Macdonald choose the Modena and Bologna highways, even though they went in the wrong direction, and it made him think he gained a lot simply by arriving on the plain, so the dangers of separation seemed much less to him.

If the rationale for this had started from the fact that a decisive battle was necessary, and if that rationale had determined what form this battle could take and how the difficulties of their own situation could be overcome to some degree, then the French would not have made that mistake. They would have been driven by true necessities and not led astray by will-o'-the-wisp erroneous principles.

Now, by simply describing the events, we will be able to show how the operation takes shape, how it deviates from the likely result yielded by our plan, and how it deviates again from the plan of the French commanders themselves.

45 MACDONALD ADVANCES OVER THE APENNINES AND BEATS HOHENZOLLERN AT MODENA

Macdonald had arrived in Florence on 25 May. It was only to be expected that the necessary discussions with Moreau, reassembling scattered corps, and reorganizing the army would take eight days before operations could begin. But Macdonald let fourteen days go by, and this delay most likely had no other reason than that General Moreau was in the middle of the crisis of his retreat and therefore unavailable for any coordinated action if Macdonald had

---

21. See Clausewitz, *Napoleon's 1796 Italian Campaign*.

wanted to cut loose sooner. We are not saying that it would have been impossible for General Moreau to cooperate if he had marched directly across the Apennines to Novi instead of just keeping his eye fixed on Loano, but only that Moreau was already focused entirely in that direction and was thus neutralized for the first eight days.

All that happened during that time was that the Austrian general Morzin, who was in Pontremoli commanding the detachments sent over the Apennines by Ott, was driven back by Dombrowsky on 29 May. Although he had been warned of the impending attack and had already begun to retreat with his corps to Borgo Val di Taro, the rear guard of two companies he had left in Pontremoli was totally wiped out. Morzin continued his retreat to Fornovo in the Taro valley, where Ott had come to receive him. Macdonald's army now kept quiet until 9 June.

Upon the news of Macdonald's arrival, General Kray had directed Prince Hohenzollern, who was about to join him from Milan with 5,000 men, to head for Casal Maggiore, cross the Po there, and take position between Klenau and Ott near Modena. According to the Austrian account,[22] General Kray thought it was not impossible that Macdonald might attack him and, by breaching Kray's blockade of Mantua, seek to create a diversion that would bring Suvorov back across the Po. Although the siege had not yet begun, the siege artillery was already in position, and Kray felt he had to observe General Macdonald closely on the far side of the Po and, if possible, hold him up for a while, so that Kray could withdraw his siege artillery. This made him decide to send Hohenzollern's corps off toward the Apennines with orders to resist Macdonald's advance for as long as possible. Thus, there were now some 18,000 Austrians facing Macdonald, but these were divided into three independent corps on a 55-mile front, serving not only to observe Macdonald but also to resist him if possible and to maintain the sieges of Bologna and Fort Urbino until the last moment.

Along with the report of Macdonald's arrival, Suvorov had received a false one stating that Moreau was expecting a reinforcement of 27,000 men from the interior, which seemed to be confirmed by Macdonald's delay. In this situation, he regarded a breakout by Moreau toward Alessandria and Tortona as very likely, and since he now had to move against Macdonald anyway, he decided to set off for the area of Alessandria on the 10th.

22. **Clausewitz** notes: "*Neue militär. Zeitschrift.* Jahrgang 1812. Vol. 6, p81."

He did not wish to give up possession of Turin or the siege of its citadel, since it was about to fall, so he left General Kaim with 8,000 men from his army and 2,000–3,000 Piedmontese with orders to shut himself up in the city and defend it to the utmost in the event Moreau advanced in superior force. General Wukassowitsch was ordered to retreat from Ceva to Nizza but to extend his outposts to Mondovi and Cuneo, from which it follows that this general remained tasked with observing the Apennines east of the Bormida. Generals Lusignan, Bagration, and Fröhlich, with the rest of the main army, were to retreat to Asti, where they were indeed concentrated by 11 June and may be estimated to have had 28,000 men.

Suvorov ordered General Ott and his corps to join General Bellegarde at Alessandria, leaving only a few light cavalry under Colonel Knesewitsch in the Parma area.

Since Suvorov rightly believed that he could never be too strong for the decisive battle that was approaching, he decided that the siege of Mantua, which had not yet properly begun, should be suspended for the period of the impending crisis.[23] He therefore wrote to General Kray to send his siege artillery to Verona and Peschiera, leaving only eight squadrons outside Mantua that, together with some thousands of Mantuan militia and the garrisons of Verona, Legnago, and Peschiera, would be sufficient to observe Mantua, and to march his corps to Piacenza to join Suvorov on the battlefield. This would have provided a reinforcement of around 12,000 men and, including the troops in the area of Alessandria and Tortona, would have produced a force of about 65,000 men. Even so, this force still would have been scarcely sufficient to cross swords with the French if Moreau had received the suspected reinforcements, in which case he easily could have sallied forth with 60,000–70,000 men.

But here we encounter one of those peculiarities of a war conducted by an alliance, in which a common threat fails to bring about unity and consistency, when different political interests come into play to cause discord and disagreement and finally create an utter shambles. The Austrian cabinet had failed to learn from the campaigns of 1796 and 1797, and in 1799 it thought matters were so infallibly on track, so far from any possible reversal of fortune, that simply ensuring a positive result was no longer of overriding importance, and

---

23. Napoleon did similarly in 1796. See Clausewitz, *Napoleon's 1796 Italian Campaign*, 114–117.

instead, the nuances of special interests could also be taken into consideration. The Austrians always regarded it as in their particular immediate interest to gain possession of Italy's fortresses, and since they saw that the Russian field marshal might not attach any such weight to this, and since they feared that his ambition and spirit of enterprise would make him strive above all else to extend his series of victories and expand the area of his conquest at the expense of its solidity (or so it appeared to the Austrian government), so they felt they had to protect themselves against this and therefore intervened by means of an order written by the emperor's own hand, commanding General Kray not to abandon the siege of Mantua on any condition.[24] Suvorov's radical idea, which we cannot praise highly enough, therefore foundered here on a rock he had not suspected, and by their truly outrageous interference in the natural operation of the machinery of war, the Austrians risked collapsing the entire edifice of the campaign on top of them. Thus General Kray remained outside Mantua and, as we have seen, contented himself with sending General Hohenzollern off to Modena.

That was how matters stood on the allied side when Macdonald began his move on 9 June.

On that day he crossed the crest of the Apennines in three columns.

His right wing, comprising Rusca's and Montrichard's divisions, 11,000 strong, together with the heavy artillery, took the highway from Florence to Bologna.

The center, comprising the advance guard and Olivier's and Watrin's divisions, 15,000 strong, followed the highway from Pistoia to Modena via Piave di Pelago and two secondary roads via San Pellegrino through the Dragone valley and via San Leone through the Panaro valley.

The left wing, formed by Dombrowsky's division of 3,500 men, moved from Fivizzano through Sassalbo into the Secchia valley.

---

24. **Clausewitz** notes: "Jomini Vol. XI, p386. General Jomini deserves to be completely taken at his word in quoting this, because he has worked from a handwritten account by General Chasteler." In addition, Milyutin quotes a letter from the emperor to Suvorov calling for the siege of Mantua to be maintained. Milyutin, *Geschichte des Krieges Russlands*, 2:28. The problem with the Austrian policy change is that the main forces trying to implement it were Russian. As such, they were unlikely to be happy fighting for something that did not match their own political objectives or that might actually be counterproductive.

The French divisions continued their maneuvers on the 10th and 11th. The right wing reached Bologna, the center Formigine with the advance guard before Modena, and the left wing Vezzano, a few leagues south of Reggio.

This march across the Apennines was accomplished without any Austrian resistance; because the Austrian accounts say it happened three days earlier, on the 6th, 7th, and 8th, we may conclude that they no longer occupied the crest or even the northern slope and that the French had already sent detachments across earlier. The only action was at Bologna, where the French advance guard drove back Hohenzollern's forward elements on the 11th and was then repulsed with loss when it pursued them.

While Macdonald thus advanced close to the great highway from Piacenza to Bologna within three days, Victor crossed the Pontremoli Pass and advanced through the Tarro valley toward Parma. No specific time is given for his maneuver, but we may well imagine that he arrived outside Parma at the same time as the other columns moved to Bologna and toward Modena and Reggio.

As far as the Austrian corps are concerned, we do not know exactly how or where they were deployed during the three days from 9 to 11 June. Klenau was busy besieging Modena and Fort Urbino. Naturally, he had to abandon this when Montrichard approached, and it seems that he concentrated at Cento on the Reno on the 11th and advanced to San Giovanni again on the 12th, occupying Nonantola to maintain communications with Hohenzollern. On the 11th Hohenzollern was at Modena facing Macdonald and decided to await his attack.

General Ott had begun his march to Alessandria, as ordered by Suvorov. On the 12th he was at Borgo San Donino on the highway from Parma to Piacenza.

Thus, on the 11th, the day before the first battle, we find both sides widely extended in three groups on a front 55 miles across; these similar errors meant that neither side was punished for them.

The Encounter at Modena on 12 June[25]

Hohenzollern had taken position outside Modena, with his infantry in the suburbs and his cavalry on the road to Rubiera. His line of retreat ran between

---

25. The original said 12 July, but clearly this was a typographical error.

the Panaro and the Secchia to Mirandola, and from there to the area of Governolo, where a pontoon bridge had been thrown across the Po. Klenau, who was at San Giovanni, was to guard the left flank and, as a last resort, cover the retreat by defending the Panaro. Since San Giovanni is 15 miles from Modena, there was no way Klenau could support General Hohenzollern against the frontal assault he would have to withstand.

Macdonald decided to attack Hohenzollern on the 12th. At the same time, his right wing under General Rusca was to operate from Bologna and cut off Hohenzollern's retreat to Mirandola. General Olivier's division was to attack frontally, the advance guard was to march to Rubiera to establish communications with Dombrowsky, and Watrin was to be held in reserve.

General Olivier attacked in three columns at 10:00 on the morning of the 12th. Although the 5,000 men of Olivier's division were not much stronger than General Hohenzollern's force, the latter was unable to resist for very long, and according to Jomini's account, Olivier lost only 300 men.[26] With this slight loss, he drove Hohenzollern out of the suburbs, onto the glacis, and from there into the city, which he penetrated at the same time as the Austrians. The most terrible confusion ensued, and of Hohenzollern's force of perhaps 4,000 men, he lost no fewer than eight guns and (according to the Austrians' own account) 2,233 men dead, wounded, and taken prisoner; he only escaped with difficulty to Mirandola with the rest. On the French side, General Forest fell, and Macdonald himself received two saber cuts from a group of Austrian light dragoons as they fought their way out.

Despite General Olivier's brilliant success, Macdonald did not achieve his aim of cutting off the enemy's retreat. General Rusca let himself be held up by Klenau. We cannot find any satisfactory details about the action there. Klenau seemingly put up his main resistance behind the bridge by which the highway from Bologna to Carpi crosses the Samoggia. At the moment when the French vanguard advanced across the bridge, Klenau charged them with four squadrons and drove them back across the river, taking one gun. The French had also sent a small detachment to advance against Nonantola, which perhaps came from Fort Urbino. Though this report of Klenau's action is sketchy, we can see that it was not significant; thus it can only be assumed that General Rusca made very poor use of his estimated two-to-one superiority. As for the overall result, we see Hohenzollern remained at Mirandola on the night of

26. Jomini, 11:347–348.

12–13 June and marched along the Secchia to the Po on the 13th; when he found that the bridge there had been prematurely demolished, he was still able to effect a crossing 5 miles further downstream, while Klenau managed to retreat along the Panaro to Ferrara.

After this first successful blow, Macdonald decided to march off to the left with his main body and approach both the allied main army and General Moreau at the same time along the Piacenza highway. He and Moreau agreed that the latter would advance to Novi and Serravalle on the 17th, sending his right wing to Bobbio, while Macdonald aimed to arrive in Piacenza the same day. Moreau thought he could then join up with Macdonald on the Trebbia, by which he meant nothing more than that his right wing would connect with Macdonald's left. These decisions were contained in a dispatch the Austrians captured after the action at Modena, so they seem to be the result of an agreement reached during the course of events. Obviously, there was no question that the two commanders wanted anything other than to establish one continuous line of deployment from the Scrivia to the Trebbia and then along the Trebbia to the Po; they assumed their opponent would then adopt an equally long parallel line or, if he did not, that they would have the advantage of being able to outflank and envelop him. They therefore saw this junction as an advantageous preparation for the decisive battle. The quest for tactical and strategic outflanking and the view that it would be a great masterstroke to attack everywhere on one and the same day all along a 70-mile front are peculiar to the early period of the revolutionary war. Bonaparte's method in 1796 was disregarded; Moreau and Macdonald were pupils of an earlier time, and even the former had not transcended its methods in any respect. So it comes as no surprise when we see them operating this way and striving toward a goal that is like a target without a bull's-eye, in accordance with arrangements that have nothing at the heart of them.[27]

It is true that to rescue General Moreau's reputation, some authors (Jo-

---

27. Clausewitz argues that outflanking should not be an end in itself, as this maneuver was sometimes viewed. Indeed, he points out that if one can outflank the enemy, it is useful, but only insofar as it aids the overall decision. If such a move allows a pursuit, which is where the real fruits of victory are found, all the better. However, it is useful only when tied to a broader purpose. See *On War*, book 1, chap. 3 ("On Military Genius"); book 3, chap. 15 ("The Geometrical Factor"); and book 4, chap. 12 ("Strategic Means of Exploiting Victory").

mini[28] and the archduke[29]) say that Macdonald did not act as Moreau intended, in that he headed first for Bologna and Modena and then chose the Piacenza highway for his main body's approach march, whereas Moreau had demanded that he stay in the mountains and meet up at Bobbio on the Trebbia. This view is inferred from Moreau's captured dispatch to Macdonald. But this dispatch, whose contents are shared in the [Austrian] military journal, contains so many contradictions that it cannot be regarded as proof on its own. It says that:

1. Moreau would await Macdonald's arrival at Piacenza.
2. He would likewise advance through the mountains from Bobbio to Piacenza at this time and join up with Macdonald at the foot of the mountains.
3. Bobbio would be occupied by Lapoype and serve as a point of support for Moreau's right wing and Macdonald's left.
4. Moreau would make every effort to pin part of Suvorov's force behind the Bormida.
5. He recommended that Macdonald stay at the foot of the mountains and use their protection to avoid any battle before they could meet up.
6. If Macdonald should be attacked by Suvorov, Moreau would attack the latter's right flank.

Who can fail to see that the third point disagrees with the second? That the fourth is in direct contradiction with the second and the fifth with the first? And that the sixth is hardly consistent with an accurate picture of the situation?

The original plan as shared by Jomini contains absolutely nothing about any intention to unite in the mountains or even at their foot; it expressly prescribes Macdonald's direction as Modena and says that during his advance, Macdonald should rest his left on the mountains and his right on the Po, which obviously leans more toward attaining the deployment given above. It is a quite characteristic bad habit of military historians, rather as it is in the nature of the French language, to mistake the part for the whole with apparent elegance as often as it pleases them. Bobbio was the point on which Moreau

28. Jomini, 11:352–354.
29. Karl, 2:52–53.

was to direct his right wing and Macdonald his left; that is enough for the historians to say that the French commanders wanted to meet up at Bobbio, so that it looks good when they then conveniently characterize the whole mass of the French forces as being combined at this point. Thus the difference arises between what Macdonald did and what he was supposed to do according to Moreau's idea, whether the blame for this false elegance lies with the dispatch writer himself or with the reader. We hold by those parts of the dispatch that conform with the general plan and with what Moreau actually did later. Accordingly, we do not feel justified in ascribing blame to Macdonald alone when both commanders should bear it jointly.

We felt this reflection was necessary to reveal the thread of strategic reasoning to the reader's eye in some degree. Let us now return to Macdonald's movements.

After Macdonald had thus driven Hohenzollern's and Klenau's corps back across the Po, he had Montrichard's division move between Carpi and Correggio to both threaten and observe that stretch of the Po between him and Mantua; he left Olivier at Modena, probably as support for Montrichard, and set off on the 13th to march to Piacenza with the other two divisions and the advance guard. He moved to Reggio, where he joined up with Dombrowsky, and the advance guard continued to Parma.

On the 14th Macdonald marched to Parma; his advance guard drove General Ott's forward elements before it and linked up with Victor at San Donino.

Before we permit Macdonald to continue his march, we must take a look at the other corps.

We have little precise or complete information about General Moreau after his retreat to the Riviera. On 6 June, as we have described, the last of his columns reached Loano. Now, with his left wing under Grenier, he adopted a position on that part of the mountain range that approaches the Tanaro at Barninetto; he sent Laboissière to the Genoa area, where Lapoype was already located; and he sent Victor to Pontremoli, whence, as we have already seen, he met up with Macdonald.

At Vado harbor (not far from Savona), Moreau found Admiral Bruix's squadron, which had no landing forces on board but was tasked only with cruising the Mediterranean. Yet still he took about 1,000 marines from it and used its presence to spread the rumor of a reinforcement of 15,000 men, to which he sought to lend credibility through some suitably calculated troop movements.

Thus at the time when Macdonald's debouchment onto the Lombardy plain is necessarily attracting the enemy's main body toward him, we see General Moreau busy sending Victor's division to join him but taking position with the rest of his force in the Apennines on a front of more than 50 miles stretching from Albenga to Genoa. General Lapoype, who had been directed to move to Bobbio, did not get there until the 16th. Since it is only three days' march from Genoa, his arrival there was probably calculated to tie in with Macdonald's movements.

Moreau himself, as we shall see, set his main body in motion a couple of days later. Until then, he contented himself with trying to keep Suvorov *en échec* [in check] by broadcasting rumors of his reinforcement.

As we have related, for a while, Suvorov actually did believe that Moreau would break out along the Scrivia or the Bormida together with Macdonald, and his order to General Ott to return to Tortona was a consequence of this. But it had no influence at all on his own movements. As we have seen, he and his army reached Alessandria on the 12th. There, he learned of Macdonald's advance along the Modena and Bologna highways, whereupon he ordered General Ott to do an immediate about-face, to advance toward Parma again, and, if possible, to stay between that place and Piacenza until the army's arrival, but without getting involved in any decisive action. Suvorov himself took a couple of thousand men from Bellegarde's troops as reinforcements but could not continue his march until the 15th; the pontoons had fallen behind on the poor roads, and the bridge over the Bormida could not be completed before then. Of course, we must wonder why there was no bridge there already, although it is understandable, given how many rivers there are in that area.

Again, we do not have precise details of General Ott's movements. Most likely he moved from Borgo San Donino to Piacenza on the 13th, received the counterorder there, and on the 14th turned back along the Parma road as far as the Nura, where he was met by Colonel Knesewitsch. As we have said, on that day Victor met up with Macdonald's advance guard at Borgo San Donino. Their forward elements had probably driven Colonel Knesewitsch back toward the Nura.

Hohenzollern's defeat at Modena had given General Kray a nasty fright. He feared a crossing of the Po, so he sent his siege artillery back to Verona and Peschiera and took serious measures for the defense of the Po, which the local people vigorously assisted. But he himself stayed before Mantua; in response to Suvorov's urgent request for reinforcements, he sent only three battalions and six squadrons that had joined him during the battle of the Trebbia.³⁰

Since the combat forces were scattered in numerous individual corps, and since the impending decisive battle develops from a great multitude of positions and maneuvers, it is doubly important to keep a constant eye on them in chronological order, so we will assemble them day by day so far as possible.

15 June

Suvorov left General Bellegarde with two brigades at San Giuliano between Tortona and Alessandria; he also attached Generals Alcaini, Seckendorff, and Wukassowitsch to him. Of these, the first was besieging the Tortona citadel, and the other two were posted toward the mountains. He instructed General Bellegarde that if the enemy moved against him in force, he should raise the siege of Tortona and hinder the enemy from operating against the rear of the army moving to Piacenza; if he had to give way, he should first move behind the Bormida and then into the camp at San Salvatore between Alessandria and Valenza, and if he could not hold there, he should shut himself up in Valenza.

Suvorov set off with thirty-two battalions, eighteen squadrons, and four regiments of Cossacks, about 30,000 strong, in two columns and moved to Castelnuovo [Castelnuovo Scrivia Alacre]. Macdonald moved to Borgo San Donino, and Victor moved to Fiorenzola [Fiorenzuola d'Arda]. Ott retreated to Piacenza, followed by the French advance guard under General Salm.

On this day, Olivier's and Montrichard's divisions apparently received the order to follow the army as far as the Tarro.³¹

On the same day, Moreau concentrated his army at Genoa, and Lapoype was on the march to Bobbio.

---

30. It is worth reminding the reader of the problems incurred when policy goals and strategy do not line up with those of all the alliance partners. See note 24 in this chapter.

31. **Clausewitz** notes: "Jomini does not allow this order to be issued to them until the 16th; but as we shall see, by midday on the 18th they had already reached the Trebbia, which was 70 miles from where they were in the Modena region, and they could not have marched that far in two days." See Jomini, 11:354.

16 June

Suvorov marches to Casteggio and sends General Chasteler to Stradella with 5,000 men to receive Ott, if necessary, and he sends General Welesky to Bobbio with 2,000 men to observe the French division that was expected there. Suvorov's march covers only 15 miles, but since he had not been able to set off until toward evening of the previous day, the troops presumably did not arrive before nightfall.

Macdonald marches on Piacenza.

Salm, Rusca, and Dombrowsky remain on the Nura, with Watrin in reserve at Fiorenzuola, while Victor moves to Piacenza itself and drives off Ott. The latter hesitated for a moment, considering whether to shut himself up in the city and await Suvorov's arrival behind its walls, but he chose instead to demolish the Po bridge and retreat first across the Trebbia and then, when the French crossed that river, behind the Tidone.

As far as the more distant corps were concerned, Olivier's and Montrichard's divisions were still three days' march from the Nura.

Lapoype arrived at Bobbio.

Moreau moved to Gavi with 14,000 men and left Generals Pérignon and Laboissière in the state of Genoa with 5,000–6,000.

On the left bank of the Po, Generals Hohenzollern and Klenau were deployed to defend the river. Suvorov was expecting two Russian battalions from Valenza, as well as three Austrian battalions from Mantua that were still on their way along the left bank of the Po.

Such was the situation on the eve of the three-day battle on the Trebbia.

Suvorov and the main body of his 26,000 men were still 25 miles from Ott, but some advanced corps had approached within a few miles of him. Ott was retreating, and Suvorov was hastening forward, so it could be anticipated that if Macdonald wanted to fight a significant battle on the 17th, he would have to deal with the larger part of the allied forces.

Macdonald had 7,000 men on the Trebbia, 12,000 men 10 miles behind them on the Nura, 6,000 another 10 miles further back at Fiorenzuola, and 11,000 more who were still two days' march behind. If he stood still, he could give battle with 25,000 men on the 17th and, if necessary, with 36,000 on the 18th—that is, with his full strength. But if he wanted to operate offensively throughout, that is, continue to advance on the 17th, he had to fear that his leading 19,000 men would have the entire allied force on their hands on the 17th.

But he could not act offensively with his own entire force before the 19th.

As was to be expected, the detachments at Bobbio in the upper valley of the Trebbia sorted matters out among themselves, without the outcome between these insignificant forces having any influence on the nine or ten times bigger battle on the lower Trebbia; they should therefore not be considered part of the combat forces delivering the decisive action.

46 THE BATTLE OF THE TREBBIA ON 17, 18, AND 19 JUNE

The first day of the battle was 17 June.[32] Macdonald probably did not think Suvorov and the main army were close enough yet to support General Ott on the 17th. He still wanted to get the better of Ott to the full extent that his superior numbers entitled him to. On the 16th, therefore, General Victor had already received the order to attack Ott the next morning, while Generals Salm, Rusca, and Dombrowsky were to support him.

Ott was behind the Tidone, which he was holding with a light chain of outposts 4 miles long from Gazzino [Agazzino] to Verato.[33] First he was attacked by Victor at Verato at 8:00 in the morning. While Ott was undecided as to whether he should continue this fight, he noticed a column advancing on Mottaziana, 2 miles beyond his right wing. This was Dombrowsky's division, constituting Macdonald's left wing. Meanwhile, Rusca moved against the center at Ponte Tidone, and General Salm joined Victor.

Thus, 19,000 French had joined the battle line, but extended on a front more than 5 miles long.

Ott was just about to begin his retreat to Stradella when General Melas arrived with several thousand Russians and Austrians, who were soon followed by Prince Bagration with the Russian advance guard.

---

32. For a more Russian-oriented view of the battle, see Duffy, *Eagles over the Alps*, 87–112.

33. The small hamlet of Veratto di Sopra no longer exists. It was to the west of Santimento (Sant'Imento) along the via Veratto, but it appears to have been swallowed by the shifting of the Po River. See https://mapire.eu/de/map/europe-19century-second survey/?layers=here-aerial%2C158%2C164&bbox=1055558.1950366166%2C5632721.231 559648%2C1067706.9052196918%2C5636543.082973908.

Generals Melas and Ott combined had only about 10,000–12,000 men available, and Melas must have thought he was dealing with Macdonald's whole army. Still, he had reservations about beginning a retreat to Stradella. The allied army had conducted an exhausting march in the heat, and the tactical organization of the march does not seem to have been particularly commendable; Melas was worried that his retreat and a rapid pursuit by the French could be bad for morale and bring dire consequences with it. On the other hand, the terrain around San Giovanni was not unsuitable for making a stand, and Suvorov's arrival was so imminent that even if this stand lasted only a little while, he might arrive in time for the decisive battle. Another reason may be added to these, and it is of the highest importance from the critic's point of view: namely, fear of Suvorov. The letter he wrote to Melas before the battle of Cassano may still have been vivid in the latter's memory.[34] Such energy in the right place is one of the most important elements in warfare; thus Suvorov's genius begins to influence the battle here.[35]

As a result of General Melas's decision, General Ott now occupied the village of Sermet [Sarmato] and the area around it with the seven battalions and fourteen squadrons of his corps, and his outposts fell back to this position. Sermet was now attacked by the French and repeatedly taken and retaken. Finally, the French were left in possession of it and, at the same time, captured a battery of eight guns that had been deployed on the highway.

Meanwhile, the troops that Melas had brought with him, plus other reinforcements that brought the total up to ten battalions and twenty squadrons, had deployed on the small plain in front of San Giovanni with their right wing at Caramel and their left at Fontana Pradosa.

---

34. This is the letter in which Suvorov reacted to Melas's perceived whining; see the text of the letter in chapter 2 at note 61. Milyutin, *Geschichte des Krieges Russlands*, 1:229–230.

35. It is important to note that Clausewitz's concept of genius entails more than simply making decisions or raw intellect; it includes psychological and moral elements too. All these factors are important. See *On War*, book 1, chap. 3. Paret's chapter in *On War* titled "The Genius of On War" (pp. 9–13) and Howard's "The Influence of Clausewitz" (pp. 27–44) are very helpful in explaining what Clausewitz is driving at and in providing context for his ideas. That being said, the concept of genius is inherent throughout *On War* and forms an integral part of his understanding of the phenomenon of war. In this case, Clausewitz is making the point that the previous exchange of letters placed Melas in the position of feeling compelled to act in a manner that would meet with his commander's approval.

Suvorov himself arrived just as Dombrowsky's French division advanced against Caramel and as Victor and Salm moved along the Po against San Giovanni.

Dombrowsky seems to have been the furthest forward. Suvorov had Prince Gortschakof attack him in the flank with two regiments of Cossacks and four battalions of infantry, while Ott attacked him in the front. The Poles were violently repulsed and escaped with difficulty across the Tidone. Ott then turned against Sermet and recaptured the village, together with the lost battery.

Meanwhile, Victor and Salm were attacked by Bagration and driven back all the sooner, as their retreat was already threatened by Dombrowsky's defeat and the loss of Sermet. While they were retreating, the cavalry that had been used against Dombrowsky rushed up, attacked Victor in the left flank, and wiped out some of the infantry that had formed square level with Castel Bosco. The remaining part of the right wing only escaped across the Trebbia with difficulty and under cover of the very broken ground. The other divisions also fell back across the Trebbia at nightfall, but Macdonald was still in a position to keep his outpost line on the left bank between Sant'Imento and Gragnano. This was possible thanks to the terrain being crisscrossed with ditches and walls, among which the allied cavalry driven forward by Suvorov in pursuit mostly had to fight dismounted; their efforts were in vain, and they lost a lot of men.

The allied infantry was happy just to take position behind the Tidone.

Meanwhile, the whole of Suvorov's army had arrived on the battlefield. It was busy sorting out its units, which had become very mixed up during the marching and fighting.[36] During the night it received the following deployment: Fröhlich's division took the left wing between Sermet and the Po; on its right was Förster's division, with Schweikowsky to the right of that at Caramel; Ott's division provided the outposts for the left wing and Prince Bagration's for the right, without crossing the Tidone.

The French position stretched from the Po to Gossolengo and was 7 miles long. Watrin's division was at Piacenza investing the citadel, and Olivier's and Montrichard's were still behind the Nura.

---

36. Judging by near contemporary maps, there is only one decent road along the allied armies' route of march, running almost due west from Piacenza via Castel San Giovanni and on to Stradella. It is likely that most of the allied troops had to march along this one road, which would have made deploying across a large area rather difficult.

We know nothing of the two sides' losses on this day.[37] We may well imagine, however, that they came to a few thousand men each and that the French lost at most 1,000 more men than the allies. Since Macdonald fought with only about half his combat forces anyway, losing this action had a much smaller effect on morale. Thus, it was true that very little had been decided on this first day, but for Macdonald, it could certainly be regarded as a bad start for the impending decisive battle.

Whether Watrin's division of some 6,000 men really arrived too late to have any impact on the action, or whether Macdonald had it halt at Piacenza out of concern for his rear, might have remained in doubt if not for the fact that on the 18th we find this division equally inactive on the very same spot.

As we have already said, the combat forces that Macdonald brought into action came to 19,000 men. Those of the allies that actually took part in the fighting may have totaled the same number. However, the whole army gradually arrived, and everything in sight of the enemy during a battle may be regarded as effective. Thus, it was actually Suvorov's whole main army that obtained this victory, which was estimated at 33,000 strong.

On this day, it seems that no fighting took place between the detachments facing one another at Bobbio.

Moreau advanced onto the plain at Novi.

18 June

The reader's eager anticipation of the history of this day will be very much disappointed.

Macdonald expects that a full third of his army will only arrive sometime during the day. He therefore decides to postpone his attack until the 19th. He has very good reasons not to continue his retreat any further, perhaps to behind the Nura: in part because doing so would add to the previous day's damaging effect on morale, and in part because there are always significant losses associated with a retrograde maneuver directly after a major battle. Besides, he could still hope that the approaching divisions would arrive in time to take part in a defensive battle if that were necessary. One would therefore expect

---

37. Duffy cites a source listing 1,000 French casualties and 1,200 prisoners. Duffy, *Eagles over the Alps*, 96.

the French commander to maintain his position behind the Trebbia and hold it as long as possible in the event of an attack.

Suvorov has won a half victory, and his forces are concentrated; one would expect him to continue his attack and make his victory complete. This was indeed the intention of both commanders, and a decisive result seemed to be the inevitable consequence; nevertheless, the business turned out otherwise, and it left the contest unresolved yet again.

Suvorov decided not to start his attack until 10:00 in the morning, probably to allow the troops time to obtain rations and cook a meal. His plan of attack was organized to strike the French left wing with his main strength, because he imagined they would attach the most weight to that because of their line of communications with Moreau and the mountains. He divided his army into three attacking columns.

General Rosenberg, with Bagration's and Schweikowsky's divisions (fourteen battalions, six squadrons, and one Cossack regiment), was to cross the Tidone at Brenno and move on Campremoldo and Rivalta, where he was to cross the Trebbia and advance through Settima toward San Giorgio [San Giorgio Piacentino] on the Nura.

The second column, under command of General Melas, comprised eight battalions and six squadrons under General Förster, followed by a reserve of ten battalions under General Fröhlich. They were to cross the Tidone at Mottaziana and move to Gragnano; from there, they were to advance across the Trebbia on Vallero, St. Bonico, and Veccari toward the Nura.

The third column comprised Ott's division of seven battalions, eight squadrons, and a Cossack regiment. It was to cross the Trebbia on the main highway and, if the other columns were successful, it was to advance on Ponte di Nura, bringing the garrison of Piacenza with it. It seems to have been charged with forming a somewhat refused flank and pinning the enemy. The reserve under Fröhlich, though, was expressly tasked by Suvorov to direct its main attention toward the right wing, to provide maximum impetus there.

In general, the troops were told to attack en masse and with the bayonet. Because it was the anniversary of the battle of Kolin,[38] their battle cry was to be "Theresia and Kolin!"

To make it easier to bring across the battalions Suvorov was still expecting

---

38. At the 1757 battle of Kolin, during the Seven Years' War, Austrian general Daun soundly defeated Frederick the Great.

from the left bank of the Po and, in the worst case, to provide another line of retreat, he had a bridge thrown across the Po near Parpanese (level with San Giovanni) [north] and protected by a bridgehead.

Suvorov's dispositions seem more like a pursuit while ready for action than an actual battle plan, and we can very well understand how the events of the 17th caused this. Rivalta is more than 9 miles away from the main highway to Piacenza, the columns advanced on diverging radii, and the combat forces were spread over such a large area that they could not apply proper pressure anywhere.

Suvorov himself was with the column on the right wing. When it reached the Casaliggio area at 3:00 in the afternoon, it ran into Dombrowsky's division. This apparently constituted the outposts for the French left wing, and it was soon in serious trouble. General Victor, who, according to Jomini,[39] was commanding the whole line in Macdonald's absence, concentrated his infantry—that is, Victor's and Rusca's divisions—as quickly as possible and crossed the Trebbia with them to support Dombrowsky. Thus the battle stabilized at this point, as both commanders had roughly equal forces of about 14,000 men. Victor made a stand around Toridella for some time, but in the end, he had to give way and retreat across the Trebbia to Settimo. Rosenberg followed as far as the Tavernasco area, which he only reached at dusk.

Rosenberg's column did not attack at Casaliggio until 3:00 in the afternoon. The plan was based on the idea that the left wing should be refused, and the maneuver would be a sort of [left] wheel, so we may imagine that the center and left wing did not rush to launch their own attacks. It is explicitly stated that General Ott did not strike the enemy at Rotto Freddo, 2 miles from Tidone, until 5:00 p.m. Thus this second decision was deferred until toward evening—so late that, first, the two French divisions expected during the course of the day surely would have arrived by then, and second, the onset of night scarcely allowed time to cross the Trebbia. This is sufficient for us to say that the allies' entire attack for the day was bound to fail.

Olivier's and Montrichard's divisions had actually arrived toward 2:00 p.m. The former had deployed astride the main Piacenza highway for Salm to fall back on. Montrichard hurried across the Trebbia to Gragnano to support the center, which presumably consisted of part of Rusca's division, as the rest of it was being used by Victor against Rosenberg. Förster's division could hardly

39. For a description of the battle, see Jomini, 11:354–373.

have broken through to the Trebbia here if it had not been that Montrichard, worried about his left flank because of Victor's retrograde maneuver, found it advisable to retreat behind the river and deploy his left wing at Gossolengo. The two sides then confined themselves to a heavy cannonade across the Trebbia.

On the French right wing, General Salm had been received by Olivier's division behind the Trebbia. But the allies' advance to the Trebbia cannot have been of a very victorious nature here. Despite Suvorov's instruction that the reserve should primarily be ready to support the first column, General Melas felt obliged to use it to cover the highway and to support General Ott.

There is no mention of Watrin's division. In the morning it was still at Piacenza and seems to have been neutralized by this place—that is, by just three Austrian companies.

Thus, by the evening of the 18th, the allies had advanced up to and across the Trebbia: the left wing and center as far as the river, and the right wing under Rosenberg 2 miles beyond it to Tavernasco. But in the endless broken and difficult terrain, this right wing consequently found itself isolated and endangered to such a degree that General Rosenberg had his entire infantry form one large square in which they spent the night; then he retreated back across the Trebbia come morning.

This day's result was again to the disadvantage of the French, since their left wing had suffered heavily and was entirely driven off the battlefield their divisions had chosen on the left bank of the Trebbia, falling back across it to the right bank. But this result was not in any way decisive; the French are said to have lost just one single cannon.

While Suvorov's orders were more suitable for a battle-ready march, and the fighting was practically an encounter battle, the French too seem to have operated entirely without a plan, relying on the division commanders' inspirations of the moment. As Jomini expressly states, on his own initiative, Victor crosses the Trebbia with the larger part of two divisions to oppose the allies' first column;[40] Montrichard does exactly the same against the second; Olivier remains on the right bank. There is not a single word about Macdonald and his orders. It is in the nature of the business that, in such broken and covered terrain as that between the Trebbia and the Tidone, the commander can intervene much less and is to some degree neutralized, but the major tactical

40. Jomini describes this as "impetuous." Jomini, 11:354.

outlines must still be imbued with his spirit. The advance across the Trebbia by Generals Victor and Montrichard could have been undertaken for two reasons: first, the general principle of always being the attacker, and second, the characteristics of the terrain. The ground is so covered with obstacles that all observation and communications are terribly impeded, and the riverbed of the Trebbia, which runs in two or three branches almost throughout and is several thousand paces across, actually constitutes the most accessible and open part of the whole area in the seasons when it is not swollen. Since, at the time of the battle, the river was very low and wadable everywhere, and since it has very gentle banks, its bed obviously presented no obstacle to movement, so we can well imagine that troops in a battle line ready to fight would prefer to have it behind them rather than in front of them because it provides easier communications to the flanks.[41] In the absence of a good map and any detailed description, we offer this guess but do not wish to attach any great value to it; other local factors or forgotten reasons could have caused it. But whatever the reasons for this advance might have been, it is impossible for us to recognize it as a laudable battle plan. The French were still in the process of concentrating their forces, and Macdonald did not want to launch his attack until the 19th; it was therefore in the French commander's interest to buy time, that is, to *delay* the decision. But the French advance *accelerated* it, and the fact that the encounter on the 18th did not turn into a decisive battle against the interests and intentions of the French commander is no thanks to his generals.

But anyway, what good could ever come from a totally unplanned confrontation with the foe in which some advance, others do not, and nobody knows anything about the enemy!

If we deduct Watrin's division and Macdonald's earlier losses, his strength at the outset on the 18th can hardly have exceeded 26,000 men. They fought on a front of 9 miles, and because the broken terrain equally limited both observation and rapid maneuver, in order to protect their flanks and maintain communications with one another, his units were extended in long, thin lines. According to the usual method of the time and certainly also to the nature of the terrain, these, in turn, were mostly dispersed into skirmish lines. Taking all these factors together, we may conclude that the form of the fighting was in no

---

41. This is because the riverbed would be relatively sheltered from the fighting and thus could act as a natural form of covered way to facilitate the movement of messages or troops to either flank.

way suited to wresting victory from the hands of a determined opponent like Suvorov, and if it did not conversely lead to utter defeat, that was only because of the defective, delayed, and halfhearted attack.[42]

To remove any last trace of plan or purpose from this day's operations, and to make it virtually just a natural phenomenon without the intervention of any thinking brain, the fighting suddenly flared up again in the bed of the Trebbia as night fell, which no one wanted, no one understood, and where no one could take charge.

At 9:00 p.m., in response to a false alarm, three French battalions on the Piacenza highway snatch up their weapons and rush forward hastily and in disorder into the bed of the Trebbia. The allied troops take this to be an attack and open up a heavy cannonade on the French. When the French begin to retreat, individual detachments rush into the riverbed after them; now the French turn about, and it turns into an infantry battle, with both sides committing reinforcements to enable their friends to disengage and to put an end to the fighting, which just fuels the fire. Thus, like a poorly doused torch, the past day's battle blazes up again of its own accord, in the very riverbed that seemed to offer the two sides some rest by serving to separate them. Since the going is easier here than anywhere else in the area, everyone calls for cavalry, which arrives from both sides and escalates the chaos of this nocturnal fight to the maximum. By the weak light of the moon, the two sides' artillery posted on the banks cannot distinguish who is who, but fire blindly into this mob of combat-trained men gone wild, salving their artillerymen's conscience with the certainty that any unlucky shot that plows destructively through their own ranks will be paid back with a similar one of the enemy's. Only two hours later, at 11:00 p.m., are the senior commanders able to put a stop to this pointless destruction, and it takes most of the night to restore order.

We cannot say that this had any effect, except that it is an indubitable truth that any losses and futile exertions weigh more heavily on he who is already at a disadvantage and whose constitution has already suffered.

At Bobbio, all was quiet again on this day, and Moreau either did not advance at all or at least did not move through Novi and Serravalle.

Hohenzollern and Klenau began to patrol along the right bank of the Po toward Parma.

---

42. Here, Clausewitz seems to be referring to Melas's decision to use the reserve to support the line rather than risk it elsewhere.

19 June

Both armies were extremely exhausted, but still nothing had been resolved. Suvorov was expecting five battalions and fourteen squadrons from the [left] bank of the Po, some of which had already arrived on the evening of the 18th.[43] Macdonald still had one division that had not yet been in action. Suvorov was not the kind of man to give up before he was absolutely forced to do so; to the French, at the time, this was something unheard of. Besides, Macdonald was tied to Moreau's operation; on the one hand, he could expect Moreau's appearance at Tortona to create an effective diversion, and on the other, if he retreated too soon, he could put Moreau in danger and be held responsible. Thus the battle had to flare up again on the 19th.

Suvorov gave no new orders. He regarded those of the 18th as yet to be completely executed, and that evening he stipulated only that the columns should advance across the Trebbia on the morrow and that the reserve should mainly be held in readiness to support General Rosenberg.

But Macdonald gave proper orders for the day, according to which the enemy army was to be outflanked on both sides, entirely in the style of the tactics of the time.[44] Dombrowsky was to move out past the allies' right wing in the direction of Niviano, then advance toward Rivalta and Tuna to get on their right flank. Victor and Rusca were to attack the right wing under General Rosenberg frontally. Thus, in this place the same corps were destined to confront one another again. Olivier and Montrichard were to advance in the center, the former along the highway and the latter against Gragnano, while Salm and Watrin advanced on the right wing between the highway and the Po. Thus, this time they were entirely lacking any significant reserve. It was felt that, on a 12-mile front, this could be dispensed with, when in fact that would have made it essential, since whatever protection this extended front guaranteed against outflanking was in turn lost by weakening the line overall. The more one overrides the natural principle of length of tactical frontage, the more important reserves become.

---

43. The original mistakenly has this as the right bank. Presumably, these are the troops mentioned earlier.

44. It is worth reminding the reader about the previous discussion regarding flank and enveloping attacks.

General Lapoype was asked to cooperate by advancing through Travo against the Russians' right flank.

Whether Macdonald really thought it possible that Moreau would appear in the allied rear on this day remains an open question. But he did try to influence the troops' morale by assuring them of it.

Since the night fighting had deprived the troops of the rest they so badly needed, neither side began to move again before 10:00 a.m.

The French left wing under Victor's command moved across the Trebbia at Gossolengo, while Dombrowsky advanced through Rivalta and appeared on the Russians' right flank. Suvorov, who was commanding here in person again, sent Bagration against Dombrowsky and drove him back across the Trebbia after a lively action. This move to the right by Bagration produced a gap of 1,500 paces between him and Schweikowsky, which Rusca and Victor used to overwhelm Schweikowsky by taking him in his right flank. He was driven back to the area of Casaliggio. But the Russians were as brave as they were steadfast. The Rosenberg regiment holding the right wing received a flank attack by forming to face in both directions and thus withstood this assault.

The essential element was not the gap that arose and opened up the flank of Schweikowsky's division but that Bagration was probably stronger than Dombrowsky, since he drove the latter back across the Trebbia again. By the same token, Rusca and Victor were able to outnumber Schweikowsky, who was now paying for Bagration's success. But Bagration completes his victory more quickly than Victor, hastens back, and falls on the latter's left flank; meanwhile, on the other side, General Chasteler arrives with a reinforcement of four battalions from Förster's division and supports Schweikowsky's front. The fighting now gains new force, the allies go over to the attack, and both Victor's and Rusca's divisions are obliged to withdraw across the Trebbia, during which the 17th and 55th Line Infantry Regiments are almost totally destroyed. The Russians try to get across the Trebbia, but in vain; the fighting comes to a standstill on the banks of the river once again.

General Melas was in command of the allied center and left wing. He had Förster's and Ott's divisions, the latter having been reinforced on the evening of the 18th by three battalions and a cavalry regiment from the left bank of the Po. In addition, Fröhlich's division of ten battalions was in reserve. In the morning before the battle began, General Melas received a repeated order from Suvorov that the reserve, together with the Lobkowitz Dragoons under the command of Prince Johann Lichtenstein, should march off to the right to support General Rosenberg. Since Melas was a fretful old man who constantly felt that wherever he happened to be was always the point under the greatest threat, yet again he would have preferred to keep the reserve with him, but Suvorov's order was too explicit, and he had to resolve to carry it out. However, he now collected his generals for a council of war in which they agreed that, in this situation, they were too weak to cross the Trebbia before the right wing had a firm foothold on the far side of the river, so they should therefore remain on the defensive.

If he had been sure the French would attack him in earnest, then this decision certainly would have contributed more profitably to winning the battle than any attack of his own; however, it was still against Suvorov's express order, and if the French did not attack, it would have neutralized a third of the allied combat forces. Clearly, Melas regarded himself not as purely and simply subordinate to Suvorov but more or less as a co-commander, and this is one of the evils that undermine the operations of every alliance.[45]

Thus, when Olivier's and Montrichard's French divisions crossed the Trebbia and attacked, they found the Austrian commander resolved to defend. Their two divisions and those of Watrin and Salm forming the French right wing were perhaps 18,000 strong altogether. Förster and Ott may be estimated at about 16,000, but as we have seen, the former had to send four battalions, which must have had at least 3,000 men, to support Schweikowsky; this left only 13,000, hardly enough to resist the French attack if the whole reserve had already gone. But as luck would have it, when Olivier's and Montrichard's divisions began their action and were optimistically promising themselves great success, Prince Lichtenstein was on the march to join Suvorov but was still close enough to perform a sudden about-face not only to support Melas but also to attack the enemy in the left flank. Prince Lichtenstein did not hesitate to join in, with the result that Montrichard's division, struck by this superior

---

45. The Austrian emperor's 3 April 1799 letter to Suvorov appointing him commander in chief of the Austrian army in Italy also contains a note stating that the Austrian government will include General Melas in the loop of correspondence between it and Suvorov. It is perhaps not surprising that Melas viewed the chain of command differently from Suvorov, and the regular interventions in the campaign by the Aulic Council surely undermined the command relationship even further. See Milyutin, *Geschichte des Krieges Russlands*, 1:544–546.

attack, was so violently defeated that it was utterly routed all the way back to Piacenza. This then exposed Olivier's and Victor's flanks. Prince Lichtenstein sensed the importance of further exploiting the success obtained here. Turning about again and marching off to the right wing would have wasted too much time, so he turned against Olivier, who, in danger of losing his line of retreat, had to hurry back to regain the right bank of the Trebbia, where he halted for the time being, steadfastly denying the allies any further advance.

The French right wing under Watrin found itself facing little opposition and advanced without difficulty to Calendasco, from where it patrolled as far as Ponte Tidone. After the dire events on the left wing and in the center, it was called back by Macdonald and had difficulty carrying out this retreat without significant loss. It too took position behind the Trebbia.

Macdonald's hope that General Lapoype would appear on Suvorov's right flank during the battle, to make a strategic impact rather than to cooperate tactically, was in vain. Lapoype received Macdonald's request only at 11:00 a.m. on the 19th, and Bobbio is about 25 miles away from the center of the battlefield. General Lapoype immediately set out to march through Travo but must have been unable to reach the battlefield, which is understandable. According to Jomini, on the 20th he was above San Giorgio, so he presumably moved into the Nura valley when he heard the news of Macdonald falling back.

Thus the French attack was beaten off everywhere, but they once again held their previous position. Although repelling an attack can be regarded as a victory in most cases, in the present one, the matter could not be viewed as decided until the French had abandoned their position on the Trebbia, for in general, Suvorov was just as much the attacker as Macdonald. The result of the three days' battle so far was that the allies had up to 6,000 men out of action, and the French 8,000. The difference is not very significant, and since the two were of almost equal strength, the remaining combat forces must still have been fairly equivalent.

Because of the long duration of this battle, it is usually thought of as an extremely tough and bloody one, and indeed, all the historians describe it this way. But we are of the opinion that this duration—in other words, the fact that it remained undecided for so long—must be ascribed more to the nature of the terrain than to uncommon bravery. Very broken and difficult terrain has the effect of delaying the forces conducting the battle and thereby weakening the principles on which they operate, that is, diluting them with time.

Of the 6,000 men the allies had out of action, probably 2,000 were missing,[46] leaving 4,000 dead and wounded, which, out of 36,000 in three separate encounters, is clearly not very many.

Obviously, none of the results produced by this three-day battle was due to geometrical or geographical elements. The forms of the opposing deployments and the terrain factors were entirely equivalent in their nature. Even the actual losses differed very little, as we have just seen.

If we look at the strategic factors, these were certainly not of the kind to oblige General Macdonald to retreat any more than Suvorov. On the 18th or 19th Moreau could have struck a blow against Bellegarde in Suvorov's rear, and he actually did so on the 19th; Suvorov then would have had no time to lose in turning against him or, in the event Macdonald's proximity did not allow this, retreating across the Po. The explanation Jomini gives for the French retreat—the threat Hohenzollern and Klenau posed to Macdonald's rear—is exaggerated, since these generals were only patrolling in his rear and did not dare show themselves on his line of retreat. Certainly, Macdonald could not have known their exact strength, since Kray might have reinforced them. But this strategic factor already existed when Macdonald began his march through Parma, and as long as there was still hope of victory, it could not become a reason to retreat.

Thus, if we see the French commander commence his retreat on the 20th, the reason for doing so must lie in the state of his army itself. Thus, in this battle, we find the principle that is primarily responsible for deciding modern battles—the principle of physical and moral exhaustion—isolated and significantly highlighted.[47] Here, there was not one point of the position lost, not one outflanked wing, no breakthrough in the center, no threatened line of retreat,

---

46. **Clausewitz** notes: "The Austrians only report 497 missing, but the 244 dead and 1,816 wounded they report gives a quite unusual ratio, so we probably have to count 800 of the wounded as missing. It is well known that junior commanders do not like to report these, and so with the best will in the world it is not possible to reach the truth. The Russians report 675 dead and 2,986 wounded, or between four and five wounded for every man dead, which is the normal ratio."

47. Clausewitz discusses the importance of this principle in "Purpose and Means in War": "Wearing down the enemy in a conflict means using *the duration of the war to bring about a gradual exhaustion of his physical and moral resistance.*" *On War*, book 1, chap. 2, 93 (emphasis in original). As such, if the French intended to continue the fight, they had to disengage to preserve their physical and moral resistance. Likewise, if the allies wished to end the war quickly, they had to maintain continuous pressure on the

not one unsuccessful cavalry charge, not one lost battery, no misunderstanding, no local confusion that could count as contributing disproportionately to losing the battle. It was purely the incremental tiring out of the forces that finally made the scales so sensitive that victory went to the one with only a slight advantage. But it is not merely a question of the physical. If anything, it is more a question of moral force than physical force. And so here the allies' advantage lay not in the couple of thousand more men they might have had, but in their moral state. The French had come off somewhat worse in each of the three encounters, which had a more destructive effect on the structure of their army; what remained was more a *caput mortuum* [worthless residue]. The impact of this triple defeat mounted and worsened until both the commanders and the army came to feel they were not strong enough, which is the one thing it always finally boils down to when a great battle is conceded.

47 MACDONALD RETREATS ACROSS THE APENNINES

20 June

Since General Macdonald had not the slightest news of either Moreau or Lapoype and could not survive another battle with Suvorov on his own, after midnight he began his retreat behind the Nura. Victor and the three divisions of the left wing moved to San Giorgio, leaving a strong rear guard on the Trebbia. Watrin moved to Piacenza with his division and Olivier's, then continued along the highway to Ponte Nura. A reserve under the command of Adjutant-General La Croix moved via Ronca between the highway and the Po. Montrichard was given the mission of hurrying to the Tarro to drive off Klenau's and Hohenzollern's patrols and occupy Parma. The baggage and the heavy artillery followed his division.

---

enemy, thereby enhancing and accelerating the process of wearing out their opponent. This ties in directly with the ideas about continuity and pursuit. Maintaining continuous pressure degrades one's own forces, but the negative effect on the enemy is even greater. Continued pressure adds to the loss of cohesion, combat power, and morale begun by the loss in battle. If that pressure is continuous, it can lead to the total collapse of an enemy. The French operations after the battle of Rivoli in 1797 are a prime example. See Clausewitz, *Napoleon's 1796 Italian Campaign*, 244–291.

On the evening of the 19th Suvorov still had no word of what had transpired between Moreau and Bellegarde that day,[48] but he had reports that the French were patrolling as far as Voghera and Casteggio. Although this must have caused him concern in connection with Bellegarde's fate and the implications for himself, and it certainly would have prompted any normal general to be satisfied with the advantages he had gained and immediately march off to face Moreau, Suvorov was determined not to let the victory to which he was entitled slip away but to force his opponent to lower his colors [i.e., take down his flag, or surrender] by striking a hearty new blow on the 20th. He was content to cover his rear by sending two squadrons and a Cossack regiment to Casteggio, an infantry battalion to Gardazza between San Giovanni and Stradella, and three more battalions to Parpanese and the bridgehead. He set off at 4:00 a.m. for a new attack in the same battle order as on the previous day.

This decision by the allied commander cannot be praised highly enough.[49] According to the false and vague reports he had received of Moreau's strength, Suvorov could expect him to arrive on the Tortona plain with 25,000–30,000 men. This was not only more than enough to drive Bellegarde back across the Po but also sufficient to force Suvorov to give battle again against some 20,000 men. After the losses his army had already suffered, and since a corps would still have to be left to face Macdonald, Suvorov certainly would not have been able to stand up to Moreau with 20,000 men of his own, so the outcome of this new decisive battle would have looked very doubtful. This would have compelled an ordinary general to march away all the sooner and get closer to his bridge at Parpanese, whatever happened. The consequence would then have been that he actually put himself between two fires and would have had no time to lose in crossing the bridge at Parpanese to gain the left bank of the Po, sacrificing his victory, abandoning his aim, and taking heavy losses. It would have been a complete strategic defeat. To reach this result would not have required the combat forces we have lent to General Moreau in accordance with the rumors, but only those that he actually had. But to Suvorov, what mattered above all else was to finish off the business with Macdonald, so it would have been a great mistake to leave too early and relinquish the advantages he

---

48. Moreau had driven Bellegarde back outside of Tortona. Karl, 2:59–61.

49. It conforms to Clausewitz's idea about concentrating force against the object one is seeking, which in this case is Macdonald's army. It also hints at Suvorov's military genius (as described earlier by Clausewitz).

had already obtained in order to fight for a new victory somewhere else. The one he had already largely achieved here needed just one more punch.[50] In his raw nature, he was always possessed by the idea, so often driven out by false theory, that *in most cases* all that matters is victory, not where it is won nor against whom. If Suvorov had always been ruled by the importance of geographical points, as Archduke Charles was, he could not have thought this way. By making his victory over Macdonald definite and complete, Suvorov would defeat General Moreau strategically. And the more glorious his victory was, the more strongly it would affect Moreau and the more it would eliminate any doubt about Suvorov's own situation.

During its crossing of the Trebbia, the allied army found that the river was held only by light troops who offered little resistance, so Suvorov immediately had the satisfaction of seeing his fixity of purpose rewarded with the certainty of victory. But just as in many cases it is the pursuit that lends real substance to the notion of victory, so it was in this case: where scarcely a single cannon was mentioned as being taken during the battle itself, the magnitude of victory could be created and realized only by the pursuit, and so it is the 20th that should be considered the actual day of victory in this respect.

Just after the allies crossed the Trebbia, an enemy spy was captured who was on his way with a letter from Macdonald to Pérignon,[51] informing him that he was retreating because of the huge losses he had suffered and the shattered state of his army. This discovery poured new fire through Suvorov's veins,[52] demanding that he strike Macdonald once more; he therefore ordered his columns to march as fast as they could, force the crossing of the Nura if need be, and advance to the Larda.

Förster's division was to join Rosenberg, who was to head via Gossolengo and Tavernasco to San Rocca, opposite San Giorgio. Melas was to move through Piacenza to Ponte Nura with Ott's and Fröhlich's divisions.

Victor had occupied the village of San Giorgio with the 17th Demi-brigade, defending the crossing with two guns and six squadrons. His corps was de-

---

50. This returns us to the idea of continuity, discussed previously.
51. Catherine-Dominique de Pérignon (1754–1818) was a marshal of France and had been commander of the French troops in Liguria since May 1799.
52. Again, this ties in with the concept of continuous pressure, and the knowledge that Macdonald's army was in a bad state understandably excited Suvorov. It also emphasizes the role of chance.

ployed behind these. It was not Victor's intention to accept battle with his main body, and he was already in the process of marching away when Suvorov's right column, accompanied by Suvorov himself, pushed forward impetuously. Not giving the foe time to pull out, Suvorov attacked the village of San Giorgio on several sides, finally cutting off the 17th Demi-brigade's retreat, forcing its 1,100 men to lay down their arms, and giving Victor's whole corps such a shock that part of it retreated in disorder along the highway to Cadeo and the rest fled into the mountains. This latter group rallied again at Castel Arquato on the Larda.

Rosenberg followed to Montenaro on the Chiavenna.

In Piacenza, General Melas found Generals Olivier, Rusca, Salm, and Cambray with 5,000 wounded but only a weak garrison otherwise. He left General Fröhlich there (apparently contrary to Suvorov's intention)[53] and then pursued to the Nura with just Ott's division. In these circumstances, he was too weak to drive off General Watrin, who did not retreat until the rout of the left wing forced him to do so, and who still had time to rescue the left wing's artillery parks. Watrin retreated to Fiorenzola.

The detachment at Ronca was not attacked at all but moved to Corte Maggiore as ordered by Macdonald.

Thus, on the first day Macdonald's retreat covered about 20 miles to behind the Larda.

General Lapoype, who, according to Jomini's account,[54] was above San Giorgio on the 20th, turned back to Bobbio, most probably at the news of Victor's hasty retreat. But he found this place already occupied by General Welesky's troops, and his attempts to recapture it were in vain. At that point, as the historians say, he scattered into the mountains, which probably means the troops moved across them in small groups along footpaths.

21 June

Victor's troops who had rallied at Castel Arquato set off for Borgo San Donino during the night. When they arrived early in the morning, they found Mon-

---

53. Given that these troops would have posed little genuine threat in the circumstances, it is easy to see why Suvorov might have been annoyed by this.

54. Jomini, 11:372.

trichard, who then set off to march to Parma, where he drove out Hohenzollern's outposts. Macdonald now found himself with all his divisions united on the highway. On this day he retreated behind the Tarro.

Suvorov only moved up to behind the Larda, while his advance guard under Ott reached Borgo San Donino.

22 June

On this day Macdonald moved to Reggio, but Victor's division presumably split off from Macdonald and took its path through Fornovo back to Pontremoli, as we find it there later without knowing any details of its march there.

Suvorov now decided to turn against Moreau, so he let his troops rest on the 22nd and entrusted further pursuit to General Ott, who was to establish communications with Hohenzollern and Klenau.

The direct effects of the battle concluded on the 21st. Including wounded, the total captured came to between 12,000 and 13,000 men and eight guns. If we reckon 3,000–4,000 dead and wounded left on the battlefield, Macdonald's losses can be assumed to be 16,000 men, which, adding in the sick and stragglers, comes to about half of the 37,000 men with which he had crossed the Apennines.[55]

Although Macdonald's subsequent retreat over the Apennines was somewhat delayed, it is too much a consequence of the battle of the Trebbia for us to ignore it here. Therefore, before we return to the Scrivia, we wish to relate the further course of events at the eastern end of the theater of operations up until Macdonald's departure for the west.

At Reggio on the 22nd, Macdonald had to reorganize his army, which now

---

55. Here, it is worth looking at these few days in terms of Clausewitz's ideas about continuity. Macdonald's army, had it been left unmolested after the first day at the Trebbia, might well have retreated with few losses (about 2,000, if the previous accounts were correct). Suvorov, by maintaining almost continuous pressure on Macdonald, was able to badly beat the French, causing extremely heavy losses to Macdonald's army and essentially removing him as a threat to allied operations in Piedmont. Had Suvorov chosen to ignore Macdonald to turn on Moreau earlier, that would have left a significant French threat to Suvorov's rear.

comprised Dombrowsky's, Montrichard's, and Watrin's divisions and a reserve under Adjutant-General La Croix.

On the 23rd Macdonald continued his move. Dombrowsky moved to Castel Novo di Monte in the Apennines to cover the approach to the Riviera, which is on a saddle in the crest at the sources of the Secchia and runs from there to Fivizzano. Watrin and La Croix marched to Modena, while Montrichard remained at Crostolo.

General Ott advanced to Reggio and established communications with Klenau and Hohenzollern, who were on his left.

On the 24th, under pressure from Ott, Montrichard retreated to Rubiera. On this day Macdonald wanted to hold his position behind the Secchia to gain time for his baggage train to cross the Apennines safely. He held the bridges at Rubiera and Pontalto (the road to Carpi) with his main body; Calvin's brigade was sent to Sassuolo, and La Croix was posted at Formigine with the reserve. Since the Seccchia is contained within high dikes and its riverbed is less firm than that of the Trebbia, it is easier to defend.

The attacks by Ott on the bridge at Rubiera and by Klenau and Hohenzollern at Pontalto were unsuccessful, and an attempt by General Ott to have the French left flank attacked by the cavalry under Colonel Knesewitsch, who crossed at a ford above Rubiera, drew the latter into a disadvantageous action with the French cavalry. A wider outflanking move had an even worse outcome. Ott had sent Major Pastori with the Warasdiner Battalion [Croat Grenzer][56] and a squadron of Reitender Jäger [*chasseurs à cheval*] to Sassuolo, instructing them to cross there and, if possible, throw themselves on the road Macdonald's baggage was following from Modena to Pistoia. Calvin's brigade at Sassuolo put up very little resistance, so Pastori easily seized that place. But now the reserve under La Croix rushed up, and the whole Austrian detachment of 700 men and two guns was captured. The Austrian account reads as though Major Pastori defended the position to the utmost to bar the road to Pistoia. But Sassuolo is not on this road but on a smaller one 3 miles east that runs from Modena to Castel Novo di Monte. We must leave Major Pastori's actual intentions and the circumstances that led to his debacle shrouded in the mystery of vague accounts, but in any case, we can probably say that it was a good intention clumsily executed.

56. These were frontiersmen serving in the Austrian army. They typically functioned as light infantry.

On the 25th Macdonald took position at Formigine at the foot of the mountains, after leaving 600 men in Fort Urbino and sending Montrichard's division to Bologna. Victor was at Pontremoli.

General Ott moved to Modena. Klenau left a detachment outside Urbino and moved against Bologna. There is no mention of Hohenzollern, who had presumably been ordered to return to Kray.

The opposing corps remained in this position in the northern foothills of the Apennines until early July, when Macdonald led his corps to Pistoia and sent an order to General Montrichard to return to Florence. We do not have complete information about his departure across the Apennines, nor his march to Genoa. On 6 July Bologna surrendered to Klenau, who granted the garrison free passage. Urbino held out against Ott so long that he had already been ordered to leave for Mantua when it surrendered to him on the same conditions on 10 July.

In Lucca, Macdonald made preparations to march along the Corniche to Genoa and set off on 8 July, while Montrichard and Victor still occupied the Apennines to cover this difficult march and then followed.

Since the coast was free of English ships, the artillery parks and heavy artillery could be transported by sea. The light artillery was carried on mules. Thus, on 17 July this army arrived in Genoa 14,000 strong but in a very poor state.[57]

48 MOREAU ATTACKS BELLEGARDE ON THE SCRIVIA

General Moreau's force came to 26,000 men, not counting the Ligurian[58] troops. As we know, he had sent 7,000 of these to join Macdonald, a few thousand under Lapoype moved to Bobbio, and General Pérignon stayed in Genoa with Laboissière's division plus three battalions. That left Moreau with a corps of just 14,000 men with which to begin his offensive.

Since there were Ligurian troops with Moreau's army and their strength is not stated anywhere, we cannot properly make out how the whole force was organized. If we take the Ligurian units to be 4,000–5,000 men and we reckon

---

57. This is all that was left of a force of 37,000 men just a few weeks earlier.
58. The Ligurian Republic was a short-lived republic founded in 1797, running along the coast adjoining Genoa.

Victor to have 7,000, Lapoype perhaps 2,000, and Moreau 14,000, that would leave 7,000–8,000 men in the state of Genoa. These last were presumably not all in Genoa itself, as the historians say, but some of them were likely covering the western approaches in the mountains.

On 16 June, as we have already said, General Moreau concentrated these 14,000 men at Gavi. He divided them into two divisions: the first under Grenier's command comprised Quesnel's, Gardanne's,[59] and Partouneaux's brigades and was 9,500 strong; the other under Grouchy had Colli's and Garreau's brigades with 4,500 men. Their total artillery was just fifteen cannon.

We have seen that out of Suvorov's and Bellegarde's combined strength of 54,000 men, 8,000 remained in Turin under Kaim and 30,000 moved to the Trebbia with Suvorov; thus, just 16,000 men stayed behind between the Scrivia and the Tanaro under Wukassowitsch, Seckendorff, and Bellegarde, who were busy besieging the Alessandria and Tortona citadels. Modest though the combat forces were with which Moreau advanced to the attack, it could be expected that, if used well, they would be sufficient to relieve both fortresses and oblige General Bellegarde to retreat across the Po. Since General Moreau could have reached the road from Tortona to Alessandria in a single day's march from Gavi, Bellegarde was not in a position to prevent his force from being split unless he was willing to abandon one of the sieges at the outset. Out of his 16,000 men, Bellegarde probably had no more than 6,000–8,000 in the San Giuliano area with which to oppose this advance and would therefore have had to give way and fall back across the Bormida; the manner of the enemy's advance could have made even this too difficult for him, and he would have been caught in a very bad situation between the Scrivia and the Tanaro. In short, when we see Bellegarde on the 17th still extended on a 25-mile-wide front from Tortona to where Wukassowitsch was at Nizza, it does not seem as though it would have been hard to deny him any possibility of successful resistance.

59. **Clausewitz** notes: "We write this according to Jomini, who not only names one brigade as Gardanne's, but even lets this general appear there in person. Since a General Gardanne remained in Alessandria as its commandant and even surrendered that fortress, either there must have been two, or else General Jomini has let himself be guilty of serious carelessness. The latter is much more likely, since only one Brigadier General Gardanne appears in the French army list for the month of March. Perhaps here he has confused Gardanne with General Grandjean, who commanded a brigade of the Army of Italy."

On 17 June Moreau had Grouchy's division advance along the highway to Novi and Grenier's move on a secondary road along the Scrivia, which he crossed below Serravalle, probably level with Novi.

On the 18th he seems to have halted.

On the 17th Bellegarde had withdrawn his infantry who were posted toward the mountains, leaving only a few cavalry facing the foe, and concentrated his central corps at Spinetta in front of the junction of the roads from Tortona and Novi to Alessandria. Wukassowitsch concentrated his troops at Nizza, Seckendorff at Castagnole delle Lanze; Alcaini was still outside Tortona.

On the 18th Bellegarde ordered Alcaini to raise the siege of Tortona and join him. On this day Wukassowitsch arrived at Cantalupo, 5 miles south of Alessandria, and occupied the line of the Bormida. Seckendorff took over command outside Alessandria.

On the 19th Moreau moved Grenier's division to Tortona; he stayed on the Scrivia with Quesnel's and Partouneaux's brigades and sent Gardanne along the Voghera road as far as Pontecurone. The latter sent his light cavalry as far as Voghera, where they were driven back by an allied detachment. On this day Grouchy moved to Bettole di Villa [Bettole], 4 miles south of Tortona, and pushed his advance guard out to Garofoldo [Torre Garofoli].

This maneuver by Moreau along both banks of the Scrivia seemed to be intended more to cause alarm and make Suvorov turn around, thus acting as a diversion, than to attain any important objective itself, since relieving the Tortona citadel could not count as one.

On the 20th Grenier was to continue his march to Voghera, leaving Partouneaux's brigade at Castelnovo [Castelnuovo Scrivia]. Meanwhile, Grouchy was to attack the Austrian outposts around San Giuliano, drive them back beyond that place, and then await new orders there. If this was completed by midday, Partouneaux's brigade that had been left at Castelnuovo was to follow General Grenier to Voghera, and the latter was to continue his march to the Trebbia, while Grouchy was to hold General Bellegarde *en échec* [in check] for the entire day on the 21st and then march during the night to catch up with Grenier.

We have copied out this plan of Moreau's from General Jomini's work, without being in a position to divest it of its immediately obvious decided stupidity. We are unwilling to conclude that a commander of repute was capable of a mode of operation that appears to have been designed by someone half asleep, but whatever angle we examine this offering from, we cannot make any sense of it. Thus, if we allow that one of the commanders whom the French rightly rated most highly operated according to such a stupid plan, it is General Jomini who is responsible.

On the 19th, which is when General Moreau must have drawn up this plan, he must at least have known that the two armies [Macdonald and the Austrians] were in the region of the Tidone and the Trebbia and that they had fought along the former river on the 17th. It is highly unlikely that he had not heard the cannon fire. But Grenier could not reach this area before the evening of the 21st, so he could not come into action until the 22nd. How could the business be expected to remain undecided for five days! And even if it remained so, Grenier and his two brigades of perhaps 6,000 men would arrive right in Suvorov's rear, thus separated from Macdonald and making coordinated action impossible. Meanwhile, Bellegarde could beat Grouchy's division and cut General Moreau off from the road to the Bocchetta Pass. But if, as could hardly be doubted, Grenier arrived in Suvorov's rear only after the battle was decided and found Suvorov victorious, nothing would have been easier than to cut Grenier off from the Apennines. Thus General Moreau exposed himself to the most definite danger on both sides for the sake of a barely conceivable good result. How can a general think of having any say in a battle that has already lasted two days and that is 45 miles away from him, and how can he not find it a thousand times more natural to attack an enemy he outnumbers who is right in front of his nose?

Even if we assume against all probability that, by the 19th, General Moreau still had not heard a single syllable about the two actions fought on the 17th and 18th 45 miles from him, and even if he could have imagined that Suvorov, who had left Casteggio on the 17th, had still not got around to attacking his opponent by the 18th, nor the 19th, nor the 20th or 21st, it still would have been stupid to send a division of 6,000 men in the exact direction that would have separated it from its own main body by the 36,000-strong enemy army.

If General Moreau had merely intended to create a diversion to make Suvorov retreat before giving battle, he would have acted differently and sent a brigade through Voghera as fast as possible. But this was certainly not a solution to the problem, since that depended on fighting Suvorov united.

It was Moreau's undeserved good fortune[60] that his expectation that

---

60. The play of chance perhaps?

Grouchy would have no trouble driving the Austrians back through San Giuliano and could then quietly take position there was not fulfilled.

On the 20th Bellegarde had 7,000–8,000 men concentrated at Spinetti, and Wukassowitsch had 6,000 at Cantalupo. When Grouchy crossed the Scrivia on the morning of the 20th and attacked the Austrian outposts in three columns, taking control of San Giuliano, Bellegarde sent four battalions in support that threw the French out again. Then Bellegarde himself arrived with the rest of his troops, and Grouchy found himself in a difficult situation that certainly would have ended in his total defeat if Moreau had not responded to his messages by immediately turning around Quesnel's brigade, which was already heading for Voghera, marching it to San Giuliano, and summoning Partouneaux. When Grenier arrived with Quesnel's brigade, he had it form up in two attack columns. These hurled themselves so determinedly upon the Austrian center that they burst through, and the Austrian right wing, which was supposed to attack Grouchy's left flank, was cut off from the road to Alessandria. When it took the road to Novi instead, it was confronted by Partouneaux coming from Tortona; surrounded on all sides, it was obliged to lay down its arms. This turning point of the battle left General Bellegarde no option but to retreat across the Bormida, which he achieved with the loss of 900 dead and wounded and 1,360 prisoners, as well as three cannon.

Wukassowitsch seems to have taken no part in this battle, having been neutralized by occupying the line of the Bormida.

Thus, in a way, fate[61] put a victory in General Moreau's pocket behind his back. But, as if he had to show himself unworthy of it, as Jomini says, he made up his mind to march away again to Piacenza, thereby losing some of the fruits of his victory, when crossing the Tanaro or the Bormida could have doubled it and relieved Alessandria. Given his lack of bridging equipment, this crossing could have been difficult, but it would not have been impossible and could even have been attempted at Acqui. Besides, as Jomini maintains, Bellegarde was already fully prepared to beat a retreat to Valenza.

But both commanders were absolved of their intentions by the same piece of news. The Turin citadel surrendered on 20 June, ten days after the approach saps were begun. Here, the allies found a huge quantity of supplies,

---

61. Recall the role of luck in war and its critical place in Clausewitz's trinity (*On War*, book 1, chap. 1).

including 618 cannon, 40,000 muskets, and 50,000 *Centner* [about 2,500 tons] of powder.

This news naturally must have made Bellegarde decide to remain behind the Bormida, even if the more important news of the victory on the Trebbia had not done so.

Moreau concentrated his little army between Alessandria and Tortona, made as if to cross the Bormida or the Tanaro, and provided the Tortona citadel with fresh supplies. On the 24th, when Suvorov approached the Scrivia, he beat a retreat to Gavi, from where he later fell back again to his previous positions.

Suvorov camped his army on the Orba to rest, sent his advance guard to Novi, and invested Tortona anew.

49 REFLECTIONS ON THE FOURTH CHAPTER

Since, in the course of our account, we have already considered most of the theoretical ideas touched on by the events in this section so as to clearly understand the origins and interrelation of those events, we have just a few remarks still to make.

The French

We cannot see General Moreau's actions during this chapter as those of a distinguished talent or a decisive character. At no point does it seem that he thought properly about what he could actually undertake with the approaching Macdonald. Initially, it seems as though all he thought about was their joining up, and that he intended this junction to happen on the Riviera; problems with this plan arose as events unfolded, and once the time and means for uniting unhindered on the plain had been squandered, all of a sudden the idea of a twin attack and combined action emerged, as though born from a higher spirit, apparently from the kind of genius that instinctively realizes the right answer without any great exposition or analysis of the situation. It is a leap of faith. Now, the idea of actually uniting before a decisive battle had completely disappeared, and the simplest and most natural thing to strive for was lost along with it. Yet again, the actual objective of this parallel action is not made explicit but is lost in fashionable florid terminology. Clearly thought out ends and means are entirely lacking.[62]

We find this lack of decisiveness mainly in Moreau's hesitant progress toward Tortona. Most likely there was nothing to stop him from concentrating his corps at Gavi a day sooner, on the 15th, and from being at Tortona on the 16th—nothing but the fear that Suvorov might face about and turn against him, but in that case, there would have been time to fall back again. This mission certainly would not have been an easy one, but similar ones arise in war that are much harder, and in any case, Moreau should have done *at least* this much for his fellow commander. If Moreau had held up Suvorov for just a few days, Macdonald would have got closer, and joining up ahead of the major battle would have become feasible. If Suvorov had continued to march against Macdonald, at least Moreau would have had time to take advantage of this against Bellegarde.

Once the business was under way, in our opinion, the only reproach against General Macdonald is that he did not keep his forces suitably concentrated for the main blow but scattered them in space and time; he did not give any particular thought to his battle dispositions but merely acted in accordance with the prevailing method of the time.[63] We believe we have already demonstrated that he did not act against Moreau's intentions by remaining on the highway. He probably made one more mistake, in that at the Trebbia he tried to use the bulk of his forces on his right wing rather than on his left. This was a mistake not so much because the latter would have better secured his communications with the mountains, for Moreau was not actually in the mountains, nor because Moreau was on his left in general, since strictly speaking, one could not say that this was the case. Rather, it was a mistake simply because the highway that was his line of retreat for three or four days' march makes a sharp bend at Piacenza, turning toward the left wing, and thus is most at risk from that side.

---

62. Clausewitz is referring to Moreau's plan mentioned earlier.

63. As previously noted, this often seemed to involve maneuver for its own sake rather than concentration of force to maximize one's chances in an engagement. Maneuver places an army in a better position to fight its enemy; by itself, maneuver does not do much to defeat an enemy, unless it places one army in a position to threaten the destruction of another. The key is the threat of destruction, not the maneuver itself.

The Allies

Above all else, we might ask: what was supposed to be achieved by sending General Hohenzollern across the Po? If he was supposed to cover the investment of Mantua together with Klenau, they could do this much better from behind the Po than in front of it. It surely cannot be claimed that the fear that genius has of river defense in general also inspired the idea here that these small corps could do much better in the open field than behind an 800-paces-wide water obstacle.[64] But why were they so worried about the investment of Mantua anyway? The siege had not yet begun, and the fortress was not short of provisions, so a breach of their blockade would cost them nothing. And did they suppose that Macdonald would have crossed the Po for such a worthless objective (for which he entirely lacked the means anyway [boats or bridging equipment]),[65] leaving Moreau in the lurch and giving up all his lines of communications and indeed any possible line of retreat? If those in the corps facing Macdonald generally felt that something like this was likely, of course, it just proves that at the time—and probably now too—among the great majority of military men as well as those outside the profession, there was still so little method for understanding and evaluating such things that the most nonsensical of ideas could exist alongside sensible ones.

We do not in any way wish to criticize Hohenzollern's and Klenau's two corps being sent across the Po to oppose Macdonald, provided the intention was not to throw them like human sacrifices to the minotaur but to allow them to retreat toward Suvorov and reinforce him. Even such a divergent retreat would have made it impossible for Macdonald to even consider crossing the Po.

The question could arise whether Suvorov might not have done better to continue to pursue Macdonald, in order to inflict even greater losses on him or drive him away from the Apennines entirely, and whether this might

---

64. Clausewitz's sarcasm is aimed at a number of generals from the eighteenth century, but particularly some of those whose armies either failed to defend a river line or deployed in front of it during the Seven Years' War. This peculiarity was noted particularly by Henry Lloyd in *The History of the Late War in Germany*, 2 vols. (London, 1781).

65. Jomini does not list bridging equipment in Macdonald's army in his chart of 26 May 1799. A small number of sappers is listed, but it is unlikely they would have had sufficient means to cross a major river like the Po. Jomini, 11:346 (chart 14).

not have offered advantages that outweighed all the disadvantages that could emerge from having Moreau in his rear. But if we consider more closely the relative lines of retreat, this was obviously not the case. In the battle itself, if Suvorov had been at liberty to use the larger part of his force on his right wing, he would have been able to drive his opponent away from the mountains and, it necessarily follows, from the Parma road. But Suvorov could not afford to expose the highway to that degree, so the quest for this extraordinary aim ruled itself out. But if Macdonald retreated along the highway, there could be no thought of cutting him off from all the routes to Florence, since for a 50-mile stretch, Macdonald had the possibility of withdrawing into the Apennines, and his units could always march faster along the highway than those sent by Suvorov could cross the foothills of the mountains to cut them off.

The number of trophies might have been significantly increased if Suvorov had continued to pursue General Macdonald for three more days, as far as the Reggio area, and if Hohenzollern and Klenau had been instructed to concentrate their forces and confront Macdonald at some point along the highway. That might have prompted him to take to the mountains sooner, and by doing so, he might have lost some of his artillery park, his heavy guns, and his baggage. But this would have taken General Suvorov eight days' march further away from the Scrivia.[66] Hohenzollern's and Klenau's cooperation was always an uncertain and indeed a risky business, so we can hardly criticize the allies' commander for this.

Finally, let us draw attention to the influence of Suvorov's spirit on these days' events. Wherever he finds himself, the allies are always clearly the victors, even though the forces they have in action are by no means superior.[67] Conversely, Melas always discovers difficulties, and without Suvorov around, he would have found even more. Any normal commander with such a threat to his rear would not have carried fighting on the 19th and 20th, still less would he have pursued as far as the Larda. Courage is always the primary factor in war, but in the higher echelons that bear great responsibility, it lasts only if it is supported by a strong mind; this is why, out of so many brave soldiers, so few succeed in becoming bold and enterprising commanders.

---

66. The distances are 45–50 miles on either side of Piacenza. If Suvorov pursued Macdonald for three days instead of turning immediately toward Moreau, it would have taken him eight days longer to reach Moreau (who was a day's march away).

67. Again, the role of moral and physical will is emphasized by Clausewitz.

5. The Allies Take Mantua and Alessandria
Suvorov Defeats Joubert at Novi

50 SUVOROV'S SITUATION AFTER THE BATTLE OF THE TREBBIA

After the losses he had taken and after leaving Ott facing Macdonald, Suvorov turns back toward the Scrivia with about 20,000 men. There he can draw about 5,000 men from Kaim if he leaves the rest behind as a garrison for Turin, and he can draw as many again from Bellegarde if he leaves just the minimum necessary before Alessandria and Tortona; he then has 30,000 men with which to attack Moreau, who can only oppose him with 20,000. It is therefore beyond doubt that he can obtain another victory, and a victory is always worth something,[1] even if one does not really know what to do with it. But if this absolute value of a victory is to be sufficient reason for a commander to expose himself to the risks and losses that are always associated with a great battle, it at least requires him to be in a very independent position and not held back from such a decision by any other considerations or circumstances. This was clearly not the case for Suvorov. For the Austrian court, capturing the fortresses was its heart's dearest desire.[2] Whatever battles might be delivered should only be for the purpose of securing and furthering these conquests; any additional offensive plans by which one might perhaps think of invading the duchy of Nice or even Provence were an abomination to it, and indeed, not without justification. Suvorov therefore received an instruction from the court that he should attend to taking the fortresses[3] and refrain from any other operations as far as possible. He must have constantly felt like a stranger at the head of the allied army, since it comprised only one-fifth Russians and four-fifths

---

1. Whether politically, morally, physically, or some combination of these factors.

2. This was because control of the fortresses would enable the Austrians to exert control over the region. For a more detailed explanation of the logic, see Murray, *Rocky Road to the Great War*, 31–44.

3. The detachment of numerous Austrian besieging forces is testament to this. See a list of detachments in Milyutin, *Geschichte des Krieges Russlands*, 1:531–532. There is also a letter (incorrectly dated 1797 when it describes events in 1799) from the Austrian emperor. Ibid., 1:582–584.

Austrians, and Russia had joined more as a supporting power that generally subjugated its own interests to those of the Austrians. In such a position, Suvorov could not operate with the independence of a Marlborough, a Eugene, or a Condé, and if he tried to do so, he ran the risk that Melas would refuse to obey him.[4] Thus, if, under the influence of his victory on the Trebbia, Suvorov had wanted to consider a new operation against Moreau straightaway, glorious and certain success would have to be guaranteed; otherwise, he risked being held seriously accountable.

If we ask what could ensue if Suvorov attacked Moreau in his position in the mountains, it would be that Moreau accepted battle, lost it, and then either sought refuge in Genoa with his main body and let his left wing retreat to Nice or garrisoned Genoa with just 12,000 men and went to Nice himself with the other 10,000; alternatively, he could do one of these two things without letting himself get into a battle first. Now it is clear that, as it indeed turned out, Suvorov would have been at the end of his road or, more accurately, beyond it, since his 30,000 men were not enough to besiege Genoa while leaving a corps facing Nice and still operating against Macdonald in Tuscany. Of course, he would have managed to divide these two armies, but in doing so, his own situation would have become a weak and threatened one. Thus, such a situation did not by any means qualify as a great enough success for Suvorov to justify his operation. Of course, we know that there was yet another thing that could have happened: Suvorov might have been able to not just beat Moreau but also inflict a decisive defeat on him, shatter his army, drive him away from Genoa, hurl the remnants toward Nice, and lean on Genoa with the moral weight of this victory. As a great Italian commercial city, Genoa was accustomed to popular movements and swift changes of party; its government was controlled by a pro-Austrian oligarchy, and its people's hatred for the French still glowed beneath the ashes. In such a city, the triumphant thunder of the Austrian artillery echoing from the mountains would work wonders and was a much surer way to conquer it than sapping, mining, or storm. But along with this first fruit of victory, a second yet more glorious would fall into the allied commander's lap, because then the impossibility of the two enemy armies combining would become clear, the battle of the Trebbia would attain its full effect, and Macdonald's army would then be in a situation from which it had hardly any way out other than a shameful negotiation.

4. This was a real possibility, given Melas's frequent inertia.

Such a victorious bounty would have intoxicated even the most cautious member of the Aulic Council,[5] and the commander's disobedience would soon be forgotten.

We will allow that such a success was possible, but it would have been down to skill and to individual strokes of brilliance in its execution rather than simply the natural consequence of the general situation. A Bonaparte might have kept this glorious aim in sight, pursued it, and attained it, but what critic would dare to formulate a reproach on the basis of this possibility? When we see historians outraged at Suvorov for not making better use of his victory on the Trebbia, it is not because they want him to exploit his subjective moral advantage for some necessary objective purpose; it is solely and simply because they have not properly considered the matter and have not seriously asked what ultimately could and should have happened. Macdonald's march toward Moreau is so difficult, the latter's position in the Apennines so weak, that it seems as if advantages for the allies must necessarily arise from them—that is, so long as the allies could let the matter take its course and not keep half their forces busy besieging three fortresses.

Thus, when we see Suvorov halt and camp quietly after returning to the Scrivia and the Bormida from the Trebbia, we can find no striking omission in that. Rather, we see the victory on the Trebbia as a repulse of the offensive undertaken against the various sieges and investments, and the position at Spinetti was further protection for these operations.

51 STRENGTH AND POSITIONS OF THE TWO SIDES

Moreau had resumed his former position in the Apennines, that is, an extended line of outposts that reached from the sources of the Tanaro to those of the Tarro. He had his headquarters in Cornigliano at the mouth of the Polcevera.

Suvorov left General Kaim in the Turin area to observe the alpine passes. He ordered General Haddick to take position at Aosta to observe the two St. Bernard Passes. Ott was ordered to reinforce Kray outside Mantua, while the latter was to commence the siege and progress it as fast as possible. Klenau

---

5. This is where the political component of a victory would assist in the campaign, even if the victory itself did not directly enhance the military object to the same extent.

was to follow Macdonald across the Apennines, Alcaini was to invest Tortona again with 3,000–4,000 men, and Bellegarde was to commence the siege of the citadel of Alessandria, which, as a bastioned regular pentagon with a garrison of 3,000 men, almost qualified as a fortress itself.

In this position, both armies waited for this stage of their operations to run its course. The French anticipated considerable reinforcements and the reorganization of their army, and they hoped both would happen soon enough to enable a new offensive that could relieve Mantua and Alessandria. Suvorov was waiting for the fortresses to fall and hoped that his newly freed-up besieging forces, as well as a new detachment of Russian troops that was approaching, would put him in a position to complete the conquest of Italy.

Within France, the four major battles lost in this three-month war, the loss of all of Italy, and the threat to its own borders had whipped up all parties and factions into a storm against the government. This led to a crisis on 18 June (30 *prairial*), which, as is usually the case, initially gave the government new strength. The Directory mustered money and men to reinforce the forces in Italy significantly. Since the borders of France itself were threatened,[6] it seemed to the Directory that nothing was more important than for a competent authority to determine exactly where the heart of the French Republic was, which had to be protected above all else. This authority was the *bureau topographique*, which was entrusted with the safekeeping of all the century's distilled strategic wisdom, so all this corps of pedants had to do was keep its dividers, sketch map, and technical pen handy, don its spectacles, and read. What they now deduced from these old rules and moldering documents was this: there should be a separate Army of the Alps to cover and protect the approaches to France through the Simplon, Great and Little St. Bernard, Mont Cenis, Mount Geneva, and Col d'Argentière Passes, while the Army of Italy should go over to the offensive again and relieve the fortresses. Trusting in this writ of wisdom filtered through pedantry, the Directory ordained that the Army of the Alps should comprise 32,000 men, while the army of Italy should be brought up to 48,000. Since Macdonald had lost the

---

6. This ties in with the idea of the value of the object and the degree of effort to be made (*On War*, book 1, chap. 2). Given that France was under an imminent threat, it makes sense that this raised the level of effort of the French government and people. With this increased effort, it was likely that political demands would also be raised. If they increased sufficiently, that might cause a reaction by their opponents, escalating the degree of effort and objectives on both sides.

Directory's confidence through his defeat on the Trebbia, and since Moreau was not regarded as sufficiently enterprising, the former was entirely relieved of his command, while the latter was nominally transferred to supreme command over the Rhine and Switzerland. But when Masséna objected, this was changed so that Moreau was only given command of the Army of the Rhine, which, at the time, had not yet been made ready for action again. Two new commanders were now selected for Italy. For the Army of Italy, it was Joubert, who had distinguished himself during his campaign in the Tyrol in 1797; his youth[7] and character promised much boldness and spirit of enterprise, so he was deemed most suitable to confront the energetic Suvorov. Championnet was chosen for the Army of the Alps. Both had previously been removed from command for similar reasons—namely, their opposition to the activities of the political commissars—and had incurred the displeasure of the Directory. It was therefore thought that their selection would butter up public opinion. The two were given positions independent of each other. The fortresses in the Alps—Geneva, Grenoble, Briançon, and Fenestrelles—were hastily made ready and provided with every necessity.

The Directory did not dare order a full mobilization of the National Guard; it believed the government's position was not strong enough for such a measure, so it limited itself to using the guard as garrisons in the first-rank fortresses.[8]

The reinforcements destined for the Army of Italy reached it toward the end of July and consisted of six demi-brigades with a strength of 12,000 men. By contrast, the establishment of the Army of the Alps lagged far behind. It was formed mainly from battalions of new conscripts and from units that had hitherto served to maintain peace and order in the interior. In the first half of August, when the next decisive battle happened at Novi, the Army of the Alps still had no more than 16,000 men.

After Macdonald had joined Moreau and General Lemoine had arrived with the 12,000 reinforcements, the Army of Italy was reorganized, though the only description we have of its new organization is the order of battle Jomini provides for the battle of Novi.[9] According to this, it consisted of:

7. **Clausewitz** notes: "He was 30 years old."
8. This is important, as it indicates that the political situation had deteriorated with the threat to France but was not yet sufficiently bad to increase the burden on the French population.
9. Jomini, 12:98 (chart 15).

Grouchy's division: 5,600 men
Lemoine's division: 6,400
Laboissière's division: 3,600
Watrin's division: 4,500
Dombrowsky's division: 2,100
Miollis's division: 3,500
Colli's brigade: 3,900
Right-wing reserve: 3,000
Left-wing reserve: 5,900
Detachment in the Bormida valley: 2,400
Detachment on the Riviera di Ponente: 2,300
Total: 43,200 men

This listing seems to give the state of the army at the start of operations, so 4,000–5,000 of these men should be assumed to be sick or on other duties.

During July, the army maintained its position in the Apennines, where St. Cyr commanded the right wing, Lemoine the left, and Pérignon the center.

A new detachment of Russian troops under General Rehbinder joined the allied army on 8 July, so that during July and up until the fall of Mantua and Alessandria, its strength and positions were as follows:

Main army at Spinetta at the mouth of the Orba: 30,600 men
Bellegarde besieging Alessandria: 11,200
Alcaini besieging Tortona: 3,300
Rosenberg facing the Apennine crossings at Bobbio, Santa Croce, and Pontremoli: 8,200
Klenau facing the eastern Apennines, later in Tuscany: 6,000
Kray outside Mantua: 27,300
Kaim at Turin and observing the alpine passes: 13,800
Haddick in the Val d'Aosta and facing Wallis: 12,000
Total: 112,400 men[10]

Among these troops were some 8,000 Piedmontese.

10. **Clausewitz** notes: "We have taken these strength reports partly from Jomini, partly from the Austrian journal, depending on which source induced more confidence where they differed. Jomini takes his figures from Chasteler's memoirs; as

In addition, the fortress garrisons comprised twenty-six battalions and two squadrons.

Since the main allied army, excluding Haddick, had been 88,000 strong in mid-June (section 43), and the encounter at Modena and the battle of the Trebbia would have weakened it by 9,000 men, it follows that it had been reinforced by 33,000 men: Haddick's corps of 12,000, the 8,000 Piedmontese, Rehbinder's division with 8,000, and a few thousand Austrians arriving from the interior who principally joined Kray outside Mantua.

Of his designated positions, Kaim occupied Susa, Pignerol, and Carignano with infantry and cavalry and Fossano and Savigliano with just cavalry.

General Haddick had Colonel Strauch with eight battalions at Oberwald in Wallis and Colonel Rohan with two and a half battalions in the Simplon Pass; Haddick was with the remaining eight battalions at Aosta, where he could observe the two St. Bernard Passes. Bard Castle in the Aosta valley was in allied hands.

Colonel Strauch's detachment can hardly be counted as part of the army in Italy; it probably took its orders from the archduke rather than Haddick. If we reckon it at 5,000 men, that leaves Haddick with about 7,000 to observe the three passes. Beyond the passes, though, there was only General Xaintrailles in Wallis and a few detachments from the left wing of the Army of the Alps, thus not a force from which there was any fear of an advance effective enough to reach Milan.

As for the main army, we only know that, in general, its outposts formed a

---

reliable though this seems, the Marquis of Chasteler could well have been mistaken concerning Haddick's far-off corps and used an earlier return as his basis, since he states its strength as 19 infantry battalions with 14,600 men, whereas the Austrian journal reports 18½ battalions with 10,990 men; the former gives about 750 men per battalion, the latter 600; the latter tallies much better with the total strength of the army and is in itself much more likely, since these battalions would have lost more than 250 men in the five months the war had lasted. On the other hand, the Austrian journal says there were only 500 Piedmontese with Kaim, while Jomini says there were 10 battalions, which gives a difference of 6,000 men. If there definitely were Piedmontese there, then it is unlikely that there would have been only 500 of them. The Austrian journal probably leaves out the battalions detailed to garrison Turin. Finally, in its strength report the Austrian journal leaves the Cossacks out entirely, when they must have comprised 1,200–1,500 men. Our strength total tallies with that given by the archduke." See also Karl, 2:67–68.

chain from Acqui through Ovada and Novi toward Bobbio. Likewise, Rosenberg was observing the Apennines from the Bobbio area to Pontremoli, but we do not know exactly where he was himself. Later on, at the time of the battle of Novi, we find him and his corps at Tortona, but not one historian notes this change of position or the reason for it.

General Klenau was tasked with advancing into Florence's territory, about which we will say more shortly.

The allies remained in this position for about six weeks through the whole of July and the beginning of August, that is, until the fall of Mantua and Alessandria. During this we see 112,000 allied troops facing 60,000–70,000 French, including Championnet's troops; but of course, 42,000 of the allies were engaged against the three fortresses, so the equilibrium expressed by this six-week lull actually reflects the size of the combat forces available.

The events that transpired north of the Apennines during these six weeks were of absolutely no account, since they entailed only a few insignificant and inconsequential outpost actions.

After being reinforced with Rehbinder's division, it seems that old Suvorov initially had some desire to continue his offensive against Moreau before Macdonald joined him. His numerically superior combat forces would have made that easy, and totally preventing their linkup was a not unimportant aim. But our observations presented in section 49 show that without some really brilliant solution, this mission would not have created a very advantageous situation because Genoa would have come into play. It is unclear whether Suvorov and his advisers themselves backed off from this idea after further consideration or whether Suvorov was deterred by a personal letter from the Austrian emperor[11] containing the specific order not to undertake any operations against Switzerland, Genoa, or the French alpine border until Mantua and the Piedmontese fortresses had fallen. Either way, he abandoned this idea.

However, he did decide to create a diversion with Haddick's corps for the benefit of Archduke Charles. He ordered Haddick, whom we left on the march to Suvorov in section 39, to move to Aosta and advance from there across the Great St. Bernard Pass to Martinach; at the same time, Prince Rohan was to push through the Simplon Pass, and Strauch was to move through Oberwald into the Rhone valley, whereby the French under Xaintrailles would then not

---

11. **Clausewitz** notes: "Jomini Vol. XII, p27." Jomini, 12:27–28.

only be obliged to vacate that valley but also, perhaps, even be cut off from their line of retreat. We do not know the date of this order; nor are we given any information as to how Haddick arrives at the head of the departing troops again, when according to his last instruction, he was supposed to remain at the St. Gotthard Pass.[12]

This plan was probably conceived as a result of Archduke Charles's complaints about Haddick's corps being taken away, since he had the fixed idea that the allies had overwhelming superiority in Italy, while failing to recognize his own superior numbers in Switzerland. When such plans arise merely out of consideration for others, they normally have no great vigor of their own; they succumb to the pressure of the tiniest difficulties, which is all the more to be expected when they are supposed to be carried out by an intermediary corps that is 90–140 miles from the main army and is itself very split up. Thus, the facts that the French had established a fortified position in the Great St. Bernard Pass, that it was too late in the summer to order troop movements across the alpine snows, and that the great dispersal of Haddick's corps made the outcome very uncertain, were sufficient reason to abstain from this operation and leave General Haddick in his position given above.

The only active progress made by the allies was General Klenau's crossing of the Apennines in the second half of July.

Although this move was only intended to occupy Tuscany and threaten Genoa from that direction and was not aimed toward Rome, to give the situation some clarity, we must cast a fleeting glance at the course of events in the kingdom of Naples and the Papal States.

52 THE STATE OF AFFAIRS IN CENTRAL AND LOWER ITALY

As we have seen, Macdonald had left 5,000 men to garrison Fort St. Elmo, Capua, and Gaeta. The Directory of the Parthenopean Republic now exerted itself, bringing the National Guard up to 20,000 men, but its actual troops in the so-called Legions amounted to only 8,000–9,000 men. That was scarcely enough to defend the capital [Naples], let alone the whole country. New in-

---

12. Karl, 1:310–311, 2:77–78.

surrections broke out everywhere, and Cardinal Ruffo approached the capital with 25,000 men, arriving outside it on 6 June.[13]

Ruffo had asked the court for more regular troops in support, and indeed, 5,000 men had already embarked; however, Admiral Bruix's appearance in the Gulf of Genoa meant that the English squadron that was supposed to escort these troops across was otherwise engaged, so they disembarked again, and Ruffo was left with only his existing forces. This apparently had an influence on his slow progress toward Naples and on the resistance he encountered there.

Castellamare [Castellamare di Stabia] was quickly taken by the English ships. But in Naples, the republicans made serious preparations. Although there were perhaps only 3,000–4,000 people, some of them refugees from Calabria and Apulia, who were sufficiently inflamed with partisan spirit and committed deeply enough to the new order that they passionately and determinedly promoted the idea of resisting to the last, and although the majority yearned not only for peace but also, some of them, for the old regime, still it happened in Naples the way it usually does: this small party holding the reins of government in its hands carried the rest along with it. Since there was no lack of the material means of defense, and since Naples possessed many strongpoints in the shape of Fort St. Elmo, Castel Novo, and Castel Ovo and plenty of buildings suitable for defense, the republicans were actually able to hold out for seventeen days and continue their resistance in the barricaded streets of the city. It was not until 23 June that the republican authorities surrendered the city on certain conditions, and a few days after that, General Nujeau capitulated in Fort St. Elmo. Capua and Gaeta only fell four weeks later, at the end of July, to the Neapolitan general Salandra, whereupon the last traces of the Parthenopean Republic disappeared.[14]

The Roman Republic fell later on. Here, the French had left General Garnier with a few thousand men. The French forces were divided between the

---

13. These men included local peasants as well as contingents of Russian and Ottoman soldiers. The story was sensationalized at the time; however, a cardinal leading an army of peasants to overthrow a republic does not need much sensationalizing. See Esdaile, *Wars of the French Revolution*, 219–220.

14. According to Esdaile, Ruffo offered very mild terms to the defenders, which facilitated their rapid surrender. This deal was almost immediately overturned by Lord Nelson (of later Trafalgar fame), who purged the republicans, hanging many prominent ones in the process. Esdaile, *Wars of the French Revolution*, 219–220.

two points of Rome and Ancona. In Ancona, General Monnier had a garrison of 3,000 French and Roman troops. General Garnier had 5,000 in Rome, with which he held Castel San Angelo as well as many other points on the northern and southern borders and on the coast. In his situation, it took uncommon courage to delay the fall of this new republic for even a few months.

On the eastern side of the Apennines, as we have already described, an insurrection had broken out in May and June under General Lahoz that threated Ancona and interrupted communications between the two French generals. Somewhat later, but still before Macdonald passed through, unrest began in the area north of Rome, and once Macdonald was gone, this insurrection broke out properly in Arezzo and Viterbo and gained such strength that it could be reckoned at 10,000 armed men. At the same time (mid-June), after taking Corfu, Admiral Utchakov sent a small Russo-Turkish squadron to the eastern coast of Italy, which landed a few hundred men and took Fano and Sinigaglia. Admittedly, these too were called away by Admiral Bruix's appearance in the Gulf of Genoa, but they returned in July and cooperated with Lahoz against Ancona. Finally, the fall of the Parthenopean Republic meant that General Garnier could soon expect to have to deal with a new enemy south of Rome.

To even the odds in the face of all these problems, Garnier tried to strengthen his hold through energetic revolutionary measures. In this he must have been quite successful because, during August, we see him fighting a few successful actions against the approaching Neapolitans and postponing the fall of the Roman Republic to the end of September. After the fall of Mantua, Suvorov was actually compelled to send General Fröhlich there with 7,000 men.

Thus, in mid-June, when Klenau crossed the Apennines with 6,000 men, the kingdom of Naples had been restored, and its troops were engaged in recapturing its last fortresses. In the Roman Republic, Ancona was besieged by Russians, Turks, and insurgents; the regions of Arezzo and Viterbo were in revolt; and Garnier was threatened from all sides.

As we have already said, Klenau's move across the Apennines was by no means intended to deliver the final blow to the Roman Republic; rather, he was supposed to occupy Tuscany and advance toward the Riviera to threaten the right flank of the French position in Genoa. Yet the revolt by the locals in the north of Rome[15] was seemingly the principal reason for this maneuver.

---

15. **Clausewitz** notes: "Östreichisch-militärische Zeitschrift. 1812; Vol. 9, p14."

Until then, it seems to have been thought that the French in the Tuscany area were still too strong and too well organized for a corps like Klenau's to be entrusted with taking control of the province. Now that the insurgents had sent emissaries to ask for assistance and revealed how easy the whole operation would be, Klenau received the order to seize the Tuscany region. He was greeted with great jubilation in Florence, Lucca, Pisa, and Livorno; took 1,100 prisoners and a rich booty in various war matériel that the French had been unable to remove; and drove the French across the Magra. On 31 July he took position at Sarzana, whereupon the French vacated Pontremoli as well, and Klenau gained a shorter line of communications with the main army.

Thus the insurgents achieved their aim only insofar as their rear was now secure; otherwise, this advance by Klenau had no decisive effect on Garnier's situation.

53 THE FALL OF MANTUA AND ALESSANDRIA

The month of July sufficed for the allies to gain possession of both major fortifications, namely, the citadel of Alessandria and the fortress of Mantua.

The former fell on 22 July. It had been besieged by Bellegarde with 11,000 men since 26 May; the approach saps were begun on 8 July and pushed forward to the covered way, and they had already opened a breach of sorts from long range. This was not yet viable, though, and no essential part of the fortress had been lost; yet the garrison surrendered as prisoners anyway, so it seems their defense was not a very stubborn one. The large number of siege guns at the allies' disposal; an unusually lively fire, especially from howitzers and mortars;[16] and a lack of casemates to shelter the garrison all contributed to the rapid success of this vigorously well-conducted siege, with a loss of no more than 200 dead and wounded. Marquis Chasteler was seriously wounded during the siege.

---

16. Clausewitz uses the word *Wurfgeschütz*, which normally refers to howitzers or mortars, but in this case he is referring to plunging fire, which is conducted at a higher angle and then plunges down, ideally landing behind the enemy's walls or entrenchments. Direct fire typically possesses a relatively flat trajectory and would therefore be blocked by a physical barrier such as a breastwork or wall. See Murray, *Rocky Road to the Great War*, 11.

The defense of Mantua, which surrendered on 28 July, was even less satisfactory for the French.

The siege of this fortress could not be begun until the victory on the Trebbia because the besieging forces numbered only about 12,000 men, since Hohenzollern, who was supposed to come from Milan to reinforce them, had to move to Modena, as we have described. After the battle of the Trebbia, Kray was joined by Hohenzollern and Ott, though the latter set off from Fort Urbino only on 8 July. Since a few battalions of reinforcements had also arrived from the interior, the besieging army grew to 29,000 men. General Zach was its chief of staff.

The garrison was close to 11,000 strong. The fortress had 600 guns, and there was no shortage of essential supplies. But Mantua's fortifications at the time consisted of just one strong wall, which was most meagerly defended by a few very small, irregular bastions and ravelins.[17] Outside the Cerese gate there was an entrenched camp serving as an outwork; outside the Pradella gate, a very poor hornwork. The fortress was supposed to derive most of its strength from the Paiolo Canal and from the marshy terrain along it. But their effectiveness was demonstrably little, and Mantua's governor, General Foissac, was a man of all too conventional character and far too well-trained an engineer to be able to do much with such a poor and irregular fortress. From the outset, he was convinced it could achieve nothing and consequently had requested urgently but in vain that General Schérer replace him with someone else. On 5 July the Austrians began their siege operations by taking some advanced works that defended the Paiolo Canal; on the 14th they opened approach saps in front of the Pradella hornwork, which the French were obliged to abandon fourteen days later. With that, General Foissac concluded his defense on 28 July. The garrison received free passage, on condition that they not serve against the allies for a year, and the general staff were taken to the Austrian provinces as hostages. The Austrians' losses came to no more than 300 men, and during the three-week siege, they had fired just 14,000 shot and shell, or one-third the amount they had fired in eight days at Alessandria. The garrison marched out 8,000 strong.

On Suvorov's order, Kray left seven battalions as garrison, sent eleven battalions and six squadrons under General Hohenzollern (from whom General

---

17. A ravelin is an outwork fortification consisting of two faces forming a salient angle, much like a redan. See Murray, *Rocky Road to the Great War*, 247.

Fröhlich later took over command) across the Apennines to Tuscany, and took twenty-three battalions via Cremona to join the main army, which he did on 12 August with just 13,600 men, as he had to leave 3,000 sick behind.

After the fall of Alessandria, Suvorov's army had commenced the sieges of the fort at Serravalle and the citadel of Tortona at the beginning of August. To that end, the main army had taken position at Rivalta on the left bank of the Scrivia, while Bellegarde remained with a corps on the Bormida.

After the fall of Alessandria and before Suvorov had yet received the news of the French army being significantly reinforced from the interior, he returned to the idea of an offensive against the French army to conquer the Riviera. Now, if he concentrated all his troops well, with the exception of the 6,000 men besieging Tortona, he could use 50,000 men for that offensive and could expect to face no more than half that number. As soon as General Zach arrived to replace General Chasteler, Suvorov occupied himself with planning for this attack. Then the news of the fall of Mantua arrived, which meant he could expect to be reinforced by the besieging force within eight days. He therefore decided to postpone his offensive for that long. Perhaps this news came at the same time as that of the recent reinforcement of the French army by General Lemoine, and this made Suvorov all the more set on awaiting his own reinforcements.

Serravalle fell on 7 August, and Kray joined the main army on 12 August. But before Tortona was taken, and before Suvorov's plan came to fruition, the French army appeared with Joubert leading it on the attack.

54 THE BATTLE OF NOVI ON 15 AUGUST

Joubert had reached the army on 5 August. He called his leading generals together to discuss what was to be done. Their conclusion was that they should wait until the Army of the Alps was capable of acting in combination with the Army of Italy; then the two armies should engage in a kind of game of offense and defense, advance and hold back, demonstrations and attacks. That is the way these things usually work out when fighting divided—not as a necessary evil, but rather as a characteristic effect of operating in this way. Since these proposals were never executed, we will not waste time on presenting them. Joubert did not think he could postpone his operation that long; the Directory had ordered an offensive everywhere without delay, and even if one did not think the fall of Mantua was imminent, one could not be sure how long it might hold out, and it was dangerous to miscalculate on such an important matter. The new commander therefore decided to concentrate his army and descend to the plain on the offensive. Of course, his opponent had 60,000 men between Turin and Tortona, but it could be anticipated that not many more than 40,000 would be available for the actual battle, since neither Turin nor Tortona could be left entirely exposed. Thus the operation was not too risky in terms of the enemy's superior numbers; it was only the enemy's great superiority in cavalry that was worrying. They had 12,000, against no more than 2,000 French.[18]

Moreau and Joubert were already acquainted. When Joubert took over command of the Army of Italy after Bonaparte's departure at the end of the 1797 campaign, Moreau, who had been relieved of his command of the Army of the Rhine, was posted to the Army of Italy as its inspector of infantry. During this period, the two became friends, so when Joubert asked Moreau not to leave the Army of Italy before the crisis was over but to stay and advise him, Moreau was noble enough to swallow his pride, wait for the impending battle, and fight in it under the orders of his young successor.

Joubert began his maneuvers on 9 August.

We must now think of the French army in two large bodies. The right wing under St. Cyr comprised:

Dombrowsky's division: 2,000
Watrin's division: 4,600
Laboissière's division: 3,700
Colli's brigade: 3,900
Reserve: 2,800
Total right wing: 17,000 men

18. Cavalry were important in two ways: they were largely the eyes and ears of the army, although that was starting to change with the increasingly widespread use of light infantry; and they were an excellent battlefield tool, as they presented the enemy with an extra set of problems to deal with and enabled rapid tactical mobility. This last element is particularly important, as cavalry were one of the best means of pursuing and destroying a defeated enemy. As Clausewitz has made clear, a distinct superiority in cavalry is vital for pursuit (*On War*, book 4, chap. 11, 261), and pursuit is the key to exploiting victory (*On War*, book 4, chap. 12). However, he also noted that cavalry cost four times more than infantry. See section 15 and note 195 in chapter 1.

The left wing under Pérignon comprised:

Lemoine's division: 6,400
Grouchy's division: 5,600
Reserve (Partouneaux's and Clausel's infantry brigades and Richepanse's cavalry brigade): 5,900
Total left wing: 18,000 men
Overall total: 35,000 men

In addition to these, there were General Miollis's division of 3,500 men in the eastern Riviera, facing General Klenau, and 5,000 men in the Bormida valleys and the western Riviera. Altogether these constitute the active force of 43,000 men we gave above.

On 9 August the right wing concentrated between Voltaggio and Ovada, the left in the Bormida valleys above the Cairo area. On the 10th and 11th the latter moved to the Bormida above Acqui; part of it crossed the Bormida at Bistagno on the 12th and again at Rivalta Bormida on the 13th and then moved toward the Orba.

The right wing remained in its position until the 13th; then on that day it moved to the area of Serravalle and Gavi.

On the 14th the French army deployed with its right wing at San Bartolomeo on the Scrivia, 3 miles below Serravalle; its center at Novi; and its left wing at Pasturana on the Lemma.

Suvorov had decided to wait for the French army on the plain, where his superiority in cavalry would give him a very significant advantage.[19] We are

---

19. The archduke is rather disparaging of Suvorov's abilities as a commander, and he is worth quoting at length: "Suvorov possessed military qualities but without the training. He had fought mostly against the Turks at higher levels where the decisiveness of the general and the courage, which he knew how to permeate his troops with through enthusiasm, are sufficient to gain victory against an enemy whose numbers and position were never taken into account because it rarely withstands a cunning assault, and in a country where rapid moves are impossible because one has to bring up everything needed. With this type of gloriously acquired war experience he entered into the conflict on a foreign soil with an as yet untried opponent. His situation was one of the most favorable that a general had ever enjoyed: the superiority in numbers, the better organization of his troops, the support of the entire country—all this gave him a decisive superiority. He should have used it to make rapid progress, to force the

not told how he intended to prepare for and conduct the battle; we only see that he did not occupy any defensive position as such but just a provisional deployment in which the individual formations were probably supposed to operate according to their circumstances to support one another or go on the attack. The deployment in which we find his army on the 14th may be thought of in that respect.[20] Kray stood between Basaluzzo and the road from Novi to Alessandria with Ott's and Bellegarde's divisions (18,000 men). General Derfelden was at Pozzolo Formigaro with Förster's and Schweikowsky's divisions (13,000). General Melas was at Rivalta Scrivia with Fröhlich's and Lichtenstein's divisions (14,000). These large formations, 44,000 strong, were ready for battle.

Apart from these, General Rosenberg was now outside Tortona with 12,700 men to besiege the place and at the same time cover the siege; 5,600 men were left in reserve at Spinetti [Spinetta Marengo], and General Kaim and his 14,000 men were in Turin and the Piedmontese alpine passes. Since the first two forces were only a few leagues away from the army, they could reasonably take part in a battle on the plain, which, if we deduct a few thousand for Tortona, where there were only 1,200 French, could thus have been fought with about 60,000 men.

The motives and reasons for Joubert's exceptionally slow advance remain entirely unknown to us. However, we can guess that the two days of the 12th

---

enemy into repeated battles and worn him down through an incessant pursuit. The seven marches from the Adda to the foot of the Cottian Alps would have soon been put behind him and Moreau would have had to flee over the borders of France with the few remnants of his army before Macdonald could reach the Po and encounter an even more unfavorable fate. Instead of this type of warfare appropriate to the enemy and country, Suvorov never pursued the decisive purpose because he did not have a definite plan. His instinct taught him to seek and attack the enemy where he was located, without taking account of the time, forces, and the move—a process, which only reveals material determination but not mental determination and just gives the impression of rapid powerful actions to those around him." Karl, 2:38–44. This, of course, ignores the fact that the Austrian commanders did not always follow Suvorov's orders, or the fact that they were frequently slow and cautious. The supreme irony, however, is that the archduke is criticizing Suvorov for lacking dynamism and aggression. One can almost hear the schoolchildren at the back of the classroom sniggering in disbelief.

20. As noted earlier, the Austrian commanders did not always obey Suvorov's orders, despite his command of the allied army in Italy. See Duffy, *Eagles over the Alps*, 115–116.

and 13th, during which his left and right wings remained 15 miles apart, were used to obtain some certainty about Suvorov's position and intentions. Perhaps Joubert feared that while the French army was concentrating between the Scrivia and the Lemmo, a significant allied corps might advance in the Acqui area and thereby produce a strategic situation with a disadvantageous effect on the intended battle. We cannot hold these couple of lost days against the French commander, since a commander who is forced by necessity to advance on the offensive against a superior foe cannot do so in any other way than cautiously.

What is more surprising is that Joubert had no official word of Mantua's surrender before the 14th. He gave no credence to unsubstantiated rumors, taking these for an enemy ruse. Until the 14th, then, his advance had the specific intention of relieving the fortress by means of a battle, and according to Jomini, it was only on this day, when Joubert saw Kray's corps encamped in front of his left wing, that he was convinced that Mantua had fallen.[21] He called his leading generals to a council of war, and they unanimously thought it would be foolish to descend to the plain and attack, so they should wait for Championnet's cooperation. Joubert himself did not express a view and told no one of the decision he had made. Jomini says Joubert would have returned to his previous position in the mountains but wanted to wait until he received the next day's reports, so he was surprised by Suvorov's attack and prevented from carrying out his intent.[22] This assertion would look more plausible if we were told what the reports he was waiting for were supposed to be about. As it is, it seems like a mere placeholder. Besides, on the morning of the 15th, we see the French left wing itself in the process of *advancing* when it comes to blows with Kray.

It is probably simplest to assume that General Joubert had decided to abandon his offensive and that retreating to his previous positions naturally followed from this, because he could not remain so concentrated and with his communications so exposed for very long; but that when he saw his opponent go over to the attack, the strong position at Novi seemed to promise so many advantages that he could not resist the desire to match himself against Suvorov there. The aim of the battle could no longer be the relief of Mantua, and any other aim could have been just as well served by a decision delivered

---

21. Jomini, 12:103.
22. Jomini, 12:103–104.

later in conjunction with Championnet; thus, given the present ratio of forces, it was certainly a mistake to seek a battle—one that a Turenne would never have delivered. But we can well understand that a fiery young general like Joubert, who probably had Bonaparte's glorious 1796 campaign constantly in his mind's eye, did not consult the dialectic of war too much but let himself be carried onward by his ambition.[23] So long as no more valid external factors are adduced to show that the battle was unavoidable, we must hold Joubert accountable for it, and we therefore consider the prophecies that were made concerning his talent as a commander to be very dubious.

The position Joubert had not yet adopted on the 14th but in which the French army fought on the 15th lies on the last foothills descending toward Pozzolo Formigaro from the high ridge that stretches east to west from Serravalle to Cristofaro and is breached by the Lemmo at the latter place. The northern slope of this ridge reaches as far as Novi, and from there to Formigaro is a flat plateau. The main arm of the slope forms a narrow ridge at its eastern end, where it creates Monte Rotondo, the name by which it is known as far as the vicinity of Novi. From this ridge the whole slope descends to the Lemmo, so that in the inner angle between the main ridge and Monte Rotondo there are five or six transverse valleys feeding the Riasco, which then runs into the Lemmo at Pasturana. As we shall see, these valleys lie in the rear of the position itself, and the lines of retreat cut across them. Since the Monte Rotondo ridge[24] as far as Novi is at a very acute angle with the Scrivia,[25] up to that point it did not offer a very good front for the position toward the Russians. But at Novi it bends back gently, turns more to the west right behind the city, and thus creates a front about 3 miles long facing Pozzolo Formigaro. But here it is barely a couple of hundred feet high and has only a gentle slope. Thus the front of the position runs from southeast to northwest behind Novi, starting a few hundred paces east of Novi and finishing about 2.5 miles west of it. If one extends it to the right, Monte Rotondo forms a refused flank lying a little further back that could be extended for 5 miles as far as the main ridge, if necessary; the terrain becomes ever more advantageous as the ridge

---

23. Joubert was under orders from the Directory to launch a counteroffensive, and he had never held army command before. Esdaile, *Wars of the French Revolution*, 285–286.

24. This is the ridge just south of Novi that runs parallel to the modern rail line.

25. Clausewitz said the Trebbia, but this is clearly an error.

becomes steadily higher and steeper. If one wishes to extend the position to the left, a series of low ridges, one behind the other, offers a flank bending back for 2 miles to the Riasco. These provide a good, coherent position because they all finish along the same line, and although they are not very high, they dominate the ground in front of them. Thus, from the left wing to the right, the position steadily increases in height and in strength, and furthermore, its front is protected for about 1,000 paces by the walled city of Novi. The area around Novi is largely covered with terraced vineyards surrounded by stone walls, which naturally makes it hard to move through. Anyone who knows how little elevation it takes to make the front of a battle line very strong will be readily convinced that in respect of its front, the Novi position can be counted among the strongest in which one might care to concentrate large masses for battle. The Riasco could serve as support for the left flank, but really the right flank had none, because the position could not be extended as far as the high ridge. However, the advantageous terrain extending the right flank could still be considered an indirect strength. If we calculate the length of the position according to the terrain the French occupied during the battle, it was close to 5 miles,[26] which is always too much for some 30,000 men, even if the nature of the ground compensates for this deficiency somewhat. But the position contained a major defect, in that the three roads suitable for wheeled traffic that led back from it to Gavi—namely, the highway to the Bocchetta Pass, a secondary road east of that running along Monte Rotondo, and a road from Pasturana to Gavi—ran at such a sharp angle to the front that the second of these roads would be lost just by overlapping on the right, and the smallest outflanking maneuver would seriously threaten the first. Since having a secure line of retreat to the Bocchetta would always be the major condition of any deployment at Novi, this position cannot be held unless it has a substantial corps in echelon on its right—given the ratio of forces present here, at least 6,000–8,000 men—that, posted on Monte Rotondo, could either deter the enemy from outflanking the right wing and then be used as a reserve, or attack an outflanking enemy in his own flank. On this condition, the Novi position can certainly be regarded as a very advantageous one.

We have seen that on the 14th the French army had its right wing on the

---

26. Clausewitz says "two French miles." We assume this means an old French league, which was roughly 2.5 miles. This would match the 5-mile French deployment based on Jomini's maps. See Jomini, maps vol., plan XXXI.

Scrivia (Dombrowsky's and Watrin's divisions under St. Cyr); Dombrowsky surrounded Serravalle, which was garrisoned by one allied battalion; Watrin was at San Bartolomeo; the center, Laboissière's division and Colli's brigade, was in position at Novi, occupying the city and the range of hills to the west of it; and the left wing was at Pasturana, apparently on the left bank of the Riasco. This position, which the French army adopted at 4:00 in the afternoon, was probably still designed to allow an advance. We have already said we do not know what General Joubert decided on the 14th, and we know just as little about his orders for the next day; nor do we know whether the full occupation of the Novi position, which only happened on the morning of the 15th, was a result of that decision or whether it only came about because he wanted the left wing to oppose Kray's advance.[27] Here again, we must make do with the facts.

Suvorov likewise revised his decision on that same day, the 14th. When he saw Joubert occupy the strong position at Novi on the 14th instead of advancing to the attack, he got the idea that Joubert intended to hold firm there and could then easily make it impregnable by means of entrenchments, thereby placing major obstacles in the path of Suvorov's own aim of making himself master of the Riviera. Suvorov therefore decided to attack Joubert early the next day and defeat him while there was still time.

Concerning Suvorov's plan of attack, all the historians find themselves very much at a loss, and us with them, mainly because of their confused accounts.[28] General Kray was supposed to set off at daybreak on 15 August to attack the French left wing at Pasturana. Prince Bagration with the Russian advance guard was to set off from Pozzolo Formigaro, bypass the Novi position, attack the French right wing on the Scrivia, and from there try to join up with Kray, which thus envisaged a complete encirclement of the enemy army.

---

27. **Clausewitz** notes: "The fact that General Jomini can neglect such major questions and leave us in the dark about how such a major event in warfare as the battle of Novi really came about demonstrates that his theory and criticism are far from robust." Jomini does not mention Joubert's orders, but he does show the French deployment in full on the map (plan XXXI). If he knew enough to place the French troops on the map, it is a little surprising that he did not know what their orders were. Of course, it is possible that he drew the map based on his best guess about the French deployment.

28. For a good overview of the battle, see Duffy, *Eagles over the Alps*, 134–149.

Derfelden was to attack Novi, and Melas was to stay in reserve. This is how Jomini presents the battle plan,[29] but of course here, where Chasteler's memoirs forsake him, he no longer deserves any great credence. But the *Österreichische Zeitschrift*, with its own constant efforts to give Suvorov's personal actions a slight sheen of the ridiculous,[30] only provides the order sent to Kray on the evening of the 14th, instructing him to attack the left wing while the Russians engaged the center and Melas the right wing.

We do not wish to involve ourselves in any further consideration of the battle plan or lack thereof; rather, we will be content to relate its course factually, and only after that ask ourselves what we ought to think of it.

Kray began his march at daybreak. Ott's division headed in such a direction that it would have marched past the left wing of the French center to Pasturana if it had not run into Lemoine's division, which, as Jomini says, was still in column of march, so perhaps it had only just arrived. This was apparently thrown into some disarray by the unexpected attack and soon gave way, so the Austrians almost got a foothold on the heights. But Joubert himself rushed up, encouraged his troops, and stemmed the spreading disorder.

Bellegarde's division moved on Ott's right. It ran into Grouchy's division, which had deployed next to Lemoine's in a bent-back formation, and with which it was soon engaged in a very lively action.

More to protect his right flank than to outflank the enemy's left, Kray had sent General Seckendorff with three battalions and three squadrons to Bassaluzzo, where he found no enemy initially.

Thus the western wings of the two armies were in full battle from 5:00 a.m. Each was about 18,000 strong. During the course of the action, the left wing's infantry reserve under Clausel and the cavalry reserve under Richepanse arrived at Pasturana behind the two French divisions.

A new crisis soon arose for Lemoine's division when Joubert was laid out unconscious by a ball[31] while he was exhorting his skirmish lines to advance. This again caused great confusion, and the troops were once again beginning to fall back when, just as Joubert had done, Moreau rushed up just at the right

---

29. Jomini, 12:104–106.
30. This matches the archduke's criticism of Suvorov in note 19 of this chapter.
31. Joubert was killed, not simply knocked unconscious. Duffy says it was a volley [musketry]. Duffy, *Eagles over the Alps*, 139–142. Clausewitz simply says *Kugel* (ball), which could mean either cannonball or musketball.

moment and, by his personal influence, restored their confidence and order, so the French held on to the heights.

Bellegarde too had not got very far with his attack on Grouchy. When he saw that he was making no progress frontally, he tried to threaten Grouchy's left flank, had his cavalry move into the Lemmo and Riasco valleys, and ordered General Seckendorff to support them. But the latter had marched further along the road from Bassaluzzo to Ovada and thought the most important thing he could do was prevent a French detachment, which had appeared in the area and he presumably took to be the head of a significant column, from joining the main army. He was thereby prevented from supporting the operation against Grouchy's left flank. The appearance of the Austrian cavalry compelled General Richepanse, covering Grouchy's left flank, to withdraw toward Pasturana. But now the French infantry reserve under Clausel came into play, not only forcing the Austrians to retreat again but also advancing against Bellegarde's right flank and obliging him to face front in that direction, preventing him from advancing any further.

Thus the battle hung in the balance from 5:00 a.m. until 8:00 a.m. In the center and on the opposite wing, profound silence still reigned. General Kray felt convinced that he could not break through. As is always the case, he thought he was facing the largest part of the enemy army and could not understand the extraordinary dispositions that meant he had been in full battle for three hours already while the center had not yet stirred. Very anxious and discouraged, he sent his adjutant to Bagration to request that he should finally join the fight. But Suvorov had not yet given the order to attack, and Bagration had reservations about acting on his own initiative. Therefore, a little more time passed. Only when the French seemed about to advance against Kray and the balance was tilting against him, and only when Kray said he would retreat entirely unless Bagration joined in quickly, did the latter decide to advance and attack Novi together with the adjacent part of the position, by which time it was 9:00 a.m.

While half their army on the left wing was holding out for four hours, but only with great effort, the French generals realized that Watrin's position on the Scrivia 3 miles from the battlefield was too dangerous. Although it had the support of the river and was protecting the road to the Bocchetta, it could easily become separated from the left wing and the center. General St. Cyr therefore ordered Watrin to move closer to Novi, with the aim of occupying the Monte Rotondo ridge to the right of the city and thus creating a refused flank. This measure was in the process of being implemented.

In the center, Gardanne's brigade was occupying Novi and apparently the suburbs facing the Russians as well. The rest of Laboissière's division and Colli's brigade had their main body on the heights left of Novi, but with one demi-brigade to its right and another as reserve on the heights behind Novi.

The Russians' first attack consisted of ten battalions led by Generals Bagration and Miloradovich and was directed straight at the front of Novi and the adjacent parts of the position. The French were strong enough and had had enough time to organize themselves, so they had nothing to fear from this attack; the Russians were repulsed everywhere with a bloody nose. Now Bagration tried to outflank Novi to the east with four battalions. This maneuver coincided with the arrival of Watrin's division; the latter took the four battalions in flank, and they were tumbled back on some of the other units, whereby these were likewise thrown into disorder and forced to retreat toward Formigaro.

Soon after Bagration and Miloradovich advanced to the attack, Suvorov also set Derfelden's division in motion, with him at its head, to support the attack; at the same time, he requested that Kray renew his own attack, while Melas was to march immediately to join the left wing of the army. He also sent an order to Rosenberg to come as fast as possible. He may have sent these orders at around 11:00 a.m.

Derfelden's division did not direct its attack against Watrin's division, as one might have assumed, given that it was the furthest forward and the easiest to defeat; rather, it attacked the position in and around Novi itself. This was presumably because of Derfelden's own position, which may already have been too far advanced when Watrin drove the left wing back on Formigaro. Derfelden's attack was again in vain. Kray's renewed assault achieved some initial success; Bellegarde seized a height on Grouchy's left flank; and, after fresh exertions, Ott, facing Lemoine, took the foremost of the range of hills that combined to form the position west of Novi. But Clausel's reserve brigade threw back Bellegarde's advanced right wing, and Partouneaux's reserve brigade, which Moreau sent against General Ott's left flank, obliged him too to fall back to the plain. General Partouneaux himself was captured while pursuing too vigorously.

General Kray was now resigned to his fate and thought only of rallying his totally exhausted infantry and reorganizing them behind his cavalry and guns. Meanwhile, to their front, a couple of light battalions still skirmished with the French among the gardens, vineyards, and houses.

So the battle continued until midday without falter, and this is no great surprise. After deducting Dombrowsky, the French were 33,000 strong and the allies 31,000; thus the former had a couple of thousand more men and were occupying a very strong position. The two sides' forces were now very fatigued, and any blow struck by a suitable fresh force was bound to produce a decisive result quickly. If the French had been able to bring just one new division of 6,000–8,000 men into the fray at midday, perhaps that could have tipped the swaying scales against the allies in such a way that neither Melas nor Rosenberg could have restored it.

During these six hours, while the thunder of battle roared 10 miles away from him, Melas waited expectantly and increasingly perturbed at Rivalta. He had sent forward only security detachments, so he must have been under specific instructions not to leave his camp until he received the order to do so. At 11:00 a.m. a forward detachment brought him news of the defeat inflicted on Bagration by Watrin and informed him that a French column—namely, Watrin's division—was descending from the heights to the road from Formigaro to Novi. Melas now felt that he could no longer wait for orders whose arrival might have been prevented by some unlucky accident; he decided to march off without delay and attack the enemy army's right flank,[32] for which he adopted the following dispositions.

General Nobili with one brigade was to march up the Scrivia and relieve Serravalle.

General Mitrowsky with another was to head between the river and Monte Rotondo, scale the ridge in the flank of the French army, and attack it in flank and rear.

Melas himself, with Laudon's and Lusignan's brigades and two regiments of cavalry under Lichtenstein, initially followed the road toward Novi but then likewise turned off to the left to attack that part of the range of hills that lay east of Novi.

So began the third and closing act of this great tragedy. Melas arrived with 14,000 fresh troops while the crisis of the major struggle was not yet over, and it may be regarded as a foregone conclusion that he would decide victory for the allies. Nothing could change this destiny: neither lack of skill nor false step on the Austrian side, nor stroke of genius or exceptional courage on the part

---

32. Clausewitz states left flank, but this is an error, albeit an easy one to make, as it was the right flank of the allied forces.

of the French. This is how the state of the battle appears to us, but of course, those commanders caught up in creating that appearance and denied the bigger picture could have had quite a different view of it.

Meanwhile, as we have described, Suvorov had sent Melas the order to move up, and when he learned that he was on the Busetto heights, sent him a request to bear right and attack Novi while the Russians and Kray renewed their assault west of the city. But Melas could no longer change his dispositions. To conform to Suvorov's intention as much as possible, Melas supported Mitrowsky with Laudon's brigade only, while he himself turned directly to the right with Lusignan's brigade of five battalions toward the edge of the plateau stretching between Novi and Formigaro.

The French had not changed the position of their right wing soon enough, which had become bent forward by Watrin's attack. Watrin's division was pinned by the Russians returning again and again to the attack. It was around 2:00 p.m., and the action here had already lasted two to three hours; it had largely destroyed both sides' original formations and turned the geometrical symmetry of their battle orders into confused turmoil. Meanwhile, Melas and his troops quietly made their way forward. When he became visible to the French, they still had just enough time to change their defective deployment. Some battalions moved to the edge of the plateau to prevent Lusignan's brigade from scaling it, while others hurried to the Monte Rotondo ridge. The resistance at the edge of the plateau did not last very long, and the hasty retreat to the heights had a bad effect on the troops. When they reached the top and discovered the black clouds of enemy advancing on them from several directions, their resolution deserted them, and instead of presenting a front to Lusignan, they rushed back toward the center of the position to escape from the ring that threatened to surround them. Thus the appearance of Mitrowsky and Laudon on Watrin's flank helped Lusignan's brigade scale Monte Rotondo. A few battalions dispersed in thin skirmish lines still made a stand, presumably in blissful ignorance of what was going on behind them, and along with the artillery, they provided the only resistance the Austrians encountered.

Laudon and Mitrowsky directed their march toward the heights behind Novi, while Lusignan moved along the ridge toward the city itself.

By its near rout, Watrin's division had already sacrificed the road to Gavi, but it was rallied by St. Cyr. With the support of the 106th Demi-brigade from Laboissière's division, he led it against the Austrians again and regained possession of the road. These units then retreated along it behind the Fornova valley, 2 miles from the battlefield, and took position there.

While this was transpiring on the allied left wing, the Russians in the center and Kray on the right wing renewed their efforts. Kray had little success, which was indeed in the nature of the business, since the French left wing was least affected by the right being outflanked. But Suvorov and the Russians were now able to drive the French out of the Novi suburbs back into the city itself. By then, it was 4:00 p.m. Moreau decided to retreat.

Watrin's division, which had already been driven from the battlefield, was ordered to occupy the higher terraces of the Medesima and the villages of Tassarolo and San Cristoforo and thereby prepare for the retreat of the rest of the troops.

Laboissière's division moved to Tassarolo; from there, covered by Watrin, it headed back toward Gavi.

Colli's brigade and 600 cavalry under Guerin were to cover the retreat of the right wing.

The divisions of the left wing retreated to Pasturana. Grouchy redeployed in the vicinity of the village initially; Lemoine covered this move.

The retreat of the right wing, followed cautiously by Melas, was completed without significant incident, but Colli's brigade was unable to follow it and was driven to the left wing.

It was Moreau's intention that Grouchy would move to Pasturana first, Lemoine would follow, and Colli would cover the retreat. But this plan and its organization could no longer be implemented as he intended. On one side, before the French had even started to leave, Bellegarde had been able to insert a battalion behind Pasturana, which caused panic and confusion; on the other, Lemoine's division was completely overwhelmed by a combined attack by the Austrians and Russians. This was the moment when wild, disorderly rout took hold, and every man sought to escape along whatever track he could find. Only Grandjean's brigade of Grouchy's division, which had found a way to bypass the village of Pasturana, remained in good order. Generals Pérignon and Grouchy[33] were still in Pasturana with one battalion, and they rallied whatever routers they could grab to hold the place for a while and gain time for the rest to escape; but they were attacked from all sides, and both generals fell into the allies' hands, Pérignon with seven wounds, and Grouchy with six.

33. Both men went on to become marshals of France.

Colli and his brigade suffered the same fate. Attacked from all sides, it was routed, and its general was seriously wounded and taken prisoner.

Thus, a battle that had begun at 5:00 in the morning ended at 8:00 in the evening. The French army had suffered an utter defeat; the left wing was completely dispersed, and only weak remnants of the right had escaped; their commander had fallen, and division generals Pérignon and Grouchy and brigadiers Colli and Partouneaux had been captured. A relentless pursuit would have allowed them no thought of any further resistance in Genoese territory nor of rallying their army.[34] However, a conventional pursuit with cavalry in this terrain was quite unfeasible, and since Rosenberg had not yet arrived, the only corps whose infantry still had the strength to do so was Melas's. But when and where do we ever see the pursuit continue beyond nightfall, after a stubborn battle, and in such difficult terrain? When even mere maneuver is obstructed and impeded by so many natural obstacles, any advance against the enemy, even one who is so scattered, seems like a new fight. To undertake such a fight in the dark with troops who feel they have already done their bit during the day demands quite uncommon energy, which could not be expected from a man like Melas. And although that energy was indeed present in Suvorov, its force soon evaporated all too easily through the wide cracks in an allied army. Thus it was inevitable that the French escaped individually during the night, and the number of trophies from this first day was much smaller than the scale of the victory entitled the allies to expect. The routed army rallied at Gavi.

The French lost thirty-seven guns, twenty-eight wagonloads of powder, 1,500 dead, 5,000 wounded, and 3,000 prisoners. The allies lost 8,000 men: 5,000 from Kray's corps, 2,500 Russians, and 500 from Melas. The French losses thus totaled between a quarter and a third of their total force, those of the allies, one-sixth. This battle therefore counts among the bloodiest in the history of war. Given the circumstances, the number of guns the French lost is modest, even if we assume that they were only weakly equipped with artillery.[35]

---

34. This brings us back once again to the concept of continuity and pursuit. This time, we refer the reader to *On War*, book 7, chaps. 6 and 7: "The Destruction of the Enemy's Forces" and "The Offensive Battle." The allied army had a significant advantage in cavalry and should have been more than able to pursue and destroy the French force completely. It is also worth consulting book 7, chap. 5, "The Culminating Point of the Attack," and book 3, chap. 16, "The Suspension of Action in War."

35. These numbers come from Jomini, 12:121–122.

All we have left to mention is that General Nobili drove General Dombrowsky out of Serravalle and forced him to retreat through Vignole to the Scrivia. Their little sideshow had no influence on the main event.

General Rosenberg had actually started his march but did not reach Pozzolo Formigaro until during the night.

55 REFLECTIONS ON THE BATTLE OF NOVI

It is truly a scandal that the Austrian history of the war does not give us more information about this day's events. Even if it is true that no written dispositions for 15 August were ever issued by Suvorov, there must be more in the Austrians' military archives than the few words the *Militärzeitschrift*'s account offers as the instruction General Kray received on the evening of the 14th. Anything that was not written in the archives must still be available in oral tradition, so it should not be difficult to uncover Suvorov's precise intention and show how this intention and the orders arising from it influenced events. It is not impossible that we might discover some genuine quirk on the part of the Russian commander, something that would have been more suitable on the Danube than on the Po. But first, it is not the role of military history to look after Suvorov's reputation, which people would not expect in a serious dialectic on war anyway; and second, it is really not likely that anything would have been left unsaid out of concern for his reputation. On the contrary, we may entertain the thought that the opening stage of the battle is deliberately treated so anecdotally in order to make Suvorov's eccentricity more prominent, since all too often we see the Austrians thinking that their victorious arms were not so much inspired as hindered by his genius.[36]

From the little the Austrian account says of Suvorov's instructions, it appears that he intended only a limited operation with Bellegarde's and Ott's two divisions to drive the French left wing out of Pasturana—where, on the 14th, it could still be regarded as a detached corps—and to take possession of that place. The rest of the force was merely to pin the French center and right wing. This view also tallies with the late commitment of the Russians and with General Melas being left at Rivalta.

36. As has previously been noted.

If we were dealing with a timid commander, such an aim would not seem unlikely to us. It would be an attempt to maneuver the French backward strategically. Whether such a measure was not somewhat clumsy and very dangerous is quite a different question, but at least it has a strategic value that we can credit to the account. But Suvorov was no timid commander,[37] and even if the stubbornness of the French resistance on the Trebbia may have made him somewhat apprehensive, he could be fairly sure of victory because of his superior numbers. In addition, the opportunity to defeat his opponent in a major battle before the Army of the Alps could join in must have seemed all too desirable. In all the accounts, the talk of an intention to attack is too definite to allow any notion of mere maneuver to stand.

Jomini's account includes an actual battle plan,[38] but we fear this was constructed after the fact from uncertain sources. First, according to this, Bagration was supposed to move outside cannon range of Novi to Serravalle and attack the French right wing there, but in the actual execution, he never leaves the Formigaro area and advances against Novi itself from there. Second, leaving General Melas at Rivalta is not in keeping with a plan for a battle, and third, during an attack, it would be just as unusual to leave an interval of 15 to 20 miles between columns.

We confess we can find no way out of these contradictions, but we are still inclined to believe that Suvorov intended only a limited operation with his right wing against the corps at Pasturana on the 15th, that he left General Melas at Rivalta because he feared part of the French force might appear on the right bank of the Scrivia, and that he wanted to wait for the French operation to develop further. We find such a notion possible simply because Suvorov was used to fighting the Turks and because that conflict, like all conflicts with semicivilized nations, was notable for its lack of internal coherence or, rather, of any organizing principle according to which the activity of the smallest part is more or less an expression of the whole. Such a war is the domain of limited operations, which take effect not by their coherence but by their cumulation.[39]

---

37. The archduke did think Suvorov was too cautious. See note 19 in this chapter.

38. Clausewitz means a map of the battle as well as the actual plan. See Jomini, map vol., plan XXXI, and 12:95–138.

39. Again, it is worth reminding the reader that the Austrians did not always fully cooperate with what Suvorov wanted.

We do not wish to attach any great worth to this guess, nor to fret over details that will probably all be revealed in the fullness of time.

If we consider the battle as it actually happened, the following circumstances strike us as noteworthy:

1. That 44,000 allies beat 35,000 French requires no explanation, so we do not need to seek any enlightenment about this from the course of the battle itself.

2. If, at the start of the battle, the French had not been deployed in three separate places—namely, at San Bartolomeo on the Scrivia, at Novi, and at Pasturana—but instead had already been established in the Novi position, they would have fought at a much greater advantage and, in that situation, might have obtained a victory over the allies. Their left wing was in a very difficult position from the outset because it was still in march order and not yet properly organized; in addition, all 18,000 of its men had to be committed against 18,000 allied troops, which would not have happened if it had been in a good position. In that case, it would have had more reserves with which to deliver a decisive blow.

If the French right wing had been on the crest of Monte Rotondo, it would have been almost unassailable and would have avoided the situation of starting an attack that it was virtually incapable of following through, since this move carried it into the Formigaro area, where Melas's advance could take it in flank and rear.

We say that if the French had held their forces concentrated at Novi with a third of them in reserve, it is quite possible that they would have repulsed Kray's attack and the Russians' and perhaps could have even properly beaten them before Melas approached. Then, when he did arrive, the situation would have been such that it no longer seemed like a good idea for him to get involved. We say this is possible, but it is not probable when we consider the great energy Suvorov demonstrated on the Trebbia. It would have taken very significant events during the actions against Kray and the Russians to bring them to such a state that Melas could not have restored the situation, and so long as he could restore it, Suvorov could not be expected to give up.

That possibility was the risk the allies exposed themselves to through the stepwise commitment of their forces. But apart from that possibility, it obviously worked to their advantage. This battle is therefore extremely noteworthy for theory because there is no other in which the advantageous effect of using successive forces is so clearly expressed.

3. It is therefore this use of successive forces that attracts our attention. Kray begins the first act at 5:00 a.m., Bagration begins the second at 9:00 a.m., and at 2:00 p.m. Melas arrives to decide it. The battle had therefore lasted nine hours by the time Melas joined in. If the Russians had been sent into action at 5:00 a.m., at the same time as Kray, it would have been very difficult for the allies to sustain the battle so long, since after five hours in action, the Russians already found themselves in a bad way and could not have held out for another four hours; but if Melas had arrived that much earlier, the whole battle would have been shortened, and the forces would not yet have been so worn out at the decisive moment.

We do totally disregard the risk that could have arisen for the allies from this, and we only wish to show that this echeloned attack was the means by which the battle could reign undecided for nine hours. Although the Russians' attack and General Kray's did not strike the same place nor consequently the same part of the enemy army, it was inevitable that they had an influence on each other. When the Russians joined the fight, Kray had already resigned himself to his fate, and without such a renewal of the battle at another point, he probably would have done nothing more. He thought he had the larger part of the enemy army to deal with, so he saw the Russians' intervention as directly assisting him. But as we know from the course of events, this was not so; none of the troops that fought the Russians had been used against Kray, so if the Russians had started at the same time as Kray, he would not have been facing any fewer and would not have been any more successful. But it is generally in men's nature that each new hope extends their strength and makes them capable of new effort. Thus the battle blazed longer because it was not ignited everywhere at once.

When Melas arrived, both sides' forces were largely exhausted. There were few or no fresh reserves available, all their initial tactical cohesion had more or less gone, and the French right wing was engaged in an attack that should have been part of the final act. In a word, all the preparations for victory had been made, and the mere advance of Melas's 14,000 men was bound to ensure it. Indeed, this corps simply appearing on Monte Rotondo was sufficient to suddenly shatter the French left wing and center—which had successfully withstood every assault until then and had held absolutely in their original positions for nine hours—and for them to buckle everywhere under the allies' new blows like a rotten wall.

This certainty of victory at the moment Melas arrived was the great benefit brought about by the use of successive forces. If we imagine the allies' three major formations all attacking simultaneously—General Melas in the same manner as he did, but outflanking the right wing from the start and appearing on the Monte Rotondo ridge—it is certainly possible that the allies still would have obtained victory through their superior numbers, but it is not such a foregone conclusion as it was when Melas turned up at 2:00 p.m.

But this certainty of victory had been earned by the risks taken up until then. These would not have existed if the Russians and Melas had been present on the spot, even without attacking any earlier; then this battle would have returned to the ranks of conventional dispositions and would be distinctive only for the successive use of combat forces on the allied side.

In our modern battles, it is certain that this successive use of combat forces of all elements of the order of battle[40] is the thing that has the most effect, on average. Therefore, anyone who knows how to outbid his opponent in doing so can virtually overcome him systematically.

However, we are not really of a mind to accept that Suvorov's dispositions were a good plan for the battle; on the contrary, we doubt that they were supposed to be a battle plan at all. The gradual commitment of his forces came about by chance owing to the non-battle-ready dispositions of his formations. This hardly would have happened if they had all been in place, which would have been no less feasible and thereby would have insured against any risks.

There is no need to prove that the 5,600 men Suvorov left at Spinetta, the better part of the 13,000 men who stayed at Tortona under Rosenberg, and the couple of thousand men Melas sent to Serravalle constituted a real dissipation of force for which there was no excuse. These deployments weakened the allies in the battle by 16,000–18,000 men, which would have been sufficient to destroy the French army utterly.[41]

---

40. Clausewitz means combined arms, as the combination of combat arms presents much greater difficulties for the opponent and greatly enhances fighting power. This is particularly the case when combined with the maintenance of continuous pressure.

41. This again serves as a reminder of the need to concentrate one's efforts against the object one is seeking, despite the risk associated with doing so.

56 SUVOROV RESTS ON THE TANARO UNTIL HIS MARCH AWAY; TORTONA FALLS

After losing 10,000 men and most of its artillery in the battle of Novi, the French army was still 31,000 strong, though not in the best shape. Using these men to defend the Genoese mountains against the 60,000 allies would have been impossible if they had continued their offensive. Moreau had even decided to retreat to Nice and had already sent his artillery to San Pietro d'Arena, a small harbor near Genoa, for embarkation. However, on the day after the battle, the allies did not pursue with their main force but contented themselves with sending a division of Russians toward Gavi.[42] The French commander therefore had no need to keep marching at full speed on the 16th and 17th but could settle for reoccupying his old positions in the mountains.[43]

Watrin occupied the villages between the Scrivia and the Orba with his division and Dombrowsky's. General Miollis, who had 3,400 men behind the Sturla in the eastern Riviera facing Klenau, was placed under his command.

The left wing under St. Cyr's command comprised Laboissière's, Lemoine's, and Grandjean's (formerly Grouchy's)[44] divisions, as well as Roguet's brigade, which had stayed in the Bormida valleys. This wing occupied the approaches to Savona, Finale Ligure, and Loano and extended its left wing as far as the Stura.

Evacuating Genoese territory must have seemed especially urgent to General Moreau because an allied attack on his left wing would have prevented most of his troops from reaching the county of Nice. In that event, they would have been obliged to shut themselves up in Genoa, which did not seem very desirable to the French commander, given the mood of its inhabitants. However, he knew that he would be held accountable for any voluntary evacuation of Genoa. There are too many conflicting views on such strategic questions for a commander to rest easy about his own convictions; what he saw as ben-

---

42. Again, this ties in with Clausewitz's ideas about continuous pressure and the role of pursuit in strategic victory.

43. The lack of continued pressure therefore allowed the French to reorganize and figure out a new defensive posture to try to maintain their position in Italy. Had the allies pursued the French, it is extremely unlikely the latter would have been able to make any organized stand outside of French territory.

44. Grouchy was wounded and captured at Novi.

eficial or even necessary might appear to the Directory as fainthearted and precipitate. Since Moreau was only the army's de facto commander, without any formal mission, he shied away from taking this decisive step on his own initiative. Because the allies had not followed him, he still hoped he could postpone a decision until his successor arrived or the Directory made one for him.[45] With this aim in mind, he asked General Championnet to concentrate a strong division from the Army of the Alps at Cuneo, and he requested the Ligurian Republic, which already had a few troops serving with the army, to raise another 12,000–15,000 men who could take over the defense of the city of Genoa. He was told there could be no question of this, since far from defending it against the allies, the inhabitants were much more likely to open the gates to them as soon as they appeared outside it.[46]

Suvorov did not follow the French army and did not even make any preparations for a new attack or for any exploitation of his victory.[47] He halted with his army at Novi, sent General Melas back to Rivalta, and had Alcaini resume the siege of Tortona, which had briefly been interrupted. The reason he gave for this inactivity was that events in the Alps caused him concern for the flank and rear of his theater of operations. Let us devote a few words to these events.

Championnet had joined the Army of the Alps at the beginning of August but found it still in a very poor state of combat readiness. The few regular troops had been sent to the Army of Italy with Lemoine and were supposed to be replaced with more from the interior. In mid-August it had just 16,000 men and still lacked all manner of military equipment. However, even before the French army advanced, Championnet had decided to create a diversion to facilitate it. Therefore, on 10 August General Compans broke out through the Little St. Bernard Pass with a couple of thousand men and took the entrenched position of La Tuile, at the foot of the pass, from General Haddick, who was at Aosta. At the same time, a detachment pushed across Mont Cenis and drove

---

45. He was right to be cautious, as on 1 September the Directory ordered the defense of a line from Genoa to Geneva. Ross, *Quest for Victory*, 251.

46. As previously noted, the Genoese were far from happy with French rule.

47. He seemed to be more interested in securing winter quarters for his army and capturing Genoa. In addition, he was exceedingly frustrated by the interference of the Austrian emperor and the Aulic Council and discussed resigning from his command. Milyutin, *Geschichte des Krieges Russlands*, 3:65–71. Given his frustration, it is perhaps no wonder that he was more interested in securing his gains.

Kaim's Austrian outposts back to Susa. These events cost the Austrians a few men and caused more alarm than they deserved.

A few days later, Lecourbe began his operation against the Austrian left wing in Switzerland. During this operation, Colonel Strauch and his eight battalions in the Wallis valley got involved in adverse actions against Xaintrailles's and Lecourbe's divisions on the 14th and 15th. Strauch was driven out of Wallis, lost half his force, and was obliged to retreat to Lake Maggiore, as we will describe in more detail in the next volume.

These were the two events that at least appeared to cause Suvorov's inactivity and, a few days after the battle of Novi, made him send General Kray to Lake Maggiore with 8,000 men while he and the main army marched to Asti on 20 August to be closer to Kaim.

But there is scarcely any doubt that these events were not the real reasons for Suvorov's inactivity.[48] He already knew that he was supposed to march to Switzerland with the Russians, unite there with the awaited 30,000 Russians under Korsakov, and relieve the archduke in Switzerland so the latter could move to the Rhine, where the French intended to form a new army under Moreau's command. One might well think that this change of role did not please General Suvorov because in Italy, all he had to do was reap the fruits of victory, whereas in Switzerland, such a victory would first have to be won. But the main reason for his disgruntlement and lack of enthusiasm for any further operation probably lay in the resentment and silent division that had already arisen between the cabinets in Vienna and St. Petersburg. The Russian commander was naturally very much involved, as much in the cause of this division as in its effect. To his mind, nothing had gone right for a long time. In particular, when he prematurely attempted to invite the king of Sardinia to return to his capital, the Austrian court had not only issued a formal disclaimer but also completely opposed the king's return.[49] We do not have the full details of these matters, but what we do know suffices for us to think that Suvorov's standstill after such a decisive victory was not the result of obvious

---

48. He also had logistical difficulties and was utterly reliant on Austrian help for his supplies, which did not always arrive in a timely manner. Furthermore, a move into the Alps required mules to navigate the mountain tracks, and he was forced to wait to assemble sufficient numbers of them. Duffy, *Eagles over the Alps*, 150.

49. Again, it is worth considering the political objectives of a war and the difficulty of achieving agreement between allies.

factors in the theater of operations but rather the effect of a counterweight lurking in the shadows, of the kind present in every campaign.

When Suvorov moved to Asti, he sent General Bellegarde to Acqui and lingered in this position until he marched away.

Around the 24th or 25th, Suvorov received the effective order to march off to Switzerland with the Russian troops and hand over command in Piedmont to General Melas. In the heat of the moment, he initially wanted to set off on the 27th, but he let himself be persuaded to postpone this for a few days so that arrangements could be made for provisions. Also, since the citadel of Tortona had just concluded an armistice treaty on the 25th, under which it was supposed to surrender on 11 September if no relief had come by then, indeed, it would not have been difficult for the Austrian generals to persuade Suvorov to wait in Italy until this deadline.

Suvorov therefore stayed another three weeks in Italy in the position at Asti, Acqui, and Rivalta, while the French remained in their positions in the mountains. During this time, the war in the field [as opposed to the siege operations] was marked by just a couple of events on the left and right wings of the allied theater of operations.

On the left wing, General Klenau sought to advance against Genoa in the eastern Riviera with a couple of thousand men at the time of the battle of Novi. He arrived on the Gulf of Spezia at the start of August and seized the forts there, with the exception of Fort Santa Maria, which had a strong garrison. On 15 August a Cossack regiment arrived, bringing Suvorov's order that Klenau should advance against the enemy's right flank. Even though he was still waiting for a couple of infantry regiments that were supposed to join him from the units sent across the Apennines by the siege corps outside Mantua, and even though he was only 1,600 strong, he decided to advance to Ricio that same day. On 16 August he attacked General Miollis's detachments around Moneglia and drove them back through Sestri, Chiavari, Rapallo, and Nervi. Since General Klenau had received the order to send both of the recently arrived regiments to Tuscany, and the French were being reinforced, he moved back behind the Stura to Chiavari and left Colonel Asper in Rapallo with a few hundred men.

He remained in this position for a few days. Meanwhile, Moreau reinforced General Miollis and ordered Watrin to move forward along the crest of the Apennines with a few thousand men and descend down the Stura through Torraglia to attack the Austrian general's right flank.

In this way, Klenau was attacked on two sides on 21 August; he put up stubborn resistance but was beaten, with the loss of 500–600 men, and forced to retreat to Sestri. Since the French did not follow him any further, Klenau was able to busy himself unhindered with taking Fort Santa Maria. He lacked siege weapons, so he found some artillery at the Florentine fortresses, bought powder and ball for them, and, with great trouble and effort, got the artillery up the mountainside overlooking the fort. He bombarded the fort from this position to great effect for a few days, and on the 27th the 600-man garrison surrendered. In addition to sixty-four guns, the fort contained considerable supplies of rations and military stores. These were the events on the allied left wing.

On the right wing, after the organization of his army had progressed somewhat, General Championnet descended from the high crest of the Cottian Alps into the Piedmontese valleys to create a diversion for the benefit of the Army of Italy. None of the accounts gives us the slightest indication of the positions occupied by General Kaim's troops. Since Turin is 40–45 miles away from most of the strongpoints in these valleys, and since Kaim's corps was only about 14,000 strong, we can imagine that these strongpoints, which were mainly half-ruined forts from olden times, were garrisoned mostly by armed Piedmontese and just a few Austrian troops. Determining what exactly transpired in the Po, Maira, and Stura valleys is quite a problem, since nowhere is it reported that Cuneo had been invested by the allies. There, the French Army of the Alps was apparently faced only by the armed bands known as Barbets [*barbetti*],[50] but further behind them was General Gottesheim with a few thousand men around Savigliano and Fossano.

An effective diversion would have had to be undertaken at the same time as the battle of Novi to immediately create a counterweight to the allies' victory through the rumors generated by the operation. This would have been the case if Championnet had continued his initial operation on 10 August and been able to descend to the plain of the Po at that time. But during that first operation, Championnet apparently felt he was still too weak, and the new op-

---

50. These bandits fought against external intruders (particularly the French) in the seventeenth and eighteenth centuries. See Michael Broers, "Revolt and Repression in Napoleonic Italy 1796–1814," in *War in an Age of Revolution 1775–1815*, ed. Roger Chickering and Stig Förster (New York: Cambridge University Press, 2010), 200. They are mentioned in Clausewitz, *Napoleon's 1796 Italian Campaign*, 162.

eration found its only motivation in Moreau's decision to linger in the Apennines.

On 25 August the French columns advanced across the Alps: the right wing under Championnet over the mountain barrier between the sources of the Var and the Stura valley, and the center under Duhesme from Briançon over Mount Geneva in two columns—the one on the right under Lessuire moved to Fenestrella and Pignerolo in the Perosa valley, and the one on the left under Molard moved into the Val d'Houlx (the Susa valley). These three columns had 12,000 men. Within six days, by 31 August, the last two had seized the valleys, relieved Fenestrella, and taken Susa and Pignerolo. The one under Championnet[51] advanced more slowly. It encountered sustained resistance from the Barbets and did not manage to reach Cuneo until 2 September.

On 6 September, twelve days after these crossings took place, General Mallet crossed the Little St. Bernard Pass on Championnet's extreme left wing. Since General Xaintrailles crossed the Simplon Pass at the same time and drove Prince Rohan out of Domodossola, Haddick thought it best to retreat to Ivrea.

Championnet remained in this position, and we shall see him continue his operations against Melas from here after Suvorov's departure.

Suvorov did not overreact to this commotion in the mountains; it had no influence on his actions, beyond recalling Kray.

Upon learning that the French had not followed Colonel Strauch any further, Kray halted at Novara[52] on 22 August and sent only Laudon's brigade to reinforce Strauch. Suvorov had General Kray stay at Novara, although we cannot see exactly why. He only ordered Kray to return to the Tanaro and deploy at Felizzano on 28 August, after it was reported that the Army of the Alps was advancing.

Suvorov's main army was ordered to stand ready to march to Savigliano, because if there really was a serious French advance, Suvorov could expect it to come there from the direction of Cuneo in the first instance.

In Genoa, in response to Seckendorff's approach and the French demand to increase its armed forces by 12,000–15,000 men, unrest broke out, and the

---

51. Clausewitz says Compans, but this must be a printer's error. Compans was in the Aosta valley at the time.

52. Clausewitz states Voghera, but this is another printer's error. Jomini has him at Novara on this date. Jomini, 12:133.

people threatened to enter into direct negotiations with the Austrians. This serious development caused General Moreau to declare Genoa to be in a state of siege and to appoint General Dessolles commandant with absolute authority. He recognized that if Genoa were to be held, the government of old patricians had to be removed from the helm and replaced by people who had little to lose[53] and were deeply committed to the democratic system. But here too, Moreau shied away from taking decisive steps and, as he prepared to depart for the Rhine, thought he could leave this difficult business to his successor as well.

By its very nature, the Tortona armistice demanded a relief attempt. Aware of Suvorov's new destination, Moreau decided to make one more such attempt, as he hoped to find the Russian commander already on the march. He gave this task to a strong division of the right wing under General Watrin, which advanced to Novi on 8 September and drove off the Austrians. Moreau asked St. Cyr and Championnet to advance toward the Stura and the Bormida to attract the allies' attention there.

In fact, given that the designated date for Tortona to fall was 11 September, Suvorov had already begun his maneuver on 8 September, moving with one column under Rosenberg from Rivalta to Alessandria and with the other from Asti to Monte Calva.

When the French first moved against Novi, Melas had General Kray set off from Felizzano toward Formigaro, while he himself hastened there from Asti. Suvorov also turned around again on the 9th and marched back to Alessandria, so that on the 9th, General Watrin was forced by Kray to retreat back through Novi again.

On the following day, Moreau carried out another reconnaissance in person and, after convincing himself that the larger part of the allied army was in front of him, ordered the retreat to the previous positions.

The Tortona garrison surrendered the fortress on 11 September after three months' investment and three weeks' siege. A thousand of the garrison were given free passage. On the same day, Suvorov set off for the St. Gotthard, while Melas left General Karaczay with 5,000 men around Novi and took the main army to the position at Bra, where the Stura flows into the Tanaro, which he occupied on 16 September.

---

53. Or everything to lose if the French lost, thus aligning their objectives with those of their occupiers.

We have already made our remarks on Suvorov's inaction in this section. Our thoughts on the dispositions the French government made for its intended new offensive, in forming the two armies in Italy as well as the allies' decision to have Suvorov's Russian army move to Switzerland, will find a more suitable place in our general reflections on the campaign as a whole. We therefore turn to the next chapter, whose subject is the events in Switzerland between the two battles of Zurich.[54]

---

54. This can be found in volume 2 of this campaign.

Bibliography

BOOKS AND ARTICLES

Abel, Jonathan. *Guibert: Father of Napoleon's Grande Armée*. Norman: University of Oklahoma Press, 2016.
Arnold, James R. *Marengo and Hohenlinden: Napoleon's Rise to Power*. Barnsley, UK: Pen & Sword Books, 2005.
Bassford, Christopher. "Clausewitz and His Works." http://www.clausewitz.com/readings/Bassford/Cworks/Works.htm#_edn40.
———. "Clausewitz's Categories of War and the Supersession of 'Absolute War.'" http://www.clausewitz.com/mobile/Bassford-Supersession5.pdf#zoom=100.
———. "Jomini and Clausewitz: Their Interaction." http://www.clausewitz.com/readings/Bassford/Jomini/JOMINIX.htm.
———. "Tip-Toe through the Trinity: The Strange Persistence of Trinitarian Warfare." https://www.clausewitz.com/mobile/trinity8.htm.
Bellinger, Vanya Eftimova. *Marie von Clausewitz: The Woman behind the Making of On War*. Oxford: Oxford University Press, 2016.
Berkovich, Ilya. *Motivation in War: The Experience of Common Soldiers in Old-Regime Europe*. Cambridge: Cambridge University Press, 2017.
Bertaud, Jean Paul. *The Army of the French Revolution: From Citizen-Soldiers to Instrument of Power*. Princeton, NJ: Princeton University Press, 1988.
Bonaparte, Napoléon. *Correspondance* Générale. 15 vols. Paris: Publiée par la Fondation Napoléon, Librairie Arthéme Fayard, 2004–2018.
Bowden, Mark. *Black Hawk Down: A Story of Modern War*. Berkeley, CA: Atlantic Monthly Press, 1999.
Broers, Michael. "Revolt and Repression in Napoleonic Italy 1796–1814." In *War in an Age of Revolution 1775–1815*, ed. Roger Chickering and Stig Förster. New York: Cambridge University Press, 2010.
Bulos, A. *Memoirs of Marshal Ney*. 2 vols. 2nd ed. London: Bull & Churton, 1834. https://archive.org/details/memoirsmarshaln02bulogoog/page/n9.
Bülow, Heinrich von. *Geist des Neuern Kriegssystems*. Hamburg: August Campe, 1835.
Casse, A., du. *Le Général Vandamme: et sa correspondence*. 2 vols. Paris: Librairie et Cte, 1870. https://books.google.com.
Clausewitz, Carl von. *La Campagne de 1799 en Italie et en Suisse*, trans. A. Niessel. 2 vols. Paris: Librairie Militaire, Chapelot et Co., 1906.
———. *The Campaign of 1812 in Russia*, trans. Francis Egerton. London: John Murray, 1843. https://www.clausewitz.com/readings/1812/Clausewitz-CampaignOf1812inRussia-EllesmereTranslation.pdf.

———. *Die Feldzüge von 1799 in Italien und der Schweiz.* 2 vols. Berlin: Ferdinand Dümmler, 1833.
———. *Napoleon's 1796 Italian Campaign,* trans. and ed. Nicholas Murray and Christopher Pringle. Lawrence: University Press of Kansas, 2018.
———. *On War,* ed. and trans. Michael Howard and Peter Paret. Princeton, NJ: Princeton University Press, 1989.
———. *On War,* trans. O. J. Matthijs Jolles. New York: Modern Library, 2000.
———. *Vom Kriege.* 3 vols. Berlin: Ferdinand Dümmler, 1832–1834.
Cuccia, Phillip. *Napoleon in Italy: The Sieges of Mantua 1796–1799.* Norman: University of Oklahoma Press, 2014.
Dedon, François L. *Relation du Passage de la Limmat.* Paris: Didot Jaune, 1801. https://books.google.com.
Douglas, Major-General Sir Howard. *An Essay on the Principles and Construction of Military Bridges, and the Passage of Rivers in Military Operations.* London: T. Egerton, 1816. https://books.google.com.
Doyle, William. *The Oxford History of the French Revolution.* Oxford: Oxford University Press, 2002.
Duffy, Christopher. *Eagles over the Alps: Suvorov in Italy and Switzerland, 1799.* Chicago: Emperor's Press, 1999.
———. *Frederick the Great: A Military Life.* London: Routledge, 1995.
Esdaile, Charles J. *The Wars of the French Revolution 1792–1801.* New York: Routledge, 2019.
———. *The Wars of Napoleon.* New York: Routledge, 1995.
"Franziszeische Landesaufnahme (1806–1869)." http://mapire.eu/de/map/secondsurvey.
Furse, Colonel George Armand. *1800: Marengo and Hohenlinden.* 1903. Reprint, Uckfield, UK: Naval & Military Press, 2005.
Gat, Azar. *A History of Military Thought: From the Enlightenment to the Cold War.* Oxford: Oxford University Press, 2001.
Generals Reglement. Vienna: Johann Thoman Edlen von Trattern, 1769.
Graham, J. M. *Histoire des Campagnes d'Italie, d'Allemagne et de Suisse en 1796, 97, 98 et 99.* Paris: Fournier, 1817.
Handel, Michael. *Masters of War: Classical Strategic Thought.* 3rd ed. London: Frank Cass, 2001.
Hertefeld, A. *The Game of Skat,* trans. and ed. Professor Hoffman. London: George Routledge & Sons, 1893.
Heuser, Beatrice. *Strategy before Clausewitz: Linking Warfare and Statecraft, 1400–1830.* Abingdon, UK: Routledge, 2018.
Honig, Jan Willem. "Clausewitz and the Politics of Early Modern Warfare." In *Clausewitz the State and War,* ed. Andreas Herberg-Rothe, Jan Willem Honig, and Daniel Moran, 29–48. Stuttgart: Franz Steiner Verlag, 2011.
Intelligence Branch. *British Minor Expeditions 1746 to 1814.* London: HMSO, 1884. https://books.google.com.

Jomini, Antoine Baron de. *Summary of the Art of War*, trans. Major O. F. Winship and Lieutenant E. E. McLean. New York: G. P. Putnam, 1854.

———. *Tableau Analytique des Principales Combinaisons de la Guerre, et de leurs apports avec la politique des états pour servir d'introduction au Traité des grandes opérations militaires*. 3rd ed. Paris: Chez Anselin, 1830.

Jomini, Lieutenant-Général [Antoine]. *Histoire Critique et Militaire des Guerres de la Révolution*. 15 vols. Paris: Chez Anselin et Pochard, 1819–1824.

Jourdan, Général. *Précis des opérations de l'armée du Danube sous les ordres du Général Jourdan. Extrait des mémoires manuscrits de ce general*. Paris: Charles, [1799]. https://archive.org/details/precisdesoperatioojour.

Kant, Immanuel. *Critique of Pure Reason*, trans. and ed. Paul Guyer and Allen W. Wood. Cambridge: Cambridge University Press, 2000.

Karl Erzherzog von Österreich. *Geschichte des Feldzuges von 1799 in Deutschland und in der Schweiz*. 3 vols. Vienna: Anton Strauss, 1819. https://www.e-rara.ch/zut/doi/10.3931/e-rara-33557.

———. *Grundsätze der Strategie erläutert durch die Darstellung des Feldzugs von 1796 in Deutschland*. 4 vols. Vienna: Anton Strauss, 1814.

Lefebvre, Georges. *The French Revolution from 1793 to 1799*, trans. John Hall Stewart and James Friguglietti. New York: Columbia University Press, 1964.

Lloyd, Henry. *Geschichte des siebenjährigen Krieges in Deutschland zwischen dem Könige von Preussen und der Kaiserin Königin mit ihren Alliirten vom General Lloyd*, trans. Georg Tempelhof. 6 vols. Berlin: Gedrukt und verlegt von Johann Friedrich Unger, 1783–1801.

———. *The History of the Late War in Germany*. 2 vols. London, 1781.

Longworth, Philip. *The Art of Victory*. New York: Holt, Rinehart & Winston, 1965.

Macksey, Piers. *Statesmen at War: The Strategy of Overthrow 1798–1799*. London: Longman Group, 1974.

Mangourit, Michel-Ange-Bernard. *Défense d'Ancone*. 2 vols. Paris: Charles Pougens, 1802. https://books.google.com.

Meyer-Weiss: Atlas of Switzerland. http://www.unibe.ch/university/services/university_library/research/special_collections/map_collections/meyer_weiss/index_eng.html.

Milyutin, D. A. *Geschichte des Krieges Russlands mit Frankreich unter der Regierung Kaiser Pauls I. im Jahre 1799*. 5 vols. Munich: Commission der Jos. Lindauer'schen Buchhandlung, 1856–1858.

Mitchell, A. Wess. *The Grand Strategy of the Habsburg Empire*. Princeton, NJ: Princeton University Press, 2018.

Montalembert, Marquis de. *Correspondance de Monsieur le Marquis de Montalembert, étant employé par le Roi de France à l'Armée Suédoise, avec Mr. le Marquis d'Havrincour... pendant les campagnes de 1757, 58, 59, 60 et 61: pour servir à l'histoire de la dernièr guerre*. 3 vols. London, 1777.

Montholon, Général, ed. *Mémoires pour servir à l'Histoire de France sous Napoléon*. 8 vols. Paris: F. Didot, Père et Fils; Bossange, Frères, 1823–1825.

Moran, Daniel, and Arthur Waldron. *The People in Arms: Military Myth and National Mobilization since the French Revolution*. Cambridge: Cambridge University Press, 2003.

Murray, Nicholas. *The Rocky Road to the Great War: The Evolution of Trench Warfare to 1914*. Washington, DC: Potomac Books, 2013.

Napoléon I. *Correspondance de Napoléon Ier*. 32 vols. Paris: Henri Plon & J. Dumaine, 1858.

Nobili, Johann. *Hungary 1848: The Winter Campaign*, trans. and ed. Christopher Pringle. Solihull, UK: Helion, 2021.

Officer of the Staff. *The Life and Campaigns of Victor Moreau: Comprehending His Trial, Justification and Other Events, till the Period of His Embarkation for the United States*, trans. John Davis. New York: I. Riley, 1806. https://books.google.com.

Ospinov, K. *Alexander Suvorov*, trans. Edith Bone. London: Hutchinson, 1944.

Page, Anthony. *Britain and the Seventy Years War, 1744–1815: Enlightenment, Revolution and Empire*. London: Palgrave Macmillan, 2015.

Palmgren, Anders. "Visions of Strategy: Following Clausewitz's Train of Thought." Doctoral diss., National Defence University, Helsinki, 2014.

Paret, Peter. *Clausewitz and the State*. New York: Oxford University Press, 1976.

———, ed. *Makers of Modern Strategy: From Machiavelli to the Nuclear Age*. Princeton, NJ: Princeton University Press, 1986.

Parlett, David. *A History of Card Games*. Oxford: Oxford University Press, 1991.

"Projekt zur Erschliessung historisch wertvoller Altkartenbestände." http://ikar.sbb.spk-berlin.de/werkzeugkasten/sonderregeln/4_3.htm.

Rapin, Ami Jacques. "Jomini at the Time of the Helvetian Republic (1798–1801)." Université de Lausanne. https://applicationspub.unil.ch/interpub/noauth/php/Un/UnPers.php?PerNum=851054&LanCode=37&menu=pub.

Rodger, A. B. *The War of the Second Coalition 1798–1801*. Oxford: Clarendon Press, 1964.

Rogers, Clifford J. "Clausewitz, Genius, and the Rules." *Journal of Military History* 66 (October 2002): 1167–1176.

Roider, Karl A., Jr. *Baron Thugut and Austria's Response to the French Revolution*. Princeton, NJ: Princeton University Press, 1987.

Ross, Steven T. *Quest for Victory: French Military Strategy 1792–1799*. London: Thomas Yoseloff, 1978.

Rothenberg, Gunther. *Napoleon's Great Adversaries: The Archduke Charles and the Austrian Army, 1792–1814*. Tiptree, UK: Anchor Press, 1982.

Ruch, Christian. "Waldstädte." *Historisches Lexikon Der Schweiz*. http://www.hls-dhs-dss.ch/textes/d/D7350.php.

Saxe, Maurice Count de. *Reveries, or, Memoirs Concerning the Art of War*, trans. unknown. Edinburgh: Sands, Donaldson, Murray & Cochran, 1759.

Schneid, Frederick C., ed. *European Armies of the French Revolution: 1789–1802*. Norman: University of Oklahoma Press, 2015.

Showalter, Dennis E. *The Wars of Frederick the Great*. New York: Longman, 1996.

Six, Georges. *Dictionnaire Biographique des Généraux & Amiraux de la Révolution et de L'Empire (1792–1814)*. 2 vols. Paris: Libraire Historique et Nobiliaire, 1934.
Smith, Digby. *The Greenhill Napoleonic Wars Data Book*. London: Greenhill Books, 1998.
Strachan, Hew. "A Clausewitz for Every Season." *American Interest* 2, 6 (1 July 2007). https://www.the-american-interest.com/2007/07/01/a-clausewitz-for-every-season/.
———. *Clausewitz's On War: A Biography*. New York: Atlantic Monthly Press, 2007.
Strachan, Hew, and Andreas Herberg-Rothe, eds. *Clausewitz in the Twenty-First Century*. Oxford: Oxford University Press, 2007.
Von Seida und Landensberg, Franz Eugen Joseph Anton. *Politisch-militärische Geschichte des merkwürdigen Feldzugs von 1799*. Stettin, 1801. https://books.google.com.
Wurzbach, Dr. Constant von. *Biographisches Lexikon des Kaiserthums Oesterreich*. 60 vols. Vienna: Universitäts Buchruderei von L. E. Zamarski, 1856–1891.
Wylie, J. C. *Military Strategy: A General Theory of Power Control*. Annapolis, MD: Naval Institute Press, 2014.
Zimmerman, F. G. *Military Vocabulary German-English and English German*. London: Hugh Rees, 1915.
Zwirner, E. J. *Die Kriegerischen Ereignisse in Vorarlberg zu Beginn des Zweiten Koalitionskriegs 1799*. Feldkirch: Druck von L. Sausgruber, 1912.

ONLINE RESOURCES

http://gallica.bnf.fr
https://www.bsb-muenchen.de/
https://www.clausewitz.com/index.htm
https://www.deutsche-biographie.de
https://www.e-rara.ch/
www.literature.at

Index

Ainoni, [General], 75, 85, 88
Alcaini, Johann, 208, 345, 369, 379, 381, 410
Alessandria
    action at, 207–210, 325, 328–331, 368, 371, 379, 383, 387–389
    strategic importance, 196, 199, 214–215, 217, 219, 224
    troop movement and disposition, 200, 204, 299, 300, 322, 325, 336, 337, 339, 344, 345, 368, 369, 372, 376, 381, 392, 415
Am-Steg, action at, 286–288, 314
Andelfingen, action at, 278n47, 279–282, 307, 309, 310
Anschauung. *See* genius: intuition
Auffenberg, Franz, 27, 71, 74–80, 86, 127–128, 292
Aulic Council, 20, 141, 142n6, 150, 249, 358n45, 378, 410n47

Bagration, Prince Peter, 7, 204, 207, 210, 324, 337, 347, 349, 351, 357, 396, 398–400, 405, 407
Barbets (*barbetti*), 413, 414
Bassignana, action at, 204–206, 210
Bellegarde, Heinrich
    Alessandria, 330–331, 376, 379, 381, 387, 389
    Army of the Tyrol, 22, 28, 50, 52, 80–82, 101, 124, 147
    as a commander, 140, 249, 300
    and Dessolles, 139, 243–245, 247, 248n6, 312
    Graubündten, 81, 82, 92, 105n152, 250, 265–271, 299, 302, 305–306
    and Lecourbe, 139, 253–257, 258, 263
    march to Italy, 271–274, 292, 303
    and Masséna, 313–316
    Modena, 337, 344, 345
    and Moreau, 367–373
    Novi, 392, 397–399, 402, 404
    St. Luciensteig, 259, 260
    Taufers, 129–130
    Trebbia, 360, 362
    troop movement and disposition, 139, 209, 212, 217, 252, 264, 284, 285, 322, 324–325, 327, 328, 392, 412
Bernadotte, Jean, 15, 21, 43, 53, 56, 59n82, 68–70, 103, 121–123, 134
Bey, Karl, 293, 294, 299, 300, 301
boldness. *See* genius: dynamism
Bonaparte, Napoleon
    as a commander, 15n11, 20, 21n26, 26, 42, 45, 49, 253, 277n45, 378
    Dresden, battle of, 138n199
    Egyptian campaign, 14, 16n16, 25, 42
    Italian campaign of 1796, 18n21, 156, 174n47, 182, 202, 203n87, 216n103, 222, 226, 335, 341, 390, 394
Bruix, Eustache, 326, 343, 385, 386
Bülow, Heinrich, 29n45, 63n87

Campo Formio, Treaty of, 9, 10, 12, 15n10, 23, 39, 69n100, 153
Carniola, 45, 141, 226
Cassano, 169, 181, 186–192, 193, 194–197, 200, 202, 224, 226, 257, 322, 348
cavalry, importance of, 21n28, 34–35, 135–136, 390n18
center of gravity, 49n74, 221n108
Chabran, Joseph, 75, 77, 78, 267, 279, 283, 289, 302
Championnet, Jean, 7, 18, 318, 380, 383, 393, 394, 410, 413–415

chance, 11n6, 22, 39n61, 40n62, 84n123, 114n168, 126n181, 169n42, 174n48, 185n60, 188, 242, 363n52, 370n60, 373n63, 408
Charles, Archduke of Austria
  as a commander, 7, 20, 25n35, 52, 66, 71, 108, 110–111, 112, 113n166, 115n169, 120n173, 123, 124, 131–139, 206–207, 249–252, 275, 283, 293, 300, 305, 307, 309–311, 363, 382, 384
  criticism of Bellegarde, 273
  criticism of Laudon, 89, 128–129
  criticism of Lecourbe, 85–86, 87n127, 89, 90n131
  crossing the Rhine, 274–283, 307, 316–317
  history of the campaign, 3–4, 7, 9n1, 21n27, 22, 29, 36n53, 38n56, 49, 68n99, 83n121, 85n124, 88, 91n133, 92, 93, 98n142, 102n147, 105n152, 118–119, 128n185, 140, 145n12, 148n18, 150n21, 152n25, 167n38, 206–207, 210n99, 244n1, 259–262, 267n31, 268n33, 270, 273, 275n44, 278n47, 279n48, 280, 285, 288nn, 290n61, 291, 292, 298n73, 301n76, 302n77, 308n85, 342
  and Jourdan, 25, 64, 69–70, 100–109, 111, 115, 122, 124, 138, 139
  and Masséna, 243, 247, 249, 262, 266, 275, 279, 280–281, 288, 293, 296, 297, 298, 302, 306–308, 310, 311
  mountain warfare, 33–34
  Osterach, 100, 102–109, 131n190
  Stockach, 109–121, 124n176, 131, 134–139, 243, 249–250
  and Suvorov, 383, 391n19, 397n30, 405, 411
  troop movement and disposition, 22, 28, 29, 46, 50, 53, 62, 71, 80n116, 81, 85–86, 103, 105, 110, 111, 118, 122, 124, 128–129, 139, 244, 247–249, 252, 265, 269, 270, 271, 272, 273, 284, 292, 301, 307–308, 309, 382n10
  Tyrol, 80–82, 101, 140
  Zurich, first battle of, 288–298, 302, 309n87
Charles Emmanuel IV, King of Sardinia, 18
Chasteler, Johann, 146, 167, 181, 183, 190, 338n24, 346, 357, 381n10, 387, 389, 397
  chief of the general staff, 143, 159, 185n61, 300
Cisalpine Republic, 9, 18, 23, 27, 39, 57, 60n82, 197, 198n80, 208n97, 244, 320n6
Clausel, Bertrand, 391, 397, 398, 399
Colli, Michelangelo, 205, 368, 381, 390, 396, 399, 402, 403
concentration of force
  importance, 29n44, 35n50, 52n79, 60n83, 75n106, 76n111, 78n114, 134, 253n16, 254n17, 307, 373n63
  in space, 177n51
  in time, 177n51
continuity
  principle of, 49n74, 299n74, 363n50, 365n55, 403n34
  pursuit, 21n28, 135, 175n50, 178n51, 341n27, 361n47, 363, 390n18, 403, 409n42
continuous pressure, 175n50, 224n110, 252n13, 360n47, 363n52, 408n40, 409n42
Corfu, 57, 386
coup d'oeil. See genius: intuition
critical analysis, 90n132, 99n142, 215n102, 333
culmination, 3, 61n85, 403n34

Daun, Leopold, 111, 351n38
Debrie, [General], 274, 284, 286, 287, 299
Decaen, Charles, 106, 107, 108, 117

decisive battle, 33, 46–47, 110, 120n173, 130n190, 133, 147, 159, 164, 189, 214, 224–225, 242–243, 253, 266, 275n43, 278, 280, 283, 288, 292, 309, 337, 341, 345, 348, 350, 354, 362, 372, 380
in French plan of attack, 325–327, 331, 333, 335
defense
mountains, 7, 32, 33–34, 71, 73, 74n106, 76n112, 78n114, 107n158, 130n188
river line, 107n158, 195, 374n64
stronger form of war, 73
Delmas, Antoine, 143, 151–153, 159–161, 162–168, 179
Demont, Joseph, 77, 91, 256
Derfelden, Wilhelm, 392, 397, 399
Dessolles, Jean, 83, 84, 87, 89, 90–94, 123–124, 130, 139, 143, 243–245, 246, 247, 249, 257–258, 306, 311, 312, 313, 415
destruction. *See* principle of destruction
Devil's Bridge, action at, 285–288, 298, 300, 301
d'Hautpoul, Jean, 68, 106, 118, 120, 121, 122
Directory
and Carnot, 42n66
invasion of Switzerland, 35–36
and Joubert, 389–390, 394n23
and Jourdan, 69, 101, 103–104, 115
and the kingdom of Naples, 16, 18, 37, 318
and Masséna, 281, 316, 380
and Moreau, 144, 410
politics, 20, 42, 50n74, 144n11, 173n46
and Schérer, 144, 174–175
strategic decisions, 40n62, 43, 54n81, 65–66, 143, 145, 379–380, 389–390
troop movement and disposition, 23, 55, 410n45
Dombrowsky, Jean, 320–321, 336, 338, 340, 343, 346, 347, 349, 352, 356, 357, 365–366, 381, 390, 395–396, 400, 404, 409

Duphot, Léonard, 13, 14n8
dynamism. *See* genius: dynamism

Egypt, 14, 15, 16n16, 20n24, 23, 25, 42
Ehrenbreitstein, 10, 13n7, 29, 38n57, 56, 57, 59n82, 70
Elsnitz, Franz, 152–153, 154, 156, 157, 159, 160, 174, 175, 180, 182
engagement, purpose of, 111, 373
envelopment, 130, 132–133, 134, 135n194, 307, 356n44
escalation, 13n7, 39n61, 209n98, 379n6
Euler, Leonard, 43n68

Feldkirch
battle of, 91, 95–100, 113, 130, 139
geography, 27–28, 32n47, 79, 82–83, 288
troop movement and disposition, 46, 67, 71, 74, 75, 76, 77, 79, 84, 104, 139, 246, 260, 265, 307
Ferdinand IV, King of Naples, 16, 17, 36–37
Férino, Pierre, 68, 102, 106, 109, 110, 113, 116, 117, 119, 122, 136, 137n197, 245
First Coalition, 25n35, 69n100, 198n80
forest towns, 69
Förster, Ivan, 204, 205, 217, 221, 222, 322, 349, 351, 352, 357, 358, 363, 392
Fra Diavolo, 320
Franz II, Holy Roman Emperor, 142, 181
Frederick the Great, 61, 222, 351n38
friction, 15n10, 84n123, 94n139, 102n146, 147n16, 158n33, 169n42, 174n48, 185n60, 186n62
Fröhlich, Michael
Cassano, 186, 188
Magnano, 162–163, 165, 166–167, 177, 178, 179
Trebbia, 349, 351, 357

Fröhlich, Michael, *continued*
    troop movement and disposition, 141, 142, 147–149, 155, 158, 159, 180, 201, 203, 205, 207, 209–210, 324, 337, 363, 364, 386, 388–389, 392
Fürstenberg, Karl, 105, 107

Gardanne, Gaspard, 155, 207, 368, 369, 399
Garnier, Pierre, 320, 321, 385, 386, 387
Gauthier, Etienne, 143, 146, 199, 200, 216, 220, 321
Gavasini, Alois, 276, 278, 283, 286, 301, 314
genius, 26n36, 27n38, 30n45, 43n68, 48–49, 111n163, 114n168, 130n189, 157n30, 158n33, 174n47, 185n60, 341n27, 348n35, 372, 374, 404
    dynamism, 22, 90n131, 195n77, 306n84, 314n90, 392n19
    intuition, 3, 27n38, 43n68, 158n33, 174n48, 185
Glarus, 67, 76, 261, 283
Gottesheim, Friedrich, 148, 149, 166, 413
Gouvion–St. Cyr, Laurent, 68, 102, 106, 107, 108, 109–110, 116, 117, 118, 119, 120–121, 122, 134, 136–138, 381, 390, 396, 398, 401, 409, 415
Grandjean, Charles, 368n59, 402, 409
Graubündten
    actions in, 70, 76, 79, 123, 124–127, 247, 302, 313
    Engadin, 80–87
    geography, 13, 27, 28, 73, 74, 98
    insurrection, 260–263
    retaking of, 92, 101, 145, 146, 149–150, 210, 264, 265–271, 274
    strategic importance, 50, 62, 63, 71–75, 96, 140, 250, 305–306, 308, 311–312
    troop movement and disposition, 22, 46, 50, 55, 69, 71, 201, 273, 283, 285, 292, 299

Grenier, Paul, 143, 151–153, 159–160, 161, 162, 165, 167, 177–179, 183, 186, 188, 190, 194, 197, 200, 204, 205, 207, 212, 343, 368, 369, 370, 371
Grey League. *See* Oberbund insurrections
Grouchy, Emmanuel, 212, 368, 369, 370, 371, 381, 391, 397–399, 402, 403, 409

Haddick, Karl, 254, 255, 256, 265, 271, 274, 277, 284–288, 298–302, 313, 322, 378, 381, 382, 383, 384, 410, 414
Hatry, Jacques, 143, 151, 154, 157, 161, 162, 165
Helvetia. *See* Switzerland
Hohenzollern-Hechingen, Prince Friedrich
    Magnano, 162, 163, 164, 166, 178–180
    minor actions in Italy, 154, 160, 264
    Modena, 335–345
    troop movement and disposition, 141, 142, 148, 149, 180, 181, 182, 183, 184, 186, 195, 196, 202, 203, 210–211, 226, 312, 327, 328, 346, 355, 360, 361, 365, 366, 367, 374, 375, 388
Holland, 10n5, 16, 19, 23, 24, 41
Hotze, Johann
    as a commander, 7, 250
    crossing the Rhine, 274–283
    Feldkirch, 79, 96, 99
    Graubündten, 70, 124, 253, 261, 265–271, 302, 305–306
    and Masséna, 279–281, 282, 307–309
    St. Luciensteig, 258–260, 286, 313
    troop movement and disposition, 22, 50, 71, 75, 77, 80, 82n119, 92, 101, 139, 247, 249, 272, 273, 299, 300
    Zurich, first battle of, 292, 293, 294, 295

Italy
    Army of, 24, 25, 37, 53n80, 54, 55, 56, 57, 60, 67, 143, 144, 156, 257, 263,

272, 287, 311–312, 315, 368n59, 379, 380, 389, 390, 410, 413
Austrian plan of operations, 39–41, 44, 45, 50–52, 146, 150, 185, 196–197, 209, 222, 225, 253, 296, 302, 338, 384
campaign of 1796, 18n21, 37n55, 52n78, 90n132, 144, 156, 171, 174n47, 182
French plan of operations, 45–46, 53, 54–57, 60, 63, 67, 76, 84, 157, 171, 201, 409n43, 416
and Germany, 32, 45, 50, 54, 63, 67, 145, 174n47, 270n35, 312n89
insurrections, 198, 211, 320n5, 384–385
politics, 12n6, 16, 18n21, 145n12, 303, 304, 377, 379
strategic importance, 18, 19, 29, 36–37, 39, 94, 209, 223, 270n35, 274n42, 302, 303, 312n89, 315
and Switzerland, 7, 29, 32, 35, 39, 40, 41, 45, 46, 55, 67, 74, 83, 84, 92, 128, 145, 174n47, 263, 266, 270n35, 302, 303, 312n89, 411
troop movement and disposition, 9, 16, 21, 22, 23, 24, 25, 28, 75, 80n116, 83, 141–142, 143, 148, 159, 164, 169, 187, 199, 210, 211, 223, 226, 244, 257, 258, 263, 266, 270, 273, 284, 292, 299, 300, 301, 312, 313, 320–321, 329, 379, 380, 382, 386, 392n20, 411, 412

Jellachich, Franz, 99, 100, 267, 283, 284, 293, 294, 299, 301, 310
Jomini, Antoine
on actions in Italy, 36, 151n23, 152n25, 155n28, 160, 167n38, 240, 380–381
Clausewitz's criticism of, 66n91, 171n45, 191n72, 338n24, 342–343, 345n31, 360, 368n59, 369–370, 396n27, 397, 405
concentration of force, 253n16
on the Directory, 65, 66n90
French plan of operations, 76n110, 146n15, 332–335

history of the campaign, 3–4, 83n122, 85n124, 86n125, 113n166, 145n12, 146n13, 148n18, 150n21, 152n23, 188–189n67, 395n26
invasion of Switzerland, 29–30, 32, 36
on key commanders, 220n107, 222n109, 273, 280, 371, 383n111, 393, 414n52
Marengo, 206, 212n101, 213, 219
mountain warfare, 63n87
offensive and defensive actions, 171n45, 188–189n67, 316n92
Trebbia, 352, 353, 359
troop movement and disposition, 21n25, 68n99, 149nn, 190, 202n86, 210n99, 245–246, 248n5, 257, 265n29, 267n31, 364, 374n65, 380–382, 403n35
Zurich, first battle of, 291, 297
Joubert, Barthélemy, 7, 18, 144–145, 376, 380, 389–390, 392–394, 396, 397
Jourdan, Jean
as a commander, 9, 23n31, 25, 43, 45, 69–70, 91, 102, 104–105, 111, 114–115, 126n183, 136–139, 242
crossing the Rhine, 121–123, 244, 250n10
and the Directory, 103–104, 115, 144
French plan of operations, 63, 64–65, 76, 114
history of the campaign, 53n80, 54, 108n159
Osterach, 95, 100–109
Stockach, 109–121, 132–133, 134, 243, 281
troop movement and disposition, 21, 47, 53, 53–53, 54–57, 63, 65, 68, 99, 104, 106, 109n160, 113, 124

Kaim, Konrad
actions in Italy, 152, 153, 165, 167, 186, 188, 207

Kaim, Konrad, *continued*
   troop movement and disposition, 141, 148, 149, 162–163, 165, 180, 201, 203, 206, 209, 222, 324–325, 337, 368, 376, 378, 381, 382, 392, 411, 413
   Verona, 150, 154, 157, 158, 159
Kant, Immanuel, 158n33
Klenau, Johann
   actions in Italy, 169, 182, 183, 327, 339, 340–341, 343, 366, 387, 412–413
   crossing the Apennines, 384, 386
   troop movement and disposition, 149, 164, 182, 186, 203, 211, 226, 322, 323, 324, 330, 331, 336, 346, 355, 360, 365, 367, 374, 375, 378, 381, 383, 391, 409
Korsakov, Alexander, 250, 289, 411
Kray, Paul
   actions in Italy, 148, 153, 155
   Austrian plan of operation, 145–146, 148
   as a commander, 7, 149–150, 154, 158, 160, 179, 184, 398, 399, 407
   Magnano, 161–168, 177, 178, 179, 180, 181
   Mantua, siege of, 211, 322, 330, 336, 337–338, 378, 388, 393
   Novi, 396, 397, 398, 399, 401, 402, 403, 404, 406, 407
   troop movement and disposition, 22, 80n116, 141, 142, 146–151, 184, 186, 322, 337, 344–345, 360, 367, 378, 381, 382, 388–389, 392, 396, 411, 414, 415
   Verona, 154, 157, 158, 159–161

Laboissière, Pierre, 188, 190, 194, 197, 343, 346, 367, 381, 390, 396, 399, 401, 402, 409
Lahoz Ortiz, Giuseppe, 211, 386
Lamarcelle, [General], 274, 284, 285, 286, 287, 299
Lapoype, Jean, 332, 342, 343, 344, 345, 346, 357, 359, 361, 364, 367, 368

Laudon, Johann, 82, 83, 86, 87, 88, 89, 90–94, 128, 129, 130, 256, 270, 400, 401, 414
Lazzaroni, 18
Lecourbe, Claude
   as a commander, 7, 90n131, 306, 314
   Engadin, 80–89, 128–129, 246, 253–257, 270, 311, 312, 313
   minor actions in Italy, 264, 272, 273, 274
   minor actions in Switzerland, 283, 411
   Nauders, 91–92, 94–95, 123, 130, 243
   St. Gotthard, 284–288
   troop movement and disposition, 75, 91, 139, 174, 210, 243, 244, 246, 247, 258, 262, 263, 265, 268, 269, 289, 298, 301, 302, 307, 316
Lefebvre, François, 68, 106, 107, 108, 116
Lemoine, Louis, 380, 381, 389, 391, 397, 399, 402
Lichtenstein, Prince Johann, 307, 358, 359, 392, 400
Ligurian Republic, 23, 57, 200, 206, 334, 363n51, 367, 410
Loison, Louis, 75, 76, 77, 91, 94, 95, 210, 257, 258, 263–265, 269, 284, 285, 286, 287, 313
Lombardy, 35, 41, 44, 141, 143, 144, 170, 196, 198, 223, 257, 302, 303, 312, 315, 329, 344
Lorge, Jean, 75, 77, 79, 246, 265, 270, 276, 279, 289, 290, 309
Lothringen, Prince Karl, 293, 294, 295
Lusignan, Franz, 207, 210, 324, 337, 400, 401

Macdonald, Jacques
   as a commander, 7, 169n41, 379–380
   marching through Italy, 169, 197, 199, 200, 203, 206, 208, 209, 211, 212, 213, 214, 215, 216, 217, 219, 220, 222, 223, 224, 225, 299, 318, 321, 322, 323, 327, 328, 330, 331, 332, 333, 334, 341, 342, 343, 344, 378, 386, 392n19

Modena, 335–339, 340
  in Naples, 319, 320, 384
  Trebbia, 345–360, 370, 372–375
  troop movement and disposition,
    325, 326, 361–367, 376, 377, 379, 380,
    383
Magnano, battle of, 161–168, 169, 177, 181,
  183, 214, 223, 226, 258n20, 322
Mainz, 10, 27, 29, 40, 54, 55, 56, 57, 70,
  246, 304n81
Malta, 14, 57
Mantua
  siege of, 203, 209, 211, 226, 322, 325,
    336, 337, 338, 344, 367, 374, 378, 379,
    383, 387–389, 390, 393
  strategic importance, 18, 29, 143–144,
    177, 199, 216n104
  troop movement and disposition,
    145, 146, 155, 159, 162, 163, 169, 180,
    182, 183, 186, 343, 346, 381, 382, 386,
    412
Marengo, battle of, 141n2, 142nn, 206–
  213, 219
Martinsbrück, 74, 81, 82, 83, 87, 88, 89,
  91, 92, 94, 95, 124n176, 129–130,
  256, 271
Masséna, André
  and Archduke Charles, 139, 249, 252,
    262, 266, 275, 277, 278, 280
  as a commander, 7, 21, 43, 45, 242, 281,
    316, 317, 380
  Feldkirch, 95–100, 113
  French plan of operation, 56, 59n82,
    63, 67, 84, 145, 243, 315
  Graubünden, 69, 71–79, 84, 101, 145
  and Jourdan, 101, 103, 113, 242
  troop movement and disposition, 53,
    91, 95, 104, 124, 128, 139, 243, 245,
    246, 247, 249, 255, 263, 272, 275,
    276, 279, 282, 283, 284, 285, 286,
    301, 312, 313, 314
  Zurich, first battle of, 288–298, 302,
    306–307, 308, 310, 311

maximum exertion of strength, 22, 49n74,
  61n85, 105n152, 111n163, 320n5
Meerfeld, [General], 109, 113, 117, 118, 119,
  134, 136, 138
Melas, Michael,
  Cassano, 186, 188, 191
  as a commander, 7, 142, 201n84, 207,
    300, 348, 355n42, 358, 375
  Novi, 397, 399, 400, 401, 402, 403, 404,
    405, 406, 407–408
  and Suvorov, 185, 300, 348, 353, 357–
    358, 375, 377
  Trebbia, 347, 348, 351, 353, 355, 357–358
  troop movement and disposition, 147,
    150, 168, 180, 184, 322, 353, 363, 364,
    392, 410, 412, 414, 415
Ménard, Jean, 75, 77, 99–100, 246, 258,
  259, 260, 261, 262, 265, 266–267,
  268, 270, 272, 276, 279, 283, 285,
  289, 290, 292, 302, 311, 313
Mercantin, Karl, 141, 148, 149, 155, 158,
  159, 162, 163, 165, 166, 167, 175, 177,
  178, 180
Miollis, Sextius, 321, 381, 391, 409, 412
Modena
  action at, 332, 334, 347, 339–341, 344,
    382, 388
  strategic importance, 18, 323, 324, 329
  troop movement and disposition,
    203, 321, 324, 335, 336, 338, 342, 343,
    345n31, 366, 367
Montalembert, Marc, 66
Monte Ceneri
  action at, 257n19, 264, 314
Montrichard, Joseph
  actions in Italy, 151, 155, 157, 158–159,
    165, 175, 323, 339, 352–353, 358–359,
    361
  as a commander, 211
  troop movement and disposition, 143,
    161, 162, 164–165, 183, 188, 199, 200,
    203, 216, 220, 321, 338, 343, 345, 346,
    349, 354, 356, 365–366, 367

moral factors
    moral and physical exhaustion, 360–361
    moral courage, 111n163, 114n168, 348n35
    morale, 26n38, 361n47
    success, 121, 130, 131, 171, 225
Moreau, Jean
    actions in Italy, 167–168, 183, 223, 315, 321, 330–331, 332, 336, 337, 342–343, 344, 360, 392n19
    and Bellegarde, 367–372
    as a commander, 7, 20, 25, 144–145, 188, 190–191, 194, 195, 199–200, 205n90, 214–220, 224–225, 327, 330–331, 334, 341–343, 369–371, 373–374, 380, 390, 409–410, 411, 415
    and the Directory, 144, 380, 409–410
    and Macdonald, 325–329, 332–334, 335–336, 341–342, 342–343, 356, 357, 361, 374, 378
    Marengo, 206–208, 212–213
    Novi, 397–398, 399, 402, 409–410
    and Suvorov, 221, 222, 225, 323, 344, 351, 362–363, 365, 374–375, 376, 377, 383, 415
    troop movement and disposition, 161, 162, 164–165, 169, 177, 178, 179, 180, 191, 192, 197, 199, 200, 212, 325, 333–334, 335–336, 337, 341, 343, 345, 346, 350, 355, 367, 372, 378, 412, 414
    Verona, 151, 154, 157, 161
mountain warfare, 32–35, 46n71, 63n87, 71, 73, 74n106, 75n108, 78n114, 86n125, 89, 107n158, 130n188, 135, 260n24, 305–306
Münster, 28, 81, 82–83, 86, 88, 89, 92–93, 94, 95, 243–245, 254, 299, 311, 312
Muotta valley, action at, 283–284, 301, 314

Näfels, action at, 283
Naples, kingdom of, 16, 17, 18, 19, 36, 37, 53, 57, 60n82, 318, 319, 320, 325, 384, 385, 386

Nauders, 28, 83, 84, 86, 90, 91, 92, 94–95, 128, 129, 130, 139, 243, 271
Nauendorf, Friedrich, 109, 113, 116, 117, 119, 276–277, 281, 282, 293, 308
Nelson, Horatio, 16, 17, 385n14
Newton, Isaac, 42n65, 43n68
Ney, Michel, 277, 280, 281
Nobili, Johann, 274, 284, 285, 286, 299, 400, 404
Novi, battle of, 144n10, 181, 207, 336, 341, 350, 355, 369, 371, 372, 376, 380, 383, 389–408, 409, 410, 411, 412, 413, 415

Oberbund insurrections, 27, 261
object
    likely cost, 14n9, 30, 40n62
    renounce, 40n62
    value, 3, 14n9, 20, 60n83, 61n86, 125n180, 198n81, 208n97, 303n78, 305n82, 379n6
objective
    Austrian political and military, 39–40, 131, 202n87, 222–223, 224, 225, 271n36, 275, 302, 303–304, 325, 327, 374
    French political and military, 39n61, 60n83, 63, 76n111, 91, 201, 333, 334, 372–373, 415n
    general political, 38, 42, 60n83, 175n49, 378n5, 411n49
    link to strategic effect, 39n60, 313
    military, 14n9, 17n17, 33, 49, 60, 61, 115n169, 125n180, 172n45, 315, 369, 378n5
    Neapolitan political and military, 17n17
    Russian political and military, 274n42, 338n24
    scale of military effort, 61, 120n, 125n180, 362n49, 379n6, 408n41
Olivier, Jean, 321, 338, 340, 343, 345, 346, 349, 352, 353, 356, 358, 359, 361, 364

Osterach, action at, 95, 100–109, 110, 111n163, 113n166, 131n190, 137, 243, 247
Ott, Peter
 as a commander, 141n4
 Cassano, 186, 188, 190
 and the French plan of attack, 330, 331, 332
 minor actions in Italy, 366, 367
 Novi, 397, 399, 404
 stopping Moreau and Macdonald, 323–324, 326–328, 343, 344, 345, 346, 365, 366
 Trebbia, 347–350, 351, 352, 353, 357, 358
 troop movement and disposition, 141, 142, 147–148, 149, 164, 180, 181, 182, 184, 201, 202, 203, 220, 222, 322, 336, 337, 339, 363, 364, 367, 378, 388, 392
Ottoman Empire, 16, 136n196, 385n13
Oudinot, Nicolas, 75, 76, 77, 79, 99, 100, 246, 276, 279, 280, 281, 290, 295

Papal States, 14n8, 17, 36, 41, 320, 384
Parma, 18, 202, 203, 219, 329, 332, 337, 339, 343, 344, 355, 360, 361, 365, 375
Parona, action at, 145, 153, 156, 159–161
Parthenopean Republic, 18, 36, 37, 318, 384–385, 386
Partouneaux, Louis, 368, 369, 371, 391, 399, 403
Pastrengo, action at, 145, 148, 149, 151–153, 155, 157, 158, 164, 174, 175
Paul I, Tsar of Russia, 14, 16, 54n81, 142, 191n72
Pérignon, Catherine-Dominique, 200, 206, 207, 212, 215, 346, 363, 367, 381, 391, 402, 403
Petrasch, Franz, 278, 280, 281, 294
Piedmont
 strategic importance of, 144, 196, 198, 199, 205n90, 208n97, 222n109, 365n55, 383
 troop movement and disposition, 23, 57, 143, 200, 202n87, 209, 272–273, 322, 325, 326, 337, 381, 382, 392, 412, 413
 See also Sardinia
principle of destruction, 40n63, 104n150, 131, 373n63, 403n34
probability. *See* chance
purpose and means, in war, 13n7, 14n9, 26n37, 39n60, 40nn, 104n150, 125n180, 360n47
pursuit. *See* continuity: pursuit

Quesnel, François, 368, 369, 371

Rastatt, Congresses of, 9, 10n5, 12, 13, 15, 28, 54
Rehbinder, Maksim, 381, 382, 383
Reichs-Contingents, 9, 10, 19, 24
Remüs, the action at, 87, 88–89, 91, 244, 252, 254–257, 305, 311, 312
result, 33, 37, 253n16
 never final, 15n12, 38n58, 198n80, 208n97, 261n26, 318n2
Reuss, Prince Heinrich, 293, 295
Reuss valley, 262, 269, 285, 286, 287, 288, 298, 301, 313, 314
Richepanse, Antoine, 391, 397, 398
river line defense. *See* defense, river line
Rivoli, battle of, 151, 152, 153, 174, 361n47
Rohan, Prince Ludwig, 201, 210, 257, 258, 263–265, 272, 273, 274, 284, 285, 286, 287, 299, 300, 312, 313, 314, 382, 383, 414
Rome
 Army of, 54, 57, 58n82, 60n82
 politics, 13, 14, 319, 386
 strategic importance, 17, 384
 troop movement and disposition, 197, 211, 222, 320, 321, 386
Rosenberg, Andrei, 181, 189, 192, 193, 204, 205, 206, 225, 322, 351, 352, 353, 356, 357, 358, 363, 364, 381, 383, 392, 399, 400, 403, 404, 408, 415

Ruby, Sebastien, 75, 76, 104, 113, 116, 122
Ruffo, Fabrizio, 319, 320, 385
Rusca, Jean, 321, 338, 340, 346, 347, 352, 356, 357, 364
Russia
   Cassano, 186, 187, 188, 189n68, 192, 195, 196
   international relations, 14, 15, 16, 19, 38, 54, 304, 305
   military cooperation, 146n14, 153n27, 182, 222, 274n42, 304, 305, 338, 376–377
   minor actions in Italy, 204–205, 207, 210
   naval operations, 211, 320, 385, 386
   Novi, 396, 397, 399, 401, 402, 403, 404, 406, 407, 408
   plan of operations, 45, 46, 48, 50, 51, 65, 66, 147, 193, 219, 250, 411, 416
   Trebbia, 346, 347, 357, 360n46
   troop movement and disposition, 19, 22, 24, 36, 142, 150, 180, 201, 202, 203, 204, 206, 212, 226, 322, 324, 376, 379, 381, 409, 412, 415

Salm, Jean, 321, 345, 346, 347, 349, 352, 353, 356, 358, 364
Sardinia, 18, 205, 411
Saxe, Maurice, 29, 63
Schérer, Barthélemy
   actions in Italy, 151–153, 162, 167, 168, 178, 179
   as a commander, 25, 43, 144, 145–146, 150, 156, 157, 160, 173, 174, 175, 188, 388
   troop movement and operations, 21, 57, 143, 145, 146, 159, 161, 169, 183
Schwarzenberg, Prince Karl, 109, 110, 112, 113, 116, 117, 119, 138n199
Schweikowsky, Yakov, 349, 351, 357, 358, 392
Schwerpunkt. See center of gravity
Schwyz, action at, 260, 261, 262, 301
Scuol, action at, 87, 88, 92, 270
Second Coalition, 8, 14, 15n12, 16, 18, 20, 24, 25n35, 36, 56, 43, 44, 65, 223, 253
Sérurier, Jean, 143, 151, 152, 153, 159–161, 162, 165, 166, 174, 178, 183, 186, 188, 190, 191, 192–193, 195, 196, 197, 199, 200
Sicily, 19, 24, 319
Souham, Joseph, 68, 106, 116, 117, 122, 136, 137n197, 246, 279
Soult, Jean, 7, 116, 117–120, 121, 122, 136, 138, 245, 246, 261, 262, 276, 279, 280, 281, 282, 284, 290, 295
Spain, 18, 19, 37n55, 126, 262n28, 319n4
St. Gotthard, action at, 7, 74, 201, 210, 263, 264, 265, 271, 272, 273, 274, 283, 284–288, 298, 299, 301, 307, 312, 313, 314, 315, 316, 384, 415
St. Julien, François, 146, 148, 149, 159, 161, 164, 166, 178, 182, 258–259, 261, 270, 271, 273, 284, 285, 286, 287, 298, 299, 301, 313, 314
St. Luciensteig, action at, 74, 76–78, 127, 128, 258–260, 261, 263, 265, 266, 267, 268, 271, 272, 275, 305, 306, 307, 311, 313
Stockach, battle of, 9, 102, 109–121, 124n176, 131, 133, 134, 135, 136, 137n197, 139, 140, 242, 243, 247, 249, 250, 252, 278n47, 281, 296, 311
strategic analysis. *See* critical analysis
Strauch, Gottfried, 169, 186, 201, 247, 257–258, 263, 264, 273, 274, 284–285, 287, 298, 300, 382, 383, 411, 414
Sublime Porte. *See* Ottoman Empire
Suchet, Louis, 267, 269, 272, 273, 276, 285, 286, 289
superiority in numbers, 17, 21, 26, 41, 51, 53, 66, 111, 115, 130, 133, 135, 149, 166, 173, 177, 190, 221, 249, 253, 299, 390–391
suspension of action, 299n74, 403n35

Süss
  action at, 256, 257, 258, 269
Suvorov, Alexander
  and Bellegarde, 252, 257, 270, 271, 273, 274, 337, 368
  as a commander, 7, 15, 20, 25, 50, 142, 150, 181–182, 183–184, 185, 195, 200, 202, 207, 208, 220, 221, 222, 223, 225, 244n1, 299, 306n84, 338, 348, 356, 362, 363, 374–375, 376–377, 378, 383, 391n19, 392n20, 403, 404–405
  Cassano, 187–189, 191, 197
  and the French plan of operations, 214, 215, 216, 217, 218, 219, 312, 326–332, 342, 373
  and Haddick, 284, 286, 299, 300, 378, 383
  and Joubert, 380, 393, 396
  and Macdonald, 347, 361, 373, 374–375
  and Melas, 185, 348, 358, 399, 401, 410, 412
  and Moreau, 344, 362, 365, 369–370, 372, 373, 377, 383, 415
  Novi, 391, 393, 396, 397, 398, 399, 401, 402, 403, 404–406, 408
  and Ott, 323, 337, 339
  Trebbia, 346, 349–353, 355, 356, 357, 358, 359, 360, 406
  troop movement and disposition, 50, 142, 147, 150, 181, 183, 186, 193, 197, 201, 202, 203, 204, 205, 206, 208, 209, 210, 212, 248n6, 252, 264, 324, 336, 337, 339, 345, 346, 362, 364, 365, 368, 372, 376, 378, 379, 386, 388, 389, 410, 411, 412, 414, 415, 416
Switzerland
  actions in, 253, 266, 270n35, 411
  Austrian plan of operations, 45–47, 50, 51, 113n166, 122, 125, 131n190, 132, 140, 250, 302, 383–384
  and Germany, 124n176, 125, 131n190, 145, 242, 270n35, 303
  insurrections, 260–263
  and Italy, 7, 32, 35, 39, 40, 41, 44, 145, 174n47, 270n35, 272, 303, 315, 411
  French invasion of, 13, 27, 29–32, 35–36, 303–304
  French plan of operations, 48, 53, 63, 113, 133, 242–243, 311
  strategic importance of, 30, 32, 34, 35, 40, 41, 44, 270n35, 303–304, 305n83, 312n89, 314, 315
  troop movement and disposition, 21, 22, 24, 26, 28, 123, 242–243, 244, 245, 246, 247, 248, 275, 380, 411, 412
  Zurich, first battle of, 288, 298
Szenasy, Johann, 163, 164, 166, 167, 177, 178, 179

Taufers
  action at, 81, 86, 90–94, 128, 129, 130, 134, 139, 193, 243–244, 257, 271, 311
Taverno
  action at, 264–265
Tharreau, Jean, 246, 276, 277, 279, 280, 282, 290, 292, 293, 298, 310, 317
Tolstoy, Alexander, 248n6, 271n36, 272n38
Tortona
  Austrian plan, 221
  French plan, 199, 206, 214, 217, 219, 220, 332, 331, 333, 356, 373
  siege of, 208, 209, 322, 325, 328, 345, 368, 369, 379, 381, 389, 392, 410, 412, 415
  troop movement and disposition, 203, 204, 205n89, 207, 208, 210, 330, 331. 336, 337, 344, 345, 362, 368, 369, 371, 372, 376, 379, 381, 383, 390, 408
Trebbia, battle of, 181, 300, 318, 323, 324, 326, 332, 341, 342, 345, 346, 347–361, 363, 365, 366, 368, 369, 370, 372, 373, 376, 377–378, 380, 382, 388, 394n25, 405, 406

trinity, wondrous fickle (paradoxical),
    11n6, 27n38, 39n61, 40n62, 42n65,
    84n123, 99n142, 114n168, 174n48,
    191n71, 221n108, 371n61
Turenne, Henri, 220, 222, 294
Turkey, 14, 19, 181, 184n57, 204, 211, 386,
    391n19, 405
Tuscany, 14, 18, 57, 67, 143, 146, 197, 206,
    212, 321, 325, 326, 377, 381, 384, 386,
    387, 389, 412
Tyrol
    actions in, 70, 92, 96, 244, 247, 380
    Army of the, 50, 52, 53n80, 56, 59n82,
        71, 80, 81, 82, 97, 104, 123, 157, 201,
        209, 244, 250, 251, 252, 257, 258n20,
        270
    Austrian plan, 46, 50, 80, 140, 146–147,
        149–150
    French plan, 48, 60–63, 67, 84, 101, 156
    geography, 27–28, 45, 80, 82
    strategic importance, 63, 126–127, 250,
        266, 274n42
    troop movement and disposition,
        9, 22, 50, 80, 82, 84, 89, 92, 148,
        157n31, 159, 168, 169, 226, 248, 249,
        265

value of the object. *See* object, value
Vandamme, Dominique, 68, 102, 106,
    109, 116, 118, 119, 120, 121, 136, 245,
    246, 276, 279, 280, 281n52, 290
Venice, 9, 10, 29, 141, 142, 169, 211
Verderio, action at, 190, 192–193, 195
Verona
    action at, 152n25, 154, 159, 160
    Austrian plan, 150, 158, 176, 180
    French plan, 57, 67, 145, 151, 156, 157–
        158, 160, 161, 173–175
    strategic importance, 29, 156–157,
        158–159, 170–171, 177–178
    troop movement and disposition, 141,
        142, 149, 153, 159, 160, 161, 162, 163,
        164, 165, 166, 167, 177, 181, 337, 344

Victor, Claude
    actions in Italy, 151, 154, 207, 346,
        363–364
    Cassano, 188, 190, 191, 194, 196
    Magnano, 162, 165, 167, 168, 177, 178, 179
    Trebbia, 347, 349, 352, 353, 354, 356,
        357, 359
    troop movement and disposition, 143,
        157, 159, 161, 183, 186, 197, 204, 212,
        215, 219, 328, 332, 333–334, 339, 343,
        344, 345, 361, 364–365, 367, 368
victory, key factors, 33, 40–41, 49n74, 61,
    111n163, 120n173, 130, 131, 133, 173,
    175n50, 363, 376, 378n5, 390n18,
    409n42
Vienna, 15, 25, 26, 41, 82, 92, 105n152, 123,
    140, 145n12, 250, 299, 411

Waldstädte. *See* forest towns
Wallis
    actions in, 246, 247, 260, 261, 262, 263,
        272, 273, 274, 287, 299, 300, 315, 381,
        382, 411
Wallis, Olivier, 105, 108, 119, 250, 295
war by geometry, 63n87
Watrin, François, 321, 338, 340, 346, 349,
    350, 353, 354, 356, 358, 359, 361, 364,
    366, 381, 390, 396, 398, 399, 400,
    401, 402, 409, 412, 415
Windisch-Grätz, Alfred, 112n165
Wukassowitsch, Joseph, 169, 180, 181, 183,
    184, 186, 188, 189, 190, 193, 202, 203,
    204, 206, 208, 209, 210, 226, 244,
    247, 270, 322, 324, 337, 345, 368,
    369, 371
Würzburg, 19, 29, 131

Xaintrailles, Charles, 75, 76, 246, 262, 287,
    298–301, 382, 383, 411, 414

Zernetz
    action at, 86, 87, 88–89, 128, 254, 255,
        256, 257, 263

Zoph, Johann, 141, 142, 147, 148, 149, 159, 162, 163, 164, 165, 166, 167, 178, 179, 180, 184, 186, 188, 190, 191, 201, 203, 207, 324

Zurich

    Austrian plan, 139, 250n10, 275n43, 278n47, 293, 296, 307, 308n85, 309–310

    first battle of, 281, 288–298, 302, 317

    French plan, 279, 288–289, 297

    strategic importance, 46, 288, 290–291, 297

    troop movement and disposition, 275, 276, 277, 282, 283, 284, 289–290, 292, 293–294, 296, 298, 313